Mathematical Analysis for Business and Economics

Custom Version for Saddleback College

Second Edition

Schelin | Bange

CENGAGE
Learning™

Australia • Brazil • Japan • Korea • Mexico • Singapore • Spain • United Kingdom • United States

CENGAGE
Learning™

Mathematical Analysis for Business and Economics: Custom Version for Saddleback College, Second Edition

Schelin | Bange

Executive Editors:
Michele Baird

Maureen Staudt

Michael Stranz

Project Development Manager:
Linda deStefano

Senior Marketing Coordinators:
Sara Mercurio

Lindsay Shapiro

Senior Production / Manufacturing Manager:
Donna M. Brown

PreMedia Services Supervisor:
Rebecca A. Walker

Rights & Permissions Specialist:
Kalina Hintz

Cover Image:
Getty Images*

* Unless otherwise noted, all cover images used by Custom Solutions, a part of Cengage Learning, have been supplied courtesy of Getty Images with the exception of the Earthview cover image, which has been supplied by the National Aeronautics and Space Administration (NASA).

For product information and technology assistance, contact us at
Cengage Learning Customer & Sales Support, 1-800-354-9706

For permission to use material from this text or product, submit all requests online at **cengage.com/permissions**
Further permissions questions can be emailed to
permissionrequest@cengage.com

ISBN-13: 978-0-495-19835-2

ISBN-10: 0-495-19835-8

Cengage Learning
5191 Natorp Boulevard
Mason, Ohio 45040
USA

Cengage Learning is a leading provider of customized learning solutions with office locations around the globe, including Singapore, the United Kingdom, Australia, Mexico, Brazil, and Japan. Locate your local office at:
international.cengage.com/region

Cengage Learning products are represented in Canada by Nelson Education, Ltd.

For your lifelong learning solutions, visit **custom.cengage.com**

Visit our corporate website at **cengage.com**

Printed in the United States of America

CONTENTS

The Sizzler Burger chain has decided to add a salad bar to its menu. It has been estimated that the daily fixed cost for operating the salad bar will be $36 and the variable cost will be $2.10 per order. The price of the salad bar is to be $2.85.
a. Determine the profit P as a function of q, the number of customers who order the salad bar.
b. How many customers must order a salad bar each day for Sizzler Burger to break even?

CHAPTER 1

Algebraic Functions for Business Models

1.1
Models and Functions of a Single Variable

In this textbook, mathematical models are used to describe a variety of situations and problems that arise in business and economics. These models are intended to show the relationships among variables such as production level, cost, price, revenue, profit, capital, and interest rate, which are important to business managers and economists. An attempt has been made to select models that are as realistic and intuitive as possible for an introductory course. We begin with a brief explanation of the modeling process itself.

A model is an abstraction or simplification of a real-world phenomenon that is created to obtain a better understanding of that phenomenon. Models may be classified either as **physical** (for example, scale models of buildings or wiring diagrams of electrical equipment) or as **conceptual** (for example, computer programs that forecast economic developments or sets of symptoms used to diagnose an illness). In all cases, the model is not reality but is intended only to illustrate or clarify some aspects of the real situation.

An existing model may be improved by altering it so that it more closely approximates reality, provided the new version does not become so complex that it obscures what the original model was built to clarify. The art of building a model and improving it is a circular process, as illustrated in Figure 1.1. The builder begins with the real-world phenomenon and proceeds by abstraction to a simple model. This model is then "tested" by using it to predict how reality will respond to various changes or by observing how the model "fits" new examples of the phenomenon. From such testing, the original model might be refined or adjusted, perhaps resulting in an improved model ready for further testing.

A **mathematical model** is a special kind of conceptual model in which the major components of the phenomenon are represented by variables and their relationships are represented by one or more equations involving these variables. The simplest mathematical models have two variables, with the value of one variable expressed so as to indicate its dependence on the value of the other.

An **independent variable** represents a quantity that can be controlled or chosen to represent input data. A **dependent variable** has its value determined by the choice of the independent variable; that is, it represents the output value. In many situations involving two variables, it is possible for the modeler to select either variable as the independent variable, depending on what the model is intended to illustrate. Consider, for example, the selling price of a commodity and the demand

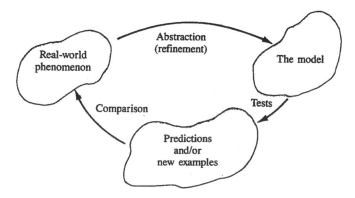

Figure 1.1
The modeling process

for that commodity: a model might be made to show that as the selling price rises, the demand for the commodity declines; on the other hand, the model could be designed to show that if the demand for the commodity is decreasing, then its selling price must be rising. Frequently, in a given relationship it is possible to solve for the independent variable, thereby converting it to the dependent variable.

We formalize our development of mathematical models with the definition of a functional relationship between two variables.

Definition 1.1

A **function** is a relationship between the values of two variables in which to each value of the independent variable there is assigned exactly one value of the dependent variable. The dependent variable is said to be a function of the independent variable.

The collection of all values the independent variable may assume is called the **domain** of the function. The set of all assigned values taken on by the dependent variable is called the **range** of the function. The manner in which a value is assigned to the dependent variable for a given value of the independent variable is often called the **rule of correspondence**. This rule may be given by a table, a graph, or a similar means, but ideally it is given as an equation that has been solved for the dependent variable.

EXAMPLE 1

Let x denote an independent variable that can assume any value in the interval $[-2, 3]$, and let y be the square of x. (Interval notation is reviewed in Appendix A.2.) Then y is a function of x with domain $[-2, 3]$ and range $[0, 9]$.

We can represent this function algebraically as $y = x^2$, $-2 \leq x \leq 3$. Using a horizontal axis for values of the independent variable x and a vertical axis for the dependent variable y, we can graph this function by plotting all points (x, y) with $-2 \leq x \leq 3$ as shown in Figure 1.2.

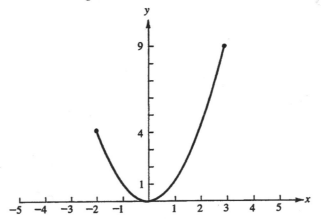

Figure 1.2
A graphical representation of the function $y = x^2$, $-2 \leq x \leq 3$

If the domain of the function $y = x^2$ was restricted to the integers $-2, -1, 0,$ 1, 2, 3, the resulting function could be represented by Table 1.1. [A graph of this function would consist of only those six (x, y) points on an axis system.]

x	-2	-1	0	1	2	3
y	4	1	0	1	4	9

Table 1.1

A tabular representation of the function $y = x^2$, $x = -2, -1, 0, 1, 2, 3$

It is important to note that the definition of a function requires that a unique value of the dependent variable be assigned to each value of the independent variable. This means that when a function is given as a graph, no vertical line may intersect the graph in more than one place; when the function is given in tabular form, if any entry for the independent variable appears more than once, the corresponding entries for the dependent variable must all be the same.

Often a separate symbol, such as f, is used to denote a function; that is, the domain, range, and rule of correspondence are simultaneously denoted by f. With this convention, if x denotes the independent variable, then $f(x)$, read "f of x," denotes the assigned value of the dependent variable. The function of Example 1 can be written as

$$f(x) = x^2, \qquad -2 \leq x \leq 3.$$

Now $f(2)$ denotes the value of the dependent variable assigned to $x = 2$ by the function; that is, $f(2) = 4$. If it is necessary to denote the dependent variable by y, we can write the function as

$$y(x) = x^2, \qquad -2 \leq x \leq 3,$$

which illustrates the dependence of y on x without introducing the symbol f.

When a function is given by an equation such as $y = f(x)$ but the domain is not specified (as was done above), the domain is assumed to be all real numbers for which the expression $f(x)$ is defined. For example, $y = 1/x$ represents a function whose domain is all real numbers other than 0; $f(x) = \sqrt{x - 5}$ denotes a function whose domain is $[5, \infty)$.

The following examples indicate the convenience and usefulness of function notation.

EXAMPLE 2

Consider the function $f(x) = 2x^2 - 5x + 3$. Find and simplify $f(4)$, $f(-2)$, $f(a)$, and $f(3 - x)$.

SOLUTION

Replacing x in the rule of correspondence for the function with the given number or expression, we get:

$$f(4) = 2(4)^2 - 5(4) + 3 = 15$$
$$f(-2) = 2(-2)^2 - 5(-2) + 3 = 21$$
$$f(a) = 2a^2 - 5a + 3$$
$$f(3 - x) = 2(3 - x)^2 - 5(3 - x) + 3$$
$$= 2(9 - 6x + x^2) - 5(3 - x) + 3$$
$$= 2x^2 - 7x + 6.$$
●

EXAMPLE 3

Consider the function $f(x) = \sqrt{3x + 10}$. Find and simplify $f(2)$, $f(1 + a)$, and $f(x + h)$.

SOLUTION

Substitution for x in the equation gives

$$f(2) = \sqrt{3(2) + 10} = 4$$
$$f(1 + a) = \sqrt{3(1 + a) + 10} = \sqrt{13 + 3a}$$
$$f(x + h) = \sqrt{3(x + h) + 10} = \sqrt{3x + 3h + 10}.$$

●

Frequently the variables that appear in a function used as a mathematical model represent quantities that are meaningful only when they are nonnegative. In such cases, the domain must be chosen so that both the independent and the dependent variables are nonnegative.

EXAMPLE 4

Let q denote the demand for some commodity and p denote the corresponding price for that commodity. If p and q are related by $p = 36 - q^2$, where q is assumed to be the independent variable, find the largest domain for which both variables will be nonnegative.

SOLUTION

To ensure that p is nonnegative, we must have

$$36 - q^2 \geq 0$$

or

$$q^2 \leq 36.$$

This inequality is satisfied for $-6 \leq q \leq 6$. Because q is required to be nonnegative, the domain must be $[0, 6]$.

●

The modeler, having created a function $y = f(x)$, may wish to alter the model to obtain a new function in which y becomes the independent variable with x depending on y. This can be done only if there is no value of y that corresponds to two values of x. If the graph of $y = f(x)$ is known, this condition is met if no horizontal line intersects the graph in more than one point. If this is the case, it may be possible to find the new function by algebraically solving for x. We give one example here, postponing further discussion of this topic until Section 1.6.

EXAMPLE 5

Let $y = (4 + x)/(3 - x)$. Obtain x as a function of y by solving for x.

SOLUTION

Multiplying by $3 - x$ gives the equation

$$y(3 - x) = 4 + x$$

or

$$3y - xy = 4 + x.$$

Rearranging the equation so that all terms with a factor of x are on the left,

$$-xy - x = 4 - 3y,$$

factoring out the $-x$,

$$-x(y + 1) = 4 - 3y,$$

and dividing by $-(y + 1)$, we get

$$x = \frac{3y - 4}{y + 1}.$$

●

Until recently many rules of correspondence could not be evaluated without the use of extensive tables or tedious calculations. Today scientific calculators perform many such evaluations and in many instances can be considered as function machines. Values of the independent variable are entered through the keypad, and the corresponding values of the dependent variable appear on the display after the appropriate function key is struck. Many examples and exercises in this text presume that the reader has a hand-held calculator and is familiar with its use. The reader is cautioned that a given function's actual domain and range will be limited by the capacity of the calculator. Consequently, a value computed for a dependent variable is often only the machine's "best approximation" to the actual value.

EXERCISES 1.1

In Exercises 1–8 use the given rule of correspondence to find $f(2), f(a), f(1 + t),$ *and* $f(x + h)$.

1. $f(x) = 7$

2. $f(x) = 2x - 5$

3. $f(x) = 5 - x + x^2$

4. $f(x) = 2x^2 + x - 6$

5. $f(x) = \dfrac{x - 2}{2x + 1}$

6. $f(x) = \dfrac{3x}{x + 1}$

7. $f(x) = \sqrt{8 - 3x}$

8. $f(x) = \sqrt{x + 7}$

In the rules of correspondence for Exercises 9–18 q *is the independent variable. If* p *and* q *must both be nonnegative, determine the domain of the function (or the possible values of* q).

9. $p = 25 - .02q$

10. $p = 420 - 3q$

11. $p = \dfrac{20}{q}$

12. $p = \dfrac{150}{2q - 5}$

13. $p = 32 - 2q^2$

14. $p = 4 - q^2$

15. $p = \dfrac{q - 8}{5 - q}$

16. $p = \dfrac{2q - 10}{q + 1}$

17. $p = \sqrt{40 - 5q}$

18. $p = \sqrt{q - 20}$

In Exercises 19–28 rearrange the rules of correspondence (if possible) so that y *is the independent variable; that is, solve for* x. *If it is not possible to solve for* x *uniquely, find two different* x-*values that correspond to the same* y-*value.*

19. $y = 15 - .01x$

20. $y = 20 + .2x$

21. $y = \dfrac{150}{x}$

22. $y = \dfrac{200}{x + 1}$

23. $y = 4 - x^2$

24. $y = 32 - 2x^2$

25. $y = \sqrt{x - 20}$

26. $y = \sqrt{12 + 3x}$

27. $y = \dfrac{2x - 10}{x + 1}$

28. $y = \dfrac{x - 8}{5 - x}$

29. The accompanying table illustrates data gathered for Frank's Diner during five recent lunch hours. The selling price of that day's special is represented by p, and the number of specials sold on that day is represented by q.

p	2.50	2.55	2.60	2.70	2.75
q	88	80	80	73	67

a. Can p be considered a function of q? If so, what are the domain and range of this function?

b. Can q be considered a function of p? If so, what are the domain and range of this function?

30. Al's Autos sells used cars and offers "no questions" financing. The data in the table show Al's annual rate of interest r and the number of cars financed q for each of six months.

r	.20	.18	.21	.18	.19	.17
q	12	23	10	25	17	24

a. Can r be considered a function of q? If so, what are the domain and range of this function?

b. Can q be considered a function of r? If so, what are the domain and range of this function?

31. The table given here is part of a "crib sheet" that is often used by merchants when calculating a 5% retail sales tax. Refer only to this table, and let S denote the amount of sale and t the sales tax.

Amount of Sale	Tax	Amount of Sale	Tax	Amount of Sale	Tax
.01– .09	.00	4.30–4.49	.22	8.70– 8.89	.44
.10– .29	.01	4.50–4.69	.23	8.90– 9.09	.45
.30– .49	.02	4.70–4.89	.24	9.10– 9.29	.46
.50– .69	.03	4.90–5.09	.25	9.30– 9.49	.47
.70– .89	.04	5.10–5.29	.26	9.50– 9.69	.48
.90–1.09	.05	5.30–5.49	.27	9.70– 9.89	.49
1.10–1.29	.06	5.50–5.69	.28	9.90–10.09	.50
1.30–1.49	.07	5.70–5.89	.29	10.10–10.29	.51
1.50–1.69	.08	5.90–6.09	.30	10.30–10.49	.52
1.70–1.89	.09	6.10–6.29	.31	10.50–10.69	.53
1.90–2.09	.10	6.30–6.49	.32	10.70–10.89	.54
2.10–2.29	.11	6.50–6.69	.33	10.90–11.09	.55
2.30–2.49	.12	6.70–6.89	.34	11.10–11.29	.56
2.50–2.69	.13	6.90–7.09	.35	11.30–11.49	.57
2.70–2.89	.14	7.10–7.29	.36	11.50–11.69	.58
2.90–3.09	.15	7.30–7.49	.37	11.70–11.89	.59
3.10–3.29	.16	7.50–7.69	.38	11.90–12.09	.60
3.30–3.49	.17	7.70–7.89	.39	12.10–12.29	.61
3.50–3.69	.18	7.90–8.09	.40	12.30–12.49	.62
3.70–3.89	.19	8.10–8.29	.41	12.50–12.69	.63
3.90–4.09	.20	8.30–8.49	.42	12.70–12.89	.64
4.10–4.29	.21	8.50–8.69	.43	12.90–13.09	.65

a. Can t be considered a function of S?

b. Can S be considered a function of t?

c. Can [.01, 13.09] be used to denote the set of all values of S that are represented in this table? Explain.

32. Let t denote the 5% tax on a sale of amount S. Assuming that S takes on all values in the interval [0, 1], sketch t as a function of S.

33. Estimate the domains and ranges of the functions with these graphs.

a.
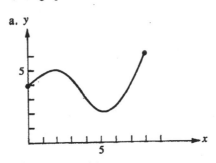

b.
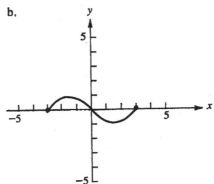

34. Could the graph given here represent a function? Why or why not?

35. Using a calculator, enter -9 and press $\boxed{\sqrt{\ }}$. What is the machine indicating about the function with rule of correspondence $y = \sqrt{x}$?

36. For the function f with rule of correspondence $f(x) = 5^x$, use a calculator with an exponentiation key $\boxed{y^x}$, to find $f(.5)$, $f(3.6)$, $f(111)$, $f(999)$, $f(-1.8)$, $f(-3.7)$, and $f(-27)$. After trying other values of x and being sympathetic with machine capabilities, what do you think the range of this function is?

1.2
Linear Functions

In this section we begin a class-by-class analysis of the elementary functions commonly used in model building. To illustrate how basic models can be developed and perhaps improved by selecting functions from the appropriate class, we will also introduce several concepts from business and economics. Starting from basic models in this section, we develop more sophisticated models of the same concepts in later sections.

The simplest functions and those most frequently used for basic models are the linear functions.

Definition 1.2

A function f is said to be a **linear** function if its rule of correspondence can be written as

$$f(x) = mx + b,$$

where m and b are constants.

If $m = 0$, the linear function f with $f(x) = b$ is called a **constant** function. When $b = 0$ and $y = f(x)$ (that is, when $y = mx$) y is said to **vary directly** with x.

The **revenue** (or income) R received by a firm from the sale of its products can often be modeled as a linear function. When the firm sells q units of a product at a price of p dollars, its revenue is $R = pq$. If the selling price p remains constant over an interval of q values, then R is a linear function of q; in particular, revenue varies directly with the number of units sold.

EXAMPLE 1

The owner of a knitting mill knows that at a price of $25 per sweater, he will be able to sell the day's output so long as that output is no more than 100 sweaters. Write the revenue for each day as a function of q, the number of sweaters available that day.

SOLUTION

At price $p = 25$, we have $R = 25q$. Technically, the domain of this function is the collection of whole numbers 0, 1, . . . , 100. Although fractional values of q are absurd for products like sweaters, for ease in analysis we will take domains to be *intervals* of *real* numbers, such as [0, 100]. Thus, we write

$$R = 25q, \qquad 0 \leq q \leq 100. \qquad \bullet$$

The **total cost** C associated with the manufacture of a product is usually divided into those costs that are **fixed** or independent of the quantity produced and those that are **variable** and depend on the quantity produced. Fixed costs typically include things like rent and heat, whereas variable costs include such things as direct labor and raw materials. Frequently C is written as a linear function of output.

EXAMPLE 2

The owner of the knitting mill in the previous example also knows that the mill can produce up to 100 sweaters each day. If fixed costs are $300 per day and variable costs are $20 per sweater, find the total cost C as a function of output q.

SOLUTION

Since the variable cost of making each sweater is $20, when q sweaters are made, these costs are $20q$. Adding the fixed cost, we have

$$C = 300 + 20q, \qquad 0 \leq q \leq 100.$$

The **profit** P earned by a firm that manufactures and sells its products is the sales revenue minus the manufacturing costs; that is, $P = R - C$. If revenue and total cost are linear functions of a quantity q, then P will also be a linear function of q. A value of q for which $P = 0$ is called a **break-even point**; at such a point the firm's revenue and total cost are equal.

EXAMPLE 3

Obtain the profit earned by the knitting mill of the previous examples as a function of q, the number of sweaters produced and sold each day. Then find the break-even point.

SOLUTION

Substituting the expressions for R and C, we have

$$P = R - C = 25q - (300 + 20q)$$
$$= 5q - 300, \qquad 0 \leq q \leq 100.$$

The break-even point occurs when $5q - 300 = 0$ or when $q = 60$. Note that at $q = 60$, both revenue and total cost are $1500.

Linear functions are so named because their graphs are straight lines. The property that distinguishes a line from graphs of other curves is that between any pair of points on a nonvertical line, the ratio of the vertical distance to the horizontal distance between these points is always the same. This ratio of vertical change to horizontal change varies between points on other curves. (See Figure 1.3.)

Figure 1.3

For a straight line the ratio of vertical change to horizontal change is constant.

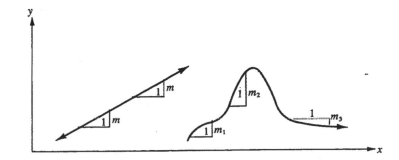

Definition 1.3

> If (x_1, y_1) and (x_2, y_2) are two distinct points on a nonvertical line, the **slope** m of the line is given by
>
> (1.1) $$m = \frac{y_2 - y_1}{x_2 - x_1}.$$

Slope is not defined for vertical lines. [For a vertical line, equation (1.1) is a ratio with 0 denominator.] Since all points on a horizontal line have the same y-coordinate, $m = 0$ for horizontal lines. When $m > 0$, the graph of the line slopes upward to the right (y increases as x increases when moving between points on the line); when $m < 0$, the line slopes downward to the right (y decreases as x increases when moving between points on the line). Figure 1.4 illustrates these cases.

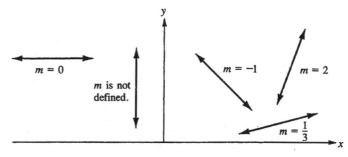

Figure 1.4

Examples of lines with various slopes

If (x_1, y_1) is a particular point on a nonvertical line, and (x, y) is any other point on that line, then from equation (1.1),

$$\frac{y - y_1}{x - x_1} = m,$$

or after multiplying through by $(x - x_1)$, we get

(1.2) $$y - y_1 = m(x - x_1).$$

Equation (1.2) is called the **point-slope form** of the equation for a nonvertical line. If the slope and the coordinates of a point on a line are known, then equation (1.2) can be used to obtain the y-coordinate for a given x-coordinate of any point on the line.

Solving equation (1.2) for y, we can write

$$y = mx + (y_1 - mx_1)$$

or more simply

(1.3) $$y = mx + b,$$

where b is the constant term $y_1 - mx_1$. Equation (1.3) is called the **slope-intercept form** of the equation of a line. Note that it explicitly identifies the slope m as well as the y-coordinate of the point $(0, b)$ at which the line intersects the y-axis. Also equation (1.3) gives y as a function of x as in Definition 1.2.

EXAMPLE 4

Find an equation of the line through the points with coordinates (1, 6) and (3, −2). Write the equation in slope-intercept form.

SOLUTION

The slope of the line through the given points is

$$m = \frac{-2 - 6}{3 - 1} = \frac{-8}{2} = -4.$$

Using $m = -4$ with the point (1, 6) in the point-slope equation (1.2), we have

$$y - 6 = -4(x - 1)$$

for any point (x, y) on the line. Solving for y, we have

$$y = -4x + 10,$$

the slope-intercept form of this line.

Note that the other point, (3, −2), could have been used to obtain the same result. ●

EXAMPLE 5

The daily cost C of producing Lustre Lamps is assumed to be a linear function of q, the number of lamps produced. Suppose it costs \$180 to produce two lamps and \$201 to produce five lamps. Find C as a function of q if it is possible to produce as many as 50 lamps per day. What are the fixed cost and variable cost per unit under these assumptions?

SOLUTION

Since q is to be the independent variable, points on the graph of the cost function take the form (q, C). From the given information, we know that (2, 180) and (5, 201) are two such points. The slope of this line is then

$$m = \frac{201 - 180}{5 - 2} = \frac{21}{3} = 7.$$

Using (2, 180) as the point (x_1, y_1) in the point-slope equation (1.2), we have

$$C - 180 = 7(q - 2)$$

for any pair (q, C). Solving for C, we obtain

(1.4)
$$C = 7q + 166, \qquad 0 \le q \le 50,$$

which gives C as a linear function of q on the domain [0, 50] (see Figure 1.5).

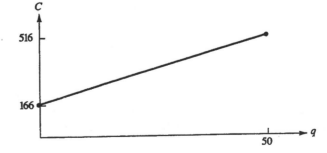

Figure 1.5
The graph of $C = 7q + 166$,
$0 \le q \le 50$

Fixed costs are the same regardless of q, so taking $q = 0$, we find that $C = 166$ is the fixed cost; that is, the constant term in a total cost function represents the fixed cost. Moreover, we can see from equation (1.4) that increasing q by one unit will cause the total cost C to rise by \$7; that is, the slope in equation (1.4) represents the variable cost per unit.   ●

EXAMPLE 6

Suppose the quantity q of a product demanded is a linear function of its selling price per unit p. If $q = 50$ when $p = 8$, and $q = 80$ when $p = 5$, and if $3 \le p \le 12$, find q as a function of p.

SOLUTION

If p is the independent variable and q is the dependent variable, then (8, 50) and (5, 80) are coordinates of points on the graph of the desired function. The slope of this line is then

$$m = \frac{80 - 50}{5 - 8} = -10.$$

From the point-slope formula we obtain

$$q - 50 = -10(p - 8)$$

or

$$q = -10p + 130, \qquad 3 \le p \le 12.$$ ●

Frequently it is convenient to write the equation of a line in **general form**; namely,

(1.5)
$$ax + by = c,$$

where a, b, and c are constants, with not both a and b equal to 0. From the general form one can solve to obtain the slope $m = -a/b$ (provided b is not 0), the x-intercept $(c/a, 0)$, and the y-intercept $(0, c/b)$. The special cases of horizontal and vertical lines occur when $a = 0$ and $b = 0$, respectively, in equation (1.5). Thus $y = c$ is a horizontal line with y-intercept $(0, c)$, and $x = c$ is a vertical line with x-intercept $(c, 0)$.

EXAMPLE 7

Find the slope, y-intercept, and x-intercept of the graph of the linear equation $2x + 3y = 12$.

SOLUTION

Solving for y, we find

$$y = -\frac{2}{3}x + 4.$$

Thus the slope is $-2/3$ and the y-intercept is (0, 4). To obtain the x-intercept, set $y = 0$ and solve to find that $x = 6$. Thus the x-intercept has coordinates (6, 0).   ●

In Example 6, we considered a **demand relationship**: the customers' demand q for a product was given as a function of the selling price p. It is usually assumed that the demand for a product will decline as its price rises; that is, if the demand function is linear, it has a negative slope. In a **supply relationship**, the sellers' willingness to provide q units of the commodity is determined by the price offered in the marketplace. Because the supply should increase with an increase in the price, a linear supply function has a positive slope. It is asserted in free market theory that there is a price p at which supply equals demand. At this value of p the market is said to be in **equilibrium** and p is called the **market-clearing price**.

EXAMPLE 8

At the Centerville Farmer's Market it has been observed that on a day when apples sell for $2.30 a peck, 10 pecks are brought to market. For each increase of $.01 in the selling price (per peck), another peck will be supplied by producers (up to a maximum of 150 pecks, when the selling price is $3.70). On the demand side, when the selling price is $4.40 per peck, 10 pecks of apples can be sold per day. For each decrease of $.02 in selling price, another peck can be sold (up to a maximum of 150 pecks, when the selling price is $1.60). Find linear supply and demand functions that give p as a function of the quantity q. Determine the market-clearing price and the corresponding value of q.

SOLUTION

For the supply relationship, we know that when $q = 10$, the price is $p = 2.30$. The observation that each rise of $.01 in p will increase the supply by 1 peck means that if p is a linear function of q, the slope of that line is .01. From the point-slope formula, the supply function is then

$$p - 2.3 = .01(q - 10)$$

or

(1.6)
$$p = 2.2 + .01q, \qquad 0 \le q \le 150.$$

In the relationship for demand, we are given that when $q = 10$, $p = 4.4$. That a $.02 decrease in the price will raise the demand by 1 peck means that if p is a linear function of q, then that line has slope $-.02$. Thus, the demand function is

$$p - 4.4 = -.02(q - 10)$$

or

(1.7)
$$p = 4.6 - .02q, \qquad 0 \le q \le 150.$$

To find the equilibrium point, the selling prices given by equations (1.6) and (1.7) must be equal. Equating these two expressions, we have

$$2.2 + .01q = 4.6 - .02q,$$

which is solved to find that $q = 80$. Substitution of this value into either the supply or the demand equation gives the market-clearing price $p = 3.0$. Graphs of equations (1.6) and (1.7) appear in Figure 1.6.

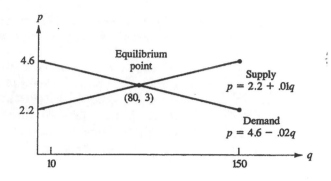

Figure 1.6
Graphs of supply and
demand functions

EXERCISES 1.2

For Exercises 1–8 find an equation (in slope-intercept form) of the line through the given point with the indicated slope. Use x and y for the independent and dependent variables, respectively.

1. $(2, 3)$, $m = \dfrac{1}{2}$ 2. $(1, 0)$, $m = 3$

3. $(-2, 5)$, $m = -3$ 4. $(5, -4)$, $m = \dfrac{2}{3}$

5. $(1, -1)$, $m = \dfrac{5}{2}$ 6. $(-3, 3)$, $m = \dfrac{9}{8}$

7. $(-6, -7)$, $m = 1$ 8. $(-2, -2)$, $m = 0$

For Exercises 9–16 find a rule of correspondence for the linear function f whose graph contains the given points.

9. $(2, 3)$ and $(-1, 0)$ 10. $(-1, 3)$ and $(4, 8)$

11. $(3, -1)$ and $(2, 3)$ 12. $(4, 7)$ and $(-1, -1)$

13. $(0, 0)$ and $(5, 10)$ 14. $(5, 0)$ and $(0, 5)$

15. $(2, 6)$ and $(5, 6)$ 16. $(3, 3)$ and $(4, 4)$

17. Find equations for the vertical and horizontal lines through the indicated point.

   a. $(2, 3)$ b. $(-1, 7)$ c. $(9, 0)$ d. $(-3, -6)$

For Exercises 18–24 sketch the graph of the given linear function.

18. $y = 2x - 5$ 19. $y = x + 3$

20. $2x + 4y = 9$ 21. $3x + y - 9 = 0$

22. $y - 3 = 5(x - 2)$ 23. $y - 1 = 2(x + 3)$

24. $y = 5$

For Exercises 25–30 find the slope m and the x- and y-intercepts of the given linear equations.

25. $2x - 3y = 6$ 26. $5x + 8y = 12$

27. $x + 2y = 16$ 28. $2x - y = 10$

29. $8y = 16$ 30. $-2x = 1$

31. A pretzel vendor sells hot pretzels for \$.80 each. On a given day the vendor may sell as many as 200 pretzels. Write daily revenue R as a function of the number of pretzels sold q.

32. The manager of a store feels that the demand function for a certain item is constant up to a level of 300 units per week (that is, the selling price p is a constant function of q). It was reported that \$948 of revenue was generated by the sale of 240 units during the previous week. Find the constant selling price and give the revenue as a function of q.

33. The vendor in Exercise 31 has daily fixed costs of \$11 and variable costs of \$.25 per pretzel. Write the total cost C as a function of the number of pretzels prepared q. Assuming that all pretzels prepared are sold, write the profit P as a function of q and find the break-even point.

34. The daily operation of a plant that produces LCD clocks entails a fixed cost of \$150. Furthermore, the production of one clock requires \$3.00 in raw materials, \$0.25 in electricity, and \$1.50 in labor. If these are the only variable

costs and the plant can produce up to 400 clocks per day, write the daily production cost C as a function of output q, with the appropriate domain.

35. Busicalc business calculators can be sold at a constant price of $30 each. Manufacturing these calculators requires fixed costs of $120 per day and variable costs of $22 per unit. Up to 40 calculators can be manufactured each day.
    a. Obtain profit P as a function of output q with a suitable domain.
    b. Determine the break-even point.
    c. If the plant is operated at capacity, what is the resulting daily profit?

36. Refer to Exercise 35. How many Busicalc calculators are manufactured on a day when total production costs are $780?

37. The weekly cost C for the manufacture of Glint Sunglasses is a linear function of the number of pairs of glasses produced q. When $q = 500$, $C = \$3050$, and when $q = 200$, $C = \$1550$. Find C in terms of q; then determine the variable cost per unit and the weekly fixed cost.

38. The daily cost C of producing Universal Umbrellas is a linear function of the number of umbrellas produced q. On a day when 80 umbrellas are produced, $C = \$1040$, and when 200 umbrellas are produced, $C = \$1280$. Find C in terms of q; then determine the variable cost per unit and the weekly fixed cost.

39. Suxion Vacuum Cleaner salespersons are paid a monthly base salary plus $50 for each cleaner they sell. During September an active seller earned $1250 by selling 15 Suxions. Determine the base salary for Suxion sellers; then write the monthly salary S as a function of the number of cleaners sold q.

40. Suppose the selling price p of a product is linearly related to the quantity demanded q. If $p = \$15$ when $q = 25$, and $p = \$10$ when $q = 100$, and if q is at least 20 but not more than 150, find p as a function of q.

41. At a farmer's market the selling price p of potatoes is thought to be a linear function of the daily demand q (in bushels). When $q = 100$, $p = \$7$, and when $q = 300$, $p = \$5$. Assuming that no more than 400 bushels are brought to market on a given day, find p in terms of q; then find q as a function of p.

42. Suppose the selling price of a product depends linearly on the quantity q supplied to market by producers. If $p = \$10$ when $q = 50$, and $p = \$20$ when $q = 150$, and if q is at least 25 but not more than 500, find p as a function of q.

43. An accountant has been asked to determine the fixed and variable costs that are incurred for the manufacture of an item. Checking total cost C and output q on two different days, the accountant finds that $C = \$331$ when $q = 22$, and $C = \$360$ when $q = 24$. What are the daily fixed cost and variable cost per unit, assuming that C is a linear function of q?

44. Suppose the value of a piece of equipment depreciates each year by 20% of its original value. If a new machine is worth $25,000, give its value V as a function of its age t (in years) for $0 \le t \le 5$. This method of determining the decreasing value of capital equipment if called **straight-line depreciation**. What are the slope and V-intercept of the graph of this linear function?

45. In a simple interest transaction, where interest is earned at annual rate r, t years after an initial investment of P dollars the investment has value $V = P + Prt$.
    a. Show that V is a linear function of t by giving the slope and V-intercept of the graph of this function.
    b. If $r = .12$ and $P = 500$, find V in terms of t.
    c. Compute the value of the investment in part b after 4 yr. After 7 yr.

46. Let
$$p = 10 + .5q, \qquad 20 \le q \le 100$$
    and
$$p = 40 - .25q, \qquad 20 \le q \le 100$$
    be the supply and demand equations, respectively, for a certain commodity. Determine the equilibrium value of q and the market-clearing price p.

47. The supply function for a certain commodity is given by
$$p = 1.50 + .03q, \qquad 30 \le q \le 200.$$
    It is also estimated that revenue R varies directly with q according to the equation
$$R = 6q, \qquad 30 \le q \le 200.$$
    Determine the equilibrium value of q and the market-clearing price p.

48. When leather belts sell for $4.00 at the Reynosa Market, handicrafters offer 200 belts for sale each day. For each increase of $.10 in the selling price, another 5 belts are supplied to the market (up to 500 belts). When belts sell for $10.00 each, 100 people will buy them each day. For each decrease of $.30 in the selling price, another 10 are

sold. Find the equilibrium value of q and the market-clearing price p.

49. When sunflower seeds sell for $8 per bushel at the Centerville Farmer's Market, 22 bushels (per day) are brought by producers. Each increase of $.05 in the selling price brings another bushel to market (up to 200 bushels). When sunflower seeds sell for $13 per bushel, consumers will buy 10 bushels per day. For each drop of $.02 in the selling price, another bushel is sold. Find the equilibrium value of q and the market-clearing price p.

1.3
Quadratic Functions

Models involving **quadratic functions**, those whose rule of correspondence takes the form

(1.8) $$y = ax^2 + bx + c,$$

where a, b, and c are constants with $a \neq 0$, often arise through the refinement of linear models. We consider two examples where this occurs, review properties of quadratic functions, and then use these properties to analyze the refined quadratic models.

EXAMPLE 1

In the linear cost function

$$C = 90 + 10q, \qquad 0 \leq q \leq 150,$$

fixed costs are $90, while the variable cost per unit is constantly $10. After considering the savings that result from mass production, bulk ordering of raw materials, and similar factors, the variable cost per unit v is found to decline from about $10 at $q = 0$, to $7 at $q = 150$. Assuming v is a linear function of q, find the revised cost function.

SOLUTION

Since v is a linear function of q, we use the pairs (0, 10) and (150, 7) with the point-slope form of the equation of a line to find

$$v = 10 - .02q, \qquad 0 \leq q \leq 150.$$

Replacing $v = 10$ by $v = 10 - .02q$ in the preceding cost function, we get the revised function

$$C = 90 + (10 - .02q)q$$

or

$$C = 90 + 10q - .02q^2, \qquad 0 \leq q \leq 150. \qquad \bullet$$

EXAMPLE 2

In the linear revenue function

$$R = 15q, \qquad 0 \leq q \leq 150,$$

the selling price is taken to be $15 regardless of the quantity sold. Under these circumstances, the demand function is constant: $p = 15$ for all q. Upon more careful analysis we find that when q is near 0, $p = 15$, but $p = 6$ when $q = 150$. Assuming p is a linear function of q, find the revised revenue function.

SOLUTION

Once again we apply the point-slope formula to the pairs (0, 15) and (150, 6) to obtain

$$p = 15 - .06q, \qquad 0 \le q \le 150,$$

as a demand function. Revising the revenue function by replacing $p = 15$ with $p = 15 - .06q$ yields

$$R = (15 - .06q)q$$

or

$$R = 15q - .06q^2, \qquad 0 \le q \le 150. \qquad \bullet$$

In both examples above, linear models were refined by replacing the slope, which is constant, with a quantity that varies as a linear function of the independent variable. This refinement of the model gives rise to a term involving the square of the independent variable.

For linear functions the rule of correspondence $y = mx + b$ contains two constants, the slope and the y-intercept, that completely determine its graph. For quadratic functions where $y = ax^2 + bx + c$, there are three coefficients a, b, and c, each of which plays a part in determining the graph. The following examples illustrate the effect each coefficient has on the graph of a quadratic function.

EXAMPLE 3

Sketch the graph of $y = x^2$; then generalize to the graph of $y = ax^2$ for any nonzero a.

SOLUTION

Here we are dealing with the special case of equation (1.8) where $b = c = 0$. First for the case $a = 1$, several x-y pairs are given in Table 1.2. We draw the graph

Table 1.2

x	0	1/2	1	2	3	-3	-2	-1	$-1/2$
y	0	1/4	1	4	9	9	4	1	1/4

of $y = x^2$ in Figure 1.7 by plotting the points in Table 1.2 and sketching between them after observing the following:

1. $y \ge 0$ for all x, since $y = x^2$ and $x^2 \ge 0$.
2. The same range value y is assigned to x and $-x$, since $x^2 = (-x)^2$.
3. As we move from left to right the curve moves "downhill" when x is negative and "uphill" when x is positive, with a turning point at (0, 0).

The graph obtained in Figure 1.7 is called a **parabola** and the turning point is its **vertex**.

To realize the effect of changing from the special case of $a = 1$ to other values of a, consider recomputing the range values in Table 1.2. All y values would be multiplied by a. As illustrated in Figure 1.8, if a is positive, the curve becomes steeper when $a > 1$ and flatter when $a < 1$. If a is negative, all y values become negative [except at the point (0, 0)] and the curve opens downward rather than

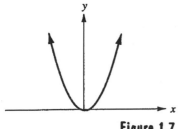

Figure 1.7

The graph of $y = x^2$

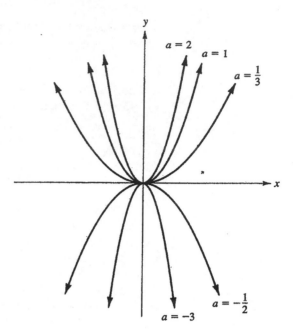

Figure 1.8

The graph of $y = ax^2$
for several values of a

upward. The vertex is not altered when a is changed; only the shape (or "spread")
of the curve is affected.   ●

EXAMPLE 4

Find the rule of correspondence for a function whose graph has the same shape
as $y = ax^2$ with every point on the graph shifted h units horizontally and k units
vertically.

SOLUTION

Geometrically, horizontal and vertical shifts are called translations. Figure 1.9
illustrates a translation of $y = ax^2$, where a, h, and k are positive. We see that the
vertex of the translated parabola is (h, k). Also, if (x_1, y_1) is a point on the translated
graph, the corresponding point on $y = ax^2$ is $(x_1 - h, y_1 - k)$ and so

$$(y_1 - k) = a(x_1 - h)^2 \quad \text{or} \quad y_1 = a(x_1 - h)^2 + k.$$

Thus, for any point (x, y) on the translated graph, we have

(1.9) $$y = a(x - h)^2 + k.$$

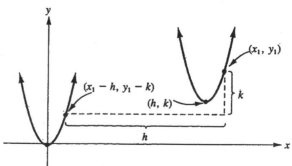

Figure 1.9

The graph of $y = ax^2$ and a
translation

That is, the graph of the quadratic function given in equation (1.9) is a parabola with the same shape as $y = ax^2$ but translated h units horizontally and k units vertically. ●

Equation (1.9) may be used to show that the graph of any quadratic function is a parabola. When the rule of correspondence is given in the standard form of equation (1.8), the vertex may be determined by first converting to the translated form of equation (1.9). This is a tedious process if it must be performed over and over again. The efficient approach is to remember that h is the x-coordinate of the vertex and then find h in terms of the given coefficients a, b, and c. A little algebra is all that is required. From

$$y = a(x - h)^2 + k,$$

we have

$$y = a(x^2 - 2hx + h^2) + k,$$

and so, collecting like terms, we get

$$y = ax^2 - 2ahx + (ah^2 + k).$$

Upon comparison to $y = ax^2 + bx + c$, we find that if both equations (1.8) and (1.9) represent the same function, the coefficients are equal, or

$$-2ah = b \quad \text{and} \quad ah^2 + k = c.$$

Solving the first condition for h yields

(1.10)
$$h = \frac{-b}{2a},$$

the x-coordinate of the vertex. This value of h may be used in the second condition, $ah^2 + k = c$, to solve for k, the y-coordinate of the vertex. Rather than remembering two formulas, it is easier to find the y-coordinate by evaluating $f(x) = ax^2 + bx + c$ at the x-coordinate of the vertex; that is,

$$k = f\left(\frac{-b}{2a}\right).$$

EXAMPLE 5

Sketch the graphs after finding the vertices.

a. $y = x^2 + 2x + 7$

b. $y = -2x^2 + x + 1$

If the domain of each of these quadratic functions is all real numbers, use the graphs to determine the respective ranges.

SOLUTION

a. Using equation (1.10), we find that

$$h = \frac{-b}{2a} = \frac{-2}{2} = -1.$$

When $x = -1$,

$$y = (-1)^2 + 2(-1) + 7 = 6,$$

so the vertex has coordinates $(-1, 6)$. The shape of the graph is the same as that of $y = x^2$. (See Figure 1.10.) Since the parabola opens upward and $y = 6$ at the vertex, the range of this function is all numbers greater than or equal to 6—that is, the interval $[6, \infty)$.

b. From equation (1.10) we find that

$$h = \frac{-b}{2a} = \frac{-1}{-4} = \frac{1}{4},$$

and then

$$y = -2\left(\frac{1}{4}\right)^2 + \frac{1}{4} + 1 = \frac{9}{8},$$

so the vertex has coordinates $(1/4, 9/8)$ and the shape of the graph is the same as that of $y = -2x^2$. (See Figure 1.11.) Since the parabola opens downward and $y = 9/8$ at the vertex, the range of this function is $(-\infty, 9/8]$.

Figure 1.10
The graph of $y = x^2 + 2x + 7$

Figure 1.11
The graph of $y = -2x^2 + x + 1$

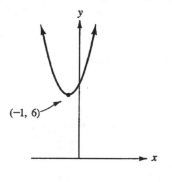

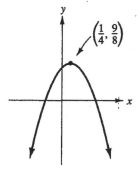

EXAMPLE 6

For the revenue function of Example 2,

$$R = 15q - .06q^2, \qquad 0 \le q \le 150,$$

find the vertex and sketch the graph. What is the maximum revenue for this model, and at what output level does it occur?

SOLUTION

R is of the form $aq^2 + bq + c$ with $a = -.06$, $b = 15$, and $c = 0$. Now from equation (1.10) we know that the q-coordinate of the vertex is $-b/(2a) = -15/(-.12) = 125$. Also, $R(125) = 15(125) - .06(125)^2 = 937.5$. To sketch the curve we plot the points $R(0) = 0$ and $R(150) = 900$ with the vertex, and remember that the parabola opens downward, since $a = -.06$. Because this parabola opens downward, the maximum range value occurs at the vertex. Here revenue attains a maximum value of $937.50 when $q = 125$ units are produced and sold. The graph appears in Figure 1.12.

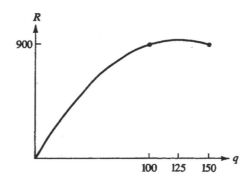

Figure 1.12

The graph of the parabola $R = 15q - .06q^2$, for $0 \le q \le 150$

The y-intercept of the graph of equation (1.8) ($y = ax^2 + bx + c$) is merely $(0, c)$. To find the x-intercepts we must find those values of x for which $y = 0$; that is, we must find solutions to the quadratic equation

(1.11)
$$ax^2 + bx + c = 0.$$

When equation (1.11) is not easily factored, the quadratic formula (see Appendix A.6) may be used to find these intercepts. If $b^2 - 4ac > 0$, the graph of equation (1.8) has x-intercepts that are given by

(1.12)
$$x = \frac{-b \pm \sqrt{b^2 - 4ac}}{2a}.$$

EXAMPLE 7

Using the cost and revenue functions of Examples 1 and 2, form the associated profit function. Find the output level that maximizes profit and the maximum profit. Find the break-even points and sketch the graph.

SOLUTION

Since profit equals revenue minus cost, we have
$$P = R - C = (15q - .06q^2) - (90 + 10q - .02q^2)$$
or
$$P = -90 + 5q - .04q^2, \qquad 0 \le q \le 150.$$

P is a quadratic function of q, and the graph of P opens downward because $a = -.04$. Thus, P is maximized at $q = -5/2(-.04) = 62.5$. Assuming that half units can be produced, we have
$$P(62.5) = -90 + 5(62.5) - .04(62.5)^2 = \$66.25$$

for the maximum profit; that is, $(62.5, 66.25)$ is the vertex of the graph of P. If half units cannot be produced, producing 62 or 63 units both yield a profit of $66.24.

To find the break-even points, we must find q so that $P = 0$; that is, the equation

$$0 = -90 + 5q - .04q^2$$

must be solved. Applying the quadratic formula,

$$q = \frac{-5 \pm \sqrt{10.6}}{-.08}$$

so $P = 0$ at approximately $q = 21.8$ or $q = 103.2$. Figure 1.13 shows the graph of P as a function of q.

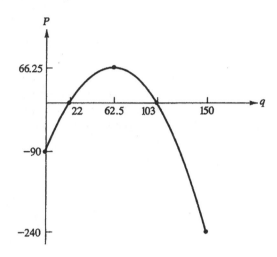

Figure 1.13
The graph of the function
$P = -90 + 5q - .04q^2$,
$0 \le q \le 150$

EXERCISES 1.3

For Exercises 1–14 sketch the graph of the given quadratic function after finding the vertex.

1. $y = 4x^2$

2. $y = \frac{1}{3}x^2$

3. $y = -\frac{1}{10}x^2$

4. $y = -x^2$

5. $y = 3x^2 - 12$

6. $y = -2x^2 + 7x - 5$

7. $y = -x^2 + 9$

8. $y = -3x^2 + 6x + 24$

9. $y = x^2 + 2x - 8$

10. $y = x^2 + 6x + 9$

11. $y = 3x^2 - 18x + 4$

12. $y = x^2 - 6x + 9$

13. $y = x^2 + x + 1$

14. $y = -5x^2 + 4x - 1$

In Exercises 15–20 find the rule of correspondence for a quadratic function whose graph has the indicated features. Write the rule in standard form.

15. Vertex at $(0, 2)$; the same shape as $y = 3x^2$

16. Vertex at $(2, 0)$; the same shape as $y = 3x^2$

17. Vertex at $(1, 4)$; the same shape as $y = -x^2$

18. x-intercepts at $(-3, 0)$ and $(1, 0)$; the same shape as $y = x^2$

19. x-intercepts at $(2, 0)$ and $(6, 0)$; the same shape as $y = 5x^2$

20. x-intercepts at $(7/2, 0)$ and $(5, 0)$; the same shape as $y = -3x^2$

21. Eastern Ceramics produces up to 200 flower pots per day with daily fixed costs of $375. On a day when q pots are produced, the variable cost per pot v is

$$v = 4 - .01q.$$

Write the total daily production cost C as a function of output q. Sketch a graph of this function.

22. At a manufacturing plant it is known that the fixed costs are $200 per week. Additionally, the variable cost per unit is estimated to be $25 - .005q$ dollars per unit when q units are being produced each week. Maximum output is 800 units per week. Obtain the total weekly production cost as a function of output q. Sketch a graph of this function.

23. Eastern Ceramics can sell up to 200 of its flower pots per day in accordance with the demand function

$$p = 13 - .04q.$$

Write revenue R as a function of the quantity sold q. Find the output level q that maximizes R and the selling price at this output level.

24. The weekly output of a manufacturing plant q can be sold for price p per unit, where

$$p = 26.60 - .007q.$$

Write revenue R as a function of the quantity sold q. Find the output level q that maximizes R and the selling price at this output level.

25. Refer to Exercises 21 and 23. Find the daily profit P in terms of the number of flower pots q made and sold by Eastern Ceramics. Determine the output level that maximizes profit and the maximum profit. Find the break-even points and then sketch a graph of this function.

26. Find the weekly profit P in terms of output q for the manufacturer in Exercises 22 and 24. Determine the output level that maximizes profit and the maximum profit. Find the break-even points and then sketch the graph of this function.

27. The daily demand q (in gallons) for bulk ice cream at Riverdale Dairy is a linear function of the selling price p. When $p = 6.30$, $q = 70$, and when $p = 6.00$, $q = 100$. Assume q is never less than 50 and never more than 400 gal.

a. Find p in terms of q (slope-intercept form).

b. Find revenue R as a function of q.

c. Determine the value of q at which revenue is maximized. What are the maximum revenue and the corresponding value of p?

28. The monthly demand q for Terri's Ties is thought to be a linear function of the selling price p. When $p = \$6$, $q = 120$, and when $p = \$8$, $q = 80$. Assume q is never less than 40 and never more than 180 ties.

a. Find p in terms of q (slope-intercept form).

b. Find revenue R as a function of q.

c. Determine the value of q at which revenue is maximized. What are the maximum revenue and the corresponding value of p?

29. Fixed costs for the production of ice cream at Riverdale Dairy are $100 per day, and the variable cost per gallon v is a linear function of the gallons produced q. When $q = 200$, $v = \$3.30$, and when $q = 80$, $v = \$3.90$. Assume $50 \le q \le 400$.

a. Find v in terms of q (slope-intercept form).

b. Find total cost C as a function of q.

30. Fixed costs for the manufacture of Terri's Ties are $200 per month, while the variable cost per tie v is thought to be a linear function of the number of ties produced q. When $q = 100$, $v = \$2$, and when $q = 60$, $v = \$2.40$. We know that $40 \le q \le 180$.

a. Find v in terms of q (slope-intercept form).

b. Find total cost C as a function of q.

31. Referring to Exercises 27 and 29, write the daily profit P for Riverdale Dairy's ice cream as a function of the gallons produced and sold q. Determine the output level that maximizes profit and the maximum profit.

32. Referring to Exercises 28 and 30, write the monthly profit P for Terri's Ties as a function of the number of ties made and sold q. Determine the output level that maximizes profit and the maximum profit.

33. An Illinois farmer will plant from 800 to 2000 acres of soybeans. The number of acres q that he will plant depends on the selling price per bushel p that is being paid in April. Suppose that if $p = \$10$, then all 2000 acres will be planted, but if $p = \$6.25$, then only 800 acres will be planted.

a. Assuming p and q are linearly related, find q as a function of p, giving a suitable domain.

b. Find the farmer's revenue as a function of p, assuming that each acre planted will produce 40 bushels of soybeans.

c. What are the maximum and minimum revenues the farmer could earn from soybeans?

34. It is known that the total cost C for producing q units of a product each day can be written as

$$C = 75 + 22q - .08q^2, \qquad 0 \le q \le 120.$$

a. Find the fixed cost and the variable cost per unit.

b. Show that the value of q that maximizes C for any $q > 0$ is not in the domain of this function. (Consequently, the cost increases with q on the interval $[0, 120]$.)

c. Sketch the graph of this function.

35. Thirty-two oil wells, each producing an average of 400 barrels of oil per day, are being operated in a Wyoming oil field. It is estimated that for each new well drilled in this field, average production per well will decrease by 8 barrels per day for each well. If n denotes the number of new wells drilled and T represents the total daily output of the field, write T as a function of n. Determine a suitable domain for this quadratic function.

36. Hawaiian Tours offers a large group excursion to the islands for 100 to 200 persons. If the group consists of 100 persons, the rate is $1200 per person. For each person beyond 100 in the group, the fee is decreased by $5. Write the total revenue R as a function of the group size n; then find a suitable domain for this function.

37. What is the range of the function $f(x) = a(x - h)^2 + k$ when $a > 0$? When $a < 0$?

38. In equation (1.10) we found that $h = -b/(2a)$ is the x-coordinate of the vertex of the graph of $y = ax^2 + bx + c$. Use this value of h to solve $ah^2 + k = c$ for k, the y-coordinate of the vertex:

39. Observe that if a and k are positive, then $y = a(x - h)^2 + k$ must also be positive; that is, the graph of this parabola is entirely above the x-axis and so has no x-intercepts. Show that $b^2 - 4ac < 0$ when $a > 0$ and $k > 0$.

40. For the special case $y = ax^2 + c$ [that is, when $b = 0$ in equation (1.8)], what are the coordinates of the vertex of the graph? What is the range of the function?

41. If the graph of $y = ax^2 + bx + c$ has vertex $(2, 1)$ and contains the point $(-2, 5)$, determine a, b, and c.

42. If the graph of $y = ax^2 + bx + c$ has vertex $(-1, 3)$ and contains the point $(3, 6)$, determine a, b, and c.

43. The **sum-of-the-digits method** models the depreciation of a piece of equipment as a quadratic function of its age. If the value V declines to 0 in n years, then the graph of V as a function of time t is a parabola (which opens upward) that contains the points $(0, V_0)$, $(n, 0)$, and $(n + 1, 0)$, where V_0 denotes the original value of the equipment. If $V_0 = \$15,000$ and $n = 5$, find $V(t)$, the value of the machine for $0 \le t \le 5$.

1.4
General Polynomial Functions

In this section we briefly consider the fine tuning of existing models in a manner that produces polynomials of degree greater than 2. We find that further refinement in this direction yields functions with characteristics, often complications, that limit their general use as models.

Definition 1.4

A polynomial function f is a function with the rule of correspondence

(1.13) $f(x) = a_n x^n + a_{n-1} x^{n-1} + \cdots + a_1 x + a_0, \qquad$ for all x,

where n is a whole number, called the **degree** of the polynomial, and $a_n, a_{n-1}, \ldots, a_1, a_0$ are constants called **coefficients,** with $a_n \ne 0$.

For example:

$$f(x) = 2x^3 - 4x^2 + 5x - 7,$$
$$g(x) = -x^4 + x^2 - 7x + 2,$$

and
$$h(x) = 7x^5 - x^3 + 15x^2 + 9$$

are rules of correspondence for polynomial functions of degrees 3, 4, and 5, respectively. Third-degree polynomial functions are often called "cubic," fourth-degree polynomials are termed "quartic," and fifth-degree "quintic."

The general form of equation (1.13) could have been used for quadratic, linear, or even constant functions because these functions are polynomials of degree 2, 1, and 0, respectively. Using equation (1.13), we would write

$$y = a_2x^2 + a_1x + a_0 \quad \text{instead of} \quad y = ax^2 + bx + c,$$
$$y = a_1x + a_0 \quad\quad\quad \text{instead of} \quad y = mx + b,$$
and $\quad\quad y = a_0 \quad\quad\quad\quad\quad \text{instead of} \quad y = k.$

Usually, however, subscripts on the coefficients are avoided for polynomial functions of degree 3 or less.

EXAMPLE 1

Returning again to the cost functions considered in Example 1 in Section 1.3, we recall that the variable cost per unit v in the first case was $v = 10$, and in the second case $v = 10 - .02q$, for $0 \le q \le 150$. In the latter case v decreases as q increases. This decrease is constant as indicated by the $-.02$ slope. At some output level, the rate of decrease should taper off, and perhaps v should even begin to increase as plant capacity is approached. Keeping the same domain, [0, 150], suppose variable cost per unit is found to "bottom out" at $q = 100$, where $v = 8$. If v is assumed to be a quadratic function of q and $v = 10$ when $q = 0$, find the rule of correspondence for v, sketch its graph, and find the resulting total cost function.

SOLUTION

(1.14)

If v is a quadratic function of q with vertex (100, 8), then using techniques from the previous section, we find

$$v = a(q - 100)^2 + 8.$$

To find a, we use the fact that $v = 10$ when $q = 0$:

$$10 = a(-100)^2 + 8,$$

and thus $a = .0002$. Substituting for a in equation (1.14), we have

$$v = .0002(q - 100)^2 + 8$$

or

$$v = .0002q^2 - .04q + 10, \quad 0 \le q \le 150.$$

The graph of this function together with the original linear function $v = 10 - .02q$ appears in Figure 1.14. The resulting total cost function is

$$C = 90 + (.0002q^2 - .04q + 10)q,$$

so

$$C = .0002q^3 - .04q^2 + 10q + 90, \quad 0 \le q \le 150.$$

Cubic polynomial functions are commonly used to model total cost.

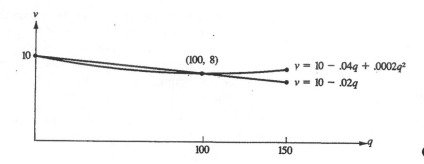

Figure 1.14

Comparison of the variable cost functions $v = 10 - .04q + .0002q^2$ and $v = 10 - .02q$, for $0 \le q \le 150$

After studying calculus we will be able to determine the important points to plot (like the vertex of a parabola) when sketching the graph of a polynomial function of degree 3 or more. Now it is worthwhile to consider an efficient scheme for computing the range values of polynomial functions.

Reading the rule of correspondence

(1.15)
$$y = ax^3 + bx^2 + cx + d$$

literally, it appears that to obtain y from a given value of x we must form x^3 and x^2, multiply them by a and b, respectively, and then form the product cx and sum the three products ax^3, bx^2, and cx with d. This process may be streamlined by considering the "nested" form of equation (1.15); namely,

(1.16)
$$y = [(ax + b)x + c]x + d.$$

Certainly if (1.16) is expanded from the innermost parentheses outward, equation (1.15) is obtained. Furthermore, if for a given value of x we evaluate from the innermost parentheses outward, the corresponding y value is obtained using only three multiplications and three additions. As an illustration suppose we evaluate

$$C = [(.0002q - .04)q + 10]q + 90$$

at $q = 150$. Working through one pair of parentheses at a time, we get:

1. $.0002(150) - .04 = -.01$
2. $-.01(150) + 10 = 8.5$
3. $8.5(150) + 90 = 1365$

Here line 1 is the value of $(.0002q - .04)$, line 2 is the value of $(.0002q - .04)q + 10$, and finally line 3 is the value of C when $q = 150$.

		Enter	150	STO	150	
Line 1	$\times$		.0002	$=$	.03	
	$-$		.04	$=$	$-.01$	Values
Line 2	$\times$		RCL	$=$	-1.5	appearing in calculator
	$+$		10	$=$	8.5	display
Line 3	$\times$		RCL	$=$	1275	
	$+$		90	$=$	1365	

Figure 1.15

Algebraic calculator evaluation of $C(150)$

This nested evaluation procedure is tailor-made for a hand calculator with memory. Suppose (STO) and (RCL) denote store and recall; then the sequence of steps in Figure 1.15 may be used to obtain $C(150)$.

As a final evaluation example suppose we seek $C(85)$. Using nested evaluation and a hand calculator, we have the sequence of steps shown in Figure 1.16. Note that $C(85) = 773.825$.

Enter	85	(STO)	85
×	.0002	=	.017
−	.04	=	−.023
×	(RCL)	=	−1.955
+	10	=	8.045
×	(RCL)	=	683.825
+	90	=	773.825

Figure 1.16

Algebraic calculator evaluation of $C(85)$ where $C(q) = .0002q^3 - .04q^2 + 10q + 90$

The nested evaluation procedure could be used on quadratic functions and should be used when evaluating polynomials of degree 3 or more. For the general nth-degree polynomial of equation (1.13), with any given x, the scheme amounts to: multiply a_n by x, add a_{n-1}; multiply by x, add a_{n-2}; ...; multiply by x, add a_0.

By considering further refinements of quadratic and cubic models, we can see how fourth- and higher-degree polynomial functions can be obtained. When the domain of a function is extended, higher-degree polynomials can be used to increase the usefulness of earlier functions by keeping the curve relatively "flat" over longer intervals. However, no polynomial of positive degree can remain "flat" as the domain is extended again and again. Eventually the term with the highest exponent will dominate all other terms. Ultimately, for larger and larger domain values, range values will grow (or decline) beyond any bound.

As an illustration, suppose the domain of the cost function in Example 1 is extended from [0, 150] to [0, 300]. For the earlier variable cost function

$$v = 10 - .02q,$$

v decreased from 10 to 7 as q moved from 0 to 150. Now as q moves to 300, v drops to 4. The term $-.02q$ is starting to dominate. Likewise, for the refined variable cost function

$$v = 10 - .04q + .0002q^2,$$

v decreases from 10 to 8 as q moves from 0 to 100. Then the term $.0002q^2$ begins to take over as v increases with q: $v(150) = 8.5$ and $v(300) = 16$. Now, if data indicated that $v(300)$ should be nearly 8, we could add the term $-.0000003q^3$ to obtain

(1.17)
$$v = 10 - .04q + .0002q^2 - .0000003q^3,$$

which would result in $v(300) = 7.9$. Clearly the new term $-.0000003q^3$ has an insignificant effect on v for small values of q. However for large values of q, this term becomes dominant and will eventually make v negative. [Check $v(10,000)$.]

There is a side effect associated with tacking on new terms, with opposite signs and higher powers of the independent variable, to control the size of v. Turning points may be introduced into the graph of the function. Note that as q increases from 0 in equation (1.17), the value of v decreases, then increases, then decreases again. It is unlikely that this "roly-poly" nature reflects reality in a variable cost function.

The graphs of a few polynomial functions are given in Figure 1.17 to illustrate the "roly-poly" and unbounded behavior of polynomial functions of degree 3 or higher. Sketching techniques that can be used to obtain these graphs will be treated in Chapter 5.

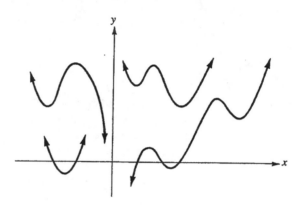

Figure 1.17
Graphs of a few polynomial functions

EXERCISES 1.4

In Exercises 1–8 use the nested evaluation procedure illustrated in equation (1.16) to evaluate each of the given rules of correspondence at the indicated domain values.

1. $f(x) = 3x^3 - 5x^2 + 6x - 2$; $x = 12$, $x = -8$

2. $g(x) = 2x^3 + x^2 - 3x - 5$; $x = 4$, $x = -5$

3. $f(x) = -x^3 + 8x^2 - .5x + 3$; $x = 7$, $x = 9.3$

4. $h(x) = -4x^3 - 3x + 7$; $x = -3$, $x = 8$

5. $f(x) = 2x^4 + 5x^3 - 7x^2 + 3x - 10$; $x = -15$, $x = 4.5$

6. $g(x) = -x^4 + 2x^3 - 4x^2 + x + 5$; $x = 6$, $x = -8$

7. $h(x) = x^5 + 2x^4 - 2x^2 + 3$; $x = 5$, $x = -10$

8. $f(x) = 2x^5 - 3x^3 + x - 12$; $x = -9$, $x = 7$

In Exercises 9–14 find the total cost function with the given fixed costs k, if variable cost per unit v is assumed to be a quadratic function with the given vertex and v-intercept on the indicated interval.

9. $k = 90$; v has vertex (100, 8) and v-intercept (0, 12) on [0, 150].

10. $k = 100$; v has vertex (200, 10) and v-intercept (0, 20) on [0, 300].

11. $k = 200$; v has vertex (50, 20) and v-intercept (0, 25) on [0, 80].

12. $k = 250$; v has vertex (250, 20) and v-intercept (0, 30) on [0, 300].

13. $k = 500$; v has vertex (100, 40) and v-intercept (0, 50) on [0, 120].

14. $k = 400$; v has vertex (80, 10) and v-intercept (0, 20) on [0, 100].

15. The Advantage Tennis racquet factory has a maximum production capacity of 500 racquets per day. It is known that the variable cost per racquet is about $30 when the output is near 0 and that the factory is most efficient when the output is 400 racquets a day. At the latter level, the variable cost is $20 per racquet, the minimum possible.

   a. Obtain the variable cost per racquet v as a quadratic function of the output level q.

   b. Find the variable cost when the factory is producing 100 units, 200 units, 300 units, and 500 units per day.

16. Refer to Exercise 15.

   a. Assuming that fixed costs are $250 per day, obtain the total cost C of a day's operation as a function of output q.

   b. Evaluate $C(0)$, $C(100)$, $C(200)$, $C(300)$, and $C(500)$.

   c. Explain why total cost increases as the output increases, even though the variable cost (per unit) is decreasing.

17. Your company has the capacity of making up to 60 units of its product each day. A consultant to your company says that you can estimate the total cost C of a day's production q from the formula

$$C = 125 + 5q - .03q^2 - .001q^3, \qquad 0 \le q \le 60.$$

   a. Obtain the fixed cost and variable cost per unit.

   b. Why should you decide that this model is unrealistic? (*Hint:* What happens to v when q nears 60?)

18. Show that if price p is a quadratic function of demand q, then revenue R is a cubic function of q. Specifically, find R

as a function of q when the demand equation is

$$p = 80 - .4q - .003q^2, \qquad 0 \le q \le 100.$$

19. At a price of $100, there is no demand for Advantage Tennis racquets. At a price of $50 per racquet, which is the minimum price that Advantage will accept, 500 racquets can be sold.

   a. Find the demand q as a quadratic function of price p with the vertex at $(100, 0)$.

   b. Find the price p as a quadratic function of demand q with the vertex at $(500, 50)$.

   c. Use the result from part b to find revenue R as a cubic function of q.

   d. Use the result from part a to find revenue R as a cubic function of p.

20. Refer to Exercises 16 and 19 and use the cost and revenue functions to form a profit function for Advantage Racquets. Assume all racquets produced are sold, and write profit P as a function of output q.

21. a. Evaluate $f_1(x) = x$, $f_2(x) = x^2$, $f_3(x) = x^3$, and $f_4(x) = x^4$ for $x = 0, .2, .4, .6, .8$, and 1.

   b. Plot the points in part a on the same axes and use them to sketch the graph of each function on the interval $[0, 1]$.

22. a. Evaluate $f_1(x) = x$, $f_2(x) = x^2$, $f_3(x) = x^3$, and $f_4(x) = x^4$ for $x = 1, 1.2, 1.4, 1.6, 1.8$, and 2.

   b. Use the data in part a to extend the graphs from Exercise 21, part b, to the interval $[0, 2]$.

1.5
Rational Functions

The rules of correspondence for polynomial functions involve only the algebraic operations of addition, subtraction, and multiplication. By including the operation of division, we obtain a new class of functions with properties that polynomials do not have. A simple rule of correspondence involving division is that of **inverse variation:**

(1.18)
$$y = \frac{k}{x} \qquad \text{for } x \ne 0,$$

where k is a nonzero constant, called the constant of variation.

EXAMPLE 1

Sketch the graph of $y = 1/x$, where $x \ne 0$, and then generalize to $y = k/x$ for any nonzero constant k.

SOLUTION

To investigate the behavior of $y = 1/x$, a few range values are calculated in Table 1.3. The pairs (x, y) in this table are plotted in Figure 1.18, and the graph of $y = 1/x$ is sketched. We see that y and x are reciprocals, so the following are true for positive x:

1. As x increases, y decreases toward 0 without ever reaching 0; the graph decays toward the x-axis.

2. As x decreases toward 0, y increases beyond any fixed number, no matter how large; the graph "blows up" as it nears the y-axis.

Also, if y is the reciprocal of x, then $-y$ is the reciprocal of $-x$, so the "branch" of the graph in the third quadrant has the same shape as the "branch" in the first quadrant.

Table 1.3

x	1/2	1	2	5	-5	-2	-1	$-1/2$
y	2	1	1/2	1/5	$-1/5$	$-1/2$	-1	-2

The graph obtained in Figure 1.18 is called a **hyperbola**. The behavior described in statements 1 and 2 is summarized by saying that the x-axis is a **horizontal asymptote** and the y-axis is a **vertical asymptote** of the hyperbola.

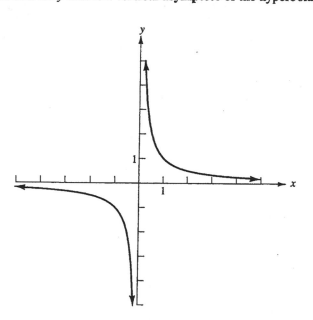

Figure 1.18
The graph of $y = 1/x$

For the more general case $y = k/x$, range values are just k times those in Table 1.3. When $k > 1$ the curve is "steeper" than $y = 1/x$; when $0 < k < 1$ it is "flatter." If $k < 0$ the two branches of the hyperbola appear in quadrants II and IV. Figures 1.19 and 1.20 illustrate the two cases of positive and negative k.

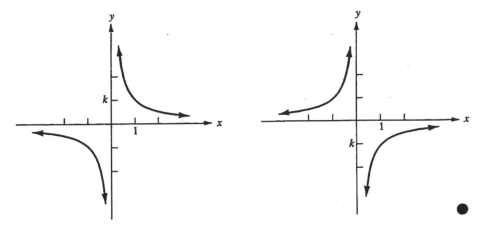

Figure 1.19
The graph of $y = k/x$ for $k > 0$

Figure 1.20
The graph of $y = k/x$ for $k < 0$

The "asymptotic" behavior of a hyperbola, the bending to approach its asymptotes, makes it very useful in modeling. The next example models the demand for a product with a function whose graph is a hyperbola.

EXAMPLE 2

The Hamilton Mint is a company that makes medals and metal figurines in limited editions for sale to collectors. To commemorate the 95th running of the Boston Marathon in 1991 it intends to issue a gold medallion. An expert on collectibles estimates that the demand for these medallions will be such that the revenue from their sale will be $800,000, provided Hamilton mints 500 to 10,000 of the medallions. Find the demand function, giving the selling price p as a function of q, the number minted.

SOLUTION

Letting $R = 800,000$ in $R = pq$, we find that $pq = 800,000$. Division by q gives the desired demand function:

$$p = \frac{800,000}{q}, \qquad 500 \le q \le 10,000.$$

This function indicates that if 500 medallions are minted, they can be sold for $1600 each. But as the company mints more of them, the price falls steadily, reaching $80 if the company mints 10,000.

Although Example 2 may seem very simple, demand functions of the type introduced—namely, $p = k/q$ with k a constant—play an important role in the theory of economics. They will reappear later in this text in the study of more advanced topics.

In other situations, we will want a function whose graph is a curve that has the same shape as $y = k/x$, but with asymptotes other than the x- and y-axes. To obtain such a hyperbola with asymptotes $y = a$ and $x = -c$, we must **translate** the graph of $y = k/x$ vertically by a units and horizontally by $-c$ units. To move a point (x, y) on the translated graph back to the original graph, we must subtract a from y and add c to x. Thus for the translated graph, we have

$$y - a = \frac{k}{x + c}, \qquad x \neq -c,$$

or

$$y = \frac{k}{x + c} + a$$

$$= \frac{k + a(x + c)}{x + c}, \qquad x \neq -c.$$

Simplifying, we obtain

(1.19)
$$y = \frac{ax + b}{x + c}, \qquad x \neq -c,$$

where b is the constant $ac + k$. Thus the graph of equation (1.19) is a hyperbola with horizontal asymptote $y = a$, vertical asymptote $x = -c$, and the same shape as $y = k/x$, where $k = b - ac$.

The rule of correspondence in equation (1.19) is an example of a rational function.

Definition 1.5

> We say that y is a **rational** function of x if y is the ratio of two polynomials in x—that is, if
>
> $$y = \frac{g(x)}{h(x)}, \qquad h(x) \neq 0,$$
>
> where $g(x)$ and $h(x)$ are polynomials.

A rational function in the form of equation (1.19) is said to be **linear-to-linear** because both the numerator and the denominator are first-degree or linear polynomials. Analogously, a **quadratic-to-linear** rational function has a quadratic numerator and a linear denominator, whereas a **quadratic-to-quadratic** rational function is the ratio of two quadratic polynomials.

When graphing a linear-to-linear rational function of the form

$$y = \frac{ax + b}{x + c}, \qquad x \neq -c,$$

we remember that the shape of this curve is similar to $y = k/x$ except the horizontal asymptote is $y = a$ and the vertical asymptote is $x = -c$. After sketching these asymptotes, we need only plot $(0, b/c)$, when $c \neq 0$, and a few other points to determine the final graph.

EXAMPLE 3

Sketch the graphs.

a. $y = \dfrac{3x + 10}{x + 2}, \qquad$ for $x \neq -2$

b. $y = \dfrac{x - 8}{x - 4}$,   for $x \neq 4$

SOLUTION

a.   After sketching the asymptotes $y = 3$ and $x = -2$, we plot $(0, 5)$ and a few other points to obtain the graph. (See Figure 1.21.)

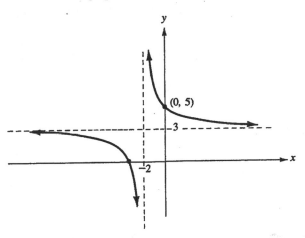

Figure 1.21
The graph of $y = (3x + 10)/(x + 2)$
for $x \neq -2$

b. We sketch the asymptotes $y = 1$ and $x = 4$ and plot $(0, 2)$ with a few other points to obtain the graph in Figure 1.22.

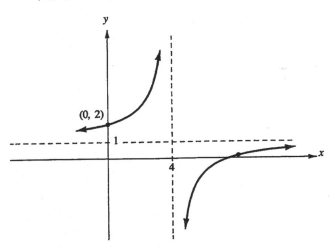

Figure 1.22
The graph of $y = (x - 8)/(x - 4)$
for $x \neq 4$

We have considered several types of functions as models for the variable cost per unit v of producing an item. We have treated v as a constant function, linear function, or quadratic function of output q. In the last section, higher-order polynomial functions were briefly considered, but it was noted that no polynomial function (other than a constant function) can remain "flat" over an interval of arbitrary length. Linear-to-linear rational functions can be used to model cases in which the variable cost per unit is continually decreasing (due to efficiencies in operation), but this cost per unit never drops below a certain level.

EXAMPLE 4

Find a linear-to-linear rational function that expresses variable cost v as a function of output q, if v is about \$10 when q is near 0, $v = \$8$ when q is 100, and v declines toward \$7 for large q.

SOLUTION

We must find a, b, and c in

$$v = \frac{aq + b}{q + c}, \qquad q \geq 0.$$

Since v tends toward 7 as q increases, the horizontal asymptote is $v = 7$, and so $a = 7$. Also, since v must equal 10 when $q = 0$, we know that $b/c = 10$ or $b = 10c$. Therefore,

$$v = \frac{7q + 10c}{q + c}, \qquad q \geq 0.$$

Now to determine c, we use the requirement that $v(100) = 8$ to get

$$8 = \frac{7(100) + 10c}{100 + c}$$

or

$$800 + 8c = 700 + 10c,$$

and thus

$$c = 50.$$

Finally, we are able to write

$$v = \frac{7q + 500}{q + 50}, \qquad q \geq 0.$$

The graph of this function appears in Figure 1.23.

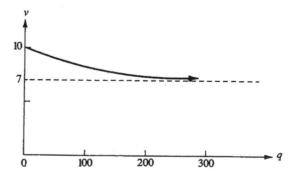

Figure 1.23
A curve showing variable cost per unit as a linear-to-linear rational function of output

A quadratic-to-linear rational function arises naturally from the setting in Example 4.

EXAMPLE 5   If the daily fixed cost of producing q units of a product is $90 per unit, while the variable cost per unit v when producing q units is given by

$$v = \frac{7q + 500}{q + 50}, \qquad q \geq 0,$$

find the total cost C as a function of q and write the rule of correspondence as a quadratic-to-linear rational function.

SOLUTION   Because

$$C = 90 + vq,$$

we have

$$C = 90 + \frac{7q + 500}{q + 50} \, q, \qquad q \geq 0.$$

We get the desired form by combining the right side over a common denominator:

$$C = \frac{90(q + 50) + (7q + 500)q}{q + 50}, \qquad q \geq 0,$$

or

$$C = \frac{7q^2 + 590q + 4500}{q + 50}, \qquad q \geq 0. \qquad \bullet$$

EXERCISES 1.5

For each of the linear-to-linear rational functions in Exercises 1–12 find the asymptotes and the point at which the graph intercepts the vertical axis (if there is such a point); then sketch the graph.

1. $y = \dfrac{2}{x}$

2. $y = \dfrac{-2}{x}$

3. $y = \dfrac{2x + 15}{x + 5}$

4. $y = \dfrac{x - 8}{x + 2}$

5. $y = \dfrac{3x + 4}{x - 2}$

6. $y = \dfrac{-2x}{x - 5}$

7. $y = \dfrac{2x}{x - 5}$

8. $y = \dfrac{2x - 1}{x + 1}$

9. $y = \dfrac{-5x + 8}{x + 1}$

10. $y = \dfrac{-2x + 10}{x - 5}$

11. $p = \dfrac{2q + 50}{q + 4}$

12. $p = \dfrac{6q + 300}{q + 15}$

In Exercises 13–20 find the linear-to-linear rational function whose graph has the indicated properties.

13. Horizontal asymptote $y = 3$; vertical asymptote $x = 5$; contains the point $(2, 1)$

14. Horizontal asymptote $y = 0$; vertical asymptote $x = -4$; contains the point $(5, 3)$

15. Horizontal asymptote $p = 18$; vertical asymptote $q = 0$; contains the point $(10, 50)$

16. Horizontal asymptote $p = 40$; vertical asymptote $q = -10$; contains the point $(5, 30)$

17. Horizontal asymptote $y = 4$; contains the points $(0, 0)$ and $(5, 2)$

18. Horizontal asymptote $y = 0$; contains the points $(2, 1)$ and $(8, -1)$

19. Vertical asymptote $x = -10$; contains the points $(0, 5)$ and $(10, 4)$

20. Vertical asymptote $x = 3$; contains the points $(0, -4)$ and $(6, 8)$

21. Tickets for a major sporting event are often available through large travel agencies even after the event is officially sold out. The maximum price p that a certain agency will ever charge is $25 per ticket; that is, $p = 25$ even if q is nearly 0. This agency will charge $20 per ticket if only five are available, but the price decreases to $10 if a lot of tickets are available. Assuming that p is a linear-to-linear rational function of q, find the rule of correspondence for this function.

22. Referring to Exercise 21, find the revenue R that the travel agency receives as a function of q, the number of tickets it has available.

23. A plant manager estimates that when the production rate q for a product is near 0, the variable cost v of making one unit is $24. For large batches, this cost is known to decrease toward $15. Finally, it is known that when q is 40, v is $19.50. Find v as a linear-to-linear function of q.

24. Refer to Exercise 23. The manager also knows that the fixed costs are $200 per day. Use this to write the total cost C of a day's production as a quadratic-to-linear function of q.

25. An accountant has been hired to find the break-even point for a manufacturer of steel castings. By checking past records of costs and output, the accountant has determined that the variable cost per casting is $30 when output is very low, is $18 when the output is 30 castings per hour, and drops toward $10 when the output is very high; the fixed cost is $300 per hour; and each casting made will be sold for $20.

    a. Write the variable cost v as a linear-to-linear rational function of output q.

    b. Write the total cost C as a quadratic-to-linear rational function of q.

    c. Determine the output level q at which the manufacturer must operate to break even.

26. Assume that the market price p for a certain item is a linear-to-linear rational function of q, the supply provided by the producers. If no units are provided at a price of $20 per unit or less, 100 units are made at $30 per unit, and the supply becomes very large as the price approaches $50, find the rule of correspondence for this function.

Find the equilibrium value of q and the market-clearing price p for each of the supply and demand functions in Exercises 27–32; then sketch their graphs.

27. $p = 3 + .1q, \ 0 \le q \le 200$ (supply)

    $p = \dfrac{10q + 190}{q + 10}, q \ge 0$ (demand)

28. $p = 5 + .025q, \ 0 \le q \le 500$ (supply)

    $p = \dfrac{6q + 400}{q + 20}, q \ge 0$ (demand)

29. $p = \dfrac{60q}{q + 80}, q \ge 0$ (supply)

    $p = \dfrac{30q + 1440}{q + 20}, q \ge 0$ (demand)

30. $p = \dfrac{8q}{q + 50}, q \ge 0$ (supply)

    $p = \dfrac{3q + 630}{q + 30}, q \ge 0$ (demand)

31. $p = \dfrac{5q + 500}{q + 200}, q \ge 0$ (supply)

    $p = \dfrac{3q + 500}{q + 50}, q \ge 0$ (demand)

32. $p = \dfrac{40q + 120}{q + 25}, q \ge 0$ (supply)

    $p = \dfrac{10q + 300}{q + 10}, q \ge 0$ (demand)

1.6
Function Composition and Inverse Functions

Having examined several types of elementary functions that are useful in modeling, we now consider an operation that may be used to build new functions from existing ones, or to break complicated functions into simpler components. The operation is called **function composition**.

To begin, consider the function h with the rule of correspondence

$$h(x) = (x - 5)^2.$$

When $h(x)$ is evaluated for a given value of x, two things must be done. First 5 is subtracted from x; then the result is squared. Each process could be performed using a separate function. Suppose g and f are functions with rules of correspondence

$$g(x) = x - 5 \quad \text{and} \quad f(x) = x^2.$$

To obtain $h(x)$ for any choice of x, we could first form $g(x)$ and then apply f to $g(x)$. In this case we say that h is the **composition** of f with g and write

$$h(x) = f(g(x)).$$

Definition 1.6

If g and f are functions and the range of g is contained in the domain of f, then the **composition** of f with g is the function h with the rule of correspondence

$$h(x) = f(g(x))$$

for all x in the domain of g.

The schematic diagram in Figure 1.24 illustrates this composition.

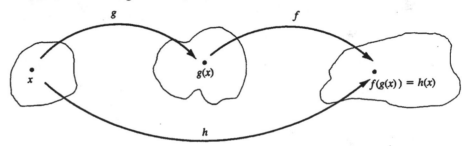

Figure 1.24
Function composition

EXAMPLE 1

If $g(x) = 5/x$ for $x > 0$, and $f(x) = 2x + 3$ for all x, find $f(g(x))$ and $g(f(x))$.

SOLUTION

The range of g is $(0, \infty)$ and the domain of f is $(-\infty, \infty)$, so for any x in the domain of g,

$$f(g(x)) = f\left(\frac{5}{x}\right) = 2\left(\frac{5}{x}\right) + 3$$

or, on simplification,

$$f(g(x)) = \frac{10 + 3x}{x}, \qquad x > 0.$$

The range of f includes 0, which is not in the domain of g, but by restricting the domain so that $x > -3/2$, we get

$$g(f(x)) = g(2x + 3) = \frac{5}{2x + 3}, \qquad x > \frac{-3}{2}. \qquad \bullet$$

EXAMPLE 2

Write $y = 3(x - 5)^2 + 7$ as the composition of three functions.

SOLUTION

Recalling the procedure of Example 4 in Section 1.3 used to translate the parabola $y = 3x^2$ five units horizontally and seven units vertically, we take

$$h(x) = x - 5, \quad g(x) = x + 7, \quad \text{and} \quad f(x) = 3x^2.$$

Then $y = g(f(h(x)))$ because

$$g(f(h(x))) = g(f(x - 5))$$
$$= g(3(x - 5)^2)$$
$$= 3(x - 5)^2 + 7. \qquad \bullet$$

Next we consider a class of functions where the dependent variable is directly proportional to some power of the independent variable. In many cases these power functions can be written as the composition of two simpler functions.

Definition 1.7

A function with the rule of correspondence

$$y = kx^p,$$

where k and p are positive constants, is called a **power function**.

When p is a nonnegative integer, a power function is just a polynomial function. Also, if n is a positive integer, $x^{1/n}$ denotes the **nth root** of x. (These roots do not exist for negative x when n is even. See Appendix A.4 for further discussion.) That is, the power function $y = x^{1/n}$ is a root function. Recall that the nth root of x may also be written as $\sqrt[n]{x}$. For a rational value of p that is not the reciprocal of an integer, a power function can be thought of as the composition of a polynomial function and a root function.

EXAMPLE 3

Write $y = 4x^{2.7}$ as a composition of a polynomial function and a root function.

SOLUTION

Let $f(x) = 4x^{27}$ and $g(x) = \sqrt[10]{x}$. Then

$$y = f(g(x)) = f(\sqrt[10]{x}) = f(x^{.1}) = 4(x^{.1})^{27} = 4x^{2.7}. \qquad \bullet$$

Evaluation of power functions for irrational values of p is a more difficult task, which will be considered in Section 4.1. However, today's scientific hand calculators offer a $\boxed{y^x}$ or exponentiation key with which x^p can be easily approximated to several decimal places. Simply enter x and press $\boxed{y^x}$; enter p and press $\boxed{=}$. For example, performing these steps for $x = 5$ and $p = 2.7$, we find that $5^{2.7} \doteq 77.13$.

Graphs of $y = kx^p$, with $p > 1$, $p = 1$, and $0 < p < 1$, are shown in Figure 1.25. In Chapter 3 we will discover the reason for the different "bends" in these curves.

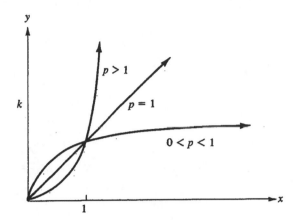

Figure 1.25
Graphs of $y = kx^p$, $x \geq 0$

In many functional relationships we have interchanged dependent and independent variables in the rule of correspondence of a function to obtain a new function. This procedure can be formalized by using function composition to define **inverse functions**.

Definition 1.8

If f and g are functions such that

$$f(g(x)) = x \qquad \text{for all } x \text{ in the domain of } g$$

and

$$g(f(x)) = x \qquad \text{for all } x \text{ in the domain of } f,$$

then g is said to be the **inverse** of f and is denoted by f^{-1}. Also, f is said to be the inverse of g, denoted by g^{-1}.

We have, then, $f^{-1}(f(x)) = x$ and $f(f^{-1}(x)) = x$ for all x in the domain and range of f, respectively.

The demand q for a commodity at price p may be expressed either by giving p as a function of q or by giving q as a function of p. However, for both to represent the same relationship, these two functions must be inverses.

EXAMPLE 4

In Example 6 in Section 1.2, we constructed the linear demand function

$$q = -10p + 130, \qquad 3 \leq p \leq 12.$$

When this is solved for the variable p, we obtain the demand function

$$p = -.1q + 13, \qquad 10 \le q \le 100.$$

Show that these functions are inverses.

SOLUTION   To avoid confusion, let x be the independent variable in both functions; that is, let

$$f(x) = -10x + 130, \qquad 3 \le x \le 12,$$

and

$$g(x) = -.1x + 13, \qquad 10 \le x \le 100.$$

Then

$$
\begin{aligned}
g(f(x)) &= g(-10x + 130) \\
&= -.1(-10x + 130) + 13 \\
&= x
\end{aligned}
$$

and

$$
\begin{aligned}
f(g(x)) &= f(-.1x + 13) \\
&= -10(-.1x + 13) + 130 \\
&= x.
\end{aligned}
$$

By Definition 1.8, $g = f^{-1}$ and $f = g^{-1}$.   ●

The procedure for finding the rule of correspondence for an inverse function usually requires solving the given rule of correspondence for the independent variable as was done in Example 4.

To each value of x in the domain of a function f there is assigned a value y in the range. The inverse function f^{-1} then sends y back to the original x. The domain and the range of f therefore become the range and the domain, respectively, of f^{-1} (see Figure 1.26).

If $y = f(x)$ and $y = f^{-1}(x)$ are graphed on the same coordinate system, their graphs are symmetric, or "mirror images" of each other, through the line $y = x$ (see Figure 1.27). This symmetry occurs because if a point (x_1, y_1) is on the graph of f, then the pair (y_1, x_1) is on the graph of f^{-1}, and vice versa. Pictorially, if the

Figure 1.26
The domains and ranges of inverse functions

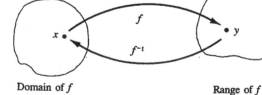

Domain of f Range of f

Range of f^{-1} Domain of f^{-1}

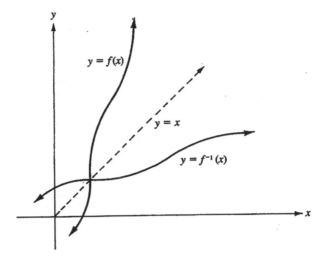

Figure 1.27

Graphs of functions $y = f(x)$ and $y = f^{-1}(x)$ are symmetric through the line $y = x$.

graph of a function is drawn in ink, and if the graph paper is folded along the line $y = x$ before the ink dries, the graph of the inverse function will be blotted onto the paper.

There is an important example of functions and their inverses in the power functions. Let n be any positive integer and consider the functions $f(x) = x^n$ and $g(x) = x^{1/n}$, where $x \geq 0$. Then composing these functions gives us

$$f(g(x)) = f(x^{1/n}) = (x^{1/n})^n = x$$

and

$$g(f(x)) = g(x^n) = (x^n)^{1/n} = x;$$

that is, f and g are inverse functions. In particular, we observe that $f(x) = x^2$, where $x \geq 0$, and $g(x) = \sqrt{x}$ are inverse functions. These functions are graphed in Figure 1.28; note that the graph of g is the upper half of a parabola opening to the right.

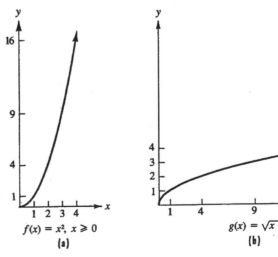

Figure 1.28

Graphs of $y = x^2 \ (x \geq 0)$ and $y = \sqrt{x}$

In general, if a quadratic function has an inverse, the inverse involves a square root function and has a parabolic graph.

Not all functions have inverses. Suppose f sends two or more different values to the same range value y. Then it is not possible for an inverse function to return y to its original x value uniquely. [The rule $y = f(x)$ cannot be solved uniquely for x.] So, in order for a function to have an inverse, it must send each domain value to a different range value. Such functions are said to be **one-to-one**.

A function is one-to-one if no horizontal line intersects its graph in two or more points: multiple intersections indicate that two or more domain values are assigned to the same range value. Using this test, nonconstant linear functions are one-to-one, but quadratic functions are not—when the domain is all real numbers (see Figure 1.29). Note that a quadratic function is one-to-one if its domain is a set of numbers, all of which are on the same side of the vertex.

Figure 1.29

(a) All horizontal lines intersect the straight line at a single point; (b) some lines intersect the parabola at two points.

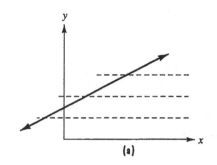
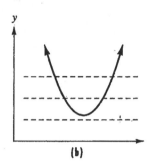

(a)   (b)

EXAMPLE 5

(1.20)

Suppose that the price p for a ton of sugar in the commodities market is related to the supply q by

$$p = \sqrt{.5q + 900}, \qquad q \geq 0.$$

Find the inverse function, giving q in terms of p. Sketch the graphs of both functions.

SOLUTION

First note that for $q \geq 0$, $p \geq 30$; thus the domain of the inverse function must be $p \geq 30$. We find the inverse by solving for q. Squaring both sides of equation (1.20), we get

$$p^2 = .5q + 900,$$

and dividing by .5 gives

(1.21)
$$q = 2p^2 - 1800, \qquad p \geq 30.$$

The graph of $q = 2p^2 - 1800$ is a parabola opening upward with vertex at $(0, -1800)$; the graph of equation (1.21) is the section of the parabola in the first quadrant. The graph of equation (1.20) can now be drawn on the q- and p-axes by reflecting the graph of equation (1.21) through the line $p = q$. (See Figure 1.30.)

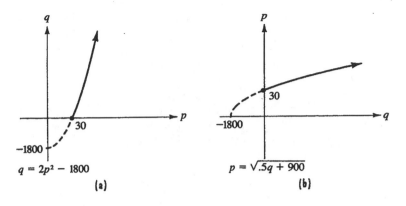

Figure 1.30

$$q = 2p^2 - 1800$$

(a)

$$p = \sqrt{.5q + 900}$$

(b)

EXERCISES 1.6

For the functions f and g in Exercises 1–8 form $f(g(x))$ and $g(f(x))$, indicating the domain of each function.

1. $f(x) = 2x + 5$ and $g(x) = x^2 - 3$

2. $f(x) = x + 8$ and $g(x) = 2x^2$

3. $f(x) = \dfrac{x}{x + 1}$ and $g(x) = 2x + 7$

4. $f(x) = x - 3$ and $g(x) = \dfrac{x + 1}{x - 1}$

5. $f(x) = x^3$ and $g(x) = \sqrt[4]{x}$

6. $f(x) = \sqrt{x}$ and $g(x) = 4x^2 + 1$

7. $f(x) = 3x^2 + 2x + 1$ and $g(x) = \sqrt{x - 1}$

8. $f(x) = \dfrac{2x + 5}{x + 2}$ and $g(x) = \dfrac{5 - 2x}{x - 2}$

In Exercises 9–16 find rules of correspondence for functions f and g so that $h(x) = f(g(x))$.

9. $h(x) = 5x + 7$

10. $h(x) = 3x + 2$

11. $h(x) = (x + 8)^2$

12. $h(x) = (3x + 1)^5$

13. $h(x) = \sqrt{x + 5}$

14. $h(x) = \sqrt{x - 7}$

15. $h(x) = x^{4/5}$

16. $h(x) = x^{4.6}$

In Exercises 17–26 show that the given functions are inverses.

17. $f(x) = x + 3$ and $g(x) = x - 3$ (all x)

18. $f(x) = 2x - 5$ and $g(x) = .5x + 2.5$ (all x)

19. $f(x) = x^2 + 1$ and $g(x) = \sqrt{x - 1}$ ($x \geq 1$)

20. $f(x) = x^2 + 4x - 11$ and $g(x) = -2 - \sqrt{x + 15}$ ($x \geq -15$)

21. $f(x) = \dfrac{10}{x}$ and $g(x) = \dfrac{10}{x}$ ($x \neq 0$)

22. $f(x) = -x$ and $g(x) = -x$ (all x)

23. $f(x) = x^{.4}$ and $g(x) = x^{2.5}$ ($x \geq 0$)

24. $f(x) = x^{2/3}$ and $g(x) = x^{3/2}$ ($x \geq 0$)

25. $f(x) = \dfrac{x - 1}{x + 1}$ and $g(x) = \dfrac{x + 1}{1 - x}$ ($x \neq 1$ and $x \neq -1$)

26. $f(x) = \dfrac{2x + 1}{x - 1}$ and $g(x) = \dfrac{x + 1}{x - 2}$ ($x \neq 1$ and $x \neq 2$)

In Exercises 27–38 find the inverse of each of the given functions by letting $y = f(x)$ and then solving for x to obtain $f^{-1}(y)$.

27. $f(x) = 2x + 6$ (all x)

28. $f(x) = 3x + 7$ (all x)

29. $f(x) = x^2 + 4$ ($x \geq 0$)

30. $f(x) = x^2 - 5$ ($x \geq 0$)

31. $f(x) = \dfrac{x - 2}{x + 2}$ ($x \neq 2$)

32. $f(x) = \dfrac{3x + 2}{x + 1}$ ($x \geq -1$)

33. $f(x) = 8x^3$ (all x)

34. $f(x) = x^3 - 8$ (all x)

35. $f(x) = \sqrt{x - 3}$ $(x \geq 3)$

36. $f(x) = \sqrt{2x - 5}$ $(x \geq 2.5)$

37. $f(x) = (x - 3)^2 + 5$ $(x \geq 3)$

38. $f(x) = x^2 - 4x + 7$ $(x \geq 2)$. [*Hint:* First determine the vertex; then write $f(x)$ in the form $(x - h)^2 + k$.]

39. We have seen that the graph of $y = (ax + b)/(x + c)$ is the graph of $y = k/x$ shifted $-c$ units horizontally and a units vertically; that is,

$$y = \frac{k}{x + c} + a$$

for some k. Use this fact to write

$$y = \frac{3x + 10}{x + 2}$$

as the composition of three functions: $y = k/x$ and two linear functions.

40. On which domains will $f(x) = (x - 3)^2 + 2$ be one-to-one?

   a. $(0, \infty)$ b. $(3, 4)$ c. $(4, \infty)$ d. $(-\infty, 2)$

In Exercises 41–44 sketch the graph of the given supply function after first sketching the graph of the inverse function.

41. $p = \sqrt{q + 9}, q \geq 0$ 42. $p = \sqrt{q + 16}, q \geq 0$

43. $p = \sqrt{4q + 36}, q \geq 0$ 44. $p = \sqrt{.5q + 25}, q \geq 0$

45. The daily demand for chocolate at Homade Candies depends on its selling price. At \$8 per pound, 40 lb are sold each day, while at \$6 per pound, 72 lb are sold.

   a. Assuming that demand q is a linear function of price p when $5 \leq p \leq 10$, find the rule of correspondence for this function.

   b. To determine profit as a function of q, revenue must be written in terms of q. Use the inverse of the function in part a to write revenue R as a function of q.

   c. The daily cost C of producing q pounds of chocolate at Homade is known to be $C = 20 + 2q$, where $0 \leq q \leq 100$. Use the revenue function from part b to write the daily profit P as a function of q.

46. Show that in special cases where revenue is constant—that is, $pq = k$ (see Example 2 of Section 1.5)—the function that gives p in terms of q and its inverse are identical.

47. The daily quantity of rice q (tons) that is supplied to an Asian market is thought to be related to the selling price by

$$p = \sqrt{.2q + 400}, \quad q \geq 0.$$

Find the inverse function, giving q in terms of p, with the appropriate domain. Sketch the graphs of both functions.

48. The number of tons q of iron ore that are produced by a mine is related to the current selling price by

$$p = \sqrt{.02q + 16}, \quad q \geq 0.$$

Find the inverse function, giving q in terms of p, with the appropriate domain. Sketch the graphs of both functions.

CH. 1 REVIEW

I. Key Terms & Concepts

Mathematics

Function
Independent Variable
Dependent Variable
Rule of Correspondence
Domain
Range
Direct Variation
Inverse Variation
Linear Function
Quadratic Function
Polynomial Function
Rational Function
Power Function
One-to-One Function
Inverse Function
Function Composition
Vertex
Asymptote

Business

Total Cost
Fixed Cost
Variable Cost per Unit
Revenue Function
Demand Function
Supply Function
Break-even Point
Equilibrium Point

II. True or False

Indicate whether each statement is true or false.

1. Every function has an inverse function.

2. The vertex of the parabola given by $y = ax^2 + bx + c$ occurs at $x = -b/a$.

3. The horizontal asymptote of the graph of

$$y = \frac{ax + b}{x + c}$$

   is the line $y = a$.

4. At the break-even point, total cost equals revenue.

5. A constant function is a linear function with 0 slope.

6. If y varies inversely as x, then $yx = k$ for some constant k.

7. No vertical line can intersect the graph of a function at more than one point.

8. The graph of $y = ax^2 + bx + c$ has two x-intercepts whenever $a < 0$.

9. If x_1 and x_2 are in the domain of the function f, then $f(x_1 + x_2) = f(x_1) + f(x_2)$.

10. If $p = f(q)$ is the demand function for a product, then the revenue function for this product is $R = q\,f(q)$.

III. Drill Problems

In Problems 1–10 sketch the graph of the given function.

1. $f(x) = 2x + 7$

2. $f(x) = 8 - 3x$

3. $g(x) = 10 + 2x + x^2$

4. $g(x) = 18 - 5x + 2x^2$

5. $f(x) = 8 - 12x - 3x^2$

6. $f(x) = 7 + 10x - x^2$

7. $g(x) = \dfrac{4x + 35}{x + 5}, x > 0$

8. $g(x) = \dfrac{2x + 1}{x + 3}, x > 0$

9. $f(x) = \sqrt{5x + 9}, x > 0$ 10. $f(x) = \sqrt{2x + 25}, x > 0$

In Problems 11–16 let $f(x) = 2x - 1$ and $g(x) = x^2 + 3$. Find the functions.

11. $f(g(x))$

12. $g(f(x))$

13. $f(x + h) - f(x)$

14. $g(x + h) - g(x)$

15. $f^{-1}(x)$

16. $f\left(\dfrac{1}{x}\right)$

In Problems 17–22 find the rule of correspondence for the function f.

17. $f(1) = 6, f(4) = 12$, and f is a linear function.

18. $f(0) = 4, f(5) = 10$, and f is a linear function.

19. $f(3) = 6$ and the graph of f is a parabola with vertex $(5, 2)$.

20. $f(4) = 8$ and the graph of f is a parabola with vertex $(1, 10)$.

21. $f(0) = 20$ and f is a linear-to-linear rational function whose graph has horizontal asymptote $y = 8$ and vertical asymptote $x = -3$.

22. $f(0) = 25$, $f(4) = 20$, and f is a linear-to-linear rational function whose graph has horizontal asymptote $y = 10$.

IV. Applications

1. The Sizzler Burger chain has decided to add a salad bar to its menu. It has been estimated that the daily fixed cost for operating the salad bar will be $36 and the variable cost will be $2.10 per order. The price of the salad bar is to be $2.85.

   a. Determine the profit P as a function of q, the number of customers who order the salad bar.

   b. How many customers must order a salad bar each day for Sizzler Burger to break even?

2. Refer to Exercise 1. As a promotion, Sizzler Burger is offering a second salad bar for $1.00 less than the regular price to each salad bar customer. Assuming that each customer is accompanied by a friend who will take advantage of the offer, find the break-even point during this promotion.

3. The manager of a tax preparation agency wants to determine the fixed and the variable costs for the business. During a recent week, when 150 returns were prepared, the total cost of running the agency was $2100; during another week, when 110 returns were done, the cost was $1860. Assuming that the total cost C is a linear function of the number of returns q, find the fixed cost and the variable cost per return.

4. Refer to Exercise 3. What flat rate per return should this tax preparation agency charge to break even in a week when 50 returns are prepared?

5. It is possible for a leather goods shop to produce as many as 200 pairs of gloves each week. Find the level of output that maximizes profit if the fixed cost is $200 per week, the variable cost per pair is $v = 6.5 - .01q$, and the demand function is $p = 17.7 - .08q$, where q is the number of pairs made each week.

6. Find the break-even points for the leather goods shop in Exercise 5.

7. MovieTime is a cable TV subscription service. It is known that in a small community, there will be 5000 subscribers if the monthly charge is $6.00. However, it is estimated that for each $.05 increase in the monthly subscription charge, MovieTime will lose 20 subscribers. Let n denote the number of $.05 increments above $6.00 that the management charges.

   a. Write the revenue R received by MovieTime as a function of n.

   b. Find n that maximizes R. What is the corresponding monthly charge? How many subscribers are there?

8. Assume that a coffee grower will supply 10 tons of beans to a coffee roaster when the price is $6 per pound, none if the price is $2 per pound or less, and as much as the roaster could ever want at $10 per pound. Model the price of the coffee p (dollars per pound) as a linear-to-linear rational function of the supply provided q (tons).

9. Refer to Exercise 8. Let the roaster's demand function for the coffee be given by $p = 8 - .5q$ for $q \geq 0$. Find the market-clearing price and the amount of coffee sold at equilibrium.

Amcraft is a supplier of materials for arts-and-crafts hobbyists. Craft shops can order q of its Knit Kits at a wholesale price of p dollars per kit, where

$$p = 8 - .02q, \qquad 0 \le q \le 100.$$

How much revenue is received by Amcraft from an order for 60 of these kits? Use the marginal revenue from the 60th kit to estimate the additional revenue from an order for 61 kits.

CHAPTER 2

Limits and Continuity

2.1
Marginal Cost and Marginal Revenue

A recurring decision that a business manager has to make is whether or not to increase the output level of some production system (an assembly line, a plant or factory, or a collection of plants). A primary consideration in the decision is whether or not the revenue generated by the additional output will exceed the cost. To introduce the mathematical concepts required to make this determination, we begin with an example.

EXAMPLE 1

Currently the Wilderness Supply Company produces 100 backpacks per day. The production manager wants to determine whether or not it is profitable to increase the daily output. At present the plant is operating near its capacity. In fact, for $90 \le q \le 120$ it is estimated that the total cost C of producing q backpacks is

$$C = 1000 + 50q + .2q^2.$$

The manager has been assured by the vice-president for marketing that more backpacks can easily be sold for $85 each. Based on this information, should the manager order an increase in the daily output?

SOLUTION

The total cost of producing 100 backpacks is

$$C(100) = 1000 + 50(100) + .2(100)^2$$
$$= 8000.$$

Dividing the total cost by 100, the quantity produced, yields $8000/100 = $80, the average cost of each of the first 100 backpacks produced. Comparing the $80 average cost with the $85 selling price, we see that Wilderness Supply Company is earning an average of $5 for each backpack. However, this does not necessarily mean that additional output is desirable. The *average* earnings of $5 per backpack could include a loss on the 100th unit (and any future units) produced.

To decide on additional output the manager should compute the average cost of each additional backpack produced beyond the current 100 (rather than including costs for those already produced), and compare this cost with the $85 selling price. To do this, let h denote the number of additional backpacks produced. The difference

$$C(100 + h) - C(100)$$

represents the extra cost of producing h more backpacks. The average cost of each of these h extra backpacks is then given by the quotient

$$\frac{C(100 + h) - C(100)}{h}.$$

For instance, if $h = 10$, the average cost of 10 extra units is

$$\frac{C(110) - C(100)}{10} = \frac{8920 - 8000}{10}$$
$$= \frac{920}{10}$$
$$= \$92.$$

Clearly it would be a bad decision to increase the output level to 110 per day, since the extra 10 backpacks can be sold for only $85 each. Their production would reduce profit by $7 ($92 − $85) each—a reduction of $70 per day in total profit.

Treating h as a small real number, the manager needs to compute

(2.1)
$$\frac{C(100 + h) - C(100)}{h}$$

as a function of h to see whether even a small increase in production would be profitable. Doing this, we find

$$\frac{C(100 + h) - C(100)}{h} = \frac{1000 + 50(100) + h) + .2(100 + h)^2 - 8000}{h}$$

$$= \frac{1000 + 5000 + 50h + 2000 + 40h + .2h^2 - 8000}{h}$$

$$= \frac{90h + .2h^2}{h}$$

$$= 90 + .2h.$$

We now see that any increase in production h, no matter how small, will reduce the profit, since the cost of additional backpacks will be more than $90. Indeed, as h gets close to 0, we see that the cost of the 100th backpack is $90. The manager should not increase output; Wilderness Supply is losing $5 on the production and sale of the 100th backpack. Output should be decreased to increase profit. ●

Observe that in the quotient (2.1) it is not actually possible to let $h = 0$ because this would involve division by 0. However, after the algebraic simplification it is apparent that the value approached by, or the limiting value of, the quotient (as h gets closer and closer to 0) is $90. This limiting value is called the marginal cost of the 100th backpack.

Definition 2.1

If $C(q)$ is the cost of producing q units of an item, then the **marginal cost of the qth unit of output** is the limiting value of the quotient

(2.2)
$$\frac{C(q + h) - C(q)}{h}$$

as h approaches 0. This limiting value is denoted by $MC(q)$.

The marginal cost of the qth unit can be interpreted as the ratio of the change in total cost to the change in production level from q units. The units of measurement in this ratio are dollars over the quantity of output. Thus, the ratio gives a rate of change in dollars per unit of output. Since marginal cost is taken as a limiting value, it represents the rate of change at this instant (or output level) and is often called the **instantaneous rate of change in cost per unit of output**.

A similar analysis can be performed for the revenue generated from the sale of additional units. The limiting value of the average revenue from the sale of extra units (as the number of extra units approaches 0) is called the marginal revenue.

Definition 2.2

If $R(q)$ is the revenue generated by the sale of q units of an item, then the **marginal revenue from the qth unit** is the limiting value of the quotient

(2.3) $$\frac{R(q + h) - R(q)}{h}$$

as h approaches 0. This limiting value is denoted by $MR(q)$.

The related concepts of marginal cost and marginal revenue are fundamental to deciding the optimal output level. For a given output level q, the marginal cost $MC(q)$ represents the (instantaneous) rate of change in total cost, whereas the marginal revenue $MR(q)$ represents the (instantaneous) rate of change in revenue. Thus we have the following rules of thumb:

1. If $MC(q) < MR(q)$, then an increase in output q will result in an increase in profit. (Equivalently a decrease in q will result in a decrease in profit.)

2. If $MC(q) > MR(q)$, then a decrease in output q will result in an increase in profit. (Equivalently an increase in q will result in a decrease in profit.)

3. If $MC(q) = MR(q)$, then profit is maximized at output level q.

EXAMPLE 2

The manager of a sporting goods plant is trying to decide whether to increase the output of certain lines of equipment. At present the plant is turning out 750 tennis racquets of a new design each week. The manager knows that when q tennis racquets are made in a given week, the total cost C is given by

$$C(q) = 500 + 100q - .03q^2, \qquad 0 \le q \le 1000.$$

It is also known that when q racquets are sold, the revenue R is given by

$$R(q) = 135q - .05q^2, \qquad 0 \le q \le 1000.$$

Determine the marginal cost and marginal revenue at $q = 750$ and decide whether or not it is profitable to increase the output of this model racquet. Use $MC(q)$ and $MR(q)$ to determine the output level that maximizes profit.

SOLUTION

To determine the marginal cost of the qth racquet, we begin with ratio (2.2), the average cost of h extra units beyond output level q:

$$\frac{C(q + h) - C(q)}{h} = \frac{[500 + 100(q + h) - .03(q + h)^2] - [500 + 100q - .03q^2]}{h}.$$

Combining like terms in the numerator of this ratio, we have

$$\frac{C(q + h) - C(q)}{h} = \frac{100h - .06qh - .03h^2}{h}$$

$$= \frac{h(100 - .06q - .03h)}{h}$$

$$= 100 - .06q - .03h.$$

Letting h shrink toward 0, we obtain the marginal cost of the qth racquet:

$$MC(q) = 100 - .06q.$$

In particular, when $q = 750$, $MC(750) = 100 - .06(750) = \$55$.

In a similar fashion we find marginal revenue by first simplifying quotient (2.3), the average revenue ratio:

$$\frac{R(q + h) - R(q)}{h} = \frac{[135(q + h) - .05(q + h)^2] - [135q - .05q^2]}{h}$$

$$= \frac{135h - .1qh - .05h^2}{h}$$

$$= \frac{h(135 - .1q - .05h)}{h}$$

$$= 135 - .1q - .05h.$$

As h shrinks toward 0, we obtain the marginal revenue from the sale of the qth racquet:

$$MR(q) = 135 - .1q.$$

When $q = 750$, $MR(750) = 135 - .1(750) = \$60$. Since the $60 marginal revenue exceeds the $55 marginal cost when $q = 750$, output should be increased to increase profit.

To find the output level that maximizes profit, we need only solve $MC(q) = MR(q)$ for q. For these racquets, marginal cost equals marginal revenue when

$$100 - .06q = 135 - .1q$$

or

$$.04q = 35.$$

Thus profit is maximized when $q = 35/.04 = 875$ racquets.　　●

The careful reader will note that the optimal output level in Example 2 could have been determined by locating the vertex of the graph of the quadratic profit function. However, marginal analysis can be applied even when the profit function is not quadratic. Before systematically finding marginal cost and marginal revenue for various functions, we must develop general results to avoid the tedious algebra encountered in the previous examples.

General results, or rules, that can be used to find marginal cost and marginal revenue are derived in Chapter 3. The remainder of Chapter 2 is devoted to the limit concept, which is an essential part of the marginal cost and marginal revenue definitions.

EXERCISES 2.1

In Exercises 1–6 find the marginal cost at the given value of q.

1. $C = 200 + 4q, q = 30$ 2. $C = 500 + .7q, q = 10$

3. $C = 24 + 30q, q = 125$

4. $C = 40 + 5q - .1q^2, q = 20$

5. $C = 600 + 25q - q^2, q = 6$

6. $C = 85 + 15q - .05q^2, q = 120$

In Exercises 7–10 find the marginal revenue at the given value of q.

7. $R = 18q, q = 100$ 8. $R = 25q, q = 8$

9. $R = 70q - .2q^2, q = 50$

10. $R = 4q - .03q^2, q = 15$

In Exercises 11–16 simplify the quotient
$$[C(q + h) - C(q)]/h;$$
then determine the marginal cost of the qth unit of output.

11. $C = 150 + 15q, q \geq 0$ 12. $C = 720 + .4q, q \geq 0$

13. $C = 1000 + 25q - .2q^2, 0 \leq q \leq 30$

14. $C = 45 + 8q + .01q^2, 100 \leq q \leq 130$

15. $C = 380 + 62q - 1.3q^2, 0 \leq q \leq 10$

16. $C = 100 + 40q - .1q^2, 0 \leq q \leq 100$

In Exercises 17–22 simplify the quotient
$$[R(q + h) - R(q)]/h;$$
then determine the marginal revenue of the qth unit.

17. $R = 35q, q \geq 0$ 18. $R = 9.20q, q \geq 0$

19. $R = 15q - .05q^2, 0 \leq q \leq 100$

20. $R = 80q - .18q^2, 0 \leq q \leq 25$

21. $R = 470q - q^2, 0 \leq q \leq 200$

22. $R = 60q - .5q^2, 0 \leq q \leq 100$

In Exercises 23–26 determine the marginal cost of the qth unit of output from the given variable cost function. Assume fixed costs are $100 per day.

23. $v = 48, q \geq 0$ 24. $v = 9.5, q \geq 0$

25. $v = 25 - .3q, 0 \leq q \leq 40$

26. $v = 70 - 1.5q, 0 \leq q \leq 30$

In Exercises 27–30 determine the marginal revenue from the qth unit of output if the selling price p is given as a function of the quantity demanded q, as indicated.

27. $p = 30, q \geq 0$ 28. $p = 22.50, q \geq 0$

29. $p = 20 - .04q, 0 \leq q \leq 200$

30. $p = 300 - 2q, 0 \leq q \leq 80$

31. At Tennessee Instruments, the variable cost of producing a programmable calculator is
$$v = 70 - .05q, \qquad 0 \leq q \leq 300,$$
when q calculators are produced each week. Fixed costs are known to be $850 per week.

  a. Write total cost as a function of q.

  b. Find the marginal cost of the qth unit of output.

  c. Find the total cost and the marginal cost when $q = 200$.

  d. If output were increased from 200 to 201 calculators, find the additional cost of producing this extra calculator. [Note that this additional cost is an estimate of $MC(200)$.]

32. During a certain week in June, the cash price p for live hogs at a midwestern farm market was
$$p = 58 - .004q,$$
$$0 \leq q \leq 1000 \text{ (dollars per hundredweight)},$$
when q hogs were offered for sale by the producers.

  a. Write the revenue R received by the producers as a function of q.

  b. Find the marginal revenue from the qth hog brought to market.

  c. Find the total revenue and the marginal revenue when $q = 800$.

  d. If sales were increased from 800 to 801 hogs per day, determine the revenue generated from the sale of the 801st hog. [Note that this additional revenue is an approximation to $MR(800)$.]

33. The accounting department at Shades Ltd. has determined that when q pairs of sunglasses are manufactured during one shift at the company's plant, the total cost C is approximately

$$C = 150 + 8q - .006q^2, \qquad 0 \le q \le 400.$$

   a. Determine the marginal cost of the qth pair.

   b. Find the average cost of the first 100 pairs and the marginal cost of the 100th pair.

34. A manager is considering a change in the current daily output level of 150 units at her company's manufacturing plant. Fixed costs are $150 per day and the variable cost per unit at output level q is estimated to be

$$v = 70 - .15q, \qquad 0 \le q \le 180.$$

   Each unit that is produced can be sold at a price of

$$p = 82 - .2q, \qquad 0 \le q \le 180.$$

   a. Find $MC(150)$ and $MR(150)$.

   b. Estimate the effect on the profit if the output is increased by one unit.

35. When q packages of Pro Slice golf balls are produced in a day, the variable cost per package is $v = 12 - .02q$. Daily plant capacity and fixed costs are 300 packages and $200, respectively. In order to sell the entire output, the price for each package of balls must be $p = 17 - .03q$.

   a. Find the marginal cost and marginal revenue as functions of q.

   b. If the current output level is $q = 225$, should output be increased or decreased to increase profit?

   c. Determine q so that $MC(q) = MR(q)$ and profit is maximized.

36. A new production facility is already nearing its capacity of 500 units of output per week. Increasing the production rate from the present 450 units per week will increase the variable cost per unit produced. In fact, the accounting department reports that for $q \ge 400$, variable cost per unit is about $v = 11 + .02q$, while the selling price of each unit is estimated to be $p = 35 - .01q$.

   a. Find the marginal cost and the marginal revenue of the 450th unit.

   b. If the goal is to increase profit, should the output level be increased or decreased?

37. RealBuck athletic shoes is considering adding a line of all-weather running suits. The plant manager has reported that it would be possible to manufacture as many as 100 such suits a day using the excess capacity in the present plant. The fixed costs would be about $200 per day, and if q suits were made each day, the variable cost per suit would be $v = 90 - .1q$. The head of marketing estimates that the revenue from each day's production would be $R = 120q - .35q^2$.

   a. Find $MC(q)$ and $MR(q)$.

   b. Determine the daily production level of running suits that will maximize profit.

38. Suppose that a commodity sells for a constant price p regardless of the quantity q available for sale. Show that the marginal revenue from the sale of the qth item equals p.

39. Suppose that the variable cost v for producing each of q units of an item is constant regardless of q. Show that the marginal cost of the qth unit is also v.

40. Suppose that the variable cost v for producing each of q units of an item is given by the linear function $v = b - mq$. Show that the marginal cost of the qth unit is given by $MC(q) = b - 2mq$.

2.2
The Limit of a Function

In the previous section we studied the quotients

$$\frac{C(q + h) - C(q)}{h} \quad \text{and} \quad \frac{R(q + h) - R(q)}{h}$$

for values of h that were near 0 but never equal to 0. Note that if $h = 0$, neither quotient is defined at all, since division by 0 is not permitted.

As another example, consider the function

$$f(x) = \frac{x^2 - 2x - 8}{x - 4}, \qquad x \ne 4.$$

x	$\dfrac{x^2 - 2x - 8}{x - 4}$
4.1	6.100
4.05	6.050
4.01	6.010
4.002	6.002
3.95	5.950
3.99	5.990
3.997	5.997

Table 2.1

This function is not defined at $x = 4$; however, it is possible to ask about the behavior of $f(x)$ as x is chosen near 4. Table 2.1 gives $f(x)$ for several such values of x. Note that it seems that if x is near 4, then $f(x)$ will be near 6 and, in fact, the closer x is to 4 the closer $f(x)$ is to 6.

We indicate this behavior of $f(x)$ for x close to 4 by writing

$$\lim_{x \to 4} f(x) = 6,$$

which is read "the limit of $f(x)$ as x approaches 4 is 6." It is important to remember that this is an entirely different statement than $f(4) = 6$. Here $f(4)$ has no meaning at all. The limit statement means that whether x is larger than 4 or smaller than 4, the closer one chooses x to 4, the closer $f(x)$ will be to 6.

Definition 2.3

> Let f be a function whose domain includes all real numbers in an open interval containing a (except possibly a itself). If $f(x)$ gets arbitrarily close to some number L as x is chosen ever closer to a, then we say that the **limit of $f(x)$ as x approaches a is L** and denote this by
>
> $$\lim_{x \to a} f(x) = L.$$

Figure 2.1 offers a geometric interpretation of $\lim_{x \to a} f(x) = L$. Values of $f(x)$ fall within the indicated interval about L whenever values of x are taken within the indicated interval about a. ($x = a$ is not considered in the limiting process.)

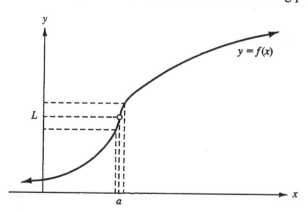

Figure 2.1
A geometric interpretation of $\lim_{x \to a} f(x) = L$

EXAMPLE 1

Find $\lim_{x \to 2}(3x + 5)$.

SOLUTION

By evaluating $f(x) = 3x + 5$ for several values of x near 2, it is apparent that $f(x)$ is approaching 11 (see Table 2.2); that is,

$$\lim_{x \to 2} (3x + 5) = 11.$$

For this function, note that it is also true that $f(2) = 11$.

x	$3x + 5$
2.1	11.30
2.02	11.06
2.001	11.003
1.94	10.82
1.99	10.97
1.998	10.994

Table 2.2

EXAMPLE 2

Find $\lim_{x \to -1} (x^2 + 2x - 3)$.

SOLUTION

The evaluation of $f(x) = x^2 + 2x - 3$ for several choices of x close to -1 is shown in Table 2.3. From this table it is apparent that the limit is -4; that is,

$$\lim_{x \to -1} (x^2 + 2x - 3) = -4.$$

For this function it is also true that $f(-1) = -4$.

x	$x^2 + 2x - 3$
$-.90$	-3.990
$-.95$	-3.998
-1.14	-3.980
-1.03	-3.999

Table 2.3

For many functions it is possible to find a limit by simply evaluating $f(x)$ at $x = a$. In Section 2.4 we will carefully study those functions f for which it is true that $f(a)$ and $\lim_{x \to a} f(x)$ are equal. For now, it is sufficient to note that this is true for all polynomial functions and all power and rational functions when a is in the domain.

The following properties of the limit are quite useful when finding the limit of a function. It is assumed that $f(x)$ and $g(x)$ are functions for which the limit as x approaches a exists. The properties are listed without proof.

1. $\lim_{x \to a} k = k$ for any constant k.
2. $\lim_{x \to a} x = a$.
3. $\lim_{x \to a} [f(x) + g(x)] = \lim_{x \to a} f(x) + \lim_{x \to a} g(x)$.
4. $\lim_{x \to a} f(x)g(x) = \lim_{x \to a} f(x) \lim_{x \to a} g(x)$.
5. $\lim_{x \to a} f(x)/g(x) = \lim_{x \to a} f(x)/\lim_{x \to a} g(x)$ [provided that $\lim_{x \to a} g(x) \neq 0$].
6. $\lim_{x \to a} \sqrt[n]{f(x)} = \sqrt[n]{\lim_{x \to a} f(x)}$ [where n is any natural number, but $f(x) > 0$ when n is even].

EXAMPLE 3

Find the limit:

$$\lim_{x \to 2} \frac{(x + 2) \sqrt{x^2 + 5}}{x^3 + 2x + 7}.$$

SOLUTION

Using the properties just given, we find

$$\lim_{x \to 2} \frac{(x + 2)\sqrt{x^2 + 5}}{x^3 + 2x + 7} = \frac{\lim_{x \to 2}(x + 2) \lim_{x \to 2}\sqrt{x^2 + 5}}{\lim_{x \to 2} x^3 + 2x + 7}$$

$$= \frac{(4)(3)}{19} = \frac{12}{19}.$$

EXAMPLE 4

Find $\lim_{x \to 5} f(x)$ and $\lim_{x \to 4} f(x)$ if

$$f(x) = \frac{x^2 - 2x - 8}{x - 4}, \qquad x \neq 4.$$

Sketch a graph of f.

SOLUTION

Using property 5, we get

$$\lim_{x \to 5} \frac{x^2 - 2x - 8}{x - 4} = \frac{\lim_{x \to 5} x^2 - 2x - 8}{\lim_{x \to 5} x - 4}$$

$$= \frac{7}{1}$$

$$= 7.$$

Since $\lim_{x \to 4} (x - 4) = 0$, property 5 does not apply to

$$\lim_{x \to 4} \frac{x^2 - 2x - 8}{x - 4}.$$

Returning to Table 2.1, we see that this limit was determined by actually evaluating $f(x)$ for values of x close to 4. Examining the numerator, we get

$$\lim_{x \to 4}(x^2 - 2x - 8) = 0,$$

suggesting that $(x - 4)$ is a factor of the numerator. In fact,

$$f(x) = \frac{x^2 - 2x - 8}{x - 4}$$

$$= \frac{(x - 4)(x + 2)}{x - 4}$$

$$= x + 2 \qquad \text{if } x \neq 4.$$

Thus, when $x \neq 4$, $f(x) = x + 2$. Since x does not equal 4 as x approaches 4, we have

$$\lim_{x \to 4} f(x) = \lim_{x \to 4} (x + 2)$$

$$= 6.$$

A graph of $y = f(x)$ appears in Figure 2.2. Observe that it is the same as the graph of $y = x + 2$ except that the point (4, 6) is missing because 4 is not in the domain of the function f.

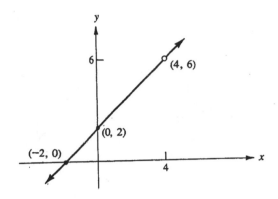

Figure 2.2
The graph of
$y = (x^2 - 2x - 8)/(x - 4)$, $x \neq 4$

EXAMPLE 5

Find the limit

$$\lim_{x \to 3} \frac{2x^2 - x - 15}{x^2 - 9}.$$

SOLUTION

Observe that once again it is not possible to find this limit by using property 5 because

$$\lim_{x \to 3} (x^2 - 9) = 0.$$

As before, the limit of the numerator is also 0, and both the numerator and denominator contain the factor $(x - 3)$. By factoring we alter the "zero over zero" form to a meaningful one:

$$\lim_{x \to 3} \frac{2x^2 - x - 15}{x^2 - 9} = \lim_{x \to 3} \frac{(x - 3)(2x + 5)}{(x - 3)(x + 3)}$$

$$= \lim_{x \to 3} \frac{(2x + 5)}{(x + 3)}$$

$$= \frac{11}{6}.$$

The cancellation in this example is permitted because x does not equal 3, and the two quotients are equal for all other values of x. The graph of $y = (2x^2 - x - 15)/(x^2 - 9)$ is the same as the graph of the linear-to-linear rational function $y = (2x + 5)/(x + 3)$ except that the point $(3, 11/6)$ is missing (see Figure 2.3).

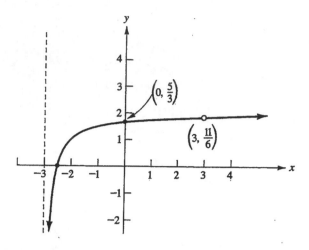

Figure 2.3
The graph of
$y = (2x^2 - x - 15)/(x^2 - 9)$;
$x > -3, x \neq 3$

In both of the preceding examples, a "zero over zero" form was altered by factoring. Often algebraic manipulations can be used to convert expressions from meaningless forms to others where limit properties can be applied and the limit can be found. In some cases, however, $f(x)$ does not approach a particular number L as x approaches a. Such cases are treated in the next section.

Recalling the work of the previous section, we can use limits to give formal definitions of marginal cost and marginal revenue.

Definition 2.4

If $C(q)$ denotes the total cost of producing q units of a product, then the marginal cost of the qth unit of output is

$$MC(q) = \lim_{h \to 0} \frac{C(q + h) - C(q)}{h}$$

provided that this limit exists. If $R(q)$ denotes the revenue generated by the sale of q units of an item, then the marginal revenue from the qth unit is

$$MR(q) = \lim_{h \to 0} \frac{R(q + h) - R(q)}{h}$$

provided that this limit exists.

It should be observed that each of these limit definitions is a zero-over-zero form. Therefore, it is necessary to simplify the quotient before letting h approach 0.

EXERCISES 2.2

In Exercises 1–24 find the indicated limit.

1. $\lim_{x \to 4} (7x - 5)$

2. $\lim_{x \to 0} \dfrac{x + 5}{3x + 2}$

3. $\lim_{y \to 2} 4$

4. $\lim_{t \to 3} \dfrac{t - 3}{t + 1}$

5. $\lim_{x \to -3} (x^2 + 5x - 1)$

6. $\lim_{u \to \sqrt{2}} (u^2 - 1)$

7. $\lim_{x \to 2} (5 - 2x)$

8. $\lim_{h \to 0} \dfrac{h + 5}{3h + 1}$

9. $\lim_{x \to 3} \dfrac{x - 3}{x + 3}$

10. $\lim_{t \to 1/2} \dfrac{1}{4t + 6}$

11. $\lim_{y \to 5} \sqrt{y^2 + 3y + 9}$

12. $\lim_{r \to 8} \dfrac{\sqrt[3]{r}}{\sqrt{r + 1}}$

13. $\lim_{x \to 0} \dfrac{x}{x^2 + 3x}$

14. $\lim_{h \to 0} \dfrac{(1 + h)^2 - 1}{h}$

15. $\lim_{x \to 0} \dfrac{x}{x^2 + 3x + 4}$

16. $\lim_{y \to 5} \dfrac{y - 5}{y^2 - 2y - 15}$

17. $\lim_{t \to 3} \dfrac{t^2 - 9}{t - 3}$

18. $\lim_{x \to 3} \dfrac{x - 3}{3 - x}$

19. $\lim_{x \to 0} \dfrac{x^2 - 2x}{x}$

20. $\lim_{u \to 1} \dfrac{u - 1}{u^2 - u + 2}$

21. $\lim_{t \to 1} \dfrac{t^2 - 1}{t - 1}$

22. $\lim_{y \to -2} \dfrac{y^2 + y - 2}{y^2 - y - 6}$

23. $\lim_{h \to 0} \dfrac{(2 + h)^2 - 4}{h}$

24. $\lim_{x \to 4} \dfrac{4 - x}{x - 4}$

25. If $f(x) = \dfrac{x^2 - 5x + 6}{x - 3}$, find

    a. $\lim_{x \to 4} f(x)$ b. $\lim_{x \to 3} f(x)$ c. $\lim_{x \to 2} f(x)$ d. $\lim_{x \to 1} f(x)$

26. Consider the function $f(x) = (\sqrt{x} - 3)/(x - 9)$, $x \neq 9$. Use a calculator with a $\boxed{\sqrt{}}$ key to complete the table; then estimate $\lim_{x \to 9} f(x)$.

x	8.9	9.1	8.99	9.001	8.999
$f(x)$					

Rewrite

$$\frac{\sqrt{x} - 3}{x - 9}$$

to algebraically determine $\lim_{x \to 9} f(x)$.

27. Consider the function $g(x) = (x^3 - 8)/(x - 2)$, $x \neq 2$. Complete the table; then estimate $\lim_{x \to 2} g(x)$. Factor $x^3 - 8$ and then find $\lim_{x \to 2} g(x)$.

x	2.1	1.9	2.01	1.99	2.001
$g(x)$					

28. Consider the function $f(x) = (1 + x)^{1/x}$, $x \neq 0$. Use a calculator with a $\boxed{y^x}$ key to complete the table, rounding to five decimal places. Rounding to three decimal places, estimate $\lim_{x \to 0} f(x)$. (This important limit will be considered in Chapter 4.)

x	.1	$-.01$	.001	$-.0001$	.00001
$f(x)$					

29. If the total cost function for a particular product is given by

$$C(q) = 500 + 3q - .01q^2, \qquad 0 \leq q \leq 200,$$

find $MC(100)$; that is, find

$$\lim_{h \to 0} \frac{C(100 + h) - C(100)}{h}.$$

30. If the revenue function for a particular product is given by

$$R(q) = 15q - .02q^2, \qquad 0 \leq q \leq 300,$$

find $MR(200)$; that is, find

$$\lim_{h \to 0} \frac{R(200 + h) - R(200)}{h}.$$

31. The demand function for a particular product is given by

$$p = 25 - .04q, \qquad 0 \leq q \leq 300.$$

Find the associated revenue function; then determine $MR(200)$.

32. The variable cost per unit for a certain product is given by

$$v = 20 - .01q, \qquad 0 \leq q \leq 500.$$

Find the total cost function and $MC(300)$.

33. Let $f(x) = x^2$. Evaluate the limit

$$\lim_{h \to 0} \frac{f(x + h) - f(x)}{h}.$$

34. Let $f(x) = 5 - 4x$. Evaluate the limit

$$\lim_{h \to 0} \frac{f(x + h) - f(x)}{h}.$$

35. Let $f(x) = 3x^2$. Evaluate the limit

$$\lim_{h \to 0} \frac{f(x + h) - f(x)}{h}.$$

36. Let $f(x) = x^2 + 3x - 1$. Evaluate the limit

$$\lim_{h \to 0} \frac{f(x + h) - f(x)}{h}.$$

2.3
Limits Involving Infinity and One-Sided Limits

In the preceding section, limits of various functions were found by judiciously applying limit properties. Here we consider some types of function behavior that are not covered by these properties. We begin with the case where $f(x)$ grows or decays beyond any given number, as x approaches a.

Definition 2.5

If $f(x)$ is defined on an open interval containing a (except perhaps at a itself) and if for any number B (no matter how large) $f(x) > B$ for x close enough to a, we say $f(x)$ **grows without bound** as x approaches a and we write

$$\lim_{x \to a} f(x) = \infty.$$

Analogously, $f(x)$ is said to **decay without bound** as x approaches a, if for any B, $f(x) < B$ for x sufficiently close to a. In this case we write

$$\lim_{x \to a} f(x) = -\infty.$$

The infinity symbol, ∞, does not represent a number, although the limits just given are often called **infinite limits** and read: "$f(x)$ approaches infinity" or "$f(x)$ approaches negative infinity." The limit concept and the ∞ symbol are used here to indicate that $f(x)$ is increasing (or decreasing) beyond any fixed numerical value as x approaches a. Figures 2.4 and 2.5 illustrate functions f with infinite limits as x approaches a.

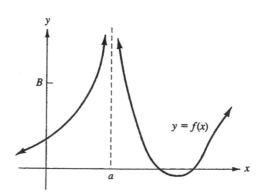

Figure 2.4

$\lim_{x \to a} f(x) = \infty$. Note that for any B, $f(x) > B$ when x is close enough to a.

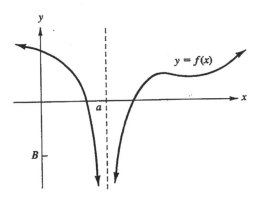

Figure 2.5

$\lim_{x \to a} f(x) = -\infty$. Note that for any $B, f(x) < B$ when x is close enough to a.

EXAMPLE 1

Examine the behavior of

$$f(x) = \frac{x^2 + 5x + 2}{x^2 - 6x + 9}, \qquad x \neq 3,$$

as x approaches 3.

SOLUTION

Checking the numerator and denominator of the function f, we find

$$\lim_{x \to 3} (x^2 + 5x + 2) = 26 \quad \text{and} \quad \lim_{x \to 3} (x^2 - 6x + 9) = 0.$$

The limit properties of the previous section do not apply here because the denominator is approaching 0. [The denominator is always positive, since it is equal to $(x - 3)^2$.] Unlike the earlier examples, the numerator is not approaching 0. As x approaches 3, the numerator approaches 26 while the denominator is nearing 0, so the ratio itself is positive and getting larger and larger (see Table 2.4). We conclude that $f(x)$ grows without bound as x approaches 3 and write

$$\lim_{x \to 3} \frac{x^2 + 5x - 2}{x^2 - 6x + 9} = \infty.$$

●

x	$\dfrac{x^2 + 5x + 2}{x^2 - 6x + 9}$
2.9	2,491
3.01	261,101
2.999	25,989,001
3.0001	2,600,110,001

Table 2.4

For some functions the behavior of $f(x)$, as x approaches a, is different when x is greater than a from when x is less than a. To distinguish between these cases, **one-sided limits** are used. We say "x approaches a from the right" and write

$$x \to a^+$$

to indicate that x is getting closer and closer to a, but that x is always greater than a (to the right of a on the number line). Similarly we say "x approaches a from the left" and write

$$x \to a^-$$

to indicate that x is getting closer and closer to a, but that x is always less than a. Figures 2.6 and 2.7 illustrate functions f with different one-sided limits. In such cases $\lim_{x \to a} f(x)$ does not exist.

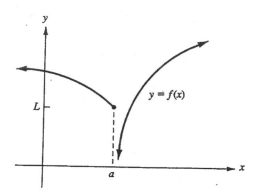

Figure 2.6

$\lim_{x \to a^-} f(x) = L$

but $\lim_{x \to a^+} f(x) = -\infty$.

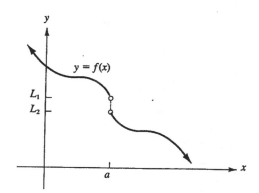

Figure 2.7

$\lim_{x \to a^-} f(x) = L_1$

but $\lim_{x \to a^+} f(x) = L_2$.

EXAMPLE 2

Examine the behavior of

$$f(x) = \frac{2x + 50}{x - 5}, \qquad x \neq 5,$$

as x approaches 5.

SOLUTION   Recall from equation (1.19) of Section 1.5 that the graph of this linear-to-linear rational function has a vertical asymptote at $x = 5$. Inspecting the numerator and denominator, we find that

$$\lim_{x \to 5} (2x + 50) = 60 \quad \text{and} \quad \lim_{x \to 5} (x - 5) = 0,$$

respectively. The ratio is getting large in magnitude as x approaches 5, but the sign of the ratio is positive when $x > 5$ and negative when $x < 5$. Using one-sided limits, we write

$$\lim_{x \to 5^+} \frac{2x + 50}{x - 5} = \infty \quad \text{and} \quad \lim_{x \to 5^-} \frac{2x + 50}{x - 5} = -\infty.$$

The graph shown in Figure 2.8 illustrates the unbounded behavior of a linear-to-linear rational function as the graph bends toward its vertical asymptote. Generally we say the graph of $y = f(x)$ has a **vertical asymptote** at $x = a$ if either

$$\lim_{x \to a^+} f(x) = \pm \infty \quad \text{or} \quad \lim_{x \to a^-} f(x) = \pm \infty.$$

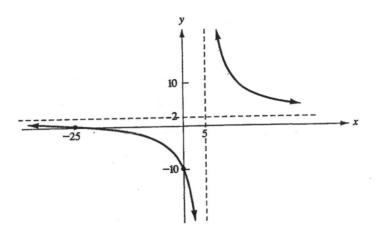

Figure 2.8
The graph of
$y = (2x + 50)/(x - 5)$

The behavior of a linear-to-linear rational function as it bends toward its horizontal asymptote can also be described using the limit concept. When the graph is approaching a horizontal asymptote, x is taking on larger and larger values (perhaps in a negative sense) while $f(x)$ is approaching some fixed value L.

Definition 2.6

The function f has the limit L as x becomes infinitely large, denoted

$$\lim_{x \to \infty} f(x) = L,$$

if $f(x)$ becomes arbitrarily close to L as ever larger values of x are chosen. Analogously, the expression

$$\lim_{x \to -\infty} f(x) = L$$

means that $f(x)$ becomes arbitrarily close to the number L as smaller (meaning negative numbers of larger magnitude) values of x are chosen.

Although these limits are often called "limits at infinity," the reader is cautioned again that ∞ is not a number. Figure 2.9 illustrates limits at infinity or horizontal asymptotes.

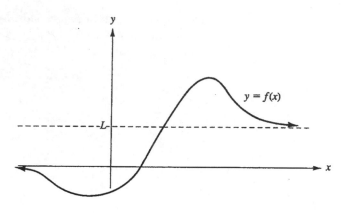

Figure 2.9

$\lim_{x \to \infty} f(x) = L$ and $\lim_{x \to -\infty} f(x) = 0$

EXAMPLE 3

Find $\lim_{x \to \infty} k/x$ and $\lim_{x \to -\infty} k/x$ where k is any constant.

SOLUTION

We know from our earlier study of rational functions that the horizontal asymptote of the hyperbola whose graph is given by $y = k/x$ is the x-axis. (See Figures 1.19 and 1.20.) This means that for large values of x, y will approach 0. Therefore,

$$\lim_{x \to \infty} \frac{k}{x} = 0 \quad \text{and} \quad \lim_{x \to -\infty} \frac{k}{x} = 0. \qquad \bullet$$

The following extensions of the result in Example 3 may be obtained using limit properties analogous to those in the previous section.

If k is any constant and n is a positive constant, then

(2.4)
$$\lim_{x \to \infty} \frac{k}{x^n} = 0$$

and

(2.5)
$$\lim_{x \to -\infty} \frac{k}{x^n} = 0.$$

Equations (2.4) and (2.5) are useful when finding limits at infinity. Examples 4, 5, and 6 illustrate their use.

EXAMPLE 4

Find the limit:

$$\lim_{x \to \infty} \frac{8x - 3}{2x + 5}.$$

SOLUTION

Examining the numerator and denominator individually, we see that as x gets large, $8x$ gets large and $8x - 3$ gets large so

$$\lim_{x \to \infty} (8x - 3) = \infty.$$

Similarly,

$$\lim_{x \to \infty} (2x + 5) = \infty.$$

Thus, we are dealing with an infinity-over-infinity form that has no meaning. If we divide the numerator and the denominator by x and then use equation (2.4), we find

$$\lim_{x \to \infty} \frac{8x - 3}{2x + 5} = \lim_{x \to \infty} \frac{8 - 3/x}{2 + 5/x}$$

$$= \frac{\lim_{x \to \infty} 8 - 3/x}{\lim_{x \to \infty} 2 + 5/x}$$

$$= \frac{8 - 0}{2 + 0}$$

$$= 4. \qquad \bullet$$

Generally the graph of $y = f(x)$ has a **horizontal asymptote** at $y = L$ if either

$$\lim_{x \to \infty} f(x) = L \quad \text{or} \quad \lim_{x \to -\infty} f(x) = L.$$

EXAMPLE 5

Find the limit:

$$\lim_{x \to -\infty} \frac{2x^2 + 5x - 3}{x^2 + 2x - 12}.$$

SOLUTION

Again, the numerator and denominator are approaching ∞. Dividing the numerator and denominator by x^2, the highest power of x that appears in the denominator, we create terms of the form k/x^n and find

$$\lim_{x \to -\infty} \frac{2x^2 + 5x - 3}{x^2 + 2x - 12} = \lim_{x \to -\infty} \frac{2 + 5/x - 3/x^2}{1 + 2/x - 12/x^2}$$

$$= \frac{2 + 0 - 0}{1 + 0 - 0}$$

$$= 2. \qquad \bullet$$

EXAMPLE 6

Find the limit:

$$\lim_{x \to \infty} \frac{3x^2 + 6x - 7}{5x + 1}.$$

SOLUTION

Dividing the numerator and denominator by x, the highest power of x that appears in the denominator, we obtain

$$\lim_{x \to \infty} \frac{3x^2 + 6x - 7}{5x + 1} = \lim_{x \to \infty} \frac{3x + 6 - 7/x}{5 + 1/x}$$

$$= \frac{\lim_{x \to \infty} 3x + 6 - 7/x}{\lim_{x \to \infty} 5 + 1/x}.$$

Since the denominator is approaching 5 while the numerator is growing without bound,

$$\lim_{x \to \infty} \frac{3x^2 + 6x - 7}{5x + 1} = \infty.$$ ●

Besides infinite limits, another instance in which $f(x)$ does not approach a particular value L, as x approaches a, is where $\lim_{x \to a^-} f(x)$ and $\lim_{x \to a^+} f(x)$ have different numerical values (see Figure 2.7). In this case we say that the (two-sided) limit $\lim_{x \to a} f(x)$ does not exist. In fact,

$\lim_{x \to a} f(x)$ exists if and only if $\lim_{x \to a^-} f(x)$ and $\lim_{x \to a^+} f(x)$ exist and are equal.

EXAMPLE 7   Let C denote the cost of a long-distance telephone call. Suppose that if the call lasts less than three minutes, the cost is $1.85 and that an additional $0.30 is charged for each additional minute or fraction of a minute. Then the cost C of a call can be given as a function of its duration t by

$$C(t) = \begin{cases} 1.85, & 0 < t < 3 \\ 2.15, & 3 \le t < 4 \\ 2.45, & 4 \le t < 5 \\ 2.75, & 5 \le t < 6 \\ \vdots & \vdots \end{cases}$$

Show that $\lim_{t \to 4} C(t)$ does not exist.

SOLUTION   If the duration of the call is nearly 4 min but less than 4 min, the cost is $2.15, but if the call lasts for even a fraction of a second over 4 min, the cost jumps to $2.45. Therefore,

$$\lim_{t \to 4^-} C(t) = 2.15 \quad \text{and} \quad \lim_{t \to 4^+} C(t) = 2.45.$$

Because the two one-sided limits are unequal $\lim_{x \to 4} C(t)$ does not exist.

The graph of C as a function of t is shown in Figure 2.10. It is an example of what is sometimes called a step function.

Figure 2.10
The graph of the cost C of a long-distance telephone call as a function of the duration of the call t

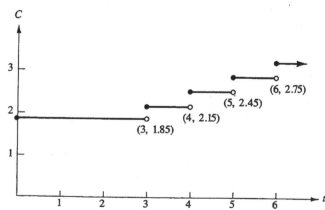

EXERCISES 2.3

In Exercises 1–30 find the limit, if it exists.

1. $\lim\limits_{x\to 0} \dfrac{5}{x^2}$

2. $\lim\limits_{x\to 0} \dfrac{-2}{x^4}$

3. $\lim\limits_{x\to 2} \dfrac{-3}{(x-2)^2}$

4. $\lim\limits_{x\to -4} \dfrac{8}{(x+4)^2}$

5. $\lim\limits_{x\to 1} \dfrac{3}{x^2 - 2x + 1}$

6. $\lim\limits_{y\to 3} \dfrac{y-5}{y^2 - 6y - 9}$

7. $\lim\limits_{x\to 2^+} \dfrac{x-1}{x-2}$

8. $\lim\limits_{x\to 2^-} \dfrac{x-1}{x-2}$

9. $\lim\limits_{x\to 3^-} \dfrac{x^2 + 9}{x-3}$

10. $\lim\limits_{x\to 3^+} \dfrac{x^2 + 9}{x-3}$

11. $\lim\limits_{x\to 4} \dfrac{x+1}{x^2 - 16}$

12. $\lim\limits_{x\to 2} \dfrac{x^2}{x^2 - 3x + 2}$

13. $\lim\limits_{y\to 5^-} \dfrac{y^2}{y^2 - 3y - 10}$

14. $\lim\limits_{x\to 3^-} \dfrac{x^2 + x - 2}{x^2 - x - 6}$

15. $\lim\limits_{x\to -2^+} \dfrac{x+2}{2x^2 + 5x + 2}$

16. $\lim\limits_{x\to 4^-} \dfrac{x^2 + x - 20}{3x^2 - 10x - 8}$

17. $\lim\limits_{x\to \infty} \dfrac{6x+4}{2x-5}$

18. $\lim\limits_{x\to \infty} \dfrac{3}{\sqrt{x}}$

19. $\lim\limits_{x\to -\infty} \dfrac{5-4x}{3-x}$

20. $\lim\limits_{t\to \infty} \dfrac{t+12}{3t-4}$

21. $\lim\limits_{r\to \infty} \dfrac{4}{3+7r}$

22. $\lim\limits_{s\to -\infty} \dfrac{4s^2 - 1}{2s^2 - s + 3}$

23. $\lim\limits_{z\to \infty} \dfrac{15z^2 + 8}{9z^2 - 7}$

24. $\lim\limits_{y\to \infty} \dfrac{y^3 - 2y}{2y^3 + 4}$

25. $\lim\limits_{x\to -\infty} \dfrac{x^2 + 3x - 8}{x^6 + x^4 - x^2 + 1}$

26. $\lim\limits_{x\to \infty} \dfrac{x^4 + 1}{x^3 - 1}$

27. $\lim\limits_{x\to \infty} 2x - 5$

28. $\lim\limits_{x\to \infty} x^2 + 8x - 12$

29. $\lim\limits_{q\to -\infty} \dfrac{q^2}{3q - 6}$

30. $\lim\limits_{p\to -\infty} \dfrac{p^2 + 8p + 7}{3p + 2}$

31. Explain why $\lim\limits_{x\to 4} \sqrt{2x - 8}$ does not exist, but $\lim\limits_{x\to 4^+} \sqrt{2x - 8} = 0$.

32. Explain why $\lim\limits_{x\to 2} \sqrt{4 - x^2}$ does not exist, but $\lim\limits_{x\to 2^-} \sqrt{4 - x^2} = 0$.

In Exercises 33–39 find $\lim\limits_{x\to 2} f(x)$, if it exists, by first finding the two one-sided limits.

33. $f(x) = \begin{cases} x^2 + 4, & x \le 2 \\ 3x + 2, & x > 2 \end{cases}$

34. $f(x) = \begin{cases} x^2 - 1, & x \ne 2 \\ 2x + 5, & x = 2 \end{cases}$

35. $f(x) = \begin{cases} \dfrac{x^2 - 4}{x - 2}, & x \ne 2 \\ 0, & x = 2 \end{cases}$

36. $f(x) = \begin{cases} \dfrac{1}{(x - 2)^2}, & x \ne 2 \\ 0, & x = 2 \end{cases}$

37. $f(x) = \begin{cases} \dfrac{1}{x - 2}, & x \ne 2 \\ 0, & x = 2 \end{cases}$

38. $f(x) = \sqrt{x - 2}$ 39. $f(x) = \sqrt[3]{x - 2}$

40. When q digital watches are produced each week, the variable cost per watch is given by

$$v = \frac{20q + 500}{q + 20}, \qquad q > 0.$$

Find $\lim\limits_{q\to 0^+} v(q)$ and $\lim\limits_{q\to \infty} v(q)$. What do these limits say about the production cost of the watch?

41. When q tons of copper ore are mined each day at the Ajax Mines, the variable cost per ton is estimated to be

$$v = \frac{75q + 4000}{3q + 80}, q > 0.$$

Find $\lim\limits_{q\to 0^+} v(q)$ and $\lim\limits_{q\to \infty} v(q)$. What do these limits say about the mining costs at Ajax?

42. The cost C (in 1987) of mailing a first-class letter that weighs w ounces in the United States is given by the function

$$C(w) = \begin{cases} .22, & 0 < w \le 1 \\ .44, & 1 < w \le 2 \\ .66, & 2 < w \le 3 \\ .88, & 3 < w \le 4 \\ 1.10, & 4 < w \le 5 \\ \vdots & \vdots \end{cases}$$

a. Find $\lim\limits_{w\to 3^-} C(w)$, $\lim\limits_{w\to 3^+} C(w)$, and $C(3)$.

b. For which values of a does $\lim_{w \to a} C(w)$ not exist?

c. Sketch the graph of $C(w)$ for $0 < w \leq 5$.

43. Consider the function $f(x) = (1 + 1/x)^x$. Use a calculator with a $\boxed{y^x}$ key to complete the table.

x	1	10	100	1000	1,000,000
$f(x)$					

Rounded to three decimal places, estimate $\lim_{x \to \infty} (1 + 1/x)^x$. (This important limit will be studied in Chapter 4.)

44. A worker is paid a regular hourly wage of $9.00 and is paid time and a half for overtime. The wages W owed the worker after t hours are then given by

$$W(t) = \begin{cases} 9t, & 0 \leq t \leq 8 \\ 72 + 13.5(t - 8), & t > 8. \end{cases}$$

a. Find $\lim_{t \to 8^-} W(t)$, $\lim_{t \to 8^+} W(t)$, and $W(8)$.

b. Sketch the graph of $W(t)$ for $0 \leq t \leq 10$. (Hint: Observe that on each part of the domain, the function is linear.)

45. A factory is in continuous operation from 8:00 A.M. to 6:00 P.M. A certain chemical is used in the production process at a fairly consistent rate of 50 lb/hr. When the factory began operation that morning, the holding tank for the chemical contained 600 lb. Just after 4:00 P.M., 300 more pounds were added to the tank. The amount A of the chemical in the tank t hours after the plant began operation can be given by the function

$$A(t) = \begin{cases} 600 - 50t, & 0 \leq t \leq 8 \\ \underline{} & 8 < t \leq 10. \end{cases}$$

a. Fill in the missing part of the relationship. (Hint: Examine the function in Exercise 44.)

b. Find $\lim_{t \to 8^-} A(t)$, $\lim_{t \to 8^+} A(t)$, and $A(8)$.

c. Sketch the graph of $A(t)$ for $0 \leq t \leq 10$. In what way does this graph differ from the graph of the function in Exercise 44?

46. Let the total cost of producing q units of some item be given by $C = vq + k$, where v is the variable cost per unit and k is the fixed cost. If the average cost per unit produced is $A = C/q$, show that $\lim_{q \to \infty} A = v$; that is, as output increases, the average cost approaches the variable cost.

2.4
Continuity

In the previous sections, we stressed that for a given function f and a given number a in the domain of f, the expressions $f(a)$ and $\lim_{x \to a} f(x)$ are quite different in concept. The first denotes the range value for f when x is chosen to equal a, whereas the second represents a value L that $f(x)$ approaches as x is chosen closer and closer to a (but without ever equaling a). Keeping this distinction in mind, we present the following definition.

Definition 2.7

> The function f is said to be **continuous** at $x = a$ if
> $$\lim_{x \to a} f(x) = f(a).$$

To elaborate, a function f is continuous at $x = a$ when three conditions are met:

1. f must be defined at a; that is, $f(a)$ exists.
2. The limit $\lim_{x \to a} f(x)$ must exist.
3. The limit as x approaches a must equal $f(a)$.

EXAMPLE 1

Show that $f(x) = x^3 + 3x^2 - 5x + 4$ is continuous at $x = 2$.

SOLUTION

Since f is a cubic polynomial, it is defined for any x and in fact $f(2) = 14$. From the properties of limits listed in the previous section, it is also true that $\lim_{x \to 2} f(x) = 14$. Since

$$\lim_{x \to 2} f(x) = 14 = f(2),$$

the function is continuous at $x = 2$. ●

The concept of continuity is best understood by looking at some functions that are not continuous at some value of x. A function is **discontinuous** at $x = a$ (or f has a discontinuity at $x = a$) if any of the three conditions listed above is not met. The following three examples illustrate common types of discontinuities.

EXAMPLE 2

Let

$$f(x) = \frac{2x^2 - x - 6}{x - 2}, \qquad x \ne 2,$$

and

$$g(x) = \begin{cases} \dfrac{2x^2 - x - 6}{x - 2}, & x \ne 2 \\ 3, & x = 2. \end{cases}$$

Show that both f and g are discontinuous at $x = 2$.

SOLUTION

The rule of correspondence for f does not cover the case where $x = 2$. Hence f is not defined at 2, or $f(2)$ does not exist, so f is discontinuous at $x = 2$.

For the function g, $g(2)$ is defined to be 3. However,

$$\lim_{x \to 2} g(x) = \lim_{x \to 2} \frac{(2x + 3)(x - 2)}{x - 2} = 7.$$

Because $g(2)$ and $\lim_{x \to 2} g(x)$ are not equal, g is discontinuous at $x = 2$.

Notice that the function h given by

$$h(x) = \begin{cases} \dfrac{2x^2 - x - 6}{x - 2}, & x \ne 2 \\ 7, & x = 2 \end{cases}$$

is continuous at $x = 2$. [In fact, $h(x) = 2x + 3$ for all x.] Graphs of f and g appear in Figure 2.11.

Figure 2.11

Graphs of the functions $y = f(x)$ and $y = g(x)$ of Example 2. Both are discontinuous at $x = 2$.

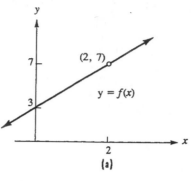

(a)

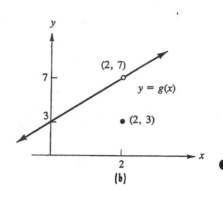

(b)

EXAMPLE 3

Suppose

$$f(x) = \begin{cases} \dfrac{2}{x^2}, & x \neq 0 \\ k, & x = 0. \end{cases}$$

Show that f is discontinuous at $x = 0$, regardless of the choice of the constant k.

SOLUTION

Because $\lim_{x \to 0} f(x) = \infty$ for any k, $f(x) > k$ when x is close enough to 0. Thus $\lim_{x \to 0} f(x)$ cannot equal $f(0)$, no matter how $f(0)$ is defined. (See Figure 2.12.)

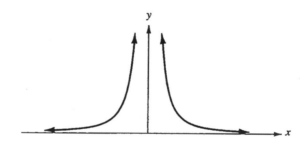

Figure 2.12

The graph of $y = 2/x^2$, $x \neq 0$

EXAMPLE 4

Let C be the cost of a long-distance telephone call that lasts for t minutes, with

$$C(t) = \begin{cases} 1.85, & 0 < t < 3 \\ 2.15, & 3 \leq t < 4 \\ 2.45, & 4 \leq t < 5 \\ 2.75, & 5 \leq t < 6 \\ \vdots & \vdots \end{cases}$$

(This function was introduced and graphed as Example 7 in Section 2.3.) Show that C is discontinuous at $t = 5$.

SOLUTION

In this example, $t = 5$ is in the domain (after all, it is possible for a telephone call to last exactly 5 min) and $C(5) = 2.75$. However, $\lim_{t \to 5} C(t)$ does not exist, since the two one-sided limits are not equal:

$$\lim_{t \to 5^-} C(t) = 2.45 \quad \text{and} \quad \lim_{t \to 5^+} C(t) = 2.75.$$

In fact, this function is discontinuous for $t = 3, 4, 5, 6, \ldots$—that is, at every point where the graph "jumps." (See Figure 2.10 in the previous section.) ●

Continuity is a pointwise property. A function can be continuous at one point and discontinuous at another. Nearly all the functions that we have used and will later use for business models are continuous at all the points in their domains (the cost of the long-distance telephone call is a notable exception). Certainly this is true for the algebraic functions, which include polynomial functions, rational functions, and power functions. A naive way to describe a function that is continuous at all points in an interval is to say that the graph of the function can be "drawn in one piece." (There are no breaks, jumps, or vertical asymptotes in the graph.) The situation is somewhat more complicated than this, but such a geometric image of a function that is continuous on an interval is suitable for our purposes in this text. For closed intervals special consideration must be given to the endpoints.

EXAMPLE 5

Suppose that the variable cost v for producing each unit of some item when q units are produced daily is modeled by the function

$$v = \frac{22q + 750}{q + 10}, \qquad q > 0.$$

According to the definition of continuity, v is not continuous at $q = 0$ for two reasons: first, v is not defined at $q = 0$ (variable cost has no meaning when there is no production at all), and second, the limit

$$\lim_{q \to 0} \frac{22q + 750}{q + 10}$$

does not exist, since the model does not permit negative values of q. We resolve both difficulties by observing that the limit from the right does exist:

$$\lim_{q \to 0^+} \frac{22q + 750}{q + 10} = 75.$$

Therefore, we extend the domain of the model to include $q = 0$:

$$v = \frac{22q + 750}{q + 10}, \qquad q \geq 0.$$

We say v is "continuous from the right" at $q = 0$ because

$$\lim_{q \to 0^+} v(q) = v(0) = 75.$$

With this description of one-sided continuity we say that v is continuous for $q \geq 0$. Observe that this is consistent with the geometric concept of continuity, for the graph of $v(q)$ can indeed be drawn in one piece (see Figure 2.13).

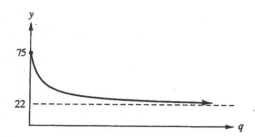

Figure 2.13

The graph of
$v = (22q + 750)/(q + 10)$, $q \geq 0$,
a continuous function for $q \geq 0$

It is worthwhile to point out that the procedure used to make v a continuous function at $q = 0$ avoids a potential problem in moving from variable cost to total cost. If the daily fixed costs for this production system are $400, then the total cost to produce q units in one day is

$$C = vq + 400$$

$$= \frac{(22q + 750)q}{q + 10} + 400$$

$$= \frac{22q^2 + 1150q + 4000}{q + 10}, \qquad q \geq 0.$$

This function is naturally defined at $q = 0$: $C(0) = 400$, the fixed costs, even though v has no real meaning for $q = 0$.   ●

Generally, a function f is said to be **continuous on the closed interval** $[a, b]$ if f is continuous at each x where $a < x < b$, and if

$$\lim_{x \to b^-} f(x) = f(b) \quad \text{and} \quad \lim_{x \to a^+} f(x) = f(a).$$

Continuous functions on closed intervals play an important role in later chapters. **If a function f is continuous on a closed interval $[a, b]$, then $f(x)$ takes on a maximum value, a minimum value, and all values in between.** This property will be explored more carefully in Chapter 5, but it is clearly reinforced by the geometric one-piece image of a continuous function. Figure 2.14 illustrates that discontinuous functions may not have this property. The graphs in Figure 2.15 show that continuous functions may not have a maximum or a minimum value on intervals that are not closed.

As a final example, we introduce a special function that is discontinuous at all integer values and we show one way in which these discontinuities can be useful.

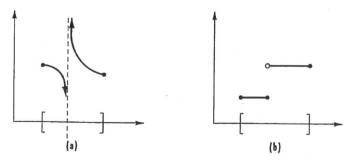

Figure 2.14

The graph of a discontinuous function on a closed interval that (a) has no maximum or minimum value and (b) has a maximum value and a minimum value but takes on none of the intermediate values

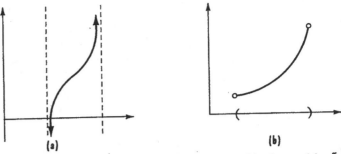

Figure 2.15

Graphs of continuous functions on open intervals that do not take on maximum or minimum values

This function is called the greatest integer function and is denoted by $[\![x]\!]$. For any real x, $[\![x]\!]$ is defined to be the largest integer that is less than or equal to x. Equivalently,

$$[\![x]\!] = \begin{cases} \vdots & \vdots \\ -2, & -2 \le x < -1 \\ -1, & -1 \le x < 0 \\ 0, & 0 \le x < 1 \\ 1, & 1 \le x < 2 \\ 2, & 2 \le x < 3 \\ \vdots & \vdots \end{cases}$$

The graph of $y = [\![x]\!]$ is shown in Figure 2.16 and is another example of a step function.

For positive values of x, $[\![x]\!]$ amounts to a crude rounding function, actually a "chopping" function. If x is positive and written in decimal form, then $[\![x]\!]$ is obtained from x by just chopping off the decimal part of x. For example,

$$[\![17.38162]\!] = 17.$$

The greatest integer function is very useful in computer programming because it permits a variety of rounding operations when it is cleverly composed with other

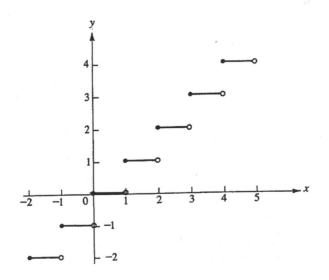

Figure 2.16

The graph of the greatest integer function $y = [\![x]\!]$

functions. For instance, for any real x, the operation $[\![x + .5]\!]$ will round x to the nearest integer. (The reader is invited to try a few values of x to be convinced of this.) When working with figures that represent amounts of money, it is often desirable to round to the nearest cent. Computer printouts that show dollar amounts like \$32.6374 are cluttered and look silly. Notice that for any x the rounding function

$$r(x) = \frac{[\![100x + .5]\!]}{100}$$

rounds x to two decimals. Within the brackets, multiplication by 100 converts the dollars to cents, the addition of .5 allows the rounding to the nearest cent, and the division by 100 converts back to dollars. For example,

$$
\begin{aligned}
r(32.6374) &= \frac{[\![100(32.6374) + .5]\!]}{100} \\
&= \frac{[\![3263.74 + .5]\!]}{100} \\
&= \frac{[\![3264.24]\!]}{100} \\
&= \frac{3264}{100} \\
&= 32.64.
\end{aligned}
$$

The greatest integer function can also be used to simplify the function $C(t)$ that gives the cost of a long-distance telephone call in Example 4. Observe that for any $t > 2$,

$$C(t) = 1.85 + .30[\![t - 2]\!].$$

For example, the cost of a call that lasts 4.75 min is

$$
\begin{aligned}
C(4.75) &= 1.85 - .30[\![4.75 - 2]\!] \\
&= 1.85 + .30[\![2.75]\!] \\
&= 1.85 + .30(2) \\
&= 2.45.
\end{aligned}
$$

Most computer programming languages contain a command for $[\![x]\!]$. In BASIC it is INT(x).

EXERCISES 2.4

In Exercises 1–20 check the given function for continuity at the specified value of a. If the function is not continuous, indicate which condition required for continuity is violated. Sketch a graph of the function.

1. $f(x) = 5x + 8$; $a = 0$

2. $f(x) = 4x^2 + 7x - 2$; $a = 2$

3. $f(x) = \sqrt{3x + 1}$; $a = 5$

4. $f(x) = \dfrac{x + 3}{2x - 1}$; $a = 0$

5. $f(x) = \dfrac{x + 3}{2x - 1}$; $a = \dfrac{1}{2}$

6. $f(x) = \begin{cases} \dfrac{x^2 - 5x + 6}{x - 2}, & x \neq 2 \\ 7, & x = 2 \end{cases}$; $a = 2$

7. $g(x) = \begin{cases} \dfrac{x^2 + x - 2}{x - 1}, & x \neq 1 \\ 5, & x = 1 \end{cases}$; $a = 1$

8. $g(x) = \begin{cases} \dfrac{x + 3}{x^2 + x - 6}, & x \neq -3, x \neq 2 \\ -1, & x = -3, x = 2 \end{cases}$; $a = -3$

9. $f(x) = \begin{cases} \dfrac{5x - 10}{x^2 + x - 6}, & x \neq -3, x \neq 2 \\ 1, & x = -3, x = 2 \end{cases}$; $a = 2$

10. $f(x) = \begin{cases} \dfrac{x^2 - 6x + 8}{x^2 - 3x - 4}, & x \neq -1, x \neq 4 \\ 1, & x = -1, x = 4 \end{cases}$; $a = 4$

11. $f(x) = \begin{cases} \dfrac{x^2 - 6x + 8}{x^2 - 3x - 4}, & x \neq -1, x \neq 4 \\ 1, & x = -1, x = 4 \end{cases}$; $a = -1$

12. $f(x) = \begin{cases} 5 - x, & x \leq 2 \\ x + 1, & x > 2 \end{cases}$; $a = 2$

13. $f(x) = \begin{cases} x - 1, & x \leq 3 \\ 2x - 1, & x > 3 \end{cases}$; $a = 3$

14. $f(x) = \begin{cases} 3x^2, & 0 \leq x < 4 \\ 5x + 8, & 4 \leq x \leq 7 \end{cases}$; $a = 4$

15. $f(x) = \begin{cases} 2x + 1, & x \leq 3 \\ x^2 - 2, & x > 3 \end{cases}$; $a = 3$

16. $f(x) = \begin{cases} 3x - 1, & x \leq 0 \\ \dfrac{x - 1}{x + 1}, & x > 0 \end{cases}$; $a = 0$

17. $f(x) = \begin{cases} \dfrac{2x - 1}{x - 1}, & x \leq 0 \\ 3x + 1, & x > 0 \end{cases}$; $a = 0$

18. $f(x) = \begin{cases} \dfrac{4x - 3}{x - 1}, & x < 1 \\ 2x - x^2, & x \geq 1 \end{cases}$; $a = 0$

19. $f(x) = \begin{cases} x^2 + 2x, & x < 0 \\ 2x - x^2, & x \geq 0 \end{cases}$; $a = 0$

20. $f(x) = \begin{cases} x^2 + 1, & x < -1 \\ 1 - x^2, & x \geq -1 \end{cases}$; $a = -1$

In Exercises 21–32 list all the discontinuities for the given function, if there are any.

21. $f(x) = 3 - 4x + 7x^2$

22. $f(x) = 12$

23. $f(x) = \dfrac{3}{5 + x}$

24. $f(x) = \dfrac{2x - 6}{x - 3}$

25. $f(x) = \dfrac{1}{x^2 - 7x + 10}$

26. $f(x) = \dfrac{x + 4}{x^2 + x}$

27. $f(x) = \dfrac{8}{x^2 - 9}$

28. $f(x) = \dfrac{8}{x^2 + 9}$

29. $f(x) = \begin{cases} 3x + 1, & x \leq 0 \\ 4, & x > 0 \end{cases}$

30. $f(x) = \begin{cases} \dfrac{15}{x + 2}, & x < 1 \\ 3, & x \geq 1 \end{cases}$

31. $f(x) = \begin{cases} \dfrac{20}{x - 3}, & x \leq 1 \\ -10, & x > 1 \end{cases}$

32. $f(x) = \begin{cases} \dfrac{x - 4}{x^2 - 5x + 4}, & x \neq 1, x \neq 4 \\ \dfrac{1}{3}, & x = 1, x = 4 \end{cases}$

33. Is the function $C(w)$ in Exercise 42 of Section 2.3 continuous at $w = 3$? Is it continuous at $w = 2.7$?

34. Let $r(x)$ be the function that rounds figures representing money to the nearest cent (see the text). Verify that $r(\$17.2547) = \$17.25$ and $r(\$17.2553) = \$17.26$. Evaluate $r(\$17.2550)$. Is r continuous at $\$17.2550$? Explain.

35. A bank collects a payment on the principal and the interest due on a commercial loan on the first banking day of each month. If the remaining balance x is $20,000 or less, the interest is 1.5% of the balance. If the balance is more than $20,000, the interest on the excess is 1.65%. The interest due I as a function of x can be written

$$I(x) = \begin{cases} .015x, & 0 \le x \le 20{,}000 \\ \underline{} & x > 20{,}000. \end{cases}$$

a. Complete the rule of correspondence for this function.

b. Is $I(x)$ a continuous function at $x = 20{,}000$?

c. Sketch a graph of $I(x)$.

36. Refer to Exercise 35. Suppose that when the remaining balance is more than $20,000, the bank adds a service charge of $10 for that month. Answer parts a, b, and c with this additional stipulation.

37. A credit union offers a new certificate of deposit that will pay 14% simple interest for any length of time t up to 2½ yr on a deposit of $1000. However, if the money is withdrawn prior to 1 yr, there is a penalty of 6 mo interest (which may be deducted from the original deposit if necessary). The amount A that is received by a depositor who withdraws the money after t years is given by

$$A(t) = \begin{cases} 930 + 140t, & 0 < t < 1 \\ 1000 + 140t, & 1 \le t \le 2.5. \end{cases}$$

a. Verify that the penalty for early withdrawal is $70.

b. Find $\lim_{t \to 1^-} A(t)$ and $\lim_{t \to 1^+} A(t)$. Is $A(t)$ continuous at $t = 1$?

c. Sketch a graph of this function.

CH. 2 REVIEW

I. Key Terms & Concepts

Mathematics

Continuous Function
Discontinuity
Greatest Integer Function
Limit
Infinite Limit
Limit at Infinity
One-Sided Limit

Business

Marginal Cost
Marginal Revenue

II. True or False

Indicate whether each statement is true or false.

1. The marginal cost of the qth unit produced is defined as a limit.

2. The maximum profit occurs at an output level where marginal cost equals marginal revenue.

3. If the selling price p of an article is constant regardless of the quantity sold q, then the marginal revenue from the qth unit is p.

4. If $\lim_{x \to \infty} f(x) = L$, then the graph of $y = f(x)$ has a vertical asymptote at $x = L$.

5. If $\lim_{x \to a^+} f(x) = \infty$, then the graph of $y = f(x)$ has a vertical asymptote at $x = a$.

6. If $\lim_{x \to a} f(x) = L$, then $\lim_{x \to a^-} f(x) = L$ and $\lim_{x \to a^+} f(x) = L$.

7. If $\lim_{x \to a} f(x) = 0$ and $\lim_{x \to a} g(x) = 0$, then $\lim_{x \to a} f(x)/g(x)$ does not exist.

8. If $f(a)$ and $\lim_{x \to a} f(x)$ are equal, then f is continuous at $x = a$.

9. Every polynomial is continuous on $(-\infty, \infty)$.

10. Every rational function is continuous on $(-\infty, \infty)$.

III. Drill Problems

In Problems 1–22 find the indicated limit, if it exists.

1. $\lim_{x \to 5} \dfrac{x^2 - 25}{3x - 15}$

2. $\lim_{x \to 2} \dfrac{x - 2}{x^2 - 4}$

3. $\lim_{x \to 2} \dfrac{x - 2}{x^2 + x + 1}$

4. $\lim_{x \to 3} \dfrac{x - 3}{x^2 + 9}$

5. $\lim_{x \to -3} \dfrac{x + 8}{x^2 + 6x + 9}$

6. $\lim_{x \to -1} \dfrac{x - 5}{x^2 + 2x + 1}$

7. $\lim_{x \to 1^+} \dfrac{3x - 7}{x - 1}$

8. $\lim_{x \to -4^-} \dfrac{2x + 1}{x - 4}$

9. $\lim_{x \to 2^-} \dfrac{x^2 + 1}{x^2 - x - 2}$

10. $\lim_{x \to 3^+} \dfrac{2x^2 - 7}{x^2 - x - 6}$

11. $\lim_{x \to 3} f(x)$ if $f(x) = \begin{cases} 6x - 10, & x \le 3 \\ x^2 - 1, & x > 3 \end{cases}$

12. $\lim_{x \to 1} g(x)$ if $g(x) = \begin{cases} 4x^2 + 1, & x \le 1 \\ 4x + 1, & x > 1 \end{cases}$

13. $\lim_{x \to -2^+} f(x)$ if $f(x) = \begin{cases} 5 - 2x, & x \le -2 \\ x^3, & x > -2 \end{cases}$

14. $\lim\limits_{x \to -2^-} f(x)$ if $f(x) = \begin{cases} 5 - 2x, & x \le -2 \\ x^3, & x > -2 \end{cases}$

15. $\lim\limits_{x \to 4^+} g(x)$ if $g(x) = \begin{cases} \dfrac{2x - 3}{x - 3}, & x \le 4 \\ \dfrac{x - 3}{2x - 3}, & x > 4 \end{cases}$

16. $\lim\limits_{x \to 4^-} g(x)$ if $g(x) = \begin{cases} \dfrac{2x - 3}{x - 3}, & x \le 4 \\ \dfrac{x - 3}{2x - 3}, & x > 4 \end{cases}$

17. $\lim\limits_{x \to \infty} \dfrac{2x^2 - 7}{x^2 - x - 6}$

18. $\lim\limits_{x \to -\infty} \dfrac{8 + 3x}{5x^2 - 2x + 1}$

19. $\lim\limits_{x \to -\infty} \dfrac{x - 2}{x^2 + x + 1}$

20. $\lim\limits_{x \to -\infty} \dfrac{x^3 + 6x^2}{x^2 + 5}$

21. $\lim\limits_{x \to \infty} \dfrac{x^2}{x + 1}$

22. $\lim\limits_{x \to \infty} \dfrac{5 + 3x - 4x^2}{x^2 + 2x + 6}$

In Problems 23–30 find all the discontinuities of the given function.

23. $f(x) = \dfrac{x}{x^3 - 4x}$

24. $f(x) = \dfrac{3 - x}{x^2 + 2x - 8}$

25. $g(x) = \dfrac{x^2 - 25}{x^2 + 9}$

26. $g(x) = \dfrac{4x}{x^2 + x + 1}$

27. $f(x) = \begin{cases} \dfrac{x + 1}{x - 1}, & x \le 0 \\ 2x + 1, & x > 0 \end{cases}$

28. $f(x) = \begin{cases} x^2 - 2, & x \le 1 \\ 2x - 3, & x > 1 \\ x + 2, & \end{cases}$

29. $f(x) = \begin{cases} 5 + 2x, & x \le -3 \\ \dfrac{10}{x^2 - 4}, & -3 < x \le 3 \\ x - 1, & x > 3 \end{cases}$

30. $f(x) = \begin{cases} \sqrt{1 - x}, & x \le 0 \\ \dfrac{1}{x - 1}, & x > 0 \end{cases}$

IV. Applications

1. The daily cost of producing q units (hundreds of pounds) of Select Sausage is known to be

$$C = 200 + 80q - .1q^2, \qquad 0 \le q \le 50.$$

Currently 2 tons ($q = 40$) of sausage are produced each day. Find the total cost of producing 2 tons of sausage, the average cost per hundred pounds, and the marginal cost of the 40th unit.

2. When a wholesaler buys q units (hundreds of pounds) of Select Sausage, the selling price per unit is

$$p = 110 - .2q, \qquad 0 \le q \le 50.$$

Find the revenue generated by the sale of 40 units of sausage, and the marginal revenue from the sale of the 40th unit.

3. Amcraft is a supplier of materials for arts-and-crafts hobbyists. Craft shops can order q of its knit kits at a

wholesale price of p dollars per kit, where

$$p = 8 - .02q, \qquad 0 \le q \le 100.$$

How much revenue is received by Amcraft from an order for 60 of these kits? Use the marginal revenue from the 60th kit to estimate the additional revenue from an order for 61 kits.

4. Amcraft can produce up to 800 knit kits each day. The daily fixed costs are $100 and the variable cost per kit v is given by

$$v = 6 - .005q, \qquad 0 \le q \le 800.$$

Find the cost of producing 500 kits, the average cost of each of the first 500 kits produced, and the marginal cost of the 500th kit.

5. The vice-president for sales has determined that the marginal revenue from the sale of the qth unit of your

company's product is given by

$$MR = 40 - .1q, \qquad 0 \leq q \leq 200.$$

As production manager you have estimated that on a day when q units are produced, the marginal cost of the qth unit is

$$MC = \frac{20q + 400}{q + 10}, \qquad q > 0.$$

a. If the current production level is $q = 150$ units per day, should you increase or decrease production in order to increase profit?

b. At what output level will profit be maximized?

6. The marginal cost and marginal revenue for a particular product are known to be

$$MC = 40 - .04q, \qquad 0 \leq q \leq 1000,$$

and

$$MR = 75 - .08q, \qquad 0 \leq q \leq 1000.$$

Find the output level q that maximizes profit.

7. The supply function for a certain commodity is given by

$$p(q) = \frac{180q + 1000}{q + 10}, \qquad q > 0.$$

Find and interpret the following limits.

a. $\lim_{q \to 0^+} p(q)$

b. $\lim_{q \to \infty} p(q)$

Precision Printers is about to produce a new letter quality printer. First estimates indicate fixed costs of $800 per day and a variable cost per unit given by

$$v = \frac{180q + 23{,}800}{q + 40}, \qquad 0 \le q \le 200.$$

Demand for letter quality printers should be

$$p = 347 - .47q, \qquad 0 \le q \le 200.$$

a. Find the marginal cost and the marginal revenue of the qth printer.
b. Determine the output level q that will maximize profit.

Differentiation

3.1
The Derivative

In Chapter 2 the concepts of marginal cost and marginal revenue were introduced as a special kind of limit that proved very useful in decision making. This limit occurs so frequently and is so important in applications of mathematics to the physical and social sciences that it is given a name and its own notation.

Definition 3.1

If f is a function defined by a rule of correspondence $y = f(x)$, then the **derivative of f with respect to x,** denoted by f', is a function defined at each x in the domain of f to be the limit

$$(3.1) \qquad f'(x) = \lim_{h \to 0} \frac{f(x + h) - f(x)}{h},$$

if this limit exists as a real number.

When we want to draw attention to the dependent variable, we call equation (3.1) the derivative of y with respect to x. The derivative may be denoted in any of the following ways:

$$f'(x), \qquad y', \qquad \frac{dy}{dx}, \qquad D_x f, \qquad D_x y.$$

If $C(q)$ denotes the total cost of producing q units of an item, then **marginal cost** is defined as

$$MC(q) = \lim_{h \to 0} \frac{C(q + h) - C(q)}{h}.$$

It follows that the derivative of total cost with respect to q is marginal cost:

$$C'(q) = \frac{dC}{dq} = MC(q).$$

Similarly, if revenue R is a function of q, then the derivative of revenue with respect to q is **marginal revenue:**

$$R'(q) = \frac{dR}{dq} = MR(q).$$

The most common interpretation of the derivative of a function f is as the **instantaneous rate of change** in the dependent variable y with respect to a change in the independent variable x. To see this, let a be a particular fixed value of x in the domain of f. If h is a nonzero number (with $a + h$ still in the domain), then the difference

$$f(a + h) - f(a)$$

is the change in the y-coordinate corresponding to a change of h in the x-coordinate (see Figure 3.1). The ratio of the change in y to the change in x,

$$\frac{f(a + h) - f(a)}{h},$$

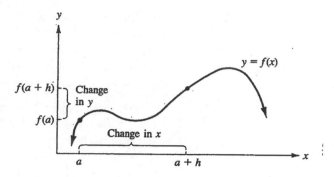

Figure 3.1

When x is changed from a by some amount h, y changes by $f(a + h) - f(a)$.

is the average rate of change in y per unit change in x from $x = a$ to $x = a + h$. Letting h tend to 0 gives the instantaneous rate of change (rather than an average rate of change) in y with respect to x when $x = a$.

Recalling the definition of the slope of a straight line, the line (called a secant line) that passes through points $(a, f(a))$ and $(a + h, f(a + h))$ on the curve $y = f(x)$ must have slope

$$\frac{f(a + h) - f(a)}{h}.$$

Generally, for different values of h, there is a different secant line and thus a different slope. If the limit as h tends toward 0 exists, these lines have as a limit a line passing through the point $(a, f(a))$ on the curve. (See Figure 3.2.) Because this point is reminiscent of the tangent line to a circle—a line that touches a circle at a single point—this limiting line is called the **tangent line** to the curve $y = f(x)$ at $(a, f(a))$. Consequently, we have another interpretation of the derivative: $f'(a)$ equals the slope of the tangent line to the curve $y = f(x)$ at the point $(a, f(a))$.

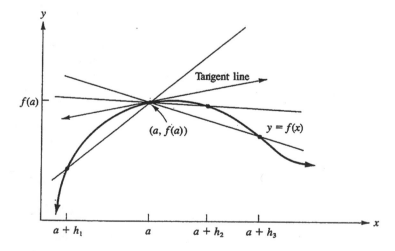

Figure 3.2

A curve $y = f(x)$ with tangent line at $(a, f(a))$ and several secant lines

EXAMPLE 1

Find the derivative of $f(x) = 7x - 6$.

SOLUTION

Since the graph of this function is a straight line with slope 7, and the derivative is the slope of the tangent line to the graph, it should be anticipated that $f'(x) = 7$ for all x. This observation may be verified by using the limit Definition 3.1:

$$f'(x) = \lim_{h \to 0} \frac{f(x + h) - f(x)}{h}$$

$$= \lim_{h \to 0} \frac{[7(x + h) - 6] - [7x - 6]}{h}$$

$$= \lim_{h \to 0} \frac{7x + 7h - 6 - 7x + 6}{h}$$

$$= \lim_{h \to 0} \frac{7h}{h}$$

$$= \lim_{h \to 0} 7$$

$$= 7.$$

●

EXAMPLE 2

Find dy/dx if $y = x^3$.

SOLUTION

This equation defines the function $y = f(x) = x^3$, and so

$$f'(x) = \lim_{h \to 0} \frac{f(x + h) - f(x)}{h}$$

$$= \lim_{h \to 0} \frac{(x + h)^3 - x^3}{h}$$

$$= \lim_{h \to 0} \frac{x^3 + 3x^2h + 3xh^2 + h^3 - x^3}{h}$$

$$= \lim_{h \to 0} \frac{3x^2h + 3xh^2 + h^3}{h}$$

$$= \lim_{h \to 0} (3x^2 + 3xh + h^2)$$

$$= 3x^2.$$

Thus $dy/dx = 3x^2$ when $y = x^3$.

●

When we wish to know the value of a derivative at a particular choice of x—say $x = a$—we can find it by evaluating $f'(x)$ at a. For instance, if $f(x) = x^3$, then we can evaluate $f'(x) = 3x^2$ at $x = 2$ to obtain $f'(2) = 12$. Using the dy/dx notation, we write

$$\left. \frac{dy}{dx} \right|_{x=2} = 12.$$

EXAMPLE 3   Find the derivative of $f(x) = \sqrt{x}$ for $x > 0$.

SOLUTION   From Definition 3.1 we have

$$
\begin{aligned}
f'(x) &= \lim_{h \to 0} \frac{\sqrt{x+h} - \sqrt{x}}{h} \\
&= \lim_{h \to 0} \frac{\sqrt{x+h} - \sqrt{x}}{h} \cdot \frac{\sqrt{x+h} + \sqrt{x}}{\sqrt{x+h} + \sqrt{x}} \\
&= \lim_{h \to 0} \frac{x+h-x}{h(\sqrt{x+h} + \sqrt{x})} \\
&= \lim_{h \to 0} \frac{1}{\sqrt{x+h} + \sqrt{x}} \\
&= \frac{1}{2\sqrt{x}}.
\end{aligned}
$$

●

EXAMPLE 4   Find the equation of the tangent line (in general form, $ax + by = c$) to the curve $y = \sqrt{x}$ at the point with coordinates $(16, 4)$.

SOLUTION   To find the equation of any line it is sufficient to know one point on the line and the slope of the line. We are given the point $(16, 4)$ and we can determine the slope from the derivative of the function $y = \sqrt{x}$. From Example 3, we know that

$$
\frac{dy}{dx} = \frac{1}{2\sqrt{x}},
$$

so

$$
\left. \frac{dy}{dx} \right|_{x=16} = \frac{1}{2\sqrt{16}} = \frac{1}{8}.
$$

The point-slope form of a line then yields

$$
y - 4 = \frac{1}{8}(x - 16)
$$

or in general form,

$$
x - 8y = -16.
$$

Figure 3.3 illustrates this tangent line.

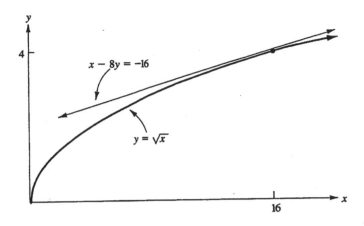

Figure 3.3

A sketch of $y = \sqrt{x}$ and its tangent line at (16, 4)

EXAMPLE 5

Find the derivative of $f(x) = 1/x$ for $x \neq 0$.

SOLUTION

Using Definition 3.1 we have

$$f'(x) = \lim_{h \to 0} \frac{\dfrac{1}{x+h} - \dfrac{1}{x}}{h} = \lim_{h \to 0} \frac{\dfrac{x - (x+h)}{x(x+h)}}{h}$$

$$= \lim_{h \to 0} \frac{-h}{hx(x+h)} = \lim_{h \to 0} \frac{-1}{x(x+h)}$$

$$= -\frac{1}{x^2}.$$

EXAMPLE 6

Find the rate of change in the reciprocal of x, with respect to x, when $x = 5$.

SOLUTION

If $y = 1/x$, then the rate of change in the reciprocal of x, with respect to x, is given by the derivative dy/dx. In Example 5 we found that

$$\frac{dy}{dx} = -\frac{1}{x^2},$$

so

$$\left.\frac{dy}{dx}\right|_{x=5} = -\frac{1}{25} = -.04.$$

Geometrically, when $x = 5$ the graph of $y = 1/x$ has a tangent line with slope $-.04$. At that point the instantaneous change in y with respect to x is $-.04$ as illustrated in Figure 3.4.

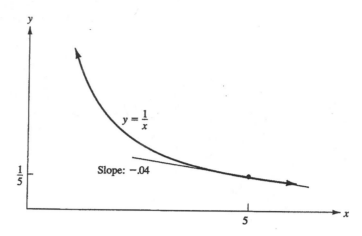

Figure 3.4

The change in the reciprocal of x, with respect to x, when $x = 5$

For later reference, we summarize the results of Examples 2, 3, and 5:

(3.2)
$$D_x[x^3] = 3x^2;$$

(3.3)
$$D_x[\sqrt{x}] = \frac{1}{2\sqrt{x}} \quad \text{or} \quad D_x[x^{1/2}] = \frac{1}{2}x^{-1/2};$$

(3.4)
$$D_x\left[\frac{1}{x}\right] = -\frac{1}{x^2} \quad \text{or} \quad D[x^{-1}] = -x^{-2}.$$

A function is said to be **differentiable** at $x = a$ if the derivative $f'(a)$ exists—that is, if the limit

$$\lim_{h \to 0} \frac{f(a + h) - f(a)}{h}$$

exists as a real number. Geometrically, a function fails to be differentiable at a point on its graph where there is a vertical tangent, or where there is no (unique) tangent—that is, at sharp corners or at breaks in the graph. Thus, a differentiable function is said to have a "smooth" graph that is in one piece.

It can be shown that if f is differentiable at $x = a$, then f is continuous at $x = a$. The converse of this statement is not true; a function can be continuous but not differentiable at a point. Figure 3.5 illustrates some of these possibilities.

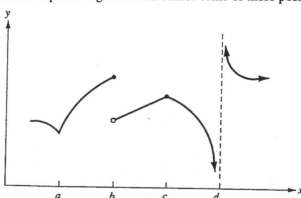

Figure 3.5

The graph of a function that is continuous but not differentiable at $x = a$ and $x = c$, and not continuous, and therefore not differentiable at $x = b$ and $x = d$

EXERCISES 3.1

In Exercises 1–12 use the limit definition of the derivative (Definition 3.1) to find $f'(x)$. Then evaluate $f'(x)$ at the given values of a to find $f'(a)$.

1. $f(x) = 3x + 6$; $a = 3, 7$

2. $f(x) = 4 - 3x$; $a = 2, -4$

3. $f(x) = 1 - 4x$; $a = 9, -3$

4. $f(x) = 7x + 2$; $a = 0, 3$

5. $f(x) = x^2$; $a = 3, 5$

6. $f(x) = 6x^2 + 4x$; $a = 0, 2$

7. $f(x) = 3x - x^2$; $a = 1, 4$

8. $f(x) = x^2 - 4x + 1$; $a = 0, 1$

9. $f(x) = 9 - x^3$; $a = -2, 3$

10. $f(x) = 4x^3$; $a = 0, 2$

11. $f(x) = \dfrac{1}{x^2}$; $a = 1, -2$

12. $f(x) = \dfrac{-1}{x}$; $a = 2, 4$

13. Find the slope of the tangent line to the curve $y = x^2$ at the point $(3, 9)$.

14. Find the slope of the tangent line to the curve $y = x^2 - 2$ at the point $(-1, -1)$.

15. Find the slope of the tangent line to the curve $y = 3x^2 + 4x + 1$ at the point $(-2, 5)$.

16. Find the slope of the tangent line to the curve $y = 6x + x^2$ at the point $(0, 0)$.

17. Find an equation of the tangent line (in general form) to the curve $y = x^3 + 2$ at the point $(1, 3)$.

18. Find an equation of the tangent line (in general form) to the curve $y = 3x^2$ at the point $(1, 3)$.

19. At which point on the curve $y = x^2 + 7x - 2$ is the tangent line horizontal?

20. At which point on the curve $y = x^2 - 3x + 5$ does the tangent line have a slope of 1?

21. Find the equation of the tangent line (in general form) to the curve $y = 1/x$ at the point $(2, .5)$. At the point $(-2, -.5)$.

22. At which point on the curve $y = 1/x$ is the slope of the tangent line equal to -9? Are there any points on the curve where the tangent line has a positive slope?

23. Expanding $(x + h)^4$, we find that

$$(x + h)^4 = x^4 + 4x^3h + 6x^2h^2 + 4xh^3 + h^4.$$

Use this result with Definition 3.1 to determine $D_x[x^4]$.

24. Referring to Exercises 5, 11, and 23, as well as equations (3.2), (3.3), and (3.4), make a conjecture about a general formula for the derivative $D_x[x^n]$, where n is a fixed real number.

25. If $y = x^2$, find the rate of change in y, with respect to x, when $x = 5$.

26. If $y = x^3$, find the rate of change in y, with respect to x, when $x = -1$.

27. If $v = 20 - .3q$, find the rate of change in v, with respect to q, when $q = 10$.

28. If $q = \sqrt{p}$, find the rate of change in q, with respect to p, when $p = 25$.

29. Let

$$C(q) = 180 + 12q - .03q^2, \qquad 0 \le q \le 50,$$

be a total cost function. What is the marginal cost of the 30th unit?

30. Let the selling price of a bushel of soybeans at a grain market be given by

$$p = 14 - .01q, \qquad 100 \le q \le 800,$$

where q is the number of bushels that are available at the market.

a. Find the revenue received by the suppliers as a function of q.

b. Find the marginal revenue function.

c. At what value of q does the marginal revenue equal 0? What is the significance of this to the suppliers?

31. The director of marketing at a small company uses the model

$$S = 60\sqrt{x}, \qquad 1 \le x \le 10,$$

to estimate the company's weekly sales S (in thousand dollars) when x (in thousand dollars) is spent each week on advertising. Find the rate at which sales are increasing as a function of advertising, dS/dx, when $x = 9$.

32. The revenue R received from the sale of a new product t months after its introduction is given by

$$R = 100t^2, \qquad 0 \le t \le 7.$$

Find the rate at which the revenue is increasing, dR/dt, 5 months after the product's introduction.

33. If s denotes the distance (in miles) a rocket has traveled from its pad t hours after launching, then ds/dt, the change in s with respect to t, represents the velocity (in miles per hour) of the rocket. Find the velocity when $t = 1/2$ if

$$s = 10{,}000t^2, \qquad 0 \le t \le 1.$$

34. Refer to Exercise 33. An auto departs from Centerville and travels due east along a straight road. If the distance s from Centerville, t hours later, is given by

$$s = 58t, \qquad 0 \le t \le 5,$$

find the velocity ds/dt of the auto.

35. Refer to Exercise 33. If an object is dropped from the top of the 400-foot Trade Building, its height H (in feet) t seconds later is given by

$$H = 400 - 16t^2, \qquad 0 \le t \le 5.$$

Find the velocity dH/dt of the object 2 sec and 4 sec after it is dropped.

36. Refer to Exercise 33. The height H (in feet) of a ball, t seconds after it is thrown vertically, is given by

$$H = 96t - 16t^2, \qquad 0 \le t \le 6.$$

Find the velocity dH/dt, 1 sec, 3 sec, and 4 sec after it is thrown.

37. The graph shows a function f. At which points of this graph is f (a) discontinuous, (b) not differentiable, (c) continuous but not differentiable, and (d) differentiable but not continuous?

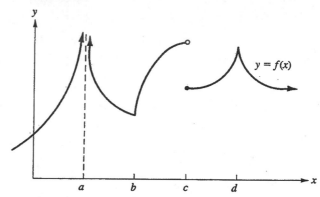

38. Show that the cube root function $f(x) = x^{1/3}$ is not differentiable at $x = 0$ by showing that

$$\lim_{h \to 0} \frac{f(0 + h) - f(0)}{h} = \infty.$$

39. Show that the absolute value function $f(x) = |x|$ is not differentiable at $x = 0$ by showing that

$$\lim_{h \to 0^+} \frac{|0 + h| - 0}{h} \ne \lim_{h \to 0^-} \frac{|0 + h| - 0}{h},$$

and thus

$$\lim_{h \to 0} \frac{f(0 + h) - f(0)}{h}$$

does not exist.

3.2
Basic Rules of Differentiation

After finding the derivatives of several functions using the limit definition of a derivative, two things become apparent: first, the process of evaluating the limit becomes tiresome and tedious, and second, certain patterns begin to emerge in the process. The remedy for the first is to take advantage of the second and develop some rules for differentiation.

The first of these rules (or theorems, for they can be proved) was observed in Example 1 of the previous section.

Theorem 3.1

If $y = f(x) = mx + b$, then $dy/dx = f'(x) = m$.

We can verify Theorem 3.1 using the limit definition:

$$f'(x) = \lim_{h \to 0} \frac{f(x + h) - f(x)}{h}$$

$$= \lim_{h \to 0} \frac{[m(x + h) + b] - [mx + b]}{h}$$

$$= \lim_{h \to 0} \frac{mx + mh + b - mx - b}{h}$$

$$= \lim_{h \to 0} \frac{mh}{h}$$

$$= m.$$

It is instructive to compare this computation with that in Example 1 of the previous section to see that the algebraic steps are the same.

Because a constant function is just a linear function with 0 slope, the following rule is a special, but important, case of Theorem 3.1.

Theorem 3.2

> If $y = f(x) = c$, where c is constant, then $dy/dx = f'(x) = 0$.

In the previous examples and exercises we have seen that

$$D_x[x^2] = 2x,$$
$$D_x[x^3] = 3x^2,$$
and
$$D_x[x^4] = 4x^3.$$

We have also determined that

$$D_x[x^{1/2}] = \frac{1}{2}x^{-1/2},$$
$$D_x[x^{-1}] = -x^{-2},$$
and
$$D_x[x^{-2}] = -2x^{-3}.$$

Each of these facts may be considered as a special case of the **power rule** for derivatives.

**Theorem 3.3
Power Rule**

> If n is a fixed real number, then
>
> $$D_x[x^n] = nx^{n-1}$$
>
> for any x at which nx^{n-1} is defined.

The power rule can be verified for any natural number n by noting that

$$(x + h)^n = x^n + nx^{n-1}h + \frac{n(n-1)}{2}x^{n-2}h^2 + \cdots + nxh^{n-1} + h^n.$$

The binomial theorem (see Appendix A.5) may be used to find each of the $n + 1$ terms in this expansion. Now if $f(x) = x^n$, then

$$f'(x) = \lim_{h \to 0} \frac{f(x + h) - f(x)}{h} = \lim_{h \to 0} \frac{(x + h)^n - x^n}{h}$$

$$= \lim_{h \to 0} \frac{\left(x^n + nx^{n-1}h + \frac{n(n - 1)}{2} x^{n-2}h^2 + \cdots + h^n \right) - x^n}{h}$$

$$= \lim_{h \to 0} nx^{n-1} + \frac{n(n - 1)}{2} x^{n-2} h + \cdots + nxh^{n-2} + h^{n-1}$$

$$= nx^{n-1}.$$

EXAMPLE 1 If $f(x) = x^6$, $g(x) = x^{1/3}$, and $p(x) = 1/x^4$, find $f'(x)$, $g'(x)$, and $p'(x)$.

SOLUTION Applying the power rule to f, g, and p, we have

$$f'(x) = 6x^5,$$

$$g'(x) = \frac{1}{3}x^{-2/3},$$

and, since $p(x) = x^{-4}$,

$$p'(x) = -4x^{-5} \quad \text{or} \quad p'(x) = -\frac{4}{x^5}. \qquad \bullet$$

Another useful result is the **constant multiple rule**.

Theorem 3.4
Constant Multiple Rule

If c is any constant and the derivative of the function f exists, then
$$D_x[cf(x)] = cD_x[f(x)] = cf'(x);$$
that is, the derivative of a constant times a function is the constant times the derivative of the function.

Theorem 3.4 may be interpreted as meaning that when a derivative is computed, constant multipliers merely carry along. The reader is cautioned not to confuse Theorem 3.4 with Theorem 3.2. To verify Theorem 3.4, observe that using earlier limit properties, we have

$$D_x[cf(x)] = \lim_{h \to 0} \frac{cf(x + h) - cf(x)}{h}$$

$$= \lim_{h \to 0} \frac{c[f(x + h) - f(x)]}{h}$$

$$= \lim_{h \to 0} c \cdot \lim_{h \to 0} \frac{f(x + h) - f(x)}{h}$$

$$= cf'(x).$$

EXAMPLE 2

Find the derivative of $y = 5x^3$.

SOLUTION

From the power rule, $D[x^3] = 3x^2$, so by Theorem 3.4, the constant multiple 5 carries along:

$$y' = 5(3x^2) = 15x^2.$$

●

EXAMPLE 3

Find the derivative of $y = -4\sqrt{x}$.

SOLUTION

Again the power rule may be used to show that

$$D_x[\sqrt{x}] = \frac{1}{2\sqrt{x}}$$

so

$$y' = -4\left(\frac{1}{2\sqrt{x}}\right) = \frac{-2}{\sqrt{x}}.$$

●

The next rule of differentiation asserts that if a function can be considered as the sum of two (or more) functions, both of which are differentiable, then the derivative of this sum equals the sum of the derivatives.

**Theorem 3.5
Sum Rule**

If f and g are two functions, each of which is differentiable, and if x is in the domain of each, then

$$D_x[f(x) + g(x)] = f'(x) + g'(x).$$

Since a difference of two functions, $f - g$, can be thought of as the sum of f and $-g$, Theorem 3.5 also applies to the difference of two functions.

EXAMPLE 4

Find the derivative of

$$y = \frac{5}{x} - 3\sqrt{x}, \qquad x > 0.$$

SOLUTION

Recalling that

$$D_x\left[\frac{1}{x}\right] = \frac{-1}{x^2}, \qquad x \neq 0,$$

we apply Theorem 3.5 as follows:

$$y' = D_x\left[\frac{5}{x} - 3\sqrt{x}\right]$$

$$= 5D_x\left[\frac{1}{x}\right] - 3D_x[\sqrt{x}]$$

$$= -\frac{5}{x^2} - \frac{3}{2\sqrt{x}}, \quad x > 0.$$

Theorem 3.5 can be verified using limit properties:

$$D_x[f(x) + g(x)] = \lim_{h \to 0} \frac{[f(x + h) + g(x + h)] - [f(x) + g(x)]}{h}$$

$$= \lim_{h \to 0} \frac{f(x + h) - f(x) + g(x + h) - g(x)}{h}$$

$$= \lim_{h \to 0} \frac{f(x + h) - f(x)}{h} + \lim_{h \to 0} \frac{g(x + h) - g(x)}{h}$$

$$= f'(x) + g'(x).$$

By using Theorems 3.1 through 3.5, it is possible to calculate the derivative of any polynomial function.

EXAMPLE 5

Find the derivative of $y = 2x^5 - 4x^3 + x^2 - 3x + 6$.

SOLUTION

The derivative is

$$y' = D_x[2x^5 - 4x^3 + x^2 - 3x + 6]$$

$$= 2D_x[x^5] - 4D_x[x^3] + D_x[x^2] - 3D_x[x] + D_x[6]$$

$$= 2(5x^4) - 4(3x^2) + (2x) - 3(1) + 0$$

$$= 10x^4 - 12x^2 + 2x - 3.$$

After a little practice you can immediately write the derivative of a polynomial function without going through the intermediate steps.

Many total cost and revenue functions are polynomial functions. For these functions we can now quickly find marginal cost and marginal revenue using differentiation rules.

EXAMPLE 6

The manager of Quality Tools wants to know whether it is profitable to increase the production of hand drills. The daily total cost C of producing q drills is

$$C = 500 + 21q - .05q^2 + .0002q^3, \quad 0 \le q \le 300,$$

and the revenue from the sale of these drills is thought to be

$$R = 40q - .02q^2, \qquad 0 \le q \le 300.$$

If the daily output is currently $q = 220$ drills, determine the marginal cost and the marginal revenue at this output level. Describe the effect of increasing production.

SOLUTION

The marginal cost of the qth unit is the derivative of the total cost function with respect to q; that is,

$$MC = \frac{dC}{dq} = 21 - .1q + .0006q^2, \qquad 0 \le q \le 300.$$

When $q = 220$, the marginal cost is

$$MC(220) = 21 - .1(220) + .0006(220)^2 = \$28.04.$$

Similarly, the marginal revenue from the sale of the qth drill is

$$MR = \frac{dR}{dq} = 40 - .04q, \qquad 0 \le q \le 300,$$

and at $q = 220$ we have

$$MR(220) = 40 - .04(220) = \$31.20.$$

Since marginal revenue exceeds marginal cost at $q = 220$, it is profitable for Quality Tools to increase the daily production of drills. Revenue will rise at a rate of \$31.20 per unit, while costs rise at a slower rate of \$28.04 per unit. These marginal quantities are illustrated geometrically as slopes in Figure 3.6.

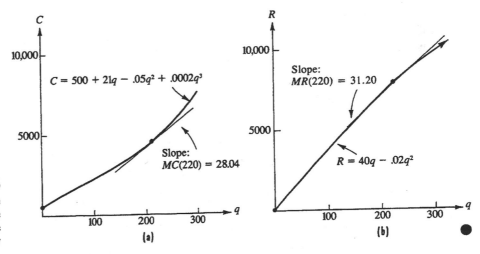

Figure 3.6

Marginal cost and marginal revenue as slopes of tangent lines to the graphs of total cost and revenue functions, respectively

The derivatives of many functions can easily be obtained if the rule of correspondence can be written as a sum of terms of the form cx^n.

EXAMPLE 7   Find the derivative of

$$y = \frac{3x^2 - \sqrt{x} + 2}{x},$$

with respect to x.

SOLUTION   It is possible to write y as the sum

$$y = \frac{3x^2}{x} - \frac{\sqrt{x}}{x} + \frac{2}{x}$$
$$= 3x - x^{-1/2} + 2x^{-1}.$$

Using Theorems 3.3 and 3.5 we find

$$y' = 3 + \frac{1}{2}x^{-3/2} - 2x^{-2}.$$

EXAMPLE 8   Find the equation of the tangent line to the curve

$$y = (x^2 + 4)(\sqrt[3]{x} + 1)$$

at the point with coordinates $(1, 10)$.

SOLUTION   To find the equation of the line, we need to know the slope—the derivative of y when $x = 1$. Writing $\sqrt[3]{x}$ as $x^{1/3}$ and expanding, we have

$$y = (x^2 + 4)(x^{1/3} + 1)$$
$$= x^{7/3} + x^2 + 4x^{1/3} + 4.$$

Using our rules to differentiate term by term, we find

$$y' = \frac{7}{3}x^{4/3} + 2x + \frac{4}{3}x^{-2/3}.$$

When $x = 1$,

$$m = y'(1) = \frac{7}{3} + 2 + \frac{4}{3} = \frac{17}{3}.$$

From the point-slope formula the tangent line is

$$y - 10 = \frac{17}{3}(x - 1)$$

or

$$3y - 30 = 17x - 17.$$

In general form,

$$17x - 3y = -13.$$

EXERCISES 3.2

In Exercises 1–8 find the derivative of the given function.

1. $f(x) = 5$

2. $g(x) = x^7$

3. $h(x) = 8x^{3/4}$

4. $f(t) = 6t^{2.4}$

5. $f(u) = \dfrac{7}{u^4}$

6. $h(w) = -\dfrac{3}{w}$

7. $g(x) = 10^{-6}$

8. $G(t) = 6t^{-1.5}$

In Exercises 9–16 find the indicated derivative.

9. $D_x[7]$

10. $D_u[6u^{-1/3}]$

11. $D_t[\sqrt[5]{t}]$

12. $D_x\left[\dfrac{-4}{x^3}\right]$

13. $D_w[.3w^{-1/3}]$

14. $D_x[\pi^2]$

15. $D_x[18x^2]$

16. $D_z[4z^{-.2}]$

In Exercises 17–24 find dy/dx.

17. $y = 2x + 7$

18. $y = x^2 + 2x + 5$

19. $y = 2x^{3/2} - 3x^{1/2} + 2$

20. $y = x^3 - 4x^2 + 3x + 7$

21. $y = \dfrac{x^2 + 2x + 5}{x}$

22. $y = \dfrac{x^4 + x^2 + 1}{x^3}$

23. $y = (3x - 2)(x^2 + 1)$

24. $y = 2x^{1/2}(x^3 + 8)$

In Exercises 25–32 find y'.

25. $y = 5x - 2$

26. $y = 3x^{-4} - 5x^{-2} + 1$

27. $y = 3\sqrt[3]{x} - 2\sqrt{x} + 8$

28. $y = x^2(x - 4)$

29. $y = -x^{4/3} + 2x^{2/3} + 5$

30. $y = \dfrac{2x^2 - 4x + 5}{x}$

31. $y = \sqrt{x}(4x^2 + 3x - 2)$

32. $y = \dfrac{2x^2 + x^{3/2} - 7}{\sqrt{x}}$

In Exercises 33–36 find the slope of the tangent line to the given curve at the given point.

33. $y = 7$; $(4, 7)$

34. $y = 3x^2 - 2x + 5$; $(2, 13)$

35. $y = 250 - .05x + .0001x^2$; $(1000, 300)$

36. $y = \dfrac{50 - x}{x^2}$; $(10, .4)$

In Exercises 37–40 find an equation of the tangent line to the given curve at the given point.

37. $y = x^2 + 6x - 7$; $(2, 9)$

38. $y = 5 - 2x + x^2 - x^3$; $(-1, 9)$

39. $y = (x + 3)(2x - 5)$; $(0, -15)$

40. $y = \dfrac{x^2 + 1}{x^{1/3}}$; $(1, 2)$

In Exercises 41–44 find the x-coordinate of the point(s) on the given curve with a horizontal tangent (if there are any).

41. $y = x^2 + 3x - 2$

42. $y = 5 - 3x$

43. $y = x^3 - 5x^2 + 3x + 7$

44. $y = x^3 + 7x^2 + 11x - 9$

45. In order for a bicycle dealer in a small town to sell q touring bikes, the price must be set according to

$$p = 350 - .08q - .002q^2, \quad 0 \le q \le 50.$$

a. What should the selling price be if the dealer intends to sell 40 bikes?

b. Find the marginal revenue from the 40th bike sold.

46. The Joggman is a miniature tape player with earphones designed to be used by joggers and bikers. Let the total cost of manufacturing q Joggmans in one day be given by

$$C = 1000 + 50q - .01q^2 + .0005q^3, \quad 0 \le q \le 500.$$

What is the marginal cost of making one of these units when 300 are made each day? How would this be affected if fixed costs were reduced from $1000 to $750?

47. A campus bookstore silkscreens T-shirts. The fixed cost for filling an order is $30; the variable cost per shirt is given by $1.50 - .002q$, $0 < q \le 500$, where q is the number of shirts ordered.

a. Find the total cost C and the average cost $A = C/q$ as functions of q.

b. Find dA/dq, the rate of change in the average cost with respect to q.

48. The U.S. per capita debt (in dollars) t years after 1980 is approximated by

$$D = 3970 + 524t + 35t^2, \qquad 0 \le t \le 10.$$

Find the rate at which D is changing with respect to t, $D'(t)$, in 1985 ($t = 5$) and in 1989 ($t = 9$).

49. The U.S. personal income P (in dollars) t years after 1980 is approximated by

$$P = 9979 + 563t + 2t^2, \qquad 0 \le t \le 10.$$

Find the rate at which P is changing, $P'(t)$, in 1983 and in 1988.

50. The number of households that have a VCR t years after 1980 is approximated by the power function

$$H = 1,000,000t^{1.4}, \qquad 0 \le t \le 10.$$

Find the rate at which H is changing, $H'(t)$, in 1988.

51. To increase sales S (in cases per week) of its flavored sparkling water, the bottler is increasing the advertising budget. The current budget is $8000 per month. If S depends on the amount x (in thousand dollars) spent each month on advertising according to

$$S = 6000 + 7200\sqrt[3]{x}, \qquad 0 \le x \le 25,$$

find the rate at which sales will increase when the budget is increased.

52. Suppose the variable cost per unit of producing q units of a product is given by

$$v = 50 - .02q + .00003q^2, \qquad 0 \le q \le 500.$$

Suppose further that fixed costs are $400 per day, and in order for every item produced to be sold, the selling price must be

$$p = 80 - .05q, \qquad 0 \le q \le 500.$$

If the current production level is 400 units per day, find the marginal cost and marginal revenue. Should the production level be increased or decreased in order to increase profit?

53. Show that the point on the parabola $y = ax^2 + bx + c$, where $a \ne 0$, with a horizontal tangent is the vertex. (*Hint:* Solve $y' = 0$ for x.)

54. Show that the cubic function $f(x) = ax^3 + bx^2 + cx + d$, where $a \ne 0$, has horizontal tangents if and only if $b^2 - 3ac > 0$, and that in this case the horizontal tangents occur at

$$x = \frac{-b \pm \sqrt{b^2 - 3ac}}{3a}.$$

(*Hint:* Solve $y' = 0$ for x using the quadratic formula.)

3.3
The Chain Rule

In this section we extend our list of differentiation rules to cover complicated functions that are the composition of simpler ones. As a first illustration suppose we wish to differentiate y with respect to x where

$$y = (x^5 + 1)^3.$$

Before expanding and differentiating, notice that y can be written as

$$y = f(g(x))$$

where $f(x) = x^3$ and $g(x) = x^5 + 1$. Furthermore, these functions can be easily differentiated: $f'(x) = 3x^2$ and $g'(x) = 5x^4$. The chain rule provides a connection between f', g', and y'.

To see this connection we expand $(x^5 + 1)^3$ to obtain

$$y = x^{15} + 3x^{10} + 3x^5 + 1.$$

Differentiating and simplifying, we have

$$\begin{aligned} y' &= 15x^{14} + 30x^9 + 15x^4 \\ &= 15x^4(x^{10} + 2x^5 + 1) \\ &= 15x^4(x^5 + 1)^2. \end{aligned}$$

Now $g'(x) = 5x^4$ is a factor of y', so y' can be written as

$$y' = 3(x^5 + 1)^2 g'(x).$$

We also note that $3(x^5 + 1)^2 = f'(g(x))$ and so

$$y' = f'(g(x))g'(x).$$

For this particular example we have seen that if $y = f(g(x))$, then $y' = f'(g(x))g'(x)$. We state the general result without proof.

Theorem 3.6 **Chain Rule**	If f and g are differentiable functions (and the range of g is contained in the domain of f), then (3.5) $\qquad D_x[f(g(x))] = f'(g(x))g'(x).$

EXAMPLE 1

If $h(x) = (x^7 + 5x)^2$, find $h'(x)$ (a) using the chain rule, and (b) after expanding $(x^7 + 5x)^2$.

SOLUTION

a. If $f(x) = x^2$ and $g(x) = x^7 + 5x$, then $h(x) = f(g(x))$. Thus by the chain rule (Theorem 3.6),

$$h'(x) = 2(x^7 + 5x)^1(7x^6 + 5)$$
$$= 2x(x^6 + 5)(7x^6 + 5).$$

b. Expanding $(x^7 + 5x)^2$, we find that

$$h(x) = x^{14} + 10x^8 + 25x^2.$$

Differentiating term by term and factoring, we obtain

$$h'(x) = 14x^{13} + 80x^7 + 50x$$
$$= 2x(7x^{12} + 40x^6 + 25)$$
$$= 2x(x^6 + 5)(7x^6 + 5). \qquad \bullet$$

In many problems where the chain rule may be applied, expanding is not an option, as illustrated in the following example.

EXAMPLE 2

If $y = \sqrt{x^3 + 5}$ for $x > 0$, find dy/dx.

SOLUTION

If $f(x) = \sqrt{x}$ and $g(x) = x^3 + 5$, then $y = f(g(x))$. Thus by equation (3.5),

$$\frac{dy}{dx} = \frac{1}{2}(x^3 + 5)^{-1/2} 3x^2$$

$$= \frac{3x^2}{2(x^3 + 5)^{1/2}}. \qquad \bullet$$

EXAMPLE 3   If $y = \sqrt[3]{3x^2 + 5x - 8}$, find dy/dx.

SOLUTION   Since $y = (3x^2 + 5x - 8)^{1/3}$,

$$y' = \frac{1}{3}(3x^2 + 5x - 8)^{-2/3}(6x + 5)$$

$$= \frac{6x + 5}{3(3x^2 + 5x - 8)^{2/3}}.$$

●

EXAMPLE 4   Find $f'(x)$ if

$$f(x) = \frac{1}{x^4 + x^2 + 1}.$$

SOLUTION   Noting that the function may be written as

$$f(x) = (x^4 + x^2 + 1)^{-1},$$

we apply the power rule and the chain rule to obtain

$$f'(x) = -1(x^4 + x^2 + 1)^{-2}(4x^3 + 2x)$$

$$= -\frac{4x^3 + 2x}{(x^4 + x^2 + 1)^2}.$$

●

Often it is easier to apply the chain rule by using an intermediate variable. For example, if $y = f(g(x))$ and we let $u = g(x)$, then $y = f(u)$. Noting that

$$\frac{dy}{dx} = f'(u) = f'(g(x)) \quad \text{and} \quad \frac{du}{dx} = g'(x),$$

we see that the chain rule can be written as

(3.6)

$$\frac{dy}{dx} = \frac{dy}{du}\frac{du}{dx}.$$

The chain rule is easily remembered in the form of equation (3.6) because it looks like the familiar cancellation rule for the multiplication of fractions.

EXAMPLE 5   Use form (3.6) of the chain rule to find the derivative of $y = (x^5 + 14)^{10}$.

SOLUTION   Let $y = u^{10}$, where $u = x^5 + 14$. Then

$$\frac{dy}{du} = 10u^9 \quad \text{and} \quad \frac{du}{dx} = 5x^4.$$

From equation (3.6) we have

$$\frac{dy}{dx} = 10u^9 \cdot 5x^4$$

$$= 10(x^5 + 14)^9 \cdot 5x^4$$

$$= 50x^4(x^5 + 14)^9.$$
●

We have seen that marginal revenue is the derivative of revenue R with respect to output q. Sometimes it is useful to write revenue as a function of the number of workers w. When this is done, the derivative of R with respect to w gives the change in revenue with respect to the number of workers and is called the **marginal revenue product**. Intuitively, the marginal revenue product dR/dw represents the value of goods that would be produced by one more worker.

EXAMPLE 6

Softright is a company that produces computer programs to be used on large computers. Suppose that the management of Softright has determined that w employees will produce q usable programs per month, where

$$q = \sqrt{w - 1}, \qquad 2 \le w \le 50.$$

If the value of each of these programs is known to be

$$p = 35{,}000 - 2000q, \qquad 0 \le q \le 7,$$

when q programs are produced each month, find the marginal revenue product dR/dw when $w = 26$.

SOLUTION

From form (3.6) of the chain rule we know that

$$\frac{dR}{dw} = \frac{dR}{dq} \frac{dq}{dw}.$$

Writing R in terms of q, we have

$$R = pq = (35{,}000 - 2000q)q = 35{,}000q - 2000q^2$$

and so

$$\frac{dR}{dq} = 35{,}000 - 4000q.$$

Differentiating the production function yields

$$\frac{dq}{dw} = \frac{1}{2}(w - 1)^{-1/2}.$$

Therefore,

$$\frac{dR}{dw} = \frac{1}{2}(35{,}000 - 4000q)(w - 1)^{-1/2}.$$

Finally, when $w = 26$, the number of programs written each month is $q = \sqrt{26 - 1} = 5$, so

$$\left.\frac{dR}{dw}\right|_{w=26} = \frac{1}{2}(35{,}000 - 4000(5))(26 - 1)^{-1/2}$$

$$= \frac{15{,}000}{2(5)}$$

$$= 1500.$$

This derivative indicates that if Softright hired an additional employee, the increase in revenue from the additional programming would be approximately \$1500 per month. ●

EXERCISES 3.3

In Exercises 1–8 find the derivative of the given function.

1. $f(x) = \sqrt{2x^2 + 1}$

2. $g(x) = \sqrt[3]{x + 5}$

3. $h(x) = (6x - 1)^8$

4. $T(x) = (x^3 - 5x + 7)^{-2}$

5. $f(x) = \sqrt{5x + 1}$

6. $g(r) = 4(2r + 5)^{2/3}$

7. $h(y) = (\sqrt{y^2 + 2y})^5$

8. $F(t) = \dfrac{20}{\sqrt{5t - 8}}$

In Exercises 9–16 find y' for the given function.

9. $y = \sqrt{6x + 2}$

10. $y = \sqrt[4]{x^2 + 2x + 5}$

11. $y = \left(3x + \dfrac{1}{x}\right)^{10}$

12. $y = \dfrac{2}{x^2 + 1}$

13. $y = 7(5x + 6)^{3/4}$

14. $y = \sqrt{3x^2 + x + 9}$

15. $y = \left(\sqrt{x} + \dfrac{3}{x}\right)^3$

16. $y = \dfrac{1}{\sqrt[3]{6x + 1}}$

In Exercises 17–22 find the indicated derivative.

17. $D_x\left[\dfrac{1}{2x + 1}\right]$

18. $D_x\left[\dfrac{-3}{3x + 2}\right]$

19. $D_x\left[\dfrac{2}{(2 - x)^2}\right]$

20. $D_x\left[\dfrac{4}{\sqrt{x^2 + 5}}\right]$

21. $D_x\left[\dfrac{1}{(4x^3 + 6x)^{2/3}}\right]$

22. $D_x\left[\dfrac{10}{(3x^2 + 7)^{10}}\right]$

In Exercises 23–28 find an equation (in general form) of the line tangent to the given curve at the indicated point.

23. $y = \sqrt{2x + 1}$; (4, 3)

24. $y = \dfrac{5}{3x - 2}$; (4, .5)

25. $y = \sqrt[3]{x^2 + 2x + 3}$; (4, 3)

26. $y = 3(5 - 4x)^{-1/2}$; $(-1, 1)$

27. $y = \dfrac{5}{x^2 + 4x + 5}$; (0, 1)

28. $y = (3 - x)^{3/2}$; $(-6, 27)$

In Exercises 29–34 find dy/dx using

$$\frac{dy}{dx} = \frac{dy}{du}\frac{du}{dx}$$

for the given pair of functions. Write the final result in terms of x.

29. $y = \sqrt{u}$; $u = x^2 + 5$

30. $y = u^{10}$; $u = x + \dfrac{1}{x}$

31. $y = \sqrt[3]{u}$; $u = 5x + 9$

32. $y = \dfrac{1}{u}$; $u = x^3 + 3x^2 - 5x + 2$

33. $y = u^3 + u$; $u = 2x + 1$

34. $y = \sqrt{u} + \dfrac{1}{\sqrt{u}}$; $u = x^2 + 5$

35. Illustrate the validity of the chain rule by differentiating $f(x) = (5x^2 + 3)^2$ two ways: first use the chain rule, and second expand the rule of correspondence and then differentiate.

36. Illustrate the validity of the chain rule by differentiating $f(g(x))$, where $f(x) = x^2$ and $g(x) = x^3$, and comparing the result with the derivative of $h(x) = x^6$.

37. Quick Homes is a construction company in the Southwest that assembles prefabricated houses on land owned by the company in the speculation that they can be sold at a profit later. The demand function for these homes is given by

$$p = 65{,}000 - 100q, \qquad 1 \le q \le 40,$$

where q is the number of houses that Quick Homes builds in 1 month. Assume that when Quick Homes has w construction workers, they are able to assemble q houses per month, where

$$q = .2w + 1.6\sqrt{w}, \qquad w > 0.$$

Find the marginal revenue product dR/dw. (See Example 6.) If the company currently employs 100 construction workers, estimate the revenue that is generated by the 100th worker.

38. Refer to Exercise 37. Find the marginal revenue product by first finding the revenue R as a function of the number of construction workers w.

39. Santo Chemical employs w workers at its herbicide plant. That plant is able to turn out q tons of the herbicide per day, with

$$q = 50(w^2 + 30w)^{1/3}, \qquad 0 \le w \le 20.$$

If the demand function for the herbicide is

$$p = 40 - .04q, \qquad 0 \le q \le 500,$$

find the marginal revenue product dR/dw and evaluate it (to the nearest dollar) when $w = 6$.

40. Rework Exercise 39 by first finding R as a function of the number of workers w.

41. A manufacturer of motorbikes can have up to 30 people working on an assembly line. When there are w workers, the weekly output q is

$$q = 2(6w - 125)^{2/3} + 10, \qquad 0 \le w \le 30.$$

If the demand for these motorbikes is

$$p = 2600 - 25q, \qquad 0 \le q \le 40,$$

find the marginal revenue product when 21 people are working on the assembly line.

42. If $f(x) = x^n$ and $g(x)$ is any differentiable function, then $f(g(x)) = [g(x)]^n$; so from the chain rule,

$$D_x\{[g(x)]^n\} = n[g(x)]^{n-1} g'(x).$$

Use this fact to derive a formula for $D_x[1/g(x)]$ when $g(x) \ne 0$.

43. If f^{-1} is the inverse of f, then $f^{-1}[f(x)] = x$ for all x in the domain of f. Assuming that f and f^{-1} are differentiable, use the chain rule to obtain a formula relating $(f^{-1})'$ and f'.

3.4
The Product and Quotient Rules

In earlier sections we were able to find the derivative of some functions that were products or quotients of other functions after rearranging their rules of correspondence. For instance, we can differentiate

$$f(x) = (x^2 + 7)(4x + 8) \quad \text{and} \quad g(x) = \frac{5}{x^3 + 4x - 9}$$

by multiplying to expand $f(x)$ and by writing $g(x)$ as

$$g(x) = 5(x^3 + 4x - 9)^{-1}$$

and applying the chain rule. To handle functions of this type more efficiently, we develop rules for differentiating the products and quotients of functions directly.

Although we have seen (Theorem 3.5 in Section 3.2) that the derivative of a sum of two functions is the sum of the individual derivatives, the derivative of a product is **not** the product of the derivatives. As an illustration, let

$$f(x) = x^2, \quad g(x) = x^3, \quad \text{and} \quad h(x) = x^5.$$

Then $h(x) = f(x)g(x)$, but

$$f'(x) = 2x, \quad g'(x) = 3x^2, \quad \text{and} \quad h'(x) = 5x^4,$$

so clearly $h'(x) \neq f'(x)g'(x)$.

To derive the product rule we return again to the derivative definition, assuming that $f'(x)$ and $g'(x)$ exist (and hence these functions are also continuous):

$$D_x[\,f(x)g(x)] = \lim_{h \to 0} \frac{f(x+h)g(x+h) - f(x)g(x)}{h}.$$

To break the quotient into quantities that can be factored, we introduce $f(x+h)g(x)$ (a hybrid of the terms in the numerator) once with a positive and once with a negative sign to obtain

$$D_x[\,f(x)g(x)] = \lim_{h \to 0} \frac{f(x+h)g(x+h) - f(x+h)g(x) + f(x+h)g(x) - f(x)g(x)}{h}$$

$$= \lim_{h \to 0} \frac{f(x+h)[g(x+h) - g(x)]}{h} + \lim_{h \to 0} \frac{g(x)[f(x+h) - f(x)]}{h}$$

$$= \lim_{h \to 0} f(x+h) \lim_{h \to 0} \frac{[g(x+h) - g(x)]}{h}$$

$$+ \lim_{h \to 0} g(x) \lim_{h \to 0} \frac{[f(x+h)) - f(x)]}{h}$$

$$= f(x)g'(x) + g(x)f'(x).$$

We now have the rule for finding the derivative of the product of two functions.

Theorem 3.7
Product Rule

If f and g are differentiable functions, then

$$D_x[\,f(x)g(x)] = f(x)g'(x) + g(x)f'(x).$$

In words, the derivative of a product of two functions is the first function times the derivative of the second plus the second function times the derivative of the first.

EXAMPLE 1

If $h(x) = 50x\sqrt{100 - x}$, find $h'(x)$.

SOLUTION

Letting $f(x) = 50x$ and $g(x) = \sqrt{100 - x}$, we have $h(x) = f(x)g(x)$, so by the product rule:

$$h'(x) = 50x \cdot \frac{1}{2}(100 - x)^{-1/2}(-1) + (100 - x)^{1/2}50.$$

(Note that the chain rule was used to differentiate g.) Simplifying by factoring out $25(100 - x)^{-1/2}$, we have

$$h'(x) = 25(100 - x)^{-1/2}[-x + 2(100 - x)]$$
$$= \frac{25(200 - 3x)}{(100 - x)^{1/2}}.$$

Note that factoring out $(100 - x)^{-1/2}$ is equivalent to writing the terms over the common denominator $(100 - x)^{1/2}$. ●

EXAMPLE 2

If $y = (2x + 5)^5(3x^2 + 7)^{1/3}$, find y'.

SOLUTION

Considering y as the product $f(x)g(x)$, where $f(x) = (2x + 5)^5$ and $g(x) = (3x^2 + 7)^{1/3}$, we apply the product rule to obtain

$$y' = (2x + 5)^5 \cdot \frac{1}{3}(3x^2 + 7)^{-2/3} \cdot 6x + (3x^2 + 7)^{1/3} \cdot 5(2x + 5)^4 \cdot 2.$$

Simplifying by factoring out $2(2x + 5)^4(3x^2 + 7)^{-2/3}$, we obtain

$$y' = 2(2x + 5)^4(3x^2 + 7)^{-2/3}[x(2x + 5) + 5(3x^2 + 7)]$$
$$= \frac{2(2x + 5)^4(17x^2 + 5x + 35)}{(3x^2 + 7)^{2/3}}.$$ ●

To derive a rule for differentiating quotients we recall that dividing $f(x)$ by $g(x)$ is equivalent to multiplying $f(x)$ by the reciprocal of $g(x)$; that is,

$$\frac{f(x)}{g(x)} = \frac{1}{g(x)}f(x),$$

so applying the product rule we have

$$D_x\left[\frac{f(x)}{g(x)}\right] = D_x\left[\frac{1}{g(x)}f(x)\right] = \frac{1}{g(x)}f'(x) + f(x)D_x\left[\frac{1}{g(x)}\right].$$

Since

$$\frac{1}{g(x)} = [g(x)]^{-1},$$

we obtain from the chain rule

$$D_x\left[\frac{1}{g(x)}\right] = -1[g(x)]^{-2}g'(x) = \frac{-g'(x)}{[g(x)]^2}.$$

Substituting and writing the result over a common denominator, we have the **quotient rule**.

Theorem 3.8 **The Quotient Rule**	If f and g are differentiable functions and if $g(x) \neq 0$, then $$D_x\left[\frac{f(x)}{g(x)}\right] = \frac{g(x)\,f'(x) - f(x)g'(x)}{[g(x)]^2}.$$

In words, the derivative of a quotient of two functions is the denominator times the derivative of the numerator minus the numerator times the derivative of the denominator, all divided by the denominator squared.

EXAMPLE 3

Find dp/dq if

$$p = \frac{10q + 40}{q + 2}.$$

SOLUTION

Using the quotient rule, we have

$$\frac{dp}{dq} = \frac{(q + 2)(10) - (10q + 40)(1)}{(q + 2)^2}$$

$$= \frac{-20}{(q + 2)^2}.$$

EXAMPLE 4

Find y' if

$$y = \left(\frac{2x - 1}{3x + 2}\right)^6.$$

SOLUTION

Using the chain and quotient rules, we get

$$y' = 6 \cdot \left(\frac{2x - 1}{3x + 2}\right)^5 \cdot \frac{(3x + 2)(2) - (2x - 1)(3)}{(3x + 2)^2}$$

$$= 6 \cdot \left(\frac{2x - 1}{3x + 2}\right)^5 \cdot \frac{7}{(3x + 2)^2}$$

$$= \frac{42(2x - 1)^5}{(3x + 2)^7}.$$

EXAMPLE 5

Find $D_x\left[\dfrac{5x^2}{\sqrt{3x^2 + 7}}\right].$

SOLUTION

Using the quotient and chain rules, we get

$$D_x\left[\frac{5x^2}{\sqrt{3x^2 + 7}}\right] = \frac{(3x^2 + 7)^{1/2}(10x) - 5x^2 \cdot \frac{1}{2}(3x^2 + 7)^{-1/2}(6x)}{3x^2 + 7}$$

$$= \frac{5x(3x^2 + 7)^{-1/2}[2(3x^2 + 7) - 3x^2]}{(3x^2 + 7)^{3/2}}$$

$$= \frac{5x(3x^2 + 14)}{(3x^2 + 7)^{3/2}}.$$

With our list of differentiation rules it is now possible to differentiate any algebraic function, no matter how complicated its rule of correspondence. This allows us to make a more subtle analysis of functions used in models. We close this section with a brief analysis of the total cost function.

Recall that total cost C is written as $C = k + vq$, where k, q, and v denote the fixed cost, the number of units produced, and the variable cost per unit, respectively. Although k is constant, v usually depends on q. Differentiating with respect to q, we obtain (using the sum and product rules)

$$\frac{dC}{dq} = D_q[k] + D_q[vq]$$

$$= 0 + v + q\frac{dv}{dq},$$

that is, $$MC = v + q\frac{dv}{dq}.$$

From this result we can observe the following:

1. MC is independent of fixed costs; $D_q[k] = 0$ regardless of the value of k.
2. If v is constant, then $MC = v$ because $dv/dq = 0$ when v is constant.

EXERCISES 3.4

In Exercises 1–20 find the derivative of the given function by using the product and/or the quotient rule.

1. $f(x) = (5x - 2)(7x^2 + 4)$

2. $f(x) = (3 - x)(1 - x^3)$

3. $g(x) = (x^2 + 3x - 4)(5 + 2x)$

4. $H(t) = t^5(t^3 + 2)$ 5. $f(x) = x^3(\sqrt{x} + 3)$

6. $R(q) = (2q + 1)(\sqrt{q} + 4)$

7. $f(x) = 3x\sqrt{2x + 1}$ 8. $f(x) = x(3x + 5)^3$

9. $g(x) = \dfrac{3x + 1}{x + 5}$

10. $h(x) = \dfrac{3x + 8}{2x + 7}$

11. $F(x) = \dfrac{x}{x^3 + 4}$

12. $G(x) = \dfrac{x^3 + 4}{x}$

13. $h(x) = \dfrac{x^2 + 1}{\sqrt{x} - 5}$

14. $f(x) = \dfrac{3x + 7}{\sqrt{7x + 2}}$

15. $C(q) = \dfrac{5q^2 + 10q + 75}{q + 20}$

16. $p(x) = \dfrac{6 - x^2}{x^2 + 3x + 5}$

17. $f(x) = [(3x^2 + 2)(x^3 + 5)]^7$

18. $g(t) = \sqrt{(3 - 8t)(1 + t^4)}$

19. $T(z) = \left(\dfrac{4z + 1}{8z - 3}\right)^5$ 20. $f(y) = \sqrt[3]{\dfrac{6y + 5}{y + 2}}$

In Exercises 21–28 find y'.

21. $y = (5x^2 + 3x + 7)(4x + 3)$

22. $y = x^3\sqrt{3 - x}$

23. $y = \dfrac{4 - 7x - 2x^2}{3x + 1}$ 24. $y = \dfrac{5x^3 + 7x}{\sqrt{x + 3}}$

25. $y = (2x^2 - 9)\sqrt{x + 3}$ 26. $y = \dfrac{\sqrt{2x + 5}}{6 - 5x}$

27. $y = \dfrac{(2 - 3x)^2}{(x + 5)^3}$ 28. $y = \dfrac{\sqrt[3]{x^2 + 7}}{\sqrt{x + 4}}$

In Exercises 29–34 find the indicated derivative.

29. $D_x[\sqrt{x + 5}(3x + 10)]$ 30. $D_x[x^{2/3}(9x + 1)^{1/3}]$

31. $D_x\left(\dfrac{x + 2}{6x + 5}\right)$ 32. $D_x\left(\dfrac{2x - 5}{3 - x}\right)^4$

33. $D_x[(x + \sqrt{x})(\sqrt{x} + x^2)]$ 34. $D_x\left[\dfrac{2x + 12}{\sqrt[3]{x^2 + 5}}\right]$

In Exercises 35–40 find an equation of the line (in general form) tangent to the given curve at the indicated point.

35. $y = (x - x^2)(4 - 2x + x^2)$; $(2, -8)$

36. $y = x^2\sqrt{10 - x}$; $(6, 72)$

37. $y = \dfrac{12x + 5}{x + 8}$; $(5, 5)$ 38. $y = \dfrac{4x - 1}{\sqrt{x^2 + 9}}$; $(4, 3)$

39. $y = (x^2 + 4)\sqrt{5x + 4}$; $(0, 8)$

40. $y = \dfrac{\sqrt{4 - x}}{2x - 5}$; $(-5, -.2)$

41. Let $f(x) = x^2$ and $g(x) = x^3$. Illustrate the validity of the product and quotient rules by differentiating

$$p(x) = f(x)g(x) \quad \text{and} \quad r(x) = \frac{f(x)}{g(x)}$$

using these rules and then comparing the results with $D_x[x^5]$ and $D_x[1/x]$, respectively.

42. Show that the graph of

$$y = \frac{ax + b}{x + c}$$

has no horizontal tangents unless $b = ac$, in which case y is a constant function.

43. The demand function for a certain product is given by

$$p = \sqrt{400 - .04q^2}, \qquad 0 \le q \le 80.$$

Find the revenue and the marginal revenue when $q = 60$.

44. Top Records has recently expanded into producing video cassettes of popular rock bands. Suppose that the variable cost per cassette when q copies of a cassette are made is given by

$$v = \frac{10q + 30}{q + 2}, \qquad q \ge 0.$$

The fixed cost of making a cassette recording is about $2000.

a. Find the total cost as a function of the number of copies q.

b. Find the marginal cost function $MC(q)$.

c. What is the marginal cost of the 20th copy? The 50th copy?

d. Find $\lim_{q \to \infty} MC(q)$.

45. Wall Balls is a company that manufactures balls for racquetball and handball. Assume that the company has fixed operating costs of $750 per day. The variable cost v for making q cases of racquetballs is given by

$$v = \frac{15q + 75}{q + 3}, \qquad q \ge 0.$$

a. Find $v(0)$ and $\lim_{q \to \infty} v(q)$.

b. Find the total cost and the marginal cost functions.

c. Compare $v(10)$ and $MC(10)$. Interpret these costs.

d. Compare $\lim_{q \to \infty} v(q)$ and $\lim_{q \to \infty} MC(q)$.

46. Refer to Exercise 45. Suppose that the demand function for the racquetballs made by Wall Balls is

$$p = \frac{14q + 180}{q + 3}, \qquad q \ge 0,$$

where p is the selling price per case.

a. Find the revenue and marginal revenue functions.

b. Compare $p(10)$ and $MR(10)$. Interpret what these values mean to Wall Balls.

c. Compare $\lim_{q \to \infty} p(q)$ and $\lim_{q \to \infty} MR(q)$.

d. At present, Wall Balls is making 10 cases of racquetballs per day. Would it be profitable to increase the output? (See the solution to Exercise 45, part b.)

e. What do the limits at infinity for $MC(q)$ and $MR(q)$ say about increasing the output indefinitely? By equating $MC(q)$ and $MR(q)$, determine the most profitable output level for the company.

47. Use the product rule to differentiate $R = pq$ with respect to q; then show that $MR = p$ when p is constant.

48. The average cost per unit A is given by $A = C/q$, where C is total cost and q represents units produced. Show that

$$\frac{dA}{dq} = \frac{dv}{dq} - \frac{k}{q^2},$$

where k and v denote fixed costs and variable cost per unit, respectively.

49. If p and v represent the selling price and the variable cost per unit for a given product, respectively, then $s = p - v$ is called the contribution to profit for the product. If P is the profit function for this product, show that

$$\frac{dP}{dq} = s + q\frac{ds}{dq}.$$

50. Suppose that a variable cost function is modeled by a linear-to-linear rational function

$$v = \frac{aq + b}{q + c}, \qquad q \geq 0, a \neq 0.$$

(See Exercises 44 and 45.) Show that

$$\lim_{q \to \infty} v(q) = \lim_{q \to \infty} MC(q) = a.$$

3.5
Increasing and Decreasing Functions

In several of the business applications for which we have built models, it is reasonable to require that the dependent variable increase (or decrease) as the independent variable increases. For example, if the total production cost C is given as a function of the output level q, then we should require that C increase as q increases; the model should reflect the reality that it costs more to produce more. As a second example, consider a model in which the demand q for a commodity is given as a function of its selling price p. Because the demand for most commodities declines if the price rises, q should decrease as p increases in such a demand model.

Definition 3.2

Let $y = f(x)$ be the rule of correspondence for a function on some interval. We say that f is an **increasing function** on the interval if $f(x_1) < f(x_2)$ for any pair x_1 and x_2 in the interval for which $x_1 < x_2$. We say that f is a **decreasing function** on the interval if $f(x_1) > f(x_2)$ whenever $x_1 < x_2$.

Intuitively, the graph of an increasing function rises from left to right and the graph of a decreasing function falls from left to right. Figure 3.7 shows the graph of a function that is increasing on the interval (a, b), and Figure 3.8 shows the graph of a decreasing function on (a, b).

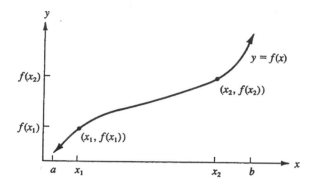

Figure 3.7

An increasing function on the
interval (a, b)

Figure 3.8

A decreasing function $y = f(x)$ on
the interval (a, b)

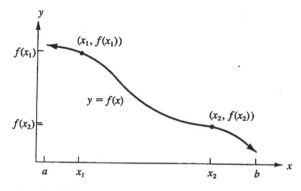

When a function is differentiable, the derivative may be used to determine
whether that function is increasing or decreasing on an interval. Recall that $f'(x)$
can be interpreted as the slope of the tangent line to the graph of $y = f(x)$ at
$(x, f(x))$. Thus, if all the tangent lines to the graph have positive slope on an
interval, then f is an increasing function on that interval; that is, where $f'(x) > 0$, f
is an increasing function. Likewise f is decreasing on an interval where $f'(x) < 0$.
Figure 3.9 illustrates these observations.

When a differentiable function f is increasing on an interval, its derivative is
nonnegative; that is, although $f'(x)$ is usually positive, there may be points on the
graph at which the tangent line is horizontal. Figure 3.10, the graph of $y = x^3$,
shows an increasing function that has a horizontal tangent line at the origin. Likewise, if f is decreasing, its derivative is nonpositive.

Figure 3.9

(a) A graph for which all tangent
lines have positive slope; it is the
graph of an increasing function.
(b) A graph for which all tangent
lines have negative slope; it is the
graph of a decreasing function.

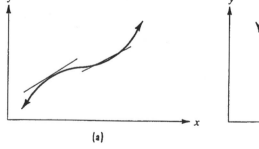

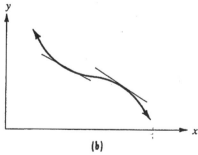

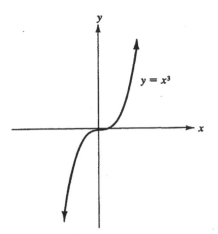

Figure 3.10

The graph of $y = x^3$, an increasing function with a horizontal tangent line at the origin

The preceding geometric observations are summarized in the following theorem, which is stated without proof.

Theorem 3.9

Suppose f is differentiable on an interval. On this interval, the following are true:

1. If $f'(x) > 0$, then f is increasing and, conversely, if f is increasing, then $f'(x) \geq 0$.

2. If $f'(x) < 0$, then f is decreasing and, conversely, if f is decreasing, then $f'(x) \leq 0$.

EXAMPLE 1

Determine whether $f(x) = x^4 - 2x^3$ is an increasing or a decreasing function on the interval $(3/2, \infty)$.

SOLUTION

The derivative of this function is

$$f'(x) = 4x^3 - 6x^2$$
$$= 2x^2(2x - 3).$$

For any x in the interval $(3/2, \infty)$, f' is positive, so by Theorem 3.9 f is an increasing function there. ●

EXAMPLE 2

Determine the intervals where the function $f(x) = 7 + 12x - 3x^2$ is increasing and the intervals where it is decreasing.

SOLUTION

Since the graph of $y = f(x)$ is a parabola that opens downward with the x-coordinate of its vertex at

$$x = -\frac{b}{2a} = \frac{-12}{-6} = 2,$$

we know that f is an increasing function on the interval $(-\infty, 2)$ and decreasing on the interval $(2, \infty)$. The derivative verifies this geometric observation, since

$$f'(x) = 12 - 6x$$

is positive if $x < 2$ and negative if $x > 2$. Note that technically f is increasing on $(-\infty, 2]$ and decreasing on $[2, \infty)$. To avoid overlapping intervals and difficulties with derivatives at endpoints of intervals, we specify the increasing or decreasing nature of a function on open intervals whenever possible. ●

EXAMPLE 3

Find the interval(s) on which the function $f(x) = x^3 - 2x^2 - 4x + 1$ is decreasing.

SOLUTION

The derivative of f is

$$f'(x) = 3x^2 - 4x - 4.$$

To find all values of x for which

$$3x^2 - 4x - 4 < 0,$$

we factor and find

$$(3x + 2)(x - 2) < 0.$$

This product is negative only when the two factors are of opposite sign. To determine when this occurs we plot the x values that make either factor 0 on a number line. The sign of each factor is then indicated on each of the resulting subintervals. The final sign chart is shown in Figure 3.11. We see that the two factors are of opposite sign on the interval $(-2/3, 2)$. Since this means that the derivative is negative on this interval, we conclude that the function is decreasing on $(-2/3, 2)$.

Figure 3.11
Determination of the sign of the product $(3x + 2)(x - 2)$

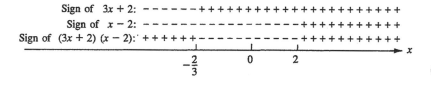

EXAMPLE 4

The manager of the Olde Coin House knows that the price at which a certain silver dollar will sell depends on how many are available for sale. Suppose that the demand function for this coin is modeled by

$$p = 50 - .08q - .4\sqrt{q}, \qquad 0 < q \le 100.$$

Show that p is a decreasing function of q; that is, as the supply of this silver dollar increases, its price decreases.

SOLUTION

Since the derivative

$$\frac{dp}{dq} = -.08 - \frac{.2}{\sqrt{q}}$$

is negative for all $q > 0$, p is a decreasing function of q on the interval $(0, 100)$. Further, because

$$p(0) = 50 \quad \text{and} \quad p(100) = 38$$

this function describes a price–demand relationship in which the price is about \$50 when the coin is scarce, but falls steadily to about \$38 when 100 are available. ●

EXAMPLE 5

Consider the rational function

$$v = \frac{5q + 800}{q + 50}, \qquad q > 0.$$

Show that if this function is used to model the variable cost per unit v of making an item, then the model describes v as a decreasing function of the output level q.

SOLUTION

The derivative of v with respect to q is

$$\frac{dv}{dq} = -\frac{550}{(q + 50)^2},$$

which is negative for any positive value of q. Therefore v is a decreasing function of q. In fact, v decreases from $v(0) = 16$ toward the limit 5 as q approaches infinity. ●

An important concept in economics, usually modeled by an increasing function, is the **consumption function**. A consumption function gives the amount C that an individual (or a group of individuals) consumes (or spends) as a function of that individual's income I. If consumption is a portion of income, then **savings** S is defined to be the amount of income that is not spent; that is,

$$S = I - C.$$

The derivative of C with respect to I represents the rate of change in the individual's spending as income increases. In other words, the derivative approximates the increase in the individual's consumption when the income goes up by a small amount. Economists call this derivative the **marginal propensity to consume**; that is, dC/dI represents the marginal propensity to consume.

If $dC/dI = 0$, then the individual does not spend anything from an increase in income; that is, extra income goes entirely to savings. If $dC/dI = 1$, then the individual spends all extra income. Therefore, in a good model for consumption as a function of income, the marginal propensity to consume should be a number between 0 and 1; that is,

(3.7)

$$0 \leq \frac{dC}{dI} \leq 1.$$

Thus consumption is modeled as an increasing function of income.

Because consumption plus savings equals income, we have

$$C + S = I.$$

Differentiating the terms with respect to I, we obtain

$$\frac{dC}{dI} + \frac{dS}{dI} = \frac{dI}{dI}.$$

Because $dI/dI = 1$, we have the relationship

$$\frac{dS}{dI} = 1 - \frac{dC}{dI}.$$

As dS/dI represents the rate of change in savings as the income increases, this derivative is called the **marginal propensity to save**. If equation (3.7) is true, it follows that savings is also an increasing function of income because

$$0 \le \frac{dS}{dI} \le 1.$$

When both the marginal propensity to consume and the marginal propensity to save are numbers between 0 and 1, they are often interpreted as the percentage of each additional dollar of income that is spent and saved, respectively.

EXAMPLE 6

Let

$$C = .90I - .04\sqrt{I} - .003I^2, \qquad 9 \le I \le 100.$$

Show that this function (with C and I measured in thousand dollars) is a suitable model for an individual's consumption of income. Determine the individual's total spending, savings, and marginal propensity to consume when the income is $16,000.

SOLUTION

The amount that the individual spends or consumes when $I = 16$ is given by

$$C(16) = .90(16) - .04\sqrt{16} - .003(16)^2$$
$$= 13.472,$$

and the savings is

$$S = 16 - 13.472$$
$$= 2.528.$$

That is, of the $16,000 income, $13,472 is spent and $2528 is saved. The marginal propensity to consume is the derivative

$$\frac{dC}{dI} = .90 - \frac{.02}{\sqrt{I}} - .006I.$$

For $9 \le I \le 100$, $.02/\sqrt{I}$ is between $.02/3 \doteq .0067$ and $.02/10 = .002$, while

$.006I$ is between $.054$ and $.6$; thus dC/dI is positive and less than 1. At an income level of $16,000, we have

$$\frac{dC}{dI}\bigg|_{I \,=\, 16} = .90 - \frac{.02}{\sqrt{16}} - .006(16)$$

$$= .799.$$

Therefore, according to this model, if this person has an income of $16,000 and gets some extra income, about 79.9% would be spent and the remaining 20.1% would be saved. ●

EXERCISES 3.5

In Exercises 1–14 determine whether the given function is increasing or decreasing on the given interval(s).

1. $f(x) = 4x - 10$; $(0, \infty)$

2. $f(x) = 4 + .03x$; $(-\infty, \infty)$

3. $f(x) = x^2 - 6x + 8$; $(-\infty, 3)$

4. $g(y) = 3y^2 + 9y - 2$; $(-1.5, \infty)$

5. $f(t) = t^3 - 3t + 4$; $(-1, 1)$, $(-\infty, -1)$, $(1, \infty)$

6. $h(x) = x^3 + 8x$; $(2, \infty)$, $(-\infty, \infty)$

7. $f(x) = \sqrt{x}$; $(0, \infty)$

8. $f(t) = \sqrt{8 + 2t}$; $(-4, \infty)$

9. $f(x) = \sqrt{16 - x^2}$; $(0, 4)$, $(-4, 0)$

10. $p(q) = \sqrt{q^2 - 400}$; $(20, \infty)$, $(-\infty, 20)$

11. $v(q) = \dfrac{30q + 1000}{q + 25}$; $(0, \infty)$

12. $f(x) = \dfrac{6}{10 - x}$; $(-\infty, 10)$, $(10, \infty)$

13. $g(t) = t^{2/3}$; $(-\infty, 0)$, $(0, \infty)$

14. $f(x) = (x - 3)^{1/3}$; $(-\infty, 3)$, $(3, \infty)$

In Exercises 15–30 determine the interval(s) on which the given function is increasing.

15. $f(x) = 5x - 12$

16. $f(x) = 1.8 - .45x$

17. $h(x) = -x^2 - 3x - 4$

18. $v(q) = 20 - .06q + .001q^2$

19. $f(x) = 2x^3 - 9x^2 + 12x - 7$

20. $f(x) = 2x^3 - 3x^2 - 72x + 101$

21. $f(t) = t^3 + t + 1$

22. $g(t) = t^3 - 75t$

23. $g(y) = \sqrt{y^2 - 9}$

24. $f(x) = (2x + 8)^{2/3}$

25. $f(x) = (3x + 1)^2(x - 5)^2$

26. $h(z) = (z - 2)^{1/3}$

27. $C(q) = 2000 + 75q^2 - q^3$

28. $h(y) = \sqrt{4 - y^2}$

29. $f(x) = \dfrac{1}{x^2 + 3}$

30. $P(q) = q^3 - 120q^2 + 2100q - 500$

31. The function

$$v = \frac{8q + 250}{q + 20}, \qquad q \geq 0,$$

is asserted to give the variable cost per unit v as a decreasing function of the output level q. Verify that this is the case. Describe specifically what happens to v as q increases.

32. The function

$$v = \frac{18q + 700}{q + 50}, \qquad q \geq 0,$$

is asserted to give the variable cost per unit v as a decreasing function of the output level q. Show that this is not the case and describe what is, in fact, happening to v.

33. Let a, b, and c be positive numbers and let

$$C = \frac{aq + b}{q + c}, \qquad q \geq 0.$$

Under what conditions on a, b, and c will v be a decreasing function of q?

34. The function

$$C = 300 + 8q - .005q^2, \qquad q \geq 0,$$

is said to represent the total cost of producing q units of a product. If the total cost is increasing as the output increases, determine the largest interval on which this model is valid.

35. Tool Masters is a company that makes sets of automotive wrenches. The company has the capability of making as many as 150 sets of wrenches each day. The plant manager knows that the variable cost of making each set decreases from about \$25 to about \$20.50 as the number of sets made increases to 150. Suppose that the variable cost v is given by

$$v = 25 - .06q + .0002q^2, \qquad q \geq 0,$$

where q is the number of sets made per day. Verify that this function has the necessary properties to model the variable cost.

36. Refer to Exercise 35. Assume that the fixed cost for Tool Masters is \$300 per day. Show that the total cost function obtained when v is modeled as given is an increasing function of q for all q. [*Hint*: Show that $C'(q)$ is positive for some value of q and that there is no real value of q at which $C'(q)$ changes sign.]

37. Suppose that the total cost C of making q units of an item is modeled by the cubic function

$$C = 400 + 24q - .27q^2 + .001q^3, \qquad q \geq 0.$$

At what value of q will C become a decreasing function of q? If, in fact, the total cost of making this item is known to be an increasing function of the output, what does this imply about the interval on which the model is useful?

38. Suppose that in the production of an item it is known that the fixed costs are \$150 per day and the variable cost per unit is constantly \$6.

a. Show that the average cost per unit A is a decreasing function of the number of units produced q, regardless of the level of output.

b. Find $\lim_{q \to \infty} A(q)$. Does this seem reasonable? Explain.

39. The function

$$p = 1000 - 2.43q + .0001q^3, \qquad q \geq 0,$$

relates the unit price p of a certain commodity to the number of units q that consumers will purchase. If p is to be a decreasing function of q, what is the longest interval on which this will remain true?

40. The demand for a silver alloy is known to fall as the price of the alloy rises. It is also known that when the price is \$16 per gram, there is a demand for 900 g of the alloy. Show that the function

$$p = \frac{48}{\sqrt{.01q}}, \qquad q > 0,$$

is a possible model that has the necessary relationships.

41. The function

$$p = \sqrt{2500 + .3q^2}, \qquad q \geq 0,$$

is intended to show the relationship between the market price p for a cord of firewood and the number of cords q that suppliers will bring to town to sell. Show that in this model whenever q increases p also increases. What is the lowest price that is required for the suppliers to provide any firewood?

42. Suppose it is known that the farmers who raise soybeans will not bring any to market unless the price is at least \$4 per bushel. However, they will provide seemingly unlimited amounts as the price rises toward \$14 per bushel. Show that the function

$$p = \frac{42q + 1000}{3q + 250}, \qquad q \geq 0,$$

gives the per-bushel price p as an increasing function of the number of bushels q that the farmers provide and has the other required properties.

43. Suppose that a person has a current income of \$25,000 per year. Determine her marginal propensity to consume if the consumption function is

$$C = .97I - .005I^2, \qquad 10 \leq I \leq 50,$$

where C and I are measured in thousand dollars. Suppose that this person receives an unexpected tax refund of \$500. Approximately how much of the refund will be saved and how much will be spent?

44. Jimmy has entered the office football pool for the first time. If he wins, he will pick up \$50. Suppose that his consumption function is given by

$$C = .93I - .002I^2 - .0001I^3, \qquad 12 \leq I \leq 30,$$

where C and I are given in thousand dollars. If Jimmy's present income is $21,000, find his marginal propensity to consume and estimate how much of the winnings he would spend.

45. Lisa has just been given a promotion and a $1200 raise. Suppose that her consumption of income is modeled by

$$C = .95I - .008I^{3/2} - .24I^{1/2}, \qquad 15 \le I \le 30,$$

where C and I are in thousand dollars. Find Lisa's marginal

propensity to save. If her previous salary was $16,000, estimate how much of the raise she will save. Approximately how much would be saved if her salary had been $25,000?

46. Refer to Exercises 43–45. Show that each of the consumption functions in these exercises is an increasing function of income; that is, as the person's income rises, so does his or her spending.

3.6
Concavity and Derivatives of Higher Order

Certain phrases are often used to describe a curve that is increasing in a special fashion. For instance, a stock analyst might refer to a company's earnings as "flattening out" even though the earnings are still on the rise; or an economist might report that unemployment figures "though still climbing, are increasing at a decreasing rate." In both cases, the curve that is being described would look like the curve in Figure 3.12(a) rather than the curve in Figure 3.12(b). Statements that might be used to describe a situation pictured by the second curve are that the company's earnings appear to be "taking off," or unemployment figures are "accelerating."

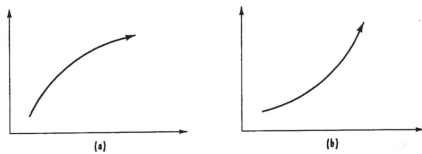

Figure 3.12

Curves representing increasing functions. The one on the left is concave downward; the one on the right is concave upward.

(a)   (b)

For curves that represent decreasing functions, phrases like "bottoming out" and "approaching a trough" are often used to describe a curve shaped like that in Figure 3.13(a), whereas "plunging" or "falling off the table" might apply to the curve in Figure 3.13(b).

Mathematicians use the concept of concavity to distinguish between the two types of curves for both increasing and decreasing functions. Geometrically, a

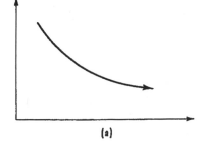
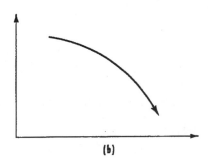

Figure 3.13

Curves representing decreasing functions. The one on the left is concave upward; the one on the right is concave downward.

(a)   (b)

smooth curve is said to be **concave upward** at a point if a segment of the tangent line to the curve at that point lies below the curve. The curve is **concave downward** if the tangent line is above the curve. Figure 3.14 illustrates both kinds of concavity. Note, however, that the function $y = f(x)$ in this figure is increasing at both $x = x_1$ and $x = x_2$, even though the concavity is reversed at these points. It is therefore apparent that the sign of the derivative is of no use in determining the concavity of a curve.

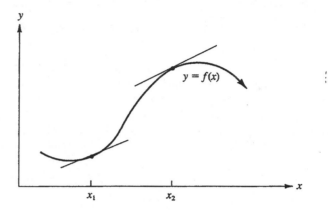

Figure 3.14

This curve is concave upward at $x = x_1$ and concave downward at $x = x_2$.

If we study how the derivative of the function f in Figure 3.15 changes as x moves from left to right through x_1 and x_2, we see that change in the derivative is linked to concavity. Observe that as x moves through x_1 the slopes of the tangent lines to the curve are increasing. [See Figure 3.15(a).] This means that near $x = x_1$ the derivative $f'(x)$ is an increasing function. It can also be observed that as x moves through x_2, the tangent lines have decreasing slopes. [See Figure 3.15(b).] That is, near $x = x_2$, the derivative $f'(x)$ is a decreasing function.

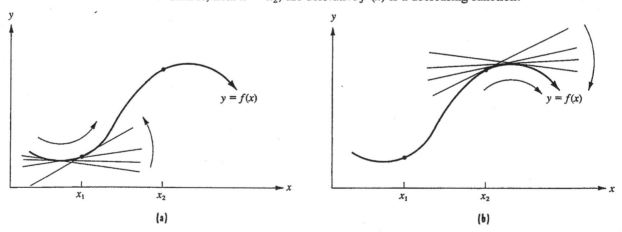

(a)   (b)

Figure 3.15

Slopes of tangent lines **(a)** *increase* where the curve is concave upward and **(b)** *decrease* where the curve is concave downward.

By considering other examples of curves, both increasing and decreasing, it becomes evident that on an interval where a smooth curve is concave upward, the slope of the tangent lines [and consequently $f'(x)$] is an increasing function of x. On intervals where the curve is concave downward, the slope of the tangent lines [and $f'(x)$] is a decreasing function.

In light of these observations, we see that in order to determine the concavity of the curve, it is necessary to know whether the derivative of the function representing the curve is an increasing or a decreasing function. Because $D_x[f'(x)] > 0$ when $f'(x)$ is an increasing function and $D_x[f'(x)] < 0$ when $f'(x)$ is a decreasing function, it is convenient to define the derivative of the derivative of a function.

Definition 3.3

> Let f be a differentiable function. Suppose that the derivative f' is also differentiable. Then the derivative of f' is called the **second derivative of f** and is denoted by f''.

Whenever there is any possibility of confusing the derivative of a function with its second derivative, we will call the former the first derivative. Just as there are several ways of denoting the first derivative, the second derivative of $y = f(x)$ may be denoted by $D_x^2[f(x)]$, or d^2y/dx^2 as well as by y'' or f''.

EXAMPLE 1

Find $f''(x)$ for the following functions.

a. $f(x) = 2x^3 - 7x^2 + 5x + 4$

b. $f(x) = \dfrac{6x + 10}{x + 3}$

c. $f(x) = \sqrt{x^2 + 7}$

SOLUTION

Each second derivative is found by taking two derivatives in succession.

a. $f'(x) = 6x^2 - 14x + 5$

$\quad f''(x) = 12x - 14$

b. $f'(x) = \dfrac{(x + 3)(6) - (6x + 10)(1)}{(x + 3)^2} = \dfrac{8}{(x + 3)^2} = 8(x + 3)^{-2}$

$\quad f''(x) = -16(x + 3)^{-3} = \dfrac{-16}{(x + 3)^3}$

c. $f'(x) = \dfrac{1}{2}(x^2 + 7)^{-1/2}(2x)$

$\quad\quad\quad = x(x^2 + 7)^{-1/2}$

$\quad f''(x) = (x^2 + 7)^{-1/2} + x\left(-\dfrac{1}{2}\right)(x^2 + 7)^{-3/2}(2x)$

$\quad\quad\quad = (x^2 + 7)^{-1/2} - x^2(x^2 + 7)^{-3/2}$

$\quad\quad\quad = (x^2 + 7)^{-3/2}[(x^2 + 7) - x^2]$

$\quad\quad\quad = 7(x^2 + 7)^{-3/2}$

Our geometric observations regarding concavity and second derivatives are summarized in the following theorem.

Theorem 3.10

Suppose f'' exists on an interval. On this interval the following are true.

1. If $f''(x) > 0$, then the graph of $y = f(x)$ is concave upward.
2. If $f''(x) < 0$, then the graph of $y = f(x)$ is concave downward.

A point on a curve at which the concavity changes is called an **inflection point** of the curve (assuming that the function is continuous at this point). Figure 3.16 shows a curve with two inflection points. The concavity changes from upward to downward at x_1 and from downward back to upward at x_2. Using Theorem 3.10, we have an intuitive test for locating points of inflection:

The curve given by $y = f(x)$ has an inflection point at $x = x_1$, if the sign of $f''(x)$ changes as x passes through x_1, and if f is continuous at x_1. If $f''(x_1)$ exists, then $f''(x_1) = 0$.

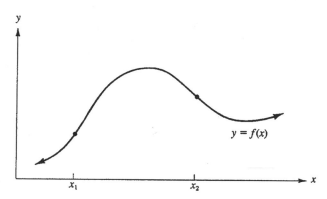

Figure 3.16
A graph with inflection points at x_1 and x_2

EXAMPLE 2

Discuss the concavity of $y = 3x^2 - 7x + 4$.

SOLUTION

Since the second derivative is constant, $y'' = 6$, the concavity does not change on the entire real line; that is, there are no points of inflection. The curve is always concave upward. ●

EXAMPLE 3

Discuss the concavity of the graph of the cubic function
$$y = 4 - 2x + 10x^2 - 5x^3.$$

SOLUTION

The second derivative is the linear function
$$y'' = 20 - 30x.$$
Since this function is positive for $x < 2/3$ and negative for $x > 2/3$, the curve is

concave upward on the interval $(-\infty, 2/3)$ and concave downward on the interval $(2/3, \infty)$. The function is continuous for all x, so in particular it is continuous at $x = 2/3$ and thus there is an inflection point at $x = 2/3$.   ●

EXAMPLE 4

Discuss the concavity of the graph of the rational function

$$y = \frac{x + 3}{x - 2}, \qquad x \neq 2.$$

SOLUTION

We find

$$y' = \frac{-5}{(x - 2)^2} = -5(x - 2)^{-2} \quad \text{and} \quad y'' = \frac{10}{(x - 2)^3} = 10(x - 2)^{-3}.$$

Since $y'' < 0$ when $x < 2$ and $y'' > 0$ when $x > 2$, the graph is concave downward on the interval $(-\infty, 2)$ and concave upward on the interval $(2, \infty)$. However, there is not a point of inflection at $x = 2$ because this point is not in the domain of the function and thus the function is not continuous at $x = 2$.   ●

In the remaining examples we show that the functions used in some of our earlier models have the appropriate concavity.

EXAMPLE 5

If the revenue R generated by the sale of q units of a commodity is graphed, it can be expected that the curve will be concave downward. This is because as q increases, the selling price of each unit should decline. Therefore, even though more revenue is generated by the sale of more units, the growth will begin to top out as the market becomes saturated.

Assume that in order for a toy store to sell q video game cartridges per day (for q up to 60) the price per cartridge p must be

$$p = 30 - .12q + .0005q^2.$$

Verify that for this demand function, the graph of the revenue function is increasing, but concave downward for $0 \leq q \leq 60$.

SOLUTION

Writing revenue as a function of q, we obtain

$$R = pq = 30q - .12q^2 + .0005q^3, \qquad 0 \leq q \leq 60.$$

The marginal revenue is then

$$MR = R' = 30 - .24q + .0015q^2, \qquad 0 \leq q \leq 60.$$

It may be verified, by finding the vertex of the graph of this function, that R' is positive in the domain. The second derivative is

$$R'' = -.24 + .003q.$$

Because $.003q < .24$ for all $q < 80$, it is true that the graph of the revenue function is concave downward on the interval $[0, 60]$.   ●

EXAMPLE 6   Let v be the variable cost per unit in the manufacture of q units of an item. Suppose that

$$v = \frac{20q + 3000}{q + 5}, \qquad q \geq 0.$$

It may be expected that although v is a decreasing function of q, the rate of decrease is declining or flattening out for large values of q. This is an example of the so-called law of diminishing returns. Verify that the graph of this function is concave upward on its domain.

SOLUTION   The graph is shown in Figure 3.17 and it does appear to be concave upward. We have that

$$v' = \frac{-2900}{(q + 5)^2} < 0, \qquad \text{for } q > 0,$$

and

$$v'' = \frac{5800}{(q + 5)^3} > 0, \qquad \text{for } q > 0.$$

Therefore, the graph is a concave upward, decreasing curve.

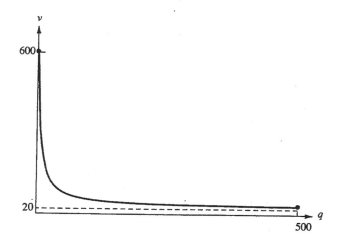

Figure 3.17
The graph of
$v = (20q + 3000)/(q + 5)$

EXAMPLE 7   Let $C = f(I)$ be a consumption function for some person. In the previous section, we required that C be an increasing function of I; that is, spending increases with income. It may also be required that the marginal propensity to consume be a decreasing function of income. This reflects a belief that as income rises, a larger proportion of the person's income will go into investments or savings.

Verify that the consumption function

$$C = .90I - .04\sqrt{I} - .003I^2, \qquad 9 \leq I \leq 100,$$

from Example 6 of Section 3.5 has a graph that is increasing and concave downward.

<hr>

SOLUTION

It was shown that the marginal propensity to consume

$$C' = .90 - .02I^{-1/2} - .006I$$

is positive on the interval [9, 100]. The second derivative

$$C'' = .01I^{-3/2} - .006$$

$$= \frac{.01}{\sqrt{I^3}} - .006$$

is negative, since the largest possible value for $.01/\sqrt{I^3}$ on the interval [9, 100] is $.00037$ at $I = 9$. ●

EXERCISES 3.6

In Exercises 1–16 find the second derivative of the given function.

1. $f(x) = 3 - 5x$

2. $g(x) = 4x^2 + 2x - 3$

3. $f(x) = x^3 + 2x - 7$

4. $r(x) = x^{1/3} + x^{-1/3}$

5. $f(x) = (5x + 4)^7$

6. $F(t) = t^2(t - 2)^6$

7. $f(x) = \sqrt{3x + 1}$

8. $g(t) = (t^2 - 3)^5$

9. $h(z) = \dfrac{z + 7}{z - 1}$

10. $v(q) = \dfrac{14q + 300}{q + 15}$

11. $C(q) = \dfrac{q^2 + 5q + 60}{q + 10}$

12. $F(q) = \dfrac{5q^2 - 3}{q^2 + 1}$

13. $f(x) = x\sqrt{2x + 3}$

14. $R(q) = \sqrt{1000 - q^2}$

15. $q(p) = \sqrt{5p^2 + 45}$

16. $s(r) = r\sqrt{3 - r^3}$

In Exercises 17–26 determine whether the graph of the given function is concave upward or concave downward on the given interval.

17. $f(x) = 4x^2 + 6x - 10; (-\infty, \infty)$

18. $g(t) = t^3 - 3t^2 + 5t - 3; \left(\dfrac{1}{2}, \infty\right)$

19. $f(x) = (5 - 3x)(7 - 2x); (-\infty, \infty)$

20. $p(q) = q^3 + 12q^2 - q + 8; (-4, \infty)$

21. $h(s) = s^5 - 80s^2 + 100; (-\infty, 2)$

22. $f(s) = s^4 - 12s^3 + 18s + 24; (0, 6)$

23. $f(z) = \dfrac{2z + 5}{3z + 2}; \left(-\infty, -\dfrac{2}{3}\right)$

24. $f(x) = \dfrac{5}{x^2 - 9}; (-3, 3)$

25. $f(x) = \sqrt{x^2 + 16}; (-4, \infty)$

26. $F(r) = (r - 3)^{5/3}; (3, \infty)$

In Exercises 27–36 find the interval(s) on which f is concave upward and the interval(s) on which it is concave downward. Find any inflection points.

27. $f(x) = x^3 + 15x + 25$

28. $f(x) = (x^2 + 2)(6 - x)$

29. $f(x) = 4x^5 - 5x^2$

30. $f(x) = x^4 - 7x^3 + 18x^2 + 3x - 9$

31. $f(x) = \dfrac{x + 5}{2x - 12}$

32. $f(x) = \dfrac{x}{x^2 - 1}$

33. $f(x) = x(x^2 + 4)^{1/2}$

34. $f(x) = x(x - 6)^3$

35. $f(x) = x^2 + \dfrac{1}{x}$

36. $f(x) = (x^2 + 6)^{-2}$

37. Show that the graph of the cubic function $y = ax^3 + bx^2 + cx + d$ always has one inflection point. At what value of x does this occur?

38. Show that the demand function

$$p = \frac{50q + 160}{q + 2}, \qquad q \geq 0,$$

is decreasing and concave upward. Show that the corresponding revenue function $R = pq$ is concave downward.

39. Show that the demand function

$$p = 100 - \sqrt{.5q + 2500}, \qquad 0 \leq q \leq 5000,$$

is decreasing and concave upward. Show that the corresponding revenue function $R = pq$ is concave downward.

40. Show that the consumption function

$$C = \sqrt{5I + 16}, \qquad 8 \leq I \leq 48,$$

is increasing and concave downward.

41. Show that the consumption function

$$C = I - .1\sqrt{I} - .002I^2, \qquad 16 \leq I \leq 36,$$

is increasing and concave downward.

42. Let the total production cost for one day's operation of a plant C be written as a function of the day's output level q. It is reasonable to expect that the graph of C will be concave downward to reflect the added efficiency gained by increasing the output (at least until the plant begins to approach capacity). Show that C is an increasing, concave downward function for $0 \leq q \leq 250$ when the fixed cost per day is known to be \$150 and the variable cost per unit is given by (a) $v = 50 - .08q + .0001q^2$ and by (b) $v = (30q + 500)/(q + 10)$.

43. Frequently it is desirable to model the variable cost with a function whose graph looks like the one shown here. Such a graph indicates that the variable cost declines gradually at first, then drops sharply when economies of scale are reached, and finally levels off. Ratios of quadratic functions can have a graph with this shape. Let v be given by the function

$$v = \frac{20q^2 + 18,000}{q^2 + 300}, \qquad q \geq 0.$$

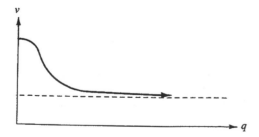

Find $v(0)$, $\lim_{q \to \infty} v(q)$, the interval where the graph is concave downward, the interval where it is concave upward, and the point of inflection. Sketch the graph of v.

44. Repeat Exercise 43 with

$$v = \frac{4q^2 + 1500}{q^2 + 120}, \qquad q \geq 0.$$

45. Sometimes the relationship between the supply of a commodity and its price is modeled by a function whose graph has the shape shown here. Such a graph indicates that price increases will bring forth large increases in supply as new producers enter the market or existing producers add to their output, until limits on natural resources eventually curtail further increases in output regardless of price.

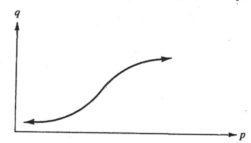

A function of the form $q = \sqrt[3]{ap^2 + b} - c$ for positive a, b, and c has such a graph. For each of the following show that q is an increasing function and find the point where the concavity changes.

a. $q = \sqrt[3]{1.5p^2 + 400} - 10$, $p \geq 20$

b. $q = \sqrt[3]{.6p^2 + 110} - 5$, $p \geq 5$.

46. S. H. McIntyre* examined a sales response function of the form

$$S = a + \frac{kx^n}{x^n + b},$$

where S is the number of sales over a given time period, x is the marketing expenditure, and a, b, k, and n are positive constants with $n > 1$. Functions of this form are positive and increasing, and they change from concave upward to concave downward with increasing x. If

$$S = 1000 + \frac{800x^{1.5}}{x^{1.5} + 40,000}, \qquad 0 \leq x \leq 500,$$

find the value of x at the inflection point on the graph of S.

*S. H. McIntyre, "An Experimental Study of the Impact of Judgement-Based Marketing Models," *Management Science* 28(1982): 17–33.

CH. 3 REVIEW

I. Key Terms & Concepts

Mathematics	Business
Derivative	Marginal Cost
Differentiable Function	Marginal Revenue
Instantaneous Rate of Change	Marginal Revenue
Tangent Line	Product
Power Rule	Consumption Function
Chain Rule	Marginal Propensity to
Product Rule	Consume
Quotient Rule	Marginal Propensity to
Increasing Function	Save
Decreasing Function	
Concavity	
Second Derivative	
Inflection Point	
Constant Multiple Rule	
Sum Rule	

II. True or False

Indicate whether each statement is true or false.

1. If $f'(x) > 0$ on an interval, then f is increasing on that interval.

2. A constant function is neither increasing nor decreasing.

3. If f is continuous at $x = a$, then f is differentiable at $x = a$.

4. If C is the total cost of producing q items and MC is the marginal cost of the qth item, then $MC(q) = C'(q)$.

5. If f and g are differentiable functions, then $D_x[f(x) + g(x)] = f'(x) + g'(x)$.

6. If f and g are differentiable functions, then $D_x[f(x)g(x)] = f'(x)g'(x)$.

7. The function $y = 1/x$ is decreasing on $(-\infty, 0)$ and on $(0, \infty)$, but not on $(-\infty, \infty)$.

8. If f is a differentiable function, then
$$\frac{f(x + h) - f(x)}{h} = f'(x).$$

9. The graph of $y = ax^2 + bx + c$ is concave upward if and only if $a > 0$.

10. The graph of the power function $y = x^n$, where n is a positive constant, is concave downward on $(0, \infty)$ if and only if $0 < n < 1$.

III. Drill Problems

In Problems 1–20 find dy/dx for the given function.

1. $y = 5x - 13$

2. $y = 7 - x + 6x^2$

3. $y = 2x + 5 + \dfrac{6}{x^2}$

4. $y = x^2 + \dfrac{1}{x}$

5. $y = (x^2 + 8)^9$

6. $y = (2x + 9)^6$

7. $y = 4x^{3/2} - 2x^{1/2} + 8$

8. $y = \sqrt{x}(x^2 + 2x + 1)$

9. $y = \dfrac{2x + 1}{4x + 3}$

10. $y = \dfrac{2x}{x^2 + 8}$

11. $y = \dfrac{5}{x^3 + 8x^2 - 2x + 1}$ 12. $y = \dfrac{3x^2 + 5}{2x + 9}$

13. $y = \dfrac{x + 9}{\sqrt{8x + 5}}$ 14. $y = \dfrac{6}{\sqrt{x^2 + 4x + 9}}$

15. $y = (6x^3 + 2x)\sqrt{5x + 7}$

16. $y = (x^2 + 1)\sqrt{4x + 7}$

17. $y = \sqrt[3]{4x^2 - 7x + 8}$ 18. $y = (\sqrt{x^2 + 8})^5$

19. $y = \left(\dfrac{6x + 1}{2x + 5}\right)^8$ 20. $y = \pi^2$

In Problems 21–26 find an equation (in general form) of the line tangent to the graph of the given function at the indicated point.

21. $y = x^3 - 3x^2 + 5x - 1$; $(2, 5)$

22. $y = \sqrt{x}(2 + x^2)$; $(1, 3)$

23. $y = \sqrt{x^2 + 16}$; $(3, 5)$ 24. $y = \dfrac{4x + 10}{2x + 5}$; $(4, 2)$

25. $y = \dfrac{x}{x^2 + 1}$; $(0, 0)$ 26. $y = \dfrac{\sqrt{2x + 1}}{x - 1}$; $(4, 1)$

In Problems 27–34 determine the intervals where the given function is (a) increasing and (b) concave upward.

27. $f(x) = 5 + 6x + x^2$ 28. $f(x) = 7 - 4x - 2x^2$

29. $g(x) = 2x^3 - 12x^2 - 48x + 5$

30. $g(x) = 8 + 45x - 3x^2 - x^3$

31. $f(x) = \dfrac{x^2}{x^2 + 12}$ 32. $f(x) = \dfrac{2x^2}{x + 1}$

33. $g(x) = \sqrt{x^2 + 25}$ 34. $g(x) = \sqrt[3]{x^2 - 64}$

IV. Applications

1. Precision Printers can make up to 200 of their dot matrix models each day. Daily fixed costs are $800, and on a day when q printers are produced, the variable cost per printer v is

$$v = 191 - .29q + .001q^2, \qquad 0 \le q \le 200.$$

All printers produced can be sold for p dollars each, where

$$p = 299 - .32q, \qquad 0 \le q \le 200.$$

a. Find the marginal cost and the marginal revenue of the qth printer.

b. Determine the output level q that maximizes profit.

2. Refer to Exercise 1. Precision Printers is about to produce a new letter quality printer. First estimates indicate fixed costs of $800 per day and a variable cost per unit given by

$$v = \dfrac{180q + 23{,}800}{q + 40}, \qquad 0 \le q \le 200.$$

Demand for letter quality printers should be

$$p = 347 - .47q, \qquad 0 \le q \le 200.$$

a. Find the marginal cost and the marginal revenue of the qth printer.

b. Determine the output level q that will maximize profit.

3. The editors of the Chartmark investment letter predict that t months from now the selling price p of a stock you own will be given by

$$p = 20 + 4.8t + .3t^2 - .05t^3, \qquad 0 \le t \le 12.$$

You wish to sell the stock next year when p stops increasing. If you believe Chartmark's prediction, in how many months should you sell?

4. Refer to Exercise 3. Although Epsilon Airways has been losing money for the past two quarters, Chartmark predicts that the selling price p of Epsilon stock will soon level off. In fact, it is estimated that in t months p will be given by

$$p = 10 - 2.88t + .12t^2 + .04t^3, \qquad 0 \le t \le 12.$$

In how many months will p stop decreasing?

5. The shelf life of Evercharge flashlight batteries is 18 mo. In fact, the current I (in amperes) generated by an Evercharge battery t months after it is produced is given by

$$I = \frac{300 + .1t^2}{300 + t^2}, \qquad 0 \le t \le 18.$$

Find the month t when the rate at which I is decreasing stops decreasing; that is, find t at the inflection point on the graph of I.

6. If the demand function for a certain product is

$$p = 3 + \frac{12}{\sqrt{2q + 9}}, \qquad q \ge 0,$$

find the values of q where p is a decreasing function of q. For what values of q is the corresponding revenue function concave downward?

7. Your assistant has devised the following consumption function to reflect the spending habits of your management trainees:

$$C = \sqrt{.9I^2 - 1.8I}, \qquad 10 \le I \le 25,$$

where I and C are measured in thousands of dollars. Find C and the marginal propensity to consume when $I = 20$.

8. Show that the consumption function in Exercise 7 is increasing and concave downward.

9. The production function for a certain manufacturer is estimated to be

$$q = 5(49w - 125)^{1/3} + 25, \qquad 3 \le w \le 20,$$

where q is the number of units produced per day and w is the number of employees. If the demand function for this product is

$$p = 135 - .3q, \qquad 0 \le q \le 75,$$

find the marginal revenue product dR/dw when $w = 13$.

A jeweler in your community is advertising that if you had purchased diamonds 10 yr ago, their value would have increased to 420% of their original value. Calculate the average effective rate of increase in the value of the diamonds during this period.

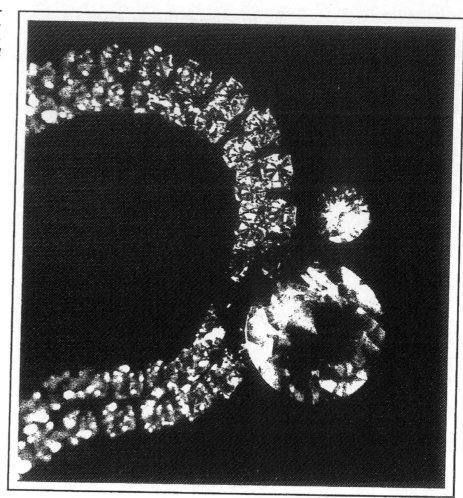

CHAPTER 4

Exponential and Logarithmic Functions

126

4.1
Exponential Growth and Decay

In this chapter we consider the growth and decay of certain things (usually amounts of money) over time. In particular, we study phenomena in which the rate of growth or decay remains constant over a time period. Growth at a constant rate implies that the change from the present size is proportional to the present size; that is, the change is a fixed percentage of the original size.

The numbers of many biological species, such as mice, bacteria, and rabbits, and the population of many cities grow (or decline) at a fairly constant rate. For example, the population of Phoenix has grown at a rate of 3% a year for the past decade, while the population of St. Louis has declined at a rate of 2% a year. Because this kind of growth (or decay) occurs so frequently in nature, it is often called **natural growth** (or **natural decay**).

There are many examples of natural growth in business: the year-to-year gain in sales and earnings of some companies, the amount of money that accumulates in a savings account, and the salary of an employee who is given annual percentage raises. On the other hand, the depreciation of equipment (where it is assumed that a fixed percentage of its value is lost each year) is an example of natural decay.

We begin with a formal definition of growth rate per year.

Definition 4.1

Let $A(t)$ denote the amount of some thing at time t, where t is measured in years. The **effective rate of growth** r of A from time $t = t_0$ to $t = t_0 + 1$ is defined to be

(4.1)
$$r = \frac{A(t_0 + 1) - A(t_0)}{A(t_0)}.$$

If this quotient is negative, r is called the **effective rate of decay**.

Notice that r is a percentage: the change in A divided by the original value of A.

EXAMPLE 1

On January 1, 1988, the price of one share of XYZ Company's stock was $24.50. By January 1, 1989, the selling price had risen to $28.25. Find the effective rate of growth in the XYZ stock price during that year.

SOLUTION

Referring to equation (4.1), we get $A(t_0) = 24.50$ and $A(t_0 + 1) = 28.25$, so

$$r = \frac{28.25 - 24.50}{24.50}$$

$$= .153.$$

Thus the effective rate of growth was 15.3%. Undoubtedly the price of the stock fluctuated considerably during the year; r measures only the net change at the end of the year relative to the value at the beginning of the year. ●

When computing effective rates of growth, we sometimes write equation (4.1) by splitting $[A(t_0 + 1) - A(t_0)]/A(t_0)$ into two terms and then simplifying to obtain

(4.2)
$$r = \frac{A(t_0 + 1)}{A(t_0)} - 1.$$

In this form, the effective rate in Example 1 can be found by forming the quotient $28.25/24.50 = 1.153$, and then mentally subtracting the 1. In many cases 1.153, or $1 + r$, itself is used as a growth factor.

Often we wish to determine a future amount when a known starting amount grows for a period of time at a known effective rate of growth. When the time period is one year, the future amount can be found by solving equation (4.2) or (4.1) for $A(t_0 + 1)$ to obtain

(4.3)
$$A(t_0 + 1) = A(t_0)[1 + r].$$

More general time periods are considered in the following example.

EXAMPLE 2   Suppose that P dollars (the principal) are invested so as to grow at an effective rate of r in each successive year. If F denotes the future value of this investment after t years, find F as a function of t.

SOLUTION   Treating F as an amount $A(t)$, we begin with $t_0 = 0$ and $A(0) = P$. From equation (4.3), after one year $t = 1$ and

$$F = A(1) = A(0)[1 + r]$$
$$= P(1 + r).$$

Considering the second year as a new investment period, we begin with $t_0 = 1$; then when $t = 2$, equation (4.3) yields

$$F = A(1)[1 + r]$$
$$= P(1 + r)[1 + r]$$
$$= P(1 + r)^2.$$

Similarly, at the beginning of the third year $t_0 = 2$, so when $t = 3$,

$$F = A(3) = A(2)[1 + r]$$
$$= P(1 + r)^3.$$

Repeating this process, we find that F, or $F(t)$, is given by

(4.4)
$$F(t) = P(1 + r)^t \qquad \text{for any nonnegative integer } t. \qquad \bullet$$

The function (4.4) in Example 2 is called an **exponential function**. As we will discover, every function that is used to model natural growth or decay is an exponential function.

Definition 4.2

An **exponential function with the base** b is a function of the form

(4.5)
$$y = ab^x \qquad \text{for all } x,$$

where a is a constant and b is a positive constant other than 1.

Notice that in the definition of an exponential function, the base cannot be 1 because then y would equal the constant a for all x. It is important to realize the difference between a function like equation (4.5) and a power function $y = ax^p$. In exponential functions the exponent (thus the name) is the independent variable, whereas in power functions the base is the independent variable.

EXAMPLE 3

Suppose that a recent accounting graduate is hired at an initial salary of $18,000 per year. If she is given a 12% salary increase each year, find her salary S as a function of the number of years t that she is employed by this company.

SOLUTION

This problem is the same in concept as Example 2. Here the initial salary corresponds to the principal P and the percentage raise is the effective growth rate. Using equation (4.4), we find her salary to be an exponential function with base 1.12:

$$S(t) = 18,000(1.12)^t, \qquad t \text{ a nonnegative integer.} \qquad \bullet$$

We next consider an example of exponential decay.

EXAMPLE 4

Assume that a machine is purchased by a company for $40,000. As the machine depreciates through age and use, each year its value declines by 20% of its value at the beginning of the year. Obtain the value V of the machine as a function of t, the number of years since its purchase.

SOLUTION

We are given that the effective rate of decay in the value of the machine is 20%; that is, its value $V(t)$ can be given by equation (4.4) where $r = -.20$. Thus,

$$V(t) = 40,000(1 - .20)^t$$
$$= 40,000(.80)^t.$$

Note that in this example V is again given as an exponential function, but the base is less than 1—in particular, $b = .80$. $\qquad \bullet$

When the base b of the exponential function $y = ab^x$ is greater than 1, as in Example 3, y will increase or grow as x increases, whereas if the base is less than 1, as in Example 4, then y will decrease or decay. To demonstrate, Table 4.1 shows the values of $(1.12)^t$ and $(.80)^t$ calculated for increasing t; the corresponding coordinates are plotted in Figures 4.1 and 4.2.

Table 4.1

t	0	2	4	6	8	10
$(1.12)^t$	1.000	1.254	1.574	1.974	2.476	3.106
$(.80)^t$	1.000	.640	.410	.262	.168	.107

In the definition of an exponential function $y = ab^x$, the domain is all the real numbers. In some of the models considered in this section, the domain must be

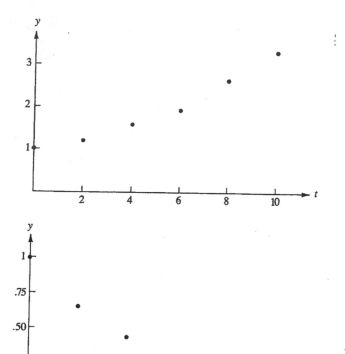

Figure 4.1

Some points that satisfy the growth function $y = (1.12)^t$

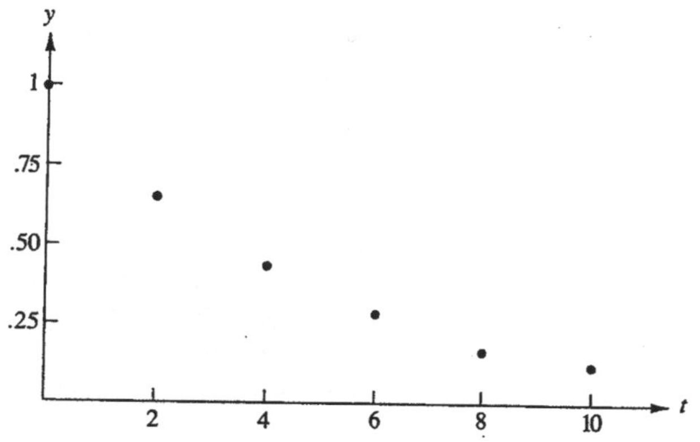

Figure 4.2

Some points that satisfy the decay function $y = (.80)^t$

restricted to nonnegative integers. For example, the accountant's salary remains constant between the times the raises are given. For other models, the domain may be all nonnegative real numbers: in the depreciation of the machine, its value decreases throughout the year, and the function $V(t) = 40,000(.80)^t$ will also give the value of the machine for any $t \geq 0$. For example, $V(2.75)$ gives the value of the machine $2\frac{3}{4}$ yr after its purchase. We can evaluate $(.80)^{2.75}$ as follows:

$$(.80)^{2.75} = (.80)^{275/100} = \sqrt[100]{(.80)^{275}} \doteq .541.$$

Thus, the value of the machine would be $V(2.75) \doteq 40,000(.541) = \$21,640$. (Such calculations are easily done using a calculator with a $\boxed{y^x}$ key.) An exponential model may even have meaning for negative values of x. For example, if the machine was purchased several years earlier, is depreciating at an effective rate of 20% per year, and is currently worth \$40,000, then $V(-2)$ would give its value two years earlier. We calculate $(.80)^{-2}$ as follows:

$$(.80)^{-2} = \frac{1}{(.80)^2} = 1.5625,$$

giving a machine value of $40,000(1.5625) = \$62,500$ two years ago.

The only real difficulty in defining an exponential function for all real numbers occurs when x is an irrational number and so cannot be written as the quotient of integers. The difficulty is overcome by using limits. For example, suppose we wanted to calculate $b^{\sqrt{2}}$ for some base b. Since 1.4, 1.41, 1.414, 1.4142, . . . are successively better approximations to $\sqrt{2}$, it can be shown that the sequence of numbers

$$b^{1.4}, \quad b^{1.41}, \quad b^{1.414}, \quad b^{1.4142}, \quad \ldots$$

has a limiting value that we denote by $b^{\sqrt{2}}$. Using limit notation, we could write this as

$$\lim_{x \to \sqrt{2}} b^x = b^{\sqrt{2}}$$

if it is understood that in this case $x \to \sqrt{2}$ means that as x is chosen closer to $\sqrt{2}$, it is always chosen as a rational number.

Because of the way we have defined b^x when x is an irrational number, the exponential functions are continuous for all x; that is,

$$\lim_{x \to c} b^x = b^c \qquad \text{for any value of } c.$$

Exponential functions can be graphed easily by plotting a few points and sketching a smoothly increasing (or decreasing) curve through those points. The graph of $y = (.80)^t$ is shown in Figure 4.3. Observe that the graph decays toward the positive t-axis as an asymptote of the curve; that is, $\lim_{t \to \infty} (.80)^t = 0$.

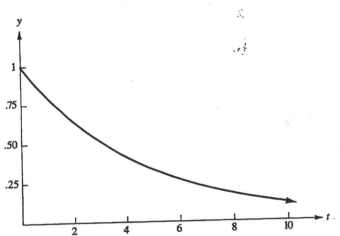

Figure 4.3
The graph of $y = (.80)^t$ for $t \geq 0$

EXAMPLE 5

Evaluate $y = 2^x$ for several values of x and use these to sketch its graph.

SOLUTION

Table 4.2 gives several pairs of x and y values, and these have been plotted to draw the graph in Figure 4.4. Observe in this case that the negative x-axis is an asymptote of the graph; that is, $\lim_{x \to -\infty} 2^x = 0$.

Table 4.2

x	0	1/2	1	3/2	2	3	-1	-2	-3
2^x	1.000	1.414	2.000	2.428	4.000	8.000	.500	.250	.125

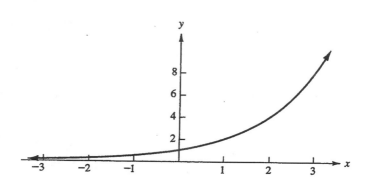

Figure 4.4
The graph of $y = 2^x$

We summarize several important properties of the exponential function $y = ab^x$, with $a > 0$, in Table 4.3. The properties are illustrated in the previous examples as well as the following ones.

	Exponential Growth	**Exponential Decay**
Function:	$y = ab^x$, for all x (with $b > 1$)	$y = ab^x$, for all x (with $0 < b < 1$)
y-intercept:	$y(0) = a$	$y(0) = a$
Range:	$y > 0$ for all x	$y > 0$ for all x
Horizontal asymptote:	$y \to 0$ as $x \to -\infty$ (negative x-axis)	$y \to 0$ as $x \to \infty$ (positive x-axis)
Effective rate:	$b - 1 > 0$ (growth)	$b - 1 < 0$ (decay)

Table 4.3

EXAMPLE 6

Suppose that

$$R(x) = 45{,}000(1.28)^x, \qquad x \geq 0,$$

gives the value of a piece of real estate x years after the original investment. Find the amount invested, the effective rate of appreciation in its value, and its value after 40 mo.

SOLUTION

The original investment is $R(0) = \$45{,}000$. The effective rate of appreciation is $1.28 - 1 = .28$, or 28% per year. Because 40 mo is $3\frac{1}{3}$ yr, the value at that time would be

$$R\left(\frac{10}{3}\right) = 45,000(1.28)^{10/3} = \$102,466.$$

●

EXAMPLE 7

Suppose that

$$D(x) = 9500\left(\frac{4}{3}\right)^{-x}, \qquad x \geq 0,$$

is used to model the value of a car x years after its purchase. Find the original price of the car, the effective rate at which it is depreciating, and its value after 1½ yr.

SOLUTION

First rewrite the given function so that it is in the form $y = ab^x$; that is,

$$D(x) = 9500\left(\frac{3}{4}\right)^x, \qquad x \geq 0.$$

Note that because the base is less than 1, the car is decreasing in value. The price of the car is $D(0) = \$9500$. The rate of depreciation is $3/4 - 1 = -1/4$—that is, a decline of 25% per year. After 1½ yr the car is worth

$$D(1.5) = 9500(.75)^{1.5} = \$6170.$$

●

EXERCISES 4.1

1. Last year the assessed value of your house was $82,000. This year the assessor has decided it is worth $84,460. What was the effective rate of growth in the value of your house over the past year?

2. The kroon, a rare coin, has risen in value from $140 to $168 over the past year. What was its effective rate of growth?

3. During one year the Blue Book value of your car decreased from $1800 to $1638. What was the effective rate of decay in its value during that year?

4. On April 1, 1988, the price of one share of Errant Corp. stock was $32.00. By April 1, 1989, the selling price had slipped to $20.80. What was the effective rate of decay in the Errant stock price during that year?

In Exercises 5–14 sketch the graph of the given function.

5. $f(x) = 3^x$

6. $g(x) = 5^x$

7. $y = \left(\frac{1}{2}\right)^t$

8. $z = \left(\frac{2}{3}\right)^x$

9. $F(s) = 7 \cdot 2^s$

10. $H(t) = 4 \cdot 3^t$

11. $F = 500(1.1)^t$

12. $P = 750(1.09)^{-t}$

13. $V(t) = 10(.9)^t$

14. $S(x) = 2(.75)^x$

For each function in Exercises 15–24 decide whether the dependent variable is growing or decaying; then find the effective rate of growth or decay.

15. $y = 4^t$

16. $y = 7(.3)^x$

17. $y = 8 \cdot 5^{-x}$

18. $z = 200(2.5)^{-t}$

19. $y = 50(.05)^t$

20. $z = 200(2.5)^t$

21. $y = \left(\frac{4}{5}\right)^x$

22. $y = \left(\frac{5}{3}\right)^{-t}$

23. $y = \left(\frac{1}{3}\right)^{-t}$

24. $y = \left(\frac{9}{8}\right)^t$

In Exercises 25–32 write an exponential function of the form $f(x) = ab^x$ that has the specified properties.

25. $f(0) = 500$, effective rate of growth 10%

26. $f(0) = 75$, effective rate of growth 100%

27. $f(0) = 120$, effective rate of decay 30%

28. $f(0) = 3000$, effective rate of decay 5%

29. $f(0) = 1$, effective rate of growth 250%

30. $f(0) = 1500$, effective rate of decay 70%

31. $f(0) = 1500$, efffective rate of growth 70%

32. $f(0) = 800$, effective rate of decay 2%

33. A savings and loan is offering an 8-year certificate of deposit that pays an interest rate of 8% per year. How much will be in an account at maturity if $1000 is invested?

34. The local credit union offers a 6-year savings certificate that pays 13% interest per year. How much will the certificate be worth in 3 yr if $500 is invested? In 6 yr? How much more is earned during the final three years than in the first three?

35. Assume that a new piece of manufacturing equipment costs $75,000. If it depreciates at an effective rate of 20% each year, what will the machine be worth in 4 yr? In 6 yr?

36. If the value of a new car that costs $12,000 depreciates at an effective rate of 35% each year, find its value after 3 yr.

37. An economist would like to compare inflation rates by showing their effect on the value of a dollar over a period of time. Assume that the value of a dollar decays at an effective rate of 5% per year. Compute the value of one dollar after 3 yr, after 6 yr, and after 10 yr. Repeat this if the effective rate of decay is 10% per year.

38. Refer to Exercise 37. An alternate approach to show the effect of inflation is to look at increases in the selling price of a familiar item. Suppose that the current price of a quarter-pound hamburger is $1.50. If prices rise at an effective rate of 5% per year, what will the hamburger cost after 3 yr, after 6 yr, and after 10 yr? Repeat this if the effective rate of growth is 10% per year.

39. Suppose that a report on the financial condition of a corporation states that the annual earnings of the company have been growing at an effective rate of 18% per year for the past 8 yr. Currently the annual earnings are reported to be $3.40 per share. Reconstruct the earnings for the previous 8 yr.

40. Refer to Exercise 39. Estimate the company's earnings for the next 5 yr if the 18% growth is maintained. How much less will the company earn 5 yr from now if the growth in earnings slips to 15% a year?

41. A common misconception can be illustrated by the following example. Let one share of common stock have a current value of $30. Assume that it increases in value at an effective rate of 20% a year for the next 6 yr and then decreases in value at a rate of 20% a year for 6 more years. Many people believe that the value of the stock will be back to $30. Show that this is false by computing $F_1 = 30(1.20)^6$ and then $F_2 = F_1(.80)^6$.

42. Refer to Exercise 41. This time assume that the value of the stock decreases for 6 yr and then increases for the next 6 yr at an effective rate of 20% a year. What is the value of the stock after 12 yr in this case?

4.2
Compound Interest and the Base e

In Example 2 of the preceding section we derived the formula (4.4)

$$F(t) = P(1 + r)^t$$

for the future value F of an investment of principal P that grows for t years at an effective rate r. This growth occurs when a bank offers an interest rate r and adds or **compounds** the interest to the principal at the end of each year. In this section we consider the effect on F of compounding more frequently.

In the following discussion and examples r will always denote the annual interest rate that would be earned if no compounding occurs except at year end. It is customary to call r the **nominal** (or stated) interest rate.

EXAMPLE 1

Assume that P dollars are invested at a nominal interest rate of 12% per year, compounded quarterly. Find the future value F of the investment in 2 yr.

<table>
<tr><td>**SOLUTION**</td><td>Let t denote the number of years since the investment was made. During the first quarter the principal P will earn $12\%/4 = 3\%$ interest. So at the end of one quarter $t = .25$ and the value of the investment is</td></tr>
</table>

$$F(.25) = P + P(.03) = P(1.03).$$

During the second quarter this sum will earn another 3% interest, so at the end of two quarters $t = .5$ and the value is

$$F(.5) = P(1.03) + P(1.03)(.03) = P(1.03)^2.$$

In general, after t years, $4t$ quarters have passed and the future value is

$$F(t) = P(1.03)^{4t}.$$

After 2 yr, then,

$$F(2) = P(1.03)^8 = 1.267P. \qquad \bullet$$

Example 1 demonstrates the following extension of compound interest formula (4.4): the **future value** F of an investment of P dollars at nominal rate r per year, compounded n times each year for t years, is

(4.6)
$$F(t) = P\left(1 + \frac{r}{n}\right)^{nt}.$$

EXAMPLE 2   A depositor puts \$5000 in a 180-day certificate of deposit that pays a nominal rate of 8%, compounded daily. How much will the certificate be worth at maturity?

SOLUTION   For daily compounding, we take $n = 365$. The interest rate per day is then

$$\frac{r}{n} = \frac{.08}{365} = .0002192.$$

There are 180 days until maturity, so from equation (4.6) we find

$$\begin{aligned}
F &= 5000(1 + .0002192)^{180} \\
&= 5000(1.0002192)^{180} \\
&= 5000(1.040236) \\
&= \$5201.18.
\end{aligned}$$

Rewriting $F(t)$ in the form of equation (4.5) for an exponential function,

$$F(t) = P\left[\left(1 + \frac{r}{n}\right)^n\right]^t,$$

we see that the base b of this function is $(1 + r/n)^n$. Referring to Table 4.3 of the previous section, we discover the effective rate of interest produced by compounding.

> The **effective rate of interest** (or growth) when the nominal rate r is compounded n times each year is
>
> (4.7)
> $$\left(1 + \frac{r}{n}\right)^n - 1.$$

The effective rate generates the same interest per year without compounding as the nominal rate generates with compounding.

EXAMPLE 3

Compute the effective interest rate when a nominal rate of 9% is compounded quarterly, monthly, and daily.

SOLUTION

For quarterly compounding the effective rate is

$$\left(1 + \frac{.09}{4}\right)^4 - 1 = (1.0225)^4 - 1$$
$$= 1.09308 - 1$$
$$= .09308$$

or 9.308%. For monthly compounding the effective interest rate is

$$\left(1 + \frac{.09}{12}\right)^{12} - 1 = (1.0075)^{12} - 1$$
$$= 1.09381 - 1$$
$$= .09381$$

or 9.381%. For daily compounding the effective rate is

$$\left(1 + \frac{.09}{365}\right)^{365} - 1 = (1.000247)^{365} - 1$$
$$= 1.09416 - 1$$
$$= .09416$$

or 9.416%.   ●

Example 3 demonstrates that more frequent compounding increases the effective interest rate earned by an investment. The natural question to ask is whether or not arbitrarily large effective rates can be obtained by compounding ever more frequently. After all, it is possible to compound every hour, every second, or every hundredth of a second. The following example shows that, in fact, there is a limit to the effective rates that can be reached.

EXAMPLE 4

Suppose that an account earns interest at a nominal rate of 100%. By taking ever larger values for n, the number of times interest is compounded, estimate to three decimal places the maximum possible effective interest rate.

SOLUTION

Referring to effective rate formula (4.7) with $r = 1$, we compute, and list in Table 4.4, several values of $(1 + 1/n)^n$ for increasing values of n. It is evident that, to three decimal places, the limiting value is 2.718. Therefore the maximum effective rate that can be achieved is approximately $2.718 - 1$, or 171.8%.

Table 4.4

n	10	100	1000	10,000	100,000	10^6	10^7
$\left(1 + \dfrac{1}{n}\right)^n$	2.59374	2.70481	2.71692	2.71815	2.71826	2.71828	2.71828

The number that was found in Example 4 is very important. Because it is used so often in the analysis of natural growth, it has been given a permanent, universal symbol—the letter e; that is

$$e = \lim_{n \to \infty} \left(1 + \frac{1}{n}\right)^n \doteq 2.71828.$$

Henceforth, e will always represent this limit. Keep in mind that, unlike x or y, it does not denote a variable—it is a constant: an irrational number whose five-decimal approximation is 2.71828.

Suppose that in Example 4 the interest rate had been some rate r other than 100%. Then it would have been necessary to compute

$$\lim_{n \to \infty} \left(1 + \frac{r}{n}\right)^n.$$

This is done by letting $1/m = r/n$ and consequently $n = mr$. This gives

(4.8)
$$\lim_{n \to \infty} \left(1 + \frac{r}{n}\right)^n = \lim_{m \to \infty} \left(1 + \frac{1}{m}\right)^{mr} \quad \text{(if } n \to \infty, \text{ then } m \to \infty)$$
$$= \left[\lim_{m \to \infty} \left(1 + \frac{1}{m}\right)^m\right]^r$$
$$= e^r.$$

Most hand-held calculators that have a $\boxed{y^x}$ key also have the ability to compute e^x for any value of x up to the limits of the particular calculator. With an $\boxed{e^x}$ key, it is only necessary to enter the desired value and press this key. In other calculators it is necessary to enter x, press an inverse key (often marked $\boxed{\text{INV}}$ or $\boxed{f^{-1}}$), and then press the key marked $\boxed{\ln x}$. The reason for the latter system will be explained in the next section. As a final comment, the reader will quickly discover that it does not take a very large value of x to overwhelm a calculator's ability to compute e^x. This serves as a reminder of the true magnitude of exponential growth.

When we take the limit as the number of compounding periods becomes infinite, the length of the compounding period approaches 0. We indicate this by saying that the nominal rate r is **compounded continuously**; there is no measurable compounding period. From expression (4.8) we can find the effective rate of interest produced by continuous compounding.

> The **effective rate of interest** (or growth) when the nominal rate r is compounded continuously is
>
> (4.9) $e^r - 1$.

EXAMPLE 5   Suppose that a bank wants to offer its depositors the highest effective rate on an account that pays a nominal 6% rate of interest. Determine that rate.

SOLUTION   Compounding continuously produces the highest effective rate of interest. From expression (4.9), we find that rate to be

$$e^{.06} - 1 = 1.06184 - 1 = .06184$$

or 6.184%.   ●

The compound interest formula (4.6) can easily be extended to include continuous compounding. When a principal P is invested at a nominal rate r for t years and the interest is compounded continuously, the future value is

$$F = P\left[\lim_{n\to\infty}\left(1 + \frac{r}{n}\right)^n\right]^t = P[e^r]^t;$$

that is,

(4.10) $F(t) = Pe^{rt}$.

In many practical problems involving compound interest it is necessary to find the principal, or **present value**, of an investment when the future value and the rate of interest are known. This "backward" compounding procedure is often called **discounting**.

EXAMPLE 6   A manager of a company knows that $250,000 will be needed in 3 yr to pay off a bond issue. The manager knows that it is possible to earn 15%, compounded quarterly, on an investment for the next 3 yr. How much must be invested to meet the bond payment?

SOLUTION   Observe that we know the values of all the variables in equation (4.6) except the present value P. Substituting, we have

$$250,000 = P\left(1 + \frac{.15}{4}\right)^{4(3)} = P(1.5555).$$

Solving for P reveals the required present investment:

$$P = \frac{\$250,000}{1.5555} = \$160,725.$$ ●

EXAMPLE 7

Suppose that the manager in Example 6 is offered a nominal interest rate of 15%, compounded continuously. Determine the investment required to yield $250,000 in 3 yr.

SOLUTION

In this case equation (4.10) is the appropriate formula and we have

$$250,000 = Pe^{.15(3)} = P(1.5683),$$

and so the required investment is

$$P = \frac{\$250,000}{1.5683} = \$159,407. \qquad \bullet$$

By solving for P in equations (4.6) and (4.10) we obtain what are sometimes referred to as "present value formulas":

$$P(t) = F\left(1 + \frac{r}{n}\right)^{-nt}, \qquad t \geq 0,$$

and

$$P(t) = Fe^{-rt}, \qquad t \geq 0.$$

EXERCISES 4.2

In Exercises 1–14 find the effective rate of interest for the indicated nominal rate of interest.

1. Nominal 5% a year, compounded quarterly
2. Nominal 5% a year, compounded monthly
3. Nominal 5% a year, compounded continuously
4. Nominal 8% a year, compounded quarterly
5. Nominal 8% a year, compounded weekly
6. Nominal 8% a year, compounded continuously
7. Nominal 10% a year, compounded semiannually
8. Nominal 10% a year, compounded daily
9. Nominal 10% a year, compounded continuously
10. Nominal 9½% a year, compounded quarterly
11. Nominal 5¼% a year, compounded monthly
12. Nominal 14.1% a year, compounded daily
13. Nominal 6.4% a year, compounded quarterly
14. Nominal 10.7% a year, compounded continuously

In Exercises 15–20 find the future value of the indicated investment.

15. $500 invested at 8%, compounded monthly for 6 yr
16. $800 invested at 7%, compounded quarterly for 5 yr
17. $1200 invested at 6.5%, compounded continuously for 2 yr
18. $1000 invested at 9%, compounded continuously for 4 yr
19. $2000 invested at 12%, compounded quarterly for 5 yr
20. $1850 invested at 11%, compounded semiannually for 3 yr

In Exercises 21–24 find the present value of the indicated investment.

21. A savings bond that grows to $50 in 10 yr through 8% nominal interest compounded monthly
22. A bond that attains a value of $3000 in 5 yr by earning a nominal interest rate of 9% with continuous compounding

23. A 2½-year certificate of deposit that will be worth $10,000 at maturity by earning a 12% nominal rate of interest, compounded continuously

24. An account whose future value in 10 yr is $7500, if 8% nominal interest is earned with monthly compounding

25. The XYZ Corporation has reported earnings of $.60 per share for the current quarter. If the earnings grow 5% each quarter, what will the earnings be in 1½ yr? In 2 yr?

26. The basic savings account at a credit union pays a nominal interest rate of 6½% per year, compounded daily. If a deposit of $1000 is made on January 1, how much will be in the account on March 31 of that year? (Assume it is not a leap year.) At the end of the year? By March 31 of the following year?

27. A savings and loan has $150 million on deposit in savings accounts that pay 5½% interest, compounded daily. How much more interest (to the nearest $10) would have to be paid to the depositors each year if the interest were compounded continuously?

28. You have the opportunity to invest money at a nominal rate of 12% with semiannual compounding or at 11% with continuous compounding. Which option yields the greater effective rate?

29. A couple has a 6-year-old child who will be ready for college in 12 yr. The couple estimates that $8500 will be needed to pay for the first year of college. To the nearest dollar, how much would have to be invested now at a nominal rate of 10%, compounded monthly, to meet this need?

30. Refer to Exercise 29. How much would have to be invested if the investment had been made at the child's birth?

31. Approximately once a month the news media report the latest increase in the Consumer Price Index and then state what this would come to if that rate of increase lasted for a whole year. A typical announcement might say that consumer prices at the retail level rose at a rate of .7 of 1% in June and that this corresponds to an annual rate of 8.4%. (This estimate is, of course, obtained by multiplying .7 by 12.) Calculate the actual annual increase that would occur if this price index did rise by .7% each month for 1 yr.

32. Money market mutual funds usually quote an "annualized rate of return." This rate is calculated by taking the interest rate that has been earned on a particular day and multiplying by 365. Suppose that one such mutual fund states that its annualized rate of return is 6.57%. Compute the effective rate of return if this rate stayed the same for the entire year.

33. Many states limit the interest that can be charged on credit cards to 1½% per month. What is the effective annual rate of interest on such credit cards?

4.3 Logarithms

In this section we consider the inverses of exponential functions. These functions are called **logarithmic functions** or simply logarithms. Logarithms are useful in analyzing exponential models and answering certain questions about exponential growth or decay. We begin with two examples that indicate the need for logarithms.

EXAMPLE 1

If an amount of money is invested at 12% a year, compounded annually, how many years does it take for the investment to double?

SOLUTION

Using the compound interest formula (4.6) from Section 4.2, we know that the future value F is related to the principal P and the years of investment t by the exponential function

$$F = P(1.12)^t.$$

If the investment has doubled, then $F = 2P$, so

$$2P = P(1.12)^t.$$

Dividing by P, we obtain the equation

$$2 = (1.12)^t,$$

which must be solved for t.

For the exponential function $y = (1.12)^t$ we have been given a value for the dependent variable and must find the value of the independent variable t. We can solve this problem for the particular value $y = 2$ by trial and error. Table 4.5 gives $(1.12)^t$ to three decimal places for several values of t. From the tabulated values we can see that the investment doubles in approximately 6 yr. Doing this for all values of y would give us the inverse function for $y = (1.12)^t$.

Table 4.5

t	2	3	4	5	6	7
$(1.12)^t$	1.254	1.405	1.574	1.762	1.974	2.211

●

EXAMPLE 2

An investor seeks an investment with an effective rate of interest of 20% a year. What nominal rate of interest with continuous compounding will yield this rate?

SOLUTION

In the previous section we learned that for a nominal rate of interest r, the effective rate yielded by continuous compounding is $e^r - 1$. Therefore, we have to solve the equation

$$e^r - 1 = .20$$

or

$$e^r = 1.2$$

for r. Again we are dealing with the inverse of an exponential function—this time $y = e^r$. We are given a range value, $y = 1.2$, and seek the corresponding domain value. Knowing that r will be less than .2 (compounding increases the effective rate), we can also solve this problem by trial and error. Table 4.6 shows e^r to three decimal places for certain values of r. The table shows that the desired nominal rate is about 18%. Continued trial and error would yield a more precise value for r.

Table 4.6

r	.20	.19	.18	.17
e^r	1.221	1.209	1.197	1.185

●

Rather than continuing to solve problems like those in Examples 1 and 2 by trial and error, we will introduce the inverse exponential functions. From the graphs sketched in Section 4.1, we see that exponential functions are one-to-one; their graphs pass the horizontal line test. The domain of an exponential function is the set of all real numbers, while the range consists of all positive numbers. With this in mind, we state the following definition.

Definition 4.3

> We say that y is the **logarithm of x, base b** (where $b > 0$, $b \neq 1$) and write
>
> (4.11) $\qquad\qquad\qquad y = \log_b x, \qquad x > 0,$
>
> if and only if $b^y = x$.

In other words, if y is the exponent we have to place on b to obtain x, then y is the logarithm of x, base b. As illustrations we have

$$3 = \log_2 8 \qquad \text{because} \quad 2^3 = 8,$$

$$2 = \log_{10} 100 \qquad \text{because} \quad 10^2 = 100,$$

$$-3 = \log_4 \frac{1}{64} \qquad \text{because} \quad 4^{-3} = \frac{1}{64},$$

$$\frac{1}{2} = \log_5 \sqrt{5} \qquad \text{because} \quad 5^{1/2} = \sqrt{5},$$

$$1 = \log_b b \qquad \text{because} \quad b^1 = b \qquad \text{for any } b,$$

$$0 = \log_b 1 \qquad \text{because} \quad b^0 = 1 \qquad \text{for any } b > 0.$$

Logarithms were developed in the early 17th century by John Napier and Henry Briggs, primarily to aid in the extensive calculations required by astronomy. Because logarithms are really exponents, they can be used to convert multiplications to additions, divisions to subtractions, and exponentiation to multiplication. Briggs constructed the first base 10 tables of logarithms in 1624 precisely for this purpose.

The following three properties of logarithms form the basis for their use in simplifying calculations. Since logarithms are special exponents, these properties are just restatements of exponent properties. (See Appendix A.4.)

Logarithm Properties

> If $b > 0$, $b \neq 1$, w and z are positive real numbers, and p is any real number, then:
>
> 1. $\log_b wz = \log_b w + \log_b z$
> 2. $\log_b w/z = \log_b w - \log_b z$
> 3. $\log_b w^p = p \log_b w$

With today's electronic computing devices, we seldom use logarithms to multiply, divide, or exponentiate. Those operations can now be performed with the touch of a button. The exponentiation key $\boxed{y^x}$, which we have frequently used, initiates a program that uses logarithm properties. When y is entered, its logarithm (in base e) is generated; when x is entered, it is multiplied by the logarithm of y to obtain a power p; and when $\boxed{=}$ is pressed, e^p, which then equals y^x, is displayed. (In Exercise 54 the reader is asked to verify that $e^p = y^x$.)

In addition to the $\boxed{y^x}$ key, most scientific and business calculators have two logarithm keys: $\boxed{\ln x}$ and $\boxed{\log x}$. Pressing the first key generates logarithms to the base e, called **natural logarithms**, which are denoted by $\ln x$ rather than $\log_e x$.

Recall that on some calculators, e^x is obtained by using $\boxed{\text{INV}}$ (or $\boxed{f^{-1}}$) and $\boxed{\ln x}$ because $y = e^x$ and $y = \ln x$ are inverse functions. The second key may be used to obtain base 10 logarithms, called **common logarithms** and frequently denoted by $\log x$ rather than $\log_{10} x$.

Using either of these keys, we can obtain logarithms to any base. Suppose that we want to calculate $\log_b w$. If $u = \log_b w$, then in exponential form $w = b^u$. If these quantities are equal, then their logarithms to any base are equal (because of the one-to-one property); so using natural logarithms and property 3, we have

$$\ln w = \ln b^u = u \ln b.$$

Solving for u, we find

$$u = \frac{\ln w}{\ln b}.$$

This verifies the so-called change of base formula:

Logarithm Base Conversion Property

$$4. \quad \log_b w = \frac{\ln w}{\ln b}$$

Property 4 holds for logarithms to any base, not just natural logarithms. We state it in this form because natural logarithms are readily available from calculators and we shall work primarily with these logarithms. It is worth noting that property 4 implies that every logarithm function is proportional to the natural logarithm function (with constant of proportionality $1/\ln b$).

We demonstrate the use of property 4 by solving Example 1.

SOLUTION TO EXAMPLE 1

Recall that we sought the value of t that satisfies the equation

$$2 = (1.12)^t.$$

In logarithmic form, the equation is

$$t = \log_{1.12} 2.$$

From property 4 we have

$$t = \log_{1.12} 2 = \frac{\ln 2}{\ln 1.12} = \frac{.6931}{.1133} = 6.12,$$

so it requires 6.12 yr for the investment to double.

This problem can also be solved using only natural logarithms. Taking the natural logarithm of both sides of the equation $2 = (1.12)^t$ and using property 3, we obtain

$$\ln 2 = t \ln 1.12$$

or

$$.6931 = .1133t.$$

Division again yields $t = 6.12$.   ●

SOLUTION TO EXAMPLE 2

This problem can be solved very easily. Recall that we had to find r so that

$$e^r = 1.20.$$

Writing this in logarithmic form, we have

$$r = \ln 1.20$$
$$= .1823.$$

Therefore, the nominal interest rate necessary to yield the 20% desired effective rate is $r = .1823$, or 18.23%.   ●

Before doing a few more examples, we list some additional properties of natural logarithms for later reference. Some of these have been noted earlier and all of them are easily derived from properties of $y = e^x$.

Additional Properties of the Natural Logarithm

> 5. $\ln x$ is defined only for $x > 0$
> 6. $\ln 1 = 0$
> 7. $\ln x < 0$ for $0 < x < 1$ and $\ln x > 0$ for $x > 1$
> 8. $\ln (e^x) = x$ for any x
> 9. $e^{\ln x} = x$ for any $x > 0$

Properties 8 and 9 are statements that $y = \ln x$ and $y = e^x$ are inverse functions. We shall use property 9 repeatedly in this and the next section.

EXAMPLE 3

Frequently inflation is described in terms of its effect on the value of the dollar. For instance, when it is said that the dollar will be worth only $.90 a year from now, it is meant that a dollar then will purchase only as much as $.90 will today. In the terminology introduced in Section 4.1, the value of the dollar will decay at an effective rate of 10%.

Suppose that the value of the dollar does decay at an effective rate of 10% a year over a long period of time. How many years will it take for today's dollar to be worth $.15 or less?

SOLUTION

The statement that the dollar's value is decaying at an effective rate of 10% per year means that after t years its value V is given by the exponential function

$$V(t) = (.9)^t.$$

To find when $V = .15$, we must solve

$$.15 = (.9)^t.$$

Taking the natural logarithm of each side of the equation, we have

$$\ln .15 = t \ln .9$$

or

$$-1.897 \doteq -.1054t.$$

Notice that both logarithms are negative; this is part of property 7. Division gives $t \doteq 17.998$, so in 18 yr the dollar will be worth about $\$.15$. ●

EXAMPLE 4

The Consumer Price Index (CPI) is a statistical average that is intended to show the change in the cost of a theoretical "basket" of consumer goods. The base year is 1967 and the index is arbitrarily set at 100 for that year. Because prices rose 4.2% the following year, the index for 1968 is 104.2. In 1969 prices rose 5.4% to put the index at 109.8 because of the compounding effect. In 1981 the CPI stood at 281.5. Compute the average effective rate of increase in prices from 1967 to 1981 based on the change in the CPI.

SOLUTION

Let i denote the average rate of increase per year in the index and t the number of years since 1967. Then

$$CPI(t) = 100(1 + i)^t.$$

In 1981 $t = 14$ and $CPI = 281.5$, so

$$281.5 = 100(1 + i)^{14}$$

or

$$2.815 = (1 + i)^{14}.$$

Taking the 14th root of each side, we get

(4.12)
$$1 + i = (2.815)^{1/14}.$$

Using a calculator with a $\boxed{\sqrt[x]{y}}$ key, we find

$$i \doteq 1.0767 - 1$$
$$= .0767.$$

The 14th root required in equation (4.12) can be found using logarithms:

$$\ln(1 + i) = \frac{1}{14} \ln 2.815$$
$$\doteq \frac{1.035}{14}$$
$$\doteq .0739.$$

Thus, in exponential form,

$$1 + i \doteq e^{.0739}$$
$$\doteq 1.0767.$$

As before, $i = .0767$, and so the average rate of increase in the CPI from 1967 to 1981 was 7.67% per year. ●

We have seen that it is possible to work exclusively with natural logarithms, so it should be expected that it is also possible (and often convenient) to write all exponential functions with the base e. To do this for $y = b^x$, observe that by property 9

$$e^{\ln b} = b.$$

Therefore,

$$b^x = [e^{\ln b}]^x = e^{(\ln b)x}.$$

We summarize this important relationship:

Exponential Base Conversion Property

$$b^x = e^{(\ln b)x}$$

EXAMPLE 5

Write the functions $y = 2^x$ and $z = 2000(.9)^t$ as exponential functions with base e.

SOLUTION

Using the exponential base conversion property, we get

$$y = 2^x = e^{(\ln 2)x} \doteq e^{.693x}.$$

Similarly,

$$z = 2000(.9)^t = 2000e^{(\ln .9)t} \doteq 2000e^{-.105t}.$$

●

EXERCISES 4.3

Convert the exponential statements in Exercises 1–8 to logarithmic form.

1. $2^3 = 8$

2. $5^2 = 25$

3. $81^{1/2} = 9$

4. $16^{1/4} = 2$

5. $7^0 = 1$

6. $9^1 = 9$

7. $3^{-1} = \dfrac{1}{3}$

8. $4^{-2} = \dfrac{1}{16}$

Convert the logarithmic statements in Exercises 9–16 to exponential form.

9. $\log_3 9 = 2$

10. $\log_5 125 = 3$

11. $\log_{27} 3 = \dfrac{1}{3}$

12. $\log_{16} 4 = \dfrac{1}{2}$

13. $\log_3 10 = 2.096$

14. $\log_{10} 3 = .301$

15. $\ln 2 = .693$

16. $\ln e = 1$

Use logarithm properties with the values $\log_b 2 = .43$ and $\log_b 3 = .68$ to find the logarithms in Exercises 17–22.

17. $\log_b 6$

18. $\log_b 16$

19. $\log_b 9$

20. $\log_b 1.5$

21. $\log_b \sqrt{3}$

22. $\log_2 3$

23. If $500 is placed in a certificate of deposit that pays a nominal rate of 9% interest, compounded monthly, how long will it take until there is $800 in this account? How long until the amount doubles?

24. Refer to Exercise 23. How long would it take in each instance if the interest is compounded continuously?

25. An employee is hired at a salary of $20,000 per year. If this employee is given a 10% salary increase each year, how long will it take for the salary to exceed $48,000 per year? If instead the employee is given a 5% raise every 6 mo, how long will it take?

26. The manager of a manufacturing plant has a new machine with a value of $360,000. It is the intention of the manager to sell the machine when it has depreciated to a value of $50,000. Assuming that the machine loses 20% of its remaining value each year, how long will it be until the machine is sold?

27. It is estimated that the cost of computers and computer equipment is decreasing at an effective rate of 9% per year. If this rate is maintained, how long will it take computer costs to decline by one-third? (*Hint:* If C denotes the present cost, the future cost will be two-thirds of C.)

28. The selling price of some Iowa farmland is currently $1500 per acre. If this price increases at an effective rate of 8% per year, how long will it take for the price to rise by 50%?

29. The Consumer Price Index at the end of 1950 was 72.1, whereas at the end of 1983 it was 298.4. Find the average annual rate of increase in the CPI over this 33-year period.

30. The decade of the 1970s is often thought of as a period of high inflation. The CPI at the end of 1959 was 87.3, at the end of 1969 it was 109.8, and at the end of 1979 it stood at 217.4. Compute the average annual increase in the CPI during the 1960s and during the 1970s.

31. During the winter of 1984–1985 a well-known mutual fund advertised that its assets in 1984 were 3800% of their value in 1951. Compute the average annual rate of growth for this fund. Compare this growth rate with the inflation rate calculated in Exercise 29.

32. Assets of the Garibaldi Fund have grown by 1727% over the past 10 yr. Find the average annual growth rate for Garibaldi.

33. An investor has $15,000 with which she plans to buy common stock. She hopes to double her money in 5 yr. What is the average annual growth rate that is necessary to accomplish this?

34. The population of a certain midwestern city was 51,500 in the 1970 census, but only 48,200 in the 1980 census. Find the average annual rate at which the city's population decreased over this period.

Solve the exponential equations in Exercises 35–44.

35. $5 = 3^x$

36. $1 = (.25)^x$

37. $7 = 5^{x+4}$

38. $10 = e^{3x-1}$

39. $20 = 8 \cdot 4^{-x}$

40. $4 = 15(.5)^{x+1}$

41. $800 = (1.5)^t$

42. $300 = 4^x 2^{3x}$

43. $15 = 10e^{-x}$

44. $72 = 3e^{2+x}$

Write the exponential functions in Exercises 45–52 in the form $y = ae^{kx}$, where k is accurate to four decimal places.

45. $y = 10^x$

46. $y = .45^x$

47. $y = 5 \cdot 2^{-x}$

48. $y = 20(1.83)^x$

49. $y = 3 \cdot 5^{2x}$

50. $y = .2 \cdot 7^{-x}$

51. $y = 50(.8)^x$

52. $y = 30(.6)^{-4x}$

53. Solve the continuous compounding formula $F = Pe^{rt}$ for t in terms of F, P, and r.

54. Verify that for any $y > 0$, $y^x = e^p$ when $p = x \ln y$.

4.4
Derivatives of Logarithmic and Exponential Functions

Having used logarithmic and exponential functions in several growth and decay models, we now determine their derivatives and further analyze their behavior. The results in our list of differentiation rules do not apply to logarithmic or exponential functions, so we return to the definition to determine the derivative of $f(x) = \ln x$.

Using properties of the natural logarithm, we have (for $x > 0$ and $x + h > 0$)

$$\frac{f(x + h) - f(x)}{h} = \frac{\ln(x + h) - \ln x}{h}$$

$$= \frac{\ln\dfrac{x + h}{x}}{h}$$

$$= \frac{1}{h}\ln\left(1 + \frac{h}{x}\right)$$

$$= \ln\left(1 + \frac{h}{x}\right)^{1/h}.$$

Substituting $n = 1/h$, we see that

$$\frac{f(x + h) - f(x)}{h} = \ln\left(1 + \frac{1/x}{n}\right)^{n}.$$

Now, recalling that

$$f'(x) = \lim_{h \to 0}\frac{f(x + h) - f(x)}{h}$$

and

$$\lim_{n \to \infty}\left(1 + \frac{r}{n}\right)^{n} = e^{r} \qquad \text{(which is also true for } n \to -\infty),$$

and noting that

$$n \to \infty \quad \text{as} \quad h \to 0^{+} \qquad \text{(and } n \to -\infty \text{ as } h \to 0^{-}),$$

we have

$$f'(x) = \ln e^{1/x} = \frac{1}{x} \qquad \text{(using the continuity of } f).$$

Summarizing, we have the following differentiation theorem:

Theorem 4.1

For any $x > 0$,

(4.13) $$D_{x}[\ln x] = \frac{1}{x}.$$

Equation (4.13) is easily extended by the chain rule to cover more complicated functions as follows: if $g(x)$ is positive and differentiable, then

(4.14) $$D_{x}[\ln g(x)] = \frac{1}{g(x)} g'(x) = \frac{g'(x)}{g(x)}.$$

EXAMPLE 1

If $f(x) = \ln(x^2 + 5)$, find $f'(x)$.

SOLUTION

Using equation (4.14) with $g(x) = x^2 + 5$, we have

$$f'(x) = \frac{1}{x^2 + 5}(2x) = \frac{2x}{x^2 + 5}.$$

EXAMPLE 2

If $f(x) = x^2 \ln(1 - x)$, find $f'(x)$.

SOLUTION

Using the product rule with equation (4.14), we have

$$f'(x) = x^2 \frac{1}{1 - x}(-1) + 2x \ln(1 - x)$$

$$= \frac{x^2}{x - 1} + 2x \ln(1 - x).$$

EXAMPLE 3

If $f(x) = \ln \sqrt{3x + 5}$, find $f'(x)$.

SOLUTION

Although the derivative can be obtained by immediately applying equation (4.14), it is easier to first simplify $f(x)$ using logarithm properties; that is,

$$f(x) = \ln \sqrt{3x + 5}$$
$$= \ln(3x + 5)^{1/2}$$
$$= \frac{1}{2} \ln(3x + 5),$$

so

$$f'(x) = \frac{1}{2} \frac{3}{3x + 5}$$

$$= \frac{3}{2(3x + 5)}.$$

EXAMPLE 4

Find y' if

$$y = \ln \frac{x + 5}{2x + 1}.$$

SOLUTION

Again using logarithm properties, we can simplify y as follows:

$$y = \ln \frac{x + 5}{2x + 1}$$
$$= \ln(x + 5) - \ln(2x + 1).$$

Thus,

$$y' = \frac{1}{x+5} - \frac{2}{2x+1}$$

$$= \frac{-9}{(x+5)(2x+1)}.$$

To obtain a differentiation formula for logarithms with other bases, we use the logarithm base conversion property from Section 4.3:

$$\log_b x = \frac{\ln x}{\ln b} = \frac{1}{\ln b}\ln x.$$

Since $1/\ln b$ is a constant, we have the following theorem.

Theorem 4.2

(4.15) $$D_x[\log_b x] = \frac{1}{\ln b}\frac{1}{x}.$$

Applying equation (4.15) to common logarithms, we see that

$$D_x[\log x] = \frac{1}{\ln 10}\frac{1}{x} \doteq \frac{.4343}{x}.$$

Clearly, the natural logarithm function is the "nicest" logarithm function to differentiate in the sense that in equation (4.15) the coefficient of $1/x$ is 1 when the base is e.

EXAMPLE 5   Show that the logarithm function $f(x) = \log_b x$, where $x > 0$, is increasing and concave downward on $(0, \infty)$ when $b > 1$, but decreasing and concave upward when $0 < b < 1$.

SOLUTION   From equation (4.15) we have

$$f'(x) = \frac{1}{\ln b}\frac{1}{x}.$$

If $b > 1$, then $\ln b > 0$, so $f'(x) > 0$ and f is increasing on $(0, \infty)$. Analogously, if $0 < b < 1$, then $\ln b < 0$, so $f'(x) < 0$ and f is decreasing on $(0, \infty)$. To determine concavity, we use the second derivative:

$$f''(x) = D_x\left[\frac{1}{\ln b}\frac{1}{x}\right] = \frac{-1}{x^2 \ln b}.$$

Here, if $b > 1$, then $\ln b > 0$, so $f''(x) < 0$ and its graph is concave downward on $(0, \infty)$. However, if $0 < b < 1$, then $\ln b < 0$, so $f''(x) > 0$ and the graph is concave upward on $(0, \infty)$. Graphs of $y = \log_b x$ for $b > 1$ and for $0 < b < 1$ are shown in Figure 4.5.

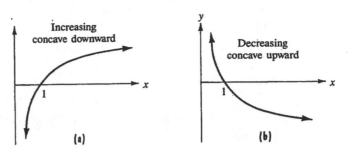

Figure 4.5
Graphs of $y = \log_b x$ for (a) $b > 1$ and (b) $0 < b < 1$

The most easily remembered differentiation formula has been saved for last. The natural exponential function turns out to be its own derivative.

Theorem 4.3

> For any x,
>
> (4.16) $$D_x[e^x] = e^x.$$

To verify equation (4.16) we begin with $y = e^x$, seeking dy/dx. Converting to logarithmic form, we obtain

$$x = \ln y.$$

If these two expressions are equal for all x, then their derivatives with respect to x are equal as well, so

$$D_x[x] = D_x[\ln y],$$

or

$$1 = \frac{1}{y}\frac{dy}{dx} \qquad \text{(using the chain rule)}.$$

Multiplying through by y, we have

$$\frac{dy}{dx} = y = e^x.$$

Once again the chain rule can be used to extend Theorem 4.3 to other exponential functions: if $g(x)$ is a differentiable function of x, then

(4.17) $$D_x[e^{g(x)}] = g'(x)e^{g(x)}.$$

EXAMPLE 6

If $G = 7000e^{.12t}$, find dG/dt.

SOLUTION

Using equation (4.17), we have

$$\frac{dG}{dt} = 7000(.12)e^{.12t} = 840e^{.12t}.$$

EXAMPLE 7

If $y = e^{x^2+5x+4}$, find y'.

SOLUTION

From equation (4.17) we have

$$y' = (2x + 5)e^{x^2+5x+4}.$$

EXAMPLE 8

Find the derivative of $f(x) = e^{-x}\sqrt{x}$.

SOLUTION

Here we use the product rule to find

$$f'(x) = \frac{1}{2\sqrt{x}}e^{-x} + \sqrt{x}\,(-1)e^{-x}$$

$$= \left(\frac{1}{2\sqrt{x}} - \sqrt{x}\right)e^{-x}.$$

To differentiate exponential functions with other bases, recall that $y = b^x$ can be written as $y = e^{kx}$, where $k = \ln b$. Therefore,

$$D_x[b^x] = D_x[e^{kx}]$$
$$= ke^{kx}$$
$$= kb^x.$$

Thus we have another differentiation theorem:

Theorem 4.4

> (4.18) $D_x[b^x] = (\ln b)b^x.$

As with logarithmic functions, when differentiating exponential functions the natural base is preferable to other bases. In equation (4.18) the coefficient of b^x is 1 when $b = e$.

EXAMPLE 9

Show that the exponential function $f(x) = b^x$, for all x, is increasing on $(-\infty, \infty)$ if $b > 1$, but decreasing if $0 < b < 1$. Furthermore, show that its graph is concave upward on $(-\infty, \infty)$ in either case.

SOLUTION

From equation (4.18) we know that

$$f'(x) = (\ln b)b^x.$$

For any x, if $b > 0$, then $b^x > 0$. If $b > 1$, then $\ln b > 0$, so $f'(x) > 0$ and f is increasing. If $0 < b < 1$, then $\ln b < 0$, so $f'(x) < 0$ and f is decreasing.

For concavity, we find the second derivative:

$$f''(x) = D_x[(\ln b)b^x] = (\ln b)^2 b^x,$$

which is positive for all x. Thus the graphs of $y = b^x$ are concave upward on $(-\infty, \infty)$ whether $b > 1$ or $0 < b < 1$. These graphs are shown in Figure 4.6.

Figure 4.6

Graphs of $y = b^x$ for (a) $b > 1$ and (b) $0 < b < 1$

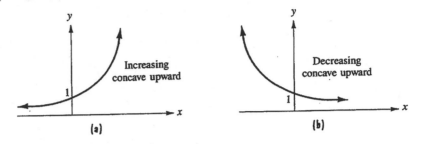

For later reference we summarize a few of the asymptotic properties of the natural exponential and logarithm functions in Table 4.7. The graphs of $y = e^x$, $y = e^{-x}$, and $y = \ln x$ are shown in Figure 4.7.

Asymptotic Properties of the Natural Exponential and Logarithmic Functions

1. $\lim_{x \to \infty} e^x = \infty$ and $\lim_{x \to -\infty} e^x = 0$; that is, $y = e^x$ grows without bound and has the negative x-axis as a horizontal asymptote.
2. $\lim_{x \to \infty} e^{-x} = 0$; that is, the positive x-axis is a horizontal asymptote of $y = e^{-x}$.
3. $\lim_{x \to 0^+} \ln x = -\infty$; that is, the negative y-axis is a vertical asymptote of $y = \ln x$.
4. $\lim_{x \to \infty} \ln x = \infty$; that is, $y = \ln x$ grows without bound.

Table 4.7

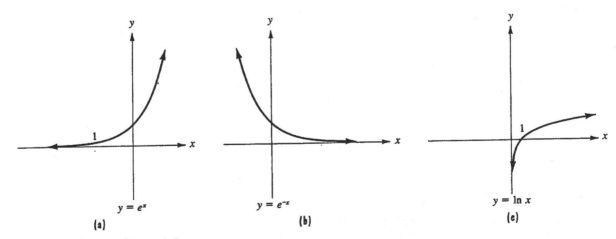

Figure 4.7

We have seen that derivatives can be used to express instantaneous rates of change in the dependent variable with respect to the independent variable. When this rate of change is compared with the value of the dependent variable, we obtain a relative (or percentage) rate of change.

Definition 4.4

> If $y = f(x)$ is a differentiable function, then the **relative rate of change** in y with respect to x is given by
>
> (4.19) $$\frac{f'(x)}{f(x)}, \qquad \text{when } f(x) \neq 0.$$
>
> If f is a function that defines the growth or decay of y, then the relative rate of change is called the **instantaneous rate of growth (or decay)** of y.

EXAMPLE 10

Let the value V (in thousand dollars) of a rental property t years from now be given by

$$V(t) = 80(1.10)^t, \qquad t \geq 0.$$

Find the effective rate of growth and the instantaneous rate of growth in the value of this property.

SOLUTION

From Table 4.3 in Section 4.1, we observe that the effective rate of growth is $1.10 - 1$, or 10% per year. From equation (4.18) we have

$$V'(t) = 80(\ln 1.10)(1.10)^t, \qquad t \geq 0.$$

Using expression (4.19), we find that the instantaneous rate of growth is

$$\frac{V'(t)}{V(t)} = \ln 1.10 = .0953$$

or 9.53%.

EXAMPLE 11

A credit union pays a nominal interest rate of 5.75%, compounded continuously, on its passbook accounts. If such an account contains $500, determine the effective rate and the instantaneous rate of growth in the account.

SOLUTION

From the future value formula $F(t) = Pe^{rt}$ developed in Section 4.2, we see that the amount in the account t years from now will be

$$F(t) = 500e^{.0575t}, \qquad t \geq 0.$$

The effective rate when the nominal rate r is continuously compounded is $e^r - 1$ or $e^{.0575} - 1 = .0592$, or 5.92%. Because $F'(t) = 500(.0575)e^{.0575t}$, the instantaneous rate of growth is

$$\frac{F'(t)}{F(t)} = .0575$$

or 5.75%

We generalize the results of Examples 10 and 11 in Table 4.8.

Table 4.8

1. If $y = ab^x$, the effective rate of growth in y is $b - 1$; the instantaneous rate of growth is $\ln b$.
2. If $y = ae^{rx}$, the effective rate of growth in y is $e^r - 1$; the instantaneous rate of growth is r.

EXAMPLE 12

Assume that the sales of record albums on compact disks are currently 250 thousand per week and growing steadily at an instantaneous rate of 20%. Find a function that will give the sales S, t years from now. What is the effective rate of growth in sales?

SOLUTION

Referring to Table 4.8, we see that the exponential function

$$S(t) = 250e^{.20t}, \qquad t \geq 0,$$

has the required 20% rate of growth and $S(0) = 250$. Moreover, the effective growth rate is $e^{.20} - 1 \doteq .2214$, or 22.14% per year. ●

EXERCISES 4.4

In Exercises 1–10 find the derivative of the given functions.

1. $f(x) = e^{5x}$

2. $f(x) = xe^{x^2}$

3. $g(x) = \ln(5x)$

4. $g(x) = x \ln x$

5. $h(x) = 5^x$

6. $h(x) = \dfrac{e^x}{x}$

7. $p(x) = \log_5 x$

8. $p(x) = \dfrac{\ln x}{x^2}$

9. $K(x) = \ln \left[\dfrac{x + 4}{x - 1} \right]^{1/2}$

10. $f(x) = \ln[(x + 5)^3(6x^2 + 2)]$

In Exercises 11–18 find the indicated derivatives.

11. $D_x[3e^{4x}]$

12. $D_x \left[\dfrac{7^x}{x^7} \right]$

13. $D_x[2x \ln(2x)]$

14. $D_x[x^2 \log_2 x]$

15. $D_x[7^{2x+1}]$

16. $D_x \left[\ln \left(\dfrac{2}{x} \right) \right]$

17. $D_x[\ln \sqrt[3]{x^2 + 5}]$

18. $D_x \left[\ln \dfrac{\sqrt{x + 2}}{x} \right]$

In Exercises 19–28 find y' or dy/dx.

19. $y = 2^x + x^2$

20. $y = \dfrac{\sqrt{e^x}}{\ln x}$

21. $y = \ln(2^x + x^2)$

22. $y = \ln(x^2 + 5x + 20)$

23. $y = x^2 e^{2x}$

24. $y = e^{20}$

25. $y = [\ln x]^7 + \ln x^7$

26. $y = e^{3/x}$

27. $y = \sqrt{\ln x}$

28. $y = \ln(e^x)$

In Exercises 29–34 find an equation of the line, in general form, tangent to the given curve at the indicated point.

29. $y = e^x$; (0, 1)

30. $y = \ln x$; (1, 0)

31. $y = \dfrac{\ln x}{x}$; (1, 0)

32. $y = x^2 e^x$; (0, 0)

33. $y = \ln(x^2 - 2x + 1)$; (2,0)

34. $y = \log_{10} x$; (1,0)

In Exercises 35–40 determine the interval(s) where the given function is increasing.

35. $y = xe^x$

36. $y = \dfrac{e^x}{x}$

37. $y = \dfrac{\ln x}{x}$

38. $y = x^2 2^x$

39. $y = x \ln x$

40. $y = \log(x^2 - 2x + 10)$

In Exercises 41–44 determine the interval(s) where the given function is concave upward.

41. $y = xe^x$

42. $y = \dfrac{e^x}{x}$

43. $y = x \ln x$

44. $y = \ln(x^2 + 2)$

For Exercises 45–50 find the relative rate of change of each function.

45. $f(x) = e^{.15x}$

46. $f(x) = 1000(1.05)^{3x}$

47. $f(x) = 2^x$

48. $f(x) = \ln x$

49. $f(x) = 5x^3$

50. $f(x) = 8\sqrt{x}$

51. Suppose that the population of a large city is 750,000 in 1987. If the population grows at an effective rate of 3% a year until 1995, find the instantaneous rate of growth in the population. Write an exponential function with the natural base that gives the population of the city during this time.

52. An investment counselor recommends the purchase of a coin collection valued at $4000. Suppose that the value of the collection appreciates at an instantaneous rate of 16% for the next 5 yr. Write the value of the collection as a function of t during this period. What is the effective rate of growth?

53. A plant manager estimates that a new piece of machinery that costs $15,000 can be used at the plant for 20 yr. If the machine's resale value declines steadily at an instantaneous rate of 7%, what is the effective rate of decay in its value? What is its resale value at the end of the 20 yr?

54. A tobacco company estimates that there are 3.5 million cigar smokers in the United States. Assume that this number is declining at an effective rate of 2% per year. What would be the instantaneous rate if this decline is occurring steadily? How many cigar smokers will there be in 15 yr if the decline continues at this rate?

55. A 5-year-old car can be sold for $1800. If it has been depreciating at an instantaneous rate of 25%, find the original value of the car. What percentage of its original value did the car lose in the first year?

4.5 More Exponential Models

Exponential functions have many financial applications that are rooted in the modeling of compound interest, as considered in Sections 4.1 and 4.2. Many of these applications are discussed in Section 9.3. In this section we consider models for **bounded exponential growth** that have marketing applications.

Exponential growth models grow without bound, and thus for many applications the domain of the growth function must be limited. Exponential decay is bounded below by the horizontal axis, however. As shown in Figure 4.8, if the values of an

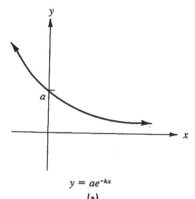

$y = ae^{-kx}$

(a)

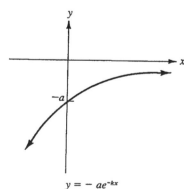

$y = -ae^{-kx}$

(b)

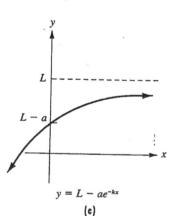

$y = L - ae^{-kx}$

(c)

Figure 4.8

Forming a bounded exponential growth function from a decaying exponential function exponential decay function are negated, the resulting function increases toward the horizontal axis. Finally if some positive value L is added to each of these function values, we obtain a function that increases toward the upper bound L. Starting with the **decaying exponential function**, $y = ae^{-kx}$, where a and k are positive constants, we have formed the bounded exponential growth function

$$y = L - ae^{-kx}.$$

Suppose that L is the number of potential consumers for a new product and S is the number of actual consumers t time units after the market has been seeded with initial sales and advertising. If the number of remaining consumers, $L - S$, is declining at an instantaneous rate k, then

$$L - S = ae^{-kt},$$

where a is a constant that depends on initial sales. Solving for S, we obtain the bounded exponential growth function

(4.20)
$$S = L - ae^{-kt}, t \geq 0.$$

A graph of equation (4.20) for $L > a > 0$ and $k > 0$ appears in Figure 4.9.

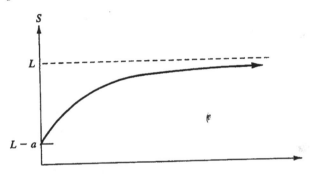

Figure 4.9

The graph of $S = L - ae^{-kt}, t \geq 0$, where $k > 0$ and $L > a > 0$

EXAMPLE 1

An analyst examines a market with 5500 potential customers (per day) for a new disposable product and determines that about 500 customers will buy the product as soon as it is brought to market. Furthermore she assumes that daily sales (customers) S will increase each day thereafter toward 5500 sales per day, with the difference between 5500 and S constantly shrinking by 4%. Find S as a function of time t (days after the product is introduced); then determine $S(30)$, $S(60)$, and $S(120)$. When will daily sales be 2750?

SOLUTION

Since $5500 - S$ is shrinking with instantaneous rate $-.04$, we know that

$$5500 - S = ae^{-.04t}.$$

To determine a we note that $S = 500$ when $t = 0$; thus,

$$5500 - 500 = a \cdot 1,$$

so $a = 5000$. Solving for S we have

$$S = 5500 - 5000e^{-.04t},$$

hence $S(30) = 3994$, $S(60) = 5046$, and $S(120) = 5459$. To determine when $S = 2750$, we must solve $2750 = 5500 - 5000e^{-.04t}$ for t. Simplifying, we get

$$e^{-.04t} = \frac{2750}{5000} = .55,$$

or in logarithmic form

$$-.04t = \ln .55.$$

Thus, $t = (\ln .55)/-.04 \doteq 15$ days. A sketch of S as a function of t appears in Figure 4.10.

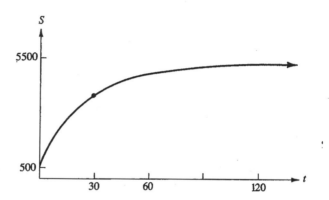

Figure 4.10
The graph of
$S = 5500 - 5000e^{-.04t}, \; t \geq 0$

Graphs of the bounded growth model of equation (4.20), appearing in Figures 4.8(c), 4.9, and 4.10, are often called "learning curves." Psychologists have found that a person's mastery of a certain subject matter begins rapidly and then slows, approaching an asymptotic plateau as modeled by these bounded exponential functions. Others believe that news, rumors, and fads spread through a population according to models of this type.

EXAMPLE 2

Creator Toys plans to saturate children's television programming with ads for the new Cozy Clone doll. Estimating a potential market of 30 million children, and assuming word of the doll spreads in accordance with a model of the form of equation (4.20), executives decide the ads are to run for 45 days during the preholiday season. At what instantaneous rate per day must new kids hear of Cozy Clones so that 20 million can in turn ask Santa for the doll?

SOLUTION

If S denotes the number of kids (in millions) who have heard the news and t denotes the number of days that the media blitz has been in effect, then

$$S = 30 - ae^{-kt}, \qquad t \geq 0.$$

Since $S = 0$ when $t = 0$, we have $a = 30$; thus,

$$S = 30(1 - e^{-kt}).$$

To find k, the desired rate, we solve $20 = 30(1 - e^{-45k})$ to obtain

$$e^{-45k} = \frac{1}{3},$$

or in logarithmic form

$$45k = \ln 3.$$

Thus $k = .0244$, and 2.44% of the remaining uninformed children must be reached each day. A sketch of the learning curve $S = 30(1 - e^{-.0244t})$ appears in Figure 4.11.

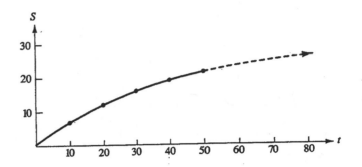

Figure 4.11
A graph of the learning curve
$S = 30(1 - e^{-.0244t})$

As seen in the preceding examples, graphs of learning curves are concave downward; that is, the second derivative is always negative so the growth rate is always decreasing. In some cases a new product does not catch on as rapidly as a learning curve model predicts. There may be a start-up time, with increasing growth rate. The **logistic growth model** accounts for such a start-up period. For logistic growth, we assume that the **relative** difference between the number of customers S and the limiting value L decreases at an instantaneous rate k; that is,

$$\frac{L - S}{S} = ae^{-kt}$$

for some constant $a > 1$. Solving for S we obtain the logistic growth model

(4.21)
$$S = \frac{L}{1 + ae^{-kt}}, \qquad t \geq 0.$$

As with the previous bounded growth model we see that $S < L$ and $\lim_{t \to \infty} S = L$. Differentiating S in equation (4.21) with respect to t, we find

$$S' = \frac{Lake^{-kt}}{(1 + e^{-kt})^2} > 0,$$

so S is an increasing function for $t > 0$. Calculating S'' we find

$$S'' = \frac{(ae^{-kt} - 1)Lak^2e^{-kt}}{(1 + ae^{-kt})^3};$$

thus $S'' = 0$ if $ae^{-kt} - 1 = 0$, or $e^{-kt} = 1/a$. Converting to logarithmic form and solving for t, we find $S'' = 0$ when

$$t = \frac{\ln a}{k}.$$

So $S'' > 0$ and the graph is concave upward when $t < (\ln a)/k$, and $S'' < 0$ and the graph is concave downward when $t > (\ln a)/k$. Thus the graph has an inflection point at $t = (\ln a)/k$ where S has the value

$$S\left(\frac{\ln a}{k}\right) = \frac{L}{1 + ae^{-\ln a}} = \frac{L}{2}.$$

Figure 4.12 illustrates a typical logistic growth function.

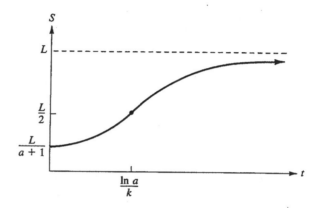

Figure 4.12
The graph of $S = L/(1 + ae^{-kt})$, $t \geq 0$, where $a > 1$ and L and k are positive

EXAMPLE 3

As in Example 1 suppose an analyst determines that a market has 5500 potential customers per day, and that 500 customers will buy the product as soon as it is brought to market. If the **relative** difference between 5500 and the daily sales S (customers) is constantly shrinking by 4%, find S as a function of t and determine $S(30)$, $S(60)$, and $S(120)$. Also determine t so that $S = 2750$.

SOLUTION

Using equation (4.21) we have

$$S = \frac{5500}{1 + ae^{-.04t}}, \qquad t \geq 0.$$

To find a, we use the fact that $S = 500$ when $t = 0$; thus,

$$500 = \frac{5500}{1 + a}.$$

Solving for a, we find $a = 10$; hence,

$$S = \frac{5500}{1 + 10e^{-.04t}}, \qquad t \geq 0.$$

Evaluating S we have $S(30) = 1371$, $S(60) = 2884$, and $S(120) = 5082$. Since $2750 = 5500/2$, we know that $S = 2750$ at the inflection point, where

$$t = \frac{\ln 10}{.04} \doteq 58 \text{ days.}$$

Recall that with the learning curve model of Example 1, $S = 2750$ after only 15 days. A sketch of the graph of this logistic model appears in Figure 4.13.

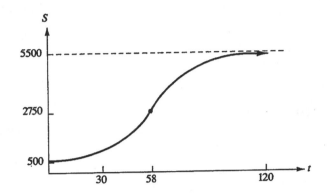

Figure 4.13
The graph of
$S = 5500/(1 + 10e^{-.04t})$, $t \geq 0$

EXERCISES 4.5

In Exercises 1–8 graph both of the given functions on the same coordinate axes.

1. $y = e^{-x}, x \geq 0$;
   $y = 1 - e^{-x}, x \geq 0$

2. $y = -3e^{-x}, x \geq 0$;
   $y = 7 - 3e^{-x}, x \geq 0$

3. $y = 5 - 2e^{-x}, x \geq 0$;
   $y = \dfrac{5x + 3}{x + 1}, x \geq 0$

4. $y = 8 - 3e^{-x}, x \geq 0$;
   $y = \dfrac{8x + 10}{x + 2}, x \geq 0$

5. $y = 5 - 4e^{-x}, x \geq 0$;
   $y = \dfrac{5}{1 + 4e^{-x}}, x \geq 0$

6. $y = 6 - 5e^{-x}, x \geq 0$;
   $y = \dfrac{6}{1 + 5e^{-x}}, x \geq 0$

7. $y = 10 - 7e^{-.1x}, x \geq 0$;
   $y = \dfrac{10}{1 + 4e^{-.1x}}, x \geq 0$

8. $y = 12 - 10e^{-.05x}, x \geq 0$;
   $y = \dfrac{12}{1 + 5e^{-.05x}}, x \geq 0$

In Exercises 9–14 use the given information to find a rule of correspondence for the function S: (a) assuming S is a learning curve model as given in equation (4.20), and (b) assuming S is a logistic model as given in equation (4.21).

9. $S(0) = 50$, $S(1) = 60$, and $\lim_{t \to \infty} S(t) = 100$

10. $S(0) = 10$, $S(1) = 11$, and $\lim_{t \to \infty} S(t) = 50$

11. $S(0) = 20$, $S(10) = 100$, and $\lim_{t \to \infty} S(t) = 200$

12. $S(0) = 8$, $S(50) = 300$, and $\lim_{t \to \infty} S(t) = 600$

13. $S(0) = 1$, $S(10) = 10$, and $\lim_{t \to \infty} S(t) = 500$

14. $S(0) = 5$, $S(10) = 10$, and $\lim_{t \to \infty} S(t) = 100$

15. The potential number of customers for a particular product is 1000, and 10 of these will purchase the product as soon as it arrives on the market. The difference between 1000 and the number of sales S continuously decreases by 2.2%.

   a. Find S as a function of t (the number of days since the product was brought to market).

   b. Determine $S(50)$ and $S(150)$.

   c. Find t so that $S(t) = 50$.

16. The rational function

$$S(t) = \frac{1000t + 125}{t + 12.5}, \qquad t \geq 0,$$

is increasing, is concave downward, and has a horizontal asymptote at $S = 1000$. Find $S(50)$ and $S(150)$; then sketch the graph of this function and that of Exercise 15 on the same set of axes.

17. Suppose the potential market for a new product consists of 5000 customers, 20 of whom will purchase the product as soon as it reaches the market. If S denotes the total number of sales and t denotes the number of days after the product is brought to market, assume the relative difference $(5000 - S)/S$ decreases continuously by 10%.

   a. Find S as a function of t.

   b. Find $S(10)$ and $S(90)$.

   c. Determine t so that $S(t) = 750$.

   d. Find the t-coordinate of the inflection point on the graph of S.

18. Find the inflection point, horizontal asymptote, and y-intercept of the logistic function

$$y = \frac{L}{1 + ae^{-kt}}, \quad t > 0,$$

   if $L = 9900$, $a = 10$, and $k = .03$.

19. Makers of Vitameg super vitamins plan to sell their products using a multilevel marketing scheme. Research indicates that the lure of quick riches attracts new distributors until 85% of the potential market has heard the Vitameg pitch. If the previously uninformed learn of Vitameg at an instantaneous rate of 3% each week, how long will it take to saturate (at the 85% level) any given market?

20. Rework Exercise 19 assuming the Vitameg market is saturated when 90%, rather than 85%, of the potential customers have been informed.

21. Bottlers of a new soft drink are beginning a 60-day summer advertising campaign to acquaint 40 million persons, out of 50 million potential customers, with their product. At what instantaneous rate per day must the uninformed learn of the beverage to achieve this goal, assuming information spreads in accordance with a learning curve model?

22. Rework Exercise 21 assuming that the ad campaign is initiated by shipping free 12 packs to 1000 randomly selected winners, and that information spreads according to a logistic model.

23. The world population at the beginning of 1970 was 3.6 billion. Find the future population P as a function of t, the number of years after 1970 if (a) the instantaneous rate of increase is 2% and a natural growth model is used, and (b) the relative difference between the actual population and a maximum supportable population of 40 billion is decreasing at a rate of 2% and a logistic growth model is used. Also, estimate the population in 1990 and 2000, using each of these models. In what year will the population be 20 billion according to each of these models?

24. For the logistic growth model given by equation (4.21), show that

$$\frac{P'}{P} = k - \frac{k}{L}P.$$

Thus the relative rate of change of P is a (decreasing) linear function of P.

CH. 4 REVIEW

I. Key Terms & Concepts

Mathematics	Business
Exponential Function	Compound Interest
Exponential Growth (Decay)	Nominal Rate of Interest
e	Effective Rate of Interest
Logarithm	Present Value
Natural Logarithm	Future Value
Bounded Exponential Growth	Continuous Compounding
Logistic Growth	Discounting
Effective Rate of Growth (Decay)	
Instantaneous Rate of Growth (Decay)	
Relative Rate of Change	

II. True or False

Indicate whether each statement is true or false.

1. In an exponential function $y = ab^x$, the base b can be any positive number.

2. For $b > 1$, if $y = ab^x$, then the effective rate of growth of y is $(b - 1) \times 100\%$.

3. For $b > 1$, if $y = ab^{-x}$, then the effective rate of decay is $(1 - b) \times 100\%$.

4. For positive x and y, $\ln(xy) = \ln x + \ln y$.

5. For all positive k, the logarithmic functions $f(x) = \ln kx$ have the same derivative.

6. $D_x[e^{\ln x}] = 0$ because $e^{\ln x}$ is a constant function.

7. If a nominal rate of interest r is compounded n times per year, then the effective rate of interest is

$$\left(1 + \frac{r}{n}\right)^n - 1.$$

8. If \$1 earns a nominal rate of interest r, compounded continuously, its value in 1 yr is e^r.

9. For positive x and y, $\log_{10}(x + y) = \log_{10} x + \log_{10} y$.

10. If $f(x) = ab^x$ and $f'(x) = ab^x$, then the base b must be e.

III. Drill Problems

In Problems 1–4 solve the given equation for x, correct to three decimal places.

1. $15 = 3^{2-x}$

2. $e^{4x+1} = 200$

3. $e^{2x} = e^{5-x}$

4. $\ln(x - 6) = -.5$

In Problems 5–14 find the derivative of the indicated function.

5. $f(x) = \ln(2 - 6x + x^3)$

6. $f(x) = x^2 e^{x^2}$

7. $G(t) = \ln \dfrac{t}{(5t + 1)(4 - 3t^2)}$

8. $F(x) = \log_{10} x^4$

9. $f(x) = e^{5x} + 10^{5x}$ 10. $f(x) = \dfrac{e^x}{e^x - e^{-x}}$

11. $h(y) = \ln(e^{3y} + y^3)$ 12. $f(x) = \sqrt[3]{\ln x}$

13. $f(x) = \ln'(1 + e^{2x})$ 14. $F(t) = \ln(\ln t)$

15. Find the effective rate of interest when a nominal rate of 10% per year is compounded daily (assuming a 365-day year).

16. What nominal rate of interest is required to provide an effective interest rate of 8% per year if the interest is compounded quarterly?

17. How long will it take for an investment to double if the interest rate is nominally 12% with monthly compounding?

18. How long will it take for an investment to double if the interest rate is nominally 12% with continuous compounding?

IV. Applications

1. A savings and loan offers three certificates of deposit. One pays 8.25% per year, the second pays 8.10% compounded quarterly, and the third pays 8% compounded continuously. Which of these has the highest effective rate of interest?

2. A mutual fund brochure claims that the value of its investments has grown at an effective rate of 22% per year for the past several years. At that rate how long does it take for the investments to triple in value?

3. A jeweler in your community is advertising that if you had purchased diamonds 10 yr ago, their value would have increased to 420% of their original value. Calculate the average effective rate of increase in the value of the diamonds during this period.

4. Refer to Exercise 4. If the increase in value had occurred at a constant rate throughout the 10 yr, what was the instantaneous rate of increase?

5. It has been reported that because of conservation efforts, the consumption of petroleum in the United States is expected to decline at an effective rate of 1½% per year for the next 5 yr. Find a function that will give the petroleum consumption P as a function of the number of years from now t if P_0 is the current level of consumption in barrels per day. Find the instantaneous rate of decline in consumption.

6. Refer to Exercise 5. Assume instead that the given rate of decline, 1½%, is an instantaneous rate. Find $P(t)$ in this case and determine the corresponding effective rate of decline.

7. A drug company has begun to market a new treatment for baldness. There is an anticipated market of 15 million men for this product, of whom 2 million will try the product immediately. If it is assumed that sales S will increase so that the difference between 15 million and S shrinks at an instantaneous rate of 10% per month thereafter, find S as a function of t, the time in months after the treatment's introduction.

8. Refer to Exercise 7. Suppose that it is the relative difference between 20 million and S that is decreasing at an instantaneous rate of 10% per month. Find $S(t)$ in this case.

The Ovens de Normandie is a French bakery whose owner models the weekly demand q for croissants by

$$q = \frac{3600}{\sqrt{1 + .5p}}, \qquad .50 \le p \le 1.00,$$

where p is the selling price for each croissant. The bakery's current price for a croissant is \$.88. Use differentials to estimate the change in the demand if the price is increased to \$.90.

CHAPTER 5

Applications of the Derivative

5.1
Relative Maximum and Minimum Values of a Function

In this chapter we begin to apply the ideas and results of calculus to fundamental business decisions. In many instances it is desirable to know the value of the independent variable that will yield the maximum (or the minimum) value of the dependent variable. For example, imagine that the manager of a textile company knows the net profit to be earned by producing and selling q bolts of some fabric. In such a case, the manager would like to know the value of q that maximizes the profit.

As a second example, an appliance dealer may order refrigerators from the manufacturer in "lots" of size q. Generally, the dealer is faced with the problem of deciding how large q should be. If q is too large, the cost of carrying the refrigerators in inventory until they can be sold will be large. On the other hand, if q is too small, the administrative cost of placing frequent orders will be excessive. The dealer would like to know the value of q so that the total inventory and ordering costs are minimized.

In the following development, we assume that f is a continuous function of x on some interval and that $y = f(x)$. We begin by making precise the notion of y, or $f(x)$, achieving a maximum or minimum value.

Definition 5.1

A function f is said to have a **relative maximum** at a point $x = c$ if $f(c) \geq f(x)$ for all x in some open interval containing c. Similarly, f is said to have a **relative minimum** at $x = c$ if $f(c) \leq f(x)$ for all x in some open interval containing c. We say that f has a **relative extreme value** to mean that it has either a relative maximum or minimum.

Intuitively, if f has a relative maximum at $x = c$, then $y = f(c)$ is larger than (or at least equal to) any other value of y "nearby." If f has a relative minimum at $x = c$, then $y = f(c)$ is smaller than the nearby values of y. Figure 5.1 shows a function that has relative maxima at $x = c_1$ and $x = c_3$ and a relative minimum at $x = c_2$. Notice that although $f(c_1) < f(c_3)$, we still say that there is a relative maximum at $x = c_1$, since $f(c_1)$ is greater than $f(x)$ for values of x chosen "near" to c_1. Similarly, there is a relative minimum at $x = c_2$ even though $f(c_2)$ is not the smallest value that $f(x)$ ever reaches.

If f is an increasing function on some open interval, then f has neither a relative

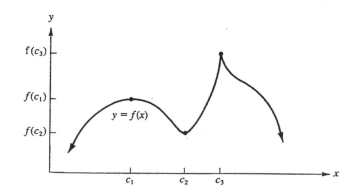

Figure 5.1
A function f with relative extreme values at $x = c_1, c_2,$ and c_3

maximum nor minimum on that interval. For any c in the interval, $f(x) < f(c)$ when $x < c$, and $f(x) > f(c)$ when $x > c$. Similarly, if f is a decreasing function on an open interval, then f has no relative extreme values in the interval. (See Figure 5.2. Note that the curves have no endpoints.)

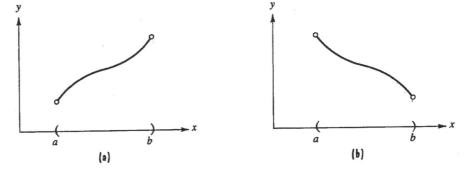

Figure 5.2

(a) Increasing or (b) decreasing functions have no relative extrema on an open interval.

Suppose the function f has a relative extreme value at $x = c$ and $f'(c)$ exists. The value $f'(c)$ cannot be positive, for then f would be increasing on some open interval containing c, contrary to f having a relative extreme value at $x = c$. Likewise, $f'(c)$ cannot be negative, otherwise f will be decreasing on some open interval containing c, and f has no relative extreme values on such intervals. Thus, we conclude that when f is differentiable, the derivative at an extreme value must be 0; that is, $f'(c) = 0$. Therefore, we can state an important theorem.

Theorem 5.1

> If the function f has a relative extreme value at $x = c$, then either
> (1) $f'(c) = 0$ or (2) f is not differentiable at $x = c$.

This theorem is easy to visualize graphically. It says that at a relative maximum or minimum point of a continuous function, there is either a horizontal tangent line to the graph of the function or no tangent line at all. Both possibilities are illustrated in Figure 5.3.

In light of Theorem 5.1, it is apparent that if we are seeking relative extreme values of a function f, we should begin by taking its derivative and looking for values of x in the domain of f for which either $f'(x) = 0$ or $f'(x)$ does not exist.

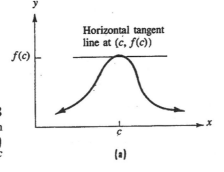
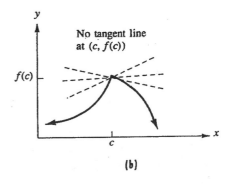

Figure 5.3

Two graphs with a relative maximum at $x = c$: (a) where $f'(c) = 0$, and (b) where f is not differentiable at $x = c$

Definition 5.2

> A number $x = c$ is said to be a **critical point** of a continuous function f if c is in the domain of f and either (1) $f'(c) = 0$ or   (2) $f'(c)$ does not exist.

Theorem 5.1 can be interpreted as stating that any relative maximum or minimum value of a function must occur at a critical point.

The first step in locating relative extreme points is to find the critical points of a function, so we conclude this section with several examples.

EXAMPLE 1

Find the critical points of

$$f(x) = 3x^2 - 5x + 8.$$

SOLUTION

Since

$$f'(x) = 6x - 5$$

exists for all x, we solve the equation

$$6x - 5 = 0$$

to find the critical points. The only critical point is $x = 5/6$. Note that the graph of $y = f(x)$ is a parabola and that the critical point is the x-coordinate of the vertex of this parabola.   ●

EXAMPLE 2

Find the critical points of

$$f(x) = 2x^3 - 7.5x^2 - 9x + 5.$$

SOLUTION

Because

$$f'(x) = 6x^2 - 15x - 9$$

exists for all x, the critical points are the solutions to

$$6x^2 - 15x - 9 = 0$$

or

$$2x^2 - 5x - 3 = 0.$$

Factoring the left side to obtain

$$(2x + 1)(x - 3) = 0,$$

it is evident that there are two critical points, $x = -.5$ and $x = 3$.   ●

EXAMPLE 3

Find all the critical points of

$$f(x) = (6 + x)(8 - 4x)^3.$$

SOLUTION

The derivative is found using the product and chain rules:

$$f'(x) = (8 - 4x)^3 - 12(6 + x)(8 - 4x)^2.$$

Setting this equal to 0 presents a formidable-looking equation:

$$(8 - 4x)^3 - 12(6 + x)(8 - 4x)^2 = 0.$$

Whenever possible, we solve such equations by writing the left side as a product of factors and then determining the values of x that make any factor 0. Here this can be done by factoring $(8 - 4x)^2$ from each term to obtain

$$(8 - 4x)^2[(8 - 4x) - 12(6 + x)] = 0$$

or

$$-16(8 - 4x)^2(4 + x) = 0.$$

In this factored form it is easy to see that $x = 2$ and $x = -4$ are the critical points. ●

EXAMPLE 4

Find the critical points of

$$f(x) = 4xe^{-2x}.$$

SOLUTION

In this problem it is necessary to recall that the exponential function $y = e^t$ is defined and positive for all choices of t. The derivative of $f(x)$ is defined for all x and

$$f'(x) = 4e^{-2x} - 8xe^{-2x}.$$

We solve the equation

$$4e^{-2x} - 8xe^{-2x} = 0$$

by factoring out $4e^{-2x}$:

$$4e^{-2x}(1 - 2x) = 0.$$

Since $4e^{-2x} > 0$ for any x, the only critical point is the solution of $1 - 2x = 0$ or $x = 1/2$. ●

EXAMPLE 5

Find the critical points of the power function $f(x) = x^{2/3}$.

SOLUTION

This function is considerably different from the previous examples. Notice that $f(x)$ is defined for any real number and, in particular, $f(0) = 0^{2/3} = 0$. For any nonzero choice of x, we see that $x^{2/3} > 0$ and so there must be a relative minimum at $x = 0$. The derivative for $x \neq 0$ is

$$f'(x) = \frac{2}{3}x^{-1/3} = \frac{2}{3\sqrt[3]{x}}.$$

For $x = 0$, this formula is undefined; using the derivative definition, it can be shown that $f'(0)$ does not exist. There are no values of x at which $f'(x) = 0$. Therefore, $x = 0$ is the only critical point. The graph of $f(x) = x^{2/3}$ is shown in Figure 5.4.

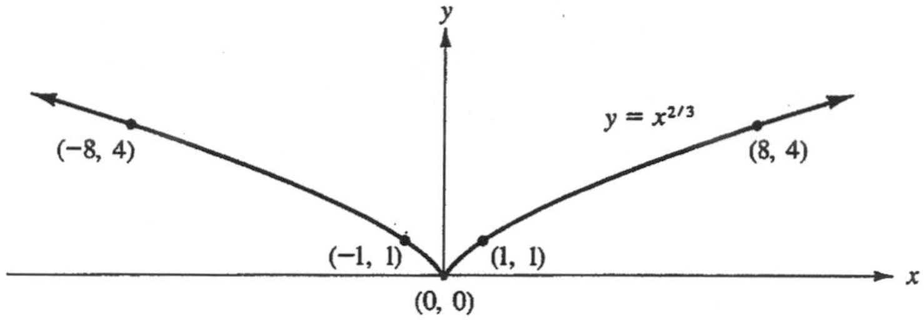

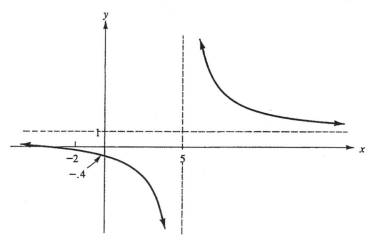

Figure 5.4

The graph of $f(x) = x^{2/3}$; there is a critical point at $x = 0$ where $f'(0)$ does not exist.

EXAMPLE 6

Find the critical points of the rational function

$$f(x) = \frac{x + 2}{x - 5}.$$

SOLUTION

The derivative is

$$f'(x) = \frac{-7}{(x - 5)^2}.$$

Although $f'(5)$ does not exist, $x = 5$ is not a critical point, since 5 is not in the domain of f; that is, $f(5)$ does not exist either. In fact, this function has no critical points: $f'(x)$ is negative for all x in the domain, so f is a decreasing function on the intervals $(-\infty, 5)$ and $(5, \infty)$. The graph of $y = (x + 2)/(x - 5)$ is shown in Figure 5.5.

Figure 5.5

The graph of $y = (x + 2)/(x - 5)$

EXAMPLE 7

Find the critical points of

$$f(x) = \ln(9 - x^2).$$

SOLUTION

First, we recall that the logarithmic function $y = \ln t$ is defined only for positive t. Therefore, $f(x) = \ln(9 - x^2)$ is defined for only $x^2 < 9$—that is, for $-3 < x < 3$. The derivative is

$$f'(x) = \frac{-2x}{9 - x^2}.$$

Again, even though $f'(3)$ and $f'(-3)$ do not exist, $x = +3$ and $x = -3$ are not considered critical points of f. The only critical point is $x = 0$, since $f'(0) = 0$. ●

EXERCISES 5.1

In Exercises 1–30 find all the critical points of f (if any).

1. $f(x) = 7x + 3$

2. $f(x) = 2 - 5x$

3. $f(x) = 3x^2 - 3x + 4$

4. $f(x) = (5 - x)(2x + 1)$

5. $f(x) = e^{4x^2}$

6. $f(x) = e^{x^2 - 5x + 1}$

7. $f(x) = x^3 + 4x^2 + 5x + 2$

8. $f(x) = x^3 - 2x^2 + x + 2$

9. $f(x) = \dfrac{x}{3} - x^{2/3}$

10. $f(x) = x^3 + x^2 - 5x + 3$

11. $f(x) = x^2(x - 8)^2$

12. $f(x) = (x + 1)^2(2x - 5)^2$

13. $f(x) = \dfrac{1}{2}x^4 + 16x$

14. $f(x) = 3x^4 - 4x^3$

15. $f(x) = 8 \ln x - x^2$

16. $f(x) = \ln x^2 - 6x$

17. $f(x) = x - 5 \ln x$

18. $f(x) = \ln(5 + x^2)$

19. $f(x) = xe^{-6x}$

20. $f(x) = x^2 e^x$

21. $f(x) = \sqrt{x} - \dfrac{1}{4}x$

22. $f(x) = \sqrt{x^2 - 9}$

23. $f(x) = \sqrt{x^2 + 9}$

24. $f(x) = x - \sqrt{x + 1}$

25. $f(x) = \dfrac{x^2 + 9}{x}$

26. $f(x) = \dfrac{x^2}{x + 5}$

27. $f(x) = \dfrac{1}{x^2 - 4x + 3}$

28. $f(x) = \dfrac{x^2}{x^2 - 1}$

29. $f(x) = x \ln x$

30. $f(x) = x^2 \ln x$

31. Which of the following functions has a critical point at $x = 3$? Explain why or why not in each case.

a. $f(x) = \sqrt{x - 3}$

b. $f(x) = (x - 3)^{-1/2}$

c. $f(x) = (x - 3)^{4/3}$

d. $f(x) = \ln(x - 3)$

e. $f(x) = \ln(x^2 - 6x)$

32. Which of the following functions has a critical point at $t = -1$? Explain why or why not in each case.

a. $g(t) = (t + 1)^{5/3}$

b. $g(t) = (t + 1)^{-5/3}$

c. $g(t) = (t + 1)^{2/3}$

d. $g(t) = \ln(t + 1)$

e. $g(t) = \ln(t^2 + 2t + 8)$

33. Let profit P, revenue R, and total cost C be differentiable functions of the output level q. Show that the critical points of the profit function occur whenever marginal cost equals marginal revenue.

34. Let C be the total cost of producing q units of any item, and let $A = C/q$ be the average cost of each unit. Show that the critical points of A occur whenever marginal cost and average cost are equal.

35. Show that a linear function $f(x) = ax + b$, $a \neq 0$, cannot have any critical points.

36. Show that a quadratic function $f(x) = ax^2 + bx + c$, $a \neq 0$, always has exactly one critical point and that this occurs at the x-coordinate of the vertex of the parabola $y = f(x)$.

37. Find conditions on the coefficients a, b, c, and d that determine whether the cubic function $f(x) = ax^3 + bx^2 + cx + d$ has no, one, or two critical points.

38. Find the critical point(s) of $f(x) = xe^{kx}$ provided that $k \neq 0$.

39. Show that the rational function $f(x) = (ax + b)/(cx + d)$, where $ad - bc \neq 0$, has no critical points.

5.2
Absolute Extreme Values

In the previous section we considered relative extreme values of a function. For applied problems we usually seek the overall or absolute maximum and minimum values of a function—the largest and smallest values of $f(x)$ for all x in the domain of f. For our models, the domain of f will always be an interval.

Definition 5.3

> The **absolute maximum** of a function f on an interval occurs at $x = c$ (in the interval) if $f(x) \leq f(c)$ for all x in the interval. Similarly, the **absolute minimum** of f occurs at $x = d$ (in the interval) if $f(x) \geq f(d)$ for all x in the interval.

Notice that for absolute extreme values an interval is specified in advance, whereas for relative extreme points there exists some open interval on which $f(c)$ is largest or smallest. Comparing the two definitions, we see that if $f(c)$ is an absolute extreme value, then $f(c)$ is also a relative extreme value unless no open interval in the domain of f contains c—that is, unless c is an endpoint of the interval. Figure 5.6 illustrates a function defined on $[a, \infty)$ with several relative extreme values and an absolute maximum, but with no absolute minimum.

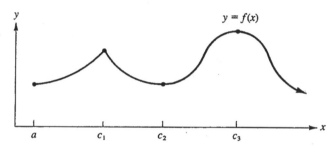

Figure 5.6

The function f has relative extreme values at $x = c_1$, $x = c_2$, and $x = c_3$, and an absolute maximum at $x = c_3$

The general problem of finding the absolute maximum and absolute minimum of a function on an interval is difficult. A function may have many relative extreme values and no absolute extreme values. However, if the function is continuous and the interval is closed, then as stated in Section 2.4, the function has an absolute maximum and an absolute minimum. This result is usually called the **extreme value theorem**. Its proof involves concepts usually considered in an advanced calculus course.

Theorem 5.2
Extreme Value Theorem

> A continuous function on a closed interval $[a, b]$ takes on an absolute maximum and an absolute minimum on that interval.

Candidates for the domain values where a continuous function assumes its absolute extreme values are those places where relative extreme values occur (thus, the critical points must be considered) and the endpoints of the closed interval. The need to consider the endpoints of a closed interval is illustrated in Figure 5.7.

Summarizing, the absolute extreme values of a continuous function f on a closed

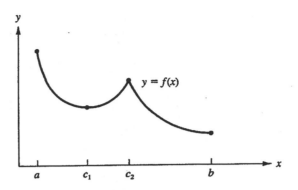

Figure 5.7

A continuous function f with relative
extreme values $x = c_1$ and $x = c_2$,
but absolute extreme values at
$x = a$ and $x = b$

interval $[a, b]$ are the largest and smallest values among $f(a), f(b)$, and $f(c)$, where
c is any critical point of f in (a, b).

EXAMPLE 1

Find the absolute maximum and absolute minimum of

$$f(x) = x^3 - 3x^2 - 9x + 7, \qquad 0 \le x \le 5.$$

SOLUTION

Clearly, the cubic polynomial f is continuous on $[0, 5]$. To find the critical points
of f, we set $f'(x)$ equal to 0 and solve:

$$f'(x) = 3x^2 - 6x - 9 = 0$$

or

$$3(x^2 - 2x - 3) = 0$$

or

$$3(x - 3)(x + 1) = 0.$$

Thus, f has a critical point at $x = 3$. ($x = -1$ is not in the interval $[0, 5]$, which
is the domain considered here.) Now $f(3) = -20$, and at the endpoints of the
interval $f(0) = 7$ and $f(5) = 12$. Thus, the absolute maximum of $f(x)$ is 12, and
this maximum occurs at $x = 5$. The absolute minimum occurs at $x = 3$ where
$f(3) = -20$. A sketch of f appears in Figure 5.8.

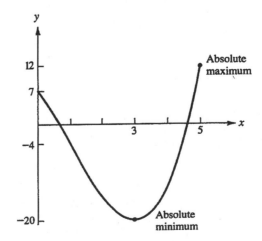

Figure 5.8

The graph of
$f(x) = x^3 - 3x^2 - 9x + 7$,
$0 \le x \le 5$, illustrating the absolute
maximum at $(5, 12)$ and the absolute
minimum at $(3, -20)$

EXAMPLE 2

The division manager of an appliance manufacturing firm must decide on the daily production level q for an electric mixer. The plant manager where these mixers are produced has reported that plant capacity is 800 units per day and daily fixed costs are \$750, while variable costs are approximately

$$v = 75 - .04q + .00008q^2 \qquad \text{(dollars per unit)}$$

when the production level is q units per day. The marketing director reports that the mixers can be sold to wholesale distributors for a price of

$$p = 85 - .03q \qquad \text{(dollars per unit)},$$

and that the market can absorb all of the plant's output at this price. Given all this information, how should the division manager select q to maximize the profit from the production and sale of these mixers?

SOLUTION

The daily total cost of producing q mixers is

$$\begin{aligned}
C &= 750 + vq \\
&= 750 + 75q - .04q^2 + .00008q^3, \qquad 0 \le q \le 800.
\end{aligned}$$

The revenue generated from the sale of q mixers is

$$\begin{aligned}
R &= pq \\
&= 85q - .03q^2, \qquad 0 \le q \le 800.
\end{aligned}$$

Therefore, profit is given by

$$\begin{aligned}
P &= R - C \\
&= (85q - .03q^2) - (750 + 75q - .04q^2 + .00008q^3) \\
&= -750 + 10q + .01q^2 - .00008q^3, \qquad 0 \le q \le 800.
\end{aligned}$$

The profit function is continuous on $[0, 800]$, and at the endpoints

$$P(0) = -750 \quad \text{and} \quad P(800) = -27{,}310.$$

Differentiating P with respect to q and setting the derivative equal to 0, we find

$$P' = 10 + .02q - .00024q^2 = 0.$$

By the quadratic formula,

$$\begin{aligned}
q &= \frac{-.02 \pm \sqrt{.0004 + 4(.00024)10}}{2(-.00024)} \\
&= \frac{-.02 \pm .10}{-.00048} \\
&= -\frac{500}{3} \quad \text{or} \quad 250.
\end{aligned}$$

Thus, P has a critical point in $[0, 800]$ at $q = 250$, and

$$P(250) = 1125.$$

Among the three candidates $P(0)$, $P(800)$, and $P(250)$, the latter is clearly the largest. Thus, profit can be maximized by producing and selling 250 mixers per day. ●

EXAMPLE 3

If the demand function for a certain product is given by

$$p = \frac{10q + 18}{q + 1}, \qquad 0 \le q \le 100,$$

find the value of q that maximizes the revenue R for this product.

SOLUTION

Total revenue R is given by

$$R = pq$$
$$= \frac{10q^2 + 18q}{q + 1}, \qquad 0 \le q \le 100.$$

This continuous function has values

$$R(0) = 0 \quad \text{and} \quad R(100) = \$1007.92$$

at the endpoints. Differentiating R with respect to q, we find

$$R' = \frac{(q + 1)(20q + 18) - (10q^2 + 18q)}{(q + 1)^2}$$
$$= \frac{10q^2 + 20q + 18}{(q + 1)^2},$$

which is positive for all q. Thus, R has no critical points and the absolute maximum of R occurs when $q = 100$. ●

EXAMPLE 4

For a new product, demand must often be generated through advertising and other marketing efforts. In a test market it is determined that if x dollars are spent per day marketing a new television video game, the sales q in response to this effort are approximated by

$$q = .8\sqrt{x}, \qquad 0 \le x \le 2500.$$

The daily fixed costs for the production of these video games are $800 and the variable costs are approximately $50 per unit for up to 40 units. If each video game can be sold for $150, find the marketing expenditure x that will maximize profit.

SOLUTION

To determine total costs we must add fixed costs, variable costs, and in this case, marketing costs (often categorized as discretionary costs). Thus,

$$C = 800 + 50q + x.$$

To write C as a function of x we substitute for q to obtain

$$C = 800 + 50(.8\sqrt{x}) + x$$
$$= 800 + 40x^{1/2} + x, \qquad 0 \le x \le 2500.$$

Revenue is given in terms of x as

$$R = 150q$$
$$= 150(.8\sqrt{x})$$
$$= 120x^{1/2}, \qquad 0 \le x \le 2500.$$

Thus, profit P as a function of marketing expenditure x is

$$P = R - C$$
$$= 120x^{1/2} - (800 + 40x^{1/2} + x)$$
$$= -800 + 80x^{1/2} - x, \qquad 0 \le x \le 2500.$$

At the endpoints,

$$P(0) = -800 \quad \text{and} \quad P(2500) = 700.$$

Differentiating P with respect to x, we have

$$P' = \frac{1}{2}(80)x^{-1/2} - 1.$$

Thus, $P' = 0$ if $40x^{-1/2} - 1 = 0$—that is, if $x^{1/2} = 40$ or $x = 1600$. Now $P(1600) = 800$; hence, the maximum profit is realized if \$1600 per day is spent on marketing. ●

EXAMPLE 5

Hawaiian Tours offers a large group excursion to the islands for 100 to 200 persons. If the group consists of 100 persons, the rate is \$1200 each. For each person beyond 100 in the group, the fee per person is decreased by \$5. For what size group does Hawaiian Tours maximize its revenue?

SOLUTION

If q denotes the size of the group, then the number of persons beyond 100 becomes $q - 100$ and the fee for each member is

$$p = 1200 - 5(q - 100)$$
$$= 1700 - 5q, \qquad 100 \le q \le 200.$$

Now the revenue R is given by

$$R = pq$$
$$= 1700q - 5q^2, \qquad 100 \le q \le 200.$$

At the endpoints, this continuous function has values

$$R(100) = 120,000 \quad \text{and} \quad R(200) = 140,000.$$

Differentiating R with respect to q, we find that

$$R' = 1700 - 10q,$$

and so R has a critical point at $q = 170$, where $R(170) = 144,500$. Thus, revenue is maximized when the group has 170 members. Note that the revenue function is a quadratic function, and the maximum value of R could be obtained at the vertex of its graph without using calculus. ●

EXERCISES 5.2

In Exercises 1–24 find the absolute maximum and absolute minimum of the given continuous function on the specified closed interval.

1. $f(x) = 3x + 2; [0, 7]$ 2. $g(x) = 5 - 2x; [-1, 4]$

3. $h(x) = 3x^2 - 3x + 4; [0,1]$

4. $p(x) = 20 + 2x - x^2; [-2, 2]$

5. $g(t) = t^3 + 3t^2 - 24t + 4; [0, 5]$

6. $h(t) = t^3 + 3t^2 - 24t + 4; [-5, 0]$

7. $f(u) = 5 + 4u + u^2 - 2u^3; [0, 2]$

8. $g(x) = 2x^3 - 15x^2 + 36x - 10; [1, 5]$

9. $p(w) = w^2(2 - w)^2; [-2, 3]$

10. $f(u) = (u + 1)^2(2u - 5)^2; [-2, 0]$

11. $p(t) = \dfrac{t}{3} - t^{2/3}; [-1, 27]$

12. $h(z) = z^{3/5}; [-1, 2]$ 13. $f(x) = \dfrac{x}{2} + \dfrac{8}{x}; [1, 5]$

14. $g(x) = x - 3 \ln x; [1, 5]$

15. $h(x) = e^{x^2}; [-1, 1]$ 16. $p(t) = 100e^{.08t}; [0, 5]$

17. $g(x) = x^2 e^x; [-3, 1]$ 18. $h(x) = \dfrac{e^x}{x^2}; [1, 4]$

19. $f(x) = 8 \ln x - x^2; [1, 4]$ 20. $g(w) = \dfrac{\ln w}{w}; [1, 4]$

21. $p(t) = \sqrt{t^2 + 9}; [-1, 4]$ 22. $f(x) = \sqrt{4x - x^2}; [0, 4]$

23. $h(x) = \dfrac{x^2}{x - 5}; [0, 4]$ 24. $p(x) = \dfrac{x - 5}{x^2}; [5, 20]$

25. Ruff Leather Products has determined that the variable cost per unit for their wallets is given by
$$v = 12 - .004q, \qquad 0 \le q \le 500,$$

while the daily fixed costs at the wallet plant are \$200. If q wallets can be sold for p dollars each when
$$p = 15 - .01q, \qquad 0 \le q \le 500,$$
find the number of wallets that should be produced and sold daily in order to maximize profit.

26. After renewing its lease, Ruff Leather's daily fixed costs at the wallet plant increased to \$510 per day. Find the output level that maximizes profit using the same variable cost and demand functions as in Exercise 25, but using the new daily fixed costs. What effect do fixed costs have on the optimal output level?

27. The demand function for Manta Mufflers is given by
$$p = 35 - .035q, \qquad 0 \le q \le 500.$$
If the daily fixed costs at the muffler assembly plant are \$100 and the variable cost per unit for the production of q units is given by
$$v = 20 - .03q + .0002q^2, \qquad 0 \le q \le 500,$$
find the daily production level that maximizes profit.

28. The demand function for Tekpac Calculators is given by
$$p = 22 - .05q, \qquad 0 \le q \le 200.$$
If daily fixed costs for the production of these calculators are \$100 and the variable cost per unit is given by
$$v = 10 - .02q + .0005q^2, \qquad 0 \le q \le 200,$$
find the daily production level that maximizes profit.

29. A division of Radink can produce up to 100 clock radios per day. Fixed costs associated with this production are \$50 per day, while variable costs are \$20 per unit. If all units produced can be sold in accordance with the demand function
$$p = \frac{19q + 350}{q + 10}, \qquad q \ge 0,$$
find the output level that maximizes profit.

30. Sprint Shoes can produce up to 300 pairs of the economy Jogger per week. Fixed costs for this production are $200 per week and variable costs are $25 per pair of Joggers. If all shoes can be sold for p dollars per pair, when

$$p = \frac{24q + 1200}{q + 20}, \qquad q \geq 0,$$

how many pairs of Joggers should Sprint produce per week in order to maximize profit?

31. The marketing division of Kitchenayds estimates that if x dollars are spent per day marketing a new food processor, the sales q in response to this effort will be approximately

$$q = .8x^{3/4}, \qquad 0 \leq x \leq 10,000.$$

The plant manager reports that the daily fixed costs for the production of the food processors are $200, and variable costs are approximately $40 per unit for up to 800 units. If each unit produced can be sold for $55, find the marketing expenditure x that results in a maximum profit. What are the daily profit and production at this optimal expenditure level?

32. If Trophy Flyrods spends x dollars per week on magazine ads, the resulting sales q are related to x by

$$q = .6x^{3/5}, \qquad 0 \leq x \leq 500.$$

If each rod produced is sold for $45, and if fixed costs are $50 per week while variable costs are $20 per rod, how much should Trophy spend per week on advertisements in order to maximize profit?

33. The daily cost of producing q Maxiwarm sweaters is given by

$$C = 100 + 12q - .01q^2, \qquad 0 \leq q \leq 100.$$

Each sweater produced can be sold for p dollars when

$$p = 40 - .11q, \qquad 0 \leq q \leq 100.$$

If x dollars are spent on daily radio advertisements, it is estimated that q sweaters will be sold when

$$q = 2\sqrt{x}, \qquad 0 \leq x \leq 625.$$

Find the value of x that yields a maximum daily profit.

34. Rework Exercise 33 by writing profit P as a function of q, finding the value of q that maximizes P and then finding the corresponding value of x.

35. Air East Airlines offers charter jet service from Chicago to Miami for groups of 200 to 300 persons. For a 200-person group the round-trip rate is $400. For larger groups the rate is decreased by $1.60 per person for each person beyond 200 in the group. Find the group size that maximizes revenue for Air East Airlines.

36. Tasty Pizza plans to open from 5 to 20 restaurants in the Los Angeles area. With 5 restaurants the estimated weekly profit per restaurant is $1000. For each restaurant beyond 5 it appears that weekly profit will decrease by $50 in all restaurants due to competition for the same customers. Find the number of restaurants Tasty Pizza should open in order to maximize profit.

37. Silverware Corp. is planning to use from 20 to 50 students to sell cutlery during the summer in Wisconsin. The students will sell door to door with no preassigned routes, and each is paid a salary of $24 per day plus commissions. With 20 students selling, it is estimated that each will average 150 sales per day. For more than 20 students, the overlapping of routes will reduce average sales by 5 items for each salesperson beyond 20. If each item is expected to generate an $.80 profit after commissions but before salaries, find the number of students that will result in a maximum profit.

38. Supermags Inc. is forming a sales force of between 10 and 25 persons to sell magazine subscriptions in towns with approximately 50,000 inhabitants. It is estimated that 10 salespersons will average 40 sales per day, and that for each additional salesperson beyond 10, the average daily sales decrease by 2 per person. If Supermags pays commissions only and makes $1.50 profit on each subscription after commissions, find the size of the sales force that yields the maximum profit.

39. The monthly output q (tons of steel girders) for Steelfab Inc. is approximated by

$$q = 1.8k^{1/3}(150 - k)^{2/3}, \qquad 0 \leq k \leq 150,$$

where k denotes thousands of dollars in capital expenditures per month (and $150 - k$ denotes thousands of dollars spent on labor per month). Find the value of k that maximizes q and the maximum value of q.

40. The weekly output for Frosto Ice Cream is approximated by

$$q = 1.6L^{3/4}(200 - L)^{1/4}, \qquad 0 \leq L \leq 200,$$

where q denotes carloads of ice cream and L represents thousands of dollars spent on labor (while $200 - L$ denotes weekly capital expenditure). Find the value of L that maximizes q.

41. A box without a top is to be made by cutting out identical squares from each corner of a 2-foot-square sheet of metal and folding up the sides as indicated in the diagram. Allow-

ing $0 \leq x \leq 12$ in., determine x so that the volume of the resulting box is maximized.

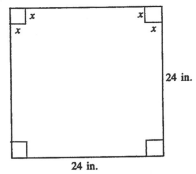

42. In general, if the sheet of metal in Exercise 41 is a square of side s and the dimension of the deleted square corner is x, then $0 \leq x \leq s/2$. In this general case find x in terms of s to maximize the volume of the resulting box.

43. A farmer wishes to fence in three sides of a rectangular pasture (see the diagram) along a straight canal, using 600 ft of fencing. Find the dimensions of the pasture of largest area that can be fenced in this fashion.

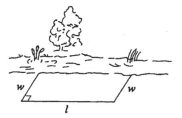

44. A farmer wishes to fence in a pasture along a straight highway. The pasture is to contain 500 sq ft of land and be rectangular, and the sides of the rectangle must be at least 10 feet long (to avoid cattle congestion). If the fencing along the highway is heavy duty and costs $3 per foot, while the material for the remaining three sides costs $2 per foot, find the dimensions of the pasture with the minimum fencing cost.

45. Judd and Weissenberger consider a model related to the problem of nuclear materials being diverted from a reactor by terrorists.* The model treats two costs: C_D, the cost to society when nuclear material is diverted, and C_S, the cost of physical safeguards to prevent diversion. These costs are considered to be functions of the probability p of detecting a diversion by an employee, where $0 < p < 1$. The costs are estimated as

$$C_D = 1.2 - .7p \quad \text{(million dollars/year)}$$
$$\text{and} \quad C_S = .0068e^{11p} \quad \text{(million dollars/year)}.$$

Find the probability p and corresponding values of C_D and C_S, where total cost $C = C_D + C_S$ is minimized.

---

*Bruce R. Judd and Stein A. Weissenberger, "A Systematic Approach to Nuclear Safeguards Decision Making," *Management Science* 28, no. 3 (March 1982): 289–302.

5.3
The First Derivative Test

In this section we use the sign of the derivative of a function to classify a critical point as a relative maximum, a relative minimum, or neither. This further analysis of relative extreme values will be especially useful in cases where the function of interest is not defined and continuous on a closed interval.

By checking for possible changes in the sign of the derivative on either side of a critical point, we can determine whether or not the critical point corresponds to a relative extreme value. Suppose that f is a differentiable function except perhaps at $x = c$ where f has a critical point. [Recall that either $f'(c) = 0$ or $f'(c)$ does not exist.] Assuming that f is continuous at $x = c$, there are four possibilities:

1. f has a relative maximum at $x = c$ and so f is increasing immediately to the left of c and decreasing immediately to the right of c.

2. f has a relative minimum at $x = c$ and so f is decreasing immediately to the left of c and increasing immediately to the right of c.

3. f is increasing on both sides of c.

4. f is decreasing on both sides of c.

Each of these possibilities is illustrated in Figure 5.9.

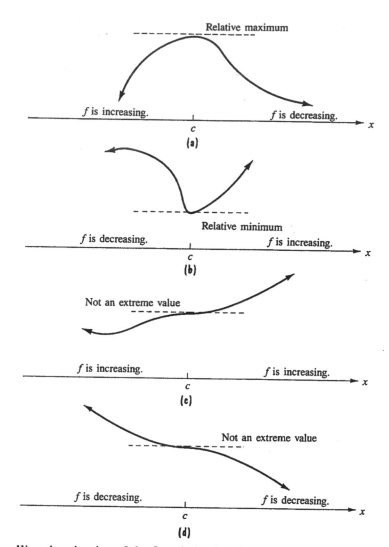

Figure 5.9

Illustrations of the possibilities for the graph of a continuous function near a critical point $x = c$ [when $f'(c) = 0$]

Recalling that the sign of the first derivative f' indicates whether f is increasing or decreasing, we summarize the preceding cases and obtain the **first derivative test**.

Theorem 5.3
The First Derivative Test

Suppose that $x = c$ is a critical point of f and that f is continuous at c. Assume (a, b) is an open interval that contains c.

1. If $f'(x) > 0$ for $a < x < c$ and $f'(x) < 0$ for $c < x < b$, then f has a **relative maximum** at $x = c$.

2. If $f'(x) < 0$ for $a < x < c$ and $f'(x) > 0$ for $c < x < b$, then f has a **relative minimum** at $x = c$.

3. If $f'(x)$ has the same sign on the intervals (a, c) and (c, b), then f does not have a relative extreme value at $x = c$.

To apply the first derivative test we must determine whether $f'(x)$ changes sign at a critical point c. This in turn means we must find points a and b so that $f'(x)$ is of constant sign on (a, c) and on (c, b). When $f'(x)$ is continuous it will maintain its sign as we move from c toward another critical point, or a discontinuity of f. Thus in this case it suffices to examine the sign of $f'(x)$ at test points a and b that are closer to c than any other critical point or point of discontinuity.

In Figure 5.10 a demonstration of this test procedure is shown. Let $x = c_1$ be the critical point to be tested. Observe that there is a discontinuity at $x = d$ to the left of c_1 and another critical point $x = c_2$ to the right of c_1. As shown, a can be chosen anywhere between d and c_1 and the value of $f'(a)$ will be negative. Similarly, when b is chosen anywhere between c_1 and c_2, $f'(b)$ will be positive. If either a or b is chosen outside these bounds, then the first derivative test would give erroneous results.

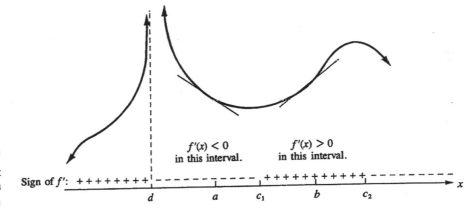

Figure 5.10

An illustration of the use of the first derivative test to show that there is a relative minimum at $x = c_1$

We now apply the first derivative test to the first five examples of Section 5.1.

EXAMPLE 1

Find and classify the critical points of
$$f(x) = 3x^2 - 5x + 8.$$

SOLUTION

The first derivative
$$f'(x) = 6x - 5$$

is 0 at $x = 5/6$. Because this is the only critical point, we can choose one test point anywhere to the left of 5/6 and another anywhere to the right of 5/6. Taking $a = 0$ and $b = 1$, we see $f'(0) = -5$ and $f'(1) = 1$, and so f has a relative minimum at $x = 5/6$ (see Figure 5.11). Since the graph of $y = 3x^2 - 5x + 8$ is a parabola that opens upward, this result is as expected. In fact, the value $f(5/6)$ is an absolute minimum of f.

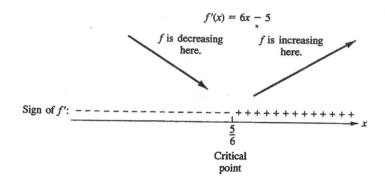

Figure 5.11
Classification of the critical point
$x = 5/6$ as a relative minimum

EXAMPLE 2   Find and classify the critical points of

$$f(x) = 2x^3 - 7.5x^2 - 9x + 5.$$

SOLUTION   We have

$$f'(x) = 6x^2 - 15x - 9$$
$$= 3(2x + 1)(x - 3),$$

so $f'(x)$ is 0 at $x = -.5$ and at $x = 3$. As shown in Figure 5.12, we can select for the test points any x less than $-.5$, any x between $-.5$ and 3, and any x greater than 3. Because $f'(-2) = 45$, f' is positive for $x < -.5$; because $f'(0) = -9$, f' is negative for $-.5 < x < 3$; and because $f'(4) = 27$, f' is positive for $x > 3$. Therefore, there is a relative maximum at $x = -.5$ and a relative minimum at $x = 3$.

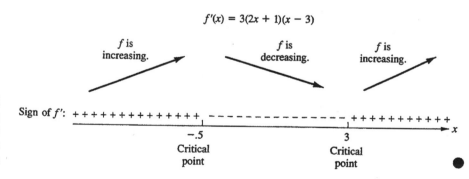

Figure 5.12
Classification of the critical point
$x = -.5$ as a relative maximum and
the critical point $x = 3$ as a relative
minimum

EXAMPLE 3   Find and classify the critical points of

$$f(x) = (6 + x)(8 - 4x)^3.$$

SOLUTION   In Section 5.1 we found that the derivative can be written as

$$f'(x) = -16(8 - 4x)^2(4 + x),$$

so there are two critical points: $x = -4$ and $x = 2$. In this instance it is a little difficult to actually evaluate f' at test points. It is easier to observe that the sign of $f'(x)$ is determined solely by the sign of the factor $(4 + x)$ because $-16(8 - 4x)^2 \leq 0$ for all x. The factor $(4 + x)$ is negative for $x < -4$ and positive for $x > 4$, so $f'(x)$ is positive to the left of $x = -4$ and negative to the right. We conclude that there is a relative maximum at $x = -4$, but there is not an extreme value at $x = 2$. The derivative is negative on each side of $x = 2$. Figure 5.13 shows this analysis.

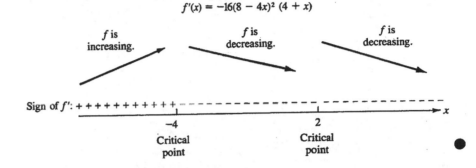

$$f'(x) = -16(8 - 4x)^2 (4 + x)$$

Figure 5.13

Classification of the critical point $x = -4$ as a relative maximum and the critical point $x = 2$ as neither a maximum nor a minimum

EXAMPLE 4

Find and classify the critical points of

$$f(x) = 4xe^{-2x}.$$

SOLUTION

The derivative

$$f'(x) = 4e^{-2x}(1 - 2x)$$

is 0 only at $x = 1/2$. In applying the first derivative test we need to recall that e^t is positive for any t. Therefore, the sign of $f'(x)$ is determined by the sign of the factor $(1 - 2x)$. If $x < 1/2$, then the derivative is positive, and if $x > 1/2$, then the derivative is negative. It follows that there is a relative maximum at $x = 1/2$. ●

EXAMPLE 5

Find and classify the critical points of $f(x) = x^{2/3}$.

SOLUTION

The derivative

$$f'(x) = \frac{2}{3}x^{-1/3}$$

fails to exist at $x = 0$, and this is the only critical point of f. As test points we can choose $a = -1$ and $b = 1$. Then $f'(-1) = -2/3$ and $f(1) = 2/3$; thus, f has a relative minimum at $x = 0$. The graph of $y = x^{2/3}$ is shown in Figure 5.4 of Section 5.1. ●

Using the first derivative test, critical points of a function are relative extreme values if the derivative of the function changes sign at the critical point ($+$ to $-$

for a relative maximum; $-$ to $+$ for a relative minimum). In fact, if f is continuous at $x = c$ and if $f'(x)$ has opposite signs on either side of $x = c$, then we may conclude that $f(c)$ is a relative extreme value without first bothering to determine whether $x = c$ is a critical point of f. Carrying this reasoning one step further, we may apply the first derivative test to any $x = c$ in the domain of a continuous function f. If $f'(x)$ does not change sign at $x = c$, then f does not have a relative extreme value at $x = c$ whether or not $x = c$ is a critical point. These observations are helpful in cases where it is suspected that $x = c$ is a critical point, but it is more work to check this suspicion than to apply the first derivative test.

EXAMPLE 6   Find the relative extreme values of f where

$$f(x) = \begin{cases} x^2 - 6x + 10 & \text{if } x \le 4 \\ x - 2 & \text{if } x > 4. \end{cases}$$

SOLUTION   When $x < 4$, $f'(x) = 2x - 6$, so $x = 3$ is a critical point of f. For $x > 4$, $f'(x) = 1$, so f has no critical points to the right of 4. At $x = 4$, f is continuous, but f may not be differentiable; we will also test $x = 4$.

Applying the first derivative test to $x = 3$, we find that f' is negative for $x < 3$ and f' is positive for $x > 3$, so f has a relative minimum at $x = 3$. To test $x = 4$, we note that f' is positive on both sides and so $f(4)$ is neither a relative maximum nor a relative minimum. (See Figure 5.14.) The careful reader will note that $x = 4$ is, in fact, a critical point, since $f'(4)$ does not exist. (See Figure 5.15.)

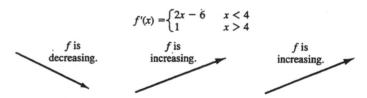

$$f'(x) = \begin{cases} 2x - 6 & x < 4 \\ 1 & x > 4 \end{cases}$$

| f is decreasing. | f is increasing. | f is increasing. |

Figure 5.14
Classification of the critical point $x = 3$ and the possible critical point $x = 4$

Sign of f': $- - - - - - - - - +$

3   4

Critical point   Critical point?

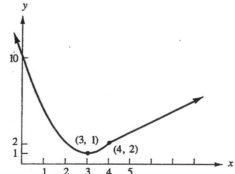

Figure 5.15
A graph of the function
$$f(x) = \begin{cases} x^2 - 6x + 10 & \text{if } x \le 4 \\ x - 2 & \text{if } x > 4 \end{cases}$$

We conclude this section with an elementary, but often useful, extension of the first derivative test. Let f be a continuous function on a closed interval $[a, b]$. Suppose that f is differentiable on the interval but has no critical points there. Then, either f' is positive on the whole interval or negative on the whole interval. If f' is positive, then f increases from a to b and so the function must have its absolute minimum at $x = a$ and its absolute maximum at $x = b$. When f' is negative, the maximum occurs at $x = a$ and the minimum at $x = b$.

EXAMPLE 7

Locate the absolute maximum value of
$$f(x) = e^{-.5x} + \frac{3}{x}$$
on the interval $[2, 10]$.

SOLUTION

The derivative is
$$f'(x) = -.5e^{-.5x} - 3x^{-2},$$
which is negative for any choice of x in $[2, 10]$. Thus, the function must be decreasing on the interval $[2, 10]$ and the maximum value has to occur when $x = 2$; that is, $f(2) = e^{-1} + 1.5$ is the largest value that f can achieve on the interval $[2, 10]$. Figure 5.16 is a graphic analysis of this observation.

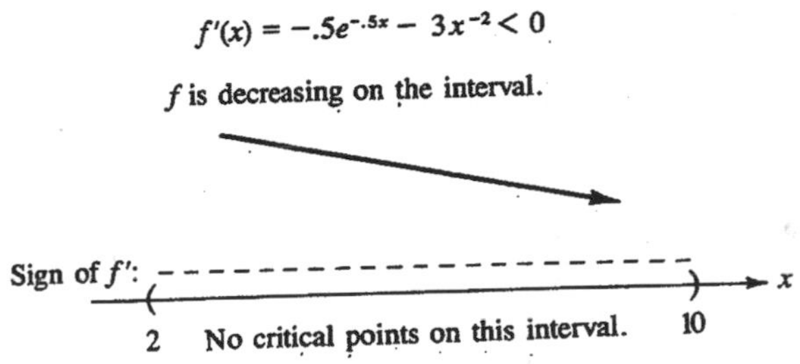

$$f'(x) = -.5e^{-.5x} - 3x^{-2} < 0$$

f is decreasing on the interval.

Figure 5.16

The maximum value of $f(x) = e^{-.5x} + 3/x$ on $[2, 10]$ occurs at the left-hand endpoint.

Sign of f': — — — — — — — — — — — — — — — — → x

2   No critical points on this interval.   10

EXERCISES 5.3

In Exercises 1–45 use the first derivative test to classify each of the critical points of the given function. (Hint: The functions in Exercises 1–20 appeared in Exercises 1–30 of Section 5.1.)

1. $f(x) = 3x^2 - 3x + 4$

2. $f(x) = (5 - x)(2x + 1)$

3. $f(x) = e^{4x^2}$

4. $f(x) = e^{x^2 - 5x + 1}$

5. $f(x) = x^3 + 4x^2 + 5x + 2$

6. $f(x) = x^3 - 2x^2 + x + 2$

7. $f(x) = x^2(x - 8)^2$

8. $f(x) = (x + 1)^2(2x - 5)^2$

9. $f(x) = \frac{1}{2}x^4 + 16x$

10. $f(x) = 3x^4 - 4x^3$

11. $f(x) = 8 \ln x - x^2$

12. $f(x) = \ln x^2 - 6x$

13. $f(x) = xe^{-6x}$

14. $f(x) = x^2 e^x$

15. $f(x) = \sqrt{x} - \frac{1}{4}x, x > 0$

16. $f(x) = x - \sqrt{x + 1}, x > -1$

17. $f(x) = \frac{1}{x^2 - 4x + 3}$

18. $f(x) = \frac{x^2}{x^2 - 1}$

19. $f(x) = x \ln x$

20. $f(x) = x^2 \ln x$

21. $f(x) = \frac{2}{3}x^3 - 5x^2 + 12x + 4$

22. $f(x) = 10 - 8x - 3x^2 - \frac{1}{3}x^3$

23. $f(x) = x^4 - 8x^2 + 8$

24. $f(x) = x^2(x^2 - 4x - 8)$

25. $f(x) = x(x - 12)^3$

26. $f(x) = xe^{3x+1}$

27. $f(x) = x^2e^{x/6}$

28. $f(x) = \frac{x^2}{3 + 2x - x^2}$

29. $f(x) = \frac{1}{\sqrt{16 - x^2}}$

30. $f(x) = \frac{x}{12 - x^2}$

31. $f(x) = (x - 7)^{4/3}$

32. $f(x) = x(8 - x)^{1/3}$

33. $f(x) = x(15 - x)^{2/3}$

34. $f(x) = \ln(x + 5) + \frac{1}{x + 5}$

35. $f(x) = x^2 - 16 \ln x$

36. $f(x) = \frac{x^2 + 12}{x - 2}$

37. $f(x) = \frac{100}{x} + 4x$

38. $f(x) = x^3e^{-6x}$

39. $f(x) = e^x - 4x$

40. $f(x) = \ln x - 2\sqrt{x}$

41. $f(x) = 24 \ln x - x^3$

42. $f(x) = \begin{cases} x^2 - 4x + 5 & \text{if } x \le 2 \\ 2x - 3 & \text{if } x > 2 \end{cases}$

43. $f(x) = \begin{cases} x^2 - 4x + 10 & \text{if } x \le 3 \\ 2x + 1 & \text{if } x > 3 \end{cases}$

44. $f(x) = \begin{cases} x^2 & \text{if } x > 0 \\ -x^2 & \text{if } x \le 0 \end{cases}$

45. $f(x) = \begin{cases} x^2 - 4x + 5 & \text{if } x < 1 \\ 6x - x^2 - 3 & \text{if } x \ge 1 \end{cases}$

46. Use the first derivative test to show that $f(x) = ax^2 + bx + c$ has an absolute maximum at $x = -b/2a$ when $a < 0$.

47. Let the profit P, revenue R, and total cost C be given as functions of the output level q. If P has a relative maximum at q_0, what does the first derivative test imply about the marginal cost and the marginal revenue on either side of $q = q_0$?

48. Let C denote the total cost of producing q units of some item and $A = C/q$ the average cost per unit. If A has a relative minimum at q_0, what does the first derivative test imply about the average cost and the marginal cost on either side of $q = q_0$?

49. Show that $f(x) = xe^{kx}$ has a relative minimum at $x = -1/k$ when k is a positive constant.

50. Use the first derivative test to classify the critical points of
$$f(x) = xe^{kx^2}, \quad \text{for } k < 0.$$

51. Show that $f(x) = (x - a)^{k/3}$ has a relative minimum at $x = a$ when k is an even positive integer and does not have an extreme value when k is an odd positive integer.

In Exercises 52–59 show that the function is either increasing or decreasing across the whole interval. Find the absolute minimum value of the function on the given interval.

52. $q(t) = t^2 + 3t + 1$; $[0, 4]$

53. $h(s) = 5 - \ln s$; $[1, 10]$

54. $f(r) = e^r$; $[-3, -1]$

55. $g(x) = \frac{2x - 5}{x + 1}$; $[0, 8]$

56. $F(p) = p^4 + 5p$; $[-1, 0]$

57. $f(x) = x^{2/3}$; $[-81, -8]$

58. $R(y) = y^2e^{4y}$; $[5, 15]$

59. $h(z) = \sqrt{25 - z^2}$; $[-4, -1]$

5.4
The Second Derivative Test

In this section we present a second method for classifying critical points. This method, which is based on the second derivative of the function, is called the **second derivative test** and is often easier to use than the first derivative test.

The basis for the method is the concavity of the graph of a function, which was discussed in Section 3.6. Recall that when the second derivative f'' of a function f is positive, the graph of $y = f(x)$ is concave upward. If $x = c$ is a point at which there is a horizontal tangent line [that is, $f'(c) = 0$] and the curve is concave upward, then there is a relative minimum at $x = c$. That is, if $f'(c) = 0$ and $f''(c) > 0$, there must be a relative minimum at $x = c$. This is shown in Figure 5.17.

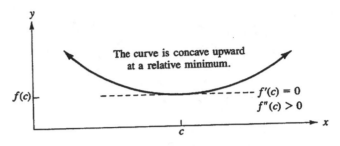

Figure 5.17

When $f'(c) = 0$ and the graph is concave upward at $x = c$, there is a relative minimum at $x = c$.

Similarly, we know that when f'' is negative, the graph of $y = f(x)$ is concave downward. It is also true that if $f'(c) = 0$ and the graph is concave downward, there is a relative maximum at $x = c$. Consequently, when $f'(c) = 0$ and $f''(c) < 0$, there must be a relative maximum at $x = c$. This is shown in Figure 5.18.

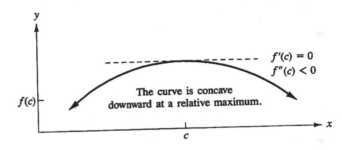

Figure 5.18

When $f'(c) = 0$ and the graph is concave downward at $x = c$, there is a relative maximum at $x = c$.

**Theorem 5.4
The Second Derivative Test**

> Suppose $x = c$ is a critical point of f at which $f'(c) = 0$. Assume $f''(c)$ exists.
> 1. If $f''(c) > 0$, then f has a **relative minimum** at $x = c$.
> 2. If $f''(c) < 0$, then f has a **relative maximum** at $x = c$.
> 3. If $f''(c) = 0$, then the test gives no information.

When we say that the second derivative test gives no information about a critical point, we mean that there may be a relative minimum, a relative maximum, or neither at that point. Exercises 36–39 illustrate this case.

The second derivative test has one advantage over the first derivative test: it is not necessary to select test points "near" the critical point; it is sufficient to check the sign of the second derivative exactly at the critical point. There are, however, some disadvantages: for many functions, especially products and quotients, the computation of the second derivative itself takes longer than just using the first derivative; it can be used only when $f''(c)$ exists; and the test may fail, forcing the use of the first derivative test anyway. As a rule of thumb, if the second derivative is easy to find, use the second derivative test. Otherwise, use the first derivative test.

EXAMPLE 1

Find and classify the critical points of

$$f(x) = x^3 - 12x^2 + 21x + 8.$$

SOLUTION

Since the derivative is

$$f'(x) = 3x^2 - 24x + 21$$
$$= 3(x - 1)(x - 7),$$

there are critical points at $x = 1$ and $x = 7$. The second derivative is

$$f''(x) = 6x - 24.$$

Because $f''(1) = -18$, there is a relative maximum at $x = 1$; also $f''(7) = +18$, so there is a relative minimum at $x = 7$.   ●

EXAMPLE 2

Find and classify the critical points of

$$f(x) = (x + 3)(2x - 10)^3.$$

SOLUTION

The derivative is

$$f'(x) = (2x - 10)^3 + 6(x + 3)(2x - 10)^2$$
$$= (2x - 10)^2(2x - 10 + 6x + 18)$$

or in factored form

$$f'(x) = 8(x + 1)(2x - 10)^2.$$

The critical points are $x = -1$ and $x = 5$. The second derivative is then

$$f''(x) = 8(2x - 10)^2 + 32(x + 1)(2x - 10)$$
$$= 8(2x - 10)(2x - 10 + 4x + 4)$$
$$= 48(2x - 10)(x - 1).$$

Since $f''(-1) = 48(-12)(-2) > 0$, we know that there is a relative minimum at $x = -1$. However, the test fails to give any information at $x = 5$ because $f''(5) = 0$. It is necessary to use the first derivative test to show that there is no relative extreme value at $x = 5$.   ●

In the preceding example, the second derivative test was probably not the best way of classifying the critical points because it took some effort to calculate the second derivative. However, had we also been looking for points of inflection (points where the concavity changes), no extra work would be required. The same comment applies to the next example.

EXAMPLE 3

Find and classify the critical points of
$$f(x) = x^2 e^{-.5x}.$$

SOLUTION

The first derivative of $f(x)$ may be written as
$$f'(x) = 2xe^{-.5x} - .5x^2 e^{-.5x}$$
$$= .5xe^{-.5x}(4 - x),$$

so there are critical points at $x = 0$ and $x = 4$. Taking the second derivative, we find
$$f''(x) = 2e^{-.5x} - xe^{-.5x} - xe^{-.5x} + .25x^2 e^{-.5x}$$
$$= .25e^{-.5x}(8 - 8x + x^2).$$

Recalling that e^x is positive for any x, we see that
$$f''(0) = .25e^0(8) > 0$$

and
$$f''(4) = .25e^{-2}(-8) < 0.$$

Therefore, f has a relative minimum at $x = 0$ and a relative maximum at $x = 4$. ●

EXAMPLE 4

Find and classify the critical points of
$$f(x) = x^3 \ln x.$$

SOLUTION

The derivative of this function is
$$f'(x) = 3x^2 \ln x + x^3\left(\frac{1}{x}\right)$$
$$= 3x^2 \ln x + x^2$$
$$= x^2(3 \ln x + 1).$$

Note that at $x = 0$, the derivative fails to exist, since $\ln 0$ is undefined. However, $x = 0$ is not a critical point because this point is not in the domain of the function. Solving $3 \ln x + 1 = 0$, we find that $\ln x = -1/3$. Thus, $x = e^{-1/3}$ is a critical point. The second derivative is
$$f''(x) = 6x \ln x + 3x^2\left(\frac{1}{x}\right) + 2x$$
$$= 6x \ln x + 5x.$$

At $x = e^{-1/3}$ we have

$$f''(e^{-1/3}) = 6e^{-1/3} \ln e^{-1/3} + 5e^{-1/3}$$

$$= 6e^{-1/3}\left(-\frac{1}{3}\right) + 5e^{-1/3}$$

$$= 3e^{-1/3} > 0.$$

Therefore, there is a relative minimum at $x = e^{-1/3}$.

EXAMPLE 5   Find and classify the critical points of

$$f(x) = x\sqrt{8 - x^2}, \qquad -\sqrt{8} < x < \sqrt{8}.$$

SOLUTION   We find that

$$f'(x) = (8 - x^2)^{1/2} - x^2(8 - x^2)^{-1/2},$$

and factoring out $(8 - x^2)^{-1/2}$ gives the derivative in the form

$$f'(x) = (8 - x^2)^{-1/2}(8 - 2x^2).$$

Therefore, the critical points are $x = 2$ and $x = -2$. The second derivative is then

$$f''(x) = x(8 - x^2)^{-3/2}(8 - 2x^2) - 4x(8 - x^2)^{-1/2}$$

$$= (8 - x^2)^{-3/2}[x(8 - 2x^2) - 4x(8 - x^2)]$$

$$= \frac{2x^3 - 24x}{(8 - x^2)^{3/2}}.$$

Because the sign of the denominator is positive for all x in the domain of the function, it can be seen that $f''(2)$ is negative and $f''(-2)$ is positive. Consequently, f has a relative maximum at $x = 2$ and a relative minimum at $x = -2$.

EXERCISES 5.4

For each of the functions in Exercises 1–35 find the critical points. Use the second derivative test to classify each as a relative maximum or a relative minimum, when this test can be applied. (Hint: Note that Exercises 1–20 are the same as those of Section 5.3.)

1. $f(x) = 3x^2 - 3x + 4$

2. $f(x) = (5 - x)(2x + 1)$

3. $f(x) = e^{4x^2}$

4. $f(x) = e^{x^2 - 5x + 1}$

5. $f(x) = x^3 + 4x^2 + 5x + 2$

6. $f(x) = x^3 - 2x^2 + x + 2$

7. $f(x) = x^2(x - 8)^2$

8. $f(x) = (x + 1)^2(2x - 5)^2$

9. $f(x) = \frac{1}{2}x^4 + 16x$

10. $f(x) = 3x^4 - 4x^3$

11. $f(x) = 8 \ln x - x^2$

12. $f(x) = \ln x^2 - 6x$

13. $f(x) = xe^{-6x}$

14. $f(x) = x^2e^x$

15. $f(x) = \sqrt{x} - \frac{1}{4}x, \quad x > 0$

16. $f(x) = x - \sqrt{x + 1}, \quad x > -1$

17. $f(x) = \frac{1}{x^2 - 4x + 3}$

18. $f(x) = \frac{x^2}{x^2 - 1}$

19. $f(x) = x \ln x$

20. $f(x) = x^2 \ln x$

21. $f(x) = x^3 + 3x^2 - 45x - 2$

22. $f(x) = 25 + 60x - 9x^2 - 2x^3$

23. $f(x) = 5x^3 - 3x^5$

24. $f(x) = \frac{1}{5}x^5 - 2x^3 - 7x + 3$

25. $f(x) = (x - 6)^2(2x + 8)^2$ 26. $f(x) = e^{1+2x+x^2}$

27. $f(x) = x^2 e^{-3x}$ 28. $f(x) = \frac{1}{x^2 - 6x + 5}$

29. $f(x) = \frac{x^2}{48 - x^2}$ 30. $f(x) = (x - 5)^{4/3}$

31. $f(x) = (2x + 9)^{8/3}$ 32. $f(x) = \ln(x + 3) + \frac{1}{x + 3}$

33. $f(x) = x^2 - 12\ln(x + 1)$

34. $f(x) = \frac{1}{\sqrt{7 + 6x - x^2}}$ 35. $f(x) = \frac{1}{\sqrt{9 - x^2}}$

36. Show that the second derivative test gives no information about the critical point in $f(x) = (x - 2)^3$, $g(x) = (x - 2)^4$, and $h(x) = -(x - 2)^6$. Then use the first derivative test to classify the critical point in each case.

37. Show that

$$f(x) = 6 \ln x + (x^3 - 9x)$$

has a critical point at $x = 1$ and that the second derivative test does not provide any information about it. Classify it with the first derivative test.

38. Show that

$$f(x) = \ln(x^2 + 1) - x^2$$

has a critical point at $x = 0$ and that the second derivative test does not provide any information about it. Classify it with the first derivative test.

39. Show that

$$f(x) = 5 + 6x - x^2 + e^{(x-3)^2}$$

has a critical point at $x = 3$ and that the second derivative test does not provide any information about it. Classify it with the first derivative test.

40. Use the second derivative test to show that for the quadratic function $f(x) = ax^2 + bx + c$ the sign of a determines whether the function has an absolute maximum or an absolute minimum.

5.5
Graphing Functions

Having developed methods for locating relative maxima, relative minima, and points of inflection, it is possible to systematically sketch graphs of many functions. Knowing the location of these points allows us to pin down the exact places where the function turns around or changes its concavity. By plotting a few other points and observing the location of any asymptotes, a fairly good sketch can be obtained, especially when the function is continuous.

Summary

Use the following steps to sketch a graph of $y = f(x)$.

1. Determine the domain of f. Plot any x-intercepts that are easily obtained and indicate any asymptotes that may exist.

2. Compute f'. Find and plot all critical points. Indicate whether f is increasing or decreasing between consecutive critical points.

3. Compute f''. Find and plot all points where $f''(x) = 0$. Indicate the concavity of f between these points.

4. Plot a few other points if needed and sketch the curve.

EXAMPLE 1

Sketch the graph of the function

$$f(x) = x^3 + 3x^2 - 24x - 20.$$

SOLUTION

1. This is a polynomial function, so it is defined and continuous for all x, but it has no asymptotes. Finding the x-intercepts of a cubic polynomial is generally a difficult task; we move to step 2.

2. The derivative of f is

$$f'(x) = 3x^2 + 6x - 24$$
$$= 3(x - 2)(x + 4).$$

Therefore, the critical points are $x = -4$ and $x = 2$. For $x < -4$, f' is positive; for $-4 < x < 2$, f' is negative; and for $x > 2$, f' is again positive. Therefore, there is a relative maximum at $x = -4$ and a relative minimum at $x = 2$. We compute $f(-4) = 60$ and $f(2) = -48$ and plot these points in Figure 5.19(a).

3. The second derivative is

$$f''(x) = 6x + 6.$$

Because f'' is negative for $x < -1$ and positive for $x > -1$, the graph has an inflection point at $x = -1$ and is concave downward to the left and concave upward to the right. We note that $f(-1) = 6$. This is shown in Figure 5.19(b).

4. The graph of $y = f(x)$ is shown in Figure 5.19(c), where a few other points have also been plotted.

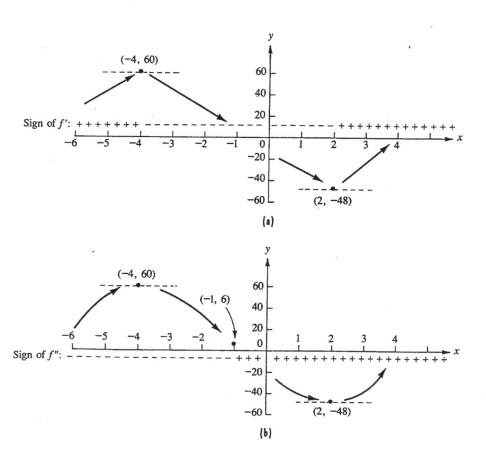

Figure 5.19
Sketching the graph of $f(x) = x^3 + 3x^2 - 24x - 20$. (a) Intervals on which f is increasing or decreasing. (b) Intervals on which f is concave upward or downward. (c) The finished graph.

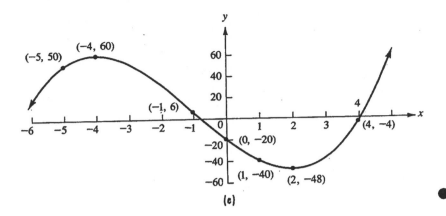

Figure 5.19
continued

EXAMPLE 2

Sketch the graph of $f(x) = 3x^4 - 16x^3 + 24x^2 + 10$.

SOLUTION

1. The function is a polynomial, so we know that it is continuous and defined for all x. Again we omit the difficult step of finding the x-intercepts for this polynomial function.

2. The derivative is

$$f'(x) = 12x^3 - 48x^2 + 48x$$

and

$$12x^3 - 48x^2 + 48x = 0$$

is solved by factoring the left side:

$$12x(x^2 - 4x + 4) = 12x(x - 2)^2 = 0.$$

The critical points are $x = 0$ and $x = 2$; at these points $f(0) = 10$ and $f(2) = 26$. These points are plotted in Figure 5.20(a). From its factored form we find that f' is negative for $x < 0$ and positive on all the other intervals. Therefore, the function is decreasing for $x < 0$ and increasing for $x > 0$.

3. The second derivative is

$$f''(x) = 36x^2 - 96x + 48.$$

Solving $f''(x) = 0$, we obtain

$$36x^2 - 96x + 48 = 12(3x - 2)(x - 2) = 0$$

or $x = 2/3$ and $x = 2$ as points where the concavity might change. These are plotted in Figure 5.20(b). Since f'' is positive for $x < 2/3$ and for $x > 2$, the graph is concave upward on these intervals. Since f'' is negative for $2/3 < x < 2$, the curve is concave downward on this interval. See Figure 5.20(b).

4. The graph is sketched in Figure 5.20(c), where a few additional points have been plotted.

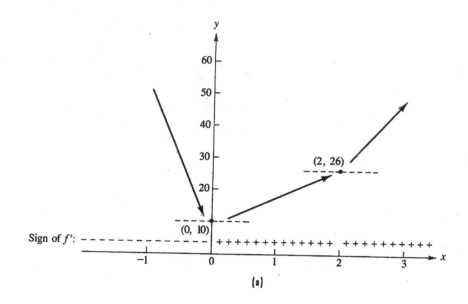

(a)

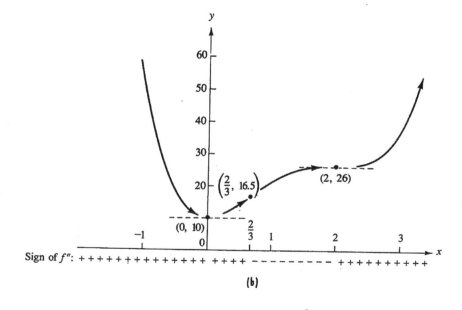

Figure 5.20
Sketching the graph of
$f(x) = 3x^4 - 16x^3 + 24x^2 + 10$.
(a) Intervals on which f is increasing
or decreasing. (b) Intervals on which f
is concave upward or downward.
(c) The finished graph.

(b)

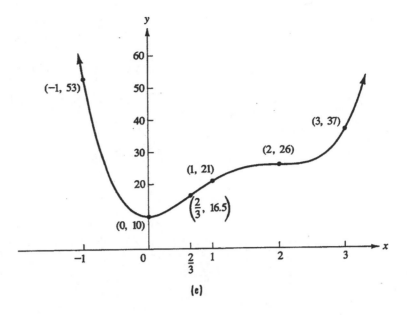

Figure 5.20
continued

(c)

EXAMPLE 3

Sketch the graph of

$$f(x) = \frac{x^2 - 1}{x^2 + 3}.$$

SOLUTION

1. This is a rational function for which the denominator is always positive. Therefore, the function is defined and continuous for all x. Also note that for $x = 1$ and $x = -1$, the function is 0, so there are x-intercepts at these points. Moreover, the limit of f at ∞ and at $-\infty$ is 1, so $y = 1$ is a horizontal asymptote of the graph.

2. The derivative of f is

$$f'(x) = \frac{(x^2 + 3)(2x) - (x^2 - 1)(2x)}{(x^2 + 3)^2}$$

$$= \frac{8x}{(x^2 + 3)^2},$$

which is 0 at $x = 0$. We see that f' is negative for $x < 0$ and is positive for $x > 0$. Therefore, the graph reaches a relative minimum at $x = 0$. Finally, we calculate $f(0) = -1/3$. This is indicated in Figure 5.21(a).

3. To check the concavity, we find that

$$f''(x) = \frac{(x^2 + 3)^2(8) - (8x)(4x)(x^2 + 3)}{(x^2 + 3)^4}$$

$$= \frac{8x^2 + 24 - 32x^2}{(x^2 + 3)^3}$$

$$= \frac{24(1 - x^2)}{(x^2 + 3)^3}.$$

We see then that the graph is concave downward for $x < -1$ and for $x > 1$. On the interval $-1 < x < 1$, the curve is concave upward. This is also shown in Figure 5.21(a).

4. The graph of the function is shown in Figure 5.21(b).

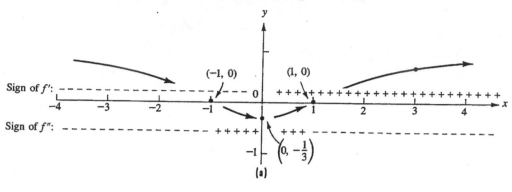

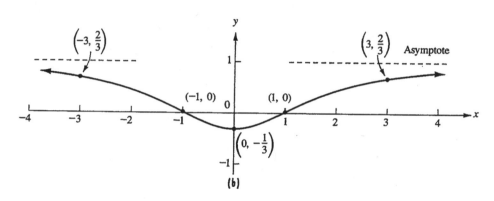

Figure 5.21

Sketching the graph of $f(x) = (x^2 - 1)/(x^2 + 3)$. (a) Intervals on which the curve is increasing and decreasing; where the curve is concave upward and downward. (b) The complete graph.

EXAMPLE 4

Sketch the graph of the function

$$f(x) = \frac{x^2}{x - 3}.$$

SOLUTION

1. This rational function is not defined at $x = 3$. The limit from the left at $x = 3$ is $-\infty$; the limit from the right is $+\infty$. Thus the graph of f has a vertical asymptote at $x = 3$. This rational function does not have horizontal asymptotes. The only x-intercept is $x = 0$.

2. The derivative of f is

$$f'(x) = \frac{(x - 3)(2x) - x^2}{(x - 3)^2}$$

$$= \frac{x^2 - 6x}{(x - 3)^2},$$

which is 0 at $x = 0$ and at $x = 6$. We find that f' is positive for $x < 0$ and for $x > 6$; it is negative for $0 < x < 3$ and $3 < x < 6$. Therefore, the function has a relative maximum at $x = 0$ and a relative minimum at $x = 6$. We calculate that $f(0) = 0$ and $f(6) = 12$. Figure 5.22(a) shows this information.

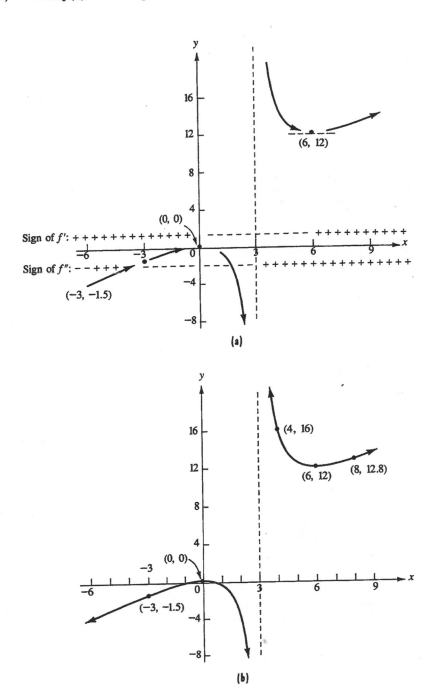

Figure 5.22
Sketching the graph of $f(x) = x^2/(x - 3)$. (a) Intervals on which the curve is increasing and decreasing; where the curve is concave upward and downward. (b) The complete graph.

3. The second derivative is

$$f''(x) = \frac{(x-3)^2(2x-6) - (x^2-6x)(2)(x-3)}{(x-3)^4}$$

$$= \frac{(x-3)(2x-6) - 2(x^2-6x)}{(x-3)^3}$$

$$= \frac{18}{(x-3)^3}.$$

Although the curve is concave downward for $x < 3$ and concave upward for $x > 3$, $x = 3$ is not an inflection point of f since 3 is not in the domain of f.

4. The complete graph of the function is shown in Figure 5.22(b). ●

EXERCISES 5.5

For Exercises 1–15 locate all relative extrema and points of inflection of the given function. Determine the intervals where the function is increasing, decreasing, concave upward, and concave downward. Use this information to sketch the graph of each function. (Hint: Each function is defined and continuous for all x.)

1. $f(x) = x^3 - 12x$

2. $f(x) = x^3 - 3x^2 - 9x + 8$

3. $f(x) = x^3 - 3x^2 + 3x + 1$

4. $f(x) = 4 - 9x + 6x^2 - x^3$

5. $f(x) = x^4 - 6x^2$

6. $f(x) = x^4 - 8x^3$

7. $f(x) = (x+1)^3(x-2)$

8. $f(x) = (x-1)^2(x-5)^2$

9. $f(x) = x^3(x+10)^2$

10. $f(x) = e^{x^2}$

11. $f(x) = xe^x$

12. $f(x) = 4xe^{.5x}$

13. $f(x) = \ln(x^2 + 16)$

14. $f(x) = \ln(x^2 - 2x + 10)$ (*Hint:* $x^2 - 2x + 10 > 0$, for all x.)

15. $f(x) = \dfrac{\sqrt{54}}{\sqrt{x^2 + 18}}$ (*Hint:* Observe that the graph will have the x-axis as a horizontal asymptote.)

In Exercises 16–24 determine the domain of the rational function and any horizontal or vertical asymptotes. Then find the intervals on which the graph is increasing, decreasing, concave upward, or concave downward. Locate all extreme points and points of inflection. Then sketch a graph of the function.

16. $f(x) = \dfrac{8-x}{x+4}$

17. $f(x) = \dfrac{4x+5}{2x-3}$

18. $f(x) = \dfrac{8}{x^2 - 6x + 5}$

19. $f(x) = \dfrac{x}{9 + x^2}$

20. $f(x) = \dfrac{x^2}{x+1}$

21. $f(x) = \dfrac{x^2 - 3}{x - 2}$

22. $f(x) = \dfrac{x^2 + 8}{x + 1}$

23. $f(x) = \dfrac{3x^2}{6 + x^2}$

24. $f(x) = \dfrac{x^2}{16 - x^2}$

5.6
More Applied Maxima and Minima

In Section 5.2 the extreme value theorem was used to maximize and minimize continuous functions on closed intervals. Now we consider cases where the domain need not be a closed interval, but the function has only one relative extreme point.

Theorem 5.5
Unique Extremum Theorem

If a continuous function f has exactly one relative extreme value on an interval, then that value is an absolute extreme value on the interval. Specifically, if the relative extreme value is a relative minimum, then it is also an absolute minimum; if the unique relative extreme value is a relative maximum, then it is also an absolute maximum.

Figure 5.23 illustrates the unique extremum theorem in the case of a relative minimum. If $f(c)$ is a relative minimum of f and if $f(x)$ were to take on a smaller value at some $x = d$, then this continuous function must turn around somewhere between c and d, giving rise to a relative maximum [contrary to $f(c)$ being the only relative extreme value of f].

Figure 5.23

The only relative extreme value of the continuous function f is a relative minimum at $x = c$; thus, $f(c)$ is the absolute minimum.

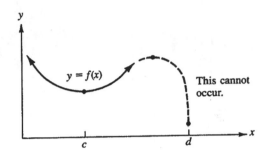

EXAMPLE 1

A closed rectangular box with a square base and a volume of 10 cu ft is to be constructed with a heavy-duty base. If the material for the base costs \$3 per square foot and the material for the top and sides costs \$2 per square foot, find the dimensions of the box that will be cheapest to build under these conditions.

SOLUTION

Letting x denote the length of a side of the base and h the height, to meet the volume requirement we must have $hx^2 = 10$; thus $h = 10/x^2$. The total cost in dollars is determined by adding the cost of the bottom, the top, and the four sides:

$$C = 3x^2 + 2x^2 + 2(4xh).$$

Substituting for h and simplifying, we have

$$C = 5x^2 + \frac{80}{x}, \qquad x > 0.$$

Since x can be any positive real number, we are working on the interval $(0, \infty)$ where the derivative of C with respect to x is

$$C' = 10x - \frac{80}{x^2}, \qquad x > 0.$$

Thus $C' = 0$ if $10x = 80/x^2$, or $x^3 = 8$; that is, $x = 2$. Applying the second derivative test, we get

$$C'' = 10 + \frac{160}{x^3} > 0 \qquad \text{for } x > 0;$$

thus C has a relative minimum at $x = 2$. Since this is the only relative extreme value of C on $(0, \infty)$, we conclude that C has an absolute minimum when $x = 2$. The dimensions of the cheapest box are thus $x = 2$ ft and $h = 2.5$ ft.   ●

EXAMPLE 2   The plant manager for Breezy Hair Dryers determines that daily fixed costs at the plant are $288, and that up to 80 dryers per day can be produced at a variable cost of $20 each. Due to crowding and other inefficiencies, for each dryer produced beyond 80 dryers per day, the variable cost increases by $.02 (for all dryers produced). Find the daily output level that minimizes the average cost of each dryer produced.

SOLUTION   Reasoning that $q - 80$ represents the number of dryers produced "beyond" 80, when $q > 80$ the variable cost per dryer v is

$$\begin{aligned} v &= 20 + .02(q - 80) \\ &= 20 + .02q - 1.6 \\ &= 18.4 + .02q. \end{aligned}$$

So the total cost function is given by the "split" rule:

$$C = \begin{cases} 288 + 20q & \text{if } 0 < q \le 80 \\ 288 + 18.4q + .02q^2 & \text{if } q > 80, \end{cases}$$

and the average cost per unit produced $A = C/q$ is given by

$$A = \begin{cases} \dfrac{288}{q} + 20 & \text{if } 0 < q \le 80 \\ \dfrac{288}{q} + 18.4 + .02q & \text{if } q > 80. \end{cases}$$

Note that A is continuous at $q = 80$, and since plant capacity is not known, we let $(0, \infty)$ be the domain of A and seek its critical points. Differentiating with respect to q, we find

$$A' = \begin{cases} -\dfrac{288}{q^2} & \text{if } 0 < q < 80 \\ -\dfrac{288}{q^2} + .02 & \text{if } q > 80. \end{cases}$$

The value of q where the rule of correspondence is split, $q = 80$, is a possible critical point. In fact, a careful analysis shows that $A'(80)$ does not exist. (See Figure 5.24.) For $0 < q < 80$, $A' < 0$ so there are no critical points between 0 and 80. To the right of 80, $A' = 0$ if

$$-\frac{288}{q^2} + .02 = 0;$$

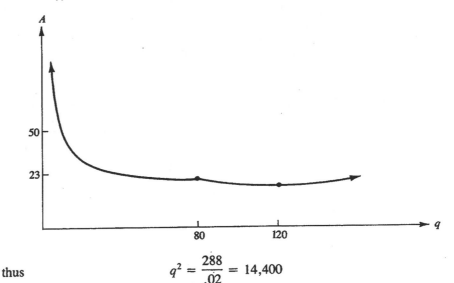

Figure 5.24

The graph of

$$A = \begin{cases} 288/q + 20 & \text{if } 0 < q \le 80 \\ 288/q + 18.4 + .02q & \text{if } q > 80. \end{cases}$$

thus
$$q^2 = \frac{288}{.02} = 14{,}400$$

or
$$q = 120.$$

Testing the critical points, we have seen that $A' < 0$ to the left of $q = 80$. Checking a value between 80 and 120, say $q = 100$, we find

$$A'(100) = -.0288 + .02 = -.0088,$$

so A' does not change sign at $q = 80$, and thus A does not have a relative extreme value at $q = 80$. To the right of 120, say at $q = 130$, $A'(130) = .00296$; hence, by the first derivative test A has a relative minimum at $q = 120$. Since this is the only relative extreme value of A on $(0, \infty)$, $A(120) = \$23.20$ is the absolute minimum average cost.   ●

EXAMPLE 3   For the annual rental value of a consumer durable, Brems* suggests a model of the form

$$E = \frac{P}{y} + Ry^a,$$

where E is the annual expenditure, y is the life of the product in years, P is the replacement cost, R denotes typical repair costs during the first year, and a is a positive constant used to reflect the increased repairs needed with increasing age of the product.

For a new automobile you have determined that

$$E = \frac{8550}{y} + 150y^{4/3}, \qquad y > 0.$$

Find the life y of the automobile that minimizes the annual expenditure E.

---

*H. Brems, *Quantitative Economic Theory: A Synthetic Approach* (New York: Wiley, 1968), p. 37.

SOLUTION

Noting that the replacement cost per year, $8550/y$, is decreasing while the repair cost, $150y^{4/3}$, is increasing, we differentiate E with respect to y to obtain

$$E' = -\frac{8550}{y^2} + 150\left(\frac{4}{3}\right)y^{1/3}$$

$$= -\frac{8550}{y^2} + 200y^{1/3}.$$

Thus $E' = 0$ if $y^{7/3} = 8550/200 = 42.75$. Using a calculator we find that $y = 42.75^{3/7} \doteq 5$ is the only critical point of E. Now,

$$E'' = \frac{17,100}{y^3} + \frac{200}{3y^{2/3}} > 0 \qquad \text{for } y > 0;$$

hence by the second derivative test and the unique extremum theorem, E has an absolute minimum value when $y = 5$.   ●

In the previous example we determined the optimal life of a durable good by striking a balance between the annual replacement cost and the annual repair cost. In the next example we consider the so-called economic order quantity (EOQ) problem in which we seek the order size that yields a trade-off between inventory or carrying costs and ordering or set-up costs.

EXAMPLE 4

Full Stride Industries annually produces and sells 8000 pairs of Winner running shoes. Demand for the Winner is uniform in the sense that sales are about the same from day to day. Production machinery could be set up once each year to produce 8000 pairs in one lot. The shoes would then be stored until they are sold. At the other extreme, the machinery could be set up to produce 32 pairs of shoes on each of the 250 working days in a year. In the first case set-up costs, which are estimated to be $24 per run, would be incurred only once. In the latter case they would be incurred 250 times. Carrying costs for such things as insurance and storage space are estimated to be 12% of the value of an average inventory. If the average cost of producing each pair of Winners is $20, find the lot size and number of runs that minimize costs.

SOLUTION

Given that the average cost per pair of Winners is $20 and that 8000 pairs are to be produced, total production cost for the shoes will be $20(8000) = \$160,000$ regardless of the lot size and number of runs. The costs we must consider are the set-up and carrying costs. If q denotes the lot size and n the number of runs,

$$nq = 8000,$$

so

$$n = \frac{8000}{q}.$$

Set-up costs are $24 per run, and thus for lot size q they amount to $24(8000/q)$. Storage costs are 12% of the value of the average inventory. This value is $20 times the average number of pairs of shoes in inventory. Since consumption is uniform, after each production run the inventory declines steadily from q to 0, so we take $q/2$ to be the average number of shoes in inventory. Carrying costs are thus $.12(20)(q/2)$. Letting S denote the combined set-up and storage costs, we have

$$S = 24\left(\frac{8000}{q}\right) + .12(20)\left(\frac{q}{2}\right)$$

$$= \frac{192,000}{q} + 1.2q, \qquad 32 \le q \le 8000.$$

Differentiating S with respect to q, we see

$$S' = -\frac{192,000}{q^2} + 1.2,$$

and so $S' = 0$ if

$$q^2 = \frac{192,000}{1.2} = 160,000;$$

thus, $q = 400$ is the only critical point of S. Furthermore,

$$S'' = \frac{384,000}{q^3} > 0 \qquad \text{for } q > 0,$$

and S has an absolute minimum when the lot size is 400 and there are $8000/400 = 20$ runs. ●

EXERCISES 5.6

For Exercises 1–12 determine whether the given function has a unique relative extreme value on the indicated interval. When this is the case draw the appropriate conclusion using the unique extremum theorem.

1. $f(x) = x^2 - 6x + 10$; $(0, 4)$

2. $g(x) = 3x^2 - 9$; $(1, 5)$

3. $h(x) = 2x^3 - 9x^2 + 12x + 5$; $(0, 5)$

4. $p(x) = x^3 - 3x + 7$; $(0, \infty)$

5. $h(x) = x^3 - 6x^2 + 9x - 5$; $(0, 2)$

6. $g(x) = 2x^3 - 3x^2 - 12x + 7$; $(-\infty, 0)$

7. $f(x) = \sqrt{x^2 - 2x + 2}$; $(0, \infty)$

8. $p(x) = \sqrt{x^2 - 8x + 17}$; $(0, \infty)$

9. $g(x) = \dfrac{x - 1}{x^2 + 24}$; $(0, 8)$

10. $h(x) = \dfrac{x + 2}{x^2 + 21}$; $(0, 10)$

11. $f(x) = e^{-x^2}$; $(-\infty, \infty)$

12. $g(x) = \ln(x^2 - 10x + 30)$; $(-\infty, \infty)$

13. A closed rectangular box with a square base and a volume of 7 cu ft is to be built using heavy-duty material for the bottom and sides. If the material for the top costs \$3 per square foot while that for the bottom and sides costs \$4 per square foot, find the dimensions of the most economical box.

14. The production division of Petty Publication Company has determined that each page of a new textbook must contain

72 sq in. of printed material. Furthermore, this rectangular region of printed material is to be bordered by ½-in. margins on each side and 1-in. margins on the top and bottom. To reduce costs, Petty wishes to make the pages as small as possible. Find the dimensions of the page with the smallest possible area that meets the given requirements.

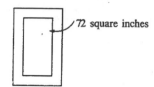
72 square inches

15. Basic Furniture Corporation can produce up to 72 three-legged stools per day at a variable cost of $12 per stool. Fixed costs are $300 per day and daily plant capacity is 150 stools. Due to crowding, for each stool beyond 72 that is produced in a day, the variable cost per stool increases by $.03 for all stools produced. Find the daily production level that minimizes the average cost per stool produced.

16. An open box with a volume of 16 cu ft is to be formed by cutting identical squares from each corner of a square sheet of metal of length s on a side and then folding up the sides. Find the length of a side of the smallest square of metal that can be used for this purpose. (*Hint:* Write s as a function of x.)

17. Tape recorders used in the Music Laboratory at Beta University have a replacement value of $80 and an average first-year repair bill of $5. Using these data the annual rental value of these machines over y years is estimated by

$$E = \frac{80}{y} + 5y^2, \qquad y > 0.$$

Find the life of the tape recorders for which E is minimized.

18. The annual rental value of Arid Clothes Dryers over y years when used in a laundromat is given by

$$E = \frac{500}{y} + 10y^{5/4}, \qquad y > 0.$$

Find the life y of Arid Dryers that minimizes E.

19. The annual rental value of Speedprint Electronic Typewriters over y years of typical office use is estimated by

$$E = \frac{1500}{y} + 200y^{1/2}, \qquad y > 0.$$

Find the life y of these typewriters that minimizes E.

20. Referring to Figure 5.23, suppose that f is continuous on an interval containing c and d, that f(c) is a relative minimum of f, and that f(d) < f(c). By the extreme value theorem, f must have an absolute maximum on [c, d]. Show that neither f(c) nor f(d) can be this maximum, so it must occur at some e where c < e < d. Finally, show that f(e) is a relative maximum.

21. Richland Rubber Mills has daily fixed costs of $432 at their hip boot plant. Up to 50 pairs of boots per day can be produced at this plant at a variable cost of $30 per pair. Beyond this output level the variable cost per pair increases by $.12 per pair for all pairs produced. Find the daily output level at which the average cost per pair of hip boots is minimized.

22. Prime Spirits Distillery annually bottles and sells 12,000 1-L bottles of gin. The average cost of producing a bottle of gin is $3 and the set-up costs associated with bottling are $100. Carrying costs are estimated to be 5% of the value of an average inventory. If gin sales are uniform, find the lot size and the number of runs that give rise to minimum set-up and carrying costs.

23. Good Sports sells 2400 golf shirts per year at a uniform rate. The shirts are ordered for $8 each plus a $4.50 handling charge per order (regardless of the size of the order). If carrying costs are estimated to be 12% of the value of an average inventory, find the lot size and number of orders that will minimize carrying and ordering costs.

24. For the general EOQ problem, if a product has an annual uniform demand of D units, ordering or set-up costs of S dollars per run, and carrying costs of I dollars per item in inventory, show that the optimum lot size is $q = \sqrt{2SD/I}$, and that for this lot size carrying and set-up costs both equal $\sqrt{SDI/2}$.

25. Pure Air Industries annually manufactures and sells 96,000 furnace filters. The average cost of producing each filter is $.30. Set-up costs for each production run are $10, while carrying costs are estimated to be 10% of the value of an average inventory. If demand for filters is uniform, find the lot size and number of runs that minimize set-up and storage costs.

26. The variable cost per unit for the production of q Express Tires in a given day is

$$v = 18 - .02q + .00002q^2, \qquad 0 < q \le 500.$$

If the demand function for Express Tires is

$$p = 34 - .028q, \qquad 0 < q \le 500,$$

find the daily production level that will result in a maximum profit. (Assume that fixed costs are $100 per day.)

27. Referring to Exercise 26, suppose that Express Tires is assessed a lump-sum tax (or license fee) that amounts to $4 per day. Treating this tax as a portion of the fixed costs, find the output level that maximizes profit after taxes. What effect does a lump-sum tax have on the optimum output level?

28. Suppose that instead of the lump-sum tax proposed in Exercise 27, Express Tires is assessed a windfall profits tax of 8%; that is, the new profit function is .92 times the old one. Find the output level that maximizes profit after this tax. What effect does the percentage profits tax have on the optimal output level?

29. Instead of the taxation schemes suggested in Exercises 27 and 28, suppose a $3.05 per tire output tax is levied against Express Tires. Treating this tax as part of the variable cost per tire produced, find the output level that maximizes profit. What effect does an output tax have on the optimal output level?

30. Suppose that R and C are the revenue and cost functions before an output tax of t dollars per unit is assessed some firm. Suppose that R and C are differentiable functions of q and that profit is maximized before the taxation at output level $q = q_0$. Show that the after-tax profit is maximized when $MR = MC + t$, and that this new output level is less than q_0.

31. The Department of Revenue is planning to assess an output tax of t dollars per tire against the Express Tires Company. (See Exercise 26.) Assuming that Express Tires always adjusts the output level to realize the maximum profit, find the value of t that will yield the maximum tax revenue. [*Hint:* If S denotes tax revenue, then $S = tq$, where q is the output level. But as shown in Exercise 30, $t = MR - MC$ so S may be written (and maximized) as a function of q.]

| 5.7 |
| Differentials |

Responsible persons in managerial positions who can change the value or level of some business variable must first estimate the effect of that change. For example, the owner of a clothing store knows that raising the price of dress shirts will decrease the demand for these shirts. However, it would be very useful to be able to estimate the actual drop in the number of shirts that would be sold. Perhaps revenue could be increased in spite of the reduced demand.

As a second example, consider the situation faced by the marketing department of a company that makes health care products. An increase in the advertising budget will increase sales, but will the additional revenue from the sales justify the extra advertising cost?

In both of these cases it is necessary to estimate the change in the dependent variable resulting from a change in the independent variable. In this section we show how the derivative of a function can be used for this purpose when there is a small change in the independent variable.

Suppose x is an independent variable and y is a dependent variable with $y = f(x)$. If x_0 is the current value of x but a change of Δx (delta x) from x_0 is contemplated, then the resulting change in y will be from $f(x_0)$ to $f(x_0 + \Delta x)$. This change in y is denoted Δy; that is,

$$\Delta y = f(x_0 + \Delta x) - f(x_0).$$

Figure 5.25 illustrates the relationship between Δx and Δy for a particular function.

If the function f relating x and y was linear, then $\Delta y / \Delta x$ would be the slope m of this linear function and $\Delta y = m \, \Delta x$ would relate the change in y to any change in x. For general functions, $\Delta y / \Delta x$ changes between different pairs of points on the

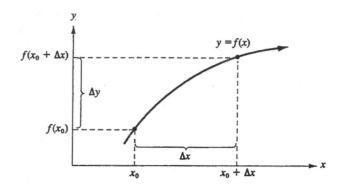

Figure 5.25
The relationship between Δx and Δy
for a particular function f

graph. However, if $f'(x_0)$ exists and Δx is small, then

$$\frac{f(x_0 + \Delta x) - f(x_0)}{\Delta x} \doteq f'(x_0),$$

so

$$\frac{\Delta y}{\Delta x} \doteq f'(x_0)$$

and thus

$$\Delta y \doteq f'(x_0)\,\Delta x.$$

In words, if x is changed from x_0 by an amount Δx, the corresponding change in y is approximately the derivative of f at x_0 times the change in x. This approximation is called the **differential** of y and is denoted dy; that is,

(5.1)

$$dy = f'(x_0)\,\Delta x.$$

Figure 5.26 illustrates the relationship between Δx, Δy, and dy. Notice that dy is the vertical change along the tangent line as x changes from x_0 to $x_0 + \Delta x$. For a small Δx, dy is a good approximation to Δy.

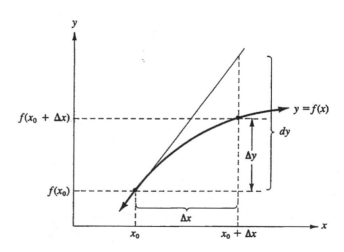

Figure 5.26
Comparing the change in y:
$\Delta y = f(x_0 + \Delta x) - f(x_0)$, to the
differential of y: $dy = f'(x_0)\,\Delta x$

EXAMPLE 1   The Shush Ski factory currently produces 40 pairs of skis per day. The plant manager has determined that the marginal cost at this production level is \$56 and would like to increase production to 42 pairs of skis per day. Approximate the additional cost associated with this additional output.

SOLUTION   If $C(q)$ is the total cost of producing q pairs of skis per day, we would like to know $\Delta C = C(42) - C(40)$. We have $C'(40) = 56$ and $\Delta q = 2$, so we can estimate ΔC using

$$dC = C'(q)\,\Delta q$$
$$= 56(2)$$
$$= \$112.$$

By using differentials, we are able to approximate the additional cost without knowing the total cost function.   ●

For consistency in notation, we let dx represent the change in x; that is, $dx = \Delta x$, whereas dy is only an approximation to Δy. Formally, we have the following definition.

Definition 5.4

Let $y = f(x)$ be a differentiable function. Then the **differential of x** is $dx = \Delta x$ for any change in x and the **differential of y** is

(5.2) $dy = f'(x)\,dx;$

that is, the differential of y is the derivative of f multiplied by the differential of x.

EXAMPLE 2   Find dy for each of the following functions.
a. $y = x^3$
b. $y = \ln(4x^2 - 5x + 2)$
c. $y = \dfrac{x + 7}{2x - 3}$

SOLUTION   a. Since $y' = 3x^2$, from equation (5.2) we have

$$dy = 3x^2\,dx.$$

b. Using the chain rule, we get

$$y' = \frac{8x - 5}{4x^2 - 5x + 2},$$

so from equation (5.2),

$$dy = \frac{8x - 5}{4x^2 - 5x + 2}\, dx.$$

c. From the quotient rule the derivative of y is

$$y' = -17(2x - 3)^{-2}.$$

By equation (5.2) we have

$$dy = -17(2x - 3)^{-2}\, dx. \qquad\bullet$$

EXAMPLE 3

Approximate $y = \sqrt{x}$ when $x = 79.8$.

SOLUTION

We begin by observing that since $\sqrt{81} = 9$, we know that $\sqrt{79.8}$ must be approximately 9. Let dx be the change in x from 81 to 79.8; that is, let $dx = 79.8 - 81 = -1.2$. (The minus sign is important; x has decreased from 81 to 79.8.) We compute the differential dy when $x = 81$ and $dx = -1.2$ and find

$$dy = \frac{1}{2\sqrt{x}}\, dx = \frac{1}{2\sqrt{81}}(-1.2)$$

$$= -.0667.$$

Now, $\sqrt{79.8} - \sqrt{81} = \Delta y$, or $\sqrt{79.8} = \sqrt{81} + \Delta y$, so the approximate value of $\sqrt{79.8}$ is

$$\sqrt{79.8} \doteq \sqrt{81} + dy = 9 + (-.0667) = 8.9333.$$

From a calculator, the value of $\sqrt{79.8}$ is 8.9331 to four decimal places. Today's calculators make approximations using differentials less important than they were in the past. $\qquad\bullet$

EXAMPLE 4

Suppose that the price p for a dress shirt is related to the monthly volume of shirts q at a clothing store by the demand function

$$q = 800 - 6p - 20\sqrt{p}, \qquad 20 \le p \le 40.$$

If the current price is \$25 per shirt, approximate the effect on the volume if the proprietor raises the price to \$28.

SOLUTION

At a price of \$25, the current monthly volume is 550 shirts. The differential is

$$dq = (-6 - 10p^{-1/2})\, dp.$$

At $p = 25$ (the original price) and $dp = +3$ (the increase), we find

$$dq = [-6 - 10(25)^{-1/2}](3)$$

$$= (-8)(3)$$

$$= -24.$$

That is, the demand for the shirts will decrease by 24 per month to approximately 526. ●

<table>
<tr><td>

EXAMPLE 5

</td><td>

The manager of a marketing department estimates that the response to television advertising is best modeled by the function

$$R = 400 + 50(x - 2)^{.65}, \qquad x \ge 2,$$

where R is the weekly national sales in thousands of dollars and x is the number of prime-time ads that appear each evening on a major network. At present the manager is running 12 ads each evening. Approximate the additional sales that would result from running 2 more ads per night.

</td></tr>
</table>

<table>
<tr><td>

SOLUTION

</td><td>

At present with 12 ads,

$$R = 400 + 50(10)^{.65} \doteq 623.3$$

so the weekly revenue is about $623,300. The differential of R is

$$dR = 32.5(x - 2)^{-.35}\, dx.$$

With $x = 12$ at present and an increase of $dx = 2$, we have

$$dR = 32.5(10)^{-.35}(2)$$
$$\doteq 32.5(.4467)(2)$$
$$\doteq 29.0.$$

</td></tr>
</table>

Thus the 2 additional ads will produce about $29,000 in additional revenue per week. ●

Sometimes we have y as a function of x, $y = f(x)$, but we want to know the approximate change in x that is required to yield some change in y. Returning to equation (5.2), $dy = f'(x)\, dx$, we see that if $f'(x) \ne 0$, we can solve for dx to obtain

(5.3)
$$dx = \frac{dy}{f'(x)}.$$

In equation (5.3) we are considering dx as depending on dy and $f'(x)$. This will be useful whenever for given values of y and dy we know or are able to find the corresponding value of x and thereby $f'(x)$.

<table>
<tr><td>

EXAMPLE 6

</td><td>

Each deer season a local tannery buys deer hides from successful hunters. Assume that when the tannery offers p dollars per hide, the hunters bring in q hides and that

$$q = 2000 + 80p + 300 \ln p, \qquad p \ge 4.$$

</td></tr>
</table>

This season the tannery offered $5 per hide and received 2883 hides. If the owner of the tannery wants to receive 3000 hides next season, approximate the price that will have to be offered.

SOLUTION

The derivative of q with respect to p is

$$\frac{dq}{dp} = 80 + \frac{300}{p},$$

and so from equation (5.3)

$$dp = \frac{dq}{80 + 300/p}.$$

Letting $q = 2883$, the present number of hides, and $dq = +117$, the desired increase, we find

$$dp = \frac{117}{80 + 300/5} = \frac{117}{140} \doteq .84.$$

(Note that it was necessary to know that $p = 5$ corresponds to $q = 2883$.) The owner of the tannery should therefore increase the offering price by about $.84. ●

As a final note the reader may have noticed that the usual notation for derivatives, $dy/dx = f'(x)$, is algebraically equivalent to the differential equations (5.2) and (5.3). Historically, dy and dx were used by Leibniz (one of the founders of the calculus) to denote the changes in y and in x (as we have used Δy and Δx). The quotient dy/dx was then the ratio of these changes. After the limit concept was carefully defined in later centuries, the distinction between Δy and dy was clarified, making the dy/dx notation legitimate. Using this notation and equation (5.3), we see that if $y = f(x)$, then

$$\frac{dy}{dx} = f'(x) \quad \text{and} \quad \frac{dx}{dy} = \frac{1}{f'(x)} \qquad \text{when } f'(x) \neq 0.$$

EXERCISES 5.7

1. DWB Life Insurance is currently selling 20 whole-life policies per day. The marginal revenue at this level of sales is $800. Estimate the additional daily revenue DWB Life would realize if sales increased to 23 policies per day.

2. Tasty Pizza currently produces 5000 pizzas per day. The marginal cost at this production level is $.85. If the output level is increased to 5500 pizzas per day, estimate the associated additional cost.

3. Cylindrical Can Company currently produces 8000 soda cans per day. The marginal cost at this production level is $.02. With slumping sales, Cylindrical has decided to reduce daily production by 1500 cans. Estimate the decrease in total cost associated with this decrease in production.

4. Each day people buy 10,000 Crunchy candy bars. The mar-

ginal revenue at this level of sales is $.20. A chemist discovered that sawdust was the principal Crunchy ingredient and sales fell to 6000 bars per day. Estimate the loss in revenue resulting from this decrease in demand.

Find dy in Exercises 5–14.

5. $y = 5x + 7$

6. $y = x^2$

7. $y = e^{4x}$

8. $y = 1 - 3x + x^2$

9. $y = \sqrt{10 - 3x^2}$

10. $y = (3x + 6)^5$

11. $y = t \ln(t - 2)$

12. $y = \dfrac{3q - 10}{q + 2}$

13. $y = se^{-s^2}$

14. $y = \ln \sqrt{\dfrac{x + 1}{2x - 1}}$

In Exercises 15–22 evaluate dy at the given values of x and Δx. Use a calculator to estimate Δy, the exact change in y, to four decimal places.

15. $y = 4 - 3x;\ x = 10,\ \Delta x = .02$

16. $y = x^2 + 4x + 4;\ x = 5,\ \Delta x = .05$

17. $y = e^{-x};\ x = 0,\ \Delta x = -.03$

18. $y = xe^{x^2-1};\ x = 1,\ \Delta x = .004$

19. $y = \sqrt{2x + 1};\ x = 12,\ \Delta x = .08$

20. $y = \dfrac{3x}{x + 1};\ x = -4,\ \Delta x = -.01$

21. $y = \ln x;\ x = 5,\ \Delta x = -.04$

22. $y = \ln\left[\dfrac{x}{x + 2}\right]^3;\ x = 1,\ \Delta x = .025$

In Exercises 23–30 use differentials to approximate $f(x_2) - f(x_1)$ for each function and each pair of domain values x_2 and x_1. Then use a calculator to find this difference to four decimal places.

23. $f(x) = 2x^2 - 6x + 1;\ x_1 = 3,\ x_2 = 2.97$

24. $f(x) = 5x - x^3;\ x_1 = -2,\ x_2 = -1.90$

25. $f(x) = 3 - x^2 + x^3;\ x_1 = 0,\ x_2 = .04$

26. $f(x) = \sqrt[3]{x};\ x_1 = 8,\ x_2 = 7.80$

27. $f(x) = \ln(x + 5);\ x_1 = -4,\ x_2 = -4.05$

28. $f(x) = \sqrt{x^2 + 2x + 10};\ x_1 = 3,\ x_2 = 3.02$

29. $f(x) = \dfrac{x - 2}{x - 1};\ x_1 = 1.5,\ x_2 = 1.51$

30. $f(x) = x^2 e^x;\ x_1 = 0,\ x_2 = -.1$

In Exercises 31–38 approximate f(x) at the given value of x using differentials. Then use a calculator to find this value to four decimal places.

31. $f(x) = -3x^2;\ x = 4.032$ 32. $f(x) = \sqrt[3]{x};\ x = 7.997$

33. $f(x) = x^4;\ x = 1.0035$ 34. $f(x) = x^{3/2};\ x = 3.985$

35. $f(x) = e^x;\ x = 1.0007$ 36. $f(x) = \sqrt{x + 2};\ x = 7.126$

37. $f(x) = \ln x;\ x = .88$ 38. $f(x) = \dfrac{x}{x + 2};\ x = -2.998$

39. A shipping crate has a square base. Suppose that the height of the crate is 30 in. and the sides of the base are 25 in. by 25 in. Use differentials to estimate the loss in the volume of the crate if the dimensions of the base are reduced by ½ in.

40. Suppose that the crate in Exercise 39 is in the shape of a cube with each side measuring 25 in. Estimate the increase in the volume of the crate if each side is increased by .75 in.

41. Microtech Electronics manufactures a floppy disk designed for use in personal computers. To produce q disks a day, Microtech spends

$$C = 300 + 18q - .002q^2,\qquad 0 \le q \le 500,$$

dollars each day in production costs. Presently the company is making 400 disks a day. Use differentials to estimate the extra cost if Microtech were to increase production to 420 disks a day.

42. Assume that when a chemical company makes a batch of q barrels of its Weed-Tox XTRA brand of herbicide, the average cost per barrel is given by

$$A = 28 - .2\sqrt{q} - .006q,\qquad 0 \le q \le 2000.$$

The company had been making Weed-Tox XTRA in batches of 1600 barrels. To reduce its inventory the company will consider making batches of 1500 barrels. Use differentials to estimate the increase in the average cost per barrel that would result from this decision.

43. The Hokah Company buys blocks of briar from a group of independent suppliers in North Africa to use for making pipes. The number of blocks of briar q that are available each month at a price of p dollars each is modeled by

$$q = 1200(3p - 6)^{2/3},\qquad p \ge 2.$$

At present Hokah is willing to pay \$11 per block and is able to buy 10,800 blocks each month.

a. Estimate how many blocks they would be able to buy if Hokah cut its offering price to \$10.50.

b. How many could be bought if the price were raised to \$11.75?

44. Refer to Exercise 43.

a. Suppose that Hokah felt it had to increase its purchase of briar to 11,500 blocks per month. Estimate how much the company would have to pay per block.

b. If Hokah had a surplus of blocks in a given month and wanted to reduce its purchase to 10,200 blocks, use differentials to estimate what price it should offer.

45. A cosmetics company is about to introduce a new perfume. Its advertising agency has estimated that the percentage of people p who will recognize $Sammi$ as the brand name of the new perfume after t minutes of television ads are aired during the first week is

$$p = 100 - 270e^{-(.01t+1)}, \qquad t \geq 0.$$

Current plans call for airing 30 min of ads during the first week. What percentage of people will recognize $Sammi$? Estimate, using differentials, how much this percentage would increase if 34 min were aired.

46. Refer to Exercise 45. The manufacturer of $Sammi$ wants to achieve a 35% recognition of the product after the first week. Estimate the amount of advertising that would be required to accomplish this.

47. At a produce market, the demand for lemons is related to the market price by the demand function

$$p = 35 - .1275q + .0001q^2, \qquad q \geq 0,$$

where q is the number of cases of lemons and p is dollars per case. At present the price of lemons is $13.50 and there is a demand for 200 cases.

a. If the growers bring 5 more cases to market, use differentials to estimate how the price will be affected.

b. Suppose that because of a drought there is a lemon shortage and the price has risen to $15 per case. Estimate the number of cases that are on the market.

48. The consumption function (see Section 3.5) for an individual is given by

$$C = .92I - .06\sqrt{I} - .00035I^2, \qquad I \geq 10,$$

where C and I are in thousands of dollars per year. Suppose the individual has a current income of $20,000 per year. Estimate how much of a $350 tax refund this individual would consume.

49. A developer is planning to build an apartment complex. Up to 40 apartments can be built on the available land. It is estimated that all the units can be rented at p dollars per month if q units are built, where

$$p = 500 - 8q - .005q^2, \qquad 10 \leq q \leq 40.$$

Current plans of the developer are to build only 25 apartments.

a. Use differentials to estimate how much the rent per unit will have to be lowered if 2 more apartments are built.

b. Write the monthly revenue that will be generated by renting all q apartments. Estimate the change in the revenue that would result from a decision to build 27 units rather than 25.

5.8
Elasticity

A frequent decision in business is whether or not to increase the price of an item. The demand for the item will almost surely drop if the price is raised. However, the revenue or the gross income received may either increase or decrease depending on how much the demand falls relative to the price increase.

The demand for an item is said to be **price elastic** at a price p if the revenue decreases in response to any increase in its price. On the other hand, the demand for a commodity is called **price inelastic** at price p if the revenue increases in response to price increases.

A visual way to remember the difference between elastic and inelastic demand is to imagine that you are holding a band stretched between your hands with one hand directly over the other. Let the upper hand represent the price and the lower one the corresponding revenue. When the band (demand) is elastic, the upper hand (price) and the lower hand (revenue) can move in opposite directions. When the band is inelastic, if the upper hand is raised, the lower hand must follow. (See Figure 5.27.)

The demand for a specific commodity is not inherently price elastic or inelastic, but its elasticity depends on the current price. To see this, imagine that you own a

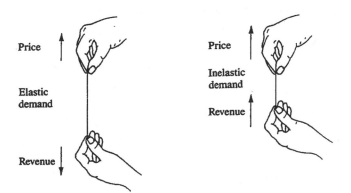

Figure 5.27
Visualizing price elasticity
of demand

restaurant that sells steak dinners. If your price is $1 per dinner, you will surely be selling a lot of steaks. Doubling the price to $2 will certainly double your revenue. (The demand is highly inelastic at a $1 price.) However, if the current price is $20 per dinner, doubling the price might cause your revenue to vanish. (The demand is elastic at a price of $20.)

The OPEC cartel had such an experience in pricing its oil: at $2 a barrel the demand for oil was so inelastic that quintupling the price to $10 a barrel in 1974 brought tremendous wealth to OPEC members. However, the 1979 attempt to push prices to $40 a barrel led to such a slump in demand for OPEC oil that the members' income fell sharply.

To mathematically define the price elasticity of demand, suppose that for some commodity the demand q is a differentiable function of its selling price p. Then revenue R, the product of p and q, may be considered a function of p. Applying the product rule to $R = pq$, we obtain

(5.4)
$$\frac{dR}{dp} = q + p\frac{dq}{dp}.$$

Recalling that demand is price elastic if revenue decreases in response to a price increase, we must have $dR/dp < 0$ or

$$q < -p\frac{dq}{dp}$$

when the demand is elastic. Dividing by q (which is positive) we see that when the demand is elastic,

$$-\frac{p}{q}\frac{dq}{dp} > 1.$$

In a similar fashion it can be shown that, when the demand is inelastic,

$$-\frac{p}{q}\frac{dq}{dp} < 1.$$

In view of these inequalities, we define elasticity.

Definition 5.5

> Let the demand q for an item be given as a function of its price p. Then the **price elasticity of the demand** for the item, denoted η, is given by
>
> (5.5)
> $$\eta = -\frac{p}{q}\frac{dq}{dp}.$$
>
> If $\eta > 1$, the demand is said to be **elastic**; if $\eta < 1$, the demand is said to be **inelastic**.

EXAMPLE 1

Find η for the demand function $q = 300 - 2p$ when $p = 40$.

SOLUTION

First, find the demand itself when $p = 40$:

$$q(40) = 300 - 2(40) = 220.$$

Next, find the derivative:

$$\frac{dq}{dp} = -2.$$

Substituting into equation (5.5), we obtain

$$\eta = -\frac{40}{220}(-2) = .364.$$

Therefore, at a price of $p = 40$, the demand is inelastic; that is, raising the price increases the revenue.   ●

EXAMPLE 2

Find η for the demand function $q = 5000 - 10p - .2p^2$ when $p = 100$.

SOLUTION

At $p = 100$, the demand is

$$q(100) = 5000 - 10(100) - .2(100)^2$$
$$= 2000.$$

The derivative of q is

$$\frac{dq}{dp} = -10 - .4p.$$

At $p = 100$, $dq/dp = -50$. Substituting into equation (5.5), we find the elasticity:

$$\eta = -\frac{100}{2000}(-50) = 2.5.$$

Therefore, the demand is elastic at the price $p = 100$. Raising the price will cause the revenue to fall.   ●

Elasticity can be used to estimate the actual change in the demand that results from a change in the price. To do so requires the use of differentials. If q is a function of p, the differential dp is the change in the price and dq is the (approximate) change in the demand. The quotients dp/p and dq/q are then the percentage change in the price and demand, respectively.

Therefore, we can rewrite the definition of elasticity (5.5) as

(5.6)
$$\eta = -\frac{dq/q}{dp/p}.$$

That is, η can be interpreted as the ratio of the percentage change in demand to the percentage change in the price. (Keep in mind that these changes will be of opposite sign and thus η will be a positive number.) In other words, η is the approximate percentage change in the demand that results from a 1% change in the price.

EXAMPLE 3

Let $q = 1000 - .5p - .02p^{3/2}$ be a demand function. Suppose the price is $400. What is the approximate effect on demand when the price is raised by 2%?

SOLUTION

At $p = 400$, the demand is

$$q = 1000 - .5(400) - .02(400)^{3/2} = 640.$$

The derivative of q at $p = 400$ is

$$\left.\frac{dq}{dp}\right|_{p=400} = \left. -.5 - .03p^{1/2}\right|_{p=400}$$

$$= -.5 - .03(400)^{1/2}$$

$$= -1.10.$$

Substitution into equation (5.5) gives

$$\eta = -\frac{400}{640}(-1.10) = .69.$$

This means that the demand will fall by approximately .69 of 1% if the price is raised by 1%. Therefore, a 2% price increase can be expected to cause the demand to decline by about $2(.69) = 1.38\%$. ●

EXAMPLE 4

Let $p = 50 - .02q^2$ be a demand function. If the present demand is $q = 20$ at a price of $p = 42$, find the approximate change in the demand if the price is cut by 3%.

SOLUTION

Note that p is given as a function of q, but we need the derivative dq/dp. We can do this by finding the differential of p:

$$dp = -.04q\, dq.$$

Then, as long as $-.04q$ is not 0, we can write

$$\frac{dq}{dp} = \frac{1}{-.04q}.$$

At $q = 20$, $dq/dp = -1.25$. Substitution into equation (5.5) gives

$$\eta = -\frac{42}{20}(-1.25) = 2.63.$$

That is, a 1% cut in price will cause demand to rise by about 2.63%. A 3% cut would produce approximately a $3(2.63) = 7.9\%$ increase in demand.   ●

Elasticity may also be used to estimate the change in the revenue R that results from a price change. To see this, we return to equation (5.4):

$$\frac{dR}{dp} = q + p\frac{dq}{dp}$$

and multiply by the differential dp to obtain

$$dR = q\,dp + p\,dq.$$

Factoring out pq, we find

$$dR = pq\left(\frac{dp}{p} + \frac{dq}{q}\right).$$

Division by $R = pq$ gives a formula for the approximate percentage change in the revenue:

(5.7) $$\frac{dR}{R} = \frac{dp}{p} + \frac{dq}{q}.$$

Because dp/p and dq/q are of opposite sign, equation (5.7) may be interpreted as: the percentage change in revenue is approximately equal to the percentage change in the price minus the percentage change in demand. A special case of equation (5.7) occurs when the change in price is a 1% increase. In this case $dq/q = -\eta$. Therefore, if the price is raised by 1%, the percentage change in revenue is

(5.8) $$\frac{dR}{R} = 1 - \eta.$$

Observe that equation (5.8) will be negative when $\eta > 1$ (when demand is elastic) and positive when $\eta < 1$ (when demand is inelastic). We can use equation (5.8) to estimate the change in the revenue for any change in price by multiplying the right side by the percentage change in p.

EXAMPLE 5   Let $q = 80 - .12p - .003p^2$ be a demand function and let $p = 60$ be the current price. Use the elasticity of demand to estimate the change in the revenue if the price is raised 5%.

SOLUTION   When $p = 60$ the demand is

$$q = 80 - .12(60) - .003(60)^2 = 62$$

and the derivative of q is

$$\left.\frac{dq}{dp}\right|_{p=60} = -.12 - .006p \left.\right|_{p=60} = -.48.$$

Substitution into equation (5.5) gives

$$\eta = -\frac{60}{62}(-.48) = .46.$$

Therefore, a 5% price increase leads to approximately a $5(.46) = 2.3\%$ decrease in the demand. From equation (5.7) the approximate percentage change in the revenue is

$$\frac{dR}{R} = 5 + (-2.3) = 2.7;$$

that is, revenue will increase by approximately 2.7%. Note that this can also be obtained by multiplying the right side of equation (5.8) by 5%:

$$(1 - \eta)5 = (1 - .46)5 = 2.7. \qquad \bullet$$

EXAMPLE 6   In 1971 the cost of using a pay telephone in La Crosse, Wisconsin, was 5 cents. A study by an economics professor at the local university found that at that price the elasticity of demand was about .24. When the local telephone corporation learned of this, it made an immediate request for a rate increase to 10 cents (at that time, the standard charge in most of the country). Estimate the effect on the revenue of the phone company from its pay phones when the rate increase was granted.

SOLUTION   The increase from 5 to 10 cents is a 100% increase. Multiplying the right side of equation (5.8) by 100, we obtain

$$(1 - \eta)100 = (1 - .24)100 = 76.$$

That is, the phone company could anticipate an increase of approximately 76% in its revenue from pay phones. $\bullet$

EXERCISES 5.8

In Exercises 1–15 find the elasticity of demand η for each demand function at the given values of p.

1. $q = 480 - 4p; p = 40, p = 80, p = 100$

2. $q = 75 - .1p; p = 375, p = 450, p = 550$

3. $q = 180 - p - .02p^2; p = 10, p = 20, p = 30$

4. $q = 1875 - 3p - .05p^2; p = 50, p = 100, p = 150$

5. $p = 1000 - 6q; p = 100, p = 400, p = 600$

6. $p = 16 - .5q; p = 6, p = 8, p = 10$

7. $p = 100 - q^2; p = 36, p = 64$

8. $p = 750 - 3q^2; p = 75, p = 450$

9. $q = \dfrac{75}{p}; p = 5, p = 15, p = 25$

10. $q = \dfrac{300}{p}; p = 20, p = 50, p = 100$

11. $q = \dfrac{200}{\sqrt{p}}; p = 400, p = 645, p = 1600$

12. $q = \dfrac{1000}{3\sqrt{p}}; p = 64, p = 1000$

13. $p = 160q^{-2}; p = .40, p = 1.60$

14. $p = 1000q^{-3/2}; p = 64, p = 125$

15. $q = 640p^{-1.25}; p = 16, p = 81$

16. Show that for any demand function of the form $q = A/p^k$, where A and $k > 0$, the elasticity is constant for any p and that, in particular, $\eta = k$.

For the demand functions in Exercises 17–24, estimate the percentage change in the demand.

17. $q = 60 - .5p$; when p is decreased 2% from $p = 40$

18. $q = 300 - 3p$; when p is increased 4% from $p = 50$

19. $q = 120 - p - .03p^2$; when p is increased ½ of 1% from $p = 20$

20. $q = 420 - 2p - .05p^2$; when p is decreased 5% from $p = 60$

21. $p = 30 - 2q$; when p is increased 3% from $p = 10$

22. $p = 26 - .04q^2$; when p is increased 2% from $p = 10$

23. $q = \sqrt{800 - p^2}$; when p is decreased 1% from $p = 20$

24. $q = 650/p$; when p is increased 6% from $p = 25$

25–32. For the demand functions in Exercises 17–24, estimate the percentage change in the revenue that results from the given price change.

33. Suppose that the number of new mortgage loans q that a savings and loan makes each week is related to the current interest rate p by the demand equation

$$q = \sqrt{9360 - 40p^2}, \qquad 8 \le p \le 15.$$

Suppose that this savings and loan has a present mortgage rate of 12%. Find the elasticity in the demand for mortgages at this rate of interest.

34. Let the weekly demand at The Little Trinket jewelry store for gold chains q be related to their price p by the demand equation

$$p = 60 - .8q - .03q^2, \qquad 5 \le q \le 30.$$

The normal price for this gold chain at The Little Trinket is $32. Find the elasticity of demand at this price. Estimate the effect on demand and revenue if the store has a sale and reduces the price by 20%.

35. The owner of Seafood Unlimited, a retail supplier of fresh fish and other seafood, knows from experience that the demand for lobster is very elastic at the present price of $7.50 per pound. A consultant has told the owner that the elasticity may be as high as $\eta = 5$. If this is the case, estimate the percentage changes in the demand and in the revenue if Seafood Unlimited had a sale on lobster with the price set at $6.75 per pound. (*Hint:* First find the percentage change in the price.)

36. Intuitively, one would suspect that the demand for table salt is rather inelastic because people will continue to use about the same amount of salt regardless of the price. Suppose that at a price of 25 cents a box, the elasticity is $\eta = .15$. Estimate the percentage changes in the demand and in the revenue for a grocer who raises the price to 30 cents a box.

37. Saudi Arabia is selling its oil at a price of $29 per barrel, the current benchmark price for OPEC oil. Suppose that the elasticity of demand for oil is $\eta = 1.30$. If OPEC were to cut its benchmark price to $27 per barrel, estimate the

effect on the demand for Saudi Arabia's oil and its oil revenue.

38. The demand to see a popular motion picture is often inelastic because people want to see it regardless of the admission. Suppose that *Raiders of the Last Park* is a very popular movie and that its elasticity is $\eta = .45$. Ordinarily, a local movie theater charges $4 for a feature film, but for this feature it plans to charge $5. Estimate the effect this increase will have on the number of admissions and on the revenue over the regular price.

Often it is possible to estimate the price elasticity by observing how the demand for an item changes when an item is put on sale. Generally if a sale creates a big increase in the demand, the demand is elastic, but if a sale draws little interest, the demand is inelastic. Exercises 39–42 can be worked using equation (5.6).

39. Tots and Teens is a clothing store that carries the Tall Texan brand of blue jeans. The normal price for these jeans is $15 a pair. When they are put on sale for $12, the weekly sales increase from 50 to 75 pairs. Estimate the elasticity based on this information.

40. Frozen orange juice usually sells at $1.15 for a 12-oz can. Recent cold weather in Florida has reduced the crop and pushed the price up to $1.22 a can. Suppose that a grocer notices that the weekly sales fall from 300 cases to 285. Estimate the elasticity of the demand for frozen orange juice at $1.15.

41. The popular home video game *Leap Frogg* generally sells at $35. One retailer who had been selling 500 *Leap Frogg* cartridges a month put the game on sale at $29.75 and increased the sales to 550 units per month. Estimate the elasticity of demand at a price of $35.

42. The Leaning Tower of Pizza sells its large pepperoni and mushroom pizza for $11.50. For a recent promotion, the Tower put coupons in the newspaper worth $2.00 off on a large pizza. That night the Tower sold 85 large pizzas rather than the usual 40. Estimate the elasticity of the demand for their pizza at the usual price.

Elasticity also offers a way to find the price at which the revenue is maximized. Recall that if $\eta < 1$, raising the price will increase the revenue, and if $\eta > 1$, lowering the price will increase the revenue. Consequently, when $\eta = 1$, the revenue is maximized. When $\eta = 1$, the corresponding price is said to provide unit elasticity. In Exercises 43–48 find p that gives unit elasticity and the corresponding demand. [Hint: Use equation (5.5) and replace q with the given function to get an expression in p. Set this expression equal to 1.]

43. $q = 600 - 4p$

44. $q = 45 - .15p$

45. $q = 450 - 3p - .1p^2$

46. $q = 30 - 6p - .5p^2$

47. $q = \sqrt{450 - p^2}$

48. $q = \sqrt{1350 - 3p^2}$

49. Show that a demand function of the form $q = b - mp$ for $b, m > 0$ has unit elasticity at $p = b/2m$.

50. Refer to Exercise 49. Write the revenue R as a function of p for the demand function. Find p such that $R'(p) = 0$ and show that R has a maximum at this value of p.

51. Show that a demand function of the form $q = A/p$ for $A > 0$ has unit elasticity for any value of p. What does this say about the revenue $R = pq$?

CH. 5 REVIEW

I. Key Terms & Concepts

Mathematics

Relative Maximum
(Minimum)
Absolute Maximum
(Minimum)
Critical Point
Extreme Value Theorem
First Derivative Test
Unique Extremum Theorem
Second Derivative Test
Differential of x
Differential of y

Business

Elastic Demand
Inelastic Demand
Economic Order Quantity
Annual Rental Value

II. True or False

Indicate whether each statement is true or false.

1. If f is a continuous function with relative maxima at distinct points $x = a$ and $x = b$, then f has a relative minimum at a point $x = c$ with $a < c < b$.

2. A discontinuous function on a closed interval must take on either an absolute maximum or an absolute minimum on that interval.

3. All points in the domain of a constant function are critical points.

4. The second derivative test will give no information at a critical point that is also a point of inflection.

5. If $x = c$ is a critical point of f at which the second deriva-tive test gives no information, then $x = c$ is a point of inflection.

6. The first derivative test can be used to classify a critical point of any differentiable function.

7. On an open interval an absolute extreme value is also a relative extreme value.

8. If $y = f(x)$, the differential of x is dx and the differential of y is $f(x)\, dx$.

9. If $y = f(x)$ is not a linear function, then $dx = \Delta x$, but $dy \neq \Delta y$.

10. If y is a linear function of x, then $dy/dx = \Delta y/\Delta x$.

III. Drill Problems

In Problems 1–8 find all critical points and classify each as a relative maximum, minimum, or neither.

1. $f(x) = x^3 + 2x^2 - 15x + 4$

2. $f(x) = x^4 + 12x^2$

3. $f(x) = x^4 - 8x^3$

4. $f(x) = \dfrac{1}{5}x^5 - x^3 - 54x$

5. $f(x) = x^2 e^{-3x}$

6. $f(x) = \dfrac{x^2}{x^2 + 5}$

7. $f(x) = \dfrac{5 + x^2}{2 + x}$

8. $f(x) = 4 \ln(x + 1) - x^2$

In Problems 9–13 find the absolute maximum and the absolute minimum of the given function on the specified interval.

9. $f(x) = 6 + 4x - 3x^2$; $[0, 3]$

10. $f(x) = x e^{1 - x^2}$; $[-1, 1]$

11. $f(x) = \dfrac{7 - 2x}{5 + x}; [-2, 2]$ 12. $f(x) = \dfrac{x^2 + 3x}{x - 1}; [2, 6]$

13. $f(x) = x^3 - 9x^2 + 15x + 5; [0, 4]$

In Problems 14–17 for each function find dy at the given value of x and Δx.

14. $y = 3x^2 - 5x + 1; x = 2, \Delta x = .05$

15. $y = \ln(x^2 + 2); x = 1, \Delta x = -.2$

16. $y = (3x + 1)^{3/2}; x = 5, \Delta x = .1$

17. $y = \dfrac{2x + 6}{3x + 1}; x = 0, \Delta x = -.25$

IV. Applications

1. Precision Printers can make up to 200 dot matrix models each day. Daily fixed costs are $800, and on a day when q printers are produced, the variable cost per printer v is

$$v = 191 - .29q + .001q^2, \qquad 0 \le q \le 200.$$

All printers produced can be sold for p dollars each, where

$$p = 299 - .32q, \qquad 0 \le q \le 200.$$

Find the profit P as a function of q and determine q so that P is maximized. (Compare this solution with that of Exercise 1 in the Applications section of the Chapter 3 Review.)

2. Refer to Exercise 1. Precision Printers is about to produce a new letter quality printer. First estimates indicate fixed costs of $800 per day and a variable cost per unit given by

$$v = \dfrac{180q + 23,800}{q + 40}, \qquad 0 \le q \le 200.$$

Demand for letter quality printers should be

$$p = 347 - .47q, \qquad 0 \le q \le 200.$$

Find profit P as a function of q and determine q so that P is maximized. (Compare this solution with that of Exercise 2 in the Applications section of the Chapter 3 Review.)

3. The manufacturer of Byte Baseball, a computer game that simulates major league baseball, intends to buy advertising time during the World Series. Commercials will cost the manufacturer $200,000 per minute. The director of marketing estimates that the company will sell $q = 160\sqrt{x + 1}$ thousand copies of the game if they advertise for x minutes. Finally, the manufacturer realizes a profit of $10 on each copy sold. How many minutes of advertising should be purchased to maximize the profit?

4. The manager of a J.D. Nichols department store wants to determine the optimum ordering policy for its line of microwave ovens. The manager estimates that annual sales will be 280 ovens. Each oven costs Nichols $300 and the accountants figure that carrying costs are 15% of average inventory. The accountants have also estimated that it costs $63 to place an order for the microwaves. Determine the order size q so that total inventory cost is minimized.

5. Let the demand function for the computer software package Locus A-B-C be given by

$$p = \dfrac{200q + 32,000}{q + 10}, \qquad q \ge 0,$$

where q is the number of copies sold per day. The company that sells the package estimates that the production and distribution costs are $50 per copy, but service and advice on its use after the sale add another $270 to the cost of each copy sold. Determine q so that profit is maximized.

6. A packaging company has been asked to design a rectangular box. These boxes will be used to ship live marine specimens. The base must be made of a very strong, waterproof material that costs $5 per square foot; the sides will still be waterproof but do not have to be as strong and can be made of material that costs $4 per square foot; the top needs only to be water resistant and so can be made from material that costs $2 per square foot. For ease of handling, it has been decided that the

length will be twice the width. Each box must have a volume of 8 cu ft. Determine the dimensions of the box that can be made for minimum cost.

7. The Ovens de Normandie is a French bakery whose owner models the weekly demand q for croissants by

$$q = \frac{3600}{\sqrt{1 + .5p}}, \qquad .50 \le p \le 1.00,$$

where p is the selling price for each croissant. The bakery's current price for a croissant is $.88. Use differentials to estimate the change in the demand if the price is increased to $.90.

8. Refer to Exercise 7. Find the price elasticity of demand for the croissants when $p = .88$. Estimate the change in the revenue that would result from a decision to increase the price to $.90.

The publisher of **The Metal Works**, *a successful new magazine for rock music fans, wants to sell more copies of each issue. Currently the publisher is distributing 50,000 copies each month. Suppose that when q thousand copies of an issue are distributed, the marginal revenue (in thousands of dollars) is given by*

$$MR(q) = 3.5 - .02q - \frac{30}{q},$$
$$40 \le q \le 80.$$

How much additional revenue would be produced by increasing the distribution to 60,000 copies per month?

CHAPTER 6

Antidifferentiation and the Definite Integral

223

6.1
Antiderivatives

In the preceding chapters we have frequently considered the situation in which a manager or a decision maker knew the total cost of producing q units of some product. As we saw, the marginal cost of the qth unit—the derivative of the total cost—is a key tool in the decision-making process. In this chapter, we will reverse the situation and assume that the manager knows the marginal cost and would like to determine the total cost function.

EXAMPLE 1

Cher's Chairs is a furniture company that specializes in making easy chairs and recliners. The plant manager is responsible for deciding how many Sunny Boy recliners to make each week. The manager knows that when q of these recliners are made in one week, the marginal cost of the qth chair is

$$MC(q) = 350 - .4q, \qquad 0 \le q \le 150.$$

It is also known that the fixed costs allocated to the Sunny Boy line are $180 per week. Find the total cost of producing q Sunny Boys each week. In particular, what is the cost to Cher's Chairs when 100 are made in one week?

SOLUTION

Since the marginal cost MC is the derivative of the total cost C, we need to find a function $C(q)$ whose derivative is $350 - .4q$. Recalling that $D_q[aq] = a$ for any constant a, and that $D_q[q^2] = 2q$, it is easy to find one such function:

$$C(q) = 350q - .2q^2.$$

Moreover, since the derivative of a constant is 0, it follows that $C(q) = 350q - .2q^2 + c$, where c is any constant, is also a function whose derivative is $350 - .2q$. (It is shown in more advanced texts that there are no other possibilities.) We can therefore write the total cost C as

(6.1) $$C(q) = 350q - .2q^2 + c, \qquad 0 \le q \le 150,$$

where c is a constant that has to be determined. The fixed cost $180 is the cost incurred when no Sunny Boys are made; that is, $C(0) = 180$. From equation (6.1) we see that $C(0) = c$, so the unknown constant is the fixed cost. We have then

$$C(q) = 350q - .2q^2 + 180, \qquad 0 \le q \le 150.$$

In particular, the total cost of making 100 chairs is

$$C(100) = 350(100) - .2(100)^2 + 180$$
$$= 33,180. \qquad \bullet$$

The same approach may be used when the marginal revenue MR is known as a function of q and we wish to find the revenue R.

EXAMPLE 2

King Lobster is a company that catches, processes, and freezes seafood for sale to restaurants. The price for its lobster tails depends on the number of lobsters that are caught that day. Assume that when q lobsters are caught and sold, the marginal revenue from the sale of the qth lobster is

$$MR(q) = 8 - .0018q^2, \qquad 0 \le q \le 60.$$

a. Find the revenue R received by King Lobster when q lobsters are caught and sold.

b. What is the selling price per lobster tail when $q = 50$?

SOLUTION

a. Recalling that $D_q[q^3] = 3q^2$, we see that one function with derivative $MR(q) = 8 - .0018q^2$ is

$$R(q) = 8q - .0006q^3.$$

Furthermore, any function with this derivative can be written as

$$R(q) = 8q - .0006q^3 + c, \qquad 0 \le q \le 60,$$

for some constant c. Because King Lobster receives no revenue on a day when no lobsters are caught, $R(0) = 0$. Therefore, we know that $c = 0$ and

(6.2)
$$R(q) = 8q - .0006q^3, \qquad 0 \le q \le 60.$$

b. The selling price p can easily be found by recalling that $R = pq$ or $p = R/q$. Dividing equation (6.2) by q, we find

$$p = 8 - .0006q^2, \qquad 0 \le q \le 60.$$

When $q = 50$, $p = 8 - .0006(50)^2 = 6.50$. ●

To develop a precise way to solve problems like these, we state a definition and introduce a new symbol.

Definition 6.1

Let f be a function defined on some interval. If F is another function such that

(6.3)
$$F'(x) = f(x)$$

for all x in this interval, we say that F is an **antiderivative** of f.

If F is an antiderivative of f, then $F + c$, for any constant c, is also an antiderivative of f. As noted, it is also true that any antiderivative G of f can be written as $G(x) = F(x) + c$ for some c. Therefore, it is convenient to speak of $F(x) + c$, where c is an arbitrary constant, as the **general antiderivative** of f.

Recall that if F is a differentiable function, then the differential of $F(x) + c$ is $dF = F'(x) \, dx$. To denote the general antiderivative of a function we introduce the symbol $\int$, which represents the inverse of the differential; that is,

(6.4)
$$\int dF = F(x) + c.$$

Combining equations (6.3) and (6.4), we have

(6.5)
$$\int f(x) \, dx = F(x) + c.$$

That is, the expression $\int f(x) \, dx$ denotes all antiderivatives of the function f (provided that f has an antiderivative).

The symbol $\int$ is usually called an **integral sign** and the function $f(x)$ is called the **integrand**. The process of finding the general antiderivative of a function is called **integration**. The constant c in equation (6.5) is called the **constant of integration**.

The following list of rules for finding antiderivatives can be verified by using a corresponding rule for differentiation.

Basic Rules of Integration

1. $\int k\, dx = kx + c$, for any constant k

2. $\int x^n\, dx = \dfrac{1}{n+1} x^{n+1} + c$, provided that $n \neq -1$

3. $\int x^{-1}\, dx = \int \dfrac{1}{x}\, dx = \ln|x| + c$

4. $\int e^x\, dx = e^x + c$

5. $\int kf(x)\, dx = k \int f(x)\, dx$, for any constant k

6. $\int [f(x) + g(x)]\, dx = \int f(x)\, dx + \int g(x)\, dx$

Except for rule 3, we will omit the verification of these rules, since they are just inverses of differentiation rules. To verify rule 3, observe that for any negative x,

$$D_x[\ln(-x)] = \frac{1}{-x}(-1) = \frac{1}{x}.$$

Therefore, for any nonzero x, the derivative of $\ln|x|$ is $1/x$.

EXAMPLE 3

Find all the antiderivatives of
$$f(x) = x^3 + 5x - 3.$$

SOLUTION

We have

$$\int f(x)\, dx = \int (x^3 + 5x - 3)\, dx$$

$$= \int x^3\, dx + \int 5x\, dx - \int 3\, dx \qquad \text{by rule 6}$$

$$= \int x^3\, dx + 5 \int x\, dx - \int 3\, dx \qquad \text{by rule 5}$$

$$= \frac{1}{4}x^4 + \frac{5}{2}x^2 - 3x + c \qquad \text{by rules 1 and 2.}$$

Note that the three constants of integration have been combined into one. This solution can be verified by taking the derivative of the final result. ●

EXAMPLE 4

Find the general antiderivative

$$\int (6e^x + 4\sqrt{x})\, dx.$$

SOLUTION

We have

$$\int (6e^x + 4\sqrt{x})\, dx = \int 6e^x\, dx + \int 4\sqrt{x}\, dx \qquad \text{by rule 6}$$

$$= 6\int e^x\, dx + 4\int x^{1/2}\, dx \qquad \text{by rule 5}$$

$$= 6e^x + \frac{8}{3}x^{3/2} + c \qquad \text{by rules 2 and 4.} \qquad ●$$

As these rules become more familiar (through repeated use), several steps may be performed at once, as illustrated in the next examples.

EXAMPLE 5

Find the general antiderivative:

$$\int \frac{x^3 - 4}{x}\, dx.$$

SOLUTION

We begin by rewriting the integrand as the sum of two terms so that the rules of integration can be applied:

$$\int \frac{x^3 - 4}{x}\, dx = \int (x^2 - 4x^{-1})\, dx$$

$$= \frac{1}{3}x^3 - 4\ln|x| + c. \qquad ●$$

EXAMPLE 6

Find the general antiderivative:

$$\int \left(\frac{2}{\sqrt[3]{x^4}} + 4\sqrt[3]{x^2} \right) dx.$$

SOLUTION

Replacing the radicals in the integrand with exponents so that the integration rules may be applied, we find

$$\int\left(\frac{2}{\sqrt[3]{x^4}} + 4\sqrt[3]{x^2}\right)dx = \int(2x^{-4/3} + 4x^{2/3})\,dx$$

$$= 2(-3)x^{-1/3} + 4\left(\frac{3}{5}\right)x^{5/3} + c$$

$$= -6x^{-1/3} + \frac{12}{5}x^{5/3} + c.$$

EXAMPLE 7

Find all the antiderivatives of

$$g(x) = (x^2 + 1)^3.$$

SOLUTION

To find the antiderivatives we first expand $(x^2 + 1)^3$. Then

$$\int g(x)\,dx = \int(x^2 + 1)^3\,dx$$

$$= \int(x^6 + 3x^4 + 3x^2 + 1)\,dx$$

$$= \frac{1}{7}x^7 + \frac{3}{5}x^5 + x^3 + x + c.$$

Using the integral notation, the total cost function in Example 1 can be found as follows:

$$C(q) = \int MC(q)\,dq = \int(350 - .4q)\,dq$$

$$= 350q - .2q^2 + c.$$

Since $C(0) = 180$ is the fixed cost, the total cost to make q Sunny Boys is

$$C(q) = 350q - .2q^2 + 180, \qquad 0 \le q \le 150.$$

The revenue function in Example 2 can be found in a similar fashion:

$$R(q) = \int MR\,dq = \int(8 - .0018q^2)\,dq$$

$$= 8q - .0006q^3 + c.$$

Because $R(0) = 0$, the revenue from the sale of q lobster tails is

$$R = 8q - .0006q^3, \qquad 0 \le q \le 60.$$

EXERCISES 6.1

In Exercises 1–30 find the indicated general antiderivatives.

1. $\int 8\,dx$

2. $\int 15\,dy$

3. $\int x^4\,dx$

4. $\int x^{-3}\,dx$

5. $\int x^{2/5}\,dx$

6. $\int z^{-3/4}\,dz$

7. $\int x^{.35}\,dx$

8. $\int y^{-3.2}\,dy$

9. $\int (5x^2 - 3x + 4)\,dx$

10. $\int (7 + 4x - x^2)\,dx$

11. $\int (x + 3)(2x - 1)\,dx$

12. $\int (3y^2 + 4)(2y - 1)\,dy$

13. $\int z^4(2 + z)\,dz$

14. $\int (y^3 + y^{-3})\,dy$

15. $\int \frac{4}{\sqrt{x}} + \frac{\sqrt{x}}{4}\,dx$

16. $\int \sqrt{8x}\,dx$

17. $\int \sqrt{x^5}\,dx$

18. $\int \sqrt[3]{x^2}\,dx$

19. $\int \frac{6}{\sqrt[5]{y^3}}\,dy$

20. $\int x^{1/3}(x + 9)\,dx$

21. $\int \sqrt{x}(x + 5)\,dx$

22. $\int \frac{x + 5}{x}\,dx$

23. $\int \frac{5x^2 + 3x + 2}{x^2}\,dx$

24. $\int \frac{x^2 + 3}{\sqrt{x}}\,dx$

25. $\int 5e^x\,dx$

26. $\int 7e^t\,dt$

27. $\int 3e^5\,dy$

28. $\int (3x - 2)^2\,dx$

29. $\int x(x + 5)^2\,dx$

30. $\int (y - 2)^3\,dy$

31. It has been estimated that if a hog farmer raises q hogs during a season, the marginal cost of the qth hog is

$$MC(q) = 700 - 1.8q - .12q^2, \qquad 0 \le q \le 50.$$

Find the total cost of raising q hogs during one season when the fixed cost to the farmer is $2000.

32. Apprentice Call is a publisher of training manuals. The editor must decide how many copies of *Beginning Carpentry* to print. It is known that if q thousand copies are printed, the marginal cost of the final thousand copies printed will be

$$MC(q) = 18{,}000 - 50q - .06q^2, \qquad 0 \le q \le 150.$$

The editor has also been told that the fixed cost to print this book is $850. Find the total cost as a function of q. What will the cost be to Apprentice Call if the editor decides to print 30,000 copies?

33. A day care center can accommodate up to 20 children a day. Suppose that the marginal cost of caring for the qth child is

$$MC(q) = 12 - .3q - .0012q^2, \qquad 0 \le q \le 20.$$

Find the average cost, $A = C/q$, of caring for each child when there are q children at the day care center if the fixed cost is $5 per day.

34. Quick Prints makes custom printed T-shirts. When a customer orders q shirts, each printed with the same design, the marginal cost of the qth shirt is

$$MC(q) = 25 - .004q - .0001q^{3/2}, \qquad 0 \le q \le 2500.$$

The manager of Quick Prints estimates that $10 of the overhead should be allocated as fixed costs to each shirt order. Find the average cost, $A = C/q$, of each shirt if q shirts are ordered.

35–38. Determine the variable cost as a function of q for each of the situations described in Exercises 31–34. (*Hint:* Subtract the fixed cost from the total cost; then divide by q.)

39. The buyer for an exclusive department store has to decide how many pairs of Kevin Kalvin designer jeans to purchase for this fall. Suppose that if q hundred pairs are purchased, these jeans will have to be priced so that the marginal revenue function is

$$MR(q) = 5000 - 20q - .27q^2, \qquad 0 \le q \le 50.$$

Find the total revenue received by the store from the sale of q hundred pairs. What would the store sell each pair for if the buyer purchases 4000 pairs?

40. A suburban auto dealer wants to sell the entire inventory of new Stingers in 30 days. Suppose that in order to do this when there are q cars in stock, the cars have to be priced so that the marginal revenue from the sale of the qth car is

$$MR(q) = 16{,}000 - 50q - 14q^{4/3}, \qquad 0 \le q \le 100.$$

Find the total revenue as a function of q. What will each car be sold for if there are 64 cars in stock?

41. Assume that the marginal propensity to consume for an individual is given as a function of this person's income I:

$$MPC(I) = .96 - .03\sqrt{I} - .005\sqrt[3]{I^2}, \qquad 0 \le I \le 30,$$

where I is in thousands of dollars per year. Assume further that this individual will spend \$7500 per year even if he or she has no income for the year. Find the consumption function for this person.

42. Assume that the marginal propensity to consume for an individual is given by

$$MPC(I) = .88 + \frac{1.2}{I} - .03\sqrt{I}, \qquad 10 \le I \le 40,$$

where I is given in thousands of dollars per year. Assume

that if the individual's income is exactly \$10,000, the entire income will be spent. Find the consumption function for this individual. [*Hint:* To determine the constant of integration, solve $C(10) = 10$.]

43. A young woman wants to be a distributor for Jackie May Cosmetics. She can order up to 100 beauty kits from Jackie May at a price of \$10 each. She is also required to pay a \$50 license fee at city hall. Assume that in order to sell q of the kits, they must be priced so that the marginal revenue from the sale of the qth kit is

$$MR = 34 - .06q - .0003q^2, \qquad 0 \le q \le 100.$$

a. Find the total cost to the woman and the revenue that she will receive if she orders and sells q beauty kits.

b. Write her profit as a function of q.

c. Find q so that her profit is maximized.

6.2
The Definite Integral

When finding the antiderivative to solve a specific problem, the solution is not complete until the constant of integration has been determined. For many problems, however, we are interested only in the change in the antiderivative. In these cases the constant of integration is immaterial.

EXAMPLE 1

At the present time, the main assembly line at Homemaker Appliances is manufacturing 200 microwave ovens each day. The manager knows that the marginal cost function is

$$MC(q) = 600 - 1.5q, \qquad 0 \le q \le 300,$$

where q is the number of ovens made each day. Find the increase in the total cost if the manager ordered the assembly line to increase the production to 220 microwaves daily.

SOLUTION

Recall that the differential dC can be used to *approximate* the additional cost. Here $dC = MC(200)\, dq = 300 \cdot 20 = 6000$. To find the *exact* increase in total cost, we first form the total cost function:

$$C(q) = \int dC = \int MC(q)\, dq = \int (600 - 1.5q)\, dq$$
$$= 600q - .75q^2 + c,$$

where c is the fixed cost, which is not known in this problem. However, as we are asked to find only the increase in the total cost, it is not necessary to know c. The change in the total cost is

$$C(220) - C(200) = [600(220) - .75(220)^2 + c] - [600(200) - .75(200)^2 + c]$$
$$= 132,000 - 36,300 + c - 120,000 + 30,000 - c$$
$$= 5700.$$

That is, the additional 20 microwaves would cost $5700 to manufacture. ●

As illustrated in Example 1, if F and G are two antiderivatives of the same function, then $G(x) = F(x) + c$ for some constant c and so

$$G(b) - G(a) = [F(b) + c] - [F(a) + c]$$
$$= F(b) - F(a).$$

That is, regardless of the antiderivative used, the change in an antiderivative from a to b is always the same. In view of this fact, it is useful to introduce notation, based on the antiderivative symbol, for this difference.

Definition 6.2

If f is a continuous function and F is an antiderivative of f, then the change in F, when the independent variable changes from $x = a$ to $x = b$, is denoted by

$$\int_a^b f(x)\, dx$$

and called the **definite integral** of f from a to b. The values a and b are called **limits of integration**.

For convenience, we also let

$$F(x) \Big]_a^b$$

denote this difference; thus,

(6.6)
$$\int_a^b f(x)\, dx = F(x) \Big]_a^b = F(b) - F(a).$$

The solution to Example 1, which was the change in total cost C when q changed from 200 to 220, can now be written as

$$\int_{200}^{220} (600 - 1.5q)\, dq = (600q - .75q^2) \Big]_{200}^{220} = 5700.$$

EXAMPLE 2

The Old Barnstormer Distillery plans to sell a "limited edition" bottle of its most expensive bourbon to commemorate the most recent presidential election. The company estimates that the marginal revenue from the sale of the qth bottle would be

$$MR(q) = 45 - .21\sqrt{q} - .01q, \qquad 0 \le q \le 1000.$$

Initially, Old Barnstormer intended to sell only 400 of these rare bottles, but the marketing department persuaded the management to sell 900. Find the additional revenue that the company will receive as a result.

SOLUTION

The revenue from the sale of q bottles can be found by taking the antiderivative of the marginal revenue function:

$$R(q) = \int MR(q) \, dq = \int (45 - .21\sqrt{q} - .01q) \, dq$$
$$= 45q - .14q^{3/2} - .005q^2.$$

In this case the constant of integration is known to be 0, but the change in the revenue would not be affected even if it were some other value. Using definite integral notation, the change in the revenue is

$$\int_{400}^{900} (45 - .21\sqrt{q} - .01q) \, dq = (45q - .14q^{3/2} - .005q^2)\Big]_{400}^{900}$$
$$= 32{,}670 - 16{,}080$$
$$= 16{,}590.$$

That is, Old Barnstormer will receive $16,590 more revenue by selling 900 bottles rather than 400. ●

EXAMPLE 3

Calculate the definite integral:

$$\int_1^6 (x^2 - 4x + 3) \, dx.$$

SOLUTION

Because $1/3x^3 - 2x^2 + 3x$ is an antiderivative of $x^2 - 4x + 3$, from equation (6.6) we have

$$\int_1^6 (x^2 - 4x + 3) \, dx = \left(\frac{1}{3}x^3 - 2x^2 + 3x\right)\Big]_1^6$$
$$= \left[\frac{1}{3}(6)^3 - 2(6)^2 + 3(6)\right] - \left[\frac{1}{3}(1)^3 - 2(1)^2 + 3(1)\right]$$
$$= 18 - \frac{4}{3}$$
$$= \frac{50}{3}. \qquad ●$$

EXAMPLE 4

Calculate the definite integral:

$$\int_4^{25} \frac{3}{\sqrt{x}} \, dx.$$

SOLUTION

We have

$$\int_4^{25} \frac{3}{\sqrt{x}}\, dx = \int_4^{25} 3x^{-1/2}\, dx = 6x^{1/2}\bigg]_4^{25}$$

$$= 6\sqrt{25} - 6\sqrt{4}$$

$$= 18.$$

EXAMPLE 5

Calculate the definite integral:

$$\int_{-5}^{-1} \frac{10}{x}\, dx.$$

SOLUTION

Recall that

$$\int x^{-1}\, dx = \ln|x| + c.$$

(In this instance the absolute value is essential because $\ln x$ is not defined for negative x.) Therefore,

$$\int_{-5}^{-1} \frac{10}{x}\, dx = \int_{-5}^{-1} 10x^{-1}\, dx = 10\ln|x|\bigg]_{-5}^{-1} = 10\ln 1 - 10\ln 5$$

$$= -10\ln 5.$$

The following theorem lists three elementary properties of the definite integral.

Theorem 6.1

Let f be continuous and have an antiderivative on the interval $[a, b]$.

1. $\displaystyle\int_a^a f(x)\, dx = 0$

2. $\displaystyle\int_b^a f(x)\, dx = -\int_a^b f(x)\, dx$

   (Interchanging the order of the limits of integration changes the sign of the integral.)

3. For any c with $a < c < b$,

   $$\int_a^b f(x)\, dx = \int_a^c f(x)\, dx + \int_c^b f(x)\, dx.$$

   (The integral from a to b can be found as the sum of the integrals from a to c and from c to b.)

Proof Let F be an antiderivative of f on $[a, b]$.

1. By equation (6.6) we have

$$\int_a^a f(x)\, dx = F(x) \Big]_a^a = F(a) - F(a) = 0.$$

2. This also follows easily from equation (6.6):

$$\int_b^a f(x)\, dx = F(x) \Big]_b^a = F(a) - F(b)$$
$$= -[F(b) - F(a)]$$
$$= -\int_a^b f(x)\, dx.$$

The proof of part 3 also follows from equation (6.6) and is left as Exercise 46.

EXAMPLE 6

Calculate the definite integral:

$$\int_6^1 (x^2 - 4x + 3)\, dx.$$

SOLUTION

From property 2 and Example 3 we know that

$$\int_6^1 (x^2 - 4x + 3)\, dx = -\int_1^6 (x^2 - 4x + 3)\, dx = -\frac{50}{3}.$$

EXAMPLE 7

Given that

$$\int_0^{10} x^{2/3}\, dx = 6\sqrt[3]{100} \quad \text{and} \quad \int_0^5 x^{2/3}\, dx = 3\sqrt[3]{25},$$

find

$$\int_5^{10} x^{2/3}\, dx.$$

SOLUTION

From property 3 we know that

$$\int_0^5 x^{2/3}\, dx + \int_5^{10} x^{2/3}\, dx = \int_0^{10} x^{2/3}\, dx.$$

Substituting the given values, we find that

$$\int_5^{10} x^{2/3}\, dx = 6\sqrt[3]{100} - 3\sqrt[3]{25}.$$

It is extremely important that the reader understand the distinction between

$$\int f(x)\, dx \quad \text{and} \quad \int_a^b f(x)\, dx.$$

The first denotes the general antiderivative of f and represents a set of functions. The second denotes the definite integral of f on the interval $[a, b]$, which is a constant: the difference $F(b) - F(a)$ for any antiderivative F of f. In the next section we give a geometric interpretation of this number.

EXERCISES 6.2

In Exercises 1–30 find the indicated definite integral.

1. $\int_0^7 4\, dx$

2. $\int_{-3}^3 5\, dx$

3. $\int_2^{10} (2x - 1)\, dx$

4. $\int_{-4}^{-1} (3 + 6x)\, dx$

5. $\int_4^0 (x + 5)\, dx$

6. $\int_8^2 (3x - 1)\, dx$

7. $\int_{-1}^1 (3x^2 - 4x + 1)\, dx$

8. $\int_2^4 (5 + x + 2x^2)\, dx$

9. $\int_0^3 (y^2 - 6y + 4)\, dy$

10. $\int_4^5 (t^2 + t + 1)\, dt$

11. $\int_0^1 x^5\, dx$

12. $\int_1^2 x^{-5}\, dx$

13. $\int_9^{16} \sqrt{x}\, dx$

14. $\int_1^{27} \sqrt[3]{x}\, dx$

15. $\int_1^5 \frac{1}{x^2}\, dx$

16. $\int_2^6 \frac{4}{x^3}\, dx$

17. $\int_5^{20} \frac{2}{x}\, dx$

18. $\int_{-10}^{-1} \frac{5}{x}\, dx$

19. $\int_0^2 e^x\, dx$

20. $\int_{-3}^3 2e^x\, dx$

21. $\int_{-1}^1 (x + 2)^2\, dx$

22. $\int_0^3 (5 - 2x)^2\, dx$

23. $\int_0^2 x^3(20x + 8)\, dx$

24. $\int_{-3}^0 x^2(6x - 1)\, dx$

25. $\int_1^3 \frac{4x^2 + 3x + 5}{x}\, dx$

26. $\int_{-2}^{-1} \frac{5x^2 + x + 3}{x^2}\, dx$

27. $\int_1^4 \sqrt{x}(10x + 3)\, dx$

28. $\int_{-1}^1 \sqrt[3]{x}(2 - x)\, dx$

29. $\int_4^9 \frac{x - 4}{\sqrt{x}}\, dx$

30. $\int_1^{25} \frac{x^2 + 3x - 1}{\sqrt{x}}\, dx$

31. Easy Eddie's is a store that sells TV sets and other appliances. At present Eddie tries to keep 7 Quinatonic color sets in stock. Assume that the marginal cost of keeping the qth set in stock is

    $$MC = 35 - .08q - .06q^2, \qquad 0 \le q \le 10.$$

    a. Find, using the definite integral, the additional cost to Eddie if he decided to raise the number in stock to 10 sets.

    b. Suppose that Eddie decided to keep only 5 Quinatonics in stock. Calculate his savings. [*Hint:* Calculate $\int_7^5 MC(q)\, dq$; the change in the cost will be negative— the absolute value of the change is his savings.]

32. Braggin and Struttin is a company that makes small engines for lawn mowers. The current output is 100 engines a day, but the management is considering increasing output to 110.

    a. If the marginal cost function is

    $$MC = 130 - .32q - .003q^2, \qquad 50 \le q \le 120,$$

    find the additional cost if this change is made.

    b. How much would Braggin and Struttin save if the output were cut from 100 to 80 engines a day?

33. At the present time, Sound-Tek makes 90 of its most popular stereo speakers per day. Assume that the marginal cost function is

    $$MC = 300 - 1.4q - 6\sqrt{q}, \qquad 50 \le q \le 120.$$

    a. The demand for this speaker has been so great that

Sound-Tek is thinking about increasing the output to 100 per day. Compute the additional cost if this is done.

b. If Sound-Tek then increased the output from 100 to 110 speakers per day, how much would the extra 10 speakers cost?

c. What is the cost of increasing the output level from 90 to 110?

d. Interpret property 3 of the definite integral in terms of the answers to parts a, b, and c.

Let the marginal cost MC be given as a function of the production level q. Then for $a < b$,

$$\frac{1}{b-a} \int_a^b MC(q) \, dq$$

represents the average cost of the additional units when the production is increased from $q = a$ to $q = b$.

34. Refer to Exercise 31. Compute the average holding cost for the additional three TV sets if Eddie increases the inventory from 7 to 10.

35. Refer to Exercise 32. Compute the average cost of the extra engines if Braggin and Struttin does increase the output from 100 to 110.

36. Refer to Exercise 33. Compute the average cost of the additional speakers if the output level is raised from 90 to 100. From 100 to 110. From 90 to 110.

37. Deerskin Leather Products makes quality hiking boots. Currently, 36 pairs are made each day. Assume that the marginal revenue function is

$$MR = 100 - .5q - 3\sqrt{q}, \qquad 10 \le q \le 50.$$

a. How much will the revenue increase if Deerskin increases production to 49 pairs a day?

b. How much would the revenue decline if the production was lowered to 25 pairs?

38. An Oregon farmer raises apples as a cash crop in a small orchard. The price per bushel that the farmer receives depends on the size of the crop that year. Assume that if the farmer has q bushels for sale, the marginal revenue is

$$MR = 10 - .003q + \frac{.1}{\sqrt{q}}, \qquad 500 \le q \le 1500.$$

Last year the crop was 900 bushels. How much more revenue will the farmer receive this year if the crop is 1200 bushels?

Let the marginal revenue MR be given as a function of the production level q. Then for $a < b$,

$$\frac{1}{b-a} \int_a^b MR(q) \, dq$$

represents the average revenue from the sale of each of the additional units when the production is increased from $q = a$ to $q = b$.

39. Refer to Exercise 37. Compute the average revenue received by Deerskin for each of the extra pairs of hiking boots if the production level is increased from 36 to 49 pairs.

40. Refer to Exercise 38. What is the average revenue received by the apple farmer for each of the extra bushels in the larger crop?

41. Suppose that an individual has a marginal propensity to consume MPC given by the function

$$MPC = .95 - .004I, \qquad 20 \le I \le 40,$$

where income I is given in thousands of dollars per year. Use a definite integral to calculate how much more this individual will spend if the annual income rises from $22,000 to $24,000.

42. A recent graduate of the college of business has a starting salary of $25,000. Assume that her marginal propensity to consume is

$$MPC = .92 + \frac{100}{I^2} - .01I, \qquad 20 \le I \le 30.$$

a. Suppose that she gets a raise to $28,000 after the first year. Find how much of this raise will be spent.

b. Suppose instead that her employer asks all employees to take a $500 salary cut because of a business slump. How much less would she spend?

43. Suppose that f is a function for which it is known that

$$\int_2^8 f(x) \, dx = 10 \quad \text{and} \quad \int_{-2}^8 f(x) \, dx = 14.$$

Find the following definite integrals.

a. $\int_2^2 f(x) \, dx$

b. $\int_{-2}^2 f(x) \, dx$

c. $\int_2^{-2} f(x) \, dx$

d. $\int_8^{-2} f(x) \, dx$

44. Suppose that f is a function for which it is known that

$$\int_6^3 f(x)\, dx = 8 \quad \text{and} \quad \int_1^6 f(x)\, dx = 2.$$

Find the following integrals.

a. $\int_1^3 f(x)\, dx$

b. $\int_3^6 f(x)\, dx$

c. $\int_6^6 f(x)\, dx$

d. $\int_3^1 f(x)\, dx$

45. Without calculating the antiderivatives, find the derivatives

$$D_x\left[\int_0^{12} (x^8 - 2x^4 + 7)\, dx\right] \text{ and } D_x\left[\int (x^8 - 2x^4 + 7)\, dx\right].$$

46. Prove property 3 of Theorem 6.1.

6.3
Area

Having considered antiderivatives and definite integrals in order to convert from *marginal* functions to *total* functions, we now consider an area function and find that it is an antiderivative of a *boundary* function. As a result, definite integrals may be used to compute areas, even areas of regions with curved boundaries. Solutions of many business problems may be interpreted as areas; thus, we briefly study this geometric topic for use in later applied problems.

We begin by considering the area of a region bounded by the x-axis, the vertical lines $x = a$ and $x = b$, and the graph of $y = f(x)$, where f is positive and continuous on an interval containing a and b. (See Figure 6.1.)

The area of the shaded region in Figure 6.1 is the definite integral

$$\int_a^b f(x)\, dx.$$

To derive this important result, suppose A is an area function for regions like those in Figure 6.1; that is, for a given x_0 let $A(x_0)$ represent the area of a region bounded by the x-axis, $y = f(x)$, $x = a$, and $x = x_0$. (See Figure 6.2.) A is clearly a

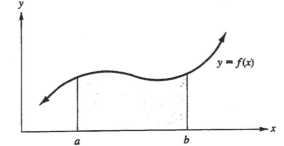

Figure 6.1

The area of a region bounded by the x-axis, $x = a$, $x = b$, and $y = f(x)$, where f is positive and continuous

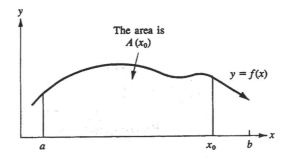

Figure 6.2

A function A, which gives the area of the region bounded by the x-axis, $y = f(x)$, $x = a$, and $x = x_0$

function. For any x_0, $A(x_0)$ is a specific, yet unknown number. In the case where $x_0 = a$ and the region has 0 width, $A(a) = 0$.

Turning to the derivative of A, we note that if $h > 0$,

$$A(x_0 + h) - A(x_0)$$

denotes the area of the shaded region in Figure 6.3. Using the extreme value theorem, the continuous function f has an absolute maximum value M and an absolute minimum value m on the interval $[x_0, x_0 + h]$. The area of the shaded region in Figure 6.3 is between the area of the rectangles with heights m and M. The base of the region and these rectangles have width h, so comparing areas, we find

$$h \cdot m \leq A(x_0 + h) - A(x_0) \leq h \cdot M$$

or

$$m \leq \frac{A(x_0 + h) - A(x_0)}{h} \leq M.$$

Now as h approaches 0, $x_0 + h$ approaches x_0, and from the continuity of f, m and M both approach $f(x_0)$. Similar reasoning follows when $h < 0$. Thus we see that

$$A'(x_0) = f(x_0);$$

that is, the derivative of our area function at any x_0 is the value of the upper boundary function at x_0. Hence A is an antiderivative of f.

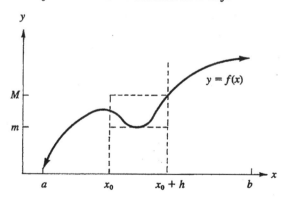

Figure 6.3

The area corresponding to $A(x_0 + h) - A(x_0)$

Recall that if F is an antiderivative of f on an interval that contains a and x_0, then

$$\int_a^{x_0} f(x)\, dx = F(x_0) - F(a),$$

so in particular

$$A(x_0) - A(a) = \int_a^{x_0} f(x)\, dx.$$

However, $A(a) = 0$ so the area function A at any x_0 is the definite integral of f from a to x_0; this value is just $F(x_0) - F(a)$ for any antiderivative F of f. Summarizing, the area in Figure 6.2 is

$$A(x_0) = \int_a^{x_0} f(x)\,dx = F(x_0) - F(a),$$

and that in Figure 6.1 is

$$\int_a^b f(x)\,dx.$$

Generally, we have the following result.

Theorem 6.2

If f is positive and continuous on $[a, b]$, then the area of the region bounded by $y = f(x)$, $x = a$, $x = b$, and the x-axis is given by the definite integral

$$\int_a^b f(x)\,dx.$$

EXAMPLE 1

Find the area bounded by $f(x) = \sqrt{x}$, the x-axis, $x = 1$, and $x = 4$.

SOLUTION

A sketch of the region appears in Figure 6.4. The area of this region is the value of the definite integral

$$\int_1^4 \sqrt{x}\,dx.$$

Now,

$$\int_1^4 \sqrt{x}\,dx = \int_1^4 x^{1/2}\,dx$$

$$= \frac{2}{3}x^{3/2}\Big]_1^4$$

$$= \frac{16}{3} - \frac{2}{3} = \frac{14}{3}\text{ square units}$$

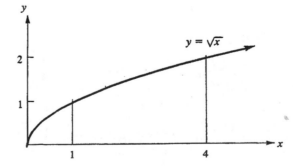

Figure 6.4

The region bounded by the x-axis, $y = \sqrt{x}$, $x = 1$, and $x = 4$

EXAMPLE 2

Find the area of the region above the x-axis bounded by the graph of $R(x) = 18x - 3x^2$.

SOLUTION

A sketch of the given region appears in Figure 6.5. Referring to the graph of R, we see that the boundaries $x = 0$ and $x = 6$ may be used for this region, so the desired area is

$$\int_0^6 (18x - 3x^2)\, dx = \left(9x^2 - x^3 \right]_0^6$$

$$= 9(36) - 216$$

$$= 108 \text{ square units.}$$

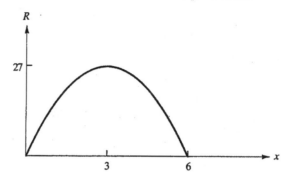

Figure 6.5

A sketch of the region bounded by $R(x) = 18x - 3x^2$ and the x-axis

EXAMPLE 3

Find the area bounded by $y = 1/x$, $x = 1$, $x = 2$, and the x-axis.

SOLUTION

Sketching the given region (see Figure 6.6), we find the desired area to be

$$\int_1^2 \frac{1}{x}\, dx = \ln x \Big]_1^2$$

$$= \ln 2 - \ln 1$$

$$= \ln 2 \text{ square units.}$$

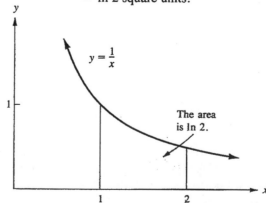

Figure 6.6

The region bounded by $y = 1/x$, $x = 1$, $x = 2$, and the x-axis

EXAMPLE 4

Find the area of the region bounded above by $y = x^{1/3}$ and below by $y = x^3$, between $x = 0$ and $x = 1$.

SOLUTION

The graphs of $y = x^{1/3}$ and $y = x^3$ appear in Figure 6.7. To obtain the area for the given region, we first find the area between the upper curve $y = x^{1/3}$ and the x-axis. From this value we then subtract the area of the region between the lower curve $y = x^3$ and the x-axis. Thus, we find the desired area to be

$$\int_0^1 x^{1/3}\, dx - \int_0^1 x^3\, dx = \int_0^1 (x^{1/3} - x^3)\, dx$$

$$= \left(\frac{3}{4}x^{4/3} - \frac{1}{4}x^4\right)\Big]_0^1$$

$$= \frac{3}{4} - \frac{1}{4} = \frac{1}{2} \text{ square unit.} \quad \bullet$$

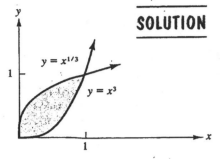

Figure 6.7

The region bounded above by $y = x^{1/3}$ and below by $y = x^3$

The procedure used in Example 4 can be applied to any region bounded above and below by graphs of continuous functions. (See Figure 6.8.)

Theorem 6.3

> If f and g are continuous functions on $[a, b]$, and if $f(x) \geq g(x)$ for all x in $[a, b]$, then the area of the region bounded above by $y = f(x)$, below by $y = g(x)$, and between $x = a$ and $x = b$ is given by the definite integral
>
> $$\int_a^b [f(x) - g(x)]\, dx.$$

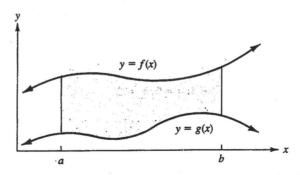

Figure 6.8

A region between $y = f(x)$ and $y = g(x)$ with area $\int_a^b [f(x) - g(x)]\, dx$

Historically, areas of the type considered in this section were found during the 16th century by summing the areas of inscribed rectangles with smaller and smaller bases. The Greeks' "method of exhaustion" became more precise with the development of the limit concept in the 17th century. In 1675, Leibniz introduced the $\int$ symbol as an elongated S for "sum." The definite integral is usually defined as a special limit of sums of terms that may be interpreted as rectangle areas. This approach will be examined in Section 7.1.

EXERCISES 6.3

For Exercises 1–8 sketch the region bounded by the x-axis, y = f(x), x = a, and x = b, for the given function f and the indicated values of a and b. Then find the area of the region.

1. $f(x) = x^2; a = 1, b = 3$

2. $f(x) = 2x + 5; a = 0, b = 4$

3. $f(x) = 1 + 3\sqrt{x}; a = 1, b = 4$

4. $f(x) = 3 + \dfrac{1}{x}; a = 1, b = 3$

5. $f(x) = x^2 - 4x + 5; a = 1, b = 4$

6. $f(x) = e^x; a = 0, b = 1$

7. $f(x) = 2 + \sqrt[3]{x}; a = 1, b = 8$

8. $f(x) = \dfrac{1}{x^3}; a = 1, b = 5$

For Exercises 9–16 find the area of the region bounded by the graphs of the given functions between x = a and x = b as indicated.

9. $f(x) = x^2, g(x) = \sqrt{x}; a = 0, b = 1$

10. $f(x) = \sqrt[4]{x}, g(x) = x^4; a = 0, b = 1$

11. $f(x) = x^2 - x + 5, g(x) = \sqrt{x}; a = 1, b = 4$

12. $f(x) = x^2 + 2x + 3, g(x) = \sqrt{x}; a = 1, b = 9$

13. $f(x) = 2x + 1, g(x) = 2e^x; a = 0, b = 1$

14. $f(x) = 1 - e^x, g(x) = \dfrac{1}{3}x^2 + 3; a = 0, b = 2$

15. $f(x) = \sqrt{x}, g(x) = \dfrac{1}{x}; a = 1, b = 9$

16. $f(x) = \dfrac{1}{x}, g(x) = \dfrac{1}{x^2}; a = 1, b = 5$

For Exercises 17–24 sketch the graphs of the given functions, locate their points of intersection, and find the area of the figure bounded by their graphs.

17. $f(x) = 20x - x^2, g(x) = 0$

18. $f(x) = x^2 - 5x, g(x) = 0$

19. $f(x) = \dfrac{1}{3}x, g(x) = \sqrt{x}$ 20. $f(x) = x + 2, g(x) = x^2$

21. $f(x) = \dfrac{1}{x}, g(x) = \dfrac{5}{4} - \dfrac{1}{4}x$ 22. $f(x) = x^3, g(x) = \sqrt{x}$

23. $f(x) = x^{1/3}, g(x) = x$

24. $f(x) = 4 - x^2, g(x) = 2x + 1$

25. It is important to remember that the area interpretation for the definite integral, $\int_a^b f(x)\, dx$, is accurate only when $f(x)$ is nonnegative for all x in $[a, b]$. The following illustrations serve as a reminder that a definite integral (unlike an area) may be negative.

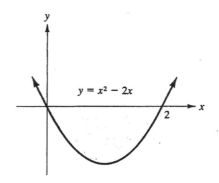

$$\int_0^2 (x^2 - 2x)\, dx = \tfrac{1}{3}x^3 - x^2\big]_0^2 = -\tfrac{4}{3}$$

(i)

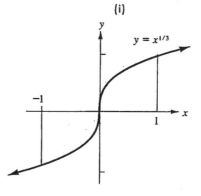

$$\int_{-1}^1 x^{1/3}\, dx = \tfrac{3}{4}x^{4/3}\big]_{-1}^1 = 0$$

(ii)

a. Find the area of the shaded region in illustration i after noting that it is bounded above by $g(x) = 0$ and below by $f(x) = x^2 - 2x$.

b. Find the area of the shaded region in illustration ii by considering it to be two separate regions. In the left region $g(x) = 0$ is the upper boundary; in the right region it is the lower boundary.

26. Use the technique suggested in Exercise 25 to find the area of the region bounded by $f(x) = x^{1/5}$ and $g(x) = x^5$ between $x = -1$ and $x = 1$.

27. Derive a formula for the area of the right triangle with legs of lengths a and b by integrating $f(x) = (a/b)x$ as indicated in the illustration.

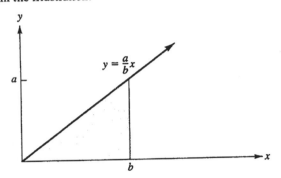

28. Derive a formula for the area of a trapezoid with bases of lengths a and b and with height h by integrating $f(x) = a + [(b - a)/h]x$ as shown in the illustration.

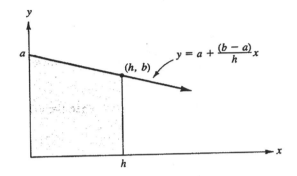

6.4
The Method of Substitution

The list of antidifferentiation formulas in Section 6.2 can be applied to more functions by using a substitution technique that depends on the chain rule for derivatives. Suppose that F is an antiderivative of the function f; that is, $F' = f$. If g is a differentiable function with $g(x)$ in the domain of F for all x, then from the chain rule we know that

$$D_x[F(g(x))] = F'(g(x))g'(x).$$

In the notation of antiderivatives, this can be written as

(6.7)
$$\int F'(g(x))g'(x)\, dx = F(g(x)) + c,$$

where c is the constant of integration. If we introduce a new variable u by defining $u = g(x)$, we have

$$du = g'(x)\, dx,$$

and substitution into equation (6.7) gives us

(6.8)
$$\int F'(u)\, du = F(u) + c.$$

As illustrated in the following examples, the task of finding an antiderivative can often be greatly simplified by making a substitution in the integrand. This procedure is called the **method of substitution** or is described as making a change of variable.

EXAMPLE 1

Find the antiderivative:

$$\int 6x(x^2 + 5)^3 \, dx.$$

SOLUTION

It is possible to work this problem by multiplying out the integrand, but it is much simpler to make a change of variable. Let

$$u = x^2 + 5.$$

Then the differential of u is $du = 2x \, dx$. Substitution into the integrand gives

$$\int 6x(x^2 + 5)^3 \, dx = \int 3(x^2 + 5)^3(2x \, dx)$$
$$= \int 3u^3 \, du$$
$$= \frac{3}{4}u^4 + c.$$

Replacing u by $x^2 + 5$ then gives us

$$\int 6x(x^2 + 5)^3 \, dx = \frac{3}{4}(x^2 + 5)^4 + c. \qquad \bullet$$

Observe that in this example the change of variable gave us the antiderivative $\int u^3 \, du$. When attempting to make a change of variable we often look for a substitution that will yield the form $\int u^n \, du$ for some n.

EXAMPLE 2

Find the antiderivative:

$$\int x^2 \sqrt{2 - x^3} \, dx.$$

SOLUTION

Rewriting the integrand as $x^2(2 - x^3)^{1/2}$, we see that we may be able to put this in the form $\int u^{1/2} \, du$. To do this let

(6.9)
$$u = 2 - x^3$$

Then the differential is

$$du = -3x^2 \, dx.$$

Division by -3 gives us

(6.10)
$$-\frac{1}{3} \, du = x^2 \, dx.$$

By equations (6.9) and (6.10) we have

$$\int x^2(2 - x^3)^{1/2} \, dx = \int (2 - x^3)^{1/2}(x^2 \, dx)$$

$$= \int u^{1/2} \left(-\frac{1}{3} \, du \right)$$

$$= -\frac{1}{3} \int u^{1/2} \, du$$

$$= -\frac{2}{9} u^{3/2} + c.$$

Returning to the original variable, we have

$$\int x^2 (2 - x^3)^{1/2} \, dx = -\frac{2}{9} (2 - x^3)^{3/2} + c. \qquad \bullet$$

EXAMPLE 3

Find the antiderivative:

$$\int \frac{3}{4x + 1} \, dx.$$

SOLUTION

Although no exponent appears explicitly, it is possible to write the integrand as $3(4x + 1)^{-1}$. Therefore, we let $u = 4x + 1$ and find

$$du = 4 \, dx.$$

Because the integrand contains a factor of $3 \, dx$, we multiply both sides of this equation by 3/4 to obtain

$$\frac{3}{4} \, du = 3 \, dx.$$

Substitution then gives us

$$\int \frac{3}{4x + 1} \, dx = \int \frac{3/4}{u} \, du = \frac{3}{4} \ln |u| + c = \frac{3}{4} \ln |4x + 1| + c. \qquad \bullet$$

When the integrand contains an exponential function, it is frequently possible to make a change of variable to obtain the form $e^u \, du$ by letting u equal the exponent.

EXAMPLE 4

Find the antiderivative:

$$\int e^{-5x} \, dx.$$

SOLUTION

We let $u = -5x$. Then $du = -5 \, dx$. Because the integrand contains only the factor dx, we divide by -5 to obtain $-1/5 \, du = dx$. Substituting in the integrand, we have

$$\int e^{-5x}\,dx = -\frac{1}{5}\int e^u\,du$$

$$= -\frac{1}{5}e^u + c$$

$$= -\frac{1}{5}e^{-5x} + c.$$

EXAMPLE 5

Find the antiderivative:

$$\int \frac{e^{\sqrt{x}}}{\sqrt{x}}\,dx.$$

SOLUTION

Here let $u = \sqrt{x}$. Then

$$du = \frac{1}{2}x^{-1/2}\,dx = \frac{1}{2\sqrt{x}}\,dx$$

or

$$2\,du = \frac{1}{\sqrt{x}}\,dx.$$

Substitution then gives

$$\int \frac{e^{\sqrt{x}}}{\sqrt{x}}\,dx = 2\int e^u\,du = 2e^u + c = 2e^{\sqrt{x}} + c.$$

EXAMPLE 6

Find the antiderivative:

$$\int \frac{\ln^3(x + 4)}{x + 4}\,dx.$$

SOLUTION

Let $u = \ln(x + 4)$. Then

$$du = \frac{1}{x + 4}\,dx.$$

Substitution gives

$$\int \frac{\ln^3(x + 4)}{x + 4}\,dx = \int u^3\,du$$

$$= \frac{1}{4}u^4 + c$$

$$= \frac{1}{4}\ln^4(x + 4) + c.$$

The three basic forms for antiderivatives that we have seen are

1. $\int u^n \, du = \dfrac{1}{n+1} u^{n+1} + c, \quad$ for $n \neq -1$;

2. $\int u^{-1} \, du = \int \dfrac{1}{u} \, du = \ln|u| + c$;

3. $\int e^u \, du = e^u + c$.

Many antiderivatives can be found by making a change of variable and using the earlier rules of antidifferentiation to reduce the problem to these basic forms. This process is not easy, and considerable practice is required to become proficient. It should also be kept in mind that many functions that have antiderivatives cannot be found by a change of variable.

We conclude this section by using the method of substitution to calculate two definite integrals.

EXAMPLE 7

Compute the definite integral:

$$\int_0^3 \frac{1}{\sqrt{5x+1}} \, dx.$$

SOLUTION

Make the change of variable $u = 5x + 1$. Then $du = 5\,dx$ or $1/5\,du = dx$. The antiderivative is

$$\int \frac{1}{\sqrt{5x+1}} \, dx = \frac{1}{5} \int \frac{1}{\sqrt{u}} du = \frac{1}{5} \int u^{-1/2} \, du$$

$$= \frac{2}{5} u^{1/2} + c$$

$$= \frac{2}{5}\sqrt{5x+1} + c.$$

Therefore

$$\int_0^3 \frac{1}{\sqrt{5x+1}} \, dx = \frac{2}{5}\sqrt{5x+1} \,\Bigg]_0^3$$

$$= \frac{2}{5}\sqrt{16} - \frac{2}{5}\sqrt{1}$$

$$= \frac{6}{5}.$$

EXAMPLE 8

Compute the integral:

$$\int_{-3}^2 \frac{3x-2}{2x+8} \, dx.$$

SOLUTION Recalling the substitution we used in Example 3, we let $u = 2x + 8$, and then $du = 2\ dx$ or $1/2\ du = dx$. To complete the substitution, it is necessary to write the numerator of the integrand $3x - 2$ in terms of u. Solving $u = 2x + 8$ for x, we find $x = 1/2u - 4$. Substituting, we get

$$3x - 2 = 3\left(\frac{1}{2}u - 4\right) - 2 = \frac{3}{2}u - 14.$$

The antiderivative is

$$\int \frac{3x - 2}{2x + 8}\ dx = \int \frac{(3/2)u - 14}{u}\left(\frac{1}{2}\ du\right)$$

$$= \int \left(\frac{3}{4} - \frac{7}{u}\right) du$$

$$= \frac{3}{4}u - 7\ \ln|u| + c$$

$$= \frac{3}{4}(2x + 8) - 7\ \ln|2x + 8| + c.$$

Therefore, the value of the definite integral is

$$\int_{-3}^{2} \frac{3x - 2}{2x + 8}\ dx = \left(\frac{3}{4}(2x + 8) - 7\ \ln|2x + 8|\right]_{-3}^{2}$$

$$= \left[\frac{3}{4}(12) - 7\ \ln 12\right] - \left[\frac{3}{4}(2) - 7\ \ln 2\right]$$

$$= \frac{15}{2} + 7(\ln 2 - \ln 12)$$

$$= \frac{15}{2} + 7\ \ln \frac{1}{6}.$$

EXERCISES 6.4

In Exercises 1–40 find the antiderivative by the method of substitution.

1. $\displaystyle\int (x - 7)^4\ dx$

2. $\displaystyle\int (3 - x)^6\ dx$

3. $\displaystyle\int (2x + 5)^3\ dx$

4. $\displaystyle\int (.4x - 10)^5\ dx$

5. $\displaystyle\int x(3x^2 + 5)^3\ dx$

6. $\displaystyle\int y(1 - y^2)^5\ dy$

7. $\displaystyle\int t^2(t^3 + 2)^4\ dt$

8. $\displaystyle\int s^5(4 - 3s^6)\ ds$

9. $\displaystyle\int x^2(x^3 + 5)^{-2}\ dx$

10. $\displaystyle\int x^3(1 - x^4)^{-3}\ dx$

11. $\displaystyle\int x^{-2}\left(4 + \frac{5}{x}\right)^2\ dx$

12. $\displaystyle\int x^{-1}(1 + \ln x)^6\ dx$

13. $\displaystyle\int 3x\sqrt{x^2 + 3}\ dx$

14. $\displaystyle\int 9x\sqrt{3x^2 + 5}\ dx$

15. $\displaystyle\int 4x(1 + x^2)^{1/3}\ dx$

16. $\displaystyle\int 8x^3(1 + x^4)^{-2/3}\ dx$

17. $\displaystyle\int (8x + 2)^{-7/4}\ dx$

18. $\displaystyle\int y(y^2 + 3)^{8/3}\ dy$

19. $\int (x - 1)(3x^2 - 6x + 2)\, dx$

20. $\int (x^2 - 2x)(3x^2 - x^3)^{-2}\, dx$

21. $\int \dfrac{x}{\sqrt{x^2 + 8}}\, dx$

22. $\int \dfrac{x^2}{\sqrt{1 - x^3}}\, dx$

23. $\int \dfrac{x + 2}{(x^2 + 4x + 5)^2}\, dx$

24. $\int \dfrac{x + 1}{(3x^2 + 6x + 1)^3}\, dx$

25. $\int \dfrac{dx}{2x + 4}$

26. $\int \dfrac{dx}{5 - 3x}$

27. $\int \dfrac{6r\, dr}{r^2 + 4}$

28. $\int \dfrac{w^2 + 2}{w^3 + 6w}\, dw$

29. $\int e^{5x}\, dx$

30. $\int e^{4 - 3x}\, dx$

31. $\int xe^{x^2}\, dx$

32. $\int \dfrac{1}{x^2}\, e^{3/x}\, dx$

33. $\int x^2 e^{-x^3}\, dx$

34. $\int (1 - x)e^{x^2 - 2x + 8}\, dx$

35. $\int \dfrac{\ln x}{x}\, dx$

36. $\int \dfrac{\sqrt{\ln x}}{x}\, dx$

37. $\int \dfrac{\ln^4(3 - x)}{3 - x}\, dx$

38. $\int \dfrac{x}{x^2 + 3}\, \ln(x^2 + 3)\, dx$

39. $\int \dfrac{e^{3x}}{e^{3x} + 2}\, dx$

40. $\int \dfrac{e^x - e^{-x}}{e^x + e^{-x}}\, dx$

In Exercises 41–54 find the value of the definite integral.

41. $\int_0^4 (x + 2)^3\, dx$

42. $\int_0^1 (4x + 1)^7\, dx$

43. $\int_0^4 \dfrac{dx}{\sqrt{2x + 1}}$

44. $\int_1^3 \sqrt{4x - 3}\, dx$

45. $\int_{-3}^3 x(x^2 - 1)^{2/3}\, dx$

46. $\int_{-2}^0 x(5 - x^2)^{-2}\, dx$

47. $\int_{-1}^1 s^2(s^3 + 1)^3\, ds$

48. $\int_0^{\sqrt{24}} \dfrac{y}{\sqrt{y^2 + 1}}\, dy$

49. $\int_0^2 \dfrac{dx}{8x + 1}$

50. $\int_3^5 \dfrac{t\, dt}{5 - t^2}$

51. $\int_0^2 xe^{x^2}\, dx$

52. $\int_1^4 \dfrac{1}{\sqrt{x}}\, e^{\sqrt{x}}\, dx$

53. $\int_1^e \dfrac{1}{x}\, \ln^2 x\, dx$

54. $\int_0^1 (1 - e^{-2x})(e^{-2x} + 2x - 1)^3\, dx$

In Exercises 55–60 find the area of the shaded region with the boundaries as indicated by the given function(s).

55.

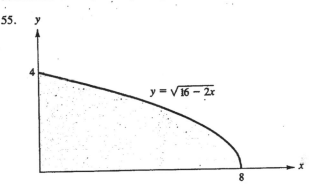

56.

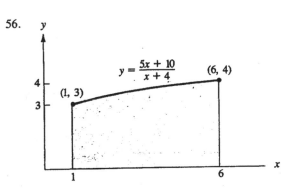

57.

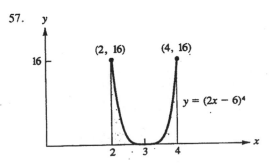

58.

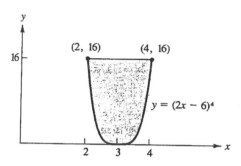

59.

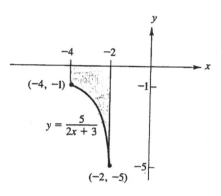

60.

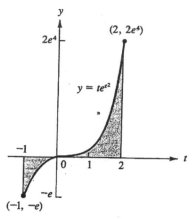

61. A department store manager must decide how many video cassette recordings of a hit movie should be ordered. Suppose that the marginal revenue from the sale of the qth recording is given by the function

$$MR = \sqrt{400 - 20q}, \qquad 5 \le q \le 20.$$

The manager orders 15 recordings of most movies. How much additional revenue would be received by the store if 20 are ordered this time?

62. Suppose that the marginal revenue function from the sale of a paperback novel is

$$MR = \frac{5q}{\sqrt{3.2q^2 - 1520}}, \qquad 25 \le q \le 100,$$

where q is the number of copies that the bookstore orders from the publisher. How much additional revenue will the bookstore receive if 60 copies are ordered rather than 40?

6.5
Applications of the Definite Integral

Our study of definite integrals began with applications. Knowing a marginal cost function, we used the definite integral to represent the increased cost associated with increased production; that is, if $MC(q)$ denotes the marginal cost of the qth unit, then the increased cost resulting from increasing output from q_0 to q_1 is given by

$$\int_{q_0}^{q_1} MC(q)\, dq.$$

Geometrically, we can now describe this additional cost as the area of the shaded region in Figure 6.9.

Areas can also be used to describe concepts related to functions other than those representing marginal quantities. For a demand function, if q_0 units are sold at price p_0, then the revenue $p_0 q_0$ can be interpreted as the area of a rectangle. (See Figure 6.10.)

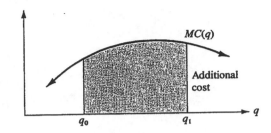

Figure 6.9

Increased total cost as the area of a region bounded by the marginal cost function

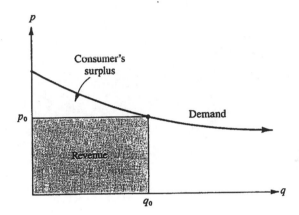

Figure 6.10

The relationship between demand, revenue, and consumer's surplus

Examining Figure 6.10 more carefully, we see that the area of the region below the demand function but above the horizontal line $p = p_0$ represents money not spent by consumers who would have been willing to pay a price higher than p_0 for the product. These savings are called the consumer's surplus at selling price p_0, or demand level q_0. More precisely, if $p = f(q)$ is a demand function, then the **consumer's surplus** CS at demand level q_0 is given by

(6.11)
$$CS = \int_0^{q_0} [f(q) - p_0] \, dq.$$

A supply curve can also be used to define two regions, one representing the actual revenue and the second a surplus income enjoyed by the producers. If p_0 is the selling price at demand level q_0, then $p_0 q_0$ is the revenue received by producers. Referring to Figure 6.11, we see in this case that the area under the supply curve is less than that of the revenue rectangle. The area of the region above the supply curve and below the horizontal line $p = p_0$ represents money that suppliers would not have received if demand had been less than q_0. This additional revenue is called the producer's surplus at demand level q_0. Specifically, if $p = f(q)$ is a supply function, then the **producer's surplus** PS at demand level q_0 is given by

(6.12)
$$PS = \int_0^{q_0} [p_0 - f(q)] \, dq.$$

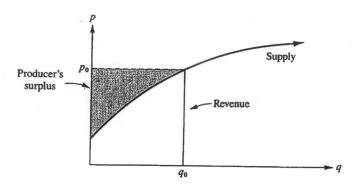

Figure 6.11
The relationship between supply, revenue, and producer's surplus

EXAMPLE 1 The daily demand and supply functions for rye flour at a local health food market are

$$p = 60 - q + .004q^2, \qquad 0 \le q \le 75,$$

and

$$p = 10 + .3q - .002q^2, \qquad 0 \le q \le 75,$$

respectively. Here q represents hundreds of pounds of flour and p represents dollars per hundred pounds. Find the market equilibrium point and the producer's and consumer's surplus at market equilibrium.

SOLUTION At equilibrium we must have

$$60 - q + .004q^2 = 10 + .3q - .002q^2$$

or

$$50 - 1.3q + .006q^2 = 0.$$

Factoring, we find

$$(50 - q)(1 - .006q) = 0;$$

thus $q = 50$ or $500/3$. Since only $q = 50$ is in the domain, the equilibrium point is $q = 50, p = 20$.

For consumer's surplus we use equation (6.11) to find

$$CS = \int_0^{50} [(60 - q + .004q^2) - 20]\, dq$$

$$= \left(40q - \frac{q^2}{2} + \frac{.004q^3}{3} \right]_0^{50}$$

$$= \$916.67.$$

Using equation (6.12) we find the producer's surplus to be

$$PS = \int_0^{50} [20 - (10 + .3q - .002q^2)]\, dq$$

$$= \left(10q - .15q^2 + \frac{.002q^3}{3} \right]_0^{50}$$

$$= \$208.33.$$

Figure 6.12 illustrates the supply and demand curves, the equilibrium point, and the regions whose areas represent consumer's and producer's surplus.

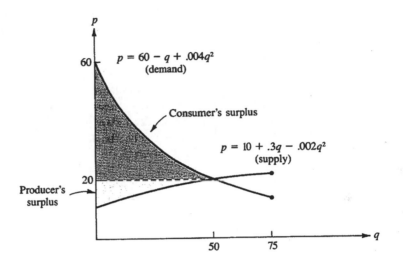

Figure 6.12

Consumer's and producer's surplus at market equilibrium.

The definite integral can also be used to determine the present value of an income stream or a cash flow over a period of time. Let I denote the income received at a time t years from the present. If future income is **discounted** at an instantaneous rate of r per year, then at time t, the present value of I is Ie^{-rt}. Suppose a project or an investment generates income at a rate of $f(t)$ per year at time t. Then the present value of the income received from the present to time T can be found by integrating $f(t)e^{-rt}$ over $[0, T]$. That is, the **present value P of an income stream** of $f(t)$ dollars per year for T years, discounted at rate r, is

(6.13)
$$P = \int_0^T f(t)e^{-rt} \, dt.$$

EXAMPLE 2

A company is considering investing \$30 million in a project that is expected to yield a profit of \$12 million per year for 4 yr. If the company discounts future earnings at an instantaneous rate of 15%, find the present value of the project. Should the company undertake this project?

SOLUTION

The rate at which the investment produces profits is $f(t) = 12$, where $0 \le t \le 4$. With $r = .15$, equation (6.13) gives the present value of the project:

$$P = \int_0^4 12e^{-.15t}\, dt$$

$$= -80e^{-.15t}\Big]_0^4$$

$$= -80e^{-.6} + 80$$

$$\doteq 36.095.$$

The project is profitable for the company: an investment of $30 million yields $36.095 million. ●

Definite integrals also provide a convenient way to express the mean (or average) value of a continuous function on a closed interval. Geometrically, the mean value of f on $[a, b]$ is equal to the height of a rectangle whose area equals that of the region bounded above by $y = f(x)$ between $x = a$ and $x = b$. (See Figure 6.13.) More precisely, the **mean value** MV of a continuous function f on the interval $[a, b]$ is given by

(6.14)
$$MV = \frac{1}{b - a} \int_a^b f(x)\, dx.$$

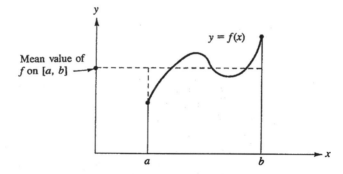

Figure 6.13

The mean value of f on $[a, b]$ as the height of a rectangle whose area equals $\int_a^b f(x)\, dx$

Recall that when averaging a finite set of n function values, we add the values and then divide by n. Here, in the case of infinitely many values, we integrate and divide by the length of the interval. As pointed out in Section 6.3, integration may be thought of as the limiting value of a summation process.

EXAMPLE 3

On the interval $[0, 2]$ find the mean value of the following:

a. $f(x) = x^2$

b. $f(x) = x^{1/2}$

c. $f(x) = x^{1/3}$

SOLUTION

Refer to equation (6.14) for each of the given functions.

a. $MV = \dfrac{\int_0^2 x^2 \, dx}{2 - 0} = \dfrac{1}{2} \cdot \dfrac{1}{3} x^3 \Big]_0^2 = \dfrac{1}{6}(8) = \dfrac{4}{3} \doteq 1.333$

b. $MV = \dfrac{\int_0^2 x^{1/2} \, dx}{2 - 0} = \dfrac{1}{2} \cdot \dfrac{2}{3} x^{3/2} \Big]_0^2 = \dfrac{1}{3} 2^{3/2} \doteq .943$

c. $MV = \dfrac{\int_0^2 x^{1/3} \, dx}{2 - 0} = \dfrac{1}{2} \cdot \dfrac{3}{4} x^{4/3} \Big]_0^2 = \dfrac{3}{8} 2^{4/3} \doteq .945$

●

EXAMPLE 4

The future value F of an investment of \$500 at 15% per annum compounded continuously for t years is

$$F = 500 e^{.15t}.$$

Find the mean value of this investment over the first 4 yr.

SOLUTION

We must find the mean of the continuous function F on the interval $[0, 4]$. Thus,

$$MV = \frac{\int_0^4 500 e^{.15t} \, dt}{4 - 0} = \frac{500}{4(.15)} e^{.15t} \Big]_0^4$$

$$= \frac{2500}{3} (e^{.6} - 1) = \$685.10.$$

●

EXERCISES 6.5

1. The marginal cost associated with the daily production of q Fresh Brew coffee makers is

$$MC(q) = 16 - .008q, \qquad 0 \le q \le 100.$$

Find the increased cost if daily production is increased from $q = 60$ to $q = 80$; then sketch the marginal cost function and shade the region whose area corresponds to this increased cost.

2. The marginal revenue when q tons of Lawn Food fertilizer are sold on a given day is

$$MR(q) = 240 - .4q, \qquad 0 \le q \le 100.$$

Find the additional revenue that results when sales increase from $q = 50$ to $q = 75$; then sketch the marginal revenue function and shade the region whose area corresponds to this increased revenue.

3. The marginal propensity to consume for an individual whose income I (in thousands of dollars) is between 20 and 30 is estimated by

$$\frac{dC}{dI} = 1 - .002I - .0003I^2, \qquad 20 \le I \le 30.$$

Find the increased consumption if an individual's income increases from $I = 25$ to $I = 28$; then sketch the marginal propensity function and shade the region whose area corresponds to this increased expenditure.

4. The marginal cost when q Steamy vacuum bottles are produced is

$$MC(q) = 10 - .08q + .006q^2, \qquad 0 \le q \le 150.$$

Find the increased cost if daily production is increased from $q = 100$ to $q = 120$; then sketch the marginal cost function and shade the region whose area corresponds to this increased cost.

For the supply and demand functions in Exercises 5–10 find the equilibrium point, producer's surplus, and consumer's surplus at equilibrium. Sketch the supply and demand functions on the same axes and shade the regions whose areas correspond to these surpluses.

5. Supply: $p = 10 + .16q$

   Demand: $p = 50 - .04q$ $0 \le q \le 300$

6. Supply: $p = 5 + .3q$

   Demand: $p = 80 - .2q$ $0 \le q \le 300$

7. Supply: $p = 2.8 + .5q - .002q^2$

   Demand: $p = 25 - .36q + .002q^2$ $0 \le q \le 90$

8. Supply: $p = 14.4 + .3q - .001q^2$

   Demand: $p = 160 - 2q + .005q^2$ $0 \le q \le 150$

9. Supply: $p = .25q + 5$

   Demand: $p = \dfrac{10q + 800}{q + 40}$ $0 \le q \le 100$

10. Supply: $p = .2q + 10$

    Demand: $p = \dfrac{20q + 4500}{q + 50}$ $0 \le q \le 300$

11. The demand function for peanuts in a local market is given by

    $$p = \frac{30q + 7000}{q + 100}, \qquad 0 \le q \le 500,$$

    where p is the price per hundred bags and q is the number of bags. If the supply function for these peanuts is

    $$p = 5\sqrt{q}, \qquad 0 \le q \le 500,$$

    then the equilibrium point is $q = 100$, $p = 50$. Find the consumer's surplus and producer's surplus at market equilibrium.

12. Your subordinates have determined that the supply and demand functions for a new line of shoes are

    $$p = 10 \sqrt[3]{q}, \qquad 0 \le q \le 500,$$

    and

    $$p = 50 + 80e^{-.01q}, \qquad 0 \le q \le 500,$$

    respectively. They have also determined that the equilibrium point is approximately $q = 208$, $p = 60$. As a market analyst you must determine the consumer's surplus and producer's surplus at market equilibrium.

13. The manager of a steel mill is considering the installation of a new smelter that uses the latest technology. If the smelter is installed, its greater efficiency will increase net profits by $10 million per year for the next 8 yr. The manager discounts future income at an instantaneous rate of 20% per year.

    a. Compute the present value of the new smelting process.

    b. If the new smelter will cost $25 million, how profitable is it for the steel mill to have the smelter installed?

14. Refer to Exercise 13. Suppose that instead of earning $10 million per year for 8 yr, the smelter will earn $10 million per year for only the first 4 yr and $5 million per year for the final 4 yr. What is the present value of the smelter in this case?

In Exercises 15–24 find the mean value of the given function on the indicated interval.

15. $f(x) = x^2$ on $[1, 4]$ 16. $f(x) = x^2 + x$ on $[0, 5]$

17. $g(x) = x^3$ on $[-1, 1]$

18. $g(x) = x^3 + x^2 - x$ on $[0, 2]$

19. $h(x) = \sqrt{2x + 1}$ on $[0, 4]$

20. $h(x) = \sqrt[3]{x + 5}$ on $[-4, 3]$

21. $r(x) = \dfrac{2x + 15}{x + 5}$ on $[0, 20]$ 22. $r(x) = \dfrac{5x + 8}{x + 2}$ on $[0, 6]$

23. $p(x) = e^{.05x}$ on $[0, 10]$ 24. $p(x) = e^{-.04x}$ on $[0, 5]$

25. If $1000 is invested in 12% per annum, compounded continuously, find the mean value of the investment over the first 5 yr.

26. Find the mean value of an investment of $600 at 10% per annum compounded continuously for 8 yr.

27. If a $50,000 machine depreciates continuously by 30%, its value at any time t (in years) is given by

    $$V = 50{,}000e^{-.3t}$$

    Find the mean value of V over the first 10 yr of use.

28. Suppose the machine in Exercise 27 has a salvage value of $4000 after 10 yr of use. If it depreciated over these 10 yr using the straight-line method, then its value V at any time t is given by

    $$V = 50{,}000 - 4600t, \qquad 0 \le t \le 10.$$

    Find the mean value of the machine over these 10 yr.

29. In the EOQ problems of Section 5.6, it was assumed that sales were uniform. Between production runs the inventory dropped from lot size q to 0 in a linear fashion; thus, as shown in illustration i, the mean or average size of an inventory was $q/2$, the area of the indicated triangle. Other demand possibilities appear in illustrations ii and iii. In case ii, sales are brisk soon after a production run when the product is fresh, but they slow down toward the end of the period. The opposite trend is suggested in case iii.

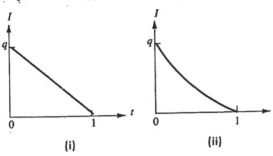

(i)   (ii)

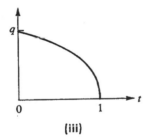

(iii)

   a. Suppose the inventory I at time t in illustration ii is
$$I(t) = q(1 - \sqrt{t}), \qquad 0 \le t \le 1.$$
   Find the mean value of I on $[0, 1]$.

   b. Suppose that
$$I(t) = q\sqrt[3]{1 - t}, \qquad 0 \le t \le 1,$$
   in illustration iii. Find the mean value of I on $[0, 1]$.

30. The distribution of a resource among members of a population is often displayed graphically using a Lorenz curve. For example, if x represents the poorest proportion of the population and y represents the proportion of total income for the population, then the curve $y = x$ indicates an equal distribution of income. (When $x = .2$, $y = .2$, so the poorest 20% of the population earns 20% of the total income. When $x = 50\%$, $y = 50\%$, and so on.) Income is not equally distributed if the Lorenz curve $y = f(x)$ takes some other form. If $y = x^2$, then $y = .04$ when $x = .2$, so the poorest 20% of the population earns only 4% of the total income. Gini's index of inequality G is defined to be twice the area between the Lorenz curve $y = f(x)$ and the equal distribution $y = x$; that is,
$$G = 2 \int_0^1 [x - f(x)]\, dx.$$

Find G for each of the following Lorenz curves.

   a. $f(x) = x^2$ b. $f(x) = x^{1.5}$

   c. $f(x) = x^{2.5}$ d. $f(x) = x^3$

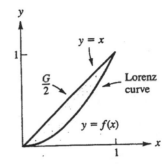

31. In Section 4.5 we found that the daily sales S of a new product, t days after its introduction to market, could be modeled using
$$S = 5500 - 5000e^{-.4t}, \qquad t \ge 0.$$

   a. Use a definite integral to determine total sales during the first month (30 days) that this product is on the market.

   b. Determine the mean sales per day during the first 10 days the product is on the market.

32. The general model used for bounded exponential growth is
$$P(t) = L - ae^{-kt}, \qquad t \ge 0,$$
where $k > 0$ and $L > a > 0$. Show that the mean value of P on $[0, T]$ is
$$L + \frac{a}{Tk}(e^{-kT} - 1).$$

33. Referring again to Section 4.5, logistic growth was modeled by
$$P = \frac{L}{1 + ae^{-kt}}, \qquad t \ge 0,$$
where $a > 1$ and L and k are positive. Find the mean value of P on the interval where the rate of growth is increasing—that is, on $[0, (\ln a)/k]$. (Hint: Multiply the numerator and denominator by e^{kt}; then substitute to evaluate the necessary integral.)

CH. 6 REVIEW

I. Key Terms & Concepts

Mathematics

Antiderivative
Integration
Definite Integral
Area Between Curves
Integration by Substitution
Mean Value of a Function

Business

Consumer's Surplus
Producer's Surplus
Present Value of an Income
　Stream

II. True or False

Indicate whether each statement is true or false.

1. $\int [f(x) - g(x)]\, dx = \int f(x)\, dx - \int g(x)\, dx$

2. $\int [f(x)g(x)]\, dx = \int f(x)\, dx \cdot \int g(x)\, dx$

3. $\int x^{-1}\, dx = x^0 + c$

4. Any antiderivative of the marginal cost is total cost.

5. For any demand and supply functions, at the equilibrium price producer's surplus equals consumer's surplus.

6. If f is continuous and positive on $[a, b]$, then $\int_a^b f(x)\, dx > 0$.

7. If f is continuous on $[a, b]$, $D_x\left[\int_a^b f(x)\, dx\right] = 0$.

8. If $\int f(x)\, dx$ exists, then $D_x\left[\int f(x)\, dx\right] = f(x)$.

9. If $F(x)$ and $G(x)$ are antiderivatives of $f(x)$, then $F(x) = G(x)$.

10. $\int e^x\, dx = \dfrac{1}{x + 1} e^{x+1} + c$

III. Drill Problems

In Problems 1–10 find the antiderivative.

1. $\int \sqrt{5x + 4}\, dx$

2. $\int \sqrt{x}(3 - x)\, dx$

3. $\int e^{-2x}\, dx$

4. $\int (x^3 - x^{-3})\, dx$

5. $\int \dfrac{x^2}{\sqrt[3]{1 - x^3}}\, dx$

6. $\int \dfrac{x - 1}{1 + 2x - x^2}\, dx$

7. $\int \dfrac{x^2 + 1}{x}\, dx$

8. $\int \dfrac{x}{x^2 + 1}\, dx$

9. $\int \left(\dfrac{1}{x} + x\right)^2 dx$

10. $\int x e^{x^2}\, dx$

In Problems 11–16 evaluate the definite integral.

11. $\int_0^3 (x^2 + 1)\, dx$

12. $\int_{-2}^2 \dfrac{x\, dx}{20 - x^2}$

13. $\int_1^5 \dfrac{dx}{8 - x}$

14. $\int_1^4 \dfrac{1}{\sqrt{x}} e^{\sqrt{x}}\, dx$

15. $\int_1^2 x(x^2 - 9)^{-2}\, dx$

16. $\int_0^1 \dfrac{e^{2x}}{1 + e^{2x}}\, dx$

17. Find the area of the figure bounded by the curves $y = x^2 + 1$ and $y = 2x + 1$.

18. Let $MC(q) = 10 - .2q - 6/\sqrt{q}$ be a marginal cost function. Find the increase in total cost if output is increased from $q = 25$ to $q = 36$ units.

19. Let $p = 10 + 4\sqrt{q}$ and $p = 80 - 2q$, where $0 \le q \le 40$, be a pair of supply and demand functions, respectively. Find the producer's surplus and the consumer's surplus at the equilibrium price, $p = 30$.

IV. Applications

1. The latest product from Dizpoz Inc. is a disposable toothbrush that contains a dab of toothpaste already on the bristles. The marginal cost (in cents) of producing the qth toothbrush is given by

$$MC(q) = 45 - .1q - .012q^2, \qquad 0 \le q \le 40,$$

where q is the number of brushes produced per minute. If the fixed cost for making the brushes is $.50 per minute, determine the total cost when the output rate is 30 brushes per minute.

2. The publisher of *The Metal Works*, a successful new magazine for rock music fans, wants to sell more copies of each issue. Currently the publisher is distributing 50,000 copies each month. Suppose that when q thousand copies of an issue are distributed, the marginal revenue (in thousands of dollars) is given by

$$MR(q) = 3.5 - .02q - \frac{30}{q}, \qquad 40 \le q \le 80.$$

How much additional revenue would be produced by increasing the distribution to 60,000 copies per month?

3. To model national savings rates for Asian countries, an economist is using

$$MPS(I) = .03 + .006\sqrt{I} + .0015\sqrt{I^3}, \quad 4 \le I \le 10,$$

where I is the gross national product in trillions of dollars and $MPS(I)$ denotes the marginal propensity to save for the aggregate economy of the country. If the economist assumes that when $I = 4$ there is no savings, deter-

mine the aggregate savings as a function of I. How much of the gross national product is saved if I is $9 trillion?

4. Refer to Exercise 3. Suppose that the economist knows that two neighboring countries in Asia have gross national products of $8 trillion and $9 trillion, respectively. If the model is accurate, how much more would be saved in the country with the larger gross national product?

5. To raise money to help cover the cost of a planned trip to Florida, a group of college students intends to hold a bake sale. They have estimated that the demand function for pies at the sale is

$$p = 8.5 - .05q, \qquad q \ge 0,$$

where q is the number of pies purchased at p dollars per pie. Assume that the number of pies these students are willing to bake is given by the supply function

$$p = \frac{3q + 15}{q + 30}, \qquad q \ge 0.$$

Find the producer's and consumer's surplus at market equilibrium.

6. An expansion is under way at a truck manufacturing plant that will double the output of lightweight trucks. The sale of these trucks will increase profits by $15 million per year for the first 2 yr, $12 million per year for the next 3 yr, and $6 million per year for 2 more years. Determine the present value of this expansion to the manufacturer if the future income is discounted at an instantaneous rate of 10% per year.

Suppose you are considering the purchase of a business that is currently making a profit of $50,000 per year. Furthermore, you think that under your management, profitability will increase by $15,000 per year indefinitely. That is, you think that t years from now, the business will be generating profits at a rate of

$$P(t) = 50 + 15t, \qquad t \geq 0$$

(in thousands of dollars per year). If you discount future earnings at an instantaneous rate of 10% per year, find the present value to you of this business.

CHAPTER 7

Further Topics in Integration

As noted earlier, the definite integral evolved historically as a means of calculating areas. During the 16th century, many scientists observed that finding the slopes of tangent lines and the areas under certain curves were inverse processes. After defining the derivative and the definite integral independently, we state this fact formally in the **fundamental theorem of calculus**:

$$\int_a^b f(x)\,dx = F(b) - F(a)$$

when f is continuous on $[a, b]$ and F is an antiderivative of f.

Up to this point, for reasons of efficiency, we have used the statement of the fundamental theorem as the definition of a definite integral. In many applications, however, antiderivatives cannot be obtained in a form that is easily evaluated. For this reason we now consider an independent definition of the definite integral that was made rigorous by Georg Bernhard Riemann, a 19th-century mathematician.

When f is continuous and positive on $[a, b]$, we have seen that $\int_a^b f(x)\,dx$ represents the area of the region shaded in Figure 7.1. To approximate this area we begin by partitioning $[a, b]$ into subintervals. Over each subinterval the graph of the function is replaced with an approximating horizontal segment. The sum of the areas of the resulting rectangles then approximates the area under the curve.

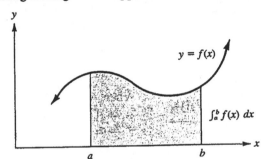

Figure 7.1
The definite integral as an area

More precisely, to construct N subdivisions of equal width Δx, take

$$\Delta x = \frac{b - a}{N}.$$

For the height of each rectangle use $f(c)$ for some c in the subinterval. The area of the rectangle is then $f(c) \cdot \Delta x$. If c_1 is selected in the first subinterval, c_2 in the second, and so on, the sum of these areas

(7.1)
$$S = f(c_1)\,\Delta x + f(c_2)\,\Delta x + \cdots + f(c_N)\,\Delta x$$

is an approximation to $\int_a^b f(x)\,dx$. See Figure 7.2.

Sums of the form (7.1) are called **Riemann sums**. For larger and larger values of N, the sum S gets closer and closer to the value of the definite integral $\int_a^b f(x)\,dx$. In fact, we may take this limit as the definition of the definite integral when f is continuous; that is,

(7.2)
$$\int_a^b f(x)\,dx = \lim_{N \to \infty} [f(c_1) + f(c_2) + \cdots + f(c_N)]\,\Delta x.$$

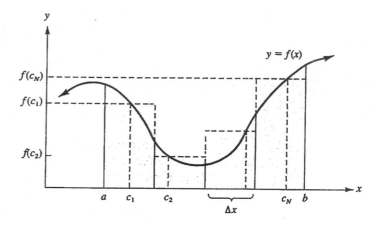

Figure 7.2

Approximating $\int_a^b f(x)\,dx$ by a sum of rectangle areas (Riemann sum)

Riemann's definition of the definite integral is more general than equation (7.2), however; it allows unequal subdivisions and applies to certain discontinuous functions.

EXAMPLE 1

Estimate $\int_1^4 x^2\,dx$ using a Riemann sum with $N = 6$ where (a) c_i is selected as the left endpoint of the ith interval, and (b) c_i is selected as the right endpoint of the ith interval. Compare these approximations with the true value of the definite integral.

SOLUTION

When $N = 6$, $\Delta x = (4 - 1)/6 = .5$, and so the subintervals are $[1, 1.5]$, $[1.5, 2]$, $[2, 2.5]$, $[2.5, 3]$, $[3, 3.5]$, and $[3.5, 4]$. In part a, $c_1 = 1$, $c_2 = 1.5$, $c_3 = 2$, $c_4 = 2.5$, $c_5 = 3$, and $c_6 = 3.5$, so the Riemann sum becomes

$$S = [f(1) + f(1.5) + f(2) + f(2.5) + f(3) + f(3.5)](.5)$$
$$= [1 + 2.25 + 4 + 6.25 + 9 + 12.25](.5)$$
$$= 34.75(.5)$$
$$= 17.375.$$

In part b the Riemann sum is

$$S = [f(1.5) + f(2) + f(2.5) + f(3) + f(3.5) + f(4)](.5)$$
$$= [2.25 + 4 + 6.25 + 9 + 12.25 + 16](.5)$$
$$= 49.75(.5)$$
$$= 24.875.$$

From the fundamental theorem,

$$\int_1^4 x^2\,dx = \frac{x^3}{3}\Bigg]_1^4 = \frac{64}{3} - \frac{1}{3} = 21.$$

Figure 7.3 illustrates the area estimates given by these Riemann sums.

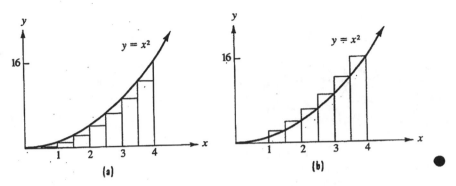

Figure 7.3
Riemann sums formed from rectangles whose heights are $f(c)$:
(a) when c is the left endpoint of each subinterval, and (b) when c is the right endpoint of each subinterval

Although Riemann sums can be formed by selecting c_i anywhere in the ith subdivision, when c_i is selected to be the left endpoint, as in the previous example, the resulting sum is called the **rectangular rule** for approximating $\int_a^b f(x)\,dx$. Another specialized Riemann sum that is often used to approximate definite integrals is the **midpoint rule**. For the midpoint rule each c_i is selected as the midpoint of the subinterval.

EXAMPLE 2

Since

$$\int \frac{1}{x}\,dx = \ln|x| + c,$$

we know that

$$\ln 2 = \ln 2 - \ln 1 = \int_1^2 \frac{1}{x}\,dx.$$

Use the midpoint rule with $N = 5$ to estimate $\ln 2$.

SOLUTION

If $N = 5$, then $\Delta x = .2$ and the subintervals are $[1, 1.2]$, $[1.2, 1.4]$, $[1.4, 1.6]$, $[1.6, 1.8]$, and $[1.8, 1]$. Thus, the midpoints are $c_1 = 1.1$, $c_2 = 1.3$, $c_3 = 1.5$, $c_4 = 1.7$, and $c_5 = 1.9$, and the Riemann sum is

$$S = \left[\frac{1}{1.1} + \frac{1}{1.3} + \frac{1}{1.5} + \frac{1}{1.7} + \frac{1}{1.9}\right](.2)$$

$$\doteq (3.4595)(.2)$$

$$= .6919.$$

To four decimal places, the true value of $\ln 2$ is .6931. Figure 7.4 illustrates this approximation.

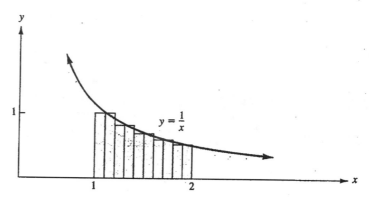

Figure 7.4
Approximating a definite integral
using the midpoint rule

The process of using special Riemann sums to approximate definite integrals is called **numerical integration**. In a careful study of numerical integration, error formulas for the rectangular rule and the midpoint rule can be derived. For a fixed number of subdivisions, the midpoint rule is generally more accurate than the rectangular rule.

EXAMPLE 3   The function $f(x) = \sqrt{1 + x^3}$ does not have an antiderivative that can be expressed in terms of well-known functions. Estimate

$$\int_0^2 \sqrt{1 + x^3}\, dx$$

using both the rectangular and midpoint rules when $N = 4$.

SOLUTION   For $N = 4$, $\Delta x = .5$, and the subintervals are $[0, .5]$, $[.5, 1]$, $[1, 1.5]$, and $[1.5, 2]$. For the rectangular rule, the Riemann sum is

$$R = [\sqrt{1 + 0^3} + \sqrt{1 + .5^3} + \sqrt{1 + 1^3} + \sqrt{1 + 1.5^3}](.5)$$
$$= 5.5665(.5)$$
$$= 2.7833.$$

For the midpoint rule, we have

$$M = [\sqrt{1 + .25^3} + \sqrt{1 + .75^3} + \sqrt{1 + 1.25^3} + \sqrt{1 + 1.75^3}](.5)$$
$$= 6.4405(.5)$$
$$= 3.2203.$$

Numerical integration schemes are used in computer programs to evaluate definite integrals. Often a rule is applied again and again, each time doubling the number of subintervals, until the Riemann sums give nearly the same numerical result. For such programs the **trapezoidal rule** is preferred over the midpoint rule for reasons of efficiency.

The trapezoidal rule can be considered an average of two Riemann sums like those formed in Example 1. Letting c_1 be the right endpoint of the first interval, c_2

the right endpoint of the second interval; and so on, we first use right endpoint values to form the Riemann sum:

$$S_R = [f(c_1) + f(c_2) + \cdots + f(c_{N-1}) + f(b)] \Delta x.$$

Left endpoint values yield the sum

$$S_L = [f(a) + f(c_1) + f(c_2) + \cdots + f(c_{N-1})] \Delta x.$$

Averaging these sums and simplifying, we obtain the trapezoidal rule:

(7.3)
$$T = \frac{S_L + S_R}{2}$$
$$= \frac{\Delta x}{2} [f(a) + 2(f(c_1) + f(c_2) + \cdots + f(c_{N-1})) + f(b)].$$

As suggested by its name, the trapezoidal rule approximates a definite integral using the sum of areas of trapezoids rather than rectangles. A geometric interpretation of the trapezoidal rule appears in Figure 7.5.

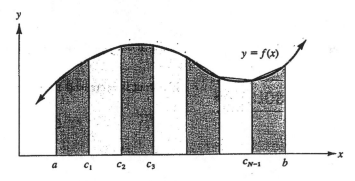

Figure 7.5

The trapezoidal rule approximation to $\int_a^b f(x)\, dx$

A feature of the trapezoidal rule that makes it favorable for numerical integration computer programs is illustrated in the next example.

EXAMPLE 4

Estimate

$$\int_1^2 \frac{1}{x}\, dx$$

using the trapezoidal rule first with five subdivisions and then doubling to ten subdivisions.

SOLUTION

When $N = 5$, $\Delta x = .2$, and the subintervals are [1, 1.2], [1.2, 1.4], [1.4, 1.6], [1.6, 1.8], and [1.8, 2]. Using equation (7.3), we get

$$T_5 = \frac{.2}{2} \left[\frac{1}{1} + 2\left(\frac{1}{1.2} + \frac{1}{1.4} + \frac{1}{1.6} + \frac{1}{1.8} \right) + \frac{1}{2} \right] = .6956.$$

When doubling N to 10, Δx becomes .1 and all of the old endpoint values are included in the new list of endpoints. Examining equation (7.3), we see that in the new sum these function values are multiplied by a new Δx that is half its former size. Thus, to form the new sum we need only multiply the old sum by .5 and add the new terms; that is,

$$T_{10} = .5T_5 + \frac{.1}{2}\left[2\left(\frac{1}{1.1} + \frac{1}{1.3} + \frac{1}{1.5} + \frac{1}{1.7} + \frac{1}{1.9}\right)\right]$$

$$= .3478 + .1(3.460)$$

$$= .6938.$$

●

In a final example we see that numerical integration can be used to approximate definite integrals from tabular data.

EXAMPLE 5

An analyst for Mayday Appliances has computed the following estimates for the marginal cost of the qth clothes dryer at Mayday's main plant:

q	20	25	30	35	40
MC	200	180	150	120	140

If the current daily output is $q = 20$, use the trapezoidal rule to approximate the increase in daily total cost if daily output is increased to $q = 40$.

SOLUTION

If output is increased from $q = 20$ to $q = 40$, the additional total cost is

$$C(40) - C(20) = \int_{20}^{40} MC(q)\, dq.$$

Since the values for q are equally spaced with $\Delta q = 5$, we have enough information to approximate this definite integral using the trapezoidal rule with $N = 4$; that is,

$$\int_{20}^{40} MC(q)\, dq \doteq \frac{\Delta q}{2}[MC(20) + 2(MC(25) + MC(30) + MC(35)) + MC(40)]$$

$$\doteq \frac{5}{2}[200 + 2(180 + 150 + 120) + 140]$$

$$= \$3100.$$

●

EXERCISES 7.1

In Exercises 1–8 evaluate the Riemann sum

$$[f(c_1) + \cdots + f(c_N)]\, \Delta x$$

for the function f on the interval [a,b] with the indicated values of N, c_1, . . . ,c_N. Compare this sum with the true value of $\int_a^b f(x)\, dx$.

1. $f(x) = 2x + 5$ on [0, 2]; $N = 4$, and $c_1 = 0$, $c_2 = .6$, $c_3 = 1.2$, $c_4 = 2$

2. $f(x) = 10 - x$ on [1, 4]; $N = 3$, and $c_1 = 1.5$, $c_2 = 2$, $c_3 = 3.3$

3. $f(x) = 3x^2 + 1$ on [0, 4]; $N = 5$, and $c_1 = 0$, $c_2 = 1$ $c_3 = 2$, $c_4 = 3$, $c_5 = 3.8$

4. $f(x) = 9 + 2x + 6x^2$ on $[-1, 1]$; $N = 5$, and $c_1 = -1$, $c_2 = -.5, c_3 = 0, c_4 = .5, c_5 = 1$

5. $f(x) = \sqrt{x}$ on $[1, 4]$; $N = 3$, and $c_1 = 1.21$, $c_2 = 2.25$, $c_3 = 3.61$

6. $f(x) = x\sqrt{x^2 + 9}$ on $[0, 4]$; $N = 4$, and $c_1 = .5$, $c_2 = 1.2$, $c_3 = 2, c_4 = 4$

7. $f(x) = \dfrac{x}{x^2 + 1}$ on $[1, 4]$; $N = 3$, and $c_1 = 1.1$, $c_2 = 2.5$, $c_3 = 3.6$

8. $f(x) = \dfrac{\ln x}{x}$ on $[1, 5]$; $N = 4$, and $c_1 = 1.6$, $c_2 = 2.5$, $c_3 = 3.3, c_4 = 4.5$

In Exercises 9–16 estimate the value of the given definite integral using the midpoint rule with the indicated value of N.

9. $\int_1^4 x^2 \, dx$, $N = 6$ (Compare this result with Example 1.)

10. $\int_1^4 \sqrt{x} \, dx$, $N = 6$

11. $\int_0^1 \dfrac{4}{1 + x^2} \, dx$, $N = 5$ (The true value of this definite integral is π.)

12. $\int_0^1 4\sqrt{1 - x^2} \, dx$, $N = 5$

13. $\int_1^3 \dfrac{1}{x} \, dx$, $N = 5$ 14. $\int_1^3 \ln x \, dx$, $N = 4$

15. $\int_0^4 2^x \, dx$, $N = 5$ 16. $\int_0^1 e^{-x} \, dx$, $N = 5$

In Exercises 17–20 use the trapezoidal rule to estimate the value of the given integral. First let $N = 5$; then $N = 10$.

17. $\int_0^1 \dfrac{4}{1 + x^2} \, dx$ 18. $\int_0^1 4\sqrt{1 - x^2} \, dx$

19. $\int_0^2 \sqrt{1 + x^3} \, dx$ 20. $\int_0^1 e^{x^2} \, dx$

In Exercises 21–24 use the trapezoidal rule to estimate the indicated definite integral from the given tabular data.

21. $\int_{50}^{100} MR(q) \, dq$

q	50	60	70	80	90	100
MR	20	15	12	8	4	2

22. $\int_{30}^{60} MC(q) \, dq$

q	30	36	42	48	54	60
MC	110	150	180	200	200	220

23. $\int_{10}^{40} p(q) \, dq$

q	10	15	20	25	30	35	40
p	40	38	35	32	30	28	27

24. $\int_0^5 f(x) \, dx$

x	0	1	2	3	4	5
$f(x)$	2	3	8	4	6	9

In statistics, normal probabilities are proportional to the area under the bell-shaped curve $f(x) = e^{-x^2/2}$ shown here. The function f does not have an antiderivative that can be written in terms of well-known functions, and so normal probability tables are built using numerical integration. In Exercises 25–28 estimate the definite integral as indicated.

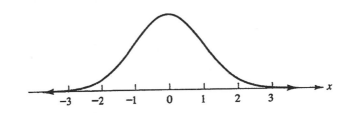

25. $\int_0^1 f(x) \, dx$; midpoint rule with $N = 4$

26. $\int_1^2 f(x) \, dx$; midpoint rule with $N = 5$

27. $\int_0^3 f(x) \, dx$; trapezoidal rule with $N = 6$

28. $\int_0^2 f(x)\, dx$; trapezoidal rule with $N = 5$

29. Recall that the mean value of a continuous function f over an interval $[a, b]$ is defined by

$$MV = \frac{1}{b - a} \int_a^b f(x)\, dx.$$

Find MV when the definite integral is approximated by the Riemann sum $[f(c_1) + f(c_2) + \cdots + f(c_N)]\, \Delta x$.

30. Derive the trapezoidal rule equation (7.3) by simplifying

$$\frac{S_L + S_R}{2}.$$

7.2
Integration Techniques

In this section we present a method for finding antiderivatives that is often useful when the integrand is a product but substitution does not yield a standard form. This method, called **integration by parts**, is based on the product rule for derivatives.

Let u and v be differentiable functions of a variable x. Then

$$\frac{d}{dx}(uv) = u'v + uv'$$

or, in terms of differentials,

$$d(uv) = (u'v + uv')\, dx$$
$$= v(u'\, dx) + u(v'\, dx).$$

We then have the product rule for differentials:

(7.4) $$d(uv) = v\, du + u\, dv.$$

Taking the antiderivative of each side of equation (7.4) yields

$$\int d(uv) = \int v\, du + \int u\, dv.$$

Since $\int d(uv) = uv$, rearrangement of the terms gives us the integration by parts formula:

(7.5) $$\int u\, dv = uv - \int v\, du.$$

To use equation (7.5) to find a particular antiderivative, it is necessary to break the integrand into a product of two functions, u and dv (the dx must be included with the dv). The formula can then be used if it is possible to find a function v whose differential is dv and if $\int v\, du$ is simpler than the original antiderivative.

EXAMPLE 1

Use integration by parts to find the antiderivative:

$$\int xe^{2x}\, dx.$$

SOLUTION

This integrand is not one of the standard forms and there is no obvious substitution that will change it to one. However, we can find an antiderivative for e^{2x}.

Therefore, we let $u = x$ and $dv = e^{2x} dx$. Then $du = dx$ and $v = 1/2e^{2x}$. Substituting into equation (7.5) gives

$$\int xe^{2x} dx = x\left(\frac{1}{2}e^{2x}\right) - \int \frac{1}{2}e^{2x} dx.$$

Finding the new antiderivative on the right gives

$$\int xe^{2x} dx = \frac{1}{2}xe^{2x} - \frac{1}{4}e^{2x} + c. \qquad \bullet$$

Because there are other ways that the integrand could have been factored, it is interesting to see what happens if u and dv are selected in another fashion. For example, let $u = e^{2x}$ and $dv = x\, dx$. Then $du = 2e^{2x} dx$ and $v = 1/2x^2$. Applying equation (7.5) gives

$$\int xe^{2x} dx = \frac{1}{2}x^2 e^{2x} - \int x^2 e^{2x} dx,$$

which is a valid equation, but the new antiderivative is more complex than the original one.

EXAMPLE 2

Find the antiderivative:

$$\int x^2 \ln x\, dx.$$

SOLUTION

Because it is easy to find an antiderivative of x^2, we let $u = \ln x$ and $dv = x^2 dx$. Then

$$du = \frac{1}{x} dx \quad \text{and} \quad v = \frac{1}{3}x^3.$$

Substituting into equation (7.5) gives

$$\int x^2 \ln x\, dx = \frac{1}{3}x^3 \ln x - \int \left(\frac{1}{3}x^3\right)\left(\frac{1}{x}dx\right)$$

$$= \frac{1}{3}x^3 \ln x - \frac{1}{3}\int x^2 dx$$

$$= \frac{1}{3}x^3 \ln x - \frac{1}{9}x^3 + c. \qquad \bullet$$

To find some antiderivatives it is necessary to use equation (7.5) more than once.

EXAMPLE 3

Find the antiderivative:

$$\int x^2 \sqrt{1 + x}\, dx.$$

SOLUTION

We know that for any n (except -1) an antiderivative of $(1 + x)^n$ is $(1 + x)^{n+1}/(n + 1)$. Therefore we will let $u = x^2$ and $dv = (1 + x)^{1/2} dx$. Then

$du = 2x\,dx$ and $v = 2/3(1 + x)^{3/2}$. From equation (7.5) we have

(7.6) $$\int x^2(1 + x)^{1/2}\,dx = \frac{2}{3}x^2(1 + x)^{3/2} - \frac{4}{3}\int x(1 + x)^{3/2}\,dx.$$

The antiderivative on the right can be found with a second integration by parts. Let $u = x$ and $dv = (1 + x)^{3/2}\,dx$. Then $du = dx$ and $v = 2/5(1 + x)^{5/2}$. Applying equation (7.5) to the right side of equation (7.6), we have

$$\int x^2(1 + x)^{1/2}\,dx = \frac{2}{3}x^2(1 + x)^{3/2} - \frac{4}{3}\left[\frac{2}{5}x(1 + x)^{5/2} - \frac{2}{5}\int (1 + x)^{5/2}\,dx\right]$$

$$= \frac{2}{3}x^2(1 + x)^{3/2} - \frac{4}{3}\left[\frac{2}{5}x(1 + x)^{5/2} - \frac{4}{35}(1 + x)^{7/2} + c\right]$$

$$= \frac{2}{3}x^2(1 + x)^{3/2} - \frac{8}{15}x(1 + x)^{5/2} + \frac{16}{105}(1 + x)^{7/2} + c. \quad\bullet$$

The next example shows that the integration by parts formula can be useful in some instances where the integrand is not actually a product.

EXAMPLE 4

Use integration by parts to find

$$\int \ln x\,dx.$$

SOLUTION

Let $u = \ln x$ and $dv = dx$. Then

$$du = \frac{1}{x}\,dx \quad\text{and}\quad v = x.$$

From equation (7.5) we have

$$\int \ln x\,dx = x \ln x - \int x\left(\frac{1}{x}\,dx\right)$$

$$= x \ln x - \int dx$$

$$= x \ln x - x + c. \quad\bullet$$

Because the process of finding the antiderivative of a function can be so difficult and time-consuming, tables that list antiderivatives have been constructed. These tables can be found in mathematics handbooks or even as separate volumes in the reference section of most libraries. To demonstrate the use of such tables, we provide a very brief list of antiderivatives in Table 7.1.

To use a table of antiderivatives it is usually necessary to make a substitution or a change of variable to put the given integrand into one of the forms that appear in the table.

1. $\int u^n \, du = \dfrac{1}{n+1} u^{n+1} + c, \qquad n \neq -1$ 2. $\int u^{-1} \, du = \ln|u| + c$

3. $\int e^u \, du = e^u + c$ 4. $\int b^u \, du = \dfrac{1}{\ln b} b^u + c$

5. $\int u e^u \, du = u e^u - e^u + c$ 6. $\int u^n e^u \, du = u^n e^u - n \int u^{n-1} e^u \, du$

7. $\int \ln u \, du = u \ln u - u + c$ 8. $\int u \ln u \, du = \dfrac{1}{2} u^2 \ln u - \dfrac{1}{4} u^2 + c$

9. $\int u^n \ln u \, du = \dfrac{1}{n+1} u^{n+1} \ln u - \dfrac{1}{(1+n)^2} u^{n+1} + c$

10. $\int \sqrt{a + bu} \, du = \dfrac{2}{3b} (a + bu)^{3/2} + c$

11. $\int u \sqrt{a + bu} \, du = \dfrac{2}{15b^2} (3bu - 2a)(a + bu)^{3/2} + c$

12. $\int \dfrac{du}{\sqrt{a + bu}} = \dfrac{2}{b} \sqrt{a + bu} + c$ 13. $\int \dfrac{u \, du}{\sqrt{a + bu}} = \dfrac{2}{3b^2} (bu - a)\sqrt{a + bu} + c$

14. $\int \dfrac{du}{u^2 - a^2} = \dfrac{1}{2a} \ln\left| \dfrac{u - a}{u + a} \right| + c$ 15. $\int \dfrac{du}{a^2 - u^2} = \dfrac{1}{2a} \ln\left| \dfrac{u + a}{u - a} \right| + c$

16. $\int \sqrt{u^2 \pm a^2} \, du = \dfrac{1}{2} u \sqrt{u^2 \pm a^2} \pm \dfrac{1}{2} a^2 \ln\left| u + \sqrt{u^2 \pm a^2} \right| + c$

17. $\int u \sqrt{u^2 \pm a^2} \, du = \dfrac{1}{3} (u^2 \pm a^2)^{3/2} + c$ 18. $\int \dfrac{du}{\sqrt{u^2 \pm a^2}} = \ln\left| u + \sqrt{u^2 \pm a^2} \right| + c$

19. $\int \dfrac{u \, du}{\sqrt{u^2 \pm a^2}} = \sqrt{u^2 \pm a^2} + c$

20. $\int \dfrac{\sqrt{u^2 + a^2}}{u} \, du = \sqrt{u^2 + a^2} - a \ln\left| \dfrac{a + \sqrt{u^2 + a^2}}{u} \right| + c$

Table 7.1

A table of antiderivatives: a and b are constants and n is a positive integer

EXAMPLE 5

Make a change of variable and use Table 7.1 to find

$$\int \frac{x}{\sqrt{9x^4 - 1}} \, dx.$$

SOLUTION

Observe that the expression under the radical is the difference of two squares. Referring to Table 7.1, we see that the integrand is of the form required by formula 18. Therefore, we let $u = 3x^2$. Then $du = 6x \, dx$ or $1/6 \, du = x \, dx$. Substitution and the use of formula 18 with $a = 1$ then give us

$$\int \frac{x}{\sqrt{9x^4 - 1}} \, dx = \frac{1}{6} \int \frac{du}{\sqrt{u^2 - 1}}$$
$$= \ln\left| u + \sqrt{u^2 - 1} \right| + c$$
$$= \ln\left(3x^2 + \sqrt{9x^4 - 1} \right) + c.$$

(The absolute value bars can be dropped because $3x^2 + \sqrt{9x^4 - 1}$ is positive for any x for which it is defined.) ●

EXAMPLE 6

Use Table 7.1 to find

$$\int x\sqrt{4 - 3x}\,dx.$$

SOLUTION

Formula 11 may be used directly with $a = 4$ and $b = -3$. Therefore

$$\int x\sqrt{4 - 3x}\,dx = \frac{2}{15(9)}[3(-3)x - 2(4)](4 - 3x)^{3/2} + c$$

$$= -\frac{2}{135}(9x + 8)(4 - 3x)^{3/2} + c. \qquad ●$$

EXAMPLE 7

Make a change of variable and use Table 7.1 to find

$$\int e^{3x}\ln(8 + e^{3x})\,dx.$$

SOLUTION

Let $u = 8 + e^{3x}$. Then $du = 3e^{3x}\,dx$ or $1/3\,du = e^{3x}\,dx$. Substitution then gives us an integrand to which formula 7 may be applied:

$$\int e^{3x}\ln(8 + e^{3x})\,dx = \frac{1}{3}\int \ln u\,du$$

$$= \frac{1}{3}(u\ln u - u) + c$$

$$= \frac{1}{3}[(8 + e^{3x})\ln(8 + e^{3x}) - (8 + e^{3x})] + c$$

$$= \left(\frac{8}{3} + \frac{1}{3}e^{3x}\right)\ln(8 + e^{3x}) - \frac{1}{3}e^{3x} + c.$$

(Note that the arbitrary constant c includes the term $-8/3$.) ●

EXERCISES 7.2

In Exercises 1–15 find the indicated antiderivative through integration by parts.

1. $\int xe^x\,dx$

2. $\int xe^{-3x}\,dx$

3. $\int x^2 e^{-x}\,dx$

4. $\int x^2 e^{4x}\,dx$

5. $\int \dfrac{x}{\sqrt{1 + x}}\,dx$

6. $\int x\sqrt{3 - x}\,dx$

7. $\int x\ln x\,dx$

8. $\int \sqrt{x}\ln x\,dx$

9. $\int x(2x + 1)^4\,dx$

10. $\int x(5 - x)^8\,dx$

11. $\int \dfrac{x^2}{\sqrt{4+x}}\,dx$

12. $\int x^2\sqrt{1-x}\,dx$

13. $\int \dfrac{x^3}{\sqrt{1+x^2}}\,dx$

14. $\int x^3 e^x\,dx$

15. $\int (\ln x)^2\,dx$

In Exercises 16–25 use the antiderivatives in Table 7.1 to find the given antiderivative.

16. $\int 5^{-3x}\,dx$

17. $\int x^2 4^{6-x^3}\,dx$

18. $\int \dfrac{dx}{25x^2-9}$

19. $\int \dfrac{x\,dx}{4-x^2}$

20. $\int e^{2x}\sqrt{e^{2x}+1}\,dx$

21. $\int e^{3x}\sqrt{e^{6x}-2}\,dx$

22. $\int (1+5x)^3 \ln(1+5x)\,dx$ 23. $\int x\ln(1+4x^2)\,dx$

24. $\int \dfrac{x}{\sqrt{1+4x^2}}\,dx$

25. $\int \dfrac{x}{\sqrt{1+9x^4}}\,dx$

In Exercises 26–32 find the indicated definite integral.

26. $\int_0^1 xe^{4x}\,dx$

27. $\int_{-1}^2 xe^{x/2}\,dx$

28. $\int_{-1}^1 x^2 e^x\,dx$

29. $\int_0^3 (x+1)\ln(x+1)\,dx$

30. $\int_1^2 x^2 \ln x\,dx$

31. $\int_{-2}^0 x(x+2)^5\,dx$

32. $\int_2^5 x\sqrt{x-1}\,dx$

33. Assume that money is deposited into an account at a rate of $f(t)$ dollars per year at time t, where $0 \le t \le T$. If interest is earned on this account at a nominal rate of r, compounded continuously, then the amount of continuous cash flow at time T is given by

$$\int_0^T f(t)e^{r(T-t)}\,dt.$$

Find the amount of continuous cash flow in these cases.

a. $f(t) = 500,\ r = .10,\ T = 4$

b. $f(t) = 500 + 10t,\ r = .10,\ T = 4$

c. $f(t) = 500t,\ r = .10,\ T = 4$

7.3
Improper Integrals

Thus far we have considered definite integrals of the form $\int_a^b f(x)\,dx$ for integrands f that are continuous on the closed interval $[a, b]$. In many cases limits can be used to extend the definition of definite integrals beyond this "proper" setting. In this section we consider so-called **improper integrals,** where the integrand or one of the limits of integration "becomes infinite."

Referring to Figure 7.6, we suppose f is continuous on the interval $(c, b]$, but $\lim_{x \to c^+} f(x) = \pm\infty$. For any a between c and b, $\int_a^b f(x)\,dx$ is a proper integral. As a approaches c, $\int_a^b f(x)\,dx$ may approach a real number. If this is the case, we say $\int_c^b f(x)\,dx$ **converges** and take

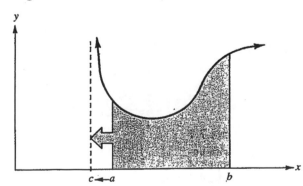

Figure 7.6
An improper integral as the limit of proper integrals

$$(7.7) \qquad \int_c^b f(x)\, dx = \lim_{a \to c^+} \int_a^b f(x)\, dx.$$

If $\lim_{a \to c^+} \int_a^b f(x)\, dx$ does not exist as a real number, we say $\int_c^b f(x)\, dx$ **diverges**.

EXAMPLE 1   Show that $\int_0^1 \dfrac{1}{x}\, dx$ diverges, whereas $\int_0^1 \dfrac{1}{\sqrt{x}}\, dx = 2$.

SOLUTION   For $0 < a < 1$ we have

$$\int_a^1 \frac{1}{x}\, dx = \ln x \bigg]_a^1 = \ln 1 - \ln a.$$

Letting a tend to 0, we find

$$\lim_{a \to 0^+} \int_a^1 \frac{1}{x}\, dx = \lim_{a \to 0^+} (-\ln a) = \infty;$$

thus, $\int_0^1 1/x\, dx$ diverges. In the second case,

$$\int_a^1 \frac{1}{\sqrt{x}}\, dx = 2\sqrt{x} \bigg]_a^1 = 2\sqrt{1} - 2\sqrt{a}.$$

Taking limits, we find

$$\lim_{a \to 0^+} \int_a^1 \frac{1}{\sqrt{x}}\, dx = 2 - \lim_{a \to 0^+} 2\sqrt{a} = 2;$$

hence, $\int_0^1 \dfrac{1}{\sqrt{x}}\, dx = 2$.   ●

The improper integrals in Example 1 may be considered as areas of "unbounded" regions, as illustrated in Figure 7.7. When the improper integral converges, the region has a finite area.

Generalizing the analysis in the previous example, we obtain the following result.

Figure 7.7
(a) an unbounded region with unbounded area, and (b) an unbounded region with finite area

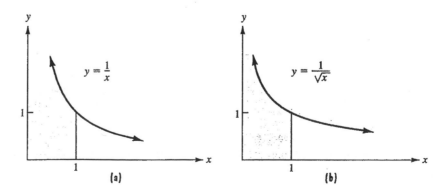

Theorem 7.1

> If p is a positive constant and b is any positive real number, then the improper integral
>
> $$\int_0^b \frac{1}{x^p}\, dx$$
>
> diverges if $p \geq 1$ and converges to $b^{1-p}/(1-p)$ if $0 < p < 1$.

EXAMPLE 2

The selling price p (per pound) for gunpowder at Shooter's Supply is related to the quantity q (in pounds) sold on a given day according to the demand function

$$p = 50q^{-1/3}, \qquad 0 < q \leq 500.$$

Find the consumer's surplus when $q = 125$.

SOLUTION

Noting that $p = 10$ when $q = 125$ and that

$$\lim_{q \to 0^+} 50q^{-1/3} = \infty,$$

we see that the consumer's surplus is represented by the improper integral

$$CS = \int_0^{125} (50q^{-1/3} - 10)\, dq.$$

Referring to Theorem 7.1, we find that

$$CS = \frac{50(125)^{2/3}}{2/3} - 1250 = \$625. \qquad \bullet$$

If the function f is continuous on the interval $[a, c)$ while $\lim_{x \to c^-} f(x) = \pm\infty$, we define the improper integral $\int_a^c f(x)\, dx$ in a fashion similar to equation (7.7); that is,

(7.8)
$$\int_a^c f(x)\, dx = \lim_{b \to c^-} \int_a^b f(x)\, dx$$

if this limit exists. Otherwise, $\int_a^c f(x)\, dx$ diverges.

Combining equations (7.7) and (7.8), if $a < c < b$ and f is continuous on $[a, b]$, except at $x = c$ where $\lim_{x \to c^+} f(x) = \pm\infty$ or $\lim_{x \to c^-} f(x) = \pm\infty$, the improper integral $\int_a^b f(x)\, dx$ is given by

(7.9)
$$\int_a^b f(x)\, dx = \lim_{d \to c^-} \int_a^d f(x)\, dx + \lim_{d \to c^+} \int_d^b f(x)\, dx,$$

provided these limits exist. If either limit fails to exist, then $\int_a^b f(x)\, dx$ diverges.

EXAMPLE 3

Determine whether $\displaystyle\int_0^6 \frac{1}{x-4}\, dx$ converges or diverges.

SOLUTION

The integrand $f(x) = 1/(x - 4)$ is continuous on $[0, 6]$, except at $x = 4$, where $\lim_{x \to 4+} f(x) = \infty$ and $\lim_{x \to 4-} f(x) = -\infty$. Integrating, with $0 < d < 4$, we find

$$\int_0^d \frac{1}{x - 4} \, dx = \ln|x - 4| \Big]_0^d = \ln|d - 4| - \ln 4.$$

Because $\lim_{d \to 4-} \ln|d - 4| = -\infty$, the integral $\int_0^4 1/(x - 4) \, dx$ diverges. We conclude that $\int_0^6 1/(x - 4) \, dx$ is also divergent. [The same conclusion would have been reached had we considered the integral of $f(x)$ on the interval $[4, 6]$.]

The careful reader should be aware that had the discontinuity in the integrand been ignored and the Fundamental Theorem of Calculus used to evaluate this definite integral immediately, an incorrect value of $\ln 6 - \ln 4$ would have been obtained. ●

A second type of improper integral arises when one of the limits of integration of a proper integral is allowed to tend toward infinity. Specifically, if f is continuous on $[a, \infty)$, then the improper integral $\int_a^\infty f(x) \, dx$ is defined by

(7.10)
$$\int_a^\infty f(x) \, dx = \lim_{b \to \infty} \int_a^b f(x) \, dx,$$

if this limit exists. Otherwise, $\int_a^\infty f(x) \, dx$ diverges. Analogously, if f is continuous on $(-\infty, b]$, then the improper integral $\int_{-\infty}^b f(x) \, dx$ is given by

(7.11)
$$\int_{-\infty}^b f(x) \, dx = \lim_{a \to -\infty} \int_a^b f(x) \, dx,$$

when this limit exists, and $\int_{-\infty}^b f(x) \, dx$ diverges otherwise.

EXAMPLE 4

Show that $\int_1^\infty \frac{1}{\sqrt{x}} \, dx$ diverges, but $\int_{-\infty}^{-2} \frac{1}{x^2} \, dx = 1/2$.

SOLUTION

For $b > 1$ we have

$$\int_1^b \frac{1}{\sqrt{x}} \, dx = 2\sqrt{x} \Big]_1^b = 2\sqrt{b} - 2.$$

As b tends to infinity,

$$\lim_{b \to \infty} (2\sqrt{b} - 2) = \infty;$$

thus, $\int_1^\infty 1/\sqrt{x} \, dx$ diverges. However, for $a < -2$,

$$\int_a^{-2} \frac{1}{x^2} \, dx = -\frac{1}{x} \Big]_a^{-2} = \frac{1}{2} + \frac{1}{a};$$

thus,

$$\int_{-\infty}^{-2} \frac{1}{x^2}\, dx = \lim_{a \to -\infty} \left(\frac{1}{2} + \frac{1}{a} \right) = \frac{1}{2}.$$ ●

Once again the analysis in Example 4 can be extended to the following general result.

Theorem 7.2

> If p is a positive constant and a is any positive real number, then the improper integral
>
> $$\int_{a}^{\infty} \frac{1}{x^p}\, dx$$
>
> diverges if $0 < p \le 1$ and converges to $a^{1-p}/(p - 1)$ if $p > 1$.

EXAMPLE 5

Suppose that an asset will yield income continuously, t years into the future, at a rate of $I(t)$ dollars per year. If the time value of money is assumed to be r per annum, then the present value P of this asset can be determined by discounting over all future years. That is,

$$P = \int_{0}^{\infty} I(t) e^{-rt}\, dt.$$

Find P if $I(t) = K$ for all t.

SOLUTION

Since $\int_{0}^{b} K e^{-rt}\, dt = K(1 - e^{-rb})/r$, we have

$$P = \lim_{b \to \infty} \frac{K}{r} (1 - e^{-rb}) = \frac{K}{r}.$$ ●

If f is continuous for all real numbers, then we can combine equations (7.10) and (7.11) to define the improper integral $\int_{-\infty}^{\infty} f(x)\, dx$ by letting c be any real number and taking

(7.12)
$$\int_{-\infty}^{\infty} f(x)\, dx = \lim_{a \to -\infty} \int_{a}^{c} f(x)\, dx + \lim_{b \to \infty} \int_{c}^{b} f(x)\, dx$$

whenever these limits exist. If either limit fails to exist, then $\int_{-\infty}^{\infty} f(x)\, dx$ diverges.

EXAMPLE 6

Determine whether $\int_{-\infty}^{\infty} |x| e^{-x^2}\, dx$ converges or diverges.

SOLUTION

Since the integrand contains the absolute value function, a convenient choice for c in equation (7.12) is $c = 0$. Integrating, we find

$$\int_0^b xe^{-x^2}\, dx = -\frac{1}{2}e^{-x^2}\bigg]_0^b = \frac{1}{2}\left(1 - e^{-b^2}\right).$$

and

$$\int_a^0 -xe^{-x^2}\, dx = \frac{1}{2}e^{-x^2}\bigg]_a^0 = \frac{1}{2}\left(1 - e^{-a^2}\right).$$

Letting $a \to -\infty$ and $b \to \infty$, we obtain

$$\int_{-\infty}^{\infty} |x|e^{-x^2}\, dx = \frac{1}{2} + \frac{1}{2} = 1.$$

The importance of letting a and b become infinite independently in equation (7.12) is illustrated in the following example.

EXAMPLE 7

Show that $\int_{-\infty}^{\infty} x\, dx$ diverges, whereas $\lim_{c \to \infty} \int_{-c}^{c} x\, dx = 0$.

SOLUTION

Breaking $\int_{-\infty}^{\infty} x\, dx$ at $x = 0$, we have

$$\lim_{b \to \infty} \int_0^b x\, dx = \lim_{b \to \infty} \frac{b^2}{2} = \infty;$$

thus, $\int_{-\infty}^{\infty} x\, dx$ diverges. However,

$$\int_{-c}^{c} x\, dx = \frac{c^2}{2} - \frac{(-c)^2}{2} = 0,$$

and so $\lim_{c \to \infty} \int_{-c}^{c} x\, dx = 0$.

EXERCISES 7.3

In Exercises 1–30 determine whether the given improper integral converges or diverges. If it is convergent, find its value.

1. $\int_0^1 \frac{1}{x^2}\, dx$

2. $\int_0^1 \frac{5}{x^5}\, dx$

3. $\int_0^4 3x^{-1/2}\, dx$

4. $\int_0^2 5x^{-1/5}\, dx$

5. $\int_{-1}^0 x^{-4/5}\, dx$

6. $\int_{-2}^0 x^{-2/3}\, dx$

7. $\int_{-9}^0 (x + 9)^{-1/2}\, dx$

8. $\int_{-1}^1 (x + 1)^{-1/3}\, dx$

9. $\int_1^e \frac{1}{x \ln x}\, dx$

10. $\int_0^1 \frac{\ln x}{x}\, dx$

11. $\int_{-1}^1 \frac{2x}{\sqrt{1 - x^2}}\, dx$

12. $\int_{-2}^2 \frac{x}{x^2 - 4}\, dx$

13. $\int_0^2 (x - 1)^{-1/3}\, dx$

14. $\int_0^5 \frac{1}{(x - 2)^{3/5}}\, dx$

15. $\displaystyle\int_0^3 \frac{1}{(5 - 3x)^2}\, dx$

16. $\displaystyle\int_{-2}^1 \frac{e^x}{e^x - 1}\, dx$

17. $\displaystyle\int_1^\infty x^{-5}\, dx$

18. $\displaystyle\int_3^\infty 2x^{-3}\, dx$

19. $\displaystyle\int_2^\infty 2^{-x}\, dx$

20. $\displaystyle\int_4^\infty 3^{-x}\, dx$

21. $\displaystyle\int_{-\infty}^0 e^x\, dx$

22. $\displaystyle\int_{-\infty}^1 10^x\, dx$

23. $\displaystyle\int_1^\infty \ln x\, dx$

24. $\displaystyle\int_1^\infty \frac{\ln x}{x}\, dx$

25. $\displaystyle\int_{-\infty}^\infty \frac{|x|}{(x^2 + 1)^3}\, dx$

26. $\displaystyle\int_{-\infty}^\infty \frac{x}{x^2 + 4}\, dx$

27. $\displaystyle\int_{-\infty}^\infty e^{-x}\, dx$

28. $\displaystyle\int_{-\infty}^\infty xe^{-x^2}\, dx$

29. $\displaystyle\int_{-\infty}^\infty x^{-1/3}\, dx$

30. $\displaystyle\int_{-\infty}^\infty \frac{1}{x}\, dx$

In Exercises 31–34 find the consumer's surplus for the given demand function and demand level q_0.

31. Demand: $p = 400q^{-3/4},\ 0 < q \le 20{,}000;\ q_0 = 10{,}000$

32. Demand: $p = 500q^{-2/3},\ 0 < q \le 500;\ q_0 = 216$

33. Demand: $p = 900q^{-.8},\ 0 < q \le 5000;\ q_0 = 3125$

34. Demand: $p = 800q^{-.4},\ 0 < q \le 2000;\ q_0 = 1024$

In Exercises 35–38 find the present value $P = \int_0^\infty I(t)e^{-rt}\,dt$ of the given income stream $I(t)$ and inflation rate r.

35. $I(t) = 900;\ r = .06$

36. $I(t) = 2500;\ r = .08$

37. $I(t) = 10{,}000e^{-.04t};\ r = .06$

38. $I(t) = 7500e^{-.05};\ r = .10$

7.4
Modeling with Differential Equations

When designing models, often the behavior of a variable is best characterized by the way it changes with respect to another variable. Formulation of the model then results in an equation involving the derivative of a function.

Definition 7.1

> An equation containing derivatives or differentials of an unknown function is called a **differential equation**. A solution to such an equation is a function that together with its derivatives satisfies the differential equation for all values of the independent variable.

As an illustration, when investments earn interest in a continuous fashion, the rate of change in the value V of the investment (with respect to time) is directly proportional to its current value; that is.

(7.13)
$$\frac{dV}{dt} = rV,$$

where r, the instantaneous interest rate, is the constant of proportionality. Equation (7.13) is called a **first-order differential equation**, since the highest order derivative in the equation is a first derivative. Earlier, by analyzing the continuous compounding process, we found that the value V is given by

(7.14)
$$V(t) = Pe^{rt}.$$

Checking the derivative, we get

$$V'(t) = rPe^{rt},$$

and clearly $rPe^{rt} = rV(t)$, so the function (7.14) is a solution to differential equation (7.13).

Actually, the rule of correspondence given in equation (7.14) is called the **general solution** of differential equation (7.13) for it describes a family or set of solutions—a different function for each choice of P. (See Figure 7.8.) Since $V(0) = Pe^0 = P$, P is called the **initial value** of V. If a value of P, or $V(0)$, is specified, then equation (7.13) together with this value of $V(0)$ is called an **initial value problem**.

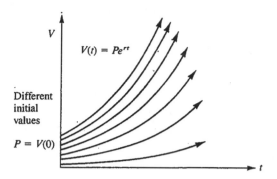

Figure 7.8
Solutions to the differential equation
$V'(t) = rV(t)$

Before considering a solution technique for differential equations, we note that the process of finding antiderivatives amounts to solving simple differential equations. For example, if we seek total cost, knowing that marginal cost is given by

$$MC = 20 - .04q \qquad 0 \le q \le 100,$$

we are really trying to solve the differential equation

$$\frac{dC}{dq} = 20 - .04q.$$

In differential form,

$$dC = (20 - .04q)\,dq,$$

so taking antiderivatives we find

$$C(q) = 20q - .02q^2 + c,$$

which represents a family of cost functions. The constant c (which represents fixed costs) is the initial value $C(0)$, so a **particular solution** is determined when the fixed costs are specified. This example illustrates that a differential equation of the form

(7.15)
$$\frac{dy}{dx} = g(x),$$

where $g(x)$ is given, has the general solution

(7.16)
$$y(x) = \int g(x)\,dx.$$

Simply taking antiderivatives would not be enough to solve equation (7.13) in its present form. The right side of this equation, $rV(t)$, is not known; it contains the unknown function V. Writing equation (7.13) in differential form, we see

$$dV = V'(t) \, dt = rV \, dt,$$

so dividing through by V to separate variables, we obtain

$$\frac{dV}{V} = r \, dt.$$

Now, taking antiderivatives we find

$$\ln|V| = rt + c.$$

Converting to exponential form:

$$|V| = e^{rt+c} = e^c e^{rt}.$$

Since V is positive, we drop the absolute value bars. Letting P denote the constant e^c, we have the general solution

$$V = Pe^{rt}.$$

The **separation of variables** technique can be used for first-order differential equations of the form

$$\frac{dy}{dx} = h(y)g(x)$$

by converting to differential form

$$dy = h(y)g(x) \, dx,$$

then dividing by $h(y)$ (when it is nonzero), and integrating:

$$\int \frac{dy}{h(y)} = \int g(x) \, dx.$$

EXAMPLE 1

The demand for a product is often treated as a function of the advertising expenditure. One school of thought claims that the change in sales with respect to advertising expenditure is directly proportional to the number of people who have not tried the product. Taking this approach, suppose there are 50,000 potential customers each week in a given market, and 1000 of these people will buy the product even if there is no advertising. If a $10,000 weekly budget results in 20,000 sales, find weekly sales in terms of weekly advertising expenditure.

SOLUTION

Letting S represent thousands of sales and x represent thousands of advertising dollars, we begin with the assumption

(7.17)
$$\frac{dS}{dx} = k(50 - S)$$

for some constant k. (When there are S customers, there are $50 - S$ who have not tried the product.) In differential form equation (7.17) becomes

$$dS = k(50 - S)\, dx,$$

so after separating variables and integrating, we find

(7.18)
$$\int \frac{dS}{50 - S} = \int k\, dx.$$

To determine the antiderivative on the left of equation (7.18), we substitute, letting $u = 50 - S$; then $du = -dS$ so

$$\int \frac{dS}{50 - S} = -\int \frac{du}{u},$$

and equation (7.18) becomes

$$\ln|50 - S| = -kx - c.$$

In exponential form,

$$50 - S = e^{-c}e^{-kx};$$

so letting $C = e^{-c}$, the general solution to equation (7.17) is

(7.19)
$$S = 50 - Ce^{-kx}.$$

To determine the value of the constant C we use the initial condition $S(0) = 1$ and find $1 = 50 - C$, so $C = 49$. To find the constant of proportionality k we use the fact that $S(10) = 20$; thus,

$$20 = 50 - 49e^{-k(10)},$$

which may be written as

$$\frac{30}{49} = e^{-k(10)};$$

thus,

$$k = -\frac{\ln(30/49)}{10} \doteq .049.$$

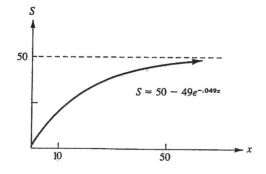

Figure 7.9
The graph of a particular solution to
$dS/dx = .049(50 - S)$

$S = 50 - 49e^{-.049x}$

Finally we have the particular solution

$$S(x) = 50 - 49e^{-.049x},$$

whose graph appears in Figure 7.9. ●

Equation (7.13) describes a function that displays natural growth, whereas equation (7.17) represents bounded exponential growth. Next we reconsider logistic growth.

EXAMPLE 2

For certain products, such as consumer durables, the change in sales with respect to advertising expenditure appears to be jointly proportional to the number of people who have tried the product and to those who have not. Under this assumption, suppose there are 50,000 potential customers each week in a given market, 1000 of whom will purchase the product without advertising. If a $10,000 weekly advertising budget results in 20,000 sales, find weekly sales as a function of advertising expenditure.

SOLUTION

As in Example 1, let S and x represent thousands of sales and thousands of advertising dollars, respectively. Here we are assuming

(7.20)
$$\frac{dS}{dx} = kS(50 - S)$$

for some constant k. In differential form we have

$$dS = kS(50 - S)\,dx;$$

so after separating variables and integrating, we obtain

(7.21)
$$\int \frac{dS}{S(50 - S)} = \int k\,dx.$$

To determine the integral on the left side of equation (7.21), we note that

$$\frac{dS}{S(50 - S)} = \frac{1}{50}\left[\frac{1}{S} + \frac{1}{50 - S}\right]dS;$$

thus integrating equation (7.21) we get

$$\ln|S| - \ln|50 - S| = 50kx + c.$$

Using logarithm properties and noting that both S and $50 - S$ are positive, we see

$$\ln \frac{S}{50 - S} = 50kx + c,$$

so in exponential form

(7.22)
$$\frac{S}{50 - S} = e^c e^{50kx}.$$

Letting $C = e^{-c}$, we solve equation (7.22) for S (see Exercise 12) to obtain the general solution to differential equation (7.20):

(7.23)
$$S = \frac{50}{1 + Ce^{-50kx}}.$$

From the initial condition $S(0) = 1$, equation (7.23) yields

$$1 = \frac{50}{1 + C};$$

thus, $C = 49$. Using the fact that $S(10) = 20$, we have

$$20 = \frac{50}{1 + 49e^{-500k}},$$

so $1 + 49e^{-500k} = 2.5$, or $e^{-500k} = 1.5/49$; thus,

$$k = \frac{-\ln(1.5/49)}{500} \doteq .007 \quad \text{and} \quad S = \frac{50}{1 + 49e^{-.35x}}.$$

A graph of this function appears in Figure 7.10.

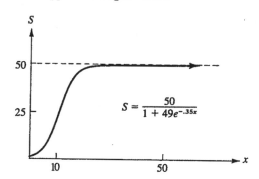

Figure 7.10

The graph of a particular solution to $dS/dx = .007S(50 - S)$

EXAMPLE 3

For certain applications, demand functions with constant elasticity are sought. Find all demand functions with constant elasticity k.

SOLUTION

Recall that elasticity of demand η is given by

$$\eta = -\frac{p}{q}\frac{dq}{dp}.$$

Thus, writing $\eta = k$ in differential form, we find

$$p \, dq = -kq \, dp.$$

Separating variables and integrating:

$$\int \frac{dq}{q} = -k \int \frac{dp}{p};$$

thus,

$$\ln|q| = -k \ln|p| + c.$$

Converting to exponential form, noting that p and q are positive, we have

$$q = e^c p^{-k}.$$

Letting $C = e^c$, all demand functions with elasticity constantly equal to k are of the form

$$q = \frac{C}{p^k}. \qquad \bullet$$

EXERCISES 7.4

In Exercises 1–10 integrate to find the general solution of the given differential equation.

1. $\dfrac{dy}{dx} = 2x - 5$

2. $\dfrac{dy}{dx} = 3 - x$

3. $\dfrac{dy}{dx} = 15 - x + .03x^2$

4. $\dfrac{dy}{dx} = 2 + x - x^2$

5. $\dfrac{dy}{dx} = \sqrt{x + 1}$

6. $\dfrac{dy}{dx} = 2 - \sqrt[3]{x}$

7. $\dfrac{dy}{dx} = \dfrac{5x + 18}{x + 2}$

8. $\dfrac{dy}{dx} = \dfrac{3x + 8}{x + 1}$

9. $\dfrac{dy}{dx} = 10e^x$

10. $\dfrac{dy}{dx} = e^{.02x}$

11. Psychologists E. H. Weber and G. T. Fechner conjectured that the increase in response r to a stimulus s is directly proportional to the increase in stimulus but inversely proportional to the starting stimulus. In differential form,

$$dr = k \frac{ds}{s}$$

for some constant k.

a. Solve this differential equation and find r as a function of s. (Assume $s \geq 1$.)

b. Consumer's preference models follow the Weber–Fechner conjecture with $s = q$, the quantity offered for sale, and $r = p$, the price a consumer is willing to pay for that quantity. If a consumer is willing to pay \$.50 for 1 lb of bananas but only \$1.00 for 3 lb, find p as a function of q (when $q \geq 1$) assuming the Weber–Fechner conjecture.

12. Derive equation (7.23) from equation (7.22) by solving for S. Simplify by multiplying the numerator and denominator by e^{-50kx}.

In Exercises 13–24 convert to differential form, separate variables, and find the particular solution to each of the given differential equations that satisfy the given conditions.

13. $\dfrac{dV}{dt} = .1V, V(0) = 100$

14. $\dfrac{dF}{dt} = .12F, F(0) = 500$

15. $\dfrac{dA}{dt} = -.05A, A(0) = 1000$

16. $\dfrac{dS}{dt} = -.2S, S(0) = 1$

17. $\dfrac{dp}{dq} = 50p^2, p(1) = 10$

18. $\dfrac{dp}{dq} = 10p^{1/2}, p(4) = 25$

19. $\dfrac{dS}{dx} = .02(100 - S), S(0) = 10$

20. $\dfrac{dS}{dx} = .08(500 - S), S(0) = 20$

21. $\dfrac{dS}{dx} = .04S(100 - S), S(0) = 10$

22. $\dfrac{dS}{dt} = .05S(500 - S), S(0) = 20$

23. $\dfrac{dy}{dx} = \dfrac{y}{x}, y(1) = 1$

24. $\dfrac{dy}{dx} = xy, y(1) = 1$

25. An investment increases continuously by 7% of its current value. If the value of the investment was \$500 at time $t = 0$, find its value at any later time t.

26. The value of a machine decreases continuously by 5% of its current value. If the initial value of the machine was $8000, find its value at any later time t.

27. In a Domar model for national income, it is assumed that investments are a fixed proportion of income Y, and also that investments are directly proportional to the change in income with respect to time. As a result,

$$h\frac{dY}{dt} = kY,$$

where h and k are positive constants (both less than 1). Find Y as a function of t.

28. Analysts for Fresh Breeze laundry detergent estimate that in a market with a potential of 100,000 customers, the change in weekly sales with respect to advertising expenditure is about 2% of those who have not yet tried their product; that is,

$$\frac{dS}{dx} = .02(100 - S),$$

where S represents thousands of customers and x represents thousands of advertising dollars. If 5000 people will buy Fresh Breeze with no advertising, find S as a function of x. How many customers will be attracted by an $80,000 weekly advertising expenditure according to this model?

29. The marketing division for Mystic Mouthwash estimates that 10,000 persons will buy their product each week if nothing is spent on advertising. They estimate further that $25,000 in weekly ads will result in 40,000 sales. Assuming a model of the form

$$\frac{dS}{dx} = k(1000 - S),$$

where S and x represent thousands of sales and advertising dollars, respectively, find the number of weekly sales corresponding to a $50,000 weekly advertising expenditure.

30. Rework Exercise 29 assuming a model of the form

$$\frac{dS}{dx} = kS(1000 - S).$$

31. Technological advances often are adopted by businesses in a manner that is jointly proportional to both the number who have adopted the innovation and those who have not. In a particular region that has 6500 grocers, only 100 had installed optical scanner checkout stations on January 1, 1980. Five months later 1000 of the grocers in this region had the scanners. Letting $N(t)$ denote the number of grocers in this region who were using optical scanners t months after January 1, 1980, and assuming

$$\frac{dN}{dt} = kN(6500 - N),$$

find the month and year when 5000 of these grocers were using optical scanners.

32. The news of a new product (or other rumor) spreads in a town of population 50,000 according to

$$\frac{dN}{dt} = kN(50 - N),$$

where N represents the thousands of persons who have heard the news t days after it occurred. If the arrival of a new product is announced at a meeting of 300 individuals, and 5000 persons have heard the news one day later, how long will it take for half the population to learn of the product?

33. The elasticity of demand for a product is known to be

$$\eta = \frac{p}{50 - p},$$

and $p = 10$ when $q = 100$. Find the demand function for this product.

34. If the elasticity of demand for a product is constantly 2, and if $p = 10$ when $q = 100$, find p as a function of q.

CH. 7 REVIEW

I. Key Terms & Concepts

Mathematics

Numerical Integration
Midpoint Rule
Trapezoidal Rule
Integration by Parts
Antiderivative Tables
Improper Integral
Differential Equation
Separation of Variables
General Solution
Particular Solution
Fundamental Theorem of
  Calculus
Riemann Sum
Rectangular Rule

Business

Present Value of an Income
  Stream
Bounded Exponential Growth
  and Logistic Growth of Sales

II. True or False

Indicate whether each statement is true or false.

1. $\int_{-1}^{1} \frac{1}{x}\, dx = 0$

2. $\int_{-1}^{1} \frac{1}{\sqrt[3]{x}}\, dx = 0$

3. If $\lim_{n \to \infty} \int_{-n}^{n} f(x)\, dx$ exists, then it equals $\int_{-\infty}^{\infty} f(x)\, dx$.

4. The average of the results obtained by using the rectangular rule on left endpoints and on right endpoints to approximate a definite integral equals that obtained from the trapezoidal rule.

5. The integration by parts formula is derived from the chain rule for derivatives.

6. Separation of variables is a technique for solving first-order differential equations.

7. There is no positive value of p for which $\int_0^{\infty} 1/x^p\, dx$ converges.

8. The trapezoidal rule is generally a more efficient numerical integration technique than the midpoint rule.

9. If f and g are differentiable on $[a, b]$, then

$$\int_a^b f(x)g'(x)\, dx + \int_a^b f'(x)g(x)\, dx = f(b)g(b) - f(a)g(a).$$

10. If $f(x)$ is positive on $[0, \infty)$, then $\int_0^{\infty} f(x)\, dx$ must diverge.

III. Drill Problems

In Problems 1–6 use integration by parts to find the antiderivative.

1. $\int xe^{-2x}\, dx$

2. $\int x^3 e^{-x}\, dx$

3. $\int x^3 e^{x^2}\, dx$

4. $\int x(3x - 5)^6\, dx$

5. $\int \frac{x^2}{\sqrt{1 + x}}\, dx$

6. $\int \frac{\ln x}{x^2}\, dx$

In Problems 7–10 use Table 7.1 to find the antiderivative.

7. $\int \frac{dx}{4x^2 - 25}$

8. $\int \sqrt{x^2 + 9}\, dx$

9. $\int x^5 \ln x^3 \, dx$

10. $\int \dfrac{x^2}{\sqrt{x^6 + 1}} \, dx$

11. Estimate $\int_0^4 \sqrt{1 + x^2} \, dx$ using the trapezoidal rule with $N = 8$.

12. Estimate $\int_1^3 x/(1 + x) \, dx$ using the trapezoidal rule with $N = 10$.

In Exercises 13–16 find the particular solution of the differential equation that satisfies the given condition.

13. $\dfrac{dy}{dx} = 3y;\ y(0) = 4$

14. $\dfrac{dy}{dx} = yx^2;\ y(0) = 1$

15. $\dfrac{dS}{dt} = .03(100 - S);\ S(0) = 5$

16. $\dfrac{dS}{dt} = .05S(200 - S);\ S(0) = 10$

IV. Applications

1. Assume that the demand for beef is modeled by
$$p = \frac{.5\sqrt{q} + 20}{\sqrt{q}}, \qquad q > 0,$$
where p is the price per pound and q is the annual per capita consumption. Find the consumer's surplus when the price is \$2.50 per pound.

2. Refer to Exercise 1. The demand for a product is modeled by a function of the form
$$p = \frac{aq^{r+b}}{q^r}, \qquad q > 0,$$
with a and b positive constants. What conditions must the exponent r satisfy to ensure that p is a decreasing function of q and that the improper integral defining the consumer's surplus will converge?

3. Consider what frequently occurs when a newly developed durable good is marketed. The initial price is very high but, because of the good's durability, as the total output of the good begins to accumulate, the price inevitably falls sharply. (For example, recall the price history of VCRs and personal computers.) Thus, if $p = f(q)$ is the demand function for the good when q units have already been sold, the integral $\int_0^\infty f(q) \, dq$ represents the total revenue received from the sale of this good.

Suppose that CWS Technologies has just developed a compact video-text reader for which the demand function is
$$p = 2000(.05q + .01)^{-3/2}, \qquad q \geq 0.$$
Find the revenue that CWS Technologies should anticipate receiving from the sale of this product.

4. Refer to Exercise 3. If the demand for a durable good is to be modeled by a function of the form
$$p = a(bq + c)^r, \qquad q \geq 0,$$
where a, b, and c are positive constants, what conditions on the exponent r will ensure that p is a decreasing function of q and that the integral representing the revenue from its sale will converge?

5. An account at a bank is earning a nominal interest rate of 8%, compounded continuously. Deposits are made into this account t years from now, at a rate of $f(t) = 4t$ thousands of dollars per year. Find the amount of continuous cash flow into this account 5 yr from now. (*Hint:* See Exercise 33 in Exercises 7.2.)

6. The financial manager of a company is considering a project that will generate profits over the next 8 yr at a rate of
$$P(t) = 4 - .5t, \qquad 0 \leq t \leq 8,$$
where $P(t)$ is millions of dollars per year t years from now. Find the present value of the project if future income is discounted at an instantaneous rate of 20% per year.

7. Suppose you are considering the purchase of a business that is currently making a profit of \$50,000 per year. Furthermore, you think that under your management, profitability will increase by \$15,000 per year indefinitely. That is, you think that t years from now, the business will be generating profits at a rate of
$$P(t) = 50 + 15t, \qquad t \geq 0$$
(in thousands of dollars per year). If you discount future earnings at an instantaneous rate of 10% per year, find the present value to you of this business.

To complete a construction project, both managers and laborers are required. Assume that managers are paid $150 per day and laborers are paid $80 per day. The time T in days to complete the project is given by

$$T = \frac{800}{M^{.2}L^{.8}}, \qquad M \geq 1, L \geq 1,$$

where M and L are the number of managers and laborers, respectively. Assume that at present, the project director has hired 3 managers and 32 laborers. Which would provide the greater reduction in time needed for completion: hiring one more manager or one more laborer? Assume that the director makes the proper decision. How are total salaries paid to all workers affected during this project?

CHAPTER 8

Multivariate Models

289

8.1
Functions of Several Variables

Most companies make and sell more than one product. We therefore expect that the total revenue, cost, and profit will depend on more than one variable. To distinguish variables that correspond to two products A and B, we will use notation as indicated in the following table:

Product	A	B
Output	q_A	q_B
Variable cost	v_A	v_B
Selling price	p_A	p_B

With this notation,

$$R = p_A q_A + p_B q_B$$

is the revenue received by the company from the sale of A and B;

$$C = v_A q_A + v_B q_B + \text{fixed cost}$$

is the total cost of manufacturing A and B; and

$$P = R - C = (p_A - v_A)q_A + (p_B - v_B)q_B - \text{fixed cost}$$

is the profit earned by the company. These functions are often called the **joint revenue, cost, and profit functions** because they are given for both products at the same time (or jointly).

EXAMPLE 1

Suppose that the demand functions for two products A and B are given by the linear functions

$$p_A = 800 - 5q_A, \qquad 0 \le q_A \le 120,$$

and

$$p_B = 600 - 3q_B, \qquad 0 \le q_B \le 120.$$

a. Find the joint revenue function.

b. Find the revenue as a function of q_A when q_B is held constant.

c. Find the revenue as a function of q_B when q_A is held constant.

SOLUTION

a. The revenue function is given by

(8.1)
$$\begin{aligned} R &= p_A q_A + p_B q_B \\ &= (800 - 5q_A)q_A + (600 - 3q_B)q_B \\ &= 800q_A - 5q_A^2 + 600q_B - 3q_B^2, \qquad 0 \le q_A, q_B \le 120. \end{aligned}$$

b. When the production of product B is held constant or fixed, the revenue from its sale is also constant. Letting K denote this constant, we can write R as a quadratic function of q_A:

$$\begin{aligned} R &= p_A q_A + K \\ &= 800q_A - 5q_A^2 + K, \qquad 0 \le q_A \le 120. \end{aligned}$$

Figure 8.1 shows the graph of this function. Note that its maximum is at $q = 80$ regardless of the production level of product B.

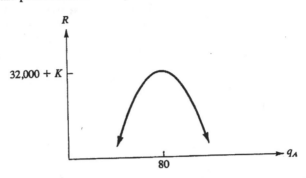

Figure 8.1

The graph of $R = 800q_A - 5q_A^2 + K$

c. When the output level of A is held constant, revenue is a quadratic function of q_B:

$$R = p_B q_B + K$$
$$= 600q_B - 3q_B^2 + K, \qquad 0 \le q_B \le 120,$$

where K now represents the constant revenue received from the sale of product A. This function, whose graph is shown in Figure 8.2, has its maximum at $q_B = 100$ regardless of the production of A.

From the results of parts b and c, the reader should note that the joint revenue function is maximized for $q_A = 80$, $q_B = 100$.

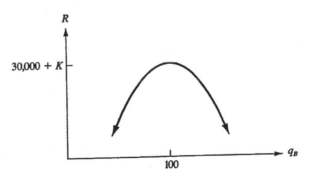

Figure 8.2

The graph of $R = 600q_B - 3q_B^2 + K$

In Example 1, the demand function for each product did not involve the output level of the other product; that is, the selling price of product A was not influenced in any way by the supply of product B, and vice versa. This enabled us to find the output levels that maximized the joint revenue function. It is also possible to have a variable cost function for a product that does not depend on the production levels of other products. In such cases, an economist would say that "there is no **inter-action** between the products." When this occurs it is possible to analyze revenue, cost, and profit for each product separately using the methods developed in the preceding chapters.

In actuality, the demand for one product is affected by the availability of other products. This is generally the case when two products are in direct competition or when one product is used along with a second. The cost of producing one product may also be influenced by the production rate of a second product when both products are made on the same equipment or require the same raw material in their manufacture. In these instances, the joint revenue and cost functions must demonstrate this interaction. The next example illustrates such a cost function.

EXAMPLE 2

CWS Technologies makes both processor and memory chips at its Denver facility. Both chips are made by the same workers using the same equipment. As a result, increasing the production level of one kind of chip will increase the variable cost of producing the other kind. Let q_A and q_B be the daily output of processor and memory chips, respectively. Assume that the variable cost for making a processor chip is

$$v_A = 35 - .05q_A + .01q_B, \qquad 0 \le q_A \le 200, 0 \le q_B \le 250,$$

and the variable cost for making a memory chip is

$$v_B = 32 + .02q_A - .04q_B, \qquad 0 \le q_A \le 200, 0 \le q_B \le 250.$$

Let the daily fixed cost at the facility be $400. Find the total cost C as a function of q_A and q_B.

SOLUTION

We have for the total cost function

$$C = v_A q_A + v_B q_B + 400$$
$$= (35 - .05q_A + .01q_B)q_A + (32 + .02q_A - .04q_B)q_B + 400$$
$$= 35q_A - .05q_A^2 + .01q_A q_B + 32q_B + .02q_A q_B - .04q_B^2 + 400$$

or finally

(8.2)
$$C(q_A, q_B) = 35q_A - .05q_A^2 + 32q_B - .04q_B^2 + .03q_A q_B + 400,$$
$$0 \le q_A \le 200, \qquad 0 \le q_B \le 250.$$

Note that the joint cost function (8.2) has an **interaction term**, $.03q_A q_B$, which reflects the way the production cost of one product is affected by altering the output level of a second product. ●

Both equations (8.1) and (8.2) are examples of functions of two variables. Similarly, when more than two products are involved, we can construct models in which revenue, cost, and profit depend on more than two variables. For simplicity we will usually restrict our attention to functions of two variables.

In general, we write $z = f(x, y)$ to indicate that the dependent variable z is a function of two independent variables x and y. For any x and y in the domain of the function, there is a unique value of z in the range.

EXAMPLE 3

Let $z = f(x, y) = x^2 - 3xy + 2y^3$. Find z when $x = 3$ and $y = -1$.

SOLUTION

We have

$$z = f(3, -1) = (3)^2 - 3(3)(-1) + 2(-1)^3 = 16.$$

●

EXAMPLE 4

Let $z = f(x, y) = 20x^{1/3}y^{2/3}$. Find z at $(27, 8)$.

SOLUTION

We have

$$z = f(27, 8) = 20(27)^{1/3}(8)^{2/3} = 20(3)(4) = 240.$$

●

Recall that to graph a function $y = f(x)$, two dimensions are required to plot pairs $(x, f(x))$ on an x,y-axis system. These axes divide the x,y-plane into four quadrants. For positive y, the point (x,y) lies y units above the point $(x, 0)$ on the x-axis; for negative y, (x, y) lies $|y|$ units below $(x, 0)$. The graph, consisting of all the pairs (x, y) is then a curve on the coordinate system—above the x-axis for $y > 0$, below it for $y < 0$. Graphing a function of two variables is similar.

To graph $z = f(x, y)$, three dimensions are required to plot the triples $(x, y, f(x, y))$ on an x,y,z-axis system. This system is usually depicted in two dimensions so that the z-axis is vertical, the positive y-axis is pointed to the right, and the positive x-axis is directed toward the viewer. (See Figure 8.3.) These axes divide three-dimensional space into eight regions or **octants**. The perspective is usually taken so that the viewer is looking at the first octant (where all the variables are positive) of the three-dimensional system.

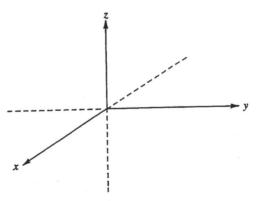

Figure 8.3
The three-dimensional coordinate system

A point (x, y, z) that satisfies the relation $z = f(x, y)$, for $z > 0$, can then be plotted on this coordinate system by finding $(x, y, 0)$ in the horizontal x,y-plane and then moving vertically upward z units to locate the point (x, y, z). [If $z < 0$, then (x, y, z) lies $|z|$ units below $(x, y, 0)$.] This is illustrated in Figure 8.4, where the points $(1, 3, 4)$ and $(4, 2, 2)$ are plotted.

The graph of a function $z = f(x, y)$ is the set of points (x, y, z) for which values of (x,y) are in the domain of f. The graph can be visualized by first thinking of the region in the x,y-plane that consists of the points $(x, y, 0)$ as the domain. The set of all points (x, y, z) then forms a **surface** in the coordinate system; for $z > 0$, the

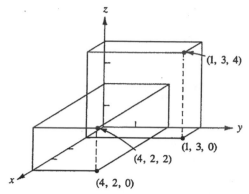

Figure 8.4
Points (1, 3, 4) and (4, 2, 2) plotted in a three-dimensional coordinate system

surface is above the x,y-plane; for $z < 0$, it is below it. Figure 8.5 is an example of such a surface where the domain of f is a rectangular region: $a \leq x \leq b$, $c \leq y \leq d$.

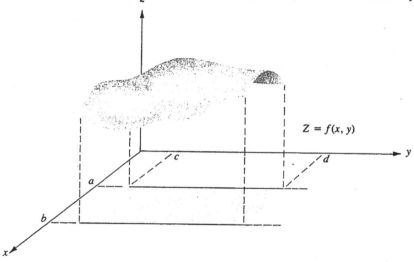

Figure 8.5
The graph of a surface defined by $z = f(x, y)$ on a rectangular domain

Figure 8.6 shows a graph of the revenue function

$$R = 800q_A - 5q_A^2 + 600q_B - 3q_B^2$$

from Example 1. Observe that, as noted, the graph reaches its highest point at $q_A = 80$, $q_B = 100$. Furthermore, the parabolas that were graphed in Figures 8.1 and 8.2 can be formed as the intersection of this graph and planes perpendicular to the R,q_B-plane and R,q_A-plane, respectively. It is possible to obtain a rough sketch of a simple function of two variables using this kind of process; that is, hold one of the variables constant and sketch the resulting function of a single variable. Doing this carefully for several values of each variable will produce an outline of a surface by giving these curves an appropriate perspective.

Fortunately, many computer programs are available that provide the user with a sketch of a function of two variables over rectangular domains. The graphs of the functions shown in Figure 8.7 were obtained by using such a program on a personal computer.

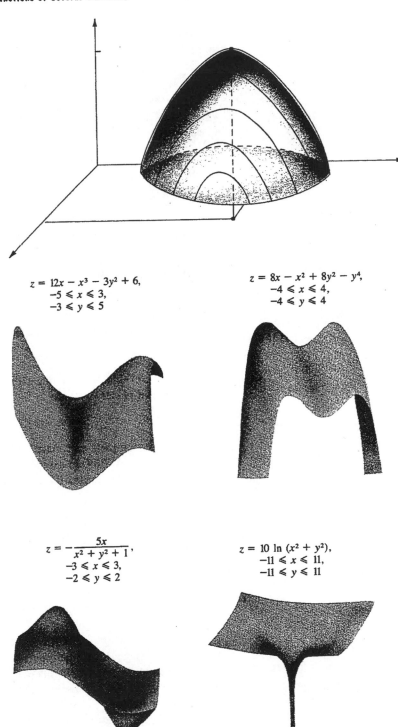

Figure 8.6
The graph of
$$R = 800q_A - 5q_A^2 + 600q_B - 3q_B^2$$

$z = 12x - x^3 - 3y^2 + 6,$
$-5 \leqslant x \leqslant 3,$
$-3 \leqslant y \leqslant 5$

$z = 8x - x^2 + 8y^2 - y^4,$
$-4 \leqslant x \leqslant 4,$
$-4 \leqslant y \leqslant 4$

$z = -\dfrac{5x}{x^2 + y^2 + 1},$
$-3 \leqslant x \leqslant 3,$
$-2 \leqslant y \leqslant 2$

$z = 10 \ln (x^2 + y^2),$
$-11 \leqslant x \leqslant 11,$
$-11 \leqslant y \leqslant 11$

Figure 8.7
Computer-generated graphs of
functions of two variables

An important example of a function of two variables is the **Cobb–Douglas production function:**

(8.3)
$$Q = f(L, K) = CL^{\alpha}K^{1-\alpha}, \qquad L, K > 0.$$

This function can be used to model the production or the output Q of a plant, a business, or a nation as a function of the inputs, labor L and capital K. In equation (8.3) C and α are constants, with $0 < \alpha < 1$.

EXAMPLE 5

Let

$$Q = 4L^{.6}K^{.4}, \qquad L, K > 0,$$

denote the number of pairs of boots made by a shoe company when it uses L worker-hours of labor and K times $100 of capital.

a. Find the output when $L = 500$ and $K = 70$.

b. What happens to the output when L and K are doubled to 1000 and 140, respectively?

SOLUTION

a. Substitution into the production function gives

$$Q = 4(500)^{.6}(70)^{.4},$$

which can be evaluated using logarithms or the $\boxed{y^x}$ key on a calculator. Rounding to two decimal places, we have

$$Q \doteq 4(41.63)(5.47) \doteq 910.92.$$

Therefore the company can make about 911 pairs of boots by using 500 worker-hours of labor and $7000 in capital.

b. Doubling the labor to 1000 hours and the capital to $14,000, we find that

$$\begin{aligned}
Q &= 4(1000)^{.6}(140)^{.4} \\
&= 4(2)^{.6}(500)^{.6}(2)^{.4}(70)^{.4} \\
&= 2 \cdot 4(500)^{.6}(70)^{.4} \\
&\doteq 2(910.92).
\end{aligned}$$

That is, the output also doubles to about 1822 pairs of boots.   ●

This example illustrates a fundamental property of the Cobb–Douglas production function. When all of the inputs (here, labor and capital) are multiplied by any positive constant n, the output is also multiplied by n (see Exercise 23). Economists describe this fact by saying that this model of an input–output system always **returns to scale**.

Other models of the Cobb–Douglas type can be built that further refine the input variables. For example, if D denotes direct labor, M management salaries, R raw materials, and F depreciation of the facilities and equipment, then assuming that output varies directly with these inputs, the production function can be written as

(8.4) $$Q = CD^{\alpha}M^{\beta}R^{\gamma}F^{\delta}, \qquad D, M, R, F \geq 0,$$

where α, β, γ, and δ are positive constants with $\alpha + \beta + \gamma + \delta = 1$.

EXERCISES 8.1

In Exercises 1–8 evaluate the given function f at the specified points.

1. $f(x, y) = 5x + 2y$; $(1, 1)$, $(-1, 3)$

2. $f(x, y) = x^2 + 4xy + 3y^2$; $(2, 0)$, $(-1, 1)$, $(0, 2)$

3. $f(x, y) = 2x^3 - x^2y + 2xy^2 + y^3$; $(1, 2)$, $(2, 1)$, $(0, 3)$, $(3, 0)$

4. $f(x, y) = xe^y$; $(3, 0)$, $(0, 4)$, $(1, -1)$, $(-1, 1)$

5. $f(x, y) = y^2 \ln x$; $(1, 2)$, $(1, 8)$, $(2, 1)$, $(2, -3)$

6. $f(x, y) = 5x^{1/4}y^{3/4}$; $(2, 0)$, $(0, 6)$, $(1, 16)$, $(16, 1)$

7. $f(x, y, z) = xy + 2yz + 3xz$; $(3, 1, -2)$, $(1, 0, 2)$, $(-1, 2, -3)$

8. $f(x, y, z) = 3x^{1/4}y^{1/2}z^{1/4}$; $(1, 4, 16)$, $(81, 16, 1/16)$

In Exercises 9–14 simplify the indicated expression.

9. $f(2 + h, 1)$ when $f(x, y) = 4x - y^2$

10. $f(5, 3 + h)$ when $f(x, y) = x^2y + 3xy^2$

11. $f(x + h, y)$ when $f(x, y) = 4xy - 2x^2y$

12. $f(x, y + h)$ when $f(x, y) = x^3y + 3x^2y^2 - 2xy$

13. $\dfrac{f(x + h, y) - f(x, y)}{h}$ when $f(x, y) = 6x + 3y$

14. $\dfrac{f(x, y + h) - f(x, y)}{h}$ when $f(x, y) = x^2 + 4xy - 2y$

15. The Nevadaco Oil Company refines both leaded and unleaded gasoline. Let q_A and q_B denote the output in hundreds of barrels of leaded and unleaded, respectively. Suppose that the variable cost of refining 100 barrels of leaded gasoline is

$$v_A = 80 - .2q_A + .1q_B, \qquad 0 \leq q_A, q_B \leq 250,$$

and the cost of refining 100 barrels of unleaded gasoline is

$$v_B = 100 + .1q_A - .2q_B, \qquad 0 \leq q_A, q_B \leq 250.$$

Suppose that the fixed cost of operating the refinery is $1000 per day. Find the total refining cost as a function of q_A and q_B.

16. Comfort-Seat Inc. produces both an easy chair and a sofa. Because of savings when fabric and other materials are ordered in larger quantities, increases in the production of either the chair or the sofa lower the variable cost of the other. If q_A and q_B denote the number of chairs and sofas, respectively, then the variable cost of each chair is

$$v_A = 350 - 4q_A - 2q_B + .1q_A^2,$$
$$0 \leq q_A \leq 15, 0 \leq q_B \leq 10,$$

and the variable cost of each sofa is

$$v_B = 720 - 3q_A - 8q_B + .3q_B^2,$$
$$0 \leq q_A \leq 15, 0 \leq q_B \leq 10.$$

Assuming that the fixed cost is $450 per day, find the total production cost as a function of q_A and q_B.

17. Refer to Exercise 15. Suppose that the selling price for 100 barrels of the leaded gasoline is given by

$$p_A = 90 - .3q_A - .1q_B, \qquad 0 \leq q_A, q_B \leq 250,$$

and the selling price for 100 barrels of the unleaded is

$$p_B = 112 - .1q_A - .4q_B, \qquad 0 \leq q_A, q_B \leq 250.$$

Find the total revenue received by Nevadaco as a function of q_A and q_B.

18. Refer to Exercise 16. Suppose that Comfort-Seat is able to sell the entire output if the price of each easy chair is

$$p_A = 420 - 6q_A + 2q_B, \qquad 0 \leq q_A \leq 15, 0 \leq q_B \leq 10,$$

and the price of each sofa is

$$p_A = 800 + q_A - 10q_B, \qquad 0 \le q_A \le 15, 0 \le q_B \le 10.$$

Find the total revenue received as a function of q_A and q_B.

19. Refer to Exercises 15 and 17. Find the profit earned by Nevadaco as a function of q_A and q_B.

20. Refer to Exercises 16 and 18. Find the profit earned by Comfort-Seat as a function of q_A and q_B.

21. Suppose that the output P from a business is modeled by the Cobb–Douglas production function

$$P = 20L^{.8}K^{.2}, \qquad L, K \ge 0.$$

a. Calculate P when $L = 40$ and $K = 40$.

b. Calculate P when $L = 60$ and $K = 40$. When $L = 40$ and $K = 60$.

c. Suppose that K is held constant at 40. How much does L have to be increased beyond 40 to double the output? If L is held at 40, how much does K have to be increased beyond 40 to double the output?

22. Suppose that the number of new drugs D marketed by a drug company in 1 yr is given by

$$D = .5L^{.15}K^{.85}, \qquad L, K \ge 0,$$

where L is in hundreds of worker-hours and K is in millions of dollars. Find D when $L = 20$ and $K = 40$. How much of an increase in labor is required to increase the number of new drugs by 50% if the capital is unchanged? How much of an increase in capital would be required to achieve the same goal?

23. Verify that the Cobb–Douglas-type model given in equation (8.3) in the text does return to scale.

8.2
Partial Derivatives

In this section we develop an analogue of the derivative for functions of more than one variable. Recall that a function of a single variable is said to be differentiable if it has a derivative at every value in its domain. Moreover, a differentiable function is continuous and its graph is a smooth curve in the x,y-plane.

The concept of continuity for a function of two variables $z = f(x, y)$ can be intuitively understood by saying that f is continuous when the surface that is its graph has no tears or holes. The concept of differentiability can be visualized by saying that the surface has no sharp creases or spikes. For convenience, we will say that such a surface is **smooth**.

At any point on a smooth surface infinitely many tangent lines can be drawn (see Figure 8.8). The slopes of these tangent lines measure the steepness of the surface in the direction of the tangent lines. **Partial derivatives** will be used to compute the slopes of the tangent lines in the direction of the x- and y-axes.

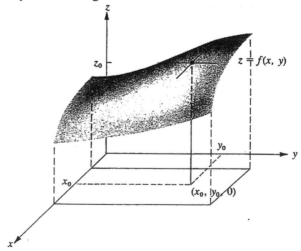

Figure 8.8
Two of the many tangent lines to the surface at the point (x_0, y_0, z_0)

We illustrate the concept of a partial derivative for a function of two variables through an example. Suppose that a plant can produce two products, A and B. Let q_A and q_B denote the current output of A and B, respectively, and assume that we know the joint cost function

$$C = f(q_A, q_B).$$

If the production level of B is held constant at q_B while the production of A is increased by h units, then the average cost of each additional unit is given by

$$\frac{f(q_A + h, q_B) - f(q_A, q_B)}{h}$$

By letting h tend toward 0 and computing the resulting limit, we can find the marginal cost of the q_Ath unit of product A when q_B units of product B are also being made. Similarly, if we want the marginal cost of the q_Bth unit of product B (this time assuming that the output of A is held constant at q_A units), we calculate the limit

$$\lim_{h \to 0} \frac{f(q_A, q_B + h) - f(q_A, q_B)}{h}.$$

Each of these limiting processes is equivalent to calculating an ordinary derivative of $C = f(q_A, q_B)$ with respect to one variable while treating the other variable as if it were a constant. We define these limits as follows.

Definition 8.1

> Let $z = f(x, y)$ be a function of two variables. The **partial derivative of f (or z) with respect to x**, denoted f_x, is given by the function
>
> $$f_x(x, y) = \lim_{h \to 0} \frac{f(x + h, y) - f(x, y)}{h}$$
>
> provided that the limit is a real number. The **partial derivative of f (or z) with respect to y**, denoted f_y, is
>
> $$f_y(x, y) = \lim_{h \to 0} \frac{f(x, y + h) - f(x, y)}{h}$$

When we want to emphasize the dependent variable z, we let $\partial z / \partial x$ denote the partial derivative with respect to x, and $\partial z / \partial y$ denotes the partial derivative with respect to y. Other notations are

$$\frac{\partial}{\partial x} [f(x, y)] \quad \text{and} \quad D_x[f(x, y)]$$

for the partial derivative with respect to x and

$$\frac{\partial}{\partial y} [f(x, y)] \quad \text{and} \quad D_y[f(x, y)]$$

for the partial derivative with respect to y.

We compute the partial derivative of $f(x, y)$ with respect to x using the usual rules of differentiation and treating y as a constant wherever it appears. Similarly, we compute the partial derivative with respect to y by treating x as a constant wherever it appears.

EXAMPLE 1

If $f(x, y) = 3x^4 + 5xy - 2y^2$, find $f_x(x, y)$ and $f_y(x, y)$.

SOLUTION

To find f_x we hold y constant. Therefore, in $f(x, y)$ the second term $5xy$ is just a constant times x and the third term $2y^2$ is just a constant. We have then

$$f_x(x, y) = D_x[3x^4] + 5y\, D_x[x] - D_x[2y^2]$$
$$= 12x^3 + 5y(1) - 0$$
$$= 12x^3 + 5y.$$

Holding x constant, we would consider the first term to be a constant and the second term as y multiplied by the constant $5x$. Then

$$f_y(x, y) = D_y[3x^4] + 5x\, D_y[y] - D_y[2y^2]$$
$$= 0 + 5x(1) - 4y$$
$$= 5x - 4y.$$

●

EXAMPLE 2

Let $z = x^2 e^{5y}$. Find $\partial z/\partial x$ and $\partial z/\partial y$.

SOLUTION

When y is held constant, e^{5y} is also constant. Therefore, we have

$$\frac{\partial z}{\partial x} = D_x[x^2 e^{5y}] = e^{5y} D_x[x^2]$$
$$= 2x e^{5y}.$$

Holding x and therefore x^2 constant, we find

$$\frac{\partial z}{\partial y} = D_y[x^2 e^{5y}] = x^2 D_y[e^{5y}]$$
$$= 5x^2 e^{5y}.$$

●

The next example extends the concept of partial derivatives to functions of three variables.

EXAMPLE 3

Let $f(x, y, z) = \ln(x^2 + 5y^3 z - 8z)$. Find $f_x(x, y, z)$, $f_y(x, y, z)$, and $f_z(x, y, z)$.

SOLUTION

To find f_x we need to hold both y and z constant. Then

$$f_x(x, y, z) = \frac{1}{x^2 + 5y^3z - 8z} D_x[x^2 + 5y^3z - 8z]$$

$$= \frac{2x}{x^2 + 5y^3z - 8z}.$$

Holding x and z constant, we find

$$f_y(x, y, z) = \frac{15y^2z}{x^2 + 5y^3z - 8z}.$$

Holding x and y constant, we find

$$f_z(x, y, z) = \frac{5y^3 - 8}{x^2 + 5y^3z - 8z}.$$

To interpret partial derivatives geometrically, let $z = f(x, y)$ be a function whose graph is a smooth surface. Let $(x_0, y_0, f(x_0, y_0))$ be a point on this surface. Consider the plane that passes through this point and is parallel to the x,z-plane. The intersection of this plane and the surface is a curve. (See Figure 8.9.) The slope of the tangent line to this curve at the point $(x_0, y_0, f(x_0, y_0))$ is $f_x(x_0, y_0)$. That is, the partial derivative with respect to x at (x_0, y_0) is the slope of the tangent line to the surface that is parallel to the x,z-plane (or the x direction).

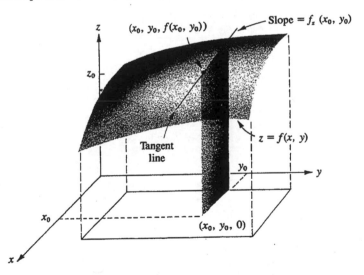

Figure 8.9

The tangent line to the surface $z = f(x, y)$ parallel to the x,z-plane

In an analogous fashion, we see that $f_y(x_0, y_0)$ is the slope of the tangent line parallel to the y,z-plane (or in the y direction). (See Figure 8.10.)

If $z = f(x, y)$ is a function of x and y, then f_x and f_y are also functions of x and y. Therefore, we can find their partial derivatives and so create **second-order**

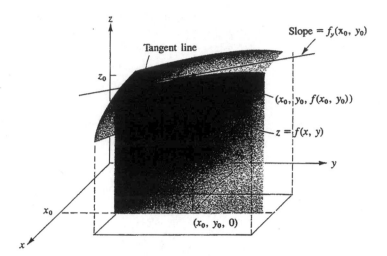

Figure 8.10

The tangent line to the surface $z = f(x, y)$ parallel to the y, z-plane

partial derivatives of f. There are four such derivatives and we denote them as follows:

$$\frac{\partial}{\partial x} [f_x] \text{ is denoted } f_{xx} \text{ or } \frac{\partial^2 z}{\partial x^2}.$$

$$\frac{\partial}{\partial y} [f_x] \text{ is denoted } f_{xy} \text{ or } \frac{\partial^2 z}{\partial y\, \partial x}.$$

$$\frac{\partial}{\partial x} [f_y] \text{ is denoted } f_{yx} \text{ or } \frac{\partial^2 z}{\partial x\, \partial y}.$$

$$\frac{\partial}{\partial y} [f_y] \text{ is denoted } f_{yy} \text{ or } \frac{\partial^2 z}{\partial y^2}.$$

EXAMPLE 4

Let $f(x, y) = 4x^2y + 2xy^3 - 3y^2$. Find all the second-order partial derivatives of f.

SOLUTION

First observe that the first-order partial derivatives are

$$f_x(x, y) = 8xy + 2y^3 \quad \text{and} \quad f_y(x, y) = 4x^2 + 6xy^2 - 6y.$$

Then,

$$f_{xx}(x, y) = D_x[8xy + 2y^3] = 8y;$$

$$f_{xy}(x, y) = D_y[8xy + 2y^3] = 8x + 6y^2;$$

$$f_{yx}(x, y) = D_x[4x^2 + 6xy^2 - 6y] = 8x + 6y^2;$$

and

$$f_{yy}(x, y) = D_y[4x^2 + 6xy^2 - 6y] = 12xy - 6.$$ ●

Note that in the previous example $f_{yx} = f_{xy}$. This is not a coincidence—it can be shown that this equality will always occur when the second-order partial derivatives are continuous. Since f_{yx} and f_{xy} are usually identical, we call this derivative the mixed second partial derivative and denote it f_{xy}.

The second partial derivative with respect to x, f_{xx}, measures the concavity of the surface $z = f(x, y)$ parallel to the x,z-plane (or in the x direction). Referring to Figure 8.8 again, we see that the surface is concave downward in the x direction. Therefore, we know that $f_{xx}(x_0, y_0)$ must be negative. Since the surface is also concave downward in the y direction (see Figure 8.9) and f_{yy} measures the concavity parallel to the y,z-plane, it is also the case that $f_{yy}(x_0, y_0)$ is negative.

EXERCISES 8.2

In Exercises 1–20 find all the first-order partial derivatives of the given function.

1. $f(x, y) = x^2 - y^2$

2. $f(x, y) = 8x + 6y^3$

3. $f(x, y) = 5x + 2xy + 3y$

4. $f(x, y) = x^2y + 3x - 5y$

5. $f(x, y) = x^2 - 3xy + y^2$

6. $f(x, y) = 4xy^2 - 2x^4y^3 - x^3y^2$

7. $f(x, y) = e^{5x-2y}$

8. $f(x, y) = e^{xy+5x}$

9. $g(s, t) = t^3 \ln(2s + 3)$

10. $C(p, q) = p^2\sqrt{4 - q}$

11. $F(x, y) = \dfrac{3x + 5}{2y - 6}$

12. $h(m, n) = \dfrac{m^2}{n - 1}$

13. $f(x, y) = \sqrt{x^2 + 3y^4}$

14. $f(x, y) = (x^2y + xy^3)^8$

15. $f(x, y, z) = x^2z + yz^3$

16. $f(x, y, z) = xe^{yz^2}$

17. $f(r, s, t) = \sqrt{rs^2 + st^2}$

18. $G(x, y, z) = \ln(5x + x^2z^5 + yz^3)$

19. $f(p, q, r) = \ln(pq^3r^5)$

20. $R(q_1, q_2, q_3) = 5q_1q_2 - q_2q_3 + 2q_1q_3$

In Exercises 21–26 evaluate f_x and f_y at the given points.

21. $f(x, y) = x^3 - xy^2 + y^3$; $(2, -1)$, $(1, 1)$

22. $f(x, y) = \ln(x - y)$; $(5, 2)$, $(4, 3)$

23. $f(x, y) = x^2e^{2-y}$; $(3, 2)$, $(1, 1)$

24. $f(x, y) = \sqrt{5x + 4y}$; $(1, 1)$, $(4, 4)$, $(8, 6)$

25. $f(x, y) = \dfrac{3y + 4}{5x + 2}$; $(0, 2)$, $(-2, 4)$

26. $f(x, y) = e^{2x-3}\ln(5 - y)$; $(2, 3)$, $(1, 2)$

27. An appliance dealer sells both washing machines and dryers. Because many people purchase both appliances at the same time, the joint profit function for these appliances will show some interaction. Suppose that when q_A washers and q_B dryers are carried in inventory, the monthly profit to the dealer from their sales is given by

$$P = 80q_A + 100q_B - q_A^2 + 2q_Aq_B - 3q_B^2,$$
$$0 \le q_A \le 25, 0 \le q_B \le 25.$$

Assume that at present the dealer has a policy of keeping 10 washers and 20 dryers in stock.

a. Find the rate of change in the profit if the number of washers is increased while the inventory of dryers is held constant.

b. Find the rate of change in the profit if the number of dryers is increased while the number of washers is held constant.

28. An individual's income comes from two sources: wages W and investments I. Assume that this individual's consumption C (the amount the individual spends) is given by

$$C = .95W + .25I - .004W^2 - .01WI - .003I^2,$$
$$0 \le W \le 40, 0 \le I \le 10,$$

where C, I, and W are in thousands of dollars. The individual's current income consists of wages of $30,000 and investment income of $2000.

a. How much is the individual presently consuming?

b. What is the rate of change in consumption with respect to wages? Estimate the change in consumption if the individual gets a $1200 raise.

c. What is the rate of change in consumption with respect to investment income? Estimate the change in consumption if the individual receives an extra $100 stock dividend.

29. Burger Villa is presently spending $3300 per month on its advertising, with $1800 spent for television, $600 for radio, and $900 for newspaper ads. Suppose the monthly demand for Burger Villa's hamburgers is given by

$$q = 2000x^{.5}y^{.3}z^{.4}, \qquad 0 \le x, y, z \le 25,$$

where x, y, and z are the monthly expenditures (in hundred dollars) for television, radio, and newspaper ads, respectively.

a. Find the current monthly demand for the hamburgers.

b. Find the rate of change in the demand with respect to the advertising expenditure for each of the three media at the current level of expenditure.

c. If Burger Villa wanted to increase its advertising budget, where should the additional money be spent to obtain the greatest increase in demand?

30. Assume that the joint cost function for the manufacture of q_A units of a product A and q_B units of another product B is given by a function of the form

$$C(q_A, q_B) = a_1 q_A + a_2 q_A^2 + a_3 q_B + a_4 q_B^2 + \text{fixed cost},$$

where a_1, a_2, a_3, and a_4 are constants. Show that the mar-

ginal cost of the q_Ath unit of A does not depend on the production level of B.

In Exercises 31–43 find all the second-order partial derivatives of the given function.

31. $f(x, y) = 5x^2 + 2y^4$

32. $f(x, y) = x^3 - 7x^2 + 3x - 2y^2 + 5y$

33. $f(x, y) = 7xy^3$ 34. $f(x, y) = 3xy^4 + 2x + y^6$

35. $f(m, n) = 2m^3n + m^2n^2 + 4mn^3$

36. $g(x, y) = e^{x^2+y^3}$

37. $T(s, t) = t^5 e^{s^2}$ 38. $f(x, y) = \ln(5x + y^2)$

39. $h(p, q) = e^{2p+1} \ln(3q + 2)$

40. $G(r, s) = \dfrac{r}{s + 2}$

41. $F(x, y, z) = x^4 z^2 + yz^3 + z^5$

42. $g(r, s, t) = re^{5t} + s^2 \ln(3t + 1)$

43. $f(p, q, r) = r\sqrt{p} + \dfrac{q}{\sqrt{p}}$

44. Suppose that $z = f(x, y)$ has no interaction terms—that is, no terms that contain both x and y. Show that the mixed partial derivative f_{xy} is 0. [*Hint:* Observe that $f(x, y)$ can be written as the sum of functions of one variable: $f(x, y) = g(x) + h(y)$.]

8.3
Applications of Partial Derivatives

As in the case of ordinary derivatives, partial derivatives represent the (instantaneous) rate of change of the dependent variable with respect to an independent variable. For partial derivatives only one independent variable is changing; the others are held fixed. As an independent variable increases, a positive partial derivative indicates an increase in the dependent variable, and a negative partial derivative reflects a decreasing dependent variable. With these similarities to ordinary derivatives in mind, marginal analysis may be applied to models involving several independent variables.

EXAMPLE 1

The attendance F (in thousands of fans) at an August Milwaukee Brewers home game is approximated by

$$F = 150\left(\frac{w}{p^2}\right)^{1/3},$$

where w is the team's winning percentage ($0 \le w \le 1$) and p is the price ($7 \le p \le 10$ dollars) of a general admission ticket. Currently, $w = .512$ and

$p = 8$, so $F = 150(.512/64)^{1/3} = 30$. Find and interpret the partial derivatives $\partial F/\partial p$ and $\partial F/\partial w$.

SOLUTION

Writing

$$F = 150w^{1/3}p^{-2/3},$$

we differentiate with respect to p to obtain

$$\frac{\partial F}{\partial p} = \left(-\frac{2}{3}\right)150w^{1/3}p^{-5/3}$$
$$= -100w^{1/3}p^{-5/3}.$$

This derivative is negative for all values of w and p, so raising the price of a ticket will decrease attendance. Currently

$$\frac{\partial F}{\partial p} = -100(.512)^{1/3}8^{-5/3}$$
$$= -2.5,$$

so each increase of $1 in the price of a general admission ticket will result in 2500 fewer people attending a game.

Differentiating F with respect to w yields

$$\frac{\partial F}{\partial w} = 150\left(\frac{1}{3}\right)w^{-2/3}p^{-2/3}$$
$$= 50(wp)^{-2/3},$$

which is positive for all values of w and p. When $p = 8$ and $w = .512$,

$$\frac{\partial F}{\partial w} = 50(4.096)^{-2/3}$$
$$\doteq 19.5,$$

which means that every increase of one unit in w (100%) results in an increase of 19,500 fans at the ballpark. More reasonably, every increase of .01 in the winning percentage results in an increase of 195 at the gate. For a 162-game season, $1/162 = .006$, so a win today should mean $.006(19,500) = 117$ more fans tomorrow. ●

EXAMPLE 2

Recall the joint cost function for CWS Technologies given in Example 2 of Section 8.1:

$$C(q_A, q_B) = 35q_A - .05q_A^2 + 32q_B - .04q_B^2 + .03q_Aq_B + 400,$$

where q_A denotes the number of processor chips and q_B the number of memory chips produced daily, with $0 \le q_A \le 200$, $0 \le q_B \le 250$. Currently $q_A = 100$ and $q_B = 150$, but the production division has decided to increase the daily output of either processor or memory chips. For which chip is the cost per unit lower for additional units?

SOLUTION

The cost per unit of additional chips at a given output level is the marginal cost at that output level. Here the marginal cost for processor chips is

$$\frac{\partial C}{\partial q_A} = 35 - .1q_A + .03q_B,$$

and the marginal cost for memory chips is

$$\frac{\partial C}{\partial q_B} = 32 - .08q_B + .03q_A.$$

When $q_A = 100$ and $q_B = 150$ we find

$$\frac{\partial C}{\partial q_A} = 35 - .1(100) + .03(150) = \$29.50,$$

while

$$\frac{\partial C}{\partial q_B} = 32 - .08(150) + .03(100) = \$23.00.$$

So at this output level, additional memory chips can be produced at a lower per unit cost than processor chips.

Geometrically, by analyzing the size of the partial derivatives we have determined the direction in which the slope of the surface representing $C = f(q_A, q_B)$ is steeper. (See Figure 8.11.)

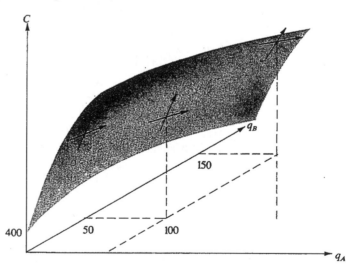

Figure 8.11

A sketch of a joint cost function

The processor and memory chips considered in Example 2 are said to be **complementary** goods. As more processor chips are used, presumably more memory chips are needed. If the price of processor chips decreases, more processor chips will be purchased and so more memory chips will be purchased. Thus, the change in demand for memory chips with respect to the price of processor chips is negative.

Some products are **competitive** rather than complementary. Pork and beef consumption is a classic example. As the price of one kind of red meat increases, consumers buy more of the other kind. Thus, the change in pork consumption with respect to the price of beef is positive, as is the change in beef consumption with respect to the price of pork. Partial derivatives are used to classify products as complementary, competitive, or neither.

Definition 8.2

If p_A, p_B and q_A, q_B represent the selling price and quantity sold for products A and B, respectively, then A and B are said to be **complementary** when

$$\frac{\partial q_A}{\partial p_B} < 0 \quad \text{and} \quad \frac{\partial q_B}{\partial p_A} < 0,$$

or **competitive** when

$$\frac{\partial q_A}{\partial p_B} > 0 \quad \text{and} \quad \frac{\partial q_B}{\partial p_A} > 0.$$

EXAMPLE 3

The electronics division of a discount department store has determined that monthly sales of cassette tapes q_A and portable cassette players q_B are related to their selling prices according to

$$q_A = 1000 - 100p_A - 10p_B^{1/2}$$

and
$$q_B = 190 - p_B + 45p_A^{-1}, \qquad 5 \le p_A \le 9, \, 50 \le p_B \le 100.$$

Determine whether these products are competitive, complementary, or neither.

SOLUTION

Examining partial derivatives, we find

$$\frac{\partial q_A}{\partial p_B} = -5p_B^{-1/2} < 0 \quad \text{and} \quad \frac{\partial q_B}{\partial p_A} = -45p_A^{-2} < 0.$$

Thus the tapes and tape players are complementary.

EXAMPLE 4

The marketing division of Jumbo Juices has derived the following joint demand functions for weekly sales (in gallons) of their tomato (q_A) and orange (q_B) juices:

$$q_A = 500 - 100p_A^2 + 50p_B^2$$

and
$$q_B = 4000 - 300p_B^{4/5} + 300p_A^{2/3},$$

where $.4 \le p_A \le .7$ and $1.5 \le p_B \le 2.8$. Show that these juices are competitive goods.

SOLUTION

Taking partial derivatives, we get

$$\frac{\partial q_A}{\partial p_B} = 100p_B > 0 \quad \text{and} \quad \frac{\partial q_B}{\partial p_A} = 200p^{-1/3} > 0.$$

Thus the juices are competitive.

In the demand functions just considered, selling price was the only marketing decision variable—the only variable under the firm's control to stimulate demand. Other marketing decision variables are advertising expenditure, product quality, service, and distribution.

EXAMPLE 5

The marketing division of Frothy Inc. estimates that weekly demand for their 12-oz. bottle of dishwashing detergent is given by

$$q = 50,000p^{-3}x^{.4}, \qquad .6 \le p \le 3, 2 \le x \le 10,$$

where p is the selling price in dollars and x is the weekly advertising expenditure in thousands of dollars. If the current selling price and weekly advertising budget are $p = \$2.00$ and $x = 5$, determine whether revenue is increased more by increasing advertising expenditure by $500 per week or by dropping the selling price by $.05 per bottle.

SOLUTION

The revenue function for this liquid detergent is

$$\begin{aligned} R &= pq \\ &= p(50,000p^{-3}x^{.4}) \\ &= 50,000p^{-2}x^{.4}. \end{aligned}$$

Differentiating, we find

$$\frac{\partial R}{\partial p} = -100,000p^{-3}x^{.4} \quad \text{and} \quad \frac{\partial R}{\partial x} = 20,000p^{-2}x^{-.6}.$$

When $p = 2$ and $x = 5$,

$$\frac{\partial R}{\partial p} = -100,000(2)^{-3}(5)^{.4} = -23,795.67,$$

while

$$\frac{\partial R}{\partial x} = 20,000(2)^{-2}(5)^{-.6} = 1903.65.$$

Interpreting $\partial R/\partial p$ as the change in weekly revenue with respect to selling price, we find that if the selling price decreases by $.05, weekly revenue will change by about $(-.05)(-23,795.67) = \$1189.78$. Reasoning in a similar fashion, if x is increased by .5, revenue will increase by $(.5)(1903.65) = \$951.83$. Thus a $.05 decrease in selling price will yield higher weekly revenues than a $500 increase in weekly advertising expenditure. (The careful reader will note that differentials were used in these approximations.) ●

The production counterparts of marketing decision variables are production decision variables. To meet a given level of demand, values of production variables such as labor and capital must be determined. The partial derivatives of output with respect to these variables are called marginal productivities.

EXAMPLE 6

For the Cobb–Douglas production function

$$Q = 4L^{.6}K^{.4}, \qquad 0 \le L \le 1000, 0 \le K \le 100,$$

find the marginal productivity with respect to labor and with respect to capital when $L = 500$ and $K = 70$. Interpret these derivatives.

SOLUTION

Differentiating we find

$$\frac{\partial Q}{\partial L} = .6(4)L^{-.4}K^{.4} = 2.4\left(\frac{K}{L}\right)^{.4}$$

and

$$\frac{\partial Q}{\partial K} = .4(4)L^{.6}K^{-.6} = 1.6\left(\frac{L}{K}\right)^{.6}.$$

When $L = 500$ and $K = 70$, we find

$$\frac{\partial Q}{\partial L} \doteq 1.1 \quad \text{and} \quad \frac{\partial Q}{\partial K} \doteq 5.2.$$

So each additional unit of labor will yield about 1.1 extra units of output, whereas each additional unit of capital will result in about 5.2 extra units of output. ●

EXERCISES 8.3

1. The attendance A (in thousands of people) at a local Food-fest is approximated by

$$A = \frac{-78 + 2.8t - .02t^2}{p}, \qquad 1 \le p \le 5, 50 \le t \le 90,$$

where t is the temperature (in degrees Fahrenheit) at noon on the day of the fest, and p (in dollars) is the price of admission. Find A, $\partial A/\partial p$, and $\partial A/\partial t$ when $p = 2$ and $t = 72$. Interpret these partial derivatives.

2. The power W (in watts) in a particular electrical circuit is determined from the voltage V and the resistance R (in ohms) according to

$$W = .8\frac{V^2}{R}, \qquad 0 \le R \le 100, 0 \le V \le 250.$$

Find and interpret the partial derivatives $\partial W/\partial R$ and $\partial W/\partial V$ when $R = 40$ and $V = 120$.

3. At Fisherman's Wharf, the daily price p (in dollars per pound) for halibut depends on the daily catch h (in

hundreds of pounds) of halibut and on the daily catch s (in hundreds of pounds) of salmon according to

$$p = \frac{3h + 8s + 4}{h + 2s}, \qquad 0 < h \le 4, 0 < s \le 8.$$

This morning after the fishing boats are unloaded, $h = 2$ and $s = 3$. Find today's price p for halibut; then find and interpret the partial derivatives $\partial p/\partial h$ and $\partial p/\partial s$.

4. Refer to Exercise 3. The daily price per pound p for salmon at Fisherman's Wharf is given by

$$p = \frac{2h + 6s + 17}{h + 3s}, \qquad 0 < h \le 4, 0 < s \le 8.$$

Find and interpret $\partial p/\partial h$ and $\partial p/\partial s$ when $h = 2$ and $s = 3$.

5. The annual salary P (in thousands of dollars) of a federal employee is determined by the employee's rank r and years of service s according to

$$P = \frac{70 - 30e^{-.2r}}{1 + e^{-.12s}}, \qquad 4 \le r \le 24, 0 \le s \le 50.$$

Find the salary of an employee with 10 yr of experience and rank $r = 8$. Use the partial derivatives $\partial P/\partial r$ and $\partial P/\partial s$ to estimate the salary increase this employee should expect with (a) an increase of one rank step to $r = 9$ and (b) another year of experience.

6. Rework Exercise 5 for a more seasoned employee for whom $r = 16$ and $s = 20$.

In Exercises 7–10 C represents a joint cost function, where x, y, and z are the units of output of products X, Y, and Z. Determine the marginal cost with respect to each output variable at the indicated output level.

7. $C(x, y) = 500 + 15x - .03x^2 + 20y - .04y^2 - .03xy$; $x = 20, y = 50$

8. $C(x, y) = 750 + 40x - .02x^2 + 35y - .03y^2 - .02xy$; $x = 100, y = 50$

9. $C(x, y, z) = 600 + 20x + 25y + 30z - .04x^2 - .05y^2 - .03z^2 - .03xy - .02xz - .03yz$; $x = 50, y = 80, z = 40$

10. $C(x, y, z) = 900 + 10x + 25y + 20z - .02x^2 - .03y^2 - .03z^2 + .01xy - .03yz$; $x = 20, y = 40, z = 50$

In Exercises 11–14 R denotes a joint revenue function where x, y, and z are the levels of sales for the products X, Y, and Z. Determine the marginal revenue with respect to each demand variable at the given level of sales. Then compare the result with the indicated cost function to determine the product whose output should be increased to realize the greatest profit increase.

11. $R(x, y) = 30x - .02x^2 + 35y - .04y^2 - .006xy$; $x = 20$, $y = 50$. Compare with the cost function in Exercise 7.

12. $R(x, y) = 50x - .03x^2 + 50y - .05y^2 - .008xy$; $x = 100$, $y = 50$. Compare with the cost function in Exercise 8.

13. $R(x, y, z) = 30x + 33y + 40z - .04x^2 - .03y^2 - .05z^2 + .006xy - .003xz + .008yz$; $x = 50, y = 80, z = 40$. Compare with the cost function in Exercise 9.

14. $R(x, y, z) = 12x + 30y + 35z - .03x^2 - .04y^2 - .02z^2 - .002xy + .001xz + .003yz$; $x = 20, y = 40, z = 50$. Compare with the cost function in Exercise 10.

15. At its main plant, the Firestorm Tire Company produces both a snow tire and a regular tire. Let s and t denote the hourly output of snow tires and regular tires, respectively. Suppose that the joint cost function is given by

$$C(s, t) = 35s + 32t - .04s^2 + .03st - .02t^2 + 50.$$

a. Find the marginal cost of the 60th snow tire when the regular tires are produced at the rate of 80 per hour.

b. Find the marginal cost of the 40th regular tire when the snow tires are produced at the rate of 70 per hour.

c. Suppose that Firestorm is presently producing 80 snow tires and 40 regular tires. If it is decided to increase the production of one of the models, which would be the less expensive to make?

16. Kamper-All Inc. makes two styles of camping vehicles— the Caravan and the Safari. Let q_A and q_B denote the number of Caravans and Safaris, respectively, that are made each week. Suppose that the joint cost function is given by

$$C(q_A, q_B) = 8000q_A + 9000q_B - 5q_A^2 + .2q_A^2 q_B - 6q_A q_B$$
$$+ .4q_A q_B^2 - 7q_B^2; \quad 0 \le q_A \le 40, 0 \le q_A \le 50.$$

a. Find the marginal cost of the 30th Caravan if the production rate for the Safari is 40 per week.

b. Find the marginal cost of the 30th Safari if the production rate for the Caravan is 40 per week.

c. Suppose that the present output is 25 Caravans and 35 Safaris. Because of a drop in demand, Kamper-All intends to cut back the production of one of the styles. Which style should be chosen to get the greater savings?

17. The Readalot Bookstore has to decide how many hardbound copies and how many paperback copies of each new novel to stock. Let the revenue that is received from the sale of these books be given by

$$R = 18h + 5s - .2h^2 - .1hs - .03s^2;$$
$$0 \le h \le 20, 0 \le s \le 100,$$

where h and s denote the number of hardbound and the number of paperbacks ordered, respectively.

a. Suppose the present policy of the store is to order 10 hardbound and 60 paperbacks. What is the marginal revenue from the 10th hardbound copy? From the 60th paperback?

b. Suppose that the store increases the number of paperbacks ordered to 70. What now is the marginal revenue from the 10th hardbound copy?

c. Suppose that the store increases the number of hardbound copies to 15 while leaving the paperbacks at 60. What then is the marginal revenue from the 60th paperback?

18. Taylormaid is a clothing company that makes two-piece and three-piece suits. Assume that when q_A and q_B of the two-piece and three-piece suits, respectively, are made each day, the revenue received by Taylormaid is

$$R(q_A, q_B) = 450q_A + 500q_B - 2q_A^2 - .01q_A^2q_B - .02q_Aq_B^2$$
$$- 3q_Aq_B - 1.5q_B^2; \quad 0 \le q_A, q_B \le 50.$$

a. If Taylormaid is currently making 30 of each type of suit, find the marginal revenue from the 30th two-piece suit. From the 30th three-piece suit.

b. Assume that Taylormaid changes its output to 40 two-piece suits and 30 three-piece suits. What is the marginal revenue from the 30th three-piece suit now?

c. If the output is changed to 30 two-piece and 40 three-piece suits, what is the marginal revenue from the 30th two-piece suit?

Analyze the demand functions in Exercises 19–26 to determine whether the associated products are competitive, complementary, or neither. (In all cases assume that $2 \le p_A \le 10$ and $5 \le p_B \le 12$.)

19. $q_A = 150 - .05p_A - .01p_B$
    $q_B = 175 - .06p_B - .005p_A$

20. $q_A = 300 - .06p_A + .01p_B$
    $q_B = 260 - .05p_B + .003p_A$

21. $q_A = 200p_A^{-.3}p_B^{.8}$
    $q_B = 150p_A^{.6}p_B^{-.2}$

22. $q_A = 100p_Bp_A^{-.5}$
    $q_B = 80p_Ap_B^{-.4}$

23. $q_A = 400\left(\dfrac{p_B}{p_A}\right)^{.6}$

    $q_B = 350\left(\dfrac{p_A}{p_B}\right)^{.8}$

24. $q_A = 250 - .05p_A^{1.5} + .002p_B^{.4}$
    $q_B = 130 - .02p_B^{1.3} - .003p_A^{.7}$

25. $q_A = \dfrac{200 + 3p_A + 8p_B}{2p_A + 7p_B}$

    $q_B = \dfrac{150 + 5p_A + 4p_B}{4p_A + 3p_B}$

26. $q_A = 500p_A^{-.8}p_B^{.3}$
    $q_B = 400p_A^{-.7}p_B^{-.2}$

For the Cobb–Douglas production functions in Exercises 27–30 find the marginal productivity with respect to capital and with respect to labor when $L = 500$ and $K = 300$.

27. $Q = .8L^{.7}K^{.3}$

28. $Q = 300L^{.2}K^{.8}$

29. $Q = 5L^{.75}K^{.25}$

30. $Q = 200L^{.9}K^{.1}$

31. Show that any Cobb–Douglas function of the form $Q = CL^{\alpha}K^{1-\alpha}$ satisfies

$$L\frac{\partial Q}{\partial L} + K\frac{\partial Q}{\partial K} = Q.$$

32. For any differentiable function of the form

$$f(x_1, x_2, \ldots, x_n) = kx_1^{a_1} x_2^{a_2}, \ldots, x_n^{a_n},$$

show that

$$\frac{\partial f}{\partial x_i} = \frac{a_i f(x_1, x_2, \ldots, x_n)}{x_i}.$$

33. The weekly demand function for Ultra-Dent toothpaste is approximated by

$$q = 100{,}000p^{-2}x^{.3},$$

where q is the number of economy-size tubes sold, p is the selling price, and x is the weekly advertising expenditure in thousands of dollars. Currently, $p = \$2.50$ and $x = 4$. Would the makers of Ultra-Dent realize a greater increase in revenue from raising the advertising budget by \$800 or from lowering the selling price by \$.10 per tube?

34. Refer to Exercise 33. Assume that the variable cost for producing a tube of Ultra-Dent toothpaste is a constant \$1.50.

a. Write the profit from the sale of this toothpaste as a function of p and x.

b. Estimate how the profit would change if the advertising budget were increased by \$800 and how it would change if the selling price were lowered by \$.10.

35. The weekly demand for Maxcaff coffee is approximated by

$$q = 80{,}000p^{-2.5}x^{.4},$$

where q is the number of 1-lb cans sold, p is the selling price, and x is the weekly advertising expenditure in thousands of dollars. Currently, $p = \$3.00$ and $x = 4$. Would Maxcaff realize a greater increase in revenue from lowering the selling price by \$.15 or from raising the advertising budget by \$1000?

36. Refer to Exercise 35. Assume that it costs the producers of Maxcaff coffee $1.75 to prepare and distribute each can.

  a. Write the profit as a function of p and x.

  b. Estimate how the profit would change if the selling price were reduced by $.15 per can and how it would change if the advertising budget were increased by $1000.

8.4
Relative Maximum and Minimum Values

The goal in this section is to provide a method for finding the maximum or the minimum of a function of two variables. Such a method can then be applied to finding the maximum of a joint profit function or the minimum of a joint cost function. Although this method will locate only relative maxima and minima, for many of the models that reflect the real world, a relative extreme value is the absolute extreme value.

Definition 8.3

Let $z = f(x, y)$ be a continuous function. We say that z has a **relative maximum (minimum)** at (x_0, y_0) if $f(x_0, y_0) \geq f(x, y)$ $[f(x_0, y_0) \leq f(x, y)]$ for all points (x, y) close to (x_0, y_0). We call $f(x_0, y_0)$ a **relative maximum (minimum) value** of z.

When the graph of $z = f(x, y)$ is a smooth surface, z has a relative maximum at the top of each hill and a relative minimum at the bottom of each valley. At these points on the surface, all of the tangent lines are parallel to the x,y-plane. (See Figure 8.12.) Consequently, these tangent lines have 0 slope. Because $f_x(x_0, y_0)$ and $f_y(x_0, y_0)$ represent the slope of the tangent lines in the x direction and the y direction, respectively, we know that when z has a relative extreme point at (x_0, y_0),

$$f_x(x_0, y_0) = 0 \quad \text{and} \quad f_y(x_0, y_0) = 0.$$

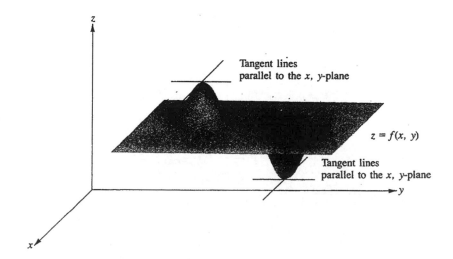

Figure 8.12
Tangent lines to a smooth surface at relative extreme points are parallel to the x,y-plane.

Definition 8.4

Let $z = f(x, y)$ be a differentiable function. We say that (x_0, y_0) is a **critical point** of f if

$$f_x(x_0, y_0) = 0 \quad \text{and} \quad f_y(x_0, y_0) = 0.$$

Note that Definition 8.4 is similar to the definition of a critical point for a function of one variable. Recall, however, that for functions of one variable, a point where the derivative does not exist is also called a critical point. Here we have required that the function be differentiable, so we will not consider such critical points for functions of two variables.

As the next examples show, finding the critical points requires solving simultaneous equations.

EXAMPLE 1

Find the critical points of

$$f(x, y) = x^2 + 6xy - 2y^2 - 12x - 14y.$$

SOLUTION

Because

$$f_x(x, y) = 2x + 6y - 12 \quad \text{and} \quad f_y(x, y) = 6x - 4y - 14,$$

to find the critical points we must solve

$$2x + 6y - 12 = 0$$

and

$$6x - 4y - 14 = 0.$$

From the first equation, we have $x = 6 - 3y$. Substituting for x in the second equation, we then have

$$6(6 - 3y) - 4y - 14 = 0$$

or

$$-22y + 22 = 0,$$

so that $y = 1$. Letting $y = 1$ in either of the original equations gives $x = 3$. Therefore, $(3, 1)$ is the only critical point of f. ●

EXAMPLE 2

Find the critical points of

$$f(x, y) = 8xy - 2x^4 - y^2.$$

SOLUTION

Since

$$f_x(x, y) = 8y - 8x^3 \quad \text{and} \quad f_y(x, y) = 8x - 2y,$$

we have to solve the equations

$$8y - 8x^3 = 0$$

and

$$8x - 2y = 0.$$

From the second equation, we see that $y = 4x$. Substituting for y in the first equation, we get

$$8(4x) - 8x^3 = 0$$

or

$$8x(4 - x^2) = 0.$$

Solving this equation, we find that $x = 0$, 2, or -2. From the relationship $y = 4x$, we obtain three critical points: $(0, 0)$, $(2, 8)$, and $(-2, -8)$. ●

After finding all the critical points of f, it is still necessary to determine whether each is a relative maximum or a relative minimum. In fact, there is a third possibility. A **saddle point** of f is a point on the surface where the tangent lines in both the x and the y directions are horizontal, but the surface is concave upward in one direction and concave downward in another direction. A saddle point can be visualized as a "pass" between two peaks that connects two valleys. Figure 8.13 shows a surface with a saddle point.

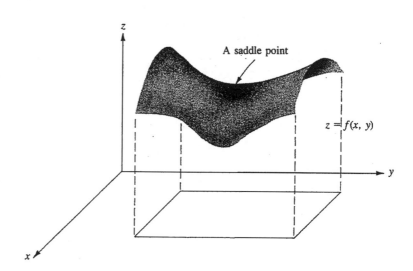

Figure 8.13
A surface with a saddle point. The surface is concave downward in the x direction and concave upward in the y direction.

EXAMPLE 3

Show that the point $(0, 0, 0)$ is a saddle point of the surface $z = y^2 - x^2$.

SOLUTION

If $f(x, y) = y^2 - x^2$, then $f_x(x, y) = -2x$ and $f_y(x, y) = 2y$. Thus, $(0, 0)$ is a critical point of f. Examining the second partial derivatives, we see that $f_{xx}(x, y) = -2$ and $f_{yy}(x, y) = 2$, so the surface is concave downward in the x direction and concave upward in the y direction and thus has a saddle point at $(0, 0, 0)$. A sketch of this surface appears in Figure 8.14.

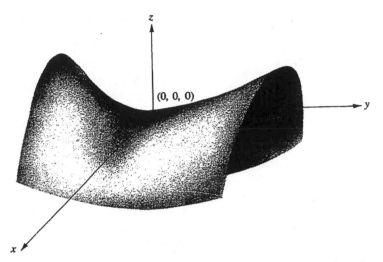

Figure 8.14
A sketch of the surface $z = y^2 - x^2$

Various concavity configurations are summarized in the following theorem, which may be used to classify a critical point as a relative maximum, relative minimum, or saddle point. This result is analogous to the second derivative test for functions of one variable.

Theorem 8.1

Suppose that all the second-order derivatives of $z = f(x, y)$ are continuous and (x_0, y_0) is a critical point of f. The test function D is defined by

$$D(x, y) = f_{xx}(x, y)f_{yy}(x, y) - [f_{xy}(x, y)]^2.$$

1. If $D(x_0, y_0) > 0$ and $f_{xx}(x_0, y_0) < 0$, then z has a relative maximum at (x_0, y_0).
2. If $D(x_0, y_0) > 0$ and $f_{xx}(x_0, y_0) > 0$, then z has a relative minimum at (x_0, y_0).
3. If $D(x_0, y_0) < 0$, then there is a saddle point at (x_0, y_0).
4. If $D(x_0, y_0) = 0$, then the test fails to give any information.

When this test fails it is necessary to analyze the behavior of the function f itself near the critical point in order to classify the point.

EXAMPLE 4

Find the critical points of $f(x, y) = x^3 - 6xy + y^2 + 5y$ and classify each as a relative maximum, relative minimum, or saddle point.

SOLUTION

The solutions to the system of equations

$$f_x(x, y) = 3x^2 - 6y = 0$$
$$f_y(x, y) = -6x + 2y + 5 = 0$$

are $x = 1$, $y = 1/2$, and $x = 5$, $y = 25/2$. The critical points to be tested are therefore $(1, 1/2)$ and $(5, 25/2)$. The second-order partial derivatives are

$$f_{xx}(x, y) = 6x, \quad f_{yy}(x, y) = 2, \quad \text{and} \quad f_{xy}(x, y) = -6.$$

Since f_{xx} and f_{yy} are positive at both critical points, the surface is concave upward in both the x and y directions at these points, and f will have a relative minimum at each of these points if the test function is positive. We have

$$D = (6x)(2) - (-6)^2 = 12x - 36,$$

so

$$D\left(5, \frac{25}{2}\right) = 60 - 36 = 24 > 0,$$

and f has a relative minimum at $(5, 25/2)$. However,

$$D\left(1, \frac{1}{2}\right) = 12 - 36 = -24 < 0;$$

hence, there is a saddle point at $(1, 1/2)$. A sketch of this surface appears in Figure 8.15.

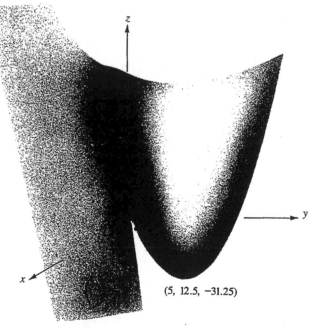

Figure 8.15

A sketch of the surface
$z = x^3 - 6xy + y^2 + 5y$

$(5, 12.5, -31.25)$

EXAMPLE 5

Find the critical points of $f(x, y) = 2x^2 - x^4 - y^2 + 6y$ and classify each as a relative maximum, relative minimum, or saddle point.

SOLUTION

To find the critical points, we solve the system

$$f_x(x, y) = 4x - 4x^3 = 0$$
$$f_y(x, y) = -2y + 6 = 0.$$

Because there are no interaction terms in f, each of these equations contains only one variable. From the first equation we find that $x = 0$, 1, or -1. From the second equation, we find that $y = 3$. The critical points are then the (x, y) pairs $(0, 3)$, $(1, 3)$, and $(-1, 3)$.

The second-order partial derivatives are

$$f_{xx}(x, y) = 4 - 12x^2, \quad f_{yy}(x, y) = -2, \quad \text{and} \quad f_{xy}(x, y) = 0.$$

The test function is

$$D(x, y) = (4 - 12x^2)(-2) - (0)^2 = 24x^2 - 8.$$

At the critical points we have

$$D(0, 3) = -8 < 0;$$
$$D(1, 3) = 16 > 0; \quad f_{xx}(1, 3) = -8 < 0;$$
$$D(-1, 3) = 16 > 0; \quad f_{xx}(-1, 3) = -8 < 0.$$

Therefore, there are relative maxima at $(1, 3)$ and $(-1, 3)$ and a saddle point at $(0, 3)$. A sketch of this surface appears in Figure 8.16.

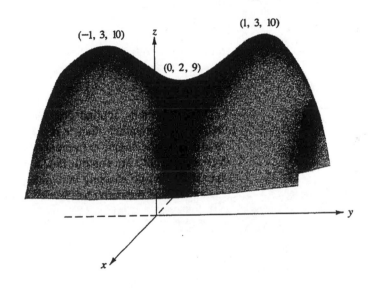

Figure 8.16

A sketch of $z = 2x^2 - x^4 - y^2 + 6y$

EXAMPLE 6

The Brite-Lite Company makes a floor lamp and a table lamp. Let s and t denote the number of floor and table lamps, respectively, that Brite-Lite makes each day. If the joint profit function for the manufacture and sale of these lamps is

$$P(s, t) = 18s + 2t - .05s^2 + .02st - .03t^2 - 100,$$
$$0 \leq s \leq 250, 0 \leq t \leq 250,$$

determine the output levels s and t where P has a relative maximum value.

SOLUTION

The critical points of the profit function P can be found by solving the system

$$P_s(s, t) = 18 - .1s + .02t = 0$$

$$P_t(s, t) = 2 + .02s - .06t = 0.$$

Solving the first equation yields $s = 180 + .2t$. Substituting this value into the second equation, we have

$$2 + .02(180 + .2t) - .06t = 0$$

or

$$5.6 - .056t = 0.$$

Therefore $t = 100$. From $s = 180 + .2t$ we find that $s = 200$.

To test the critical point $s = 200$, $t = 100$, we first calculate the second-order partial derivatives:

$$P_{ss}(s, t) = -.1, \quad P_{tt}(s, t) = -.06, \quad \text{and} \quad P_{st}(s, t) = .02.$$

These derivatives are constant and P_{ss} and P_{tt} are both negative, so the graph of P is concave downward in the s and t directions for all values of s and t. The test function

$$D(s, t) = (-.1)(-.06) - (.02)^2 = .006 - .0004 = .0056$$

is positive, so P has a (relative) maximum at $s = 200$, $t = 100$, where $P = 1800$. It can be shown that 1800 is the absolute maximum value of P for $0 \leq s \leq 250$, $0 \leq t \leq 250$. ●

To solve many applied problems like Example 6, we must find an **absolute** extreme value rather than a **relative** extreme value. Unfortunately, there is no analogue of the unique extremum theorem (see Section 5.6) for functions of several variables. There are smooth functions of two variables that have a unique relative maximum but no absolute maximum value.* There are, however, analogues of the extreme value theorem (see Section 5.2) for continuous functions of several variables. One such result is given here.

Theorem 8.2

> If $z = f(x, y)$ is a differentiable function on the closed rectangular domain $a \leq x \leq b$, $c \leq y \leq d$, then f assumes an absolute maximum value and an absolute minimum value on that domain. These extreme values occur at critical points of f, or on the **boundary** of the domain—those pairs of values (x, y) where $x = a$, $x = b$, $y = c$, or $y = d$.

EXAMPLE 7

Find the absolute extreme values of the function

$$P(s, t) = 18s + 2t - .05s^2 + .02st - .03t^2 - 100;$$
$$0 \leq s \leq 250, 0 \leq t \leq 250.$$

*See J. Ash and H. Sexton, "A Surface with One Local Minimum," *Mathematics Magazine* 58, no. 3 (May 1985): 147–149.

SOLUTION

In Example 6, we found that the only critical point of P was (200, 100), where $P = 1800$. We examine the boundary of the domain in Figure 8.17.

If $s = 0$, then $P(0, t) = g(t) = 2t - .03t^2 - 100, 0 \le t \le 250$. This quadratic function of t has maximum value $g(100/3) = -200/3$ and minimum value $g(250) = -1475$.

If $s = 250$, then $P(250, t) = g(t) = 1275 + 7t - .03t^2, 0 \le t \le 250$. Here the resulting quadratic function has maximum value $g(350/3) = 1683.33$ and minimum value $g(250) = 1150$.

If $t = 0$, then $P(s, 0) = g(s) = 18s - .05s^2 - 100, 0 \le s \le 250$. The maximum value of g is $g(180) = 1520$, and the minimum value is $g(0) = -100$.

If $t = 250$, then $P(s, 250) = g(s) = -1475 + 23s - .05s^2, 0 \le s \le 250$. The maximum value of g is $g(230) = 1170$, and the minimum value is $g(0) = -1475$.

Sorting through all the candidates for absolute extreme values, we find that the absolute maximum value of P is 1800, and this value occurs at the critical point (200, 100). The absolute minimum value of P is -1475, and this value occurs at the boundary point (0, 250).

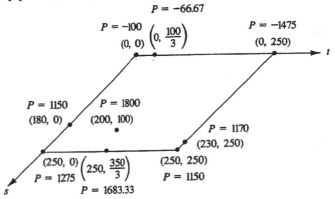

Figure 8.17

Finding the absolute extrema of P on the domain $0 \le s \le 250$, $0 \le t \le 250$

EXERCISES 8.4

In Exercises 1–10 find all the critical points of the given function.

1. $f(x, y) = 3x^2 + 4xy - y^2$

2. $f(x, y) = 2x^2 - 5xy + 4y^2$

3. $f(x, y) = x^2 + 4xy - 8y$

4. $f(x, y) = 3xy + 2y^2 + 6x$

5. $f(x, y) = x^3 + 3xy - 6y$

6. $f(x, y) = 8x - 4xy + 3y^4$

7. $f(x, y) = \dfrac{1}{x} + xy - \dfrac{1}{3}y^3$

8. $f(x, y) = x^2 - 2xy + y^3$

9. $f(x, y) = (x - 5) \ln xy$

10. $f(x, y) = e^{2y}(x^2 + 2x + y)$

In Exercises 11–28 find all the critical points and classify each as a relative maximum, relative minimum, or saddle point.

11. $f(x, y) = xy$

12. $f(x, y) = x^3 + y^3 - 12xy$

13. $f(x, y) = 4x^2 - 2xy + 6y^2$

14. $f(x, y) = 2xy - 4x^2 - y^2$

15. $f(x, y) = 3x^2 - xy - 4y$

16. $f(x, y) = x^2 + 3xy + y^2 - x - 4y$

17. $f(x, y) = x^2 - 2xy + 4y^2 + 8x - 14y$

18. $f(x, y) = 2x^3 + y^3 - 6x - 12y$

19. $f(x, y) = x^3 - 6xy + 3y^2$

20. $f(x, y) = x^2y - xy^2 + \frac{1}{3}y^3 - 9y$

21. $f(x, y) = 2xy - y^2 - x^4$

22. $f(x, y) = x^2 - 6xy + y^3 + 15y$

23. $f(x, y) = 12x^2 - 3x^2y + \frac{3}{2}y^2$

24. $f(x, y) = 12xy - x^3 - 3y^2$

25. $f(x, y) = 2x^2 + 8xy + \ln y$

26. $f(x, y) = \ln x + 2 \ln y - x^2y + 3x$

27. $f(x, y) = x^4 + \frac{1}{3}y^3 - 2x^2 - y^2 - 3y$

28. $f(x, y) = x^4 - 8x^2 + y^2 - 8y$

29. Spinaway makes washing machines and clothes dryers at the same manufacturing plant. Let w and z be the number of washers and dryers, respectively, that are made each day. Suppose that the profit earned by Spinaway is given by

$$P(w, z) = 100w + 170z - 2w^2 + wz - 5z^2 - 300,$$
$$0 \le w \le 40, 0 \le z \le 25.$$

Find the level of output that will maximize the profit.

30. Sound-Around Technology makes two kinds of portable radios—a basic AM model and an AM/FM model. Let q_A and q_B denote the number of AM models and AM/FM models, respectively, that the company makes each day. Assume

that the joint cost function is given by

$$C(q_A, q_B) = 20q_A + 45q_B - .2q_A^2 - .1q_B^2,$$
$$0 \le q_A, q_B \le 225,$$

and the joint revenue function is given by

$$R(q_A, q_B) = 50q_A + 70q_B - .3q_A^2 - .05q_Aq_B - .15q_B^2,$$
$$0 \le q_A, q_B \le 225.$$

Determine the daily production rates that will maximize profit.

31. The manager of an appliance store must decide how many 19-inch and 21-inch television sets to order each month. Each 19-inch set costs the manager $250, and each 21-inch set costs $300. The demand function for the 19-inch sets is given by

$$p_A = 410 - 3q_A - q_B, \qquad 0 \le q_A, q_B \le 25,$$

where q_A and q_B are the number of 19- and 21-inch sets, respectively, that are ordered. The demand function for the 21-inch sets is

$$p_B = 500 - q_A - 4q_B, \qquad 0 \le q_A, q_B \le 25.$$

Find q_A and q_B to maximize profit.

32. Commander Computers makes the HC-1000, a basic home computer, and the HC-2000, a similar model with extra memory. Assume that each of the HC-1000s can be sold for $800 and each of the HC-2000s for $1000. The joint cost function to make q_A and q_B HC-1000s and HC-2000s, respectively, per week is given by

$$C(q_A, q_B) = 610q_A + 860q_B + .25q_A^2 - .2q_Aq_B + .4q_B^2$$
$$+ 5000, \quad 0 \le q_A \le 500, 0 \le q_B \le 400.$$

How many of each model should be made each week so that Commander Computer earns the maximum profit?

33. Packit Containers has a contract to make 800 topless rectangular storage cartons, each with a capacity of 4 cu ft. As the Packit designer, you must build the required cartons with the smallest possible surface area. What are the dimensions of the required cartons?

34. Refer to Exercise 33. Packit must build a rectangular storage crate with a heavy-duty base and a volume of 36 cu ft. The material for the base costs $5 per square foot, whereas that used for the top and sides costs $3 per square foot. Find the dimensions of the least expensive crate with these specifications.

35. Sonic Transit specializes in next-day delivery throughout the United States. For $25, Sonic Transit will deliver a rectangular container, the sum of whose length x and girth $2y + 2z$ is at most 120 in. Find the dimensions of the rectangular container with maximum volume that Sonic will deliver for $25.

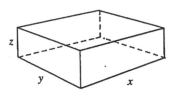

36. Refer to Exercise 35. Due to an abundance of long, narrow packages, Sonic Transit has changed its overnight special. They will now ship for $25 any rectangular carton, the sum of whose length, width, and depth is at most 90 in. Find the dimensions of the carton with maximum volume that Sonic will now ship for $25.

37. An efficiency expert has gathered productivity data on Sonic Transit shipping clerks. This expert used the data to express the number of orders N processed by a clerk during any given day as a function of the number of hours t the clerk had been working that day and the number of weeks w since the clerk's last raise. The expert's function is

$$N = \frac{(9t^2 - t^3)(w^2 - 8w + 22)}{w^2 - 8w + 19},$$
$$0 \le t \le 8, 0 \le w \le 52.$$

If a clerk's productivity is measured by the number of orders processed per hour N_t, find t and w when the clerk is most productive.

38. Suppose the demand q for a product can be modeled using a function of the form

$$q = kp^\alpha a^\beta d^\gamma,$$

where p, a, and d represent the selling price, advertising expenditure, and distribution expenditure, respectively. Assume further that the total cost for this product can be modeled using the linear cost function

$$C = vq + a + d + f,$$

where v denotes the (constant) variable cost per unit and f denotes fixed costs. Show that profit is maximized when

$$p = \frac{\alpha v}{1 + \alpha},$$

and thus the optimal selling price is independent of the other marketing decision variables.

39. Show that $z = ax + bxy + cy$, where $b \ne 0$, always has a saddle point at $(-c/b, -a/b)$.

8.5
Constrained Optimization and Lagrange Multipliers

In applied optimization problems there are usually limits on the values of the independent variables. Consider, for example, some of the factors that can affect the development of a new product: there may be a deadline for the introduction of the product, the total expenditure on labor and equipment in its manufacture may be fixed, and advertising and promotion expenses must meet budgets. Limitations on values of the independent variables are called **constraints**. Constraints restrict or determine the domain of the function to be optimized. Finding the maximum or the minimum of a function subjected to constraints is called a **constrained optimization problem**.

For functions of a single variable in a constrained optimization problem, the choices for the independent variable were usually constrained to a closed interval. For functions of several variables, constraints may take several forms. In this section we consider so-called **equality constraints**. For independent variables x_1, x_2, ..., x_n, an equality constraint can be written in the form

(8.5) $$g(x_1, x_2, ..., x_n) = 0$$

for some function g.

The simplest approach to optimizing functions of several variables subject to an equality constraint is the **method of substitution**. In this method, we begin by solving constraint (8.5) for one of the variables in terms of the others. This variable is then eliminated from consideration through substitution into the function to be optimized.

EXAMPLE 1   Community Computer is a retailer that sells two kinds of personal computers—the PC-XL and the AP-II. The manager is planning to purchase 50 personal computers in the next order from the manufacturers. Letting x and y denote the number of PC-XLs and AP-IIs ordered, respectively, assume that the profit earned from the sale of these computers is given by

$$P = 160x + 100y - 2x^2 - 2xy - y^2, \qquad 0 \le x, y \le 50.$$

How many of each model should the manager order to maximize the profit?

SOLUTION   Because a total of 50 personal computers will be ordered, the solution must satisfy the constraint

$$x + y - 50 = 0.$$

Solving this for y, we get $y = 50 - x$. Substituting into the profit function, we obtain P as a function of x alone:

$$
\begin{aligned}
P &= 160x + 100(50 - x) - 2x^2 - 2x(50 - x) - (50 - x)^2 \\
&= 160x + 5000 - 100x - 2x^2 - 100x + 2x^2 - 2500 + 100x - x^2 \\
&= -x^2 + 60x + 2500.
\end{aligned}
$$

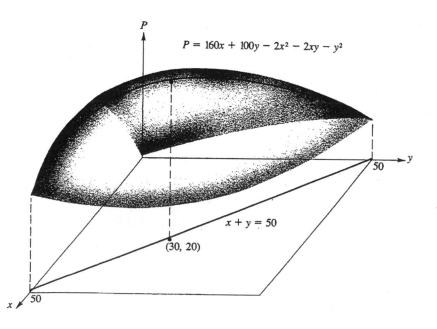

Figure 8.18
The maximum of P for $x + y = 50$ is the highest point of the curve on the surface above that line segment.

The graph of this function is a downward-opening parabola with a maximum at $x = 30$. From the constraint, we also find that $y = 20$. For these values the corresponding profit is $3400.

Geometrically, the constraint $x + y - 50 = 0$ is a line segment in the x,y-plane. By restricting x and y to this line segment, we are seeking the highest point of a curve on the surface

$$P = 160x + 100y - 2x^2 - 2xy - y^2,$$

as illustrated in Figure 8.18.

●

EXAMPLE 2

The weekly production function for a rural cheese factory is given by

$$Q = 30L^{.25}K^{.75},$$

where Q denotes pounds of cheese, L denotes worker-hours of labor, and K denotes hundreds of dollars of capital expenditure. If the factory has set a goal of producing 3000 lb of cheese per week, find the values of L and K that will minimize the weekly cost in meeting this goal. Assume that each worker-hour of labor costs $10.

SOLUTION

The weekly expenditure in dollars for labor and capital is given by

$$E = 10L + 100K.$$

We wish to minimize E subject to the constraint

$$30L^{.25}K^{.75} = 3000.$$

Solving the constraint for L, we find

$$L^{.25} = 100K^{-.75},$$

so after raising both sides of this equation to the fourth power,

$$L = 10^8 K^{-3}.$$

Substituting for L, we get

$$E = 10^9 K^{-3} + 100K.$$

Thus,

$$\frac{dE}{dK} = -3(10)^9 K^{-4} + 100,$$

and we see that $dE/dK = 0$ if $K^4 = 3(10)^7$, or

$$K = 3^{.25} (10)^{1.75} \doteq 74.$$

The second derivative test can be used to verify that E has an absolute minimum at $K = 74$ ($7400 in capital expenditures per week). From the constraint we also find that

$$L = 10^8 K^{-3} \doteq 247 \text{ worker-hours.}$$

The minimum weekly cost in meeting the factory's goal is thus

$$E = 10(247) + 100(74) = \$9870.$$ ●

In some constrained optimization problems the constraint cannot be easily solved for one of the variables. In these cases the method of **Lagrange multipliers** may be used. This scheme begins by appending the constraint (8.5) to the function $f(x_1, x_2, \ldots, x_n)$, which is to be optimized, to form a new function:

(8.6) $$F(x_1, x_2, \ldots, x_n, \lambda) = f(x_1, x_2, \ldots, x_n) + \lambda g(x_1, x_2, \ldots, x_n),$$

called the **Lagrangian**. Here λ is called a Lagrange multiplier and it is considered to be another independent variable. Notice that when $x_1, x_2, \ldots, x_n$ satisfy the constraint $g(x_1, x_2, \ldots, x_n) = 0$, the value of F is the same as the value of f regardless of the value of λ.

Critical points of F are now found by solving the system of $n + 1$ equations in $n + 1$ unknowns:

(8.7)

$$1: \quad \frac{\partial F}{\partial x_1} = 0,$$

$$2: \quad \frac{\partial F}{\partial x_2} = 0,$$

$$\vdots \quad \vdots$$

$$n: \quad \frac{\partial F}{\partial x_n} = 0,$$

$$n + 1: \quad \frac{\partial F}{\partial \lambda} = 0.$$

The last of these equations is just the constraint (8.5). Since F and f have the same value when the constraint is satisfied, it can be shown that if there is an extreme value of f subject to the constraint, it occurs at a critical point of F.

The solutions to the system (8.7) are candidates for points at which f attains extreme values. If f has a constrained maximum or minimum, it must occur at one of these points. Methods by which the critical points can be classified as maxima or minima are not included in this text. We will rely on inspection of the function f along the constraint equation at the critical points to determine the maximum or minimum.

EXAMPLE 3

Use the method of Lagrange multipliers to find the maximum of $f(x, y) = xy^2$ when x and y are constrained to satisfy $x^2 + y^2 = 9$.

SOLUTION

Writing the constraint as $x^2 + y^2 - 9 = 0$, equation (8.6), the Lagrangian, is

$$F(x, y, \lambda) = xy^2 + \lambda(x^2 + y^2 - 9).$$

Setting the partial derivatives of F with respect to x, y, and λ equal to 0, we obtain the system of equations

(1)
$$\frac{\partial F}{\partial x} = y^2 + 2\lambda x = 0,$$

(2)
$$\frac{\partial F}{\partial y} = 2xy + 2\lambda y = 0,$$

(3)
$$\frac{\partial F}{\partial \lambda} = x^2 + y^2 - 9 = 0.$$

From equation (2), we see that $2y(x + \lambda) = 0$, so either $y = 0$ or $x = -\lambda$. If $y = 0$, then from equation (3) either $x = 3$ or $x = -3$. Thus two critical points of F are (3, 0) and (−3, 0). Taking $x = -\lambda$ in equation (1), we find that $y^2 = 2\lambda^2$. Substitution for x and y in equation (3), then gives $\lambda^2 + 2\lambda^2 - 9 = 0$. Thus, $\lambda = \pm\sqrt{3}$. Using these values for λ yields four more critical points: $(\sqrt{3}, \pm2\sqrt{3})$ and $(-\sqrt{3}, \pm2\sqrt{3})$. Referring to Figure 8.19, we see that f achieves a maximum of $12\sqrt{3}$ at $(\sqrt{3}, 2\sqrt{3})$ and at $(\sqrt{3}, -2\sqrt{3})$.

Figure 8.19

Values of $f(x, y) = xy^2$ at points that satisfy $x^2 + y^2 = 9$

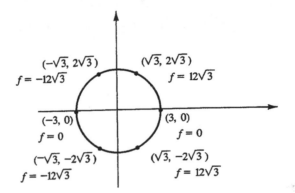

$(-\sqrt{3}, 2\sqrt{3})$
$f = -12\sqrt{3}$

$(\sqrt{3}, 2\sqrt{3})$
$f = 12\sqrt{3}$

$(-3, 0)$
$f = 0$

$(3, 0)$
$f = 0$

$(-\sqrt{3}, -2\sqrt{3})$
$f = -12\sqrt{3}$

$(\sqrt{3}, -2\sqrt{3})$
$f = 12\sqrt{3}$

EXAMPLE 4

Watersports Inc. has decided to begin production of two types of life jackets—a life vest and a life belt. Letting x and y denote the number of life vests and life belts, respectively, assume that the weekly joint cost function for these life jackets is estimated to be

$$C(x, y) = 504 + 20x - .05x^2 + 16y - .05y^2 + .01xy, \qquad 0 \le x, y \le 100.$$

Due to cash flow problems, Watersports has decided to spend only $3000 per week for the production of these jackets. If the selling prices are $25 and $20 for the life vests and the life belts, respectively, find x and y to maximize revenue subject to the $3000 cost constraint.

SOLUTION

We wish to maximize

$$R(x, y) = 25x + 20y$$

subject to

$$504 + 20x - .05x^2 + 16y - .05y^2 + .01xy = 3000$$

or

$$20x - .05x^2 + 16y - .05y^2 + .01xy - 2496 = 0.$$

Using the Lagrange multiplier technique we define the Lagrangian:

$$F(x, y, \lambda) = 25x + 20y + \lambda(20x - .05x^2 + 16y - .05y^2 + .01xy - 2496)$$

and seek its critical points. Equating the partial derivatives of F to 0, we have the system of equations

(1)
$$\frac{\partial F}{\partial x} = 25 + \lambda(20 - .1x + .01y) = 0,$$

(2)
$$\frac{\partial F}{\partial y} = 20 + \lambda(16 - .1y + .01x) = 0,$$

(3)
$$\frac{\partial F}{\partial \lambda} = 20x - .05x^2 + 16y - .05y^2 + .01xy - 2496 = 0.$$

To solve this system, we begin by solving the first two equations for λ:

$$\lambda = \frac{25}{.1x - .01y - 20}$$

and

$$\lambda = \frac{20}{.1y - .01x - 16}.$$

Equating these expressions for λ, we find that

$$\frac{25}{.1x - .01y - 20} = \frac{20}{.1y - .01x - 16},$$

so

$$25(.1y - .01x - 16) = 20(.1x - .01y - 20),$$

which reduces to $2.25x = 2.7y$ and thus $x = 1.2y$. Substituting for x in equation (3), we find that

$$20(1.2y) - .05(1.2y)^2 + 16y - .05y^2 + .01(1.2)y^2 - 2496 = 0,$$

which simplifies to

$$-.11y^2 + 40y - 2496 = 0.$$

From the quadratic formula, we find that either $y = 80$ or $y = 284$. Because $y = 284$ is not in the domain, it can be ignored. The only critical point is therefore $y = 80$ and $x = 1.2(80) = 96$. It can be checked that at this production level revenue is maximized, with

$$R = 25(96) + 20(80) = \$4000$$

and Watersports realizing a profit of $1000 per week.   ●

The final example is an optimization problem with three independent variables.

EXAMPLE 5

The makers of Chevelure Shampoo produce and sell their product in three cities: one large, one moderate sized, and one small. It is believed that sales depend largely on television advertising in each of the markets. Let x, y, and z denote the number of minutes of advertising that appear each week on television in each of the three cities, respectively. Earlier data indicate that the weekly profit from sales of the shampoo in each of these markets can be approximated by

$$PS = 12{,}000x^{1/3}, \quad PM = 1200y^{2/3}, \quad \text{and} \quad PL = 600z^{2/3},$$

respectively. It is also known the advertising costs are $500 per minute in the large city, $200 per minute in the moderate-sized city, and $100 per minute in the small city. The company's total advertising budget is $25,000 per week for these markets. How should the advertising budget be allocated among the cities so that the total weekly profit from the shampoo is maximized?

SOLUTION

We want to find the maximum weekly profit: $PS + PM + PL$. For x minutes of advertising in the large city, the company must spend $500x$ dollars. Similar reasoning for the other markets leads to the budgetary constraint $500x + 200y + 100z = 25{,}000$. The problem can therefore be stated as:

maximize: $P = 12{,}000x^{1/3} + 1200y^{2/3} + 600z^{2/3}$

subject to: $5x + 2y + z = 250$.

The Lagrangian is

$$F(x, y, z, \lambda) = 12{,}000x^{1/3} + 1200y^{2/3} + 600z^{2/3} + \lambda(5x + 2y + z - 250).$$

Equating the partial derivatives of F to 0, we obtain the system of equations

(1)
$$\frac{\partial F}{\partial x} = 4000x^{-2/3} + 5\lambda = 0,$$

(2)
$$\frac{\partial F}{\partial y} = 800y^{-1/3} + 2\lambda = 0,$$

(3)
$$\frac{\partial F}{\partial z} = 400z^{-1/3} + \lambda = 0,$$

(4)
$$\frac{\partial F}{\partial \lambda} = 5x + 2y + z - 250 = 0.$$

Eliminating λ from equations (1) and (2) gives

$$800x^{-2/3} = 400y^{-1/3},$$

and solving for y, we get

$$y = \frac{1}{8}x^2.$$

Eliminating λ from equations (1) and (3) gives

$$800x^{-2/3} = 400z^{-1/3},$$

and solving for z, we get

$$z = \frac{1}{8}x^2.$$

Substitution for y and z in equation (4) gives

$$\frac{3}{8}x^2 + 5x - 250 = 0,$$

an equation in x alone. From the quadratic formula, we find one positive root, $x = 20$. Substitution into the expressions for y and z yields $y = z = 50$.

Allocating $500(20) = \$10,000$ to the large city, $200(50) = \$10,000$ to the moderate-sized city, and $100(50) = \$5000$ to the small city yields a weekly profit of

$$P = 12,000(20)^{1/3} + 1200(50)^{2/3} + 600(50)^{2/3} = \$57,003.$$

It can be verified that this is, in fact, the constrained maximum of P. ●

EXERCISES 8.5

In Exercises 1–8 use the method of substitution to optimize each function subject to the given constraint.

1. Maximize $f(x, y) = 5xy$ subject to $x + y = 6$.

2. Maximize $f(x, y) = 2xy$ subject to $2x + y = 24$.

3. Minimize $g(L, K) = 10L + 20K$ subject to $LK = 18$, where $L, K > 0$.

4. Minimize $h(x_1, x_2) = 5x_1 + 8x_2$ subject to $x_1 x_2 = 10$.

5. Minimize $C(q_1, q_2) = 2q_1^2 + q_1 q_2 + q_2^2 + 100$ subject to $q_1 + q_2 = 100$.

6. Maximize $P(q_A, q_B) = 50q_A - .04q_A^2 + 40q_B - .03q_B^2 - .01q_A q_B$ subject to $q_A + q_B = 40$.

7. Maximize $f(x, y) = 800 - x^2 - y^2$ subject to $x + 2y = 50$.

8. Minimize $g(x, y) = 2x^2 + 3y^2 - xy$ subject to $x + y = 120$.

9–16. Rework Exercises 1–8 using the method of Lagrange multipliers.

17. The makers of Spectrum paints plan to spend $20,000 per week for labor and capital in the production of their oil-based primer. The weekly output Q (in gallons) depends on the expenditure for capital K and labor L according to

$$Q = .4L^{.2}K^{.8}.$$

Determine the values of L and K that maximize Q, and the maximum value of Q.

18. Refer to Exercise 17. If the makers of Spectrum paints decide to produce exactly 4000 gal of primer each week, determine the values of L and K that minimize the cost in meeting this production goal.

19. The weekly production function for a yogurt factory is given by

$$Q = 50L^{1/3}K^{2/3},$$

where Q denotes pounds of yogurt, L denotes worker-hours of labor, and K denotes hundreds of dollars of capital expenditure. If each hour of labor costs $12 and the owner of the factory has set a goal of producing 5000 lb of yogurt per week, find the values of L and K that minimize the weekly cost in meeting this goal.

20. Refer to Exercise 19. The production division of the factory has been budgeted $8000 each week for labor and capital in the production of yogurt. Find the values of L and K that maximize output Q subject to this constraint. Find the maximum output.

21. Kitchenayds Inc. produces mixers and blenders at the same plant. The mixers sell for $50 each and the blenders sell for $40 each. The weekly cost of producing x mixers and y blenders is

$$C = 560 + 40x + 32y - .07x^2 - .05y^2 - .1xy,$$

where $0 \le x \le 200$ and $0 \le y \le 150$. If $5000 is spent each week to produce mixers and blenders, find x and y to maximize revenue assuming that all products produced are sold. Find the corresponding weekly profit.

22. Refer to Exercise 21. The production division of Kitchenayds has decided to produce a total of 120 units each week at the blender–mixer plant. Find x and y to minimize cost subject to this constraint.

23. Located in a college town, VanGo Pizza specializes in the delivery of pizza to dormitories. It can advertise on three radio stations: the first plays classical music, the second hard rock, and the third country/western. The cost of advertising on these stations is $20, $10, and $40 per spot, respectively. VanGo has an advertising budget of $3100 per week. It is believed that the number of pizzas ordered in response to radio ads is $200x^{1/3}$, $100y^{2/3}$, and $200z^{2/3}$ per week, where x, y, and z are the number of ads run each week on the classical, rock, and C/W station, respectively. How many ads should be run on each station to maximize the number of pizzas sold? Approximately how many pizzas will be sold in response to this advertising?

24. An insurance company has 21 sales representatives who can be assigned to any of three districts. The company estimates that the number of policies N that can be sold each month is given by

$$N = 200x^{3/4} + 100y^{3/4} + 300z^{1/2},$$

where x, y, and z are the number of representatives assigned to the first, second, and third districts, respectively. How should the company allocate the sales representatives to maximize the number of policies sold each month? How many policies are estimated to be sold with this allocation?

25. Show that the Cobb–Douglas production function

$$Q = cL^a K^{1-a}$$

is maximized subject to the linear cost constraint $aL + bK = T$ when

$$\frac{K}{L} = \frac{(1 - \alpha)a}{\alpha b}.$$

CH. 8 REVIEW

I. Key Terms & Concepts

Mathematics	Business
Function of Several Variables	Joint Cost (Revenue,
Three-Dimensional Coordinate	Profit) Function
System	Interaction Terms
Three-Dimensional Surface	Cobb–Douglas Production
Partial Derivative	Function
Second-Order Partial	Complementary Goods
Derivative	Competitive Goods
Relative Maximum (Minimum)	Marginal Productivity
Saddle Point	
Equality Constraint	
Lagrange Multiplier	

II. True or False

Indicate whether each statement is true or false.

1. At a relative extreme point of a differentiable function, the first-order partial derivatives are equal.

2. If f is a continuous function of two variables, then it is differentiable.

3. If the second-order partial derivatives of f are continuous, then f_{xy} and f_{yx} are equal.

4. A Cobb–Douglas type of function, $Q = CL^{\alpha}K^{\beta}$, in which $\alpha + \beta \neq 1$, still has the property of modeling an input–output system that returns to scale.

5. If $z = f(x, y)$ has two relative minimum points, then it must also have at least one relative maximum point.

6. If f_{xx} and f_{yy} are opposite in sign at a critical point, then the point is a saddle point.

7. Any two goods must be either complementary or competitive.

8. If $C = f(q_A, q_B)$ is a joint cost function with no interaction terms, then there are functions g and h for which $f(q_A, q_B) = g(q_A) + h(q_B)$.

9. If $z = f(x, y)$ has no terms that contain both x and y, then $\partial^2 z / \partial x\, \partial y = 0$.

10. At any point on a smooth surface given by $z = f(x, y)$, there can be drawn only two tangent lines, one with slope $f_x(x, y)$ and the other with slope $f_y(x, y)$.

III. Drill Problems

In Problems 1–6 find $f_x(x, y)$, $f_y(x, y)$, $f_{xx}(x, y)$, $f_{yy}(x, y)$, and $f_{xy}(x, y)$.

1. $f(x, y) = x^3 y + xy^2$

2. $f(x, y) = \sqrt{5x - 3y^2}$

3. $f(x, y) = \ln \dfrac{x}{y + 1}$

4. $f(x, y) = x^2 e^{-3y}$

5. $f(x, y) = y \sqrt{x + y}$

6. $f(x, y) = \dfrac{2x - y}{x + 3y}$

In Problems 7–14 locate all critical points and classify each as a relative maximum, relative minimum, or saddle point.

7. $f(x, y) = x^2 - 6xy + 2y^2 - 16x + 34y$

8. $f(x, y) = 3xy - 6x^2 - y^2 + 4x - 2y$

9. $f(x, y) = y^3 + 2x^2 - 3y - 12x$

10. $f(x, y) = x^3 - 2xy + y^2$

11. $f(x, y) = x^4 + y^2 - 8x^2 - 8y$

12. $f(x, y) = 16xy + 2x^4$

13. $f(x, y) = 3x^2 + 24y^2 - 12xy^2$

14. $f(x, y) = 2x^3 y + y^2 + 3x^2$

IV. Applications

1. Sudsweiser Brewing makes both a regular and a light beer at its Florida brewery. Let q_A and q_B denote the number of barrels of regular and light beer, respectively, produced each day. Assume that the variable cost functions are given by

$$v_A = 29 - .01q_A, \qquad 0 \le q_A \le 1000,$$
$$\text{and} \quad v_B = 26 - .01q_B, \qquad 0 \le q_B \le 1000.$$

Furthermore, assume that to sell all the beer made, Sudsweiser must set the prices per barrel according to

$$p_A = 60 - .03q_A - .01q_B, \qquad 0 \le q_A, q_B \le 1000,$$
$$\text{and}$$
$$p_B = 45 - .01q_A - .02q_B, \qquad 0 \le q_A, q_B \le 1000.$$

Determine how many barrels of each kind should be brewed to maximize profit.

2. Refer to Exercise 1. Assume that currently Sudsweiser is brewing 600 barrels of regular beer and 200 barrels of light beer per day. Assuming that the brewmaster intends to keep the output of regular beer constant while increasing the output of light beer, estimate the change in profit that results from each additional barrel of light beer produced.

3. Assume that the owner of a health club models the membership M in the club by

$$M = 16{,}000p^{-1.5}x^{.2},$$
$$25 \le p \le 50, \; 200 \le x \le 1500,$$

where p is the monthly fee paid by members and x is the amount spent on advertising each month. If the current fee is $36, and $1000 per month is spent on advertising, use partial derivatives to determine which would cause the larger increase in membership: a $2 cut in the fee or a $100 increase in advertising expenditures.

4. Economists frequently make use of a **utility function** to study the choices made by an individual. Utility functions frequently have units of desirable goods as the independent variable. The dependent variable measures the relative happiness of the individual as the mix of goods changes. The purpose of the utility function is to see how the individual chooses to trade off one good for another in the pursuit of happiness.

Assume that an individual has utility U for wealth w (in dollars) and leisure time ℓ (in hours) measured by

$$U = w^{3/4}\ell^{1/4}, \qquad w \ge 0, \, \ell \ge 0.$$

This individual has available 60 hr per week that can be used for either leisure or work and that will earn him $16 per hour. How will this individual allocate time to maximize his utility?

5. To complete a construction project, both managers and laborers are required. Assume that managers are paid $150 per day and laborers are paid $80 per day. The time T in days to complete the project is given by

$$T = \frac{800}{M^{.2}L^{.8}}, \qquad M \ge 1, L \ge 1,$$

where M and L are the number of managers and laborers, respectively. Assume that at present, the project director has hired 3 managers and 32 laborers. Which would provide the greater reduction in time needed for completion: hiring one more manager or one more laborer? Assume that the director makes the proper decision. How are total salaries paid to all workers affected during this project?

6. Refer to Exercise 5. Assume that the project director has $6760 per day to spend on salaries. How many managers and how many laborers should be hired so that the project is finished in the shortest time?

7. To draw attention to its 3-week-long grand opening, a discount store plans to run 70 commercials on a local television station. By airing x commercials in the first week, y in the second week, and z in the third week, the store's manager expects to attract N people to the store during the grand opening, where

$$N = 8000x^{3/4} + 4000y^{3/4} + 6000z^{1/2}.$$

How many commercials should be aired each week to maximize the number of people who come to the store?

There is a 15-member club of Boston Celtics fans, some of whom want to attend the NBA playoff games in Los Angeles. A travel agent has put together a tour package for them. The cost for each member of the club who decides to go will be $600 if ten or fewer go; for each additional member who goes, however, the cost will drop by $20 per person. Suppose that the probabilities that x members actually go are given in the table.

x_i	8	9	10	11	12	13
$p(x_i)$	.10	.20	.25	.25	.15	.05

Find the expected cost for a member who decides to go and the standard deviation of that cost.

Probability

10.1
Discrete Random Variables

The concept of a variable has been used throughout this text. When a function was used as a mathematical model, values for one or more independent variables were used to calculate a value for the dependent variable. It was implicitly assumed that the independent variable was known or chosen with certainty by the user of the model; consequently the dependent variable was also known with certainty.

Unfortunately, as everyone knows, the real world is an uncertain place. An entrepreneur may start a business expecting to produce q units per day of some product and then sell them for p dollars per unit, yielding revenue of $R = pq$ dollars per day. However, unanticipated factors (quality of the labor force, availability of material, actions of competitors, and so forth) can cause the values for p and q to be quite different from those expected. Thus, p, q, and, consequently, R may be determined by chance, rather than by the entrepreneur; that is, their values depend on apparently random factors, uncontrolled by a decision maker.

To handle situations where a decision maker faces such uncertainty, we introduce the concept of a **random variable**. Because a formal definition is beyond the scope of this text, we will simply say that a random variable is a variable whose value is determined by chance. We will let capital letters such as X and Y denote random variables to distinguish them from ordinary variables, denoted by lowercase letters such as x and y.

A random variable is said to be **discrete** if it can take on only values from a set whose members can be enumerated or listed (even though that list may be infinitely long). Discrete random variables often involve counting random occurrences of an object or event. A random variable is said to be **continuous** if it can take on any value in some interval. Continuous random variables often arise as measurements of time, weight, length, or some other characteristic.

EXAMPLE 1

Classify each of the following random variables as discrete or continuous:

a. The number of customers who enter a shop during the next hour

b. The change in the price of a share of IBM stock at the end of a day of trading

c. The weight in ounces of a randomly chosen package

d. The length of time it takes a student to read this example

e. The number of baseball games that the St. Louis Cardinals will win in 1990

SOLUTION

Discrete random variables are described in a, b, and e. In a, the number of customers must be a nonnegative integer. In b, changes in the stock price are measured in eighths of a dollar. In e, the number of wins by a baseball team must be an integer between 0 and 162. The examples in c and d are considered to be continuous random variables; both are measurements that can, in theory, be made to any number of decimal places, depending on the instrument used for measurement. ●

For the rest of this section we will restrict our attention to discrete random variables. Associated with a random variable X is a **probability density function**, which indicates the likelihood or probability that X will actually take on values from a specified set called the **outcome set**. If X is a discrete random variable, we can denote this set by $\{x_i\}_{i=1}^n$ or $\{x_i\}_{i=1}^\infty$, where x_i denotes a possible value for X. The outcome set may be denoted by $\{x_i\}$ when it is not necessary to indicate the number of possible outcomes.

Definition 10.1

Let X be a discrete random variable with outcome set $\{x_i\}$. A function p with domain $\{x_i\}$ is called a **probability density function** (or **PDF**) for X if the following conditions are met:

1. $p(x_i) \geq 0$ for all x_i in $\{x_i\}$.

2. $\Sigma p(x_i) = 1$, where the summation is taken over all members in the outcome set.

Suppose X is a discrete random variable and p is a PDF for X. Then $p(x_i)$ denotes the probability that X will equal x_i. If $p(x_i) = 0$, then the outcome x_i is impossible; if $p(x_i) = 1$, then the outcome x_i is certain. An **event** E is a subset of the outcome set. The **probability of an event** E, denoted $Pr(E)$, is defined by

(10.1)
$$Pr(E) = \Sigma p(x_i),$$

where the summation is taken over all x_i in the subset E.

EXAMPLE 2

Let X be the number that appears on the upper face of an ordinary die after it is rolled. Then $\{1, 2, 3, 4, 5, 6\}$ is the outcome set. Let the PDF be given by $p(x_i) = 1/6$ for $i = 1, 2, \ldots, 6$; that is, assume all six possible outcomes are equally likely. Let E_1 be the event that the number is odd; let E_2 be the event that the number is less than 5. Find $Pr(E_1)$ and $Pr(E_2)$. What is the probability that both E_1 and E_2 occur?

SOLUTION

Because $E_1 = \{1, 3, 5\}$, by equation (10.1) we have

$$Pr(E_1) = p(x_1) + p(x_3) + p(x_5) = \frac{1}{2}.$$

Because $E_2 = \{1, 2, 3, 4\}$, we have

$$Pr(E_2) = p(x_1) + p(x_2) + p(x_3) + p(x_4) = \frac{2}{3}.$$

If both events occur, then X is a member of the subset $\{1, 3\}$; the probability of this event is 1/3.   ●

There is a well-developed theory of probability, closely connected to the theory of sets, that enables us to compute probabilities for complex events. We will confine our attention to properties of random variables, however, and take their PDFs as given or known through prior experience.

Definition 10.2

Let X be a discrete random variable with PDF p and outcome set $\{x_i\}$. The **mean** or **expected value** of X, denoted μ_X or $E(X)$, is given by

(10.2) $$\mu_X = E(X) = \Sigma x_i p(x_i),$$

provided that the sum converges if the outcome set is infinite. The **variance** of X, denoted σ_X^2 or $V(X)$, is given by

(10.3) $$\sigma_X^2 = V(X) = \Sigma(x_i - \mu_X)^2 p(x_i),$$

provided that the sum converges if the outcome set is infinite. If the variance of X exists, then the **standard deviation** of X, denoted σ_X, is the positive square root of the variance.

EXAMPLE 3

Let X be a random variable with PDF given in the table.

x_i	0	1	2	5	10
$p(x_i)$	.20	.40	.25	.10	.05

Compute μ_X and σ_X.

SOLUTION

From equation (10.2), the mean or expected value of X is

$$\mu_X = 0(.20) + 1(.40) + 2(.25) + 5(.10) + 10(.05)$$
$$= 1.9$$

From equation (10.3), the variance of X is

$$\sigma_X^2 = (0 - 1.9)^2(.20) + (1 - 1.9)^2(.40) + (2 - 1.9)^2(.25)$$
$$+ (5 - 1.9)^2(.10) + (10 - 1.9)^2(.05)$$
$$= 5.29.$$

Then $\sigma_X = \sqrt{5.29} = 2.3$.

    We can give an intuitive interpretation of μ_X and σ_X as follows. Let $\{y_i\}_{i=1}^n$ be a set of n numbers. The mean of the set is denoted by $\bar{y}$ and defined by $\bar{y} = (\Sigma y_i)/n$. The variance of this set of numbers is defined to be an average of their squared deviations from the mean; that is, the variance of $\{y_i\}_{i=i}^n$ is defined by $s^2 = \Sigma(y_i - \bar{y})^2/(n - 1)$. The square root of this variance is called the standard deviation of the set $\{y_i\}_{i=1}^n$. The standard deviation measures the scattering or spread of the numbers in the set. Now let X be a random variable. Suppose that values for X are generated repeatedly from a set with n members; we would anticipate that the proportion of times an outcome x_i would appear would be $p(x_i)$. Therefore as n increases, μ_X and σ_X^2 should approximate the mean and the variance of the set of numbers generated by X.

A computationally superior formula for computing the variance of a random variable is

(10.4)
$$\sigma_X^2 = V(X) = [\Sigma x_i^2 p(x_i)] - \mu_X^2.$$

Generally equation (10.4) is preferable to (10.3) because there is only a single subtraction, which reduces the number of steps involved and the potential for round-off error. We demonstrate its use by recalculating the variance of the random variable from Example 3:

$$V(X) = 0^2(.20) + 1^2(.40) + 2^2(.25) + 5^2(.10) + 10^2(.05) - (1.9)^2$$
$$= 8.9 - 3.61 = 5.29,$$

which agrees with the earlier computation.

In applications, a random variable X will generally have some unit of measurement. The definitions of the mean μ_X and the standard deviation σ_X ensure that they also have this unit of measurement. The variance σ_X^2, however, will not have a meaningful unit of measurement and should be treated as a real number.

EXAMPLE 4

Let X denote the number of cars that a dealer sells on a randomly chosen day. Assume that the PDF for X is given in the table.

x_i	0	1	2	3	4	5	6
$p(x_i)$	.05	.10	.30	.30	.15	.05	.05

Find μ_X and σ_X.

SOLUTION

From equation (10.2), the mean value of X is

$$\mu_X = 0(.05) + 1(.10) + 2(.30) + 3(.30) + 4(.15) + 5(.05) + 6(.05)$$
$$= 2.75 \text{ cars.}$$

This means that the average number of cars sold per day by the dealer is 2.75. From equation (10.4) the variance of X is

$$\sigma_X^2 = 0^2(.05) + 1^2(.10) + 2^2(.30) + 3^2(.30) + 4^2(.15) + 5^2(.05)$$
$$+ 6^2(.05) - (2.75)^2$$
$$= 9.45 - 7.5625 = 1.8875.$$

The standard deviation of X is then $\sqrt{1.8875} = 1.374$ cars.   ●

It is often desirable to give a graphical representation of a probability density function. This can be done by a **relative frequency histogram**. The histogram is formed by listing the elements of the outcome set along a horizontal axis and constructing a rectangle whose height is proportional to the probability of that outcome. Figures 10.1 and 10.2 show histograms for the PDFs in Examples 3 and 4, respectively.

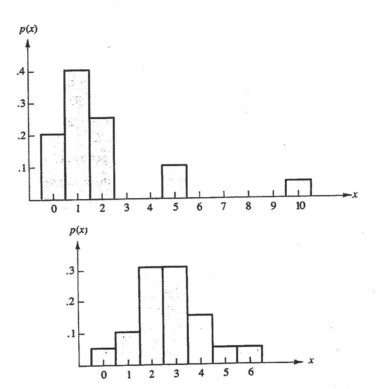

Figure 10.1
A relative frequency histogram for the random variable of Example 3

Figure 10.2
A relative frequency histogram for the random variable of Example 4

Let a function f be defined by some rule of correspondence $y = f(x)$. If X is a random variable with an outcome set contained in the domain of f, then a new random variable Y can be defined by $Y = f(X)$. When this is done, we say that Y is a **function of the random variable** X. The mean or expected value of Y can be obtained by

(10.5)
$$\mu_Y = E(Y) = \Sigma f(x_i)p(x_i),$$

and the variance of Y can be obtained by

(10.6)
$$\sigma_Y^2 = [\Sigma f(x_i)^2 p(x_i)] - \mu_Y^2,$$

where the summations are taken over all members of the outcome set for X. Equations (10.5) and (10.6) are equivalent to (10.2) and (10.4), but they avoid the necessity of determining the PDF for the random variable Y.

EXAMPLE 5

Salespeople for an insurance company frequently work on a salary plus commission basis. Assume that at one company, the weekly wages received are $100 plus $75 for each life insurance policy sold that week. It is known by the company that if X is the number of policies sold by a salesperson per week, then the PDF of X is as shown in the table.

x_i	2	3	4	5	6	7	8
$p(x_i)$	.10	.20	.25	.20	.10	.10	.05

Determine the expected weekly salary of a salesperson at this company and the standard deviation of the salaries.

SOLUTION   The weekly salary of a person who sells X policies is $Y = 75X + 100$. The expected or mean salary can then be found by using equation (10.5):

$$\mu_Y = 250(.10) + 325(.20) + 400(.25) + 475(.20) + 550(.10) + 625(.10)$$
$$+ 700(.05)$$
$$= \$437.5 \text{ per week.}$$

The variance of these salaries is found by using equation (10.6):

$$\sigma_Y^2 = 250^2(.10) + 325^2(.20) + 400^2(.25) + 475^2(.20) + 550^2(.10) + 625^2(.10)$$
$$+ 700^2(.05) - (437.5)^2$$
$$= 14,906.25.$$

The standard deviation of the weekly salaries is therefore $122.09.   ●

If μ_X and σ_X^2 are known and Y is a *linear function* of X—that is, $Y = aX + b$—then the mean and variance of Y are given by

(10.7)
$$\mu_Y = a\mu_X + b$$

and

(10.8)
$$\sigma_Y^2 = a^2\sigma_X^2.$$

These formulas are illustrated by returning to Example 5. From equations (10.2) and (10.4), the mean and variance of X, the number of policies sold per week, are $\mu_X = 4.5$ and $\sigma_X^2 = 2.65$. From equations (10.7) and (10.8) we find that

$$\mu_Y = 75(4.5) + 100 = 437.5$$

and

$$\sigma_Y^2 = 75^2(2.65) = 14,906.25,$$

which agree with the earlier values.

EXERCISES 10.1

1. For each of the following, indicate whether the random variable described is discrete or continuous.

   a. The number of shares of General Electric stock traded in one day

   b. The number of new orders received by a manufacturing company

   c. The gasoline mileage that a randomly chosen car gets

   d. The number of phone calls you receive today

   e. The distance in miles that a traveling salesperson goes in a given day

2. For each of the following, indicate whether the random variable described is discrete or continuous.

   a. The number of defective units in shipment of electrical parts

b. The time it takes for a waiter to take your order in a restaurant

c. The bill for a dinner for two at a restaurant

d. The height in meters of a randomly chosen utility pole

e. The height, to the nearest centimeter, of a randomly chosen utility pole

3. Let X be a random variable with PDF given in the table.

x_i	-5	-2	-1	1	2	5
$p(x_i)$	.15	.05	...	.10	.25	.30

a. Fill in the missing probability value.

b. Sketch a relative frequency histogram for this random variable.

c. Find $Pr(X = -2$ or $1)$.

d. Find $Pr(X \le 2)$.

e. Find $Pr(|X| \le 2)$.

4. Let X be a random variable with PDF given in the table.

x_i	0	1	2	4	7	15
$p(x_i)$	.17	.25	.02	.05	...	.34

a. Fill in the missing probability value.

b. Sketch a relative frequency histogram for this random variable.

c. Find $Pr(X \ge 4)$.

d. Find $Pr(X < 2)$.

e. Find $Pr(1 \le X < 15)$.

5. Let X be a random variable with PDF given by

$$p(x_i) = \begin{cases} .05, & x_i = 0, 1, 3 \\ .10, & x_i = 4, 6 \\ .15, & x_i = -3, -2, -1 \\ .20, & x_i = 8. \end{cases}$$

a. List the outcome set for X.

b. Verify that this is a PDF by showing that $\Sigma p(x_i) = 1$.

c. Sketch the relative frequency histogram for X.

d. Find $Pr(X \ge 3)$.

e. Find $Pr(X$ is negative$)$.

6. Let X be a random variable with PDF given by

$$p(x_i) = \frac{1}{12}x_i, \qquad x_i = 0, 2, 4, 6.$$

a. List the outcome set for X.

b. Verify that this is a PDF by showing that $\Sigma p(x_i) = 1$.

c. Sketch the relative frequency histogram for X.

d. Find $Pr(X \le 2)$.

e. Find $Pr(X \ne 0)$.

7. Compute the mean value, the variance, and the standard deviation for the random variable in Exercise 3.

8. Compute the mean value, the variance, and the standard deviation for the random variable in Exercise 4.

9. Compute the mean value, the variance, and the standard deviation for the random variable in Exercise 5.

10. Compute the mean value, the variance, and the standard deviation for the random variable in Exercise 6.

11. Let X be a random variable with PDF given in the table.

x_i	1	2	3	5	10	20
$p(x_i)$	.01	.02	.05	.07	.35	.50

a. Find μ_X and σ_X.

b. Find $Pr(\mu_X - \sigma_X \le X \le \mu_X + \sigma_X)$.

c. Find $Pr(\mu_X - 2\sigma_X \le X \le \mu_X + 2\sigma_X)$.

12. Let X be a random variable with PDF given in the table.

x_i	0	5	10	15	20	25	30
$p(x_i)$	.02	.03	.08	.65	.17	.03	.02

a. Find μ_X and σ_X.

b. Find $Pr(\mu_X - \sigma_X \le X \le \mu_X + \sigma_X)$.

c. Find $Pr(\mu_X - 2\sigma_X \le X \le \mu_X + 2\sigma_X)$.

13. Let X be a random variable with PDF given in the table.

x_i	0	2	4	6	8	10
$p(x_i)$	.10	.10	.15	.25	.30	.10

Let Y be a random variable defined by $Y = 3X - 2$.

a. Find μ_Y and σ_Y^2 by using equations (10.5) and (10.6).

b. Find μ_Y and σ_Y^2 by first finding μ_X and σ_X^2 and then using equations (10.7) and (10.8).

14. Let X be a random variable with PDF given in the table.

x_i	-3	-1	0	1	3
$p(x_i)$	.05	.20	.50	.20	.05

Let Y be a random variable defined by $Y = 10 - 2X$.

a. Find μ_Y and σ_Y^2 by using equations (10.5) and (10.6).

b. Find μ_Y and σ_Y^2 by first finding μ_X and σ_X^2 and then using equations (10.7) and (10.8).

15. Let X be a random variable with PDF given by

$$p(x_i) = \frac{1}{15}x_i, \qquad x_i = 1, 2, 3, 4, 5.$$

Let Y be a random variable defined by $Y = 1/X$. List the outcome set for Y. Find $E(Y)$ and $V(Y)$.

16. Let X be a random variable with PDF given by

$$p(x_i) = .1x_i^2, \qquad x_i = -2, -1, 0, 1, 2.$$

Let Y be a random variable defined by $Y = X^3$. List the outcome set for Y. Find the mean value and the standard deviation of Y.

17. An automobile dealer figures that if a customer takes a car for a test drive there is a one-third chance that he or she will purchase the car. Let X be the number of customers who take a test drive before the dealer makes a sale on a given day. The PDF may be written as

$$p(x_i) = \frac{1}{3}\left(\frac{2}{3}\right)^{x_i-1}, \qquad x_i = 1, 2, 3, 4, \ldots .$$

a. Compute $p(1)$, $p(2)$, and $p(3)$.

b. Verify that this is a PDF by showing that $\Sigma p(x_i) = 1$. (*Hint:* The summation is a geometric series.)

c. What is the probability that test drives will be given to at least four customers before a sale is made?

18. Refer to Exercise 17. Suppose that on a given day only three customers take a test drive. Let Y denote the number of sales that are made that day. Then Y is a random variable with outcome set $\{0, 1, 2, 3\}$ whose PDF can be written as

$$p(y_i) = \frac{3!}{y_i!(3 - y_i)!}\left(\frac{1}{3}\right)^{y_i}\left(\frac{2}{3}\right)^{3-y_i}, \qquad y_i = 0, 1, 2, 3.$$

a. Write the PDF of Y in table form.

b. Sketch the relative frequency distribution for Y.

c. Find the mean value of Y.

d. Find the standard deviation of Y.

19. Suppose that a salesperson earns \$200 per week and a \$25 commission for each sale made that week. Let X, the number of sales made per week, be a random variable with PDF given in the table.

x_i	5	6	7	8	9	10	11	12
$p(x_i)$	.04	.08	.15	.20	.20	.16	.12	.05

a. Find $E(X)$ and $V(X)$.

b. If Y denotes the earnings of a salesperson during a given week, find $E(Y)$ and $V(Y)$.

c. What is the probability that during any given week, the earnings will be within 1 standard deviation of the mean earnings?

20. A company plans to purchase a new computer for \$600,000. At the end of each year, a decision will be made to either keep the computer or replace it with a newer model. Let X denote the number of years that the computer is kept and assume that X has a PDF given in the table.

x_i	1	2	3	4	5
$p(x_i)$	.10	.30	.35	.20	.05

a. Find μ_X and σ_X.

b. The cost of the computer per year of service is the random variable $Y = 600,000/X$. Find μ_Y and σ_Y.

21. A savings and loan offers certificates of deposit for \$1000 that pay a nominal interest rate of 8%, compounded continuously. These certificates may be purchased for a term of 6 mo, 1 yr, 2 yr, 3 yr, or 6 yr. Let X denote the term selected by any given customer and suppose that X has the PDF given in the table.

x_i	.5	1	2	3	6
$p(x_i)$	.20	.30	.25	.20	.05

a. Find μ_X and σ_X.

b. The value of that customer's certificate at maturity is a random variable $Y = 1000e^{.08X}$. Find μ_Y and σ_Y.

10.2 Continuous Random Variables

Suppose a local radio station runs an advertisement for your business every day between 9:00 and 10:00 A.M., but it might run at any time during that hour with equal likelihood. Let X denote the number of minutes past 9:00 A.M. at which the ad begins on a randomly chosen day. Because time can be measured as accurately as our timing device will permit, X is a continuous random variable that will take on values in the interval $[0, 60]$. The assumption that the ad can be run at any time means that, given any subinterval $[c, d]$, the probability that X falls in $[c, d]$ must be $(d - c)/60$. For example, the probability that the ad begins at some time between 9:15 and 9:30—that is, $15 \le X \le 30$—is $(30 - 15)/60$ or $1/4$. On the other hand, if k is any number in $[0, 60]$, we say that the probability that X will equal k is 0. For example, the probability that the ad is run at precisely 28 min, 46 sec after 9:00 A.M.—that is, $X = 28.76\overline{6}$—is 0. This is reasonable if the reader recalls that for X to equal k, the random variable must agree with the prechosen value at every entry in its decimal expansion.

The previous example illustrates some aspects of working with continuous random variables. Let X be a continuous random variable. For simplicity, we restrict the outcome set for X to intervals of the form $[a, b]$, $(-\infty, b]$, $[a, \infty)$, or $(-\infty, \infty)$. We assign positive probabilities to subintervals of values for X in the outcome set. If $[c, d]$ is such an interval, we write $Pr(c \le X \le d)$ to denote the probability that X is between c and d. The probability that X equals a particular value k, denoted $Pr(X = k)$, is 0. As a result, note that the probability that X lies in the open interval (c, d) equals the probability that it lies in the closed interval $[c, d]$.

To enable us to calculate the probability of an event involving a continuous random variable, we need to define the concept of a probability density function for continuous random variables.

Definition 10.3

Let X be a continuous random variable with outcome set $[a, b]$. A function f is said to be a **probability density function** (or **PDF**) for X if the following conditions are met:

1. $f(x) \ge 0$, $a \le x \le b$; and
2. $\int_a^b f(x)\, dx = 1$.

When the outcome set is of the form $(\infty, b]$, $[a, \infty)$, or (∞, ∞), the integral in condition 2 is an improper integral.

EXAMPLE 1

Show that the following functions are PDFs for the indicated random variables:

a. $f(x) = (1/21)x^2$, where X has $[1, 4]$ as an outcome set

b. $f(x) = 2e^{-x/2}$, where X has $[0, \infty)$ as an outcome set

SOLUTION

a. Because $x^2 \ge 0$ for all x, $f(x)$ is certainly nonnegative on $[1, 4]$. Moreover,

$$\int_1^4 \frac{1}{21} x^2\, dx = \frac{1}{63} x^3 \bigg]_1^4 = 1.$$

b. Because e^t is positive for any t, $f(x)$ is nonnegative on the interval $[0, \infty)$. Moreover,

$$\int_0^\infty 2e^{-x/2} \, dx = \lim_{b \to \infty} -e^{-x/2} \Big]_0^b = 1 - \lim_{b \to \infty} e^{-b/2} = 1. \qquad \bullet$$

Geometrically, a PDF for a continuous random variable X is a nonnegative function for which the area of the region bounded by $y = f(x)$ and the x-axis is exactly one square unit. The probability that X will lie between two specified values, c and d, may then be thought of as the proportion of that region between $x = c$ and $x = d$. The next definition makes this precise.

Definition 10.4

> Let X be a continuous random variable. If f is the PDF for X and $[c, d]$ is a subinterval of the outcome set, then
>
> (10.9) $$Pr(c \leq X \leq d) = \int_c^d f(x) \, dx.$$

Definition 10.4 can be extended to events described by intervals of infinite length by using improper integrals. For example, the probability that X is greater than or equal to some number c is defined by

$$Pr(X \geq c) = \int_c^\infty f(x) \, dx.$$

Recall that this is also equal to $Pr(X > c)$, the probability that X is greater than c. If an event is described by two or more disjoint intervals, the probability of that event is defined as the sum of the definite integrals over those intervals.

EXAMPLE 2

Let X be a continuous random variable with PDF given by

$$f(x) = \frac{3}{16}x^2, \qquad -2 \leq x \leq 2.$$

a. Find the probability that X is greater than -1.

b. Find the probability that the absolute value of X is at least 1.

SOLUTION

a. From equation (10.9) we have that

$$Pr(X > -1) = Pr(-1 < X \leq 2)$$
$$= \int_{-1}^2 \frac{3}{16}x^2 \, dx = \frac{1}{16}x^3 \Big]_{-1}^2 = \frac{9}{16}.$$

b. If the absolute value of X is at least 1, then either $X \leq -1$ or $X \geq 1$. Therefore the probability of this event is found by

$$Pr(|X| \geq 1) = Pr(-2 \leq X \leq -1 \text{ or } 1 \leq X \leq 2)$$

$$= \int_{-2}^{-1} \frac{3}{16}x^2 \, dx + \int_{1}^{2} \frac{3}{16}x^2 \, dx$$

$$= \frac{1}{16}x^3 \Big]_{-2}^{-1} + \frac{1}{16}x^3 \Big]_{1}^{2}$$

$$= \frac{7}{16} + \frac{7}{16} = \frac{7}{8}.$$

Figure 10.3 illustrates the probability of the events in Example 2 graphically. The area of the figure bounded by $y = (3/16)\,x^2$ and the x-axis between $x = -2$ and $x = 2$ is 1; the shaded regions have areas equal to 9/16 and 7/8, the probabilities of the corresponding events.

Figure 10.3

Graphical representation of the PDF $f(x) = (3/16)\,x^2$, $-2 \leq x \leq 2$, and the probabilities $Pr(X \geq -1)$ and $Pr(|X| \geq 1)$

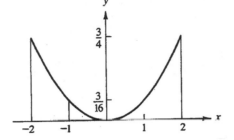 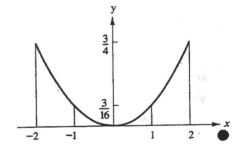

It is important to notice the similarities between discrete and continuous random variables. The probability of an event based on a discrete random variable can also be viewed as an area—the sum of the areas in the rectangles of the relative frequency histogram. These similarities become more apparent by comparing Definition 10.1 and equation (10.1) with Definition 10.2 and equation (10.9) and recalling that in Chapter 7 it was shown how definite integrals can be approximated by Riemann sums.

The mean, the variance, and the standard deviation of a continuous random variable are defined as definite integrals, analogous to the summation definitions given for a discrete random variable.

Definition 10.5

Let X be a continuous random variable with PDF f on the interval $[a, b]$. The **mean** or **expected value** of X is given by

(10.10) $$E(X) = \mu_X = \int_a^b xf(x) \, dx.$$

The **variance** of X is given by

(10.11) $$V(X) = \sigma_X^2 = \int_a^b (x - \mu_X)^2 f(x) \, dx.$$

The **standard deviation** of X, σ_X, is the square root of the variance.

As earlier, Definition 10.5 is extended to random variables with an infinite interval for its outcome set by using improper integrals. Also if we let Y depend on X by a continuous function $y = g(x)$, where $a \leq x \leq b$, then Y is also a continuous random variable with mean

(10.12)
$$E(Y) = \mu_Y = \int_a^b g(x)f(x) \, dx$$

and variance

$$V(Y) = \sigma_Y^2 = \int_b^a [g(x) - \mu_Y]^2 f(x) \, dx.$$

In the special case where Y is a linear function of X—that is, $Y = aX + b$—the mean and the variance of Y can be found by

(10.13)
$$E(Y) = aE(X) + b \quad \text{and} \quad V(Y) = a^2 V(X).$$

EXAMPLE 3

Find the mean value and the variance of the random variable X that has the PDF

$$f(x) = \frac{2}{9}x, \quad 0 \leq x \leq 3.$$

SOLUTION

From equation (10.10) we have that the mean value of X is

$$\mu_X = \int_0^3 x\left(\frac{2}{9}x\right) dx = \frac{2}{9} \int_0^3 x^2 \, dx$$

$$= \frac{2}{27}x^3 \Big]_0^3 = 2.$$

Using $\mu_X = 2$ in equation (10.11), we find the variance to be

$$\sigma_X^2 = \int_0^3 (x - 2)^2 \left(\frac{2}{9}x\right) dx = \frac{2}{9} \int_0^3 (x^3 - 4x^2 + 4x) \, dx$$

$$= \frac{2}{9}\left(\frac{1}{4}x^4 - \frac{4}{3}x^3 + 2x^2\right)\Big]_0^3 = \frac{1}{2}.$$

The standard deviation of X is therefore $\sigma_X = \sqrt{.5} = \sqrt{2}/2$.   ●

EXAMPLE 4

Let X be the random variable of Example 3. Find the probability that X will lie within 2 standard deviations of its mean. Illustrate this probability graphically.

SOLUTION

From the solution to Example 3, we see that the desired probability may be written as

$$Pr(\mu_X - 2\sigma_X \leq X \leq \mu_X + 2\sigma_X) = Pr(2 - \sqrt{2} \leq X \leq 2 + \sqrt{2}).$$

However, because X can take on only values in the interval $[0, 3]$, this reduces to $Pr(2 - \sqrt{2} \leq X \leq 3)$. From equation (10.9), this probability is

$$\int_{2-\sqrt{2}}^{3} \frac{2}{9}x \, dx = \frac{1}{9}x^2 \Big]_{2-\sqrt{2}}^{3} = \frac{1}{9}[(3)^2 - (2 - \sqrt{2})^2] = \frac{3 + 4\sqrt{2}}{9}.$$

The illustration of the probability of this event is shown in Figure 10.4.

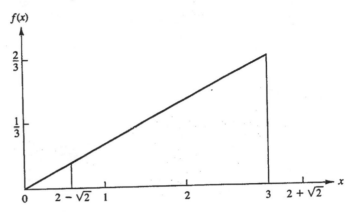

Figure 10.4
The probability
$Pr(2 - \sqrt{2} \leq X \leq 3)$,
where X has the PDF
$f(x) = 2x/9, \; 0 \leq x \leq 3$

EXAMPLE 5   A firm that supplies electronic components offers free replacement for any component that fails within 1 yr of purchase. Thus if X denotes the life (in years) of a component purchased from that firm, the outcome set is $[1, \infty)$. Assume that the PDF of X is given by

$$f(x) = 1.5x^{-5/2}, \qquad x \geq 1.$$

A purchasing manager is considering buying components from this firm. If the cost of one component is $100, find the expected life of the components and the expected annual cost per component.

SOLUTION   The expected life of the component is $E(X)$, the mean value of X. From equation (10.10) we have

$$E(X) = \int_{1}^{\infty} x(1.5x^{-5/2}) \, dx = 1.5\int_{1}^{\infty} x^{-3/2} \, dx$$

$$= \lim_{b \to \infty} -3x^{-1/2} \Big]_{1}^{b} = 3 \text{ yr.}$$

The annual cost of a component with a life of X years is $100/X$. Thus the expected annual cost of a component is $E(100/X)$. From equation (10.12), this is found by

$$E\left(\frac{100}{X}\right) = \int_{1}^{\infty} \left(\frac{100}{x}\right)(1.5x^{-5/2}) \, dx = 150\int_{1}^{\infty} x^{-7/2} \, dx$$

$$= \lim_{b \to \infty} -60x^{-5/2} \Big]_{1}^{b} = \$60.$$

It should be noted that $E(100/X) \neq 100/E(X)$; compare this with the relationship (10.13) that holds for linear functions of random variables.

EXERCISES 10.2

1. Let X be a continuous random variable with PDF given by $f(x) = 1/5$ where $3 \leq x \leq 8$.

   a. Verify that f is a PDF.

   b. Find $Pr(4 \leq X \leq 6)$.

   c. Find $Pr(X \leq 7)$.

2. Let X be a continuous random variable with PDF given by $f(x) = (2/75)x$, where $5 \leq x \leq 10$.

   a. Verify that f is a PDF.

   b. Find $Pr(5 \leq X \leq 8)$.

   c. Find $Pr(X \geq 9)$.

3. Let X be a continuous random variable with PDF given by $f(x) = (1/4)x^3$, where $0 \leq x \leq 2$.

   a. Find $Pr(X \leq 1)$.

   b. Find $Pr(X \geq 1)$.

   c. Sketch the graph of this PDF, indicating the above probabilities as areas of the appropriate regions.

4. Let X be a continuous random variable with PDF given by $f(x) = \sqrt{x}/18$, where $0 \leq x \leq 9$.

   a. Verify that f is a PDF.

   b. Find $Pr(0 \leq X \leq 1)$.

   c. Find $Pr(0 \leq X \leq 4)$.

   d. Find b so that $Pr(0 \leq X \leq b) = .5$.

5. Find the mean and the variance of the random variable in Exercise 1.

6. Find the mean and the standard deviation of the random variable in Exercise 2.

7. For the random variable in Exercise 3, find μ_X and σ_X.

8. For the random variable in Exercise 4, find $E(X)$ and $V(X)$.

9. Find the value of c for which $f(x) = cx^2$ is the PDF of a continuous random variable with outcome set $[-3, 3]$.

10. Find the value of c for which $f(x) = ce^{-5x}$ is the PDF of a continuous random variable with outcome set $[0, \infty)$.

11. Let c be a positive constant and let $f(x) = c$, where $a \leq x \leq b$.

    a. Determine c so that f is a PDF for X on $[a, b]$.

    b. Find μ_X and σ_X^2.

12. Let $f(x) = (x - 5)^2$, where $5 - c \leq x \leq 5 + c$. Find c so that f is a PDF for X on $[5 - c, 5 + c]$.

13. Is there any c for which $f(x) = cx^3$ would be a PDF for a continuous random variable with outcome set $[-1, 2]$? Explain.

14. Let X be a continuous random variable with PDF $f(x) = .005x$, where $0 \leq x \leq 20$. Let Y be a random variable defined by $Y = 4X + 6$.

    a. Find $E(X)$ and $V(X)$.

    b. Find $E(Y)$ and $V(Y)$.

15. Let X be a continuous random variable with PDF given by $f(x) = (3/64)x^2$, where $0 \leq x \leq 4$. Let Y be a random variable defined by $Y = \sqrt{X}$. Find μ_X and μ_Y.

16. Let X be a continuous random variable with PDF given by $f(x) = (3/2)\sqrt{x}$, where $0 \leq x \leq 1$.

    a. If $S = 1/X$, find $E(S)$ and $V(S)$.

    b. If $T = X^2$, find $E(T)$ and $V(T)$.

17. Assume that a machine has a value of $10,000 but it is depreciating so that after x years its value is

    $$V(x) = 2000(5 - x), \qquad 0 \leq x \leq 5.$$

    Let the number of years that the machine is kept be a random variable X with PDF given by

    $$f(x) = \frac{2}{9}(x - 2), \qquad 2 \leq x \leq 5.$$

    Find the expected number of years that the machine will be kept and its expected value at that time.

18. A plant manager would like the output of the plant to be 100 units per day. However, the actual daily output is a random variable with PDF given by

$$f(x) = \frac{3}{2000}(x - 100)^2, \qquad 90 \le x \le 110.$$

The manager knows that the fixed cost is $200 per day and the variable cost is $10 per unit.

a. Find the expected daily output of the plant.

b. Find the expected total cost of a day's production.

c. Find the expected average cost per unit.

19. Suppose that the government issues a savings bond for an initial investment of $500 that pays a 5% rate of interest compounded continuously. Let X denote the length of time (in years) that such a bond is held and assume that X has a PDF given by

$$f(x) = .25e^{-.25x}, \qquad x \ge 0.$$

Find the expected future value of such a bond at redemption.

10.3
The Normal Random Variable

In the examples and exercises of the previous sections an outcome set and a PDF for a random variable X were simply given. In practice, even if the outcome set for a random variable is known, it is usually impossible to know its exact PDF. Instead, from experience or knowledge about the random variable, the PDF is approximated by one of several theoretical density functions that have well-known properties. In this section, we introduce the most important of these, the **normal probability density function**.

A random variable X frequently has a PDF that is approximately normal when its graph is symmetric and mound- or bell-shaped. Such PDFs may occur when X is a measurement that is likely to be close to a central value, with an occurrence on either side of this value being equally likely—for instance, the true weight of the contents of a package of potato chips labeled as containing 18 oz, the exact diameter of a ball bearing that is intended to be 50 mm, or the gas mileage of a car that has a rating of 27 mi/gal.

Definition 10.6

Let μ be any real number and let σ be any positive real number. Then X is said to have a **normal distribution** with mean value μ and standard deviation σ if the PDF for X is

(10.14) $$f(x) = \frac{1}{\sqrt{2\pi}\,\sigma}e^{-(x-\mu)^2/2\sigma^2}, \qquad -\infty < x < \infty.$$

The values of μ and σ for a normal random variable determine the location and the shape of the graph of its PDF. This graph is frequently called the **normal curve** with mean μ and standard deviation σ. Figure 10.5 shows the graphs of three such normal curves.

If X has a normal distribution with mean μ and standard deviation σ, then the probability that X will fall in the interval $[a, b]$ is defined by the integral

$$Pr(a \le X \le b) = \int_a^b f(x)\, dx$$

where $f(x)$ is given by equation (10.14). However, because $f(x)$ does not have an elementary antiderivative, it is difficult to evaluate such an integral using the fun-

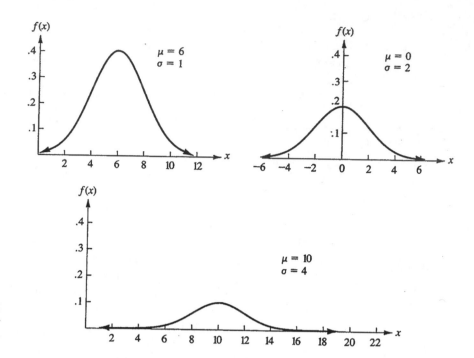

Figure 10.5
Normal curves for three values of μ and σ

damental theorem of calculus. The computation of such probabilities is simplified by the following theorem, which is stated without proof.

Theorem 10.1

> Let X have a normal distribution with mean μ and standard deviation σ. If $Y = aX + b$, where $a \neq 0$, then Y has a normal distribution with mean $a\mu + b$ and standard deviation $a\sigma$.

It follows from Theorem 10.1 that if X has a normal distribution with mean μ and standard deviation σ, then the random variable Z defined by

$$Z = \frac{X - \mu}{\sigma}$$

has a normal distribution with mean 0 and standard deviation 1. We call Z the **standard normal random variable**. The PDF for Z is given by

$$f(z) = \frac{1}{\sqrt{2\pi}}e^{-z^2/2}, \qquad -\infty < z < \infty.$$

Figure 10.6 shows the graph of $y = f(z)$. The probability that X is in an interval $[a, b]$ may be converted to an equivalent probability for the standard normal random variable; that is,

(10.15)
$$Pr(a \leq X \leq b) = Pr\left(\frac{a - \mu}{\sigma} \leq Z \leq \frac{b - \mu}{\sigma}\right).$$

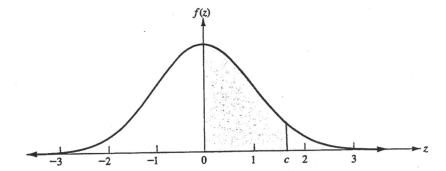

Figure 10.6

The graph of the standard normal PDF with the area representing $Pr(0 \leq Z \leq c)$ shaded

Thus the problem of calculating probabilities for normal random variables is reduced to finding probabilities for the standard normal random variable. In Figure 10.6, the area represented by the probability that Z is between 0 and a positive number c has been shaded. From the symmetry of the PDF and the fact that the area under the entire curve is 1, we can compute $Pr(a \leq Z \leq b)$ for any a and b from such areas. We do this by making the following observations:

1. For $c > 0$, $P(Z \geq c) = .5 - Pr(0 \leq Z \leq c)$;
$$P(Z \leq -c) = .5 - Pr(0 \leq Z \leq c);$$
$$P(Z \geq -c) = .5 + Pr(0 \leq Z \leq c); \text{ and}$$
$$P(Z \leq c) = .5 + Pr(0 \leq Z \leq c).$$

2. For $0 < a < b$, $Pr(a \leq Z \leq b) = Pr(0 \leq Z \leq b) - Pr(0 \leq Z \leq a)$.

3. For $a < 0 < b$, $Pr(a \leq Z \leq b) = Pr(0 \leq Z \leq -a) + Pr(0 \leq Z \leq b)$.

4. For $a < b < 0$, $Pr(a \leq Z \leq b) = Pr(0 \leq Z \leq -a) - Pr(0 \leq Z \leq -b)$.

Table 10.1 gives the probabilities $Pr(0 \leq Z \leq c)$ for several values of c, accurate to four decimal places. For $c > 3.09$, the probability $Pr(0 \leq Z \leq c)$ is approximately .500. The first example demonstrates the use of Table 10.1 on page 390.

EXAMPLE 1

Evaluate the following:

a. $Pr(0 \leq Z \leq 1.35)$

b. $Pr(-.82 \leq Z \leq 2.14)$

c. $Pr(Z \geq .61)$

d. $Pr(Z \leq .25)$

SOLUTION

a. This probability is read directly from Table 10.1:
$$Pr(0 \leq Z \leq 1.35) = .4115.$$

b. From Figure 10.7(a), we see that
$$Pr(-.82 \leq Z \leq 2.14) = Pr(-.82 \leq Z \leq 0) + Pr(0 \leq Z \leq 2.14).$$

From the symmetry of the normal distribution, $Pr(-.82 \leq Z \leq 0)$ equals $Pr(0 \leq Z \leq .82)$. Thus, from Table 10.1 we have
$$Pr(-.82 \leq Z \leq 2.14) = .2939 + .4838 = .7777.$$

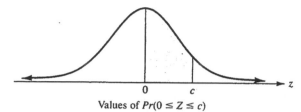

Values of $Pr(0 \le Z \le c)$

c	.00	.01	.02	.03	.04	.05	.06	.07	.08	.09
.0	.0000	.0040	.0080	.0120	.0160	.0199	.0239	.0279	.0319	.0359
.1	.0398	.0438	.0478	.0517	.0557	.0596	.0636	.0675	.0714	.0753
.2	.0793	.0832	.0871	.0910	.0948	.0987	.1026	.1064	.1103	.1141
.3	.1179	.1217	.1255	.1293	.1331	.1368	.1406	.1443	.1480	.1517
.4	.1554	.1591	.1628	.1664	.1700	.1736	.1772	.1808	.1844	.1879
.5	.1915	.1950	.1985	.2019	.2054	.2088	.2123	.2157	.2190	.2224
.6	.2257	.2291	.2324	.2357	.2389	.2422	.2454	.2486	.2517	.2549
.7	.2580	.2611	.2642	.2673	.2704	.2734	.2764	.2794	.2823	.2853
.8	.2881	.2910	.2939	.2967	.2995	.3023	.3051	.3078	.3106	.3133
.9	.3159	.3186	.3212	.3238	.3264	.3289	.3315	.3340	.3365	.3389
1.0	.3413	.3438	.3461	.3485	.3508	.3531	.3554	.3577	.3599	.3521
1.1	.3643	.3665	.3686	.3708	.3728	.3749	.3770	.3790	.3810	.3830
1.2	.3849	.3869	.3888	.3907	.3925	.3944	.3962	.3980	.3997	.4015
1.3	.4032	.4049	.4066	.4082	.4099	.4115	.4131	.4147	.4162	.4177
1.4	.4192	.4207	.4222	.4236	.4251	.4265	.4279	.4292	.4306	.4319
1.5	.4332	.4345	.4357	.4370	.4382	.4394	.4406	.4418	.4429	.4441
1.6	.4451	.4463	.4474	.4484	.4495	.4505	.4515	.4525	.4535	.4545
1.7	.4554	.4564	.4573	.4582	.4591	.4599	.4608	.4616	.4625	.4633
1.8	.4641	.4649	.4656	.4664	.4671	.4678	.4686	.4693	.4699	.4706
1.9	.4713	.4719	.4726	.4732	.4738	.4744	.4750	.4756	.4761	.4767
2.0	.4772	.4778	.4783	.4788	.4793	.4798	.4803	.4808	.4812	.4817
2.1	.4821	.4826	.4830	.4834	.4838	.4842	.4846	.4850	.4854	.4857
2.2	.4861	.4864	.4868	.4871	.4875	.4878	.4881	.4884	.4887	.4890
2.3	.4893	.4896	.4898	.4901	.4904	.4906	.4909	.4911	.4913	.4916
2.4	.4918	.4920	.4922	.4925	.4927	.4929	.4931	.4932	.4934	.4936
2.5	.4938	.4940	.4941	.4943	.4945	.4946	.4948	.4949	.4951	.4952
2.6	.4953	.4955	.4956	.4957	.4959	.4960	.4961	.4962	.4963	.4964
2.7	.4965	.4966	.4967	.4968	.4969	.4970	.4971	.4972	.4973	.4974
2.8	.4974	.4975	.4976	.4977	.4977	.4978	.4979	.4979	.4980	.4981
2.9	.4981	.4982	.4982	.4983	.4984	.4984	.4985	.4985	.4986	.4986
3.0	.4987	.4987	.4987	.4988	.4988	.4989	.4989	.4989	.4990	.4990

Table 10.1

c. Noting that $Pr(0 \le Z) = .5$, we see from Figure 10.7(b) that

$$Pr(Z \ge .61) = Pr(0 \le Z) - Pr(0 \le Z \le .61)$$
$$= .5 - Pr(0 \le Z \le .61)$$
$$= .5 - .2291 \quad \text{(from Table 10.1)}$$
$$= .2709.$$

d. From Figure 10.7(c), we have

$$Pr(Z \le .25) = Pr(Z \le 0) + Pr(0 \le Z \le .25).$$

By symmetry $Pr(Z \le 0) = .5$. Thus from Table 10.1 we find that

$$Pr(Z \le .25) = .5 + .0987 = .5987.$$

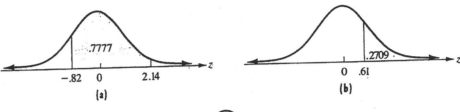

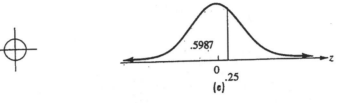

Figure 10.7

Graphical representation of the probabilities for (a) $Pr(-.82 \le Z \le 2.14)$, (b) $Pr(Z \ge .61)$, and (c) $Pr(Z \le .25)$

The next example demonstrates the use of equation (10.15).

EXAMPLE 2

Let X be a normal random variable with mean $\mu = 15$ and standard deviation $\sigma = 6$. Find the following:

a. $Pr(9 \le X \le 12)$

b. $Pr(X \ge 22)$

c. $Pr(X \le 19)$

SOLUTION

a. From equation (10.15), we have

$$Pr(9 \le X \le 12) = Pr\left(\frac{9 - 15}{6} \le Z \le \frac{12 - 15}{6}\right)$$
$$= Pr(-1.00 \le Z \le -.50)$$

From Figure 10.8 and Table 10.1, we see that

$$Pr(-1.00 \le Z \le -.50) = Pr(0 \le Z \le 1.00) - Pr(0 \le Z \le .50)$$
$$= .3413 - .1915$$
$$= .1498.$$

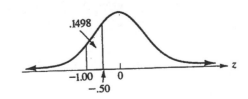

Figure 10.8

A graphical representation of $Pr(-1.00 \le Z \le -.50)$

b. Converting from X to the standard normal, we have

$$Pr(X \geq 22) = Pr\left(Z \geq \frac{22 - 15}{6}\right) = Pr(Z \geq 1.17).$$

From Table 10.1, we then find that

$$Pr(Z \geq 1.17) = .5 - .3790$$
$$= .1210.$$

c. Converting from X to the standard normal, we have

$$Pr(X \leq 19) = Pr\left(Z \leq \frac{19 - 15}{6}\right) = Pr(Z \leq .67).$$

From Table 10.1, we then find that

$$Pr(Z \leq .67) = .5 + .2486$$
$$= .7486.$$
●

EXAMPLE 3   Assume that the length of time it takes for a worker on a production line to assemble one unit is a random variable X. Suppose that X is approximately normally distributed with a mean μ of 20 min and a standard deviation σ of .75 min.

a. Find the probability that the next assembly performed will take at least 21 min.

b. Find the percentage of assemblies that are performed within 1 standard deviation of the mean.

SOLUTION   a. To evaluate $Pr(X \geq 21)$, we convert it to the standard normal:

$$Pr(X \geq 21) = Pr\left(Z \geq \frac{21 - 20}{.75}\right) = Pr(Z \geq 1.33).$$

From Table 10.1 we find that $Pr(Z \geq 1.33) = .5 - .4082 = .0918$; that is, there is only about a 9% chance that a given assembly will require 21 min or longer.

b. The required percentage is the same as the probability that X is between 19.25 and 20.75 min. Converting to the standard normal, we have

$$Pr(19.25 \leq X \leq 20.75) = Pr(-1.00 \leq Z \leq 1.00)$$
$$= 2 \cdot Pr(0 \leq Z \leq 1.00)$$
$$= .6826.$$
●

It may be observed that the solution to part b of Example 3 does not depend on the mean or the standard deviation of X. In other words, for any normal random variable X with mean μ and standard deviation σ,

$$Pr(\mu - \sigma \leq X \leq \mu + \sigma) = .6826.$$

From Table 10.1 it may also be shown that

$$Pr(\mu - 2\sigma \leq X \leq \mu + 2\sigma) = .9544$$

and

$$Pr(\mu - 3\sigma \leq X \leq \mu + 3\sigma) = .9974.$$

Sometimes it is desirable to find an interval for X so that there is a predetermined probability that X will lie within that interval. This can be done by using Table 10.1 "backwards." The next example demonstrates this process.

EXAMPLE 4   A personnel director for a corporation is on the campus of a major university to recruit recent graduates. The director wishes to offer positions to only graduates whose grade point averages (GPAs) place them in the top 20% of their class. If the GPAs are approximately normal with mean $\mu = 2.84$ and standard deviation $\sigma = .32$, find the lowest GPA that the director is willing to consider.

SOLUTION   Let X denote the GPA of a randomly selected graduate. We wish to find x_0 so that 20% of the GPAs are greater than x_0; that is, we want $Pr(X \geq x_0) = .20$. In terms of the standard normal, this may be written

$$Pr\left(Z \geq \frac{x_0 - 2.84}{.32}\right) = .20.$$

As indicated by Figure 10.9, if c is a number for which $Pr(Z \geq c) = .20$, then also $Pr(0 \leq Z \leq c) = .30$. From Table 10.1, we find that c is approximately .84. We then solve the equation

$$\frac{x_0 - 2.84}{.32} = .84$$

to find $x_0 = 3.11$, the lowest acceptable GPA.

Figure 10.9
A graphical representation of
$Pr(Z \geq .84) = .20$

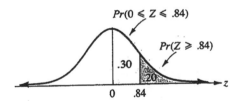

EXERCISES 10.3

In Exercises 1–8 Z denotes the standard normal random variable. Use Table 10.1 to find the indicated probabilities.

1. $Pr(.35 \leq Z \leq 2.13)$

2. $Pr(Z \geq -1.37)$

3. $Pr(Z \leq .62)$

4. $Pr(-2.45 \leq Z \leq 1.04)$

5. $Pr(-.75 \leq Z \leq -.19)$

6. $Pr(Z \geq 1.24)$

7. $Pr(-2.36 \leq Z \leq 3.40)$

8. $Pr(Z \leq -.92)$

In Exercises 9–16 Z denotes the standard normal random variable. Use Table 10.1 to find the value of c that satisfies the stated condition.

9. $Pr(0 \leq Z \leq c) = .4265$

10. $Pr(0 \leq Z \leq c) = .2291$

11. $Pr(Z \geq c) = .0495$ 12. $Pr(Z \geq c) = .4761$

13. $Pr(Z \leq c) = .8790$ 14. $Pr(Z \leq c) = .2090$

15. $Pr(-c \leq Z \leq c) = .9850$ 16. $Pr(-c \leq Z \leq c) = .4908$

In Exercises 17–20 X is a normal random variable with $\mu_X = 30$ *and* $\sigma_X = 4$. *Find each of the indicated probabilities.*

17. $Pr(27 \leq X \leq 31)$ 18. $Pr(31.4 \leq X \leq 37.8)$

19. $Pr(X \leq 26.4)$ 20. $Pr(X \geq 29.2)$

In Exercises 21–24 X is a normal random variable with $\mu_X = 6$ *and* $\sigma_X^2 = 144$. *Find each of the indicated probabilities.*

21. $Pr(1.2 \leq X \leq 3)$ 22. $Pr(-6.6 \leq X \leq 10.8)$

23. $Pr(X \leq 0)$ 24. $Pr(X \geq -9)$

In Exercises 25–28 X is a normal random variable with $\mu_X = -5$ *and* $\sigma_X = 10$. *Find each of the indicated probabilities.*

25. $Pr(-20 \leq X \leq 30)$ 26. $Pr(-15 \leq X \leq -12)$

27. $Pr(X \leq 2.5)$ 28. $Pr(X \geq 0)$

29. Assume that the exact weight of a "12-oz" package of potato chips is a normal random variable with mean 12.1 oz and variance .04.

   a. Find the probability that a given package weighs less than 12 oz.

   b. Find the probability that the package weighs at least 11.9 oz.

30. Van Go Pizza promises to deliver a pizza to your home within 20 min. Suppose that the actual time is a normal random variable with a mean of 16 min and a standard deviation of 1.5 min.

   a. What proportion of the pizzas are actually delivered within 20 min?

   b. What proportion of the pizzas are delivered between 18 and 20 min?

31. Suppose that the bill for a dinner for two at a local restaurant is a random variable that is approximately normal with a mean of $26.45 and a standard deviation of $3.85.

   a. What is the probability that a bill will be at most $30.00?

   b. What proportion of the bills are less than $20.00?

32. To meet contract specifications, a circular hole drilled in a metal unit must have a diameter between 4.95 and 5.05 cm. An employee operating the drilling machine produces holes with diameters that have a normal distribution with a mean of 5.01 cm and a variance of .0016; a computer-controlled drill produces holes with diameters having a normal distribution with a mean of 4.98 cm and a variance of .0004. Find the proportion of holes drilled by each that will meet specifications.

33. A manufacturer of automobile tires knows that the useful life of a tire is a normal random variable with mean 35,600 mi and a standard deviation of 550 mi. The manufacturer would like to offer a warranty on the tires. How much useful life should be guaranteed so that only approximately 10% of the tires sold will fail before the warranty expires?

34. Assume that the weights of chicken eggs are normally distributed with a mean of .75 oz and a standard deviation of .12 oz. If it is decided that only the heaviest 15% of the eggs should be graded as "large," find the minimum acceptable weight of a large egg.

35. A statistics instructor bases final grades on the total number of points a student earns throughout the semester on tests and assignments. Suppose that these point totals are approximately normal with mean 653 and standard deviation 38. The instructor wishes to give a grade of C to those students whose point totals comprise the middle 60% of the distribution of grades. Find the lowest and the highest point totals that will earn a C.

36. A soft drink bottler uses a machine to fill bottles. The exact amount of liquid that the machine puts in each bottle is a normal random variable. Assume that the machine can be adjusted so that the mean is any desired number but the variance is .0016. How should the mean be chosen so that approximately 98% of the bottles will contain at least 12 fluid oz of soft drink?

37. Use Theorem 10.1 to verify that if X is a normal random variable with mean μ_X and variance σ_X^2, then $Z = (X - \mu_X)/\sigma_X$ has mean 0 and variance 1.

10.4 Other Random Variables

In the previous section, we introduced the normal random variable, a theoretical random variable, and observed that it can be used to model continuous random variables whose PDFs are symmetric and mound-shaped. In this section, we briefly discuss three more theoretical random variables that are often used as models.

The first of these is the **binomial random variable**, a discrete random variable. We begin with the concept of a **Bernoulli trial**: a random event for which there are only two possible outcomes. In practice, these outcomes may be designated win or lose, yes or no, heads or tails, or similar expressions. For consistency, we will designate the two outcomes as success and failure.

We define the binomial random variable using repeated Bernoulli trials.

Definition 10.7

Let a Bernoulli trial be repeated n times. Assume that (1) the trials are independent of one another, and (2) the probability of a success in each of the trials is p. Let X be the number of successes that occur. Then X is a **binomial random variable on n trials with probability of success p**.

For brevity, we will write X is b(n, p) to indicate that X is binomial on n trials with probability of success p. The following theorem, whose proof depends on the binomial theorem (see Appendix A.5), gives the PDF for X. (The formula for the PDF uses factorial notation, which is also reviewed in the appendix.)

Theorem 10.2

Suppose that X is b(n, p). Then the probability that X equals k is computed by

$$(10.16) \quad Pr(X = k) = \frac{k!}{k!(n-k)!} p^k (1-p)^{n-k}, \quad k = 0, 1, 2, \ldots, n.$$

EXAMPLE 1

The owner of a knitting mill knows that 5% of the sweaters that are turned out will have a noticeable flaw in the pattern and will have to be sold as "seconds." The owner randomly chooses six of these sweaters for inspection.

a. Find the probability that none of the sweaters is flawed.

b. Determine the probability that one is flawed.

c. Find the probability that at least one is flawed.

SOLUTION

To use a binomial random variable, it must be reasonable to assume that flawed sweaters occur independently, with each sweater having a 5% chance of containing a flaw. If we make this assumption and let X be the number of sweaters among the six that have a flaw, then X is b(6, .05).

a. From equation (10.16), we have

$$Pr(X = 0) = \frac{6!}{0!6!}(.05)^0(.95)^6$$

$$= \frac{720}{720}(1)(.7351)$$

$$= .7351.$$

b. From equation (10.16), we have

$$Pr(X = 1) = \frac{6!}{1!5!}(.05)^1(.95)^5$$

$$= \frac{720}{120}(.05)(.7738)$$

$$= .2321.$$

c. We are asked to find $Pr(X \geq 1)$. This can be done by evaluating and summing $Pr(X = 1)$, $Pr(X = 2)$, $Pr(X = 3)$, $Pr(X = 4)$, $Pr(X = 5)$, and $Pr(X = 6)$. It is more efficient, however, to make use of the fact that $\Sigma_{k=0}^{6}Pr(X = k) = 1$ to obtain

$$Pr(X \geq 1) = 1 - Pr(X = 0)$$

$$= 1 - .7351$$

$$= .2649.$$ ●

The mean and variance of a binomial random variable are given by the next theorem.

Theorem 10.3

Let X be $b(n, p)$. Then the mean value of X is $\mu_X = np$ and the variance is $\sigma_X^2 = np(1 - p)$.

EXAMPLE 2

The director of an advertising campaign hopes that when the campaign is over, 60% of the general public will recognize the name of the product advertised. After the campaign, the director intends to survey eight people at random. Let X be the number of these people who recognize the product.

a. If the director's hopes are met, find μ_X and σ_X.

b. Find the probability that X is within 1 standard deviation of its mean value.

SOLUTION

a. Assuming that the probability that any given person will recognize the product is $p = .6$, X is $b(8, .6)$. From Theorem 10.3

$$\mu_X = 8(.6) = 4.8 \quad \text{and} \quad \sigma_X^2 = 8(.6)(.4) = 1.92.$$

Thus $\sigma_X = \sqrt{1.92} = 1.39$.

b. We have that

$$Pr(\mu - \sigma \leq X \leq \mu + \sigma) = Pr(3.41 \leq X \leq 6.19)$$
$$= Pr(X = 4) + Pr(X = 5) + Pr(X = 6).$$

From equation (10.16) we have

$$Pr(X = 4) = \frac{8!}{4!4!}(.6)^4(.4)^4 = 70(.1296)(.0256) = .232;$$

$$Pr(X = 5) = \frac{8!}{5!3!}(.6)^5(.4)^3 = 56(.0778)(.064) = .279;$$

$$Pr(X = 6) = \frac{8!}{6!2!}(.6)^6(.4)^2 = 28(.0467)(.16) = .209.$$

Summing these, we find that $Pr(\mu - \sigma \leq X \leq \mu + \sigma) = .720.$ ●

A simple continuous random variable is the **uniform random variable**. A random variable X is said to have a uniform distribution on its outcome set $[a, b]$ when all the outcomes are equally likely. For this to occur, the PDF must be constant on $[a, b]$. The requirement that the area of the region bounded by the graph of the PDF be one square unit implies that the PDF is

$$f(x) = \frac{1}{b - a}, \qquad a \leq x \leq b.$$

If X has a uniform distribution on $[a, b]$, then the mean value of X is

(10.17)
$$\mu_X = \frac{a + b}{2}$$

and the variance of X is

(10.18)
$$\sigma_X^2 = \frac{(b - a)^2}{12}.$$

The verification of equations (10.17) and (10.18) is left to the exercises. It should be noted that because this is such a simple random variable, there are very few real-world random variables that can be modeled accurately with a uniform distribution.

EXAMPLE 3

Assume that juice oranges are graded as "select" if the amount of juice that can be squeezed from them is between 2.0 and 2.5 fluid oz. Let X be the actual amount of juice that is obtained from a "select" orange, and assume X is uniformly distributed.

a. Determine the mean, variance, and standard deviation of X.

b. Find $Pr(2.3 \leq X \leq 2.45)$.

c. Find $Pr(X \geq 2.2)$.

SOLUTION

a. From equation (10.17), we have

$$\mu_X = \frac{2.0 + 2.5}{2} = 2.25 \text{ fluid oz}$$

and from equation (10.18)

$$\sigma_X^2 = \frac{(2.5 - 2.0)^2}{12} = .0208.$$

Thus $\sigma_X = .1443$ fluid oz.

b. Because X is a continuous random variable with PDF $f(x) = 2$, where $2.0 \le x \le 2.5$,

$$Pr(2.3 \le X \le 2.45) = \int_{2.3}^{2.45} 2 \, dx = .30.$$

c. We observe that $Pr(X \ge 2.2)$ is equivalent to $Pr(2.2 \le X \le 2.5)$. Thus,

$$Pr(X \ge 2.2) = \int_{2.2}^{2.5} 2 \, dx = .60. \qquad \bullet$$

To introduce another theoretical distribution, consider these random variables: the time a bank teller takes to wait on a customer, the time between successive arrivals of customers at a department store, and the time required for someone to answer a telephone. In each of these cases the graph of the PDF may look like that in Figure 10.10. The outcome set is $[0, \infty)$; there is a high likelihood that the value of X will be close to a small central value; but there is also a small probability that X will be quite large.

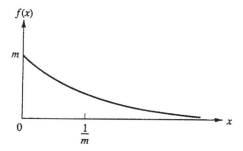

Figure 10.10
The graph of the PDF $f(x) = me^{-mx}$, where $0 \le x < \infty$

Exponential functions are frequently used for the PDFs of random variables with these properties. Let m be any positive number; then the **exponential random variable with parameter** m has outcome set $[0, \infty)$ and the PDF

$$f(x) = me^{-mx}, \qquad 0 \le x \le \infty.$$

It can be shown that the mean value and the variance of this random variable are $\mu_X = 1/m$ and $\sigma_X^2 = 1/m^2$, respectively. Verification is left to the exercises. It is noteworthy that for an exponential random variable, the mean and the standard deviation are equal.

EXAMPLE 4

Let X denote the length of time in minutes that it takes an employee of McKwik Chicken to fill a customer's order. Assume that X has a mean value of 40 sec and has an exponential distribution.

a. Give the PDF of X.

b. Find the probability that a customer will be served within 30 sec.

c. What percentage of customers have to wait longer than 2 min to have their order filled?

SOLUTION

a. Because the mean is known to be $\mu_X = 2/3$ min, we take $m = 3/2 = 1.5$ to get the PDF:

$$f(x) = 1.5e^{-1.5x}, \qquad 0 \le x < \infty.$$

b. Changing 30 sec to .5 min, we must find $Pr(0 \le X \le .5)$. Integrating the PDF yields

$$\int_0^{.5} 1.5e^{-1.5x}\, dx = -e^{-1.5x}\Big]_0^{.5}$$

$$= 1 - e^{-.75}$$

$$= .5276.$$

Thus the probability that an order is filled within 30 sec is approximately .53.

c. To find $Pr(X \ge 2)$, compute the integral

$$\int_2^{\infty} 1.5e^{-1.5x}\, dx = \lim_{b \to \infty} -e^{-1.5x}\Big]_2^{b}$$

$$= e^{-3}$$

$$= .0498.$$

Thus about 5% of the customers will not have their order filled within 2 min. ●

It is interesting to note from Example 4 that although the mean time required to fill a customer's order is 40 sec, there is a greater than .50 chance that the order will be filled within 30 sec. This is typical of the exponential distribution. In fact, if X is an exponential random variable with parameter m, then the probability that X is less than its mean value is

$$Pr\left(0 \le X \le \frac{1}{m}\right) = \int_0^{1/m} me^{-mx}\, dx$$

$$= -e^{-mx}\Big]_0^{1/m}$$

$$= 1 - e^{-1}$$

$$= .6321.$$

That is, 63% of the time X will lie below its mean, and only 37% of the time it will lie above it.

EXERCISES 10.4

1. Let X be a binomial random variable on four trials with probability of success .30. Find the indicated probabilities.

   a. $Pr(X = 3)$ b. $Pr(X = 0)$ c. $Pr(X \leq 2)$

2. Let X be a binomial random variable on seven trials with probability of success .60. Find the indicated probabilities.

   a. $Pr(X = 5)$ b. $Pr(X = 0 \text{ or } 7)$ c. $Pr(X \geq 6)$

3. Let X be a binomial random variable on six trials with probability of success .10. Find the indicated probabilities.

   a. $Pr(X = 3)$ b. $Pr(2 \leq X \leq 4)$ c. $Pr(X > 5)$

4. Let X be a binomial random variable on three trials with probability of success .95. Find the indicated probabilities.

   a. $Pr(X = 1)$ b. $Pr(X < 3)$ c. $Pr(X = 1 \text{ or } 2)$

5. Refer to Exercise 1. Find μ_X and σ_X; then compute $Pr(\mu_X - \sigma_X < X < \mu_X + \sigma_X)$.

6. Refer to Exercise 3. Find μ_X and σ_X; then compute $Pr(\mu_X - 2\sigma_X < X < \mu_X + 2\sigma_X)$.

7. Let X be a uniformly distributed random variable on $[5, 10]$.

   a. Write the PDF of X.   b. Find μ_X and σ_X^2.

   c. Find $Pr(6 \leq X \leq 8)$.   d. Find $Pr(X \leq 7)$.

8. Let X be a uniformly distributed random variable on $[-8, 8]$.

   a. Write the PDF of X.   b. Find μ_X and σ_X^2.

   c. Find $Pr(-3 \leq X \leq 5)$.   d. Find $Pr(|X| \geq 6)$.

9. Let X be a uniformly distributed random variable on $[0, 100]$.

   a. Write the PDF of X.   b. Find μ_X and σ_X^2.

   c. Find $Pr(X \geq 35)$.   d. Find $Pr(X \geq \pi)$.

10. Let X be a uniformly distributed random variable on $[0, 1]$.

   a. Write the PDF of X.   b. Find μ_X and σ_X^2.

   c. Find $Pr(.3 \leq X \leq 2)$.   d. Find $Pr(X = .5)$.

11. Let X have an exponential distribution with parameter $m = 3$.

   a. Write the PDF of X.   b. Find μ_X and σ_X.

   c. Find $Pr(X \leq 2)$.   d. Find $Pr(X \geq 2/3)$.

12. Let X have an exponential distribution with parameter $m = 2/5$.

   a. Write the PDF of X.   b. Find μ_X and σ_X.

   c. Find $Pr(1 \leq X \leq 5)$.   d. Find $Pr(X \geq 7.5)$.

13. Let X have an exponential distribution with a mean value of 8.

   a. Write the PDF of X.   b. Find $Pr(4 \leq X \leq 12)$.

   c. Find σ_X and $Pr(X \geq \sigma_X)$.   d. Find $Pr(X \geq 2\sigma_X)$.

14. Let X have an exponential distribution with a mean value of .25.

   a. Write the PDF of X.   b. Find $Pr(X \leq .75)$.

   c. Find $Pr(X \geq .1)$.

   d. Find σ_X and $Pr(X \geq 1.5\sigma_X)$.

15. A buyer for a women's dress shop has placed an order for ten dresses from a new company. The buyer has a policy that if more than one of these dresses is flawed, no future orders will be placed with that company. Assume that, in fact, there is a 15% chance that any given dress from this company will be flawed. Find the probability that the buyer will place future orders with this company.

16. A stockbroker is recommending that clients purchase stock in XYZ Products. Assume that the broker speaks with eight clients that afternoon. If there is a 25% probability that any given client will follow the recommendation, find the probability that at least two of the clients purchase the stock.

17. The marketing division of Barry's Yogurt is testing consumer reaction to a proposed new flavor: peanut butter. Assume that 35% of adults strongly dislike peanut butter. The director of marketing intends to assemble a randomly drawn panel of eight adults and have each sample the new flavor. If more than three of these indicate a strong dislike, the product will be scrapped. What is the probability that the world will see peanut butter yogurt?

18. Assume that 15% of the potential customers who walk into a new car dealership will buy a car from that dealer on the same day. If nine people walk into the dealership this

morning, let X be the number of those who buy a car that day. Find μ_X and σ_X. Find the probability that X is within 2 standard deviations of its mean.

19. There is an intersection through which you drive each day that is controlled by a stoplight. Assume that the light is red for 40 sec on each cycle. If the time that you reach the intersection is random and you have to stop for the red light, then the time you wait is a uniform random variable on [0, 40]. Find the mean and the standard deviation of your waiting time. Find the probability that your wait will be less than 15 sec.

20. A local radio station is conducting a contest in which a song by the Rolling Stones is played at a random time between noon and 5:00 P.M. The first person to call will win a collection of Stones albums. Let X be the number of hours past noon at which the song begins. Assume that X has a uniform distribution.

    a. Write the PDF of X.

    b. Find μ_X and σ_X.

    c. If you listen to this station from 3:00 to 4:15 P.M., find the probability that you hear the song.

21. Assume the time X that a car spends at a drive-up teller window at a bank has an exponential distribution with a mean of 70 sec.

    a. Write the PDF of X.

    b. Find the proportion of cars that spend longer than 2 min at the window.

22. Assume that the time X (in minutes) between successive arrivals of customers at a fast food restaurant has an exponential distribution with PDF

$$f(x) = \frac{1}{3}e^{x/3}, \qquad 0 \le x < \infty.$$

    a. Find μ_X and σ_X.

    b. What is the probability that if you enter this restaurant, the next customer will enter within 15 sec?

23. Oil Slick is an auto maintenance center that advertises it can change a car's oil and give it a simple lube in 10 min. Assume the actual time X that is required to perform these services has an exponential distribution with a mean of 8.5 min. Find the probability that Oil Slick lives up to its claim.

24. You are driving along a two-lane highway at night. Let X be the distance between two successive cars that you meet driving in the opposite direction. Assume that X has an exponential distribution with mean .2 mi.

    a. Write the PDF of X.

    b. What is σ_X?

    c. If you have just met a car, what is the probability that you will meet a second car in .05 to .25 mi?

25. Prove that if X is uniformly distributed on $[a, b]$, then its mean value is $(a + b)/2$ and its variance is $(b - a)^2/12$.

26. Prove that if X has an exponential distribution with parameter m, then $\mu_X = 1/m$. (*Hint:* Use integration by parts and see Example 5 in Section 9.5 for $\lim_{x \to \infty} xe^{-x}$.)

CH. 10 REVIEW

I. Key Terms & Concepts

Mathematics

Discrete Random Variable
Continuous Random Variable
Probability Density Function (PDF)
Mean Value
Variance
Standard Deviation
Relative Frequency Histogram
Normal Random Variable
Binomial Random Variable
Uniform Random Variable
Exponential Random Variable

II. True or False

Indicate whether each statement is true or false.

1. If X is a continuous random variable, then $Pr(a < X < b)$ and $Pr(a \leq X \leq b)$ are equal.

2. If X is a discrete random variable, then $Pr(a < X < b)$ and $Pr(a \leq X \leq b)$ are equal.

3. If X is a random variable for which the outcome set has infinitely many values, then X must be a continuous random variable.

4. The function $f(x) = x + 1/2$ may be used as a PDF for a random variable whose outcome set is $[-1, 1]$.

5. The standard deviation of a random variable must be nonnegative.

6. If X is an exponential random variable, then $\mu_x = \sigma_x$.

7. It is not possible for a random variable to be uniformly distributed on the interval $[0, \infty)$.

8. If Z is the standard normal random variable, then $Pr(0 \leq Z \leq c) = .5 - Pr(z \geq c)$.

9. If X is normal with mean μ, then $Pr(Z = \mu) = 0$.

10. If X is b$(n, .5)$ and $k \leq n$, then $Pr(X = k) = Pr(X = n - k)$.

III. Drill Problems

1. Let X be a discrete random variable with outcome set $\{0, 1, 2, 3, 4\}$. Find c so that $f(x) = cx_i(x_i + 1)$, for x_i in the outcome set, is a PDF for X.

2. Find μ_x and σ_x for the random variable X in Problem 1.

3. Find c so that $f(x) = cx^{-2}$ is the PDF of a continuous random variable with outcome set $[1, 4]$.

4. Find μ_x and σ_x^2 for the random variable whose PDF is given by
$$f(x) = \frac{3}{26}x^2, \qquad 1 \leq x \leq 3.$$

In Problems 5–8 Z is the standard normal random variable. Find the indicated probabilities.

5. $Pr(-2.36 \leq Z \leq 1.28)$ 6. $Pr(-.86 \leq Z \leq -.07)$

7. $Pr(Z \leq -1.72)$ 8. $Pr(Z \geq 2.15)$

In Problems 9–12 X is a normal random variable with mean 15 and standard deviation 3.5. Find the indicated probabilities.

9. $Pr(X \geq 16.4)$ 10. $Pr(10.8 \leq X \leq 14.3)$

11. $Pr(15 \leq X \leq 22.3)$ 12. $Pr(X \leq 19.9)$

In Problems 13–16 X is a binomial random variable on five trials with probability of success .6. Find the indicated probabilities.

13. $Pr(X = 2)$

14. $Pr(X = 2 \text{ or } 3)$

15. $Pr(X > 4)$

16. $Pr(X \neq 4)$

In Problems 17–20 X is an exponential random variable with parameter 2. Find the indicated probabilities.

17. $Pr(X \leq .25)$

18. $Pr(.6 \leq X \leq 1.1)$

19. $Pr(X \leq .4)$

20. $Pr(X \geq \mu_X - \sigma_X)$

21. Let X be a uniform random variable with a mean value of 5.

   a. If the largest possible value for X is 20, find the PDF of X.

   b. What is the variance of X?

   c. Find $Pr(X \geq 10.)$

IV. Applications

1. There is a 15-member club of Boston Celtics fans, some of whom want to attend the NBA playoff games in Los Angeles. A travel agent has put together a tour package for them. The cost for each member of the club who decides to go will be $600 if ten or fewer go; for each additional member who goes, however, the cost will drop by $20 per person. Suppose that the probabilities that x members actually go are given in the table.

x_i	8	9	10	11	12	13
$p(x_i)$	.10	.20	.25	.25	.15	.05

Find the expected cost for a member who decides to go and the standard deviation of that cost.

2. Refer to Exercise 1. Find the expected revenue that the travel agent will receive and the standard deviation of this revenue.

3. The owner of Dave's Diner knows that on Saturday nights, receipts have a distribution that is approximately normal with mean $\mu = \$2350$ and standard deviation $\sigma = \$320$. Recently, Dave has begun an advertising campaign on the radio to try to boost Saturday night business. If receipts this coming Saturday top $2600, he will believe that the ads were successful. What is the probability that this event could occur strictly by chance?

4. Refer to Exercise 3. Believing that the outcome from a single Saturday is not very convincing, Dave's accoun-

tant persuades him to check the receipts for the next four Saturdays. What is the probability that on exactly three of these days the receipts top $2600?

5. A loan officer at a bank needs to decide how much money to loan the operator of a small business. The banker believes that the amount of new debt that can be successfully carried by the business based on current profitability has a normal distribution with a mean of $55,000 and a standard deviation of $7300. What is the maximum loan that the banker would be willing to make if she wants to have at least an 85% chance that the business can carry that much new debt?

6. A personnel director of a company wants to use an exponential distribution to model X, the random variable giving the length of time in years that a newly hired employee will remain with the company.

   a. If the director knows that the mean length of employment at the company is 18 mo, find the PDF for X.

   b. Using the PDF from part a, estimate the proportion of employees who remain with the company longer than 1 yr.

7. Let X be a continuous random variable whose possible values lie on the interval [a, b] with m, a point in that interval, the most likely value. A triangular distribution for X is a continuous PDF whose graph is a triangle with base on [a, b] and peak at x = m.

   A manager must decide whether to undertake a proposed project. The manager believes that the project will generate at least $5000 and perhaps as much as $125,000. The most likely outcome, however, is thought to be a profit of $75,000. Find a triangular PDF for X, the actual profit generated by the project. (*Hint:* First locate the coordinates of the peak of the triangle by using the fact that the triangle must have an area of one square unit.)

8. Refer to Exercise 7. What decision should the manager reach if, in order to undertake the project, there must be at least an 80% chance of earning $25,000 or more?

You are the distributor for a certain brand of wine. The manager of a local liquor store has just called, wanting to know why this week's order had not yet come in. You try to explain that your route driver called in ill this morning, but the manager demands the usual order and wants it delivered within the hour. Unfortunately, you do not know what the usual order is and you cannot reach the driver. A check of your accounts shows that during the months of April, May, June, and July, this customer was billed for $456, $474, $499, and $511, respectively. The following matrix gives the price per case of each of your four kinds of wine during those months. Find how many cases of each kind of wine constitute this store's usual order.

	Rosé	Burgundy	Rhine	Chablis
April	20	24	18	22
May	20	24	21	22
June	25	24	21	22
July	25	28	21	22

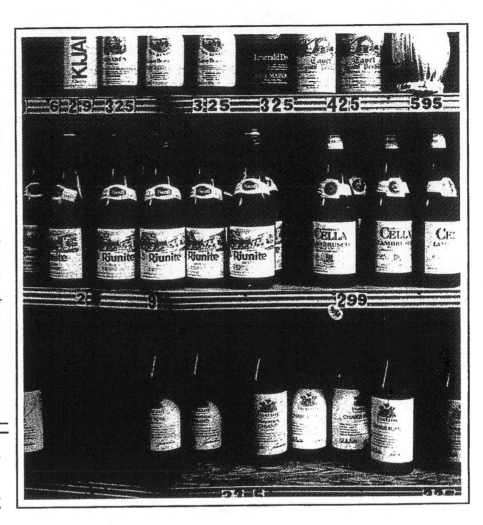

CHAPTER 11

Matrices and Linear Systems

11.1
Matrices and Matrix Operations

Many business records, forms, and worksheets consist of rows and columns of data. The rows and columns offer a natural system for organizing and indexing the data. Mathematically, a rectangular array of numbers is called a **matrix**. The numbers within the matrix are called **entries**. By studying the algebra of matrices we find systematic approaches to analyzing tables of business data.

As a mathematical entity, a matrix is denoted by a single capital letter, such as A. Each entry is denoted by a lowercase letter with double subscripts, such as a_{ij}. The subscripts serve as an address for the entry—the first denoting the row and the second the column in which the entry is located. When a matrix has m rows and n columns it is said to have **dimension** (or **size**) $m \times n$ (read "m by n").

EXAMPLE 1

For the matrix

$$A = \begin{bmatrix} 7 & 2 & 4 \\ 3 & 0 & -5 \end{bmatrix},$$

identify each entry using the a_{ij} notation.

SOLUTION

The dimension of A is 2×3; thus, A has six entries that may be denoted

$$a_{11} = 7, \quad a_{12} = 2, \quad a_{13} = 4,$$
$$a_{21} = 3, \quad a_{22} = 0, \quad a_{23} = -5. \qquad \bullet$$

Addition and **scalar multiplication** are two operations that are commonly used to combine or alter matrices.

Definition 11.1

> If A and B are two matrices with the same dimension and entries a_{ij} and b_{ij}, respectively, then their **sum** is denoted $A + B$, where
>
> $$A + B \text{ is the matrix with entries } a_{ij} + b_{ij}.$$
>
> (In words, $A + B$ is formed by adding corresponding entries of A and B.)
>   If k is a constant, then the **scalar product** of k and A is denoted kA, where
>
> $$kA \text{ is the matrix with entries } ka_{ij}.$$
>
> (In words, kA is formed by multiplying each entry of A by k.)

EXAMPLE 2

If

$$A = \begin{bmatrix} 2 & -1 \\ 3 & 5 \\ 0 & 4 \end{bmatrix} \quad \text{and} \quad B = \begin{bmatrix} 7 & 2 \\ -2 & 8 \\ 9 & -4 \end{bmatrix},$$

find $A + B$, $2A$, and $(-1)B$.

SOLUTION

Since A and B are both 3×2 matrices, we can add corresponding entries to obtain

$$A + B = \begin{bmatrix} 9 & 1 \\ 1 & 13 \\ 9 & 0 \end{bmatrix}.$$

Multiplying each entry of A by 2 yields

$$2A = \begin{bmatrix} 4 & -2 \\ 6 & 10 \\ 0 & 8 \end{bmatrix},$$

and multiplying each entry of B by -1 produces

$$(-1)B = \begin{bmatrix} -7 & -2 \\ 2 & -8 \\ -9 & 4 \end{bmatrix}.$$

●

The **subtraction** of matrices may be defined using addition and scalar multiplication as follows:

(11.1)
$$A - B = A + (-1)B,$$

whenever A and B have the same dimension.

EXAMPLE 3

The expenses for four rental properties during 1988 are given in matrix R:

	Taxes	Insurance	Management and Maintenance	Utilities	Misc.	
	850	300	2500	750	1800	Unit 1
$R =$	800	275	2200	800	1500	Unit 2
	900	350	2800	900	2000	Unit 3
	950	400	3200	950	2300	Unit 4

As the labels indicate, each row details the expenses for a different property, whereas each column represents a different expense. Similar expenses for these properties during 1987 are given in matrix L.

$$L = \begin{bmatrix} 820 & 280 & 2000 & 740 & 1500 \\ 750 & 220 & 1800 & 760 & 1200 \\ 850 & 300 & 2500 & 850 & 1600 \\ 910 & 375 & 3000 & 900 & 2000 \end{bmatrix}$$

Use matrix addition to compute $R + L$ (the matrix containing the total expenses for each property over the years 1987 and 1988). Use matrix subtraction to compute $R - L$ (the matrix of increases in expenses for each property from 1987 to 1988). Finally, if it is estimated that all expenses will increase by 8% from 1988 to 1989, use scalar multiplication to form a matrix of estimated rental expenses for 1989.

SOLUTION

Adding entries term by term, we find

$$R + L = \begin{bmatrix} 1670 & 580 & 4500 & 1490 & 3300 \\ 1550 & 495 & 4000 & 1560 & 2700 \\ 1750 & 650 & 5300 & 1750 & 3600 \\ 1860 & 775 & 6200 & 1850 & 4300 \end{bmatrix}.$$

Term-by-term subtraction yields

$$R - L = \begin{bmatrix} 30 & 20 & 500 & 10 & 300 \\ 50 & 55 & 400 & 40 & 300 \\ 50 & 50 & 300 & 50 & 400 \\ 40 & 25 & 200 & 50 & 300 \end{bmatrix}.$$

The estimated expenses for 1989 may be determined by multiplying each of the 1988 expenses by 1.08. Thus the desired matrix is

$$(1.08)R = \begin{bmatrix} 918 & 324 & 2700 & 810 & 1944 \\ 864 & 297 & 2376 & 864 & 1620 \\ 972 & 378 & 3024 & 972 & 2160 \\ 1026 & 432 & 3456 & 1026 & 2484 \end{bmatrix}.$$

Often a matrix consists of only a single row or column. In these cases the matrix is called a row or column **vector**. The entries of a vector are usually labeled with single subscripts, and a vector's dimension is referred to as its length. An n-component row vector is thus a $1 \times n$ matrix, and an n-component column vector is an $n \times 1$ matrix. A useful operation defined for row and column vectors is the **inner product**.

Definition 11.2

If X is an n-component row vector with entries x_i and Y is an n-component column vector with entries y_i, then the **inner product** of X and Y, denoted XY, is the number given by

$$XY = x_1y_1 + x_2y_2 + \cdots + x_ny_n.$$

EXAMPLE 4

Find XY if

$$X = \begin{bmatrix} 2 & -1 & 3 & 4 & 0 \end{bmatrix} \quad \text{and} \quad Y = \begin{bmatrix} 1 \\ 5 \\ 2 \\ -2 \\ 7 \end{bmatrix}.$$

SOLUTION

X and Y are both 5-component vectors, so by Definition 11.2

$$\begin{aligned} XY &= (2)(1) + (-1)(5) + (3)(2) + (4)(-2) + (0)(7) \\ &= 2 - 5 + 6 - 8 + 0 \\ &= -5. \end{aligned}$$

EXAMPLE 5

At Gamma University, the colleges are allocated funds for university services based on the percentage of those services they use. Row vector A indicates the percentage of use by the College of Arts and Sciences of the total work performed by each of the four service units.

	Buildings and Grounds	Business Services	Instructional Services	Maintenance	
$A = [$	.4	.65	.5	.6	$]$

In a similar fashion, row vectors

$$B = [.3 \quad .2 \quad .3 \quad .15]$$

and

$$E = [.3 \quad .15 \quad .2 \quad .25]$$

represent the percentage of use of the service units by the Colleges of Business and Education, respectively. If the total expenditure of the service units for academic year 1988 is given by the column vector

$$T = \begin{bmatrix} 500,000 \\ 600,000 \\ 300,000 \\ 800,000 \end{bmatrix} \begin{array}{l} \text{Buildings and Grounds} \\ \text{Business Services} \\ \text{Instructional Services} \\ \text{Maintenance} \end{array}$$

use inner products to determine the amount allocated to each college budget for service units.

SOLUTION

Assuming that funds are allocated to colleges according to the percentage of use of each service unit, the College of Arts and Sciences receives .4(500,000) for Buildings and Grounds, .65(600,000) for Business Services, .5(300,000) for Instructional Services, and .6(800,000) for Maintenance. Summing these amounts, we form the inner product

$$AT = .4(500,000) + .65(600,000) + .5(300,000) + .6(800,000)$$
$$= 200,000 + 390,000 + 150,000 + 480,000$$
$$= 1,220,000.$$

Thus the College of Arts and Sciences is allocated $1.22 million for service units.

Proceeding in a similar fashion, the service portion of the College of Business's budget is given by the inner product

$$BT = .3(500,000) + .2(600,000) + .3(300,000) + .15(800,000)$$
$$= 150,000 + 120,000 + 90,000 + 120,000$$
$$= 480,000,$$

and that of the College of Education is given by the inner product

$$ET = .3(500,000) + .15(600,000) + .2(300,000) + .25(800,000)$$
$$= 150,000 + 90,000 + 60,000 + 200,000$$
$$= 500,000.$$

The final matrix operation considered in this section, **matrix multiplication**, is defined using inner products. To use this definition we will consider a matrix as a collection of either row or column vectors.

Definition 11.3

If A is an $m \times n$ matrix and B is an $n \times k$ matrix, then the **product** AB is an $m \times k$ matrix whose ijth entry is formed from the inner product of the ith row of A and the jth column of B.

Figure 11.1 illustrates the inner product used in forming a typical entry in the product matrix. (Entries of the product matrix are denoted c_{ij}.)

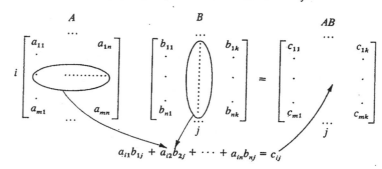

Figure 11.1
Forming the ijth entry c_{ij} of a product matrix

EXAMPLE 6

Find AB if

$$A = \begin{bmatrix} 1 & -2 & 4 \\ 3 & 1 & 0 \end{bmatrix} \quad \text{and} \quad B = \begin{bmatrix} 4 & 0 & -1 \\ 2 & 1 & 5 \\ 6 & 2 & 1 \end{bmatrix}.$$

SOLUTION

Since A is 2×3 and B is 3×3, the product AB is 2×3. If C denotes the product and C has entries c_{ij}, then c_{11} is the inner product of the first row of A and the first column of B; thus,

$$c_{11} = (1)(4) + (-2)(2) + (4)(6)$$
$$= 4 - 4 + 24 = 24.$$

Similarly,

$$c_{12} = (1)(0) + (-2)(1) + (4)(2) = 6$$

and

$$c_{13} = (1)(-1) + (-2)(5) + (4)(1) = -7.$$

The entries in the second row of the product are $c_{21} = 14$, $c_{22} = 1$, and $c_{23} = 2$; thus

$$\begin{bmatrix} 1 & -2 & 4 \\ 3 & 1 & 0 \end{bmatrix} \begin{bmatrix} 4 & 0 & -1 \\ 2 & 1 & 5 \\ 6 & 2 & 1 \end{bmatrix} = \begin{bmatrix} 24 & 6 & -7 \\ 14 & 1 & 2 \end{bmatrix}.$$

●

EXAMPLE 7

Referring to the budgeting procedure in Example 5, form a "utilization" matrix U whose rows are the vectors A, B, and E. Then use matrix multiplication to form a service vector S with amounts budgeted to the colleges for service as entries.

SOLUTION

With A, B, and E used as rows, the utilization matrix becomes

$$U = \begin{bmatrix} .4 & .65 & .5 & .6 \\ .3 & .2 & .3 & .15 \\ .3 & .15 & .2 & .25 \end{bmatrix}.$$

Now recalling that the amounts budgeted to the colleges were determined from the inner products AT, BT, and ET, we see that $UT = S$; that is,

$$\underbrace{\begin{bmatrix} .4 & .65 & .5 & .6 \\ .3 & .2 & .3 & .15 \\ .3 & .15 & .2 & .25 \end{bmatrix}}_{U} \underbrace{\begin{bmatrix} 500,000 \\ 600,000 \\ 300,000 \\ 800,000 \end{bmatrix}}_{T} = \underbrace{\begin{bmatrix} 1,220,000 \\ 480,000 \\ 500,000 \end{bmatrix}}_{S}.$$

EXERCISES 11.1

In Exercises 1–10 find $A + B$, $A - B$, kA, and kB for the given constant k and matrices A and B.

1. $A = \begin{bmatrix} 2 & 1 \\ -1 & 3 \end{bmatrix}$, $B = \begin{bmatrix} 4 & 3 \\ 5 & -2 \end{bmatrix}$, $k = 3$

2. $A = \begin{bmatrix} -7 & 8 \\ 9 & 0 \end{bmatrix}$, $B = \begin{bmatrix} 2 & -6 \\ 3 & 3 \end{bmatrix}$, $k = 5$

3. $A = \begin{bmatrix} 3 & 6 \\ 2 & 2 \\ -5 & 8 \end{bmatrix}$, $B = \begin{bmatrix} 1 & -8 \\ -2 & 4 \\ -6 & 0 \end{bmatrix}$, $k = .1$

4. $A = \begin{bmatrix} -2 & 4 \\ 3 & 1 \\ 6 & -6 \end{bmatrix}$, $B = \begin{bmatrix} -3 & -2 \\ 4 & 7 \\ -4 & 5 \end{bmatrix}$, $k = .5$

5. $A = \begin{bmatrix} 4 & 6 & -3 \\ 5 & -2 & 0 \end{bmatrix}$, $B = \begin{bmatrix} 7 & 2 & 8 \\ 3 & -4 & 9 \end{bmatrix}$, $k = 10$

6. $A = [2 \quad 3 \quad 4]$, $B = [1 \quad -1 \quad 6]$, $k = -2$

7. $A = \begin{bmatrix} 0 & 1 & 0 & 1 \\ 1 & 0 & 1 & 0 \\ 0 & 1 & 0 & 1 \end{bmatrix}$,

$B = \begin{bmatrix} 1 & 0 & 1 & 0 \\ 0 & 1 & 0 & 1 \\ 0 & 0 & 1 & 0 \end{bmatrix}$, $k = -1$

8. $A = \begin{bmatrix} 1 \\ 2 \end{bmatrix}$, $B = \begin{bmatrix} 2 \\ 1 \end{bmatrix}$, $k = 0$

9. $A = \begin{bmatrix} 1 & 2 & 3 \\ 4 & 5 & 6 \\ 7 & 8 & 9 \end{bmatrix}$, $B = \begin{bmatrix} 0 & 0 & 0 \\ 0 & 0 & 0 \\ 0 & 0 & 0 \end{bmatrix}$, $k = .01$

10. $A = \begin{bmatrix} 2 & 3 & 4 & 5 \\ 5 & 4 & 3 & 2 \end{bmatrix}$,

$B = \begin{bmatrix} -2 & -3 & -4 & -5 \\ -5 & -4 & -3 & -2 \end{bmatrix}$, $k = -10$

In Exercises 11–16 find the inner product XY for the given vectors X and Y.

11. $X = [2 \quad 1]$, $Y = \begin{bmatrix} -3 \\ 5 \end{bmatrix}$

12. $X = [-1 \quad 4]$, $Y = \begin{bmatrix} -2 \\ -1 \end{bmatrix}$

13. $X = [1 \quad -1 \quad 5]$, $Y = \begin{bmatrix} 8 \\ 3 \\ -1 \end{bmatrix}$

14. $X = [2 \quad 1 \quad -3]$, $\quad Y = \begin{bmatrix} -5 \\ 7 \\ -2 \end{bmatrix}$

15. $X = [1 \quad 3 \quad 2 \quad -4]$, $\quad Y = \begin{bmatrix} -2 \\ -1 \\ 0 \\ 1 \end{bmatrix}$

16. $X = [3 \quad 5 \quad 7 \quad 9]$, $\quad Y = \begin{bmatrix} 2 \\ -4 \\ 6 \\ -8 \end{bmatrix}$

For the matrices A and B given in Exercises 17–26, form the products AB and BA whenever they are defined.

17. $A = \begin{bmatrix} 5 & -2 \\ 4 & 1 \end{bmatrix}$, $\quad B = \begin{bmatrix} 0 & 1 \\ 3 & 6 \end{bmatrix}$

18. $A = \begin{bmatrix} 2 & -1 \\ -2 & 5 \end{bmatrix}$, $\quad B = \begin{bmatrix} 3 & 4 \\ 2 & -1 \end{bmatrix}$

19. $A = \begin{bmatrix} 1 & -4 & 7 \\ 3 & 0 & 2 \end{bmatrix}$, $\quad B = \begin{bmatrix} 4 & 5 \\ 3 & -1 \\ -2 & 8 \end{bmatrix}$

20. $A = \begin{bmatrix} 3 & -2 \\ 5 & 9 \\ 1 & 4 \end{bmatrix}$, $\quad B = \begin{bmatrix} 0 & 7 & 2 \\ 1 & -6 & 8 \end{bmatrix}$

21. $A = \begin{bmatrix} 4 & 1 & 2 \\ 2 & 0 & 1 \\ 3 & -1 & 2 \end{bmatrix}$, $\quad B = \begin{bmatrix} 1 \\ 4 \\ -2 \end{bmatrix}$

22. $A = \begin{bmatrix} 4 & 2 & 9 \\ 3 & 1 & -2 \end{bmatrix}$, $\quad B = \begin{bmatrix} 2 \\ -3 \\ 5 \end{bmatrix}$

23. $A = \begin{bmatrix} 4 \\ 2 \end{bmatrix}$, $\quad B = \begin{bmatrix} 5 & -3 \\ 2 & 6 \\ 1 & 8 \end{bmatrix}$

24. $A = \begin{bmatrix} 8 & -1 \\ 2 & 5 \end{bmatrix}$, $\quad B = \begin{bmatrix} 3 \\ 5 \end{bmatrix}$

25. $A = \begin{bmatrix} 3 & 2 & 1 \\ 1 & 0 & 1 \\ 4 & -8 & 9 \end{bmatrix}$, $\quad B = \begin{bmatrix} 5 & 6 \\ 3 & -7 \end{bmatrix}$

26. $A = \begin{bmatrix} 5 & 7 \\ 2 & 8 \end{bmatrix}$, $\quad B = [2 \quad 3 \quad -5]$

27. Sales of various 8-ft boards at Mortise Lumber during June are recorded in matrix J:

	$1 \times 4s$	$1 \times 6s$	$1 \times 8s$	$2 \times 4s$	$2 \times 6s$	
	20	4	0	8	12	Ash
	30	24	12	0	0	Cedar
$J =$	10	0	0	90	50	Fir
	80	75	60	8	12	Pine
	40	10	2	0	0	Walnut

Similar sales for the month of May are listed in matrix M:

$$M = \begin{bmatrix} 15 & 3 & 0 & 5 & 8 \\ 22 & 20 & 10 & 0 & 0 \\ 8 & 0 & 0 & 70 & 40 \\ 75 & 80 & 50 & 6 & 10 \\ 30 & 10 & 3 & 0 & 0 \end{bmatrix}$$

Use matrix addition to find $J + M$, the matrix of total sales for May and June. Use matrix subtraction to find $J - M$, and if demand is estimated to increase by 10% from June to July for all lumber products, use scalar multiplication to form an estimated sales matrix for July.

28. Travel expenses for five employees during September are recorded in matrix S:

	Lodging	Meals	Transportation	Misc.	
	350	120	800	180	Adams
	500	300	1400	320	Brown
$S =$	200	80	300	50	Clark
	400	160	1000	200	Davis
	600	360	1600	380	Evans

Similar travel expenses for November are listed in matrix N:

$$N = \begin{bmatrix} 300 & 100 & 700 & 150 \\ 400 & 250 & 1000 & 300 \\ 220 & 100 & 500 & 80 \\ 700 & 380 & 1800 & 500 \\ 500 & 320 & 1200 & 350 \end{bmatrix}.$$

Form a matrix of average travel expenses for these two months by computing $.5(S + N)$. Compare this matrix to the matrix $.5S + .5N$. [For any constant k and any pair of matrices A and B with the same dimension, it can be shown that $k(A + B) = kA + kB$.]

29. Unit prices of staple food products (during January) at various cities are listed in matrix A:

	Bread	Coffee	Ground Beef	Milk	Oranges	Peanut Butter	
	1.30	1.20	1.90	.80	2.00	.90	Atlanta
	1.50	1.30	2.20	.90	2.60	1.10	Boston
$A =$	1.20	1.20	1.60	.70	2.50	1.00	Chicago
	1.10	1.00	1.50	.80	2.00	1.00	Dallas
	1.40	1.10	2.00	.90	2.00	1.20	Seattle

The monthly consumption of staple food products by a family of four (measured in the appropriate units) is listed in vector V:

$$V = \begin{bmatrix} 8 \\ 3 \\ 12 \\ 20 \\ 5 \\ 2 \end{bmatrix} \begin{array}{l} \text{Bread (loaves)} \\ \text{Coffee (pounds)} \\ \text{Ground Beef (pounds)} \\ \text{Milk (quarts)} \\ \text{Oranges (dozen)} \\ \text{Peanut Butter (pounds)} \end{array}$$

Find the matrix whose entries represent the total monthly expenditure by a family of four (in each of the five cities) for staple food products, by computing the product AV.

30. Refer to Exercise 29. In addition to families of size four, matrix C details the consumption of staple food products by families of size three, five, and six:

Family Size:

	Three	Four	Five	Six	
	6	8	10	12	Bread
	2	3	4	5	Coffee
$C =$	10	12	15	19	Ground Beef
	16	20	25	30	Milk
	4	5	7	8	Oranges
	2	2	3	4	Peanut Butter

Form the product AC and explain what the entries of this matrix represent.

31. Quality Construction Company uses estimation matrix E for bidding on jobs. The entries of the matrix represent per-unit prices for "rough in" or complete projects. Units vary among the types of work but include such things as square feet of floor space, number of electrical outlets, and number of sewer openings.

	Carpentry	Electrical	Plumbing	Painting	
$E =$	10	15	25	0	Rough In
	18	20	32	8	Complete

This week the estimator visited five job sites and determined that the units listed in matrix U would be needed for each project:

	Job 1	Job 2	Job 3	Job 4	Job 5	
	1000	1200	800	600	400	Carpentry
$U =$	1000	800	600	500	300	Electrical
	700	500	300	250	200	Plumbing
	800	600	300	400	500	Painting

Form the matrix product EU to obtain the rough in and complete job bids. Label the rows and columns of this matrix.

32. Refer to Exercise 27. Mortise Lumber has decided to sell boards by pricing them per unit volume. An 8-ft, 1×4 board has volume 2/9 cu ft, and 8-ft 1×6 has volume 1/3 cu ft, and so on. Vector V contains these conversion factors:

Cubic Feet

$$V = \begin{bmatrix} 2/9 \\ 1/3 \\ 4/9 \\ 4/9 \\ 2/3 \end{bmatrix} \begin{array}{l} 1'' \times 4'' \times 8' \\ 1'' \times 6'' \times 8' \\ 1'' \times 8'' \times 8' \\ 2'' \times 4'' \times 8' \\ 2'' \times 6'' \times 8' \end{array}$$

Compute JV to obtain a column vector that contains the cubic feet of each type of lumber sold during June. The selling price (in dollars) per cubic foot for each type of lumber is given in row vector P:

	Ash	Cedar	Fir	Pine	Walnut
$P =$	[27	27	18	18	72].

Compute the inner product $P(JV)$ to determine the revenue from the sale of this lumber. Also compute PJ and then $(PJ)V$ and compare the result to $P(JV)$. [For any three matrices A, B, and C, it can be shown that $A(BC) = (AB)C$, whenever these products are defined.]

33. Three manufacturers, Alpha, Beta, and Gamma, dominate the personal computer market. Matrix S lists the share of the market held by each company in three different geographic regions:

	Region 1	Region 2	Region 3	
	.60	.50	.40	Alpha
$S =$	.20	.30	.40	Beta
	.10	.15	.05	Gamma
	.10	.05	.15	Others

If vectors A and M represent total personal computer sales by region for April and May, respectively, find the individual sales for each manufacturer by forming the matrix products SA and SM.

$$A = \begin{bmatrix} 800 \\ 500 \\ 600 \end{bmatrix} \quad \text{and} \quad M = \begin{bmatrix} 900 \\ 400 \\ 500 \end{bmatrix}.$$

34. Refer to Exercise 33. Find the individual sales for each of the three companies for both April and May by computing $SA + SM$. Compare this matrix to $S(A + M)$. [For any three matrices A, B, and C, it can be shown that $A(B + C) = AB + AC$ so long as the matrix products are defined.]

11.2
Matrices and Systems of Linear Equations

Systems of linear equations can be conveniently represented using matrix notation and operations. In this section theoretical solutions to systems of linear equations are considered. Then in the next section a practical solution scheme is presented.

In Section 1.2 the general form for the equation of a line was given as

(11.2)
$$ax + by = c,$$

where a, b, and c are constants. Because the graph of all pairs (x, y) that satisfy equation (11.2) is a line, the equation is said to be **linear** in the variables x and y. Generally, a **linear equation** in the n variables $x_1, x_2, \ldots, x_n$ can be written in the form

(11.3)
$$a_1 x_1 + a_2 x_2 + \cdots + a_n x_n = b$$

for some constants $a_1, a_2, \ldots, a_n, b$. The constants $a_1, \ldots, a_n$ are called **coefficients**, while b is called the **constant term** of the equation.

Notice that the left side of equation (11.3) is an inner product. If A is taken as a row vector containing the coefficients of equation (11.3) and X represents a column vector containing the variables—that is,

$$A = [a_1 \quad a_2 \ldots a_n] \quad \text{and} \quad X = \begin{bmatrix} x_1 \\ \vdots \\ x_n \end{bmatrix},$$

then the matrix form of equation (11.3) is

(11.4)
$$AX = b.$$

A **system of linear equations** is a collection of two or more equations in the form of equation (11.3), all involving the same variables. Each equation in a system can have different coefficients. Double subscripts are used on each coefficient to identify both the equation in which it is used and the variable it multiplies. A system of m linear equations in the n variables $x_1, \ldots, x_n$ can be written as

(11.5)
$$\begin{aligned}
a_{11} x_1 + a_{12} x_2 + \cdots + a_{1n} x_n &= b_1 \\
a_{21} x_1 + a_{22} x_2 + \cdots + a_{2n} x_n &= b_2 \\
\vdots \qquad \vdots \qquad\qquad \vdots \qquad\; \vdots \\
a_{m1} x_1 + a_{m2} x_2 + \cdots + a_{mn} x_n &= b_m.
\end{aligned}$$

Notice that a_{ij} is the coefficient of x_j in equation i, while b_i is the constant term in that equation.

The system of linear equations, or linear system, shown in (11.5) can be written in matrix form in the same way that the single equation (11.3) was converted to matrix form (11.4). If A represents the $m \times n$ matrix of coefficients a_{ij}, B represents a column vector containing the constant terms, and, as before, X is the column of variables, then system (11.5) has **matrix form**

(11.6)
$$AX = B.$$

A linear system of m equations in n variables has an $m \times n$ coefficient matrix and thus is called an $m \times n$ **system**. When $m = n$ the system is said to be **square**.

In this section we will consider only square systems. Nonsquare systems are treated in Section 11.4.

EXAMPLE 1

Determine matrices A, X, and B so that the given linear systems can be written in matrix form (11.6):

a. $2x + 3y = 5$

    $4x - y = 7$

b. $6x_1 - 2x_2 + 3x_3 = 9$

    $x_1 + 2x_2 - x_3 = 0$

    $-x_1 + 4x_3 = -1$

SOLUTION

a. Referring to system (11.5), we find that $a_{11} = 2$, $a_{12} = 3$, $a_{21} = 4$, and $a_{22} = -1$. Thus if

$$A = \begin{bmatrix} 2 & 3 \\ 4 & -1 \end{bmatrix}, \quad X = \begin{bmatrix} x \\ y \end{bmatrix}, \quad \text{and} \quad B = \begin{bmatrix} 5 \\ 7 \end{bmatrix},$$

this linear system can be written as $AX = B$—specifically,

$$\begin{bmatrix} 2 & 3 \\ 4 & -1 \end{bmatrix}\begin{bmatrix} x \\ y \end{bmatrix} = \begin{bmatrix} 5 \\ 7 \end{bmatrix}.$$

b. Again matching the coefficients of this system with those in the general system (11.5), we obtain the matrix form

$$\underset{A}{\begin{bmatrix} 6 & -2 & 3 \\ 1 & 2 & -1 \\ -1 & 0 & 4 \end{bmatrix}}\underset{X}{\begin{bmatrix} x_1 \\ x_2 \\ x_3 \end{bmatrix}} = \underset{B}{\begin{bmatrix} 9 \\ 0 \\ -1 \end{bmatrix}}.$$

Notice that since x_2 does not appear in the third equation, a_{32} is taken to be 0. ●

EXAMPLE 2

Convert the matrix equation to the form of system (11.5):

$$\underset{A}{\begin{bmatrix} 1 & 0 & 5 \\ 2 & -3 & 8 \\ 6 & 2 & -2 \end{bmatrix}}\underset{X}{\begin{bmatrix} x \\ y \\ z \end{bmatrix}} = \underset{B}{\begin{bmatrix} 7 \\ 4 \\ -3 \end{bmatrix}}.$$

SOLUTION

Noting that this is a matrix multiplication problem, we form inner products to obtain

$$\begin{bmatrix} (1)x + (0)y + (5)z \\ (2)x + (-3)y + (8)z \\ (6)x + (2)y + (-2)z \end{bmatrix} = \begin{bmatrix} 7 \\ 4 \\ -3 \end{bmatrix}.$$

Now these two 3×1 matrices are equal if and only if all of their corresponding entries are equal; thus, we have

$$x \qquad + 5z = 7$$
$$2x - 3y + 8z = 4$$
$$6x + 2y - 2z = -3.$$

Recall that a solution to equation (11.3) for given $a_1, \ldots, a_n$, and b is a vector of values for the variables $x_1, \ldots, x_n$ that makes equation (11.3) a true statement (satisfies the equation). A **solution** to the system of linear equations (11.5) is a vector of values for these variables that satisfy all equations in the system simultaneously.

EXAMPLE 3

Show that $\begin{bmatrix} 2 \\ -3 \\ 5 \end{bmatrix}$ is a solution to the linear system

$$x - y - z = 0$$
$$5x + y - z = 2$$
$$3x + 2y + z = 5.$$

SOLUTION

If $x = 2$, $y = -3$, and $z = 5$, then the first equation of the system becomes

$$2 - (-3) - 5 = 0,$$

the second becomes

$$5(2) + (-3) - 5 = 2,$$

and the third becomes

$$3(2) + 2(-3) + 5 = 5.$$

Since all three of these statements are true, $x = 2$, $y = -3$, and $z = 5$ is a solution to the system. In matrix form

$$\underset{A}{\begin{bmatrix} 1 & -1 & -1 \\ 5 & 1 & -1 \\ 3 & 2 & 1 \end{bmatrix}} \underset{X}{\begin{bmatrix} 2 \\ -3 \\ 5 \end{bmatrix}} = \underset{B}{\begin{bmatrix} 0 \\ 2 \\ 5 \end{bmatrix}}$$

is a true statement for this selection of the vector X.

Two special types of matrices, **identities** and **inverses**, are important in developing theoretical solutions to square linear systems.

Definition 11.4

The $n \times n$ **identity matrix**, denoted I, has entries e_{ij} where $e_{ii} = 1$ and $e_{ij} = 0$ when $i \neq j$. That is,

$$I = \begin{bmatrix} 1 & 0 & 0 & 0 & \cdots & 0 \\ 0 & 1 & 0 & 0 & \cdots & 0 \\ 0 & 0 & 1 & 0 & \cdots & 0 \\ \cdot & \cdot & \cdot & \cdot & \cdots & \cdot \\ 0 & 0 & 0 & 0 & \cdots & 1 \end{bmatrix}.$$

The identity matrix behaves under matrix multiplication as one behaves with respect to ordinary multiplication. If I is the $n \times n$ identity matrix and A is any other $n \times n$ matrix, then

(11.7)
$$AI = A \quad \text{and} \quad IA = A.$$

Definition 11.5

> If A is an $n \times n$ matrix, then an **inverse** of A, denoted A^{-1}, is another $n \times n$ matrix such that
>
> (11.8)
> $$AA^{-1} = I \quad \text{and} \quad A^{-1}A = I,$$
>
> where I is the $n \times n$ identity matrix. If A has an inverse, then A is said to be an **invertible** matrix.

An inverse matrix behaves under matrix multiplication as a reciprocal behaves with respect to ordinary multiplication. Not all square matrices have inverses, but when a matrix has an inverse it has exactly one. These and other details are left for the exercises. Next we show that an inverse can be used to solve a square linear system.

Remember that to solve the linear equation

$$ax = b,$$

when a and b are constants, we divide by a (or multiply by the reciprocal of a), when a is not 0, to obtain

$$x = \frac{b}{a} = a^{-1}b.$$

Starting with a square linear system such as (11.6):

$$AX = B,$$

if A^{-1} were available, both sides of this matrix equation could be multiplied by A^{-1} to obtain

$$A^{-1}AX = A^{-1}B.$$

But $A^{-1}A = I$ and $IX = X$; thus, we have

$$IX = A^{-1}B$$

or

(11.9)
$$X = A^{-1}B,$$

which is a solution to the system (11.6). In fact, this is the only solution to system (11.6) when A^{-1} exists because if both X and Y satisfy equation (11.6), then proceeding as above, $AX = B$ and $AY = B$ can be converted to $X = A^{-1}B$ and $Y = A^{-1}B$ and so $X = Y$. We may conclude that a square linear system has a unique solution when the coefficient matrix has an inverse.

Although $a^{-1}b = b/a$ for real numbers a and b, $A^{-1}B \neq B/A$. Matrix division is not defined.

EXAMPLE 4

Show that if

$$A = \begin{bmatrix} 3 & 8 \\ 2 & 5 \end{bmatrix}, \quad \text{then} \quad A^{-1} = \begin{bmatrix} -5 & 8 \\ 2 & -3 \end{bmatrix}.$$

Use this fact to solve the linear system

$$3x + 8y = 2$$
$$2x + 5y = 2.$$

SOLUTION

Multiplying the two matrices, we find

$$\begin{bmatrix} 3 & 8 \\ 2 & 5 \end{bmatrix} \begin{bmatrix} -5 & 8 \\ 2 & -3 \end{bmatrix} = \begin{bmatrix} 1 & 0 \\ 0 & 1 \end{bmatrix}$$

and

$$\begin{bmatrix} -5 & 8 \\ 2 & -3 \end{bmatrix} \begin{bmatrix} 3 & 8 \\ 2 & 5 \end{bmatrix} = \begin{bmatrix} 1 & 0 \\ 0 & 1 \end{bmatrix},$$

so the matrices are inverses. The linear system takes the form $AX = B$ if

$$B = \begin{bmatrix} 2 \\ 2 \end{bmatrix}.$$

Using equation (11.9),

$$X = \begin{bmatrix} -5 & 8 \\ 2 & -3 \end{bmatrix} \begin{bmatrix} 2 \\ 2 \end{bmatrix} = \begin{bmatrix} 6 \\ -2 \end{bmatrix}$$

is the unique solution to this system; that is, $x = 6$ and $y = -2$ are the only values of x and y that satisfy both equations in the system simultaneously. ●

Although inverse matrices can be used to solve certain linear systems, this is a very inefficient procedure. In Section 11.3, we shall see that finding a matrix inverse requires more computation than solving the linear system directly.

The inverse matrix given in Example 4 can be found using the following theorem.

Theorem 11.1

If

$$A = \begin{bmatrix} a_{11} & a_{12} \\ a_{21} & a_{22} \end{bmatrix},$$

and if $d = a_{11}a_{22} - a_{12}a_{21}$, then A^{-1} exists and is given by

(11.10) $$A^{-1} = \frac{1}{d} \begin{bmatrix} a_{22} & -a_{12} \\ -a_{21} & a_{11} \end{bmatrix}$$

whenever $d \neq 0$.

Proof: We verify $A^{-1}A = I$ and leave $AA^{-1} = I$ as an exercise. Forming the necessary inner products, we find:

$$\begin{bmatrix} a_{22} & -a_{12} \\ -a_{21} & a_{11} \end{bmatrix} \begin{bmatrix} a_{11} & a_{12} \\ a_{21} & a_{22} \end{bmatrix} = \begin{bmatrix} (a_{22}a_{11} - a_{12}a_{21}) & (a_{22}a_{12} - a_{12}a_{22}) \\ (-a_{21}a_{11} + a_{11}a_{21}) & (-a_{21}a_{12} + a_{11}a_{22}) \end{bmatrix}$$

$$= \begin{bmatrix} d & 0 \\ 0 & d \end{bmatrix}.$$

Thus from equation (11.10) we have

$$A^{-1}A = \frac{1}{d} \begin{bmatrix} a_{22} & -a_{12} \\ -a_{21} & a_{11} \end{bmatrix} \begin{bmatrix} a_{11} & a_{12} \\ a_{21} & a_{22} \end{bmatrix} = \frac{1}{d} \begin{bmatrix} d & 0 \\ 0 & d \end{bmatrix}$$

$$= \begin{bmatrix} 1 & 0 \\ 0 & 1 \end{bmatrix},$$

as required.

EXAMPLE 5

Use Theorem 11.1, if it applies, to find the inverse of each of the given matrices:

a. $\begin{bmatrix} 3 & 4 \\ 1 & 2 \end{bmatrix}$ b. $\begin{bmatrix} 2 & 3 \\ 4 & 6 \end{bmatrix}$

SOLUTION

a. $d = (3)(2) - (4)(1) = 2$, so from equation (11.10),

$$\begin{bmatrix} 3 & 4 \\ 1 & 2 \end{bmatrix}^{-1} = \frac{1}{2} \begin{bmatrix} 2 & -4 \\ -1 & 3 \end{bmatrix} = \begin{bmatrix} 1 & -2 \\ -1/2 & 3/2 \end{bmatrix}.$$

b. $d = (2)(6) - (4)(3) = 0$, so Theorem 11.1 does not apply.

The value $d = a_{11}a_{22} - a_{12}a_{21}$ is called the **determinant** of the 2×2 matrix.

$$A = \begin{bmatrix} a_{11} & a_{12} \\ a_{21} & a_{22} \end{bmatrix}.$$

Theorem 11.1 shows that A^{-1} exists if its determinant is not 0. By considering the geometry of 2×2 linear systems, we can determine that A^{-1} *exists if and only if its determinant is not 0*. So the value of d "determines" whether or not A has an inverse.

Geometrically, the 2×2 linear system

(11.11)
$$\begin{aligned} a_{11}x + a_{12}y &= b_1 \\ a_{21}x + a_{22}y &= b_2 \end{aligned}$$

consists of two lines in the x–y coordinate plane. As illustrated in Figure 11.2, these lines may (a) intersect in a point, (b) coincide, or (c) be parallel. Because intersections of the lines represent solutions to system (11.11), these configurations correspond to three solution possibilities for a 2×2 linear system: in case a the system has a **unique solution**, in case b it has **infinitely many solutions**, and in case c it has **no solution**. In the latter cases, if A is the coefficient matrix of system

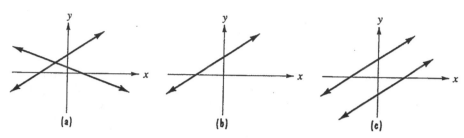

Figure 11.2

The three possible configurations for
two lines in a plane

(a)   (b)   (c)

(11.11), then A^{-1} cannot exist, for if A^{-1} exists we have seen that the system has a solution but only one solution. By comparing the slopes of the lines it can be shown that the determinant of A is 0 in cases b and c. (See Exercises 36 and 38.)

It can be shown that any $m \times n$ system of linear equations has the same solution possibilities: a unique solution, infinitely many solutions, or no solution. In particular, if the system $AX = B$ is square, then the coefficient matrix A has a determinant; if the determinant is not 0, then A^{-1} exists and the system has a unique solution. Determinants of $n \times n$ matrices are considered in Section 11.6.

EXERCISES 11.2

Specify matrices A, X, and B so that each system of linear equations in Exercises 1–10 can be written in matrix form AX = B.

1. $2x - 3y = 7$
   $4x + y = 8$

2. $3x + 5y = 6$
   $x - 9y = 0$

3. $x_1 + 3x_2 - 5x_3 = 3$
   $3x_1 + 6x_2 + x_3 = 8$
   $5x_1 - 3x_2 = 4$

4. $2x_1 - x_2 + 4x_3 = 3$
   $-x_1 + 7x_2 - 2x_3 = 12$
   $6x_1 + 7x_3 = -3$

5. $x + 8z = -2$
   $2x - 3y - 8z = 14$

6. $5x + 2y = -4$
   $-4x + 3y = 6$
   $x - 8y = 0$

7. $2x + 8y = -3$
   $-3x - 5y = 8$
   $6x + y = 12$
   $x - 2y = 0$

8. $3x + 2y - 5z = 18$
   $2x - 4y = 7$

9. $x_1 + 3x_2 - 4x_3 + 2x_4 = 21$
   $-x_1 - 4x_2 + 7x_4 = -8$
   $2x_1 + 5x_2 - 3x_3 + 6x_4 = 3$
   $6x_1 - 4x_2 + 5x_3 = 10$

10. $-3x + 4y - 5z + w = 4$
    $x - 3y + 5w = 0$
    $5x - 2y + 3z - w = 7$
    $2x + 5y - 6z - 4w = 8$

In Exercises 11–16 write each matrix equation as a system of linear equations.

11. $\begin{bmatrix} 3 & 5 \\ 7 & -2 \end{bmatrix} \begin{bmatrix} x \\ y \end{bmatrix} = \begin{bmatrix} 8 \\ 6 \end{bmatrix}$

12. $\begin{bmatrix} 1 & 0 \\ 3 & 5 \end{bmatrix} \begin{bmatrix} u \\ v \end{bmatrix} = \begin{bmatrix} -3 \\ 9 \end{bmatrix}$

13. $\begin{bmatrix} 2 & 4 & 5 & -1 \\ 3 & -2 & 0 & 8 \\ 1 & 0 & -7 & 9 \end{bmatrix} \begin{bmatrix} x \\ y \\ z \\ w \end{bmatrix} = \begin{bmatrix} -7 \\ 13 \\ 6 \end{bmatrix}$

14. $\begin{bmatrix} 2 & 3 & -4 \\ -3 & 5 & 2 \\ 0 & -6 & 1 \\ 7 & 3 & 9 \end{bmatrix} \begin{bmatrix} x_1 \\ x_2 \\ x_3 \end{bmatrix} = \begin{bmatrix} 1 \\ 0 \\ 2 \\ 3 \end{bmatrix}$

15. $\begin{bmatrix} 1 & 0 & 1 \\ 2 & -1 & 5 \\ 3 & 4 & 0 \end{bmatrix} \begin{bmatrix} x_1 \\ x_2 \\ x_3 \end{bmatrix} = \begin{bmatrix} -3 \\ 8 \\ -6 \end{bmatrix}$

16. $\begin{bmatrix} 0 & 5 & 6 & 0 \\ 1 & -2 & 3 & -5 \\ 6 & 0 & 0 & 8 \\ -3 & -1 & 7 & 9 \end{bmatrix} \begin{bmatrix} x \\ y \\ z \\ w \end{bmatrix} = \begin{bmatrix} -11 \\ 25 \\ 4 \\ 20 \end{bmatrix}$

Verify that the matrices A and B in Exercises 17–22 are inverses by showing that $AB = I$ and $BA = I$.

17. $A = \begin{bmatrix} 5 & 7 \\ 2 & 3 \end{bmatrix}$, $B = \begin{bmatrix} 3 & -7 \\ -2 & 5 \end{bmatrix}$

18. $A = \begin{bmatrix} 3 & 2 \\ 2 & -2 \end{bmatrix}$, $B = \begin{bmatrix} .2 & .2 \\ .2 & -.3 \end{bmatrix}$

19. $A = \begin{bmatrix} 1 & 2 & -1 \\ 0 & 1 & 3 \\ 1 & 2 & 0 \end{bmatrix}$, $B = \begin{bmatrix} -6 & -2 & 7 \\ 3 & 1 & -3 \\ -1 & 0 & 1 \end{bmatrix}$

20. $A = \begin{bmatrix} 1 & 1 & -1 \\ 4 & -1 & 3 \\ 1 & 3 & -4 \end{bmatrix}$, $B = \begin{bmatrix} -5 & 1 & 2 \\ 19 & -3 & -7 \\ 13 & -2 & -5 \end{bmatrix}$

21. $A = \begin{bmatrix} 5 & 0 & 1 \\ 2 & -1 & 3 \\ 4 & 1 & -2 \end{bmatrix}$, $B = \begin{bmatrix} -1 & 1 & 1 \\ 16 & -14 & -13 \\ 6 & -5 & -5 \end{bmatrix}$

22. $A = \begin{bmatrix} 1 & 2 & 3 & 4 \\ 0 & 1 & -1 & 2 \\ 0 & 0 & 1 & 5 \\ 0 & 0 & 0 & 1 \end{bmatrix}$, $B = \begin{bmatrix} 1 & -2 & -5 & 25 \\ 0 & 1 & 1 & -7 \\ 0 & 0 & 1 & -5 \\ 0 & 0 & 0 & 1 \end{bmatrix}$

23. Use an inverse matrix given in Exercise 17 to solve the linear system:
$$5x_1 + 7x_2 = 8$$
$$2x_1 + 3x_2 = 3.$$

24. Use an inverse matrix given in Exercise 18 to solve the linear system:
$$3x + 2y = -5$$
$$2x - 2y = 9.$$

25. Use an inverse matrix given in Exercise 19 to solve the linear system:
$$x + 2y - z = -7$$
$$y + 3z = 13$$
$$x + 2y = -2.$$

26. Use an inverse matrix given in Exercise 20 to solve the linear system:
$$x_1 + x_2 - x_3 = 5$$
$$4x_1 - x_2 + 3x_3 = 38$$
$$x_1 + 3x_2 - 4x_3 = -3.$$

27. Use an inverse matrix given in Exercise 21 to solve the linear system:

$$-x_1 + x_2 + x_3 = 2$$
$$16x_1 - 14x_2 - 13x_3 = -17$$
$$6x_1 - 5x_2 - 5x_3 = -5.$$

28. Use an inverse matrix given in Exercise 22 to solve the linear system:
$$x - 2y - 5z + 25w = 11$$
$$y + z - 7w = -1$$
$$z - 5w = -2$$
$$w = 0.$$

For the matrices in Exercises 29–34 find the determinant and the inverse (if it exists).

29. $\begin{bmatrix} 8 & 5 \\ 3 & 2 \end{bmatrix}$

30. $\begin{bmatrix} 1 & -2 \\ 3 & -5 \end{bmatrix}$

31. $\begin{bmatrix} 5 & 4 \\ -2 & -2 \end{bmatrix}$

32. $\begin{bmatrix} 1 & 2 \\ 3 & 4 \end{bmatrix}$

33. $\begin{bmatrix} 8 & 4 \\ 6 & 3 \end{bmatrix}$

34. $\begin{bmatrix} 4 & 2 \\ 6 & 3 \end{bmatrix}$

35. Compute the product
$$\begin{bmatrix} a_{11} & a_{12} \\ a_{21} & a_{22} \end{bmatrix} \begin{bmatrix} a_{22} & -a_{12} \\ -a_{21} & a_{11} \end{bmatrix}$$
and complete the proof of Theorem 11.1.

36. Assuming that the lines in system (11.11) are not vertical, find their slopes m_1 and m_2 in terms of a_{11}, a_{12}, a_{21}, and a_{22}. In cases b and c the lines have the same slope. Starting with $m_1 = m_2$ show that the determinant of A is 0.

37. Show that a square matrix A has at most one inverse by assuming that B and C are both inverses of A and then by considering the products $B(AC)$ and $(BA)C$.

38. Refer to Exercise 36. If both lines in system (11.11) are vertical, show that the determinant of A is 0.

39. For the linear system
$$\begin{bmatrix} 1 & 2 \\ 3 & a \end{bmatrix} \begin{bmatrix} x \\ y \end{bmatrix} = \begin{bmatrix} 1 \\ b \end{bmatrix},$$
give values of a and b so that the system has (a) a unique solution, (b) infinitely many solutions, and (c) no solution.

40. Refer to Exercise 39. Sketch the graphs of the lines that result from your choices of a and b in parts a, b, and c.

11.3
Augmented Matrices and the Reduction Method

Realizing that a system of linear equations can have one solution, infinitely many solutions, or no solution, we now consider an efficient scheme for finding solutions when they exist. In this section we treat **square systems** with a **unique solution**, leaving the more general case for the next section.

Certain linear systems are in a form that makes them easy to solve. Triangular systems are a case in point. A system is in **upper-triangular form** if the last equation involves only the last variable, the next to last equation involves at most the last two variables, the equation before that involves at most the last three variables, and so on. The following example illustrates how **back-substitution** may be used to solve upper-triangular systems.

EXAMPLE 1

Solve the following linear system:

$$
\begin{aligned}
x - 2y - 5z + 25w &= 11 \\
y + z - 7w &= -1 \\
z - 5w &= -2 \\
w &= 0.
\end{aligned}
$$

SOLUTION

Note that the given system is in upper-triangular form because the last equation involves only w, the next to last involves only w and z, and so on. In this form the last equation is solved for the last variable—that is, $w = 0$. Using this value for w in the preceding equation, we find

$$z - 5(0) = -2,$$

so $z = -2$. Using the values for w and z in the second equation, we have

$$y + (-2) - 7(0) = -1,$$

thus $y = 1$. Now back-substituting the values for w, z, and y into the first equation yields

$$x - 2(1) - 5(-2) + 25(0) = 11,$$

or $x = 3$. Thus the solution to this system is

$$x = 3, \quad y = 1, \quad z = -2, \quad \text{and} \quad w = 0. \qquad \bullet$$

A given linear system may not be in upper-triangular form. To convert a linear system from one form to another without changing the solutions (that is, to create **equivalent** systems), we use the **elementary row operations**. The solutions of a linear system are not altered when the system is changed by:

1. reordering the equations,
2. multiplying an equation by a nonzero constant, or
3. adding a multiple of one equation to another equation.

Addition and multiplication properties of the real numbers may be used to prove that elementary row operations 1, 2, and 3 yield equivalent linear systems. The following example illustrates how these operations may be used to convert a linear system to upper-triangular form.

EXAMPLE 2

Convert the given linear system to upper-triangular form; then find its solution:

$$x + 2y = 2$$
$$3x + 4y = -2.$$

SOLUTION

To be in upper-triangular form the last equation of the given system should involve only y. To eliminate x from the last equation, row operation 3 may be used as follows: multiply the first equation by -3 and add the result to the second equation. The revised second equation is

$$\begin{array}{r} -3x - 6y = -6 \\ 3x + 4y = -2 \\ \hline -2y = -8 \end{array}$$

and so the system

$$x + 2y = 2$$
$$-2y = -8$$

is equivalent to the original system. Finally, multiplying the new second equation by $-1/2$, we have

$$x + 2y = 2$$
$$y = 4.$$

The last equation is solved for y, and if $y = 4$ is substituted into the first equation, we find $x + 2(4) = 2$; thus, $x = -6$. ●

Before carefully specifying the steps in a solution scheme, we again use matrices to store the constants of a linear system. Since the row operations are performed on the coefficients and constant terms of the system, we collect all constants in one matrix and then perform the elementary row operations on the rows of this matrix. The $m \times n$ linear system

(11.12)
$$\begin{array}{cccc} a_{11}x_1 + a_{12}x_2 + \cdots + a_{1n}x_n = b_1 \\ \vdots \qquad \vdots \qquad\qquad \vdots \qquad \vdots \\ a_{m1}x_1 + a_{m2}x_2 + \cdots + a_{mn}x_n = b_m \end{array}$$

can be represented by the $m \times (n + 1)$ matrix

(11.13)
$$[A \mid B] = \begin{bmatrix} a_{11} & a_{12} & \cdots & a_{1n} & \vdots & b_1 \\ \vdots & \vdots & & \vdots & \vdots & \vdots \\ a_{m1} & a_{m2} & \cdots & a_{mn} & \vdots & b_m \end{bmatrix},$$

which is called the **augmented matrix** for system (11.12). In the augmented matrix, the first column contains the coefficients of the first variable, the second column contains the coefficients of the second variable, and so on, with the last column containing the constant terms.

When altering augmented matrices, the symbol $\sim$ (tilde) is used to indicate that two augmented matrices are equivalent—that they represent two linear systems with identical solutions.

EXAMPLE 3

Use augmented matrices to summarize the steps performed in Example 2.

SOLUTION

Referring to Example 2 and equation (11.13), we find

$$\begin{bmatrix} 1 & 2 & | & 2 \\ 3 & 4 & | & -2 \end{bmatrix} \sim \begin{bmatrix} 1 & 2 & | & 2 \\ 0 & -2 & | & -8 \end{bmatrix} \sim \begin{bmatrix} 1 & 2 & | & 2 \\ 0 & 1 & | & 4 \end{bmatrix}. \quad \bullet$$

The **reduction method** is a solution scheme that involves the systematic application of elementary row operations to an augmented matrix until a "reduced" matrix of the form

(11.14)

$$\begin{bmatrix} 1 & * & * & * & \cdots & * & | & * \\ 0 & 1 & * & * & \cdots & * & | & * \\ 0 & 0 & 1 & * & \cdots & * & | & * \\ \vdots & \vdots & \vdots & \vdots & \cdots & \vdots & | & \vdots \\ 0 & 0 & 0 & 0 & \cdots & 1 & | & * \end{bmatrix}$$

is obtained. (The entries denoted by * may be any real number.)

To convert a given square system to the reduced form (11.14) using the reduction method, the following sequence of steps is performed column by column (from first to last).

(11.15)   Within column k, follow these steps:

1. Convert the entry in row k to 1 (multiply row k by a constant, perhaps after interchanging rows).

2. Convert all entries in rows below row k to 0 (multiply row k by a constant and add to the lower row).

The procedure described in steps 1 and 2 is often called "pivoting" about the "diagonal" entries (those entries with the same row and column subscripts). The following example illustrates the use of the reduction method.

EXAMPLE 4

Use the reduction method to solve the system:

$$x_1 - x_2 + 4x_3 = -9$$
$$2x_1 + 2x_2 + 4x_3 = 2$$
$$3x_1 + 6x_2 + 2x_3 = 21.$$

SOLUTION

The augmented matrix for this system is

$$\begin{bmatrix} 1 & -1 & 4 & | & -9 \\ 2 & 2 & 4 & | & 2 \\ 3 & 6 & 2 & | & 21 \end{bmatrix}.$$

Starting with the first column, we see that the entry in the first row is already 1.

SOLUTION   The reduction method is applied to the first column of the augmented matrix as follows:

$$\left[\begin{array}{cccc|c} 1 & -4 & 2 & 5 & 5 \\ 1 & -4 & 0 & 1 & 1 \\ 3 & -8 & 4 & 7 & 7 \\ 2 & -5 & 1 & 2 & 3 \end{array}\right] \sim \left[\begin{array}{cccc|c} 1 & -4 & 2 & 5 & 5 \\ 0 & 0 & -2 & -4 & -4 \\ 0 & 4 & -2 & -8 & -8 \\ 0 & 3 & -3 & -8 & -7 \end{array}\right].$$

Elementary row operations: 1. (-1) (row 1) added to row 2
2. (-3) (row 1) added to row 3
3. (-2) (row 1) added to row 4

Moving to the second column, the entry in row 2 is 0. In order to produce a 1 in this position we must first interchange row 2 with some other (lower) row that has a nonzero entry in column 2. Here row 2 can be interchanged with either row 3 or row 4. We interchange rows 2 and 3, and then multiply the new row 2 by 1/4:

$$\left[\begin{array}{cccc|c} 1 & -4 & 2 & 5 & 5 \\ 0 & 0 & -2 & -4 & -4 \\ 0 & 4 & -2 & -8 & -8 \\ 0 & 3 & -3 & -8 & -7 \end{array}\right] \sim \left[\begin{array}{cccc|c} 1 & -4 & 2 & 5 & 5 \\ 0 & 1 & -1/2 & -2 & -2 \\ 0 & 0 & -2 & -4 & -4 \\ 0 & 3 & -3 & -8 & -7 \end{array}\right].$$

Elementary row operations: 1. Interchange row 2 and row 3
2. $(1/4)$ (row 2)

To complete work on the second column, we add (-3) (row 2) to row 4. Looking ahead to the third column, we also multiply row 3 by $-1/2$:

$$\left[\begin{array}{cccc|c} 1 & -4 & 2 & 5 & 5 \\ 0 & 1 & -1/2 & -2 & -2 \\ 0 & 0 & -2 & -4 & -4 \\ 0 & 3 & -3 & -8 & -7 \end{array}\right] \sim \left[\begin{array}{cccc|c} 1 & -4 & 2 & 5 & 5 \\ 0 & 1 & -1/2 & -2 & -2 \\ 0 & 0 & 1 & 2 & 2 \\ 0 & 0 & -3/2 & -2 & -1 \end{array}\right].$$

Elementary row operations: 1. (-3) (row 2) added to row 4
2. $(-1/2)$ (row 3)

Finally, $-3/2$ is eliminated from the third column to obtain the reduced matrix:

$$\left[\begin{array}{cccc|c} 1 & -4 & 2 & 5 & 5 \\ 0 & 1 & -1/2 & -2 & -2 \\ 0 & 0 & 1 & 2 & 2 \\ 0 & 0 & -3/2 & -2 & -1 \end{array}\right] \sim \left[\begin{array}{cccc|c} 1 & -4 & 2 & 5 & 5 \\ 0 & 1 & -1/2 & -2 & -2 \\ 0 & 0 & 1 & 2 & 2 \\ 0 & 0 & 0 & 1 & 2 \end{array}\right].$$

Elementary row operation: $(3/2)$ (row 3) added to row 4

Back-substituting in the reduced matrix, we find $w = 2$, $z = -2$, $y = 1$, and $x = 3$.   ●

The reduction method can be streamlined a bit by changing step 1 in (11.15). Instead of converting the diagonal entry to 1, we need only be sure that this entry is nonzero so it can be used in the eliminations of step 2. This revision is often made in computer programs for large linear systems; the resulting scheme is called **Gaussian elimination**.

To eliminate the 2 in row 2 (of column 1), we multiply r
row 2. Similarly, to eliminate the 3 in row 3, we multiply
row 3. The resulting equivalent matrix is

$$\begin{bmatrix} 1 & -1 & 4 & | & -9 \\ 0 & 4 & -4 & | & 20 \\ 0 & 9 & -10 & | & 48 \end{bmatrix}.$$

Moving to the second column, the entry in the second row
2 by 1/4 (or divide by 4) to convert this entry to 1. The
row has entries: 0 1 −1 5. To eliminate the 9 in r
revised second row can be multiplied by −9 and added to

$$\begin{bmatrix} 1 & -1 & 4 & | & -9 \\ 0 & 1 & -1 & | & 5 \\ 0 & 0 & -1 & | & 3 \end{bmatrix}.$$

Multiplying row 3 by −1 produces the desired reduced
steps may be summarized by

$$\begin{bmatrix} 1 & -1 & 4 & | & -9 \\ 2 & 2 & 4 & | & 2 \\ 3 & 6 & 2 & | & 21 \end{bmatrix} \sim \begin{bmatrix} 1 & -1 & 4 & | & -9 \\ 0 & 4 & -4 & | & 20 \\ 0 & 9 & -10 & | & 48 \end{bmatrix} \sim \begin{bmatrix} \end{bmatrix}$$

The reduced matrix represents an upper-triangular system
for x_3; that is, $x_3 = -3$. Using this value in row 2 we see
that

$$x_2 - 1(-3) = 5,$$

or $x_2 = 2$. Back-substituting for x_3 and x_2, the first row y

$$x_1 - 1(2) + 4(-3) = -9,$$

so $x_1 = 5$. Thus the solution to the given linear syste
and $x_3 = -3$.

The reduction steps in (11.15) can always be carried
consideration has a unique solution. If the diagonal entry
plying by a constant will never change its value, so ro
changed with some later row where the entry in colum
entries in column k are 0 as well, the system has eithe
many solutions, as we shall see in the next section.

EXAMPLE 5

Solve the linear system

$$\begin{aligned} x - 4y + 2z + 5w &= 5 \\ x - 4y \quad\quad + w &= 1 \\ 3x - 8y + 4z + 7w &= 7 \\ 2x - 5y + z + 2w &= 3. \end{aligned}$$

To eliminate the 2 in row 2 (of column 1), we multiply row 1 by -2 and add to row 2. Similarly, to eliminate the 3 in row 3, we multiply row 1 by -3 and add to row 3. The resulting equivalent matrix is

$$\left[\begin{array}{ccc|c} 1 & -1 & 4 & -9 \\ 0 & 4 & -4 & 20 \\ 0 & 9 & -10 & 48 \end{array}\right].$$

Moving to the second column, the entry in the second row is 4, so we multiply row 2 by 1/4 (or divide by 4) to convert this entry to 1. The resulting revised second row has entries: 0 1 -1 5. To eliminate the 9 in row 3 (of column 2), the revised second row can be multiplied by -9 and added to row 3 to yield:

$$\left[\begin{array}{ccc|c} 1 & -1 & 4 & -9 \\ 0 & 1 & -1 & 5 \\ 0 & 0 & -1 & 3 \end{array}\right].$$

Multiplying row 3 by -1 produces the desired reduced matrix. The elimination steps may be summarized by

$$\left[\begin{array}{ccc|c} 1 & -1 & 4 & -9 \\ 2 & 2 & 4 & 2 \\ 3 & 6 & 2 & 21 \end{array}\right] \sim \left[\begin{array}{ccc|c} 1 & -1 & 4 & -9 \\ 0 & 4 & -4 & 20 \\ 0 & 9 & -10 & 48 \end{array}\right] \sim \left[\begin{array}{ccc|c} 1 & -1 & 4 & -9 \\ 0 & 1 & -1 & 5 \\ 0 & 0 & 1 & -3 \end{array}\right].$$

The reduced matrix represents an upper-triangular system and the last row is solved for x_3; that is, $x_3 = -3$. Using this value in row 2 we see from the reduced matrix that

$$x_2 - 1(-3) = 5,$$

or $x_2 = 2$. Back-substituting for x_3 and x_2, the first row yields

$$x_1 - 1(2) + 4(-3) = -9,$$

so $x_1 = 5$. Thus the solution to the given linear system is $x_1 = 5$, $x_2 = 2$, and $x_3 = -3$. ●

The reduction steps in (11.15) can always be carried out if the system under consideration has a unique solution. If the diagonal entry in column k is 0, multiplying by a constant will never change its value, so row k should first be interchanged with some later row where the entry in column k is not 0. If all later entries in column k are 0 as well, the system has either no solution or infinitely many solutions, as we shall see in the next section.

EXAMPLE 5

Solve the linear system

$$\begin{aligned} x - 4y + 2z + 5w &= 5 \\ x - 4y \qquad\quad + w &= 1 \\ 3x - 8y + 4z + 7w &= 7 \\ 2x - 5y + z + 2w &= 3. \end{aligned}$$

SOLUTION   The reduction method is applied to the first column of the augmented matrix as follows:

$$\left[\begin{array}{cccc|c} 1 & -4 & 2 & 5 & 5 \\ 1 & -4 & 0 & 1 & 1 \\ 3 & -8 & 4 & 7 & 7 \\ 2 & -5 & 1 & 2 & 3 \end{array}\right] \sim \left[\begin{array}{cccc|c} 1 & -4 & 2 & 5 & 5 \\ 0 & 0 & -2 & -4 & -4 \\ 0 & 4 & -2 & -8 & -8 \\ 0 & 3 & -3 & -8 & -7 \end{array}\right].$$

Elementary row operations: 1. (-1) (row 1) added to row 2
2. (-3) (row 1) added to row 3
3. (-2) (row 1) added to row 4

Moving to the second column, the entry in row 2 is 0. In order to produce a 1 in this position we must first interchange row 2 with some other (lower) row that has a nonzero entry in column 2. Here row 2 can be interchanged with either row 3 or row 4. We interchange rows 2 and 3, and then multiply the new row 2 by 1/4:

$$\left[\begin{array}{cccc|c} 1 & -4 & 2 & 5 & 5 \\ 0 & 0 & -2 & -4 & -4 \\ 0 & 4 & -2 & -8 & -8 \\ 0 & 3 & -3 & -8 & -7 \end{array}\right] \sim \left[\begin{array}{cccc|c} 1 & -4 & 2 & 5 & 5 \\ 0 & 1 & -1/2 & -2 & -2 \\ 0 & 0 & -2 & -4 & -4 \\ 0 & 3 & -3 & -8 & -7 \end{array}\right].$$

Elementary row operations: 1. Interchange row 2 and row 3
2. $(1/4)$ (row 2)

To complete work on the second column, we add (-3) (row 2) to row 4. Looking ahead to the third column, we also multiply row 3 by $-1/2$:

$$\left[\begin{array}{cccc|c} 1 & -4 & 2 & 5 & 5 \\ 0 & 1 & -1/2 & -2 & -2 \\ 0 & 0 & -2 & -4 & -4 \\ 0 & 3 & -3 & -8 & -7 \end{array}\right] \sim \left[\begin{array}{cccc|c} 1 & -4 & 2 & 5 & 5 \\ 0 & 1 & -1/2 & -2 & -2 \\ 0 & 0 & 1 & 2 & 2 \\ 0 & 0 & -3/2 & -2 & -1 \end{array}\right].$$

Elementary row operations: 1. (-3) (row 2) added to row 4
2. $(-1/2)$ (row 3)

Finally, $-3/2$ is eliminated from the third column to obtain the reduced matrix:

$$\left[\begin{array}{cccc|c} 1 & -4 & 2 & 5 & 5 \\ 0 & 1 & -1/2 & -2 & -2 \\ 0 & 0 & 1 & 2 & 2 \\ 0 & 0 & -3/2 & -2 & -1 \end{array}\right] \sim \left[\begin{array}{cccc|c} 1 & -4 & 2 & 5 & 5 \\ 0 & 1 & -1/2 & -2 & -2 \\ 0 & 0 & 1 & 2 & 2 \\ 0 & 0 & 0 & 1 & 2 \end{array}\right].$$

Elementary row operation: $(3/2)$ (row 3) added to row 4

Back-substituting in the reduced matrix, we find $w = 2$, $z = -2$, $y = 1$, and $x = 3$. ●

The reduction method can be streamlined a bit by changing step 1 in (11.15). Instead of converting the diagonal entry to 1, we need only be sure that this entry is nonzero so it can be used in the eliminations of step 2. This revision is often made in computer programs for large linear systems; the resulting scheme is called **Gaussian elimination**.

Many software packages are available for solving systems of linear equations on a personal computer. The MATLAB* and Numerical Methods Toolkit[†] packages have been designed using state-of-the-art techniques for controlling round-off error. Many spreadsheet programs, such as Lotus 1-2-3[‡], also have system-solving capabilities.

Another alteration often made in the reduction method (by persons who must solve systems "by hand") is to apply step 2 in (11.15) to rows above row k as well as to those below row k. With this approach, the resulting "reduced" matrix is the identity matrix, so each row is solved for a variable and no back-substitution is needed. This scheme is called **Gauss–Jordan elimination**, and although it is less efficient than the reduction method, it is often used to compute the inverse of a matrix.

To use an elimination scheme to find the inverse of an $n \times n$ matrix A, we reason as follows. If $C_1, C_2, \ldots, C_n$ denote the columns of the identity matrix I, and we solve $AX = C_1$ to find X_1, $AX = C_2$ to find X_2, and so on, then A^{-1} is the matrix with columns $X_1, X_2, \ldots, X_n$. Thus to find A^{-1} we must solve n linear systems $AX = B$ where B is, in turn, each column of I. These systems can all be solved at once starting with the augmented matrix $[A|I]$. If Gauss–Jordan elimination is used we proceed until the matrix $[I|A^{-1}]$ is obtained.

EXAMPLE 6

Find the inverse of the matrix

$$A = \begin{bmatrix} 1 & 1 & -1 \\ 4 & -1 & 3 \\ 1 & 3 & -4 \end{bmatrix}.$$

SOLUTION

Beginning with $[A|I]$, the elimination steps are described column by column:

Elementary row operations:　1. (-4) (row 1) added to row 2
　　　　　　　　　　　　　　　2. (-1) (row 1) added to row 3

$$\begin{bmatrix} 1 & 1 & -1 & | & 1 & 0 & 0 \\ 4 & -1 & 3 & | & 0 & 1 & 0 \\ 1 & 3 & -4 & | & 0 & 0 & 1 \end{bmatrix} \sim \begin{bmatrix} 1 & 1 & -1 & | & 1 & 0 & 0 \\ 0 & -5 & 7 & | & -4 & 1 & 0 \\ 0 & 2 & -3 & | & -1 & 0 & 1 \end{bmatrix}$$

Elementary row operations:　1. $(-1/5)$ (row 2)
　　　　　　　　　　　　　　　2. (-1) (row 2) added to row 1
　　　　　　　　　　　　　　　3. (-2) (row 2) added to row 3

$$\sim \begin{bmatrix} 1 & 0 & 2/5 & | & 1/5 & 1/5 & 0 \\ 0 & 1 & -7/5 & | & 4/5 & -1/5 & 0 \\ 0 & 0 & -1/5 & | & -13/5 & 2/5 & 1 \end{bmatrix}$$

*The Math Works, Inc., Sherborn, MA.

[†]Borland International, Scotts Valley, CA.

[‡]Lotus Development Corp., Atlanta, GA.

Elementary row operations: 1. (-5) (row 3)
                             2. $(7/5)$ (row 3) added to row 2
                             3. $(-2/5)$ (row 3) added to row 1

$$\sim \begin{bmatrix} 1 & 0 & 0 & \vdots & -5 & 1 & 2 \\ 0 & 1 & 0 & \vdots & 19 & -3 & -7 \\ 0 & 0 & 1 & \vdots & 13 & -2 & -5 \end{bmatrix}.$$

Thus

$$A^{-1} = \begin{bmatrix} -5 & 1 & 2 \\ 19 & -3 & -7 \\ 13 & -2 & -5 \end{bmatrix}.$$

●

Although the scheme illustrated in Example 6 is a systematic method for finding an inverse matrix, inverses are of more theoretical value than practical value when solving $AX = B$. Finding A^{-1} was equivalent to solving three linear systems. However, to get the solution to $AX = B$, we still have to compute the product $A^{-1}B$. Clearly $AX = B$ can be solved with much less effort using the reduction method.

EXERCISES 11.3

Use back-substitution to solve the upper-triangular linear systems in Exercises 1–8.

1. $x + 2y - z = 5$
   $\quad\quad y + 2z = 15$
   $\quad\quad\quad\quad z = 4$

2. $x - 3y + 2z = 13$
   $\quad\quad y - 4z = 10$
   $\quad\quad\quad\quad z = -2$

3. $2x_1 - x_2 + 3x_3 = -5$
   $\quad\quad 3x_2 + 2x_3 = 31$
   $\quad\quad\quad\quad 2x_3 = -8$

4. $3x_1 + 2x_2 - x_3 = 2$
   $\quad\quad -x_2 + 4x_3 = 22$
   $\quad\quad\quad\quad 5x_3 = 35$

5. $2x - y + 3z + w = 10$
   $\quad\quad 6y + 2z - 5w = -28$
   $\quad\quad\quad\quad z - 4w = 28$
   $\quad\quad\quad\quad\quad\quad 3w = -18$

6. $3x + 2y - z + 7w = 16$
   $\quad\quad 2y + 3z - w = 0$
   $\quad\quad\quad\quad -z + 2w = 1$
   $\quad\quad\quad\quad\quad\quad 4w = 12$

7. $\begin{bmatrix} 1 & -2 & 3 & 1 \\ 0 & 2 & 1 & -1 \\ 0 & 0 & 1 & 5 \\ 0 & 0 & 0 & 1 \end{bmatrix} \begin{bmatrix} x_1 \\ x_2 \\ x_3 \\ x_4 \end{bmatrix} = \begin{bmatrix} 50 \\ 0 \\ -8 \\ -4 \end{bmatrix}$

8. $\begin{bmatrix} 2 & 0 & 0 & 0 \\ 0 & 3 & 0 & 0 \\ 0 & 0 & 1 & 0 \\ 0 & 0 & 0 & 1 \end{bmatrix} \begin{bmatrix} x_1 \\ x_2 \\ x_3 \\ x_4 \end{bmatrix} = \begin{bmatrix} 8 \\ -9 \\ 7 \\ -3 \end{bmatrix}$

Use the reduction method to solve the linear systems in Exercises 9–24.

9. $x + 4y = 18$
   $\quad 3x - y = -11$

10. $x - 2y = 16$
    $\quad 4x + 3y = 20$

11. $2x_1 + 4x_2 = 24$
    $\quad 3x_1 - 2x_2 = -20$

12. $5x_1 - 4x_2 = -1$
    $\quad 6x_1 - 5x_2 = -2$

13. $\begin{bmatrix} 2 & -1 \\ 5 & -3 \end{bmatrix} \begin{bmatrix} x \\ y \end{bmatrix} = \begin{bmatrix} 2 \\ 4 \end{bmatrix}$

14. $\begin{bmatrix} 3 & 4 \\ 2 & 1 \end{bmatrix} \begin{bmatrix} x \\ y \end{bmatrix} = \begin{bmatrix} -1 \\ 1 \end{bmatrix}$

15. $x + 2y - 3z = -4$
    $\quad 2x - y + 4z = 7$
    $\quad 3x - 2y + 5z = 4$

16. $x - y + 3z = 2$
    $\quad 4x - 2y + 2z = 2$
    $\quad 5x - y + 5z = 18$

17. $2x_1 - 4x_2 + 6x_3 = 16$
    $\quad 3x_1 + 2x_2 - x_3 = -4$
    $\quad 4x_1 - 2x_2 + 3x_3 = 8$

18. $3x_1 + 6x_2 - 3x_3 = 9$
    $\quad 5x_1 + 4x_2 - x_3 = 7$
    $\quad 7x_1 - 2x_2 + 3x_3 = 1$

19. $\begin{bmatrix} 0 & 4 & 8 \\ 1 & -3 & -5 \\ 2 & 4 & 1 \end{bmatrix} \begin{bmatrix} x \\ y \\ z \end{bmatrix} = \begin{bmatrix} 4 \\ 4 \\ 0 \end{bmatrix}$

20. $\begin{bmatrix} 2 & 3 & -1 \\ 3 & 2 & 1 \\ -5 & 2 & 4 \end{bmatrix} \begin{bmatrix} x \\ y \\ z \end{bmatrix} = \begin{bmatrix} -3 \\ 8 \\ -18 \end{bmatrix}$

21.
$$4y - 8z = 20$$
$$2x - y + 5z + 2w = 1$$
$$x + y - 2z + 4w = 20$$
$$3x - 2y + 4z - w = -9$$

22.
$$x + 2y - z + 3w = -14$$
$$x + 2y + 4z + 2w = 9$$
$$3x - 4y + 2z + 5w = 10$$
$$5x + 2z - 3w = 32$$

23. $\begin{bmatrix} 2 & 0 & -2 & 4 \\ 3 & 4 & 3 & 3 \\ -2 & 2 & -1 & 2 \\ 4 & -6 & -1 & 1 \end{bmatrix} \begin{bmatrix} x_1 \\ x_2 \\ x_3 \\ x_4 \end{bmatrix} = \begin{bmatrix} -10 \\ 5 \\ -13 \\ 9 \end{bmatrix}$

24. $\begin{bmatrix} 3 & -2 & 0 & 1 \\ 2 & 1 & 4 & 5 \\ -4 & 5 & -1 & -1 \\ 3 & -2 & 2 & 3 \end{bmatrix} \begin{bmatrix} x_1 \\ x_2 \\ x_3 \\ x_4 \end{bmatrix} = \begin{bmatrix} 0 \\ 6 \\ 13 \\ -2 \end{bmatrix}$

Use Gauss–Jordan elimination to find inverses of the matrices in Exercises 25–31.

25. $\begin{bmatrix} 2 & -1 \\ 3 & -2 \end{bmatrix}$

26. $\begin{bmatrix} 5 & 3 \\ 8 & 5 \end{bmatrix}$

27. $\begin{bmatrix} 2 & -3 & 3 \\ 2 & -1 & 2 \\ 1 & 2 & 0 \end{bmatrix}$

28. $\begin{bmatrix} 3 & 1 & -2 \\ 2 & -1 & 1 \\ 4 & 5 & -8 \end{bmatrix}$

29. $\begin{bmatrix} 2 & -1 & 3 \\ 1 & 4 & 1 \\ 3 & 4 & 4 \end{bmatrix}$

30. $\begin{bmatrix} 2 & -3 & 5 \\ 1 & 0 & 2 \\ 4 & -3 & 3 \end{bmatrix}$

31. $\begin{bmatrix} 1 & 2 & 0 & -1 \\ 2 & 1 & -1 & 3 \\ 4 & -2 & 3 & 1 \\ 0 & -1 & 0 & 1 \end{bmatrix}$

32. Assume the determinant of the matrix

$$A = \begin{bmatrix} a_{11} & a_{12} \\ a_{21} & a_{22} \end{bmatrix}$$

is not 0 and use Gauss–Jordan elimination to find A^{-1}, as in Theorem 11.1 of Section 11.2, under the following conditions:

a. $a_{11} \neq 0$ b. $a_{11} = 0$

33. Outsider Camping sells 3-lb, 4-lb, and 5-lb down-filled sleeping bags at their Augusta, Bend, and Casper outlets. The number of bags sold at each outlet during June is given in matrix B:

$$B = \begin{matrix} & \begin{matrix} 3\text{ lb} & 4\text{ lb} & 5\text{ lb} \end{matrix} & \\ \begin{bmatrix} 20 & 30 & 50 \\ 10 & 40 & 60 \\ 20 & 10 & 80 \end{bmatrix} & \begin{matrix} \text{Augusta} \\ \text{Bend} \\ \text{Casper} \end{matrix} \end{matrix}$$

The selling price for each type of bag is the same at each outlet, and the revenue generated from bag sales during June is given in vector R:

$$R = \begin{bmatrix} 11{,}600 \\ 13{,}200 \\ 13{,}800 \end{bmatrix} \begin{matrix} \text{Augusta} \\ \text{Bend} \\ \text{Casper} \end{matrix}$$

Solve the linear system $BX = R$ to determine the selling price of each sleeping bag.

34. Fast Finance offers new car loans, used car loans, and quick cash loans each at a different monthly interest rate. The totals for loans of each type made last month at Fast Finance's three branch offices are recorded (in thousands of dollars) in matrix T:

$$T = \begin{matrix} & \begin{matrix} \text{New Car} & \text{Used Car} & \text{Quick Cash} \end{matrix} & \\ \begin{bmatrix} 80 & 60 & 50 \\ 50 & 60 & 40 \\ 70 & 80 & 80 \end{bmatrix} & \begin{matrix} \text{North Branch} \\ \text{Central Branch} \\ \text{South Branch} \end{matrix} \end{matrix}$$

The interest earned on these loans during the month is listed branch by branch (in dollars) in vector E:

$$E = \begin{bmatrix} 3000 \\ 2200 \\ 3500 \end{bmatrix} \begin{matrix} \text{North Branch} \\ \text{Central Branch} \\ \text{South Branch} \end{matrix}$$

Solve the linear system $TX = E$ to determine the monthly interest rate for each type of loan.

35. Prima Produce sells fresh vegetables to local restaurants. Matrix P contains the price per pound for celery, cucumbers, peppers, and tomatoes during January, February, March, and April:

$$P = \begin{matrix} & \begin{matrix} \text{Celery} & \text{Cucumbers} & \text{Peppers} & \text{Tomatoes} \end{matrix} & \\ \begin{bmatrix} 1.00 & .80 & 1.00 & 2.00 \\ 1.00 & 1.00 & 1.20 & 2.40 \\ .80 & .80 & .80 & 1.50 \\ .80 & .50 & .70 & 1.20 \end{bmatrix} & \begin{matrix} \text{January} \\ \text{February} \\ \text{March} \\ \text{April} \end{matrix} \end{matrix}$$

Downtown Restaurant has a standing order for the same quantity of vegetables each month, but this order has been misplaced. However, Downtown's monthly bills for the past four months are given in vector B:

$$B = \begin{bmatrix} 726 \\ 846 \\ 580 \\ 476 \end{bmatrix} \begin{array}{l} \text{January} \\ \text{February} \\ \text{March} \\ \text{April} \end{array}$$

Solve the linear system $PX = B$ to determine the number of pounds of celery, cucumbers, peppers, and tomatoes ordered each month by Downtown Restaurant.

36. Refer to Exercise 35. The standing monthly orders for Northtown and Southtown Diners have also been misplaced by Prima Produce. Matrix D lists the monthly bills for these diners:

$$D = \begin{matrix} \text{Northtown} \quad \text{Southtown} \\ \begin{bmatrix} 620 & 670 \\ 720 & 768 \\ 496 & 540 \\ 410 & 459 \end{bmatrix} \begin{array}{l} \text{January} \\ \text{February} \\ \text{March} \\ \text{April} \end{array} \end{matrix}$$

Determine the monthly quantities of vegetables ordered by each of the diners by starting with the augmented matrix $[P|D]$ and reducing two linear systems simultaneously.

11.4
More on Linear Systems of Equations

In Section 11.3 we considered systems of linear equations of the form $AX = B$ in which A is a square, invertible matrix. For such a system there is a unique solution that can be written

(11.16) $$X = A^{-1}B,$$

where A^{-1} is the inverse of A. In this section we will consider systems in which A either is not square or is not invertible. Like any linear system, it is possible for these systems to have a unique solution, infinitely many solutions, or no solution at all. Fortunately, the method of matrix reduction can still be used to find the solution(s) (or to show that there is no solution) of such systems even if the solution cannot be written in the form of equation (11.16).

EXAMPLE 1

Use matrix reduction to solve the system

$$\begin{aligned} 3x - 4y &= 8 \\ -9x + 12y &= 6. \end{aligned}$$

SOLUTION

The augmented matrix for this system is

$$\begin{bmatrix} 3 & -4 & | & 8 \\ -9 & 12 & | & 6 \end{bmatrix}.$$

Dividing the first row by 3, we have

$$\begin{bmatrix} 1 & -4/3 & | & 8/3 \\ -9 & 12 & | & 6 \end{bmatrix}.$$

When the first row is multiplied by 9 and added to the second row, we obtain the matrix

$$\begin{bmatrix} 1 & -4/3 & | & 8/3 \\ 0 & 0 & | & 30 \end{bmatrix}.$$

In equation form, the second row asserts that $0x + 0y = 30$ or that $0 = 30$, which is false regardless of x and y. Therefore the system has no solution. ●

Example 1 illustrates what will occur when the augmented matrix of a linear system is reduced if that system has no solution: *If at any step in the reduction process, a matrix is formed that has a row in which every entry is 0 except the constant term, the system has no solution.* (See Figure 11.3.)

Figure 11.3

A system of equations has no solution if any row i in its reduced augmented matrix has 0s for every entry except the constant term b_i.

$$
\begin{array}{c}
\begin{array}{ccccc} x_1 & x_2 & x_3 & \cdots & x_n \end{array} \\
\text{Row } i \begin{bmatrix}
1 & a_{12} & a_{13} & \cdots & a_{1n} & b_1 \\
0 & 1 & a_{23} & \cdots & a_{2n} & b_2 \\
0 & 0 & 1 & \cdots & a_{3n} & b_3 \\
\cdots & \cdots & \cdots & \cdots & \cdots & \cdots \\
0 & 0 & 0 & \cdots & 0 & b_i \\
\cdots & \cdots & \cdots & \cdots & \cdots & \cdots \\
0 & 0 & 0 & \cdots & a_{mn} & b_m
\end{bmatrix}
\end{array}
$$

A system of linear equations that has no solution is said to be **inconsistent**. If the system consists of two equations in two variables, then the graphs of the equations are parallel lines. (The graphs of the equations in Example 1 are shown in Figure 11.4.)

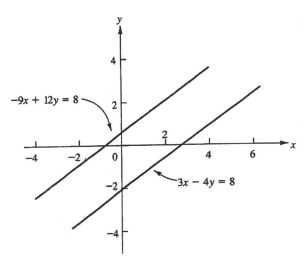

Figure 11.4

The system of equations $3x - 4y = 8$, $-9x + 12y = 8$ has no solution; their graphs are parallel lines.

When the graphs of two linear equations in two variables are identical, then every point on the line is a solution. In this case, we can determine one of the variables in terms of the other. We say that the second variable is a **free variable** or that it can be **chosen arbitrarily**.

EXAMPLE 2

Solve the linear system

$$10x - 5y = 20$$
$$6x - 3y = 12.$$

SOLUTION

The augmented matrix for this system is

$$\begin{bmatrix} 10 & -5 & | & 20 \\ 6 & -3 & | & 12 \end{bmatrix}.$$

Dividing the first row by 10 gives the matrix

$$\begin{bmatrix} 1 & -1/2 & | & 2 \\ 6 & -3 & | & 12 \end{bmatrix}.$$

When the first row is multiplied by -6 and added to the second row, we obtain a reduced matrix in which every entry in the last row is 0:

$$\begin{bmatrix} 1 & -1/2 & | & 2 \\ 0 & 0 & | & 0 \end{bmatrix}.$$

This matrix indicates that the system is equivalent to a system that has only a single equation, $x - (1/2)y = 2$. Therefore all the solutions to the system could be written as

$$x = 2 + \frac{1}{2}y, \qquad y \text{ arbitrary}$$

(or, by solving for y, as $y = 2x - 4$, x arbitrary).   ●

When solving a system of m equations in n variables with $m < n$, if there is a solution, then at least $n - m$ of the variables can be chosen arbitrarily. Moreover, when solving the system by the reduction method, if a row that has only 0 entries is formed, it should be placed at the bottom of the matrix (by interchanging rows). A row of 0s indicates that the system is equivalent to another system with one less equation. Consequently, another of the variables can be chosen arbitrarily. As illustrated in the example of a reduced matrix in Figure 11.5, the number of free variables will be $n - m$ plus the number of all-zero rows.

When a matrix is in reduced form, all nonzero rows contain an initial 1. If some column does not contain one of the initial 1s, then we cannot solve for the variable that heads that column. *A variable is free if its column in the reduced matrix contains no initial 1*. When a variable's column contains an initial 1, it is not free; there is an equation that can be solved for such a variable.

Figure 11.5

A reduced matrix from a system of five equations in six variables. There are two free variables, x_3 and x_6; columns 3 and 6 do not contain an initial 1

$$\begin{array}{cccccc} x_1 & x_2 & x_3 & x_4 & x_5 & x_6 \end{array}$$

$$\begin{bmatrix} 1 & a_{12} & a_{13} & a_{14} & a_{15} & a_{16} & | & b_1 \\ 0 & 1 & a_{23} & a_{24} & a_{25} & a_{26} & | & b_2 \\ 0 & 0 & 0 & 1 & a_{35} & a_{36} & | & b_3 \\ 0 & 0 & 0 & 0 & 1 & a_{46} & | & b_4 \\ 0 & 0 & 0 & 0 & 0 & 0 & | & 0 \end{bmatrix}$$

EXAMPLE 3

Solve the system of equations

$$\begin{aligned} x + 2y - z &= 5 \\ 3x + 6y - z &= 11 \\ -x - 2y &= -3. \end{aligned}$$

SOLUTION

The augmented matrix is

$$\begin{bmatrix} 1 & 2 & -1 & | & 5 \\ 3 & 6 & -1 & | & 11 \\ -1 & -2 & 0 & | & -3 \end{bmatrix}.$$

When this matrix is reduced, the following sequence of matrices is obtained:

$$\begin{matrix} x & y & z \end{matrix}$$
$$\begin{bmatrix} 1 & 2 & -1 & | & 5 \\ 3 & 6 & -1 & | & 11 \\ -1 & -2 & 0 & | & -3 \end{bmatrix} \sim \begin{bmatrix} 1 & 2 & -1 & | & 5 \\ 0 & 0 & 2 & | & -4 \\ 0 & 0 & -1 & | & 2 \end{bmatrix} \sim \begin{bmatrix} 1 & 2 & -1 & | & 5 \\ 0 & 0 & 1 & | & -2 \\ 0 & 0 & 0 & | & 0 \end{bmatrix}.$$

Because the final row has 0s for every entry, one of the variables can be chosen arbitrarily. The 1 in the first row under the x label and the 1 in the second row under the z label indicate that it is possible to solve for x and z, perhaps in terms of the free variable y. The two equations are

$$x + 2y - z = 5 \quad \text{and} \quad z = -2.$$

Substituting for z in the first equation, we can write the solutions to the system as

$$x = 3 - 2y, \quad z = -2, \quad y \text{ arbitrary.} \qquad \bullet$$

In summary, the following outcomes are possible when using the reduction method to solve a system of m equations in n variables.

1. If the reduced matrix has n rows with nonzero entries (except for the constant column), then the system has a unique solution. That is, in the final matrix there is exactly one row with a 1 as the first nonzero entry for each variable.

2. If the reduced matrix has a row in which every element is 0 except for the constant term, then the system has no solution.

3. If the matrix has fewer nonzero rows than variables, then the system has infinitely many solutions. The free variables (which can be chosen arbitrarily) are those whose column does not contain an initial 1.

EXAMPLE 4

Solve the system of four linear equations in three variables:

$$\begin{aligned} 2x + 3y + z &= 7 \\ 4x - y - z &= -2 \\ -2x + y + 2z &= 6 \\ 6x + 2y - 2z &= -1. \end{aligned}$$

SOLUTION

Because there are more equations than variables in this system, we may suspect that it will have no solution. The final row in the reduced matrix will have 0s for the first three entries, so there is a solution only if the constant term is also 0 in that row. The matrix reduction on the augmented matrix can be performed as follows:

$$\begin{bmatrix} 2 & 3 & 1 & | & 7 \\ 4 & -1 & -1 & | & -2 \\ -2 & 1 & 2 & | & 6 \\ 6 & 2 & -2 & | & -1 \end{bmatrix} \sim \begin{bmatrix} 1 & 3/2 & 1/2 & | & 7/2 \\ 4 & -1 & -1 & | & -2 \\ -2 & 1 & 2 & | & 6 \\ 6 & 2 & -2 & | & -1 \end{bmatrix}$$

$$\sim \begin{bmatrix} 1 & 3/2 & 1/2 & | & 7/2 \\ 0 & -7 & -3 & | & -16 \\ 0 & 4 & 3 & | & 13 \\ 0 & -7 & -5 & | & -22 \end{bmatrix} \sim \begin{bmatrix} 1 & 3/2 & 1/2 & | & 7/2 \\ 0 & 1 & 3/7 & | & 16/7 \\ 0 & 4 & 3 & | & 13 \\ 0 & -7 & -5 & | & -22 \end{bmatrix}$$

$$\sim \begin{bmatrix} 1 & 3/2 & 1/2 & | & 7/2 \\ 0 & 1 & 3/7 & | & 16/7 \\ 0 & 0 & 9/7 & | & 27/7 \\ 0 & 0 & -2 & | & -6 \end{bmatrix} \sim \begin{bmatrix} 1 & 3/2 & 1/2 & | & 7/2 \\ 0 & 1 & 3/7 & | & 16/7 \\ 0 & 0 & 1 & | & 3 \\ 0 & 0 & -2 & | & -6 \end{bmatrix}$$

with the reduced matrix

$$\begin{array}{ccc} x & y & z \end{array}$$
$$\begin{bmatrix} 1 & 3/2 & 1/2 & | & 7/2 \\ 0 & 1 & 3/7 & | & 16/7 \\ 0 & 0 & 1 & | & 3 \\ 0 & 0 & 0 & | & 0 \end{bmatrix}.$$

Because there are three variables and three nonzero rows, the system has a unique solution. The equations corresponding to the reduced matrix are

$$x + \frac{3}{2}y + \frac{1}{2}z = \frac{7}{2}, \qquad y + \frac{3}{7}z = \frac{16}{7}, \qquad z = 3.$$

Substituting for z in the second equation yields $y = 1$. Finally, substituting for y and z in the first equation gives $x = 1/2$.   ●

EXAMPLE 5

Find all solutions to the system of equations

$$\begin{aligned} x + y + 2z + v - 2w &= 3 \\ -x + 3y + 6z - 5v + w &= 1 \\ 3x - y - 2z + 7v - 5w &= 5 \end{aligned}$$

and find one specific solution.

SOLUTION

Because there are five unknowns and only three variables, we know that if this system has a solution, then at least two of the variables will be free. The matrix reduction is accomplished as follows:

$$\begin{bmatrix} 1 & 1 & 2 & 1 & -2 & | & 3 \\ -1 & 3 & 6 & -5 & 1 & | & 1 \\ 3 & -1 & -2 & 7 & -5 & | & 5 \end{bmatrix} \sim \begin{bmatrix} 1 & 1 & 2 & 1 & -2 & | & 3 \\ 0 & 4 & 8 & -4 & -1 & | & 4 \\ 0 & -4 & -8 & 4 & 1 & | & -4 \end{bmatrix}$$

$$\sim \begin{bmatrix} 1 & 1 & 2 & 1 & -2 & | & 3 \\ 0 & 1 & 2 & -1 & -1/4 & | & 1 \\ 0 & -4 & -8 & 4 & 1 & | & -4 \end{bmatrix}$$

$$\begin{array}{ccccc} x & y & z & v & w \end{array}$$

$$\sim \begin{bmatrix} 1 & 1 & 2 & 1 & -2 & | & 3 \\ 0 & 1 & 2 & -1 & -1/4 & | & 1 \\ 0 & 0 & 0 & 0 & 0 & | & 0 \end{bmatrix}.$$

Because the last row has every entry 0, there are three free variables. We can choose z, v, and w arbitrarily and write the first two equations as

$$x = 3 - y - 2z - v + 2w, \qquad y = 1 - 2z + v + \frac{1}{4}w.$$

Substituting for y in the first equation, we have

$$x = 3 - \left(1 - 2z + v + \frac{1}{4}w\right) - 2z - v + 2w$$

$$= 2 - 2v + \frac{7}{4}w.$$

The solutions to this system can be written as

(11.17) $\qquad y = 2 - 2v + \frac{7}{4}w, \quad y = 1 - 2z + v + \frac{1}{4}w, \qquad z, v, w \text{ arbitrary.}$

A specific solution may be obtained by choosing, for example, $z = 1$, $v = -1$, and $w = 4$. Then from (11.17), $x = 11$ and $y = -1$.   ●

EXERCISES 11.4

Find all solutions to the systems of linear equations in Exercises 1–18.

1. $-6x + 4y = -10$
   $9x - 6y = 15$

2. $2x + y = 70$
   $6x + 3y = 210$

3. $3x - 3y = 9$
   $-2x + 2y = 6$

4. $12s - 8t = 60$
   $9s - 6t = 50$

5. $x + 2y = 5$
   $3x - y = 1$
   $-x + y = 1$

6. $2x - 4y = 2$
   $x + 2y = 0$
   $3x + 3y = 1$
   $5x + y = 3$

7. $4a - 8b + 2c = 3$
   $2a + b - c = 5$

8. $3r + 2s + 6t = 0$
   $-2r + 4s + t = 0$

9. $2x_1 - x_2 + x_3 = 4$
   $-x_1 - 3x_2 + 2x_3 = 3$
   $3x_1 + 2x_2 - x_3 = 1$

10. $2x + 3y - z = 6$
    $6x + y + 3z = 0$
    $2x - y + 2z = 1$

11. $x + y - 2z = 1$
    $y + 4z = 5$
    $x - y = -4$
    $3x + y + 6z = 2$

12. $2p + q - r = 4$
    $-p + 3q + r = 1$
    $5p - q - 3r = 7$
    $p + 4q = 5$

13. $2x + 3y - 4z + w = 1$
    $3x + 5y - 6z - w = 2$

14. $y + z + w = 0$
    $2x - y + z = 3$
    $-x + 2y + z - w = 1$

15. $\begin{aligned} x_1 + 2x_2 \quad\quad + x_4 &= 5 \\ -x_1 + x_2 + 3x_3 + 2x_4 &= -2 \\ x_2 + 2x_3 + x_4 &= 0 \\ -x_1 + 3x_2 + x_3 + 4x_4 &= 4 \end{aligned}$

16. $\begin{aligned} 2a + b \quad\quad - d &= 4 \\ a \quad\quad + c + d &= 0 \\ -a + 2b + 2c - d &= 1 \\ 3b + c - 3d &= 2 \end{aligned}$

17. $\begin{aligned} w + 2y - z &= 0 \\ 2v + x + y + 2z &= 0 \\ v + 3w + x - y \quad &= 0 \end{aligned}$

18. $\begin{aligned} x_1 + x_2 - x_3 + 2x_4 + x_5 &= 4 \\ 2x_2 - 4x_3 + x_4 + 2x_5 &= 2 \\ 2x_1 + 2x_3 \quad\quad - x_5 &= 3 \\ -x_1 - 2x_2 + 3x_3 + x_4 + 2x_5 &= 7 \end{aligned}$

In Exercises 19–22, use the reduction method to show that the specified matrix is not invertible.

19. The coefficient matrix for the linear system in Exercise 1.

20. The coefficient matrix for the linear system in Exercise 2.

21. The coefficient matrix for the linear system in Exercise 9.

22. The coefficient matrix for the linear system in Exercise 10.

23. Find k so that the linear system has infinitely many solutions:

$$\begin{aligned} 12x - 9y &= 6 \\ -8x + 6y &= k. \end{aligned}$$

24. Find k so that the linear system has infinitely many solutions:

$$\begin{aligned} 2x - 2y + z &= 6 \\ -x + 2y - 3z &= 1 \\ 3x - 2y - z &= k. \end{aligned}$$

25. Find k so that the linear system has infinitely many solutions:

$$\begin{aligned} x - y - z &= k \\ -2x + y + 2z &= -8 \\ -x - y + z &= 14. \end{aligned}$$

26. Consider the system of two equations in three variables

$$\begin{aligned} 2x + y + z &= 5 \\ 6x - y + 3z &= 7. \end{aligned}$$

a. Show that the solutions to this system can be written with x or with z as the free variable.

b. Show, however, that y cannot be chosen arbitrarily in a solution to this system. What value must y have?

27. A young couple has $10,000 that is to be divided among a checking account, a savings account, and a certificate of deposit. Assume that the checking account earns 5% interest annually, the savings account earns 6% and the certificate earns 9%. The couple would like to have the money divided so that it earns 8% interest overall. Determine all solutions to this problem. What is the solution if they have decided that $7000 will be put in a certificate of deposit?

28. The manager of The Candy Road plans to produce and sell a nut mixture at $4.50 per pound. He would like to make 200 lb of the mix by combining peanuts worth $2 per pound, cashews worth $6 per pound, and almonds worth $7 per pound.

a. Determine all the ways in which the mix could be made.

b. How should the nuts be mixed if the manager wants to use 40 lb of almonds? 20 lb of almonds?

29. The vice-president of the EZ-UP Construction Company has 80 workers who have to be assigned to four construction projects. All workers on project A are to be paid $10 per hour, workers on project B $12 per hour, workers on project C $9 per hour, and workers on project D $10 per hour. The vice-president knows that EZ-UP has budgeted $850 per hour for total wage costs. Finally, the president of the company has said that projects A and C should have an equal number of workers so that work on them proceeds at the same pace.

a. Find all possible ways that the vice-president can assign the workers to these projects.

b. What is the solution if 30 workers are put on project D?

11.5 Input–Output Analysis

An interesting and useful application of matrices was developed by the economist Wassily Leontief. This application is called the **input–output model** of an economic system, and Leontief was awarded the 1973 Nobel Prize in economics for its development. We introduce the concept with a simple example.

EXAMPLE 1

Vitalex is a small company that makes computer equipment and writes programs to make this equipment compatible with machines made by large manufacturers. Vitalex has two divisions: Hardware, which makes the equipment, and Software, which writes the programs.

To make the equipment, it is necessary for Hardware to use some of its own equipment and some computer programs that were written by Vitalex's Software Division. The accountant for Vitalex estimates that to make one unit of output (say, $10,000 worth of equipment or programming) the Hardware Division must use .05 unit of their equipment and .1 unit of programming from Software.

Similarly, Software needs existing Vitalex equipment and software to develop more programming. It has been estimated that this division requires .25 unit of equipment and .1 unit of software to produce one unit of new programming.

This information can be displayed in a matrix A as follows:

$$A = \begin{matrix} \text{Hardware} & \text{Software} \\ \begin{bmatrix} .05 & .25 \\ .1 & .1 \end{bmatrix} & \begin{matrix} \text{Hardware} \\ \text{Software} \end{matrix} \end{matrix}$$

This matrix is called an **input–output matrix** because each column gives the number of units of input, from each of the divisions, required to produce one unit of output in that division.

Determine what level of activity is required in Hardware and Software so that Vitalex will have 40 units ($400,000 worth) of equipment and 30 units ($300,000 worth) of programming that can be sold to its customers.

SOLUTION

Let X denote the 2-component vector that gives the level of activity required in each department; that is, let

$$X = \begin{bmatrix} x_1 \\ x_2 \end{bmatrix},$$

where x_1 and x_2 denote the number of units of production in Hardware and Software, respectively. Then the matrix product AX will denote the internal consumption of the activity levels in X. If

$$B = \begin{bmatrix} 40 \\ 30 \end{bmatrix}$$

is the vector of desired external outputs from each department, then in order to meet this output level, we must have $X = AX + B$, or

(11.18)
$$X - AX = B.$$

Equation (11.18) implies that the activity in the divisions less the inputs required to support that activity will equal the production that is available to be consumed or sold to Vitalex customers. This equation may be rewritten in the more compact form

(11.19)
$$(I - A)X = B$$

where I denotes the identity matrix (a 2×2 matrix in this example).

Because

$$I - A = \begin{bmatrix} 1 & 0 \\ 0 & 1 \end{bmatrix} - \begin{bmatrix} .05 & .25 \\ .1 & .1 \end{bmatrix} = \begin{bmatrix} .95 & -.25 \\ -.1 & .9 \end{bmatrix},$$

matrix equation (11.19) is the system of linear equations

$$.95x_1 - .25x_2 = 40$$

$$-.10x_1 + .90x_2 = 30.$$

This system can be solved using the reduction method as follows:

$$\begin{bmatrix} .95 & -.25 & | & 40 \\ -.1 & .9 & | & 30 \end{bmatrix} \sim \begin{bmatrix} 1 & -.263 & | & 42.105 \\ -.1 & .9 & | & 30 \end{bmatrix}$$

$$\sim \begin{bmatrix} 1 & -.263 & | & 42.105 \\ 0 & .874 & | & 34.211 \end{bmatrix}$$

$$\sim \begin{bmatrix} 1 & -.263 & | & 42.105 \\ 0 & 1 & | & 39.143 \end{bmatrix}.$$

Therefore we have $x_2 = 39.143$ units and

$$x_1 = 42.105 + .263x_2 = 42.105 + .263(39.143) = 52.400 \text{ units.}$$

That is, Vitalex will have to require that hardware produce 52.4 units of output and Software 39.143 units of output in order to have 40 units of equipment and 30 units of programming available for sale.   ●

Definition 11.6

> Suppose that there are n activities, each of which produces some resource or commodity. Let a_{ij} be the number of units of the ith resource required by the jth activity to produce one unit of that resource. Then the $n \times n$ matrix A with elements a_{ij} is called the **input–output matrix** for this system of activities.

An n-component vector X whose ith entry shows the number of units of output produced by activity i is called an **activity vector**. This vector can be thought of as showing all the levels of activity in an economic system. The product AX is an n-component vector whose ith entry is the number of units of resource i that are required to support the activity of the economic system at output level X. We call AX the **input vector**.

When $AX = X$, the level of activity in the system consumes all of the output of the system. In such a case the economic system is said to be **in equilibrium**. The system is able to maintain itself with its own production but will not provide any output for use outside the system itself. For a system that is not in equilibrium, we form a nonzero vector B by subtracting the inputs from the activity level:

$$X - AX = (I - A)X = B,$$

where I denotes the $n \times n$ identity matrix. We will call B the **output vector** of the system. Each positive entry in B indicates the amount of that resource that is available for use outside the system. Each negative entry indicates the amount of that resource that must be provided from outside the system to support the activity level X.

EXAMPLE 2

The NVS&T Company is a large brokerage and financial services company. It can trade in stocks, bonds, and precious metals and can sell life insurance or retirement annuities. As well as providing these services to its clients, it provides them to its own employees at cost. In addition, the company manages its own portfolio of investments. Consequently, much of NVS&T's financial activity goes to support itself and its employees and does not earn revenue for the company.

The following input–output matrix shows the number of units of activity in each division that go to support one unit of activity in another division of NVS&T.

$$A = \begin{bmatrix} .2 & .1 & .05 & .15 & .2 \\ .1 & .15 & .05 & .1 & .1 \\ .05 & .05 & .1 & .1 & .05 \\ .1 & .2 & 0 & .15 & .2 \\ .05 & .2 & 0 & .2 & .25 \end{bmatrix} \begin{matrix} \text{Stocks} \\ \text{Bonds} \\ \text{Precious Metals} \\ \text{Insurance} \\ \text{Annuities} \end{matrix}$$

with columns labeled Stocks, Bonds, Precious Metals, Insurance, Annuities.

An audit of the work being done in each of the divisions shows the following levels of activity during a recent month:

$$X = \begin{bmatrix} 1200 \\ 800 \\ 300 \\ 500 \\ 600 \end{bmatrix} \begin{matrix} \text{Stocks} \\ \text{Bonds} \\ \text{Precious Metals} \\ \text{Insurance} \\ \text{Annuities} \end{matrix} \begin{matrix} (1 \text{ unit} = 100,000 \text{ shares traded}) \\ (1 \text{ unit} = 100 \text{ bonds traded}) \\ (1 \text{ unit} = 100 \text{ oz traded}) \\ (1 \text{ unit} = 1 \text{ policy sold}) \\ (1 \text{ unit} = 1 \text{ annuity sold}) \end{matrix}$$

Determine how much of this activity is actually going to the clients of the NVS&T Company and how much is being used internally.

SOLUTION

The product AX will tell us how much of each activity is being used internally. We have

$$\begin{bmatrix} .2 & .1 & .05 & .15 & .2 \\ .1 & .15 & .05 & .1 & .1 \\ .05 & .05 & .1 & .1 & .05 \\ .1 & .2 & 0 & .15 & .2 \\ .05 & .2 & 0 & .2 & .25 \end{bmatrix} \begin{bmatrix} 1200 \\ 800 \\ 300 \\ 500 \\ 600 \end{bmatrix} = \begin{bmatrix} 530 \\ 365 \\ 210 \\ 475 \\ 470 \end{bmatrix}.$$

The difference $X - AX$ will show how much of each activity is provided for the clients. This is summarized in Table 11.1. The table provides the management of NVS&T with some useful information. Only in the trading in stocks and bonds is a majority of the work being performed for clients. The large majority of life insurance policies are sold to the company's employees at cost; if this is a typical month, NVS&T should consider dropping this service.

Table 11.1

	Activity Level	Internal Use	Client Use
Stocks	1200	530	670
Bonds	800	365	435
Precious Metals	300	210	90
Insurance	500	475	25
Annuities	600	470	130

EXAMPLE 3

Assume that all the workers in a particular state can be classified according to the sector of the economy in which they are employed: Services and Administration, Agriculture, or Manufacturing. Suppose that this state is viewed primarily as an agricultural state because it is not a net provider of manufactured goods to other states. Its goal is to provide 100 units of agricultural products to other states each year without importing manufactured goods. Finally assume that all services are provided and consumed within the state. The input–output matrix for the economic system of the state is given here:

$$A = \begin{array}{c} \\ \\ \\ \end{array} \overset{\text{Services} \quad \text{Agriculture} \quad \text{Manufacturing}}{\begin{bmatrix} .2 & .1 & .2 \\ .3 & .2 & .3 \\ .1 & .5 & .4 \end{bmatrix}} \begin{array}{l} \text{Services} \\ \text{Agriculture} \\ \text{Manufacturing} \end{array}$$

Find the level of activity for each sector of the state's economy required to achieve the goal.

SOLUTION

Let the vector X denote the economic activity in the state, with x_1, x_2, and x_3 denoting the levels of activity in Services and Administration, Agriculture, and Manufacturing, respectively. The desired output vector of the state's economic system is

$$B = \begin{bmatrix} 0 \\ 100 \\ 0 \end{bmatrix} \begin{array}{l} \text{Services} \\ \text{Agriculture} \\ \text{Manufacturing} \end{array}$$

We therefore need to solve the system of linear equations

$$(I - A)X = B$$

or

$$
\begin{array}{rrrr}
(1 - .2)x_1 & - .1x_2 & - .2x_3 & = 0 \\
- .3x_1 + (1 - .2)x_2 & & - .3x_3 & = 100 \\
- .1x_1 & - .5x_2 + (1 - .4)x_3 & & = 0.
\end{array}
$$

We reduce the augmented matrix for this system as follows:

$$
\left[\begin{array}{ccc|c}
.8 & -.1 & -.2 & 0 \\
-.3 & .8 & -.3 & 100 \\
-.1 & -.5 & .6 & 0
\end{array}\right]
\sim
\left[\begin{array}{ccc|c}
1 & -.1250 & -.2500 & 0 \\
-.3 & .8 & -.3 & 100 \\
-.1 & -.5 & .6 & 0
\end{array}\right]
$$

$$
\sim
\left[\begin{array}{ccc|c}
1 & -.1250 & -.2500 & 0 \\
0 & .7625 & -.3750 & 100 \\
0 & -.5125 & .5750 & 0
\end{array}\right]
\sim
\left[\begin{array}{ccc|c}
1 & -.1250 & -.2500 & 0 \\
0 & 1 & -.4918 & 131.15 \\
0 & -.5125 & .5750 & 0
\end{array}\right]
$$

$$
\sim
\left[\begin{array}{ccc|c}
1 & -.1250 & -.2500 & 0 \\
0 & 1 & -.4918 & 131.15 \\
0 & 0 & .3230 & 67.21
\end{array}\right]
\sim
\left[\begin{array}{ccc|c}
\overset{x_1}{1} & \overset{x_2}{-.1250} & \overset{x_3}{-.2500} & 0 \\
0 & 1 & -.4918 & 131.15 \\
0 & 0 & 1 & 208.08
\end{array}\right].
$$

From the reduced matrix we find that there is a unique solution to the problem. The state must produce

$$x_3 = 208.08 \text{ units of manufactured goods}$$

$$x_2 = 131.15 + .4918(208.08)$$

$$= 233.48 \text{ units of agricultural products}$$

and $\qquad x_1 = .125(233.48) + .250(208.08)$

$$= 81.21 \text{ units of services and administration} \qquad \bullet$$

If it is necessary to determine the activity vector X for several different outputs from an economic system when the input–output matrix A does not change, it may be more convenient to calculate the inverse of $I - A$ and find X by the matrix multiplication $X = (I - A)^{-1}B$. Ordinarily, however, it is easier to simply solve the linear system using the matrix reduction method as done in Examples 1 and 3.

EXERCISES 11.5

In Exercises 1–8, for the given input–output matrix A, find the activity vector X that is required to produce the given system output vector B.

1. $A = \begin{bmatrix} .1 & .2 \\ .2 & .3 \end{bmatrix}, \quad B = \begin{bmatrix} 60 \\ 40 \end{bmatrix}$

2. $A = \begin{bmatrix} .04 & .01 \\ .02 & .05 \end{bmatrix}, \quad B = \begin{bmatrix} 100 \\ 120 \end{bmatrix}$

3. $A = \begin{bmatrix} 0 & .2 \\ .15 & .3 \end{bmatrix}, \quad B = \begin{bmatrix} 80 \\ 75 \end{bmatrix}$

4. $A = \begin{bmatrix} .3 & .05 \\ .05 & .1 \end{bmatrix}, \quad B = \begin{bmatrix} 20 \\ 20 \end{bmatrix}$

5. $A = \begin{bmatrix} .1 & 0 & .2 \\ .1 & .2 & .1 \\ .2 & .1 & .1 \end{bmatrix}, \quad B = \begin{bmatrix} 100 \\ 50 \\ 80 \end{bmatrix}$

6. $A = \begin{bmatrix} .05 & .1 & .05 \\ 0 & .05 & .2 \\ .1 & .05 & .1 \end{bmatrix}, \quad B = \begin{bmatrix} 40 \\ 10 \\ 20 \end{bmatrix}$

7. $A = \begin{bmatrix} 0 & .2 & .3 \\ .1 & 0 & .2 \\ .3 & .2 & 0 \end{bmatrix}, \quad B = \begin{bmatrix} 1000 \\ 800 \\ 1500 \end{bmatrix}$

8. $A = \begin{bmatrix} .02 & .01 & .04 \\ .01 & .01 & .02 \\ .02 & .05 & .03 \end{bmatrix}, \quad B = \begin{bmatrix} 400 \\ 400 \\ 300 \end{bmatrix}$

Recall that an economic system with input–output matrix A is in equilibrium at the activity level X when AX = X—that is, when all the production of the system is required to support the system at that level. Observe that for any A, the system is in equilibrium when every component of X is 0. If there is a nonzero vector X for which the system is in equilibrium, then the linear system (I − A)X = 0 has infinitely many nonzero solutions. This observation is demonstrated in Exercises 9–12.

9. Let an economic system with three activities have the input–output matrix

$$A = \begin{bmatrix} .2 & .5 & .3 \\ .4 & .2 & .4 \\ .6 & .1 & .3 \end{bmatrix}.$$

Find all nonzero activity vectors X for which the system is in equilibrium.

10. Let an economic system with three activities have the input–output matrix

$$A = \begin{bmatrix} .2 & .1 & .2 \\ .2 & .3 & .4 \\ .6 & .6 & .4 \end{bmatrix}.$$

Find all nonzero activity vectors X for which the system is in equilibrium.

11. Let an economic system with four activities have the input–output matrix

$$A = \begin{bmatrix} .2 & .5 & .4 & .2 \\ .3 & .4 & .2 & .4 \\ 0 & .3 & .3 & .1 \\ .2 & .2 & 0 & .2 \end{bmatrix}.$$

Find all nonzero activity vectors X for which the system is in equilibrium.

12. Construct a 3 × 3 matrix A with positive entries for which each row sums to 1. (See Exercise 9.) Show that for an activity vector

$$X = \begin{bmatrix} k \\ k \\ k \end{bmatrix},$$

where k is any positive constant, the system is in equilibrium.

13. In Example 3 it was assumed that the goal of the state was to export 100 units of agricultural products without importing any manufactured goods. If instead the state was willing to import 30 units of manufactured goods from outside, determine how much the activities within the state could be reduced. (*Hint:* Let $b_3 = -30$ in the output vector B.)

14. Suppose that a goal for the state in Example 3 is to replace some of its agricultural exports with manufactured goods. In particular, assume that the goal is to export 20 units of manufactured goods and only 80 units of agricultural products. How is the economic activity within the state affected?

15. A cattle ranch raises some grain to feed the cattle and sells the rest. Some of the cattle are not sold but kept for breeding. The input–output matrix for the past year for this ranch is given by

$$\begin{array}{cc} & \text{Grain} \quad \text{Cattle} \\ A = & \begin{bmatrix} .05 & 1.2 \\ 0 & .1 \end{bmatrix} \begin{array}{l} \text{Grain} \quad (1 \text{ unit} = 1 \text{ ton}) \\ \text{Cattle} \quad (1 \text{ unit} = 1 \text{ head}) \end{array} \end{array}$$

a. Suppose that during the past year, the rancher grew 1000 tons of grain and raised 200 head of cattle. How much of this was available to sell?

b. If the rancher wanted to be able to sell 1000 tons of grain and 200 head of cattle, how much would have to be produced?

16. Refer to Exercise 15. Suppose that the rancher decided that next year he would grow only enough grain to feed his own cattle. How much grain would have to be grown in order for him to be able to sell 240 head of cattle?

17. At the administrative offices of the DWB Company the service functions are divided into three areas: Repair, Maintenance, and Custodial. The input–output matrix for this system is given by the following (where each unit is 1 worker-hour of labor):

$$\begin{array}{cccc} & \text{Repair} & \text{Maintenance} & \text{Custodial} \\ A = & \begin{bmatrix} .1 & .1 & .05 \\ .2 & .1 & .1 \\ .05 & .1 & .05 \end{bmatrix} & \begin{array}{l} \text{Repair} \\ \text{Maintenance} \\ \text{Custodial} \end{array} \end{array}$$

Suppose that at the present time the company employs workers in these areas who provide 40 hr of repair, 60 hr of maintenance, and 120 hr of custodial services per week at the administrative offices.

a. For each area, determine how many hours per week are actually being provided to other occupants in the building.

b. Suppose the building director felt that these units needed to provide the other occupants with 30 hr of repairs, 40 hr of maintenance, and 100 hr of custodial services. How will the activity of each service area be affected?

18. The prime minister of the state of Pandemonia has grouped the industrial production of the country into four categories: machine tools, communication equipment, construction equipment, and vehicles. The input–output matrix for the system of industrial production is

Machine Tools	Com. Equip.	Const. Equip.	Vehicles	
.1	.05	.2	.2	Machine Tools
.05	.1	.05	.05	Com. Equip.
.05	0	.1	.05	Const. Equip.
.2	.3	.4	.2	Vehicles

Suppose that at present, the country is producing 140 units of machine tools, 20 units of communication equipment, 100 units of construction equipment, and 40 units of vehicles. Determine what must be imported to support this system and how much this system provides for export at these levels of production.

19. Refer to Exercise 18. The prime minister would like to see

Pandemonia's economy be able to export 100 units of machine tools and 80 units of construction equipment, while being self-sufficient in communication equipment and needing to import only 40 units of vehicles. Determine the level of production in each category necessary to accomplish this goal.

20. Let

$$A = \begin{bmatrix} .2 & .4 & .4 \\ .1 & .5 & .4 \\ .6 & .2 & .2 \end{bmatrix}$$

be the input–output matrix for an economic system.

a. Verify that there are nonzero vectors X for which the system is in equilibrium. (See Exercise 12.)

b. Show, however, that there is no activity vector X for which $X - AX = B$ when

$$B = \begin{bmatrix} 1 \\ 0 \\ 0 \end{bmatrix}, \quad \begin{bmatrix} 0 \\ 1 \\ 0 \end{bmatrix}, \quad \text{or} \quad \begin{bmatrix} 0 \\ 0 \\ 1 \end{bmatrix}.$$

c. Explain what this implies about an economic system with such an input–output matrix.

11.6
Determinants and
Cramer's Rule

The determinant played a central role in the classical study of matrices and linear systems. Numerous techniques have been devised to calculate the determinant of a square matrix and to calculate matrix inverses using determinants. Today, determinants are given less consideration. A lot of computational effort is expended in finding the determinant of a large matrix. After this numerical value is obtained, except for knowing whether or not the matrix has an inverse, very little information has been gained about the matrix. There are, however, instances where theoretical results can be obtained or verified by considering determinants of a class of matrices. For this reason we briefly consider determinants of $n \times n$ matrices.

In Section 11.2 we defined the determinant of the general 2×2 matrix

$$A = \begin{bmatrix} a_{11} & a_{12} \\ a_{21} & a_{22} \end{bmatrix}$$

to be the number $d = a_{11}a_{22} - a_{21}a_{12}$. We now use **det** A to denote the determinant of a square matrix A. It is also common to represent the determinant by enclosing the matrix entries with vertical bars; that is,

$$\det A = \begin{vmatrix} a_{11} & a_{12} \\ a_{21} & a_{22} \end{vmatrix}.$$

The "arrow diagram" in Figure 11.6 can be used to remember the formula for det A. The arrows join the factors in each term of det A; the upward-pointing arrow is associated with the term that is affixed a negative sign.

$$\det A = a_{11}a_{22} - a_{21}a_{22}$$

From Figure 11.6 we see that if I is the 2×2 identity matrix, then $\det I = 1$; if A is a 2×2 upper-triangular matrix, then $\det A$ is the product of the diagonal entries $a_{11}a_{22}$. The determinant of a general 3×3 matrix A is defined to preserve these two properties and to ensure A will have an inverse if and only if $\det A \neq 0$.

Definition 11.7

The 3×3 matrix

$$A = \begin{bmatrix} a_{11} & a_{12} & a_{13} \\ a_{21} & a_{22} & a_{23} \\ a_{31} & a_{32} & a_{33} \end{bmatrix}$$

has determinant

$$\det A = a_{11}a_{22}a_{33} + a_{12}a_{23}a_{31} + a_{13}a_{32}a_{21}$$
$$- a_{31}a_{22}a_{13} - a_{21}a_{12}a_{33} - a_{11}a_{23}a_{32}.$$

The arrow diagram in Figure 11.7 can be used to remember the formula for a 3×3 determinant.

Figure 11.7

Arrows joining the factors in each term of det A

$$a_{11}a_{22}a_{33} + a_{12}a_{23}a_{31} + a_{13}a_{32}a_{21} - a_{31}a_{22}a_{13} - a_{21}a_{12}a_{33} - a_{11}a_{23}a_{32}$$

EXAMPLE 1

Find the determinant of the matrix

$$A = \begin{bmatrix} 1 & 2 & 3 \\ 4 & 5 & 6 \\ 7 & 8 & 9 \end{bmatrix}.$$

SOLUTION

Referring to Figure 11.7, we get

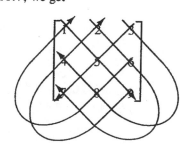

$$\begin{aligned}
\det A &= 1 \cdot 5 \cdot 9 + 2 \cdot 6 \cdot 7 + 3 \cdot 8 \cdot 4 - 7 \cdot 5 \cdot 3 - 4 \cdot 2 \cdot 9 - 1 \cdot 6 \cdot 8 \\
&= 45 + 84 + 96 - 105 - 72 - 48 \\
&= 225 - 225 \\
&= 0.
\end{aligned}$$

Matrix A does not have an inverse.

EXAMPLE 2

Find the determinant of the matrix

$$B = \begin{bmatrix} 8 & -7 & 17 \\ 0 & 2 & -1 \\ 0 & 0 & -3 \end{bmatrix}.$$

SOLUTION

Referring to Figure 11.7, we see that the only arrow that does not pass through a 0 in the upper-triangular matrix B is the arrow that joins the terms on the diagonal. Thus,

$$\det B = 8 \cdot 2 \cdot (-3) = -48.$$

The reasoning applied in Example 2 may be used to show that the determinant of any 3×3 upper-triangular matrix is the product of the diagonal entries $a_{11}a_{22}a_{33}$. In Sections 11.3 and 11.4, we changed augmented matrices to upper-triangular form using elementary row operations. The effect of these operations on the determinant of a matrix is summarized in the following theorem, which is given without proof.

Theorem 11.2

> Assume A is a 3×3 matrix.
>
> 1. If A' is obtained from A by interchanging two rows of A, then $\det A' = -\det A$.
>
> 2. If A' is obtained from A by multiplying one row of A by the constant k, then $\det A' = k \det A$.
>
> 3. If A' is obtained from A by adding a multiple of one row to another row, then $\det A' = \det A$.

Knowing the effect of elementary row operations on the determinant of a matrix, we can find determinants by transforming a matrix to upper-triangular form, recording the use of any constant multiples or row interchanges, and then forming the product of the diagonal entries in the upper-triangular matrix.

EXAMPLE 3

Find the determinant of the matrix

$$C = \begin{bmatrix} 1 & 2 & 4 \\ 3 & 5 & -2 \\ 5 & -1 & 5 \end{bmatrix}$$

after transforming it to upper-triangular form.

SOLUTION   Applying elementary row operations to matrix C yields

$$\begin{vmatrix} 1 & 2 & 4 \\ 3 & 5 & -2 \\ 5 & -1 & 5 \end{vmatrix} = \begin{vmatrix} 1 & 2 & 4 \\ 0 & -1 & -14 \\ 0 & -11 & -15 \end{vmatrix} \qquad \begin{array}{l}(-3)\ (row\ 1)\ added\ to\ row\ 2 \\ \\ (-5)\ (row\ 1)\ added\ to\ row\ 3\end{array}$$

$$= \begin{vmatrix} 1 & 2 & 4 \\ 0 & -1 & -14 \\ 0 & 0 & 139 \end{vmatrix} \qquad (-11)\ (row\ 2)\ added\ to\ row\ 3.$$

From Theorem 11.2 we have

$$\det C = \begin{vmatrix} 1 & 2 & 4 \\ 0 & -1 & -14 \\ 0 & 0 & 139 \end{vmatrix}$$

$$= -139.$$

The procedure used in Example 3 can be used to find $n \times n$ determinants for $n > 3$. Taking the determinant of an $n \times n$ upper-triangular matrix A to be the product of the diagonal entries $a_{11}a_{22}a_{33} \cdots a_{nn}$, and assuming that the results of Theorem 11.2 are true for any $n \times n$ matrix, we have a working definition for the determinant of any $n \times n$ matrix.

EXAMPLE 4   Find the determinant of the matrix

$$A = \begin{bmatrix} 1 & 1 & 2 & 2 \\ 2 & 2 & 8 & 7 \\ 1 & 3 & 1 & 6 \\ 3 & 5 & 8 & 5 \end{bmatrix}.$$

SOLUTION   Performing the necessary elementary row operations to eliminate entries in the first column of A, we obtain

$$\begin{vmatrix} 1 & 1 & 2 & 2 \\ 2 & 2 & 8 & 7 \\ 1 & 3 & 1 & 6 \\ 3 & 5 & 8 & 5 \end{vmatrix} = \begin{vmatrix} 1 & 1 & 2 & 2 \\ 0 & 0 & 4 & 3 \\ 0 & 2 & -1 & 4 \\ 0 & 2 & 2 & -1 \end{vmatrix}.$$

Interchanging rows 2 and 3 and multiplying the new row 2 by -1 and adding to row 4 yield

$$\begin{vmatrix} 1 & 1 & 2 & 2 \\ 0 & 0 & 4 & 3 \\ 0 & 2 & -1 & 4 \\ 0 & 2 & 2 & -1 \end{vmatrix} = -\begin{vmatrix} 1 & 1 & 2 & 2 \\ 0 & 2 & -1 & 4 \\ 0 & 0 & 4 & 3 \\ 0 & 0 & 3 & -5 \end{vmatrix},$$

where the minus sign appears because of the interchange of two rows. Finally, to eliminate the 3 in the last row, we multiply row 3 by $-3/4$ and add the result to row 4 to obtain

$$\det A = - \begin{vmatrix} 1 & 1 & 2 & 2 \\ 0 & 2 & -1 & 4 \\ 0 & 0 & 4 & 3 \\ 0 & 0 & 0 & -29/4 \end{vmatrix}$$

$$= -1 \cdot 2 \cdot 4 \cdot \frac{-29}{4}$$

$$= 58.$$

The following theorem directly links determinants and solutions to systems of linear equations.

**Theorem 11.3
Cramer's Rule**

Suppose that A is an $n \times n$ matrix with $\det A \neq 0$, and B is an $n \times 1$ column vector. Then, the kth component of the solution X to the linear system $AX = B$ is given by

$$x_k = \frac{\det A_k}{\det A},$$

where A_k is the matrix obtained from A by replacing its kth column with B, for $k = 1, 2, \ldots, n$.

Cramer's rule is frequently used as a theoretical tool; it is very inefficient computationally for solving $n \times n$ linear systems when $n > 2$.

EXAMPLE 5

Use Cramer's rule to solve the linear system

$$3x_1 + 4x_2 = 5$$
$$2x_1 + 2x_2 = 8.$$

SOLUTION

Letting

$$A = \begin{bmatrix} 3 & 4 \\ 2 & 2 \end{bmatrix}, \quad X = \begin{bmatrix} x_1 \\ x_2 \end{bmatrix}, \quad \text{and} \quad B = \begin{bmatrix} 5 \\ 8 \end{bmatrix},$$

we can write the given linear system as $AX = B$. Referring to Cramer's rule, we get

$$A_1 = \begin{bmatrix} 5 & 4 \\ 8 & 2 \end{bmatrix} \quad \text{and} \quad A_2 = \begin{bmatrix} 3 & 5 \\ 2 & 8 \end{bmatrix};$$

thus,

$$x_1 = \frac{\det A_1}{\det A} = \frac{\begin{vmatrix} 5 & 4 \\ 8 & 2 \end{vmatrix}}{\begin{vmatrix} 3 & 4 \\ 2 & 2 \end{vmatrix}} = \frac{-22}{-2} = 11$$

and

$$x_2 = \frac{\det A_2}{\det A} = \frac{\begin{vmatrix} 3 & 5 \\ 2 & 8 \end{vmatrix}}{\begin{vmatrix} 3 & 4 \\ 2 & 2 \end{vmatrix}} = \frac{14}{-2} = -7.$$

Cramer's rule can be used to find the value of just one variable in the solution to a linear system.

EXAMPLE 6

Find the value of y in the solution to the linear system

$$
\begin{aligned}
2x - y + z &= 0 \\
3x - 2y - 2z &= 5 \\
5x + y + 9z &= 1.
\end{aligned}
$$

SOLUTION

Using Cramer's rule, we get

$$y = \frac{\begin{vmatrix} 2 & 0 & 1 \\ 3 & 5 & -2 \\ 5 & 1 & 9 \end{vmatrix}}{\begin{vmatrix} 2 & -1 & 1 \\ 3 & -2 & -2 \\ 5 & 1 & 9 \end{vmatrix}}.$$

From Figure 11.7,

$$
\begin{aligned}
\begin{vmatrix} 2 & 0 & 1 \\ 3 & 5 & -2 \\ 5 & 1 & 9 \end{vmatrix} &= 2 \cdot 5 \cdot 9 + 1 \cdot 1 \cdot 3 - 5 \cdot 5 \cdot 1 - 2(-2)1 \\
&= 97 - 25 \\
&= 72.
\end{aligned}
$$

Also,

$$
\begin{aligned}
\begin{vmatrix} 2 & -1 & 1 \\ 3 & -2 & -2 \\ 5 & 1 & 9 \end{vmatrix} &= 2(-2)9 + (-1)(-2)5 + 1 \cdot 1 \cdot 3 - 5(-2)1 \\
&\quad - 3(-1)9 - 2(-2)1 \\
&= 54 - 36 \\
&= 18.
\end{aligned}
$$

Thus, $y = 72/18 = 4$.

EXERCISES 11.6

In Exercises 1–12 evaluate each of the given determinants.

1. $\begin{vmatrix} 1 & 2 \\ 2 & 1 \end{vmatrix}$

2. $\begin{vmatrix} 3 & 5 \\ -1 & 2 \end{vmatrix}$

3. $\begin{vmatrix} 1 & 2 & 3 \\ 4 & 3 & 2 \\ 1 & 5 & 6 \end{vmatrix}$

4. $\begin{vmatrix} 1 & -1 & 8 \\ 4 & 2 & 4 \\ 7 & 3 & 0 \end{vmatrix}$

5. $\begin{vmatrix} 2 & -1 & 3 \\ 4 & 0 & -5 \\ 6 & 2 & 3 \end{vmatrix}$

6. $\begin{vmatrix} 2 & -1 & -1 \\ 3 & 4 & -5 \\ -1 & 6 & -4 \end{vmatrix}$

7. $\begin{vmatrix} 3 & 1 & -2 \\ 1 & -2 & 5 \\ 4 & -1 & 3 \end{vmatrix}$

8. $\begin{vmatrix} -4 & 5 & 1 \\ 3 & -2 & 1 \\ 4 & 1 & 5 \end{vmatrix}$

9. $\begin{vmatrix} 1 & 2 & -1 & 1 \\ 3 & -2 & 4 & 2 \\ 0 & 1 & -2 & 5 \\ 4 & -1 & 2 & 3 \end{vmatrix}$

10. $\begin{vmatrix} -2 & 7 & 1 & 4 \\ 3 & -3 & 0 & 2 \\ 1 & 4 & 1 & 6 \\ 4 & 2 & -2 & 1 \end{vmatrix}$

11. $\begin{vmatrix} 1 & -1 & 1 & -1 \\ -1 & 2 & 1 & 0 \\ 1 & 1 & 1 & -1 \\ 2 & -2 & 3 & 4 \end{vmatrix}$

12. $\begin{vmatrix} -3 & 0 & 0 & 1 \\ 4 & 1 & 4 & -1 \\ 1 & 2 & -2 & 1 \\ -1 & 4 & -3 & 5 \end{vmatrix}$

In Exercises 13–20 use Cramer's rule to solve the given linear system, if it has a unique solution.

13. $3x + 5y = 9$
    $5x + 3y = -1$

14. $2x + y = 2$
    $3x + 2y = 1$

15. $4x + 3y = -1$
    $5x + 2y = 11$

16. $5x + 7y = -10$
    $-3x + 2y = 6$

17. $3x + 9y = -4$
    $2x + 6y = 7$

18. $7x + 5y = 9$
    $4x + 3y = 6$

19. $5x + 7y + 2z = 7$
    $3x - 4y + z = 3$
    $2x + y + z = 4$

20. $2x + y - 2z = 0$
    $4x - 3y + z = 5$
    $-2x + 3y - z = 1$

CH. 11 REVIEW

I. Key Terms & Concepts

Mathematics

Matrix
Inner Product
Matrix Multiplication
System of Linear Equations
Identity Matrix
Inverse Matrix
Coefficient Matrix
Determinant of a Matrix
Augmented Matrix
Reduction Method
Gaussian Elimination
Gauss–Jordan Elimination
Cramer's Rule

Business

Data Matrix
Input–Output Analysis
Economic Equilibrium

II. True or False

Indicate whether each statement is true or false.

1. If A and B are matrices for which $AB = BA$, then A and B are square matrices.

2. If the system $AX = 0$ has a solution, then $AX = B$ has a solution.

3. If A is an invertible matrix, then $X = 0$ is the only solution to the system $AX = 0$.

4. Matrices of different dimension can be added only if one of them is the 0 matrix.

5. The identity matrix is invertible.

6. If X is an n-component row vector and Y is an n-component column vector, then the inner product of X and Y is XY.

7. If A is any square matrix, then $\det(-A) = -\det(A)$.

8. If $AX = B$ is any system of equations with a unique solution, then Cramer's rule can be used to solve it.

9. In a system of linear equations, replacing any equation by the sum of all the equations creates an equivalent system.

10. If A is an input–output matrix, a nonzero solution to $AX - X = 0$ corresponds to a level of activity at which the economy is in equilibrium.

III. Drill Problems

In Problems 1–6 find the indicated matrix or number where

$$A = \begin{bmatrix} 3 & -6 & 5 \\ 1 & -2 & 1 \\ -2 & 5 & 1 \end{bmatrix}, \quad B = \begin{bmatrix} 2 \\ -3 \\ 4 \end{bmatrix},$$

$$C = \begin{bmatrix} -2 & 4 & -5 \\ 0 & 7 & 2 \end{bmatrix}, \quad D = \begin{bmatrix} 2 & 1 & 0 \end{bmatrix}.$$

1. $3A - 2BD$

2. DB

3. CB

4. ABD

5. A^{-1}

6. $\det BD$

7. Let

$$A = \begin{bmatrix} 2 & 0 & -3 \\ -4 & 2 & 7 \\ 2 & -1 & -3 \end{bmatrix} \quad \text{and} \quad B = \begin{bmatrix} 1/2 & 3/2 & 3 \\ 1 & 0 & -1 \\ 0 & 1 & 2 \end{bmatrix}.$$

Show that A and B are inverses of each other; then verify that $\det A$ is the reciprocal of $\det B$.

8. Let

$$A = \begin{bmatrix} 3 & -1 & 2 \\ 1 & 0 & 4 \\ 2 & -1 & 5 \end{bmatrix} \quad \text{and} \quad B = \begin{bmatrix} -2 & -2 & 1 \\ 3 & 1 & 4 \\ 0 & 1 & -3 \end{bmatrix}.$$

Show that det AB equals the product of det A and det B.

In Problems 9–12 use the reduction method to find all solutions to the system of equations.

9. $4x + y - z = 8$
   $-2x + 3y + 2z = 10$

10. $x + 2y - z = -3$
    $-2x + 3y + 5z = -1$
    $2x - 4y - 2z = 5$

11. $8x - 2y + 5z = 2$
    $-3x + y + 2z = -6$
    $5x - 3y - 7z = 4$
    $2x - y - 5z = 8$

12. $x + 2y - z + w = 5$
    $-x + 2z - w = 4$
    $2x + y + z = -3$
    $3x + 4y + 5z - w = 3$

In Problems 13 and 14, for the given input–output matrix A, find the activity vector X required to produce the output vector B.

13. $A = \begin{bmatrix} .2 & .4 \\ .6 & .2 \end{bmatrix}$, $B = \begin{bmatrix} 80 \\ 140 \end{bmatrix}$

14. $A = \begin{bmatrix} .6 & .2 & .4 \\ .1 & .2 & .1 \\ 0 & .2 & .3 \end{bmatrix}$, $B = \begin{bmatrix} 200 \\ 80 \\ 30 \end{bmatrix}$

15. Find all nonzero activity vectors X for which the economic system with this input–output matrix is in equilibrium:

$$A = \begin{bmatrix} .1 & .1 & .3 \\ .2 & .6 & .2 \\ .5 & .7 & .3 \end{bmatrix}.$$

IV. Applications

1. There are three types of life insurance policies that a sales representative can sell: term, whole life, and universal life. The following matrix gives the number of policies sold by three different representatives during a recent month:

	Term	Whole Life	Universal Life
Rep. A	30	8	40
Rep. B	24	10	32
Rep. C	34	6	38

Assume representatives A, B, and C earned $4400, $4060, and $4160, respectively, in commissions for these sales. If the commission earned depends only on the type of policy sold and is the same for all representatives, find the commission that is earned for selling a policy of each type.

2. Each Monday, Wednesday, and Friday, the workers in a downtown office send someone out to buy lunches at a nearby fast-food restaurant. The following matrix shows the total orders for the three days last week:

	Monday	Wednesday	Friday
Regular Burgers	10	8	5
Deluxe Burgers	15	12	4
Chicken Bites	7	8	12
French Fries	26	20	14
Salad Bowl	6	10	18

The following matrix shows the cost of these items at each of the four local fast-food restaurants:

	Regular Burger	Deluxe Burger	Chicken Bites	French Bites	Salad Bowl
Burger Lord	1.05	1.70	2.20	.55	1.45
Chardy's	.90	1.80	1.85	.55	1.55
Mack's	1.00	1.55	1.90	.60	1.60
Wyndee's	.95	1.60	2.00	.50	1.50

Find the matrix whose entries are the total cost of each day's order if it had been placed at any of the four restaurants.

3. You are the distributor for a certain brand of wine. The manager of a local liquor store has just called, wanting

to know why this week's order had not yet come in. You try to explain that your route driver called in ill this morning, but the manager demands the usual order and wants it delivered within the hour. Unfortunately, you do not know what the usual order is and you cannot reach the driver. A check of your accounts shows that during the months of April, May, June, and July, this customer was billed for $456, $474, $499, and $511, respectively. The following matrix gives the price per case of each of your four kinds of wine during those months. Find how many cases of each kind of wine constitute this store's usual order.

$$
\begin{array}{c}
\text{April} \\
\text{May} \\
\text{June} \\
\text{July}
\end{array}
\begin{array}{cccc}
\text{Rosé} & \text{Burgundy} & \text{Rhine} & \text{Chablis} \\
\begin{bmatrix}
20 & 24 & 18 & 22 \\
20 & 24 & 21 & 22 \\
25 & 24 & 21 & 22 \\
25 & 28 & 21 & 22
\end{bmatrix}
\end{array}
$$

4. Your boss has just given you a $450 budget to buy food for the company picnic. You figure that, including condiments, it will cost $2.80 for enough hamburger for one person and $2.40 for enough chicken for one person. You expect that it will be necessary to buy enough meat for 120 people. Potato salad costs $2.20 per pound and cole slaw costs $2.70 per pound. You have already decided that you will buy twice as much potato salad as cole slaw. Set up a system of equations whose solutions include all the possible ways for you to spend your budget on the food. Write all the solutions in terms of the amount of cole slaw you buy.

5. Assume that the following is an input–output matrix for four commodities exported by Texas:

	Oil/Gas	Cotton	Cattle	Grain
Oil/Gas	.1	.2	.05	.2
Cotton	0	.2	.1	.05
Cattle	.05	.1	.2	.1
Grain	.05	.1	.3	.1

If Texas exported 100, 50, 150, and 40 units of oil and gas, cotton, cattle, and grain last year, determine the number of units of these commodities that were actually produced in that state last year.

The total cost C of manufacturing Schuss Skis is a cubic function of the pairs produced q. Find the cubic function that passes through the Schuss cost data in the table:

q	20	40	50	100
C	1144	2072	2575	6200

CHAPTER 13

Curve Fitting

13.1
Exact Fits and Error Measurements

One of the important steps in mathematical modeling is determining a relationship between the variables of interest. Once data have been collected and plotted, a curve or rule of correspondence must be found to "fit" the data. The modeler must decide on the kind of function or curve to be used, be it a polynomial, rational function, exponential function, or some other function or combination of functions. After making this determination, a curve-fitting scheme is used to find the coefficients in the rule of correspondence for the desired function. The modeler, rather than the fitting scheme, determines the type of fitting function.

In most of the examples we have considered, just enough data were given to yield an exact fit between dependent and independent variables. When cost was assumed to be a linear function of quantity produced, two data points were considered (two points determine a line). For quadratic functions three data values were given, and so on. Often many points that are not collinear must nonetheless be approximated by a line. Before considering fitting curves that come "near" data points, we treat exact polynomial fits.

Theorem 13.1

> Given the $n + 1$ data points (x_0, y_0), (x_1, y_1), ..., (x_n, y_n), where all the x_i are distinct, there exists a polynomial p of degree n, or less, such that $p(x_i) = y_i$ for $i = 0, 1, ..., n$. (Polynomial p is called an **interpolating polynomial** through the data.)

To find the interpolating polynomial of least degree through (x_0, y_0), ..., (x_n, y_n) let

$$p(x) = a_0 + a_1 x + a_2 x^2 + \cdots + a_n x^n$$

where the coefficients are yet to be determined. Evaluating $p(x)$ at each data point, we must have:

$$(13.1) \quad \begin{aligned} p(x_0) &= a_0 + a_1 x_0 + a_2 x_0^2 + \cdots + a_n x_0^n = y_0 \\ p(x_1) &= a_0 + a_1 x_1 + a_2 x_1^2 + \cdots + a_n x_1^n = y_1 \\ &\overline{} \\ p(x_n) &= a_0 + a_1 x_n + a_2 x_n^2 + \cdots + a_n x_n^n = y_n. \end{aligned}$$

Now (13.1) is an $(n + 1) \times (n + 1)$ system of linear equations for the coefficients $a_0, a_1, ..., a_n$. This linear system, called the **Vandermonde system**, has matrix form:

$$(13.2) \quad \begin{bmatrix} 1 & x_0 & x_0^2 & \cdots & x_0^n \\ 1 & x_1 & x_1^2 & \cdots & x_1^n \\ \hline 1 & x_n & x_n^2 & \cdots & x_n^n \end{bmatrix} \begin{bmatrix} a_0 \\ a_1 \\ \hline a_n \end{bmatrix} = \begin{bmatrix} y_0 \\ y_1 \\ \hline y_n \end{bmatrix}.$$

Vandermonde showed that system (13.2) has a unique solution so long as $x_0, x_1, ..., x_n$ are all different.

EXAMPLE 1

The daily total cost C of producing Daisy Donuts is assumed to be a cubic function of the quantity q (in dozens) produced. On a day when 40 dozen are produced, the total cost is \$66.80; when 50 dozen are produced, the total cost is

$75; when 80 dozen are produced, the total cost is $128.40; and when 100 dozen are produced, the total cost is $200. If Daisy can produce up to 120 dozen per day, find C in terms of q.

SOLUTION

If $C = a_0 + a_1q + a_2q^2 + a_3q^3$, then the Vandermonde system for the data $(40, 66.8)$, $(50, 75)$, $(80, 128.4)$, $(100, 200)$ is:

$$\begin{bmatrix} 1 & 40 & 40^2 & 40^3 \\ 1 & 50 & 50^2 & 50^3 \\ 1 & 80 & 80^2 & 80^3 \\ 1 & 100 & 100^2 & 100^3 \end{bmatrix} \begin{bmatrix} a_0 \\ a_1 \\ a_2 \\ a_3 \end{bmatrix} = \begin{bmatrix} 66.8 \\ 75 \\ 128.4 \\ 200 \end{bmatrix}.$$

Using the reduction method on the augmented matrix, we find:

$$\begin{bmatrix} 1 & 40 & 40^2 & 40^2 & | & 66.8 \\ 1 & 50 & 50^2 & 50^3 & | & 75 \\ 1 & 80 & 80^2 & 80^3 & | & 128.4 \\ 1 & 100 & 100^2 & 100^3 & | & 200 \end{bmatrix} \sim \begin{bmatrix} 1 & 40 & 40^2 & 40^3 & | & 66.8 \\ 0 & 1 & 90 & 6100 & | & 8.2 \\ 0 & 1 & 120 & 11{,}200 & | & 1.54 \\ 0 & 1 & 140 & 15{,}600 & | & 2.22 \end{bmatrix}$$

$$\sim \begin{bmatrix} 1 & 40 & 40^2 & 40^3 & | & 66.8 \\ 0 & 1 & 90 & 6100 & | & 8.2 \\ 0 & 0 & 1 & 170 & | & .024 \\ 0 & 0 & 1 & 190 & | & .028 \end{bmatrix}$$

$$\sim \begin{bmatrix} 1 & 40 & 40^2 & 40^3 & | & 66.8 \\ 0 & 1 & 90 & 6100 & | & 8.2 \\ 0 & 0 & 1 & 170 & | & .024 \\ 0 & 0 & 0 & 1 & | & .0002 \end{bmatrix}.$$

Back-substituting, we find $a_3 = .0002$, $a_2 = -.01$, $a_1 = .5$, and $a_0 = 50$; thus,

$$C = 50 + .5q - .01q^2 + .0002q^3, \qquad 0 \le q \le 120.$$

Figure 13.1 illustrates this cubic function that fits the four given data points.

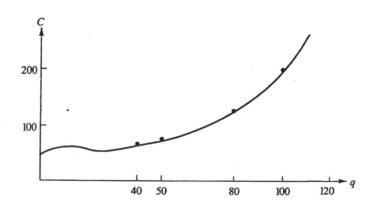

Figure 13.1

The cubic interpolating polynomial through the data points (40, 66.8), (50, 75), (80, 128.4), and (100, 200)

Although there are more efficient schemes, solving the Vandermonde system (13.2) provides a direct method for finding the interpolating polynomial of least degree through given data points.

If more than 4 pairs of data values were given in Example 1, there may not be a cubic polynomial that passes through the data. If eight data points are given, we know that an interpolating polynomial of degree no more than 7 can be found to fit the data exactly. As illustrated in Figure 13.2(a), such a polynomial could have as many as six relative extreme values, giving rise to a "roly-poly" cost function.

According to our earlier reasoning, cubic cost functions allow for a variable cost per unit that decreases as output q increases, up to a point, but beyond that point, variable cost per unit increases as output approaches plant capacity. If a cubic cost function is our choice, but if no such function passing through the data exists, we must settle for one that comes close (in some sense) to the data, as illustrated in Figure 13.2(b). Although this alternative may at first seem undesirable, total cost probably depends on other things besides output q. The curve then can be thought to fit an average or expected value of C. This kind of reasoning is the basis for a statistical approach to curve fitting.

Figure 13.2

(a) An interpolating polynomial through eight data points.
(b) A cubic polynomial passing near eight data points

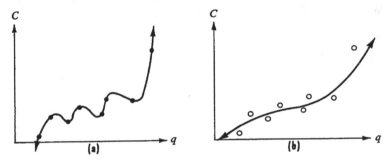

If fitting curves are to come as close as possible to data points, we must determine a way to measure closeness. We begin by measuring the **deviation** of the fitting curve at each data point. For the curve $y = f(x)$, the deviation d_i at data point (x_i, y_i) is given by

$$d_i = f(x_i) - y_i,$$

the vertical distance from the curve to the point. A deviation is positive if the curve is above the point, and negative if the curve is below the point. (See Figure 13.3).

Figure 13.3

Deviations of a fitting function from data points

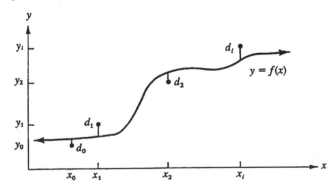

To measure the overall deviation of a function from the data points, merely adding the individual deviations is not a good idea. Since the deviations may be positive or negative, a sum of 0 can be obtained by adding large positive and large negative deviations. For a curve that is 100 units above the first data point and 100 units below the second data point, the sum of the first two deviations is 0, even though the curve is not "near" either point. One alternative to adding the deviations over all data points is to add their absolute values, all of which are nonnegative. Then for a "best" fit of $n + 1$ given data points among all functions of a certain type (perhaps cubic polynomials), we would require a function for which the sum of the absolute deviations

(13.3)
$$A = |d_0| + |d_1| + \cdots + |d_n|$$

is as small as possible.

Another way to measure the overall deviation of the function is to sum the squares of the deviations:

(13.4)
$$S = d_0^2 + d_1^2 + \cdots + d_n^2.$$

It can be shown that S, the sum of the squared deviations, has desirable analytic and statistical properties that the sum of the absolute deviations A does not have. Consequently, in the next section we will consider least squares fitted curves—that is, curves of a specified type for which S is as small as possible.

The sums in error measurements (13.3) and (13.4) are more conveniently expressed using sigma notation. (See Section 9.2.) Using this notation, we can write equation (13.3) as

$$A = \sum_{i=0}^{n} |d_i|,$$

and equation (13.4) becomes

$$S = \sum_{i=0}^{n} d_i^2.$$

EXAMPLE 2

For the data points $(x_0, y_0) = (40, 66.8)$, $(x_1, y_1) = (50, 75)$, $(x_2, y_2) = (80, 128.4)$, $(x_3, y_3) = (100, 200)$, and the linear fitting function $f(x) = 2x - 30$, evaluate the sum of the absolute deviations and the sum of the squared deviations as given in equations (13.3) and (13.4), respectively.

SOLUTION

Computing the four deviations, we have

$$d_0 = f(x_0) - y_0 = 50 - 66.8 = -16.8,$$
$$d_1 = f(x_1) - y_1 = 70 - 75 = -5,$$
$$d_2 = f(x_2) - y_2 = 130 - 128.4 = 1.6,$$

and

$$d_3 = f(x_3) - y_3 = 170 - 200 = -30.$$

Now

$$A = \sum_{i=0}^{3} |d_i| = 16.8 + 5 + 1.6 + 30 = 53.4,$$

while

$$S = \sum_{i=0}^{3} d_i^2 = 282.24 + 25 + 2.56 + 900 = 1209.8.$$

In instances where the units of measurement are important, $\sqrt{S}$ is used in place of S because $\sqrt{S}$ is given in the same units as the data. Here $\sqrt{S} \doteq 34.78$. ●

EXERCISES 13.1

In Exercises 1–8 find the interpolating polynomial of least degree through the given data by setting up and solving the Vandermonde system.

1. $(x_0, y_0) = (1, 14)$, $(x_1, y_1) = (2, 16)$, $(x_2, y_2) = (4, 14)$

2. $(x_0, y_0) = (2, 37)$, $(x_1, y_1) = (5, 25)$, $(x_2, y_2) = (8, -13)$

3. $(x_0, y_0) = (10, 380)$, $(x_1, y_1) = (30, 820)$, $(x_2, y_2) = (50, 1100)$

4. $(x_0, y_0) = (20, 1160)$, $(x_1, y_1) = (40, 2040)$, $(x_2, y_2) = (70, 3210)$

5.

i	0	1	2	3
x_i	1	2	5	10
y_i	10	12	78	748

6.

i	0	1	2	3
x_i	1	3	4	5
y_i	30	86	92	270

7.

i	0	1	2	3
x_i	10	20	40	60
y_i	110	150	170	650

8.

i	0	1	2	3
x_i	4	10	12	20
y_i	70	760	1242	6710

For the data and fitting functions in Exercises 9–14 find the sum of the absolute deviations and the sum of the squared deviations. Sketch a graph of the data with the fitting function.

9.

x	1	3	5	6	7
y	2	5	3	8	6

$f(x) = 2x - 4$

10. Same data as Exercise 9 but $f(x) = -44 + 35x - 4x^2$

11.

x	0	10	20	30	40
y	70	100	150	200	300

$f(x) = 72 + 1.6x + .1x^2$

12. Same data as Exercise 11 but $f(x) = 52 + 5.6x$

13.

x	10	20	30	50
y	100	90	85	80

$$f(x) = \frac{70x + 1300}{x + 10}$$

14. Same data as Exercise 13 but $f(x) = .0135x^2 - 1.3x + 111$

15. The variable cost per unit v for Tastee Pizzas is a quadratic function of the number of pizzas made per day q. Last week on Wednesday 200 pizzas were made at a variable cost per unit of $2. On Thursday $q = 280$ with $v = 1.5$, and on Friday $q = 400$ with $v = 1.6$. If up to 500 Tastee Pizzas can be made per day, give v as a quadratic function of q.

16. The variable cost per unit v of producing Flick lighters is thought to be a quadratic function of output q. On a day when $q = 5000$, $v = .3$; when $q = 10,000$, $v = .2$; and when $q = 25,000$, $v = .25$. If up to 30,000 Flick lighters can be produced per day, give v as a quadratic function of q.

17. The profit P from the manufacture and sale of Logo jackets is thought to be a cubic function of the quantity q produced and sold. Find the cubic polynomial that interpolates the Logo sales data in the table:

q	10	20	50	100
P	408	924	2400	3900

18. The total cost C of manufacturing Schuss Skis is a cubic function of the pairs produced q. Find the cubic function that passes through the Schuss cost data in the table:

q	20	40	50	100
C	1144	2072	2575	6200

19. Given three noncollinear points (x_0, y_0), (x_1, y_1), and (x_2, y_2), coefficients for the linear-to-linear rational function

$$f(x) = \frac{ax + b}{x + c}$$

that passes through these points may be found by solving the linear system:

$$\begin{bmatrix} 1 & x_0 & -y_0 \\ 1 & x_1 & -y_1 \\ 1 & x_2 & -y_2 \end{bmatrix} \begin{bmatrix} b \\ a \\ c \end{bmatrix} = \begin{bmatrix} x_0 y_0 \\ x_1 y_1 \\ x_2 y_2 \end{bmatrix}.$$

If the demand q (in tons) for peanuts at a farmer's market is a linear-to-linear rational function of the selling price p (per ton), use the linear system given above to fit the peanut demand data in the table:

p	1000	800	600
q	40	50	80

20. The variable cost per unit v of producing Inscent bath soap is assumed to be a linear-to-linear rational function of the quantity q (in pounds) produced. When $q = 10$, $v = 2$; when $q = 50$, $v = 1.68$; and when $q = 100$, $v = 1.46$. Use the linear system given in Exercise 19 to write v in terms of q.

13.2
First-Degree Least Squares Fits

Usually a good first approximation to a relationship between two variables is a linear one. One variable is assumed to be a first-degree, or linear, function of the other. If y is a linear function of x, then we know that $y = f(x)$, with

(13.5)
$$f(x) = a_0 + a_1 x$$

for some coefficients a_0 and a_1. As we have seen, if the linear function (13.5) is to pass through the data, then two data points completely determine the coefficients. In most modeling problems we have more than two data points, however, and the points are not collinear. Under these circumstances we could select the two best data points, use a different type of fitting function, or relax the requirement that the function fit the data. When all data are considered equally good and a linear fitting function is desired, a first-degree least squares fit of the data may be used. This fit is the first-degree polynomial for which the sum of the squared deviations over the given data is as small as possible.

To determine the first-degree least squares fit of the m data points (x_1, y_1), (x_2, y_2), ..., (x_m, y_m), where $m > 2$, we let f be of the form of equation (13.5) and examine the sum of the squared deviations over the data:

(13.6)
$$S = \sum_{i=1}^{m} d_i^2 = \sum_{i=1}^{m} [f(x_i) - y_i]^2$$
$$= \sum_{i=1}^{m} [a_0 + a_1 x_i - y_i]^2.$$

The sum S is a function of the two coefficients, a_0 and a_1, of the fitting function f. We seek values of a_0 and a_1 that minimize S.

As a function of two variables, the extreme values of S occur at its critical points: those points where the first partial derivatives of S are 0. Differentiating S term by term with respect to a_0, we find

(13.7)
$$\frac{\partial S}{\partial a_0} = \sum_{i=1}^{m} 2[a_0 + a_1 x_i - y_i],$$

whereas differentiating S with respect to a_1 yields

(13.8)
$$\frac{\partial S}{\partial a_1} = \sum_{i=1}^{m} 2[a_0 + a_1 x_i - y_i]x_i.$$

Setting equations (13.7) and (13.8) equal to 0, dividing by 2, and using properties of sigma notation to simplify, we have:

(13.9)
$$a_0 \sum_{i=1}^{m} 1 + a_1 \sum_{i=1}^{m} x_i = \sum_{i=1}^{m} y_i$$
$$a_0 \sum_{i=1}^{m} x_i + a_1 \sum_{i=1}^{m} x_i^2 = \sum_{i=1}^{m} x_i y_i.$$

Solutions to system (13.9) are critical points of S. So long as all x_i are not identical, it can be shown that (13.9) has a unique solution and that S has an absolute minimum at this solution. The 2×2 linear system (13.9) is called the system of **normal equations** for the first-degree least squares polynomial over the data $(x_1, y_1), (x_2, y_2), \ldots, (x_m, y_m)$. In matrix form, with the summation index omitted for simplicity, the normal equations become

(13.10)
$$\begin{bmatrix} m & \Sigma x_i \\ \Sigma x_i & \Sigma x_i^2 \end{bmatrix} \begin{bmatrix} a_0 \\ a_1 \end{bmatrix} = \begin{bmatrix} \Sigma y_i \\ \Sigma x_i y_i \end{bmatrix}.$$

EXAMPLE 1

The data in the table were gathered for Blast Beer at the airport lounge. They reflect the weekly sales of q bottles at selling price p dollars per bottle. Assume that q is a linear function of p, and find the first-degree least squares fit of these data. Then compute the deviation at each data point.

p	1.00	1.50	1.80	2.00	2.10
q	200	160	130	100	100

SOLUTION

From equation (13.10) the normal equations for the linear least squares fitting function

$$q = a_0 + a_1 p$$

take the form

$$\begin{bmatrix} 5 & \Sigma p_i \\ \Sigma p_i & \Sigma p_i^2 \end{bmatrix} \begin{bmatrix} a_0 \\ a_1 \end{bmatrix} = \begin{bmatrix} \Sigma q_i \\ \Sigma p_i q_i \end{bmatrix}.$$

The needed sums are computed in the table:

p_i^2	p_i	q_i	$p_i q_i$
1.0	1.0	200	200
2.25	1.5	160	240
3.24	1.8	130	234
4.0	2.0	100	200
4.41	2.1	100	210
(Σ) 14.9	8.4	690	1084

Applying the reduction method to the augmented matrix for the normal equations, we find

$$\begin{bmatrix} 5 & 8.4 & | & 690 \\ 8.4 & 14.9 & | & 1084 \end{bmatrix} \sim \begin{bmatrix} 1 & 1.68 & | & 138 \\ 0 & .788 & | & -75.2 \end{bmatrix}.$$

Back-substitution yields (to the nearest tenth)

$$a_1 = -\frac{75.2}{.788} = -95.4$$

and

$$a_0 = 138 - (1.68)(-95.4) = 298.3;$$

thus, the least squares fit is

$$q = f(p) = 298.3 - 95.4p.$$

Evaluating the deviations, we get

$$f(1.0) - 200 = 202.9 - 200 = 2.9$$
$$f(1.5) - 160 = 155.2 - 160 = -4.8$$
$$f(1.8) - 130 = 126.6 - 130 = -3.4$$
$$f(2.0) - 100 = 107.5 - 100 = 7.5$$
$$f(2.1) - 100 = 98 - 100 = -2.$$

Figure 13.4 illustrates the least squares fit of these data—the closest line (in the least squares sense) to all the data points.

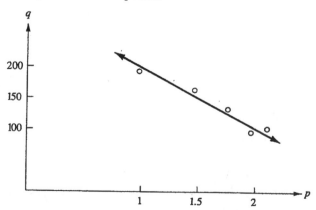

Figure 13.4
A linear least squares fit of
demand data

EXAMPLE 2

An accountant has been asked to determine the fixed and variable costs that are incurred in the manufacture of an item. Assuming that total cost C is a linear function of output q, fit the given data, which were gathered on six recent days, with a first-degree least squares polynomial to determine fixed and variable costs.

q	22	24	29	25	26	30
C	331	360	417	373	385	428

SOLUTION

Recall that if $C = a_0 + a_1 q$, then a_0 represents fixed costs and a_1 represents the variable cost per unit produced. First we compute the sums that are needed in the normal equations:

q_i^2	q_i	C_i	$q_i C_i$
484	22	331	7282
576	24	360	8640
841	29	417	12,093
625	25	373	9325
676	26	385	10,010
900	30	428	12,840
(Σ) 4102	156	2294	60,190

Next we set up the normal equations:

$$\begin{bmatrix} 6 & 156 \\ 156 & 4102 \end{bmatrix} \begin{bmatrix} a_0 \\ a_1 \end{bmatrix} = \begin{bmatrix} 2294 \\ 60,190 \end{bmatrix}$$

and apply the reduction method to the augmented matrix of this system:

$$\begin{bmatrix} 6 & 156 & | & 2294 \\ 156 & 4102 & | & 60,190 \end{bmatrix} \sim \begin{bmatrix} 1 & 26 & | & 382.33 \\ 0 & 46 & | & 546 \end{bmatrix}.$$

Upon back-substitution, $a_1 = 11.87$ and $a_0 = 73.72$, so

$$C = 73.72 + 11.87q$$

and daily fixed costs are \$73.72, while the variable cost per unit is \$11.87. Figure 13.5 illustrates this linear least squares fit.

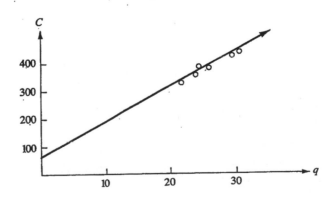

Figure 13.5

A linear least squares fit of total cost data

In statistics, a first-degree least squares fit is called a least squares **regression line**. By fitting raw data with a least squares linear function the data are regressed, or moved to a more primitive form. Solving the system of normal equations (13.10) in general, we obtain the coefficient formulas as they are listed in most statistics textbooks:

(13.11)

$$a_1 = \frac{m\Sigma x_i y_i - (\Sigma x_i)(\Sigma y_i)}{m\Sigma x_i^2 - (\Sigma x_i)^2}$$

$$a_0 = \frac{\Sigma y_i - a_1 \Sigma x_i}{m}.$$

Calculators with a $\boxed{\Sigma}$ key will simultaneously form Σx_i and Σx_i^2. Those with a statistics package will also form Σy_i, $\Sigma x_i y_i$, and even the coefficients a_0 and a_1.

EXAMPLE 3   The annual U.S. rate of inflation computed from the Consumer Price Index for each year in the decade of the 1970s is given in the table. If r denotes the annual inflation rate and t the number of years after 1970, find the least squares regression line that gives r as a function of t. Use this function to predict the annual inflation rate for 1980, 1982, and 1985.

1970	1971	1972	1973	1974	1975	1976	1977	1978	1979
5.9	4.3	3.3	6.2	11	9.1	5.8	6.5	7.6	11.5

SOLUTION   Forming the needed sums, we find

$$\Sigma t_i = 45, \quad \Sigma t_i^2 = 285, \quad \Sigma r_i = 71.2, \quad \Sigma t_i r_i = 363.6,$$

so from equations (13.11),

$$a_1 = \frac{10(363.6) - (45)(71.2)}{10(285) - (45)^2}$$

$$= .524$$

and

$$a_0 = \frac{71.2 - (.524)(45)}{10}$$

$$= 4.76$$

Thus the first-degree least squares fit of this data yields

$$r = 4.76 + .524t.$$

For 1980, $t = 10$, so $r = 4.76 + 5.24 = 10$. (The actual rate was 13.4%.) For 1982, $t = 12$, so $r = 11$ (actual rate, 6.0%), and, for 1985, $t = 15$, with $r = 12.6$ (actual rate, 3.6%). (See Figure 13.6.) Since the fitting function has positive slope (.524), all future predicted values must increase.

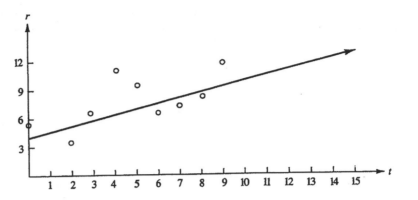

Figure 13.6

A linear least squares fit of the annual U.S. inflation rate during the 1970s

Fits of economic indicators are helpful in summarizing past trends, but they may be of questionable value in predicting the future. Generally, fitting functions lose their accuracy as one moves away from the data values. This use of fitting functions is called **extrapolation**; its skillful practice requires considerable judgment and experience on the part of the user.

EXERCISES 13.2

In Exercises 1–10 fit the given x, y data with a first-degree least squares function. Plot the data and the fitting function on the same coordinate axes.

1. $(1, 5), (2, 8), (3, 8)$

2. $(5, 5), (10, 12), (20, 50)$

3. $(2, 5), (4, 3), (6, 7), (9, 8)$

4. $(1, -2), (3, 5), (4, 8), (5, 6)$

5.

x	10	20	30	40	50
y	5	8	10	15	20

6.

x	.1	.3	.5	.7	.9
y	60	90	100	130	160

7.

x	0	1	2	3	4	5	6	7
y	.3	.5	.4	.6	.1	.9	1	.8

8.

x	1	2	3	4	5	6	7	8	9
y	10	15	13	20	28	40	37	50	45

9.

x	1.0	1.2	1.5	1.7	2.0	2.3	2.8
y	40	28	25	22	20	18	12

10.

x	100	200	300	400	500	600	700	800
y	72	80	80	95	90	120	180	200

11. Supply data for the tons of barley q brought to market when the selling price was p (in dollars per bushel) during five different days are recorded in the table. Using a linear least squares fit of these data, find q as a function of p. Estimate the tons of barley brought to market when $p = 3.80$, $p = 4.25$, and $p = 4.50$ using this function.

p	3.75	3.90	4.00	4.20	4.30
q	10	40	50	75	100

12. A livestock auction's selling prices are quoted in dollars per hundred pounds. The revenue R (in hundreds of dollars) received from the sale of W hundreds of pounds of steers on each day last week is given in the table. Find R as a linear function of W by fitting these data with a least

squares regression line. Use the fitting function to estimate R when $W = 500$ and when $W = 600$. What is the approximate price per hundredweight for the steers sold during this week? What is wrong with this fitting function when $W = 0$?

W	540	520	480	610	570
R	350	334	310	393	372

13. A producer of auto accessories wishes to determine the fixed and variable costs associated with the production of sunroof vents. Total cost C and output data q for five different days are given in the table. Assuming C is a linear function of q, find the least squares fit of these data and the resulting fixed cost and variable cost per unit.

q	50	80	70	90	100
C	3100	5700	4800	6000	6200

14. The variable cost per unit v of producing Keen pocket knives is thought to be a linear function of output q. Fit the given data with a least squares regression line. At what output level does the fitting function predict $v = 0$ and thus become meaningless?

q	80	100	130	150	200	250
v	2.5	2.2	2.0	1.9	1.7	1.5

15. A film processor wishes to determine the fixed and variable costs associated with developing 35-mm film. Total cost C and the number of rolls of film developed q for eight different days are recorded in the table. Assuming that C is a linear function of q, find the daily fixed cost and the variable cost per roll for developing this film.

q	50	80	100	150	120	90	130	70
C	160	200	260	360	300	220	325	200

16. The demand q for watermelon at a local market is thought to be a linear function of its selling price per pound p. For the data in the table fit q to p with a linear least squares function.

q (melons)	20	30	40	80	130	200
p (cents per pound)	18	16	15	12	10	7

17. The U.S. Gross National Product (GNP) in trillions of dollars is given in the table for the years 1975–1980. Let t denote the number of years after 1975, and let G denote the GNP. Then use a least squares regression line to fit the data and give G as a function of t. Use this function to estimate the GNP in 1969 (actual value .931) and in 1985 (actual value 3.988). What yearly increase in the GNP is built into this fitting function?

Year	1975	1976	1977	1978	1979	1980
GNP	1.529	1.708	1.918	2.156	2.414	2.633

18. The density of population in the United States (inhabitants per square mile of land area) at the beginning of each decade of the first half of the 20th century is given in the table. Fit these data with a least squares regression line to give population density D as a function of years t after 1900. Use this function to estimate D in the years 1880 (16.9 actual), 1925, and 1960 (lower 48 states only).

Year	1900	1910	1920	1930	1940	1950
Density	25.6	31.0	35.5	41.2	44.2	50.7

19. The average hourly earnings for workers in all manufacturing industries between 1960 and 1980 are recorded in the table. Fit the hourly wage W as a linear least squares function of t, the number of years after 1960. Use this function to estimate the hourly wage in 1968, 1978, and 1988. During what year is the hourly wage predicted to reach $10?

Year	1960	1965	1970	1975	1980
Wage	2.26	2.61	3.36	4.81	7.27

20. The table summarizes the U.S. per capita national debt from 1950 to 1980. Fit the per capita national debt D as a linear least squares function of t, the number of years after 1950. Using this function, estimate the year when the per capita national debt will be $6000.

Year	1950	1955	1960	1965	1970	1975	1980
Debt	1688	1650	1572	1613	1807	2497	4063

21. The percentage of consumers' incomes spent on food for years between 1950 and 1980 is summarized in the table. Fit the percentage of income spent on food F as a linear least squares function of t, the number of years after 1950. At what rate does this percentage seem to be decreasing each year?

Year	1950	1960	1970	1975	1980
Food %	24	22	19	18	18

22. The percentage of consumers' incomes spent on housing for years between 1950 and 1980 is summarized in the table. Fit the percentage of income spent on housing H as a linear least squares function of t, the number of years after 1950. By what rate does this percentage seem to be increasing each year? Referring to Exercise 21, in what year are the percentages of income spent on food and housing predicted to be equal?

Year	1950	1960	1970	1975	1980
Housing %	11	15	15	15	16

23. The TV percentages of total advertising expenditures for years between 1960 and 1980 are given in the table. Find the least squares regression line that gives the TV percentage of total advertising expenditure T as a function of y, the years after 1960. If the trend suggested by this function continues, in what year will TV have 25% of the total expenditures?

Year	1960	1965	1970	1975	1980
TV %	13.3	16.5	18.7	18.6	20.7

24. The newspaper percentages of total advertising expenditures for years between 1960 and 1980 are given in the table. Find the least squares regression line that gives the newspaper percentage of total advertising expenditure as a function of y, the years after 1960. What percentage of total expenditures is predicted for newspapers in 1990 by this function? Referring to Exercise 23, in what year are the percentages for TV and newspaper advertising predicted to be equal?

Year	1960	1965	1970	1975	1980
Newspaper %	31.0	29.2	29.3	29.9	28.5

25. U.S. oil imports B (in thousands of barrels per day) from OPEC countries for several years between 1970 and 1980 are given in the table. Fit the linear least squares fit of these data, giving B as a function of t, the number of years

after 1970. Use this function to estimate B in 1973, 1975, and 1979. For which of these years is the estimated value probably most accurate? Why?

Year	1970	1972	1974	1976	1978	1980
B	1334	2063	3280	5066	5751	4233

26. U.S. energy consumption C (in quadrillion Btus) for years from 1960 to 1980 are given in the table. Find the linear least squares fit of these data, giving C as a function of t, the number of years after 1960. What annual increase in consumption is built into this function? Over which of the four given five-year periods is this increase most accurate?

Year	1960	1965	1970	1975	1980
C	44	53	67	71	76

A measurement used in statistics to decide whether the data $(x_1, y_1), \ldots, (x_m, y_m)$ can be well fit by a least squares regression line is the coefficient of determination, denoted r^2. This measurement compares the summed squared deviations S to similar summed squared deviations of the y values to their average

$$\bar{y} = \frac{1}{m}\sum_{i=1}^{m} y_i.$$

If D is defined by

$$D = \sum_{i=1}^{m}(y_i - \bar{y})^2,$$

then the coefficient of determination is given by

$$r^2 = 1 - \frac{S}{D}.$$

When r^2 is near 1, the data are well fit by a linear regression line. When r^2 is near 0, the data are not well fit by such a function.

27–52. Compute r^2 for the data in Exercises 1–26.

13.3

Least Squares Polynomial Fits

Section 13.2 treated the mechanics of computing first-degree least squares data fits. Although a linear function is often a good approximation to a relationship between two variables, in many instances other fitting functions are more appropriate. In this section higher-degree polynomial least squares fits are considered.

When selecting a fitting function, the modeler should begin with heuristic reasons for the selection. After data are collected, they should be plotted to see whether they agree with the heuristics, at least in general terms. This visual exam-

CHAPTER 13   Curve Fitting

ination of the data often takes a trained eye, but gross inconsistencies between theory and this sample of reality can usually be identified. For example, if the d: seem to be part of a curve with relative extreme points or inflection points, do the proposed fitting function allow for these points? Is a function that accomm dates these apparent properties of the data more desirable for this model than or that describes only the general trend of the data?

EXAMPLE 1   Examine the data and their first-degree least squares fit for each of the sketches in Figure 13.7. Each of these examples is from an exercise or example in Section 13.2. Determine whether a polynomial function other than the linear fit might be more appropriate.

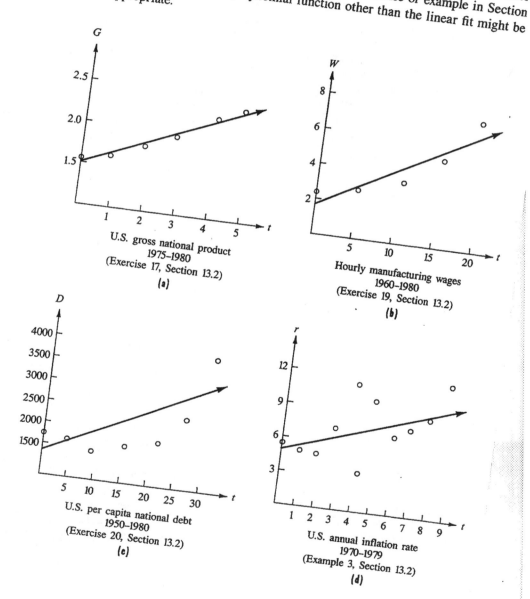

Figure 13.7
Four linear least squares fits

SOLUTION

In Figure 13.7(a), the data seem to be part of an increasing function with no apparent extreme values or inflection points. A linear fit seems appropriate.

The data in Figure 13.7(b) appear to be concave upward and increasing more rapidly than the regression line at most data points. A parabola or quadratic function may be a better fitting function.

Figure 13.7(c) illustrates data that appear to have a relative minimum and change concavity. If a fit is to be used to fill in values between the data points, a cubic function may be a good choice. If only a general trend is required, the linear least squares fit is sufficient.

If a fitting function is to portray the three apparent relative extreme values and the changes in concavity that appear in the data of Figure 13.7(d), then a fourth-degree polynomial may be used. For a general trend, the regression line is sufficient.   ●

The observations regarding the concavity and extreme points of the data in Example 1 could be verified by differentiation if the data were part of a function whose rule of correspondence was known. In place of derivatives, **divided differences** formed from the data can be used as representative derivative values. For any two data points (x_1, y_1) and (x_2, y_2), the **first divided difference** between these points is denoted $y_{1, 2}$ and defined by

(13.12)
$$y_{1, 2} = \frac{y_2 - y_1}{x_2 - x_1}.$$

The first divided difference between two points is just the slope of the line through these points. The slope, in turn, is the mean value of the derivative of a function passing through the data points, so we treat a first divided difference as a representative value of the first derivative of a fitting function.

Second divided differences between three data points are defined as divided differences of first divided differences. Specifically, the **second divided difference** between the data points (x_1, y_1), (x_2, y_2), and (x_3, y_3) is denoted $y_{1, 2, 3}$ and defined by

(13.13)
$$y_{1, 2, 3} = \frac{y_{2, 3} - y_{1, 2}}{x_3 - x_1}.$$

A second divided difference can be shown to equal half the second derivative of a function passing through the data points, somewhere between these points. As (half of) a representative value of the second derivative, the second divided difference can be used for concavity considerations.

EXAMPLE 2

Form and interpret the first and second divided differences between adjacent data points for the following data:

x	0	10	25	40	50	80
y	100	400	730	1030	1270	2020

SOLUTION

(13.14)

Divided differences between adjacent data points are often tabulated in a **divided difference table**:

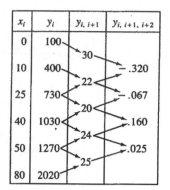

x_i	y_i	$y_{i,\,i+1}$	$y_{i,\,i+1,\,i+2}$
0	100		
		30	
10	400		.320
		22	
25	730		.067
		20	
40	1030		.160
		24	
50	1270		.025
		25	
80	2020		

The third column of this table contains first divided differences between pairs of points to the left. The fourth column contains second divided differences formed by subtracting the first differences in the third column and dividing by the x_i values in the first column as prescribed by equation (13.13) and indicated by the diagonal lines. The positive first divided differences suggest that a fitting function should be increasing; the second divided differences indicate a possible inflection point between the third and fourth data points. ●

Besides serving as a numerical check on observations made from graphs of data points, divided differences often serve as an aid when determining the appropriate degree of a polynomial fitting function. First, general nth divided differences between $n + 1$ data points can be shown to be proportional to values of nth derivatives of functions that pass through the data. Second, the nth derivative of an nth-degree polynomial is constant. As a result of these two facts, the nth divided difference of any $n + 1$ different data points on the graph of an nth-degree polynomial will have the same value. Thus when examining divided differences of data, if the nth divided differences are "nearly" constant, an nth-degree polynomial should be a good fitting function. Since the first divided differences in table (13.14) are nearly constant, a linear function will serve as a good fitting function. However, if the apparent inflection point is to be part of the fitting function, a polynomial of at least third degree is necessary.

Generally, nth divided differences are defined as divided differences of $(n - 1)$st divided differences. Precisely, the **nth divided difference** between the data points $(x_1, y_1), \ldots, (x_{n+1}, y_{n+1})$ is denoted $y_{1,\,2,\,\ldots,\,n+1}$ and defined by

$$y_{1,\,2,\,\ldots,\,n+1} = \frac{y_{2,\,3,\,\ldots,\,n+1} - y_{1,\,2,\,\ldots,\,n}}{x_{n+1} - x_1}.$$

EXAMPLE 3

Form divided differences of the data considered in Example 1, and examine the observations made from the graphs of these data.

SOLUTION

The Gross National Product data in Figure 13.7(a) are

t	0	1	2	3	4	5
G	1.529	1.708	1.918	2.156	2.414	2.633

Forming a divided difference table for these data, we have

t_i	G_i	$G_{i,\,i+1}$	$G_{i,\,i+1,\,i+2}$
0	1.529		
		.179	
1	1.708		−.016
		.210	
2	1.918		.014
		.238	
3	2.156		.010
		.258	
4	2.414		−.020
		.219	
5	2.633		

The first divided differences are very nearly constant, so as observed earlier, a linear fitting function is a good choice. The second divided differences have sign changes, but the absolute value of these differences is too small to seriously consider a curve that has inflection points.

The hourly wage data in Figure 13.7(b) are

t	0	5	10	15	20
W	2.26	2.61	3.36	4.81	7.27

Computing divided differences, we find

t_i	W_i	$W_{i,\,i+1}$	$W_{i,\,i+1,\,i+2}$	$W_{i,\,\ldots,\,i+3}$
0	2.26			
		.07		
5	2.61		.008	
		.15		.0004
10	3.36		.014	
		.29		.0004
15	4.81		.020	
		.492		
20	7.27			

The first divided differences are all less than 1, but they are increasing in magnitude with the last difference, .492, about 7 times the first, .07. It is difficult to argue that they are nearly constant. The second divided differences are positive, reinforcing the concavity observation in Example 1. Also the second divided differences are all about the same size, the largest being 2.5 times the smallest, indicating that a second-degree polynomial is a good fitting function. The (rounded) third divided differences are equal, so a third-degree polynomial will interpolate the data.

The per capita national debt data of Figure 13.7(c) are

t	0	5	10	15	20	25	30
D	1688	1650	1572	1613	1807	2497	4063

Forming divided differences:

t_i	D_i	$D_{i,\,i+1}$	$D_{i,\,i+1,\,i+2}$	$D_{i,\,\ldots,\,i+3}$
0	1688			
		−7.6		
5	1650		−.80	
		−15.6		.212
10	1572		2.38	
		8.2		.045
15	1613		3.06	
		38.8		.457
20	1807		9.92	
		138.0		.507
25	2497		17.52	
		313.2		
30	4063			

The inflection point observed in Example 1 is indicated between the second and third data points, where the second divided differences change from negative to positive. The use of a third-degree polynomial fit is also reinforced by the nearly constant third divided differences.

The annual inflation rate data in Figure 13.7(d) are

t	0	1	2	3	4	5	6	7	8	9
r	5.9	4.3	3.3	6.2	11	9.1	5.8	6.5	7.6	11.5

Forming a divided difference table, we find

t_i	r_i	$r_{i,\,i+1}$	$r_{i,\,i+1,\,i+2}$	$r_{i,\,\ldots,\,i+3}$	$r_{i,\,\ldots,\,i+4}$	$r_{i,\,\ldots,\,i+5}$
0	5.9					
		−1.6				
1	4.3		.3			
		−1.0		.55		
2	3.3		1.95		−.220	
		2.9		−.33		−.011
3	6.2		.95		−.275	
		4.8		−1.43		.171
4	11.0		−3.35		.578	
		−1.9		.88		−.114
5	9.1		−.7		.005	
		−3.3		.90		−.076
6	5.8		2.0		−.375	
		.7		−.60		.125
7	6.5		.2		.250	
		1.1		.40		
8	7.6		1.4			
		3.9				
9	11.5					

Scanning the columns of this table, we see that none of the divided differences seem to be nearly constant. Although a fourth-degree fit would allow for three relative extrema, it would not portray the apparent cyclic nature of the data for future values. Trigonometric functions may be more appropriate in this case. The first-degree fit does indicate the general trend of the data and is probably as good ● as any other polynomial fit.

Having considered techniques that aid in deciding on the degree of a polynomial fitting function, we now derive the normal equations for an **nth-degree least squares fit** of m data points, where $m > n + 1$. (If $m \leq n + 1$, the least squares fit is an interpolating polynomial.) For the m data points $(x_1, y_1), \ldots, (x_m, y_m)$ and fitting polynomial

$$f(x) = a_0 + a_1 x + a_2 x^2 + \cdots + a_n x^n,$$

the summed squared deviations are

(13.15)
$$S = \sum_{i=1}^{m} [f(x_i) - y_i]^2$$
$$= \sum_{i=1}^{m} [a_0 + a_1 x_i + a_2 x_i^2 + \cdots + a_n x_i^n - y_i]^2.$$

The sum S is a function of the coefficients $a_0, \ldots, a_n$, and so the minimum value of S, if there is one, will occur where all first derivatives of S are 0. Differentiating with respect to a typical coefficient a_k, we find

(13.16)
$$\frac{\partial S}{\partial a_k} = \sum_{i=1}^{m} 2[a_0 + a_1 x_i + \cdots + a_n x_i^n - y_i] x_i^k.$$

Setting this derivative equal to 0, dividing by 2, and using summation properties to rearrange terms, we have (with summation indices omitted)

(13.17)
$$(\Sigma x_i^k) a_0 + (\Sigma x_i^{k+1}) a_1 + \cdots + (\Sigma x_i^{k+n}) a_n = \Sigma x_i^k y_i,$$

for $k = 0, 1, 2, \ldots, n$. In matrix form, equation (13.17) amounts to the **normal equations** for the coefficients of the nth-degree polynomial fit of the m data points $(x_1, y_1), \ldots, (x_m, y_m)$:

(13.18)
$$\begin{bmatrix} m & \Sigma x_i & \Sigma x_i^2 & \cdots & \Sigma x_i^n \\ \Sigma x_i & \Sigma x_i^2 & \Sigma x_i^3 & \cdots & \Sigma x_i^{n+1} \\ \hline \Sigma x_i^n & \Sigma x_i^{n+1} & \Sigma x_i^{n+2} & \cdots & \Sigma x_i^{2n} \end{bmatrix} \begin{bmatrix} a_0 \\ a_1 \\ \hline a_n \end{bmatrix} = \begin{bmatrix} \Sigma y_i \\ \Sigma x_i y_i \\ \hline \Sigma x_i^n y_i \end{bmatrix}.$$

EXAMPLE 4   Fit the hourly wage data considered in Example 3 with a second-degree least squares fitting function.

SOLUTION   From the hourly wage data, the needed sums are computed in the following table:

	x_i^4	x_i^3	x_i^2	x_i	y_i	$x_i y_i$	$x_i^2 y_i$
	0	0	0	0	2.26	0	0
	625	125	25	5	2.61	13.05	65.25
	10,000	1000	100	10	3.36	33.6	336
	50,625	3375	225	15	4.81	72.15	1082.25
	160,000	8000	400	20	7.27	145.4	2908
(Σ)	221,250	12,500	750	50	20.31	264.2	4391.5

Applying the reduction method to the augmented matrix for the normal equations, we find

$$\begin{bmatrix} 5 & 50 & 750 & 20.31 \\ 50 & 750 & 12,500 & 264.2 \\ 750 & 12,500 & 221,250 & 4391.5 \end{bmatrix} \sim \begin{bmatrix} 1 & 10 & 150 & 4.062 \\ 0 & 1 & 20 & .2444 \\ 0 & 0 & 1.75 & .0246 \end{bmatrix}.$$

Upon back-substitution, $a_2 = .0141$, $a_1 = -.0367$, and $a_0 = 2.3209$, so

$$f(x) = 2.3209 - .0367x + .0141x^2$$

is the least squares quadratic fit of the data. A sketch of this curve with the data points appears in Figure 13.8.

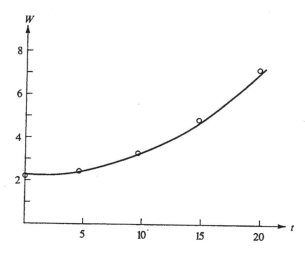

Figure 13.8

A quadratic least squares fit of hourly wage data

EXAMPLE 5   Fit the per capita national debt data, considered in Example 3, with a third-degree least squares function.

SOLUTION   For the per capita debt data, the diligent reader can verify that the needed sums are

$\Sigma x_i = 105$ $\Sigma y_i = 14,890$

$\Sigma x_i^2 = 2275$ $\Sigma x_i y_i = 268,620$

$\Sigma x_i^3 = 55,125$ $\Sigma x_i^2 y_i = 6,501,500$

$\Sigma x_i^4 = 1,421,875$ $\Sigma x_i^3 y_i = 170,394,750$

$\Sigma x_i^5 = 38,128,125$ $\Sigma x_i^6 = 1,049,546,875.$

Using these values to form the normal equations, we find upon solving these equations for a_0, a_1, a_2, and a_3 that the third-degree least squares fit of these data is

$$f(x) = 1666 + 34.47x - 7.131x^2 + .2872x^3.$$

A sketch of this fitting function along with the data appears in Figure 13.9.

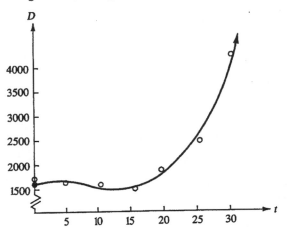

Figure 13.9

A cubic least squares fit of the per capita national debt data

Solving the normal equations is not the most efficient scheme for computing the coefficients of least squares fits for polynomials of degree 3 or higher. As illustrated in the previous example, problems of this size are too cumbersome to work by hand. Most computer systems have software packages for least squares fitting.

Least squares fits are also used for functions of several independent variables. The normal equations for the coefficients of a multivariate least squares polynomial are analogous to those in (13.18). Such fits are not considered here due to their complexity and the need for careful statistical analysis when selecting independent variables for such fits.

EXERCISES 13.3

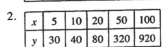

In Exercises 1–10 plot and form a divided difference table for the given data; then decide whether a first-, second-, or third-degree least squares fit would be most appropriate.

1.

q	10	20	30	50	100
C	300	600	1000	1900	5000

(C is a function of q.)

2.

x	5	10	20	50	100
y	30	40	80	320	920

(y is a function of x.)

3.

q	6	12	24	48	144
C	100	180	320	580	1020

(C is a function of q.)

4.

u	0	1	2	3	4	5
v	6	100	236	418	638	898

(v is a function of u.)

5.

x	0	1	2	3	4	5
y	20	100	146	176	196	236

(y is a function of x.)

6.

x	0	2	3	5	8	10
y	150	120	90	220	20	150

(y is a function of x.)

7.

q	0	5	10	15	20	50
C	50	144	230	266	410	520

(C is a function of q.)

8.

x	2	5	8	10	12
y	50	250	160	120	200

(y is a function of x.)

9.

x	5	8	10	15	20	25
y	8	7	12	12	25	15

(y is a function of x.)

10.

x	10	15	30	40	50	80
y	600	585	360	280	400	100

(y is a function of x.)

11–14. Fit the data in Exercises 1–4 with a least squares quadratic polynomial.

15. Plot and form a divided difference table for the given variable cost data. Decide whether these data would be better fit by a linear or quadratic function.

q	10	30	50	80	120
v	78	73	70	72	80

16. Plot and form a divided difference table for the given demand data. Decide whether these data would be better fit by a linear or quadratic function, when treating p as the dependent variable.

q	10	15	25	40	150
p	80	70	65	60	50

17. Plot and form a divided difference table for the given total cost data. Decide whether total cost should be considered a linear or quadratic function of output.

q	20	30	40	50	100
C	340	460	560	640	1150

18. Plot and form a divided difference table for the given revenue data. Decide whether revenue should be considered a linear or quadratic function of the quantity sold.

q	0	5	10	15	25	30
R	0	240	510	730	1300	1480

19–22. Find the quadratic least squares fits of the data in Exercises 15–18. Graph these functions on coordinate axes with the given data.

23. Millions of new housing starts in the United States between 1960 and 1980 are listed in the table. Form a divided difference table for these data and decide whether a quadratic fit is more appropriate than a linear one.

Year	1960	1965	1970	1975	1980
Starts	1.296	1.510	1.469	1.171	1.299

24. The number of civilian federal employees (in millions) for years between 1950 and 1980 are listed in the table. Form a divided difference table for these data and decide whether a quadratic fit is more appropriate than a linear one.

Year	1950	1955	1960	1965	1970	1975	1980
Employees	2.117	2.378	2.421	2.588	2.881	2.890	2.907

25. U.S. median family income for years between 1960 and 1978 is recorded in the table. Let M denote median family income and let t represent years after 1960; then fit M to t with a quadratic least squares function.

Year	1960	1970	1972	1974	1976	1978
Income	5620	9867	11,116	12,902	14,958	17,640

26. U.S. per capita personal income for years between 1950 and 1980 is given in the table. Let P denote per capita income and let t represent years after 1950; then fit P to t with a quadratic least squares function.

Year	1950	1955	1960	1965	1970	1975	1980
Income	1501	1881	2219	2773	3893	5851	9458

27. Millions of vehicles produced by U.S. auto makers during 1965–1980 are listed in the table. Let V denote vehicles produced and let t represent years after 1965; then fit V to t with a cubic least squares function.

Year	1965	1970	1975	1978	1979	1980
Vehicles	9.335	6.550	6.717	9.120	8.418	6.378

28. The percentages of U.S. personal income saved for years between 1950 and 1980 are given in the table. Let S denote the percentage of income saved and let t represent years after 1950; then fit S to t with a cubic least squares function.

Year	1950	1955	1960	1965	1970	1975	1980
% Saved	6.3	5.4	4.9	6.4	8.1	7.7	5.6

29. Fit the OPEC data in Exercise 25 of Section 13.2 with a quadratic least squares function.

30. The use of divided differences to help determine the degree of a polynomial fitting function depends on the fact that the nth derivative of an nth-degree polynomial is constant. Determine the nth and $(n + 1)$st derivative of the nth-degree polynomial

$$f(x) = a_0 + a_1x + a_2x^2 + \cdots + a_nx^n.$$

31. The Vandermonde system used for polynomial interpolation is related to the system of normal equations used for least squares fitting. If $AX = B$ is the Vandermonde system for the nth-degree interpolating polynomial through m data points $(m > n + 1)$, then this system has more equations than variables and probably does not have a solution. The system of normal equations for the nth-degree least squares

polynomial through these data is

$$A'AX = A'B,$$

where A' (A transpose) is the matrix obtained from A by interchanging rows and columns. Form the Vandermonde system for the quadratic polynomial through the following data:

x	1	2	3	4	5
y	2	4	8	5	1

Identify the 3×5 Vandermonde matrix A and the constant column B. Form $A'A$ and $A'B$ and compare these matrices to those for the least squares quadratic normal equations for these data.

32. When deciding on the degree of a least squares polynomial fitting function, reducing S, the summed squared deviations, was not considered as a criterion in this selection. Show that S can never increase when the degree of the least squares fitting polynomial increases.

13.4 Linearizable Least Squares Fits

The normal equations derived in the previous section for least squares polynomial fitting functions were linear. Each equation in the system was a linear equation in the unknown coefficients. The procedure used to derive these normal equations may be used for nonpolynomial fits as well; however, the resulting system of equations for the coefficients usually is not linear and thus is more difficult to solve.

Sometimes nonlinear normal equations can be avoided by first transforming the data and then fitting the transformed data with a least squares polynomial fit. The so-called **log-log** and **semilog** fits are of this type. Log-log fitting is used with power functions of the form

(13.19)
$$y = ax^p,$$

where the constants a and p are selected so that this function approximates the data.

Taking logarithms on both sides of equation (13.19), we find

(13.20)
$$\ln y = \ln a + p(\ln x).$$

Because $\ln a$ and p are constants, equation (13.20) expresses $\ln y$ as a linear function of $\ln x$. For the log-log fit of $(x_1, y_1), \ldots, (x_m, y_m)$ by a power function of the form (13.19), we fit the transformed data $(\ln x_1, \ln y_1), \ldots, (\ln x_m, \ln y_m)$ with a least squares regression line. If

(13.21)
$$f(x) = a_0 + a_1(\ln x)$$

is this linear least squares fitting function, then

(13.22) $$p = a_1 \quad \text{and} \quad \ln a = a_0, \quad \text{so} \quad a = e^{a_0}.$$

Summarizing, the coefficients a and p for a log-log least squares fit with a power function of the form (13.19) may be found by taking logarithms of the data and fitting the transformed data with a linear regression line. The slope of the regression line is then p, and the y-intercept is the logarithm of a.

EXAMPLE 1   Total monthly sales S of K-9 dog food are thought to be proportional to some power of the monthly advertising expenditure x. Sales advertising data (in thousands of dollars) for 6 mo of last year are recorded in the table.

x	750	600	800	1000	700	900
S	2500	2100	2600	3150	2370	2900

Make a log-log fit of these data with a power function of the form (13.19).

SOLUTION   The needed logarithms and sums are calculated to three decimal places in the table:

$(\ln x_i)^2$	$\ln x_i$	x_i	S_i	$\ln S_i$	$(\ln x_i)(\ln S_i)$
43.824	6.620	750	2500	7.824	51.795
40.922	6.397	600	2100	7.650	48.937
44.689	6.685	800	2600	7.863	52.564
47.720	6.908	1000	3150	8.055	55.643
42.916	6.551	700	2370	7.771	50.908
46.267	6.802	900	2900	7.972	54.226
266.338	39.963			47.135	314.073

From equations (13.11) the coefficients of the least squares regression line are

$$a_1 = \frac{6(314.073) - (39.963)(47.135)}{6(266.338) - (39.963)^2}$$
$$= .793$$

and

$$a_0 = \frac{47.135 - .793(39.936)}{6}$$
$$= 2.578.$$

The coefficients for the log-log power function fit are thus

$$p = .793 \quad \text{and} \quad a = e^{2.578} = 13.17,$$

and we have

$$S = 13.17x^{.793}.$$

See Figure 13.10 for a sketch of this figure and the data points.

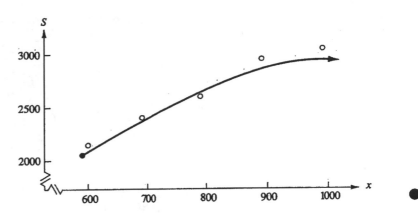

Figure 13.10
A log-log least squares
fitting function

Semilog least squares fits arise from exponential fitting functions of the form

(13.23)
$$y = ae^{kx},$$

where a and k are constants. Taking logarithms on both sides of equation (13.23) yields

(13.24)
$$\ln y = \ln a + kx.$$

In equation (13.24) we see that $\ln y$ is given as a linear function of x. To find the constants a and k for a function of the form (13.23) that fits the data (x_1, y_1), $\dots$, (x_m, y_m) in the semilog sense, the data $(x_1, \ln y_1)$, $\dots$, $(x_m, \ln y_m)$ are fit with a least squares regression line. The slope of this line is then the constant k, and the y-intercept is the logarithm of a.

EXAMPLE 2

To summarize several investments made over different lengths of time, an accountant wishes to find a typical principal P and a typical interest rate r so that all future values F of these investments can be approximated by an exponential growth function of the form

$$F = Pe^{rt},$$

where t is the number of years of the investment. Find P and r by fitting the data

t	5	3	8	7	10
F	5200	4200	7200	6400	9000

with a function of the form (13.23) in the semilog sense.

SOLUTION

Calculating the needed logarithms and sums, we have

t_i^2	t_i	F_i	$\ln F_i$	$(t_i)(\ln F_i)$
25	5	5200	8.556	42.780
9	3	4200	8.343	25.029
64	8	7200	8.882	71.056
49	7	6400	8.764	61.348
100	10	9000	9.105	91.05
247	33		43.65	291.263

Thus the coefficients for the regression line are

$$a_1 = \frac{5(291.263) - (43.65)(33)}{5(247) - (33)^2}$$

$$= .109$$

and

$$a_0 = \frac{43.65 - .109(33)}{5}$$

$$= 8.01.$$

So the needed interest rate is $r = .109$, while the principal is $P = e^{8.01} = 3011$, giving rise to the fitting function

$$F = 3011e^{.109x}.$$

A sketch of this function and the data it fits appears in Figure 13.11.

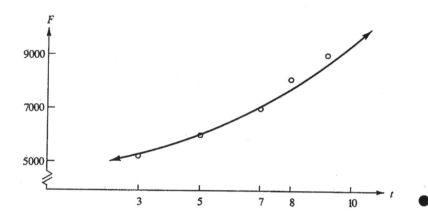

Figure 13.11

A semilog least squares fit

EXAMPLE 3   In Exercise 26 of Section 13.3, the following personal income data were fitted with a least squares quadratic function:

Year	1950	1955	1960	1965	1970	1975	1980
Income	1501	1881	2219	2773	3893	5851	9458

Examine first divided differences to determine whether a fitting function either of the form (13.19) (log-log fit) or of the form (13.23) (semilog fit) would be appropriate for these data.

SOLUTION   Let P denote personal income and let t represent the number of years after 1949 so that $\ln t$ is defined in all cases. The divided difference tables for the log-log and semilog data are then

Log-log Data		
$\ln t_i$	$\ln P_i$	
0	7.314	
		.126
1.792	7.540	
		.272
2.398	7.705	
		.595
2.773	7.928	
		1.246
3.045	8.267	
		1.911
3.258	8.674	
		2.733
3.434	9.155	

Semilog Data		
t_i	$\ln P_i$	
1	7.314	
		.0452
6	7.540	
		.033
11	7.705	
		.0446
16	7.928	
		.0678
21	8.267	
		.0814
26	8.674	
		.0962
31	9.155	

The first divided differences for the log-log data are increasing, with the largest difference about 22 times the smallest. However, the first divided differences for the semilog data are nearly constant, so a fitting function of the form $P = ae^{kt}$ would be appropriate for these data.

The sums needed for this fit are $\Sigma t_i = 112$, $\Sigma t_i^2 = 2492$, $\Sigma \ln P_i = 56.583$, and $\Sigma t_i \ln P_i = 947.093$, so the slope of the regression line is

$$a_1 = \frac{7(947.093) - (112)(56.583)}{7(2492) - (112)^2}$$

$$= .0597,$$

and the y-intercept is

$$a_0 = \frac{56.583 - .0597(112)}{7}$$

$$= 7.128.$$

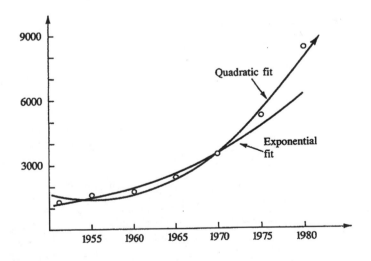

Figure 13.12

Least squares quadratic and exponential function fits of personal income data

Thus $k = .0597$ and $a = e^{7.128} = 1246$, and the desired fitting function is

$$P = 1246e^{.0597t}.$$

A sketch of this function, the data points, and the least squares quadratic fit of the data appear in Figure 13.12.   ●

A variety of other techniques are used to avoid nonlinear normal equations for certain fitting functions. Among these techniques are fixing special data points, replacing variables with their reciprocals, and interchanging dependent variables. In spite of the many sophisticated fitting techniques that may be used in modeling, most business data are reported as indicated in Figure 13.13.

Technically, the "follow the dot" approach used on the data in Figure 13.13 is called **piecewise linear interpolation**. Fits of this type are fine for displaying data. However, most data points are critical points for such a fitting, and the fits offer only crude estimates of intermediate values.

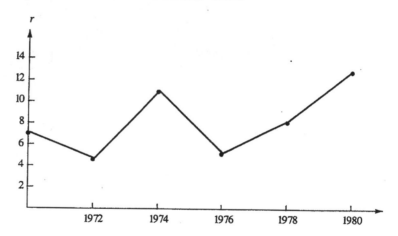

Figure 13.13
Money market rates, 1970–1980

EXERCISES 13.4

Find the log-log least squares fit of the data in Exercises 1–8. Plot the fitting function with the data on the same coordinate axes.

1.

x	2	5	8	10	20
y	12	16	19	20	25

2.

x	2	5	8	10	20
y	23	39	52	60	90

3.

x	5	10	15	20	25	30
y	14	32	52	73	95	118

4.

x	2	4	6	8	10	12
y	17	61	126	211	315	440

5.

x	3	5	7	9	11	15
y	39	58	76	93	110	140

6.

x	10	20	30	40	50	60	100
y	47	55	59	63	66	68	75

7.

x	2	4	6	8	10	12
y	40	194	493	955	1600	2430

8.

x	3	5	7	9	11	13	15
y	4	15	38	75	130	204	300

In Exercises 9–16 form the first divided differences for $(x_i, \ln y_i)$; *then find the semilog least squares fit of the data.*

9.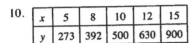

x	5	8	10	12	15
y	165	223	272	313	448

10.

x	5	8	10	12	15
y	273	392	500	630	900

11.

x	2	5	8	10	15	20
y	587	746	950	1110	1660	2480

12.

x	2	5	8	10	15	20
y	845	1013	1212	1370	1850	2490

13.

x	2	3	4	5	8	10
y	1000	916	835	765	585	490

14.

x	2	3	4	5	8	10
y	7400	6380	5490	4720	3010	2230

15.

x	5	10	15	20	25	30
y	7360	2710	1000	370	135	50

16.

x	5	10	15	20	25	30
y	6605	3680	2230	1350	820	500

17. Sales and TV advertising expenditure data for Dixie Chicken over the past 5 yr are recorded in the table (each in millions of dollars). Fit S to X using a log-log fit. Use this function to approximate total sales next year when an estimated \$50 million will be spent on TV advertising.

X	10	18	25	32	42
S	800	1200	1600	1900	2400

18. The following are advertising–sales data:

X	90	180	270	360
S	258	352	409	434

Fit these data with a power function in the log-log sense.

19. Sales–advertising data for Ole Mexican Foods (in millions of dollars) over the past 5 yr are listed in the table. Fit sales S to advertising expenditure X with a power function in the log-log sense.

X	18	13	11	9	8
S	100	80	70	60	50

20. Profit–advertising expenditure data for Misty Cosmetics (in millions of dollars) during the past 6 yr are given in the table. Fit profit P to advertising expenditure X using a log-log fit.

X	10	12	15	25	28	40
P	15	17	20	29	31	40

21. The value V of an investment after t years is given in the table for several values of t. Fit V to t using an exponential function of the form $V = Pe^{rt}$ in the semilog sense. If the value of this investment is treated as a principal accumulating continuous interest, what are the principal and the nominal interest rate?

t	2	5	8	10	15
V	17,850	28,560	41,300	54,750	110,250

22. To consider the monthly profit of a growing business as a continuous cash flow, an accountant wishes to fit the data in the table with an exponential function of the form $P = P_0 e^{kt}$ in the semilog sense. Find P_0 and k for these data.

t	1	2	3	4	5	6
P	8160	8320	8500	8700	9000	9020

23. The assessed value of a single-family residence (in thousands of dollars) during the 1970s was:

Year	1971	1973	1975	1977	1979
Value	42	51	63	77	93

Fit the value V to the years after 1970, t, using a semilog fit. Estimate the value of the home in 1970 and the annual rate of appreciation suggested by this function.

24. The value V of a "soft-whip" ice milk machine (in thousands of dollars) t years after its purchase is given in the table. Fit V to t using a semilog fit. Estimate the original

value of this machine as well as the annual rate of depreciation.

t	1	2	3	4	5
V	10.3	8.9	7.7	6.6	5.7

25. The value V of a Mike truck (in thousands of dollars) t years after its purchase is given in the table. Fit V to t using a semilog fit. Estimate the original value and annual rate of depreciation for this truck.

t	1	3	5	7
V	53	36	24	16

26. Form a log-log fit of the Mike truck data in Exercise 25.

27. For the hourly wages W of manufacturing employees, t years after 1959:

t	1	6	11	16	21
W	2.26	2.61	3.36	4.81	7.27

form divided difference tables for a log-log and a semilog fit. Find the function that yields a better fit of these data.

Appendix C: Answers to Selected Exercises

Section 1.1

1. $7, 7, 7, 7$

3. $7, 5 - a + a^2, 5 + t + t^2, 5 - x - h + x^2 + 2xh + h^2$

5. $0, \dfrac{a - 2}{2a + 1}, \dfrac{t - 1}{2t + 3}, \dfrac{x + h - 2}{2x + 2h + 1}$

7. $\sqrt{2}, \sqrt{8 - 3a}, \sqrt{5 - 3t}, \sqrt{8 - 3x - 3h}$

9. $0 \le q \le 1250$

11. $q > 0$

13. $0 \le q \le 4$

15. $5 < q \le 8$

17. $0 \le q \le 8$

19. $x = 1500 - 100y$

21. $x = \dfrac{150}{y}$

23. Not possible to solve for x uniquely—for example, $y = 0$, $x = \pm 2$

25. $x = y^2 + 20$

27. $x = \dfrac{y + 10}{-y + 2}$

29. a. No; b. Yes; domain = $\{2.50, 2.55, 2.60, 2.70, 2.75\}$; range = $\{67, 73, 80, 88\}$

31. a. Yes; b. No; c. No, the interval contains real numbers not in the table—for example, .015.

33. a. Domain = $\{x \mid 0 \le x \le 8\}$; range = $\{y \mid 2 \le y \le 6\}$
    b. Domain = $\{x \mid -3 \le x \le 3\}$; range = $\{y \mid -1 \le y \le 1\}$

35. The domain is the set of nonnegative real numbers.

Section 1.2

1. $y = \dfrac{1}{2}x + 2$

3. $y = -3x - 1$

5. $y = \dfrac{5}{2}x - \dfrac{7}{2}$

7. $y = x - 1$

9. $f(x) = x + 1$

11. $f(x) = -4x + 11$

13. $f(x) = 2x$

15. $f(x) = 6$

17. a. Vertical: $x = 2$; horizontal: $y = 3$
    b. Vertical: $x = -1$; horizontal: $y = 7$
    c. Vertical: $x = 9$; horizontal: $y = 0$
    d. Vertical: $x = -3$; horizontal: $y = -6$

19.
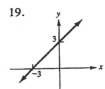

21.

23.
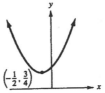

13.
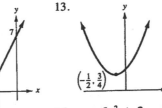

25. $m = \dfrac{2}{3}$; y-intercept: $(0, -2)$; x-intercept: $(3, 0)$

27. $m = -\dfrac{1}{2}$; y-intercept: $(0, 8)$; x-intercept: $(16, 0)$

29. $m = 0$; y-intercept: $(0, 2)$; no x-intercept

31. $R = .80q, 0 \le q \le 200$

33. $C = .25q + 11$; $P = .55q - 11, 0 \le q \le 200$; $P = 0$ when $q = 20$

35. a. $P = 8q - 120, 0 \le q \le 40$;   b. 15;   c. \$200

37. $C = 5q + 550, q \ge 0$; variable cost = \$5; fixed cost = \$550

39. Base salary = \$500; $S = 50q + 500, q \ge 0$

41. $p = -.01q + 8, 0 \le q \le 400$; $q = -100p + 800$, $4 \le p \le 8$

43. Variable cost = \$14.50; fixed cost = \$12; $C = 14.5q + 12, q \ge 0$

45. a. Slope: Pr; V-intercept: P;   b. $V = 500 + 60t$; c. \$740, \$920

47. $p = 6, q = 150$ 49. $q = 90, p = \$11.40$

Section 1.3

1.

3.

5.

7.

9.
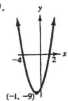

11.
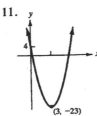

15. $y = 3x^2 + 2$ 17. $y = -x^2 + 2x + 3$

19. $y = 5x^2 - 40x + 60$

21. $C = 375 + 4q - .01q^2, 0 \le q \le 200$

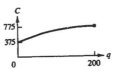

23. $R = -.04q^2 + 13q, 0 \le q \le 200$; $q = 162.5$ maximizes R; $p = \$6.50$

25. $P = -.03q^2 + 9q - 375, 0 \le q \le 200$; maximum profit is $P = \$300$ per day, which occurs at $q = 150$ units; break-even point is $q = 50$.

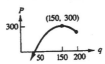

27. a. $p = -.01q + 7, 50 \le q \le 400$
    b. $R = -.01q^2 + 7q, 50 \le q \le 400$
    c. $q = 350$ gal per day; $R = \$1225$; $p = \$3.50$ per gallon

29. a. $v = -.005q + 4.30, 50 \le q \le 400$
    b. $C = -.005q^2 + 4.3q + 100, 50 \le q \le 400$

31. $P = -.005q^2 + 2.7q - 100, 50 \le q \le 400$; profit is maximized at $q = 270$ gal per day, at which $P = \$264.50$ per day.

33. a. $q = 320p - 1200, 6.25 \le p \le 10$
    b. $R = 12,800p^2 - 48,000p, 6.25 \le p \le 10$
    c. Maximum is \$800,000; minimum is \$200,000.

35. $T = 12,800 + 144n - 8n^2, 0 \le n \le 50$

37. For $a > 0$, the range is $[k, \infty)$; for $a < 0$, the range is $(-\infty, k]$.

41. $y = \dfrac{1}{4}x^2 - x + 2$

43. $V(t) = 500(t - 5)(t - 6) = 500t^2 - 5500t + 15,000$, $0 \le t \le 5$

Section 1.4

1. $f(x) = [(3x - 5)x + 6]x - 2$;
   $f(12) = 4534, f(-8) = -1906$

3. $f(x) = [(-x + 8)x - .5]x + 3$;
   $f(7) = 48.5, f(9.3) = -114.087$

5. $f(x) = \{[(2x + 5)x - 7]x + 3\}x - 10;$
$f(-15) = 82{,}745, f(4.5) = 1137.5$

7. $h(x) = \{\{[(x + 2)x]x - 2\}x + 3;$
$h(5) = 4328, h(-10) = -80{,}197$

9. $v = .0004q^2 - .08q + 12;$
$C = .0004q^3 - .08q^2 + 12q + 90, 0 \le q \le 150$

11. $v = .002q^2 - .2q + 25;$
$C = .002q^3 - .2q^2 + 25q + 200, 0 \le q \le 80$

13. $v = .001q^2 - .2q + 50;$
$C = .001q^3 - .2q^2 + 50q + 500, 0 \le q \le 120$

15. a. $v = .0000625q^2 - .05q + 30, 0 \le q \le 500;$
b. \$25.63, \$22.50, \$20.63, \$20.63

17. a. Fixed cost = \$150;
variable cost = $5 - .03q - .001q^2, 0 \le q \le 60$
b. Variable cost cannot be negative.

19. a. $q = .2p^2 - 40p + 2000, 50 \le p \le 100$
b. $p = .0002q^2 - .2q + 100, 0 \le q \le 500$
c. $R = .0002q^3 - .2q^2 + 100q, 0 \le q \le 500$
d. $R = .2p^3 - 40p^2 + 2000p, 50 \le p \le 100$

21. a. For f_1 the values are 0, .2, .4, .6, .8, and 1.
For f_2 the values are 0, .04, .16, .36, .64, and 1.
For f_3 the values are 0, .008, .064, .216, .512, and 1.
For f_4 the values are 0, .0016, .0256, .1296, .4096, and 1.

b.

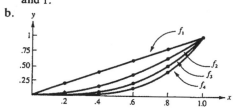

Section 1.5

1. Horizontal asymptote: $y = 0$,
vertical asymptote: $x = 0$,
y-intercept: none

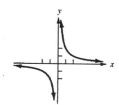

3. Horizontal asymptote: $y = 2$,
vertical asymptote: $x = -5$,
y-intercept: (0, 3)

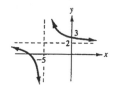

5. Horizontal asymptote: $y = 3$,
vertical asymptote: $x = 2$,
y-intercept: (0, -2)

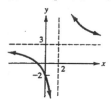

7. Horizontal asymptote: $y = 2$,
vertical asymptote: $x = 5$,
y-intercept: (0, 0)

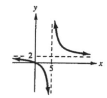

9. Horizontal asymptote: $y = -5$,
vertical asymptote: $x = -1$,
y-intercept: (0, 8)

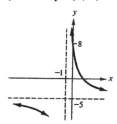

11. Horizontal asymptote: $p = 2$,
vertical asymptote: $q = -4$,
p-intercept: (0, 12.5)

13. $y = \dfrac{3x - 9}{x - 5}$

15. $p = \dfrac{18q + 320}{q}$

17. $y = \dfrac{4x}{x + 5}$

19. $y = \dfrac{3x + 50}{x + 10}$

21. $p = \dfrac{10q + 250}{q + 10}$

23. $v = \dfrac{15q + 960}{q + 40}, q \ge 0$

25. a. $v = \dfrac{10q + 600}{q + 20}, q \geq 0$

b. $C = \dfrac{10q^2 + 900q + 6000}{q + 20}, q \geq 0$

c. $q = 60$ units per hour

27. Equilibrium $q = 80, p = 11$

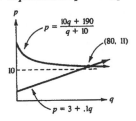

29. Equilibrium $q = 120, p = 36$

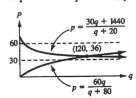

31. Equilibrium $q = 300, p = 4$

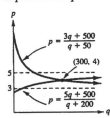

Section 1.6

1. $f(g(x)) = 2x^2 - 1$, all x; $g(f(x)) = 4x^2 + 20x + 22$, all x

3. $f(g(x)) = \dfrac{2x + 7}{2x + 8}, x \neq -4$; $g(f(x)) = \dfrac{9x + 7}{x + 1}, x \neq -1$

5. $f(g(x)) = x^{3/4}, x \geq 0$; $g(f(x)) = x^{3/4}, x \geq 0$

7. $f(g(x)) = 2\sqrt{x - 1} + 3x - 2, x \geq 1$;
   $g(f(x)) = \sqrt{3x^2 + 2x}, x \leq -2/3$ or $x \geq 0$

9. $f(x) = x + 7; g(x) = 5x$ 11. $f(x) = x^2; g(x) = x + 8$

13. $f(x) = \sqrt{x}; g(x) = x + 5$ 15. $f(x) = x^4; g(x) = \sqrt[5]{x}$

17.–25. Verify that $f(g(x)) = x$ and $g(f(x)) = x$ for each pair of functions.

27. $f^{-1}(y) = \dfrac{1}{2}y - 3$, all y

29. $f^{-1}(y) = \sqrt{y - 4}, y \geq 4$

31. $f^{-1}(y) = \dfrac{2y + 2}{-y + 1}, y \neq 1$

33. $f^{-1}(y) = \dfrac{1}{2}y^{1/3}$, all y

35. $f^{-1}(y) = y^2 + 3, y \geq 0$

37. $f^{-1}(y) = 3 + \sqrt{y - 5}, y \geq 5$

39. If $h(x) = x + 2, g(x) = \dfrac{4}{x}$, and $f(x) = x + 3$,
   then $y = f(g(h(x)))$.

41. The inverse function is $q = p^2 - 9, p \geq 3$.

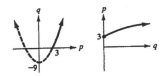

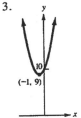

43. The inverse function is $q = .25p^2 - 9, p \geq 6$.

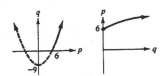

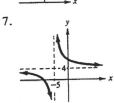

45. a. $q = -16p + 168, 5 \leq p \leq 10$

b. $R = 10.5q - .0625q^2, 8 \leq q \leq 88$

c. $P = -20 + 8.5q - .0625q^2, 8 \leq q \leq 88$

47. $q = 5p^2 - 2000, p \geq 20$

Chapter 1 Review
Drill Problems

1.

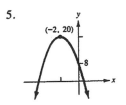

3.

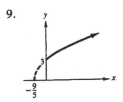

5.

7.

9.

11. $2x^2 + 5$

13. $2h$

15. $f^{-1}(x) = \dfrac{1}{2}x + \dfrac{1}{2}$ 17. $f(x) = 2x + 4$

19. $f(x) = x^2 - 10x + 27$ 21. $f(x) = \dfrac{8x + 60}{x + 3}$

Applications

1. a. $P = .75q - 36, q \geq 0$;   b. $q = 48$ orders
3. Fixed cost: \$1200 per week; variable cost: \$6 per return
5. 80 pairs per week
7. a. $R = 30,000 + 130n - n^2$;   b. $n = 65$, charge \$9.25, 3700 subscribers
9. $p = \$5$ per pound; $q = 6$ tons

Section 2.1

1. 4   3. 30   5. 13   7. 18
9. 50   11. $MC(q) = 15, q \geq 0$
13. $MC(q) = 25 - .4q, 0 \leq q \leq 30$
15. $MC(q) = 62 - 2.6q, 0 \leq q \leq 10$
17. $MR(q) = 35, q \geq 0$
19. $MR(q) = 15 - .1q, 0 \leq q \leq 100$
21. $MR(q) = 470 - 2q, 0 \leq q \leq 200$
23. $MC(q) = 48, q \geq 0$
25. $MC(q) = 25 - .6q, 0 \leq q \leq 40$
27. $MR(q) = 30, q \geq 0$
29. $MR(q) = 20 - .08q, 0 \leq q \leq 200$
31. a. $C = 850 + 70q - .05q^2, 0 \leq q \leq 300$
    b. $MC = 70 - .1q, 0 \leq q \leq 300$
    c. $C(200) = \$12,850; MC(200) = \$50$
    d. $C(201) - C(200) = \$49.95$
33. a. $MC = 8 - .012q, 0 \leq q \leq 400$
    b. $\dfrac{C(100)}{100} = \dfrac{890}{100} = \$8.90; MC(100) = \$6.80$
35. a. $MC = 12 - .04q; MR = 17 - .06q; 0 \leq q \leq 300$
    b. Increased; $MR(225) = \$3.50$ and $MC(225) = \$3.20$
    c. $q = 250$ packages
37. a. $MC = 90 - .2q; MR = 120 - .7q; 0 \leq q \leq 100$
    b. $MC(225) = \$3.00$

Section 2.2

1. 23   3. 4   5. -7 7. 1
9. 0   11. 7   13. $\dfrac{1}{3}$ 15. 0
17. 6   19. -2 21. 2   23. 4
25. a. 2;   b. 1;   c. 0;   d. -1
27.

x	2.1	1.9	2.01	1.99	2.001
$g(x)$	12.61	11.41	12.0601	11.9401	12.006001

The limit is 12.

29. 1   31. $R = 25q - .04q^2, 0 \leq q \leq 300; MR(200) = 9$
33. $2x$ 35. $6x$

Section 2.3

1. ∞ 3. $-\infty$ 5. ∞ 7. ∞
9. $-\infty$ 11. Does not exist   13. $-\infty$
15. $-\dfrac{1}{3}$ 17. 3   19. 4   21. 0
23. $\dfrac{5}{3}$ 25. 0   27. ∞ 29. $-\infty$
31. The function is undefined for $x < 4$, so there is no limit from the left.
33. Both one-sided limits are 8, so $\lim_{x \to 2} f(x) = 8$.
35. Both one-sided limits are 4, so $\lim_{x \to 2} f(x) = 4$.
37. $\lim_{x \to 2^-} f(x) = -\infty$ and $\lim_{x \to 2^+} f(x) = \infty$, so $\lim_{x \to 2} f(x)$ does not exist.
39. Both one-sided limits are 0, so $\lim_{x \to 2} f(x) = 0$.
41. $\lim_{q \to 0^+} v(q) = 50$; $\lim_{q \to \infty} v(q) = 25$. When the output is very low, the variable cost is about \$50 per ton; as the output increases, this cost declines toward \$25 per ton.
43. 2.718
45. a. $A(t) = 500 - 50(t - 8), 8 < t \leq 10$
    b. $\lim_{t \to 8^-} A(t) = 200, \lim_{t \to 8^+} A(t) = 500, A(8) = 200$
    c.

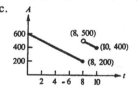

Section 2.4

1. Continuous

3. Continuous

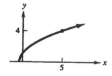

5. Discontinuous;
   $\lim_{x \to 1/2} f(x)$ does not exist.

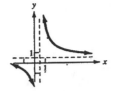

7. Discontinuous;
   $\lim_{x \to 1} f(x) \neq f(1)$.

9. Continuous

11. Discontinuous;
    $\lim_{x \to -1} f(x)$ does not exist.

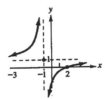

13. Discontinuous;
    $\lim_{x \to 3} f(x)$ does not exist.

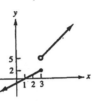

15. Continuous

17. Continuous

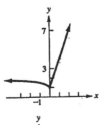

19. Continuous

21. None   23. -5
25. 2, 5   27. $-3, 3$
29. 0   31. None
33. It is not continuous at $w = 3$; it is continuous at $w = 2.7$.
35. a. $I(x) = 300 + .0165(x - 20,000)$, $x > 20,000$; b. Yes
    c.

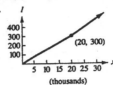

37. b. $\lim_{t \to 1^-} A(t) = 1070$; $\lim_{t \to 1^+} A(t) = 1140$; discontinuous at $t = 1$
    c.

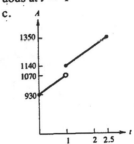

Chapter 2 Review

Drill Problems

1. $\dfrac{10}{3}$ 3. 0   5. ∞ 7. $-\infty$

9. $-\infty$ 11. 8   13. -8 15. $\dfrac{1}{5}$

17. 2   19. 0   21. ∞ 23. $-2, 0, 2$

25. None   27. 0   29. $-3, -2, 2$

Applications

1. $C(40) = \$3240$; $C(40)/40 = \$81$; $MC(40) = \$72$
3. $R(60) = \$408$; $MR(60) = \$5.60$
5. a. Increase; $MR(150) = 25$ and $MC(150) = 21.25$
   b. $q = 190$
7. a. 100; the selling price must be greater than 100 per unit before suppliers will bring the commodity to market.
   b. 180; consumers will never pay 180 or more per unit for the product.

Section 3.1

1. $f'(x) = 3$; 3, 3   3. $f'(x) = -4$; $-4, -4$
5. $f'(x) = 2x$; 6, 10   7. $f'(x) = 3 - 2x$; 1, -5
9. $f'(x) = -3x^2$; $-12, -27$

11. $f'(x) = -\dfrac{2}{x^3}; -2, \dfrac{1}{4}$

13. 6   15. -8

17. $3x - y = 0$ 19. $\left(-\dfrac{7}{2}, -\dfrac{57}{4}\right)$

21. $x + 4y = 4; x + 4y = -4$

23. $4x^3$ 25. 10   27. $-.3$ 29. 10.2

31. $10,000 in sales per $1000 of advertising

33. 10,000 mi/hr   35. -64 and -128 ft/sec

37. a. $x = a, c$;   b. $x = a, b, c, d$;   c. $x = b, d$;
    d. No such points are possible.

Section 3.2

1. 0   3. $6x^{-1/4}$ 5. $-28u^{-5}$ 7. 0

9. 0   11. $\dfrac{1}{5}t^{-4/5}$ 13. $-.1w^{-4/3}$ 15. $36x$

17. 2   19. $3x^{1/2} - \dfrac{3}{2}x^{-1/2}$ 21. $1 - \dfrac{5}{x^2}$

23. $9x^2 - 4x + 3$ 25. 5

27. $x^{-2/3} - x^{-1/2}$ 29. $-\dfrac{4}{3}x^{1/3} + \dfrac{4}{3}x^{-1/3}$

31. $10x^{3/2} + \dfrac{9}{2}x^{-1/2} - x^{-1/2}$ 33. 0

35. .15   37. $y = 10x - 11$

39. $y = x - 15$ 41. $x = -\dfrac{3}{2}$

43. $x = \dfrac{1}{3}, 3$ 45. a. $343.60; b. $334

47. a. $C = 30 + 1.5q - .002q^2, 0 \le q \le 500$;

$A = \dfrac{30}{q} + 1.5 - .002q; 0 < q \le 500$

b. $-30q^{-2} - .002, 0 < q \le 500$

49. $575 per year; $595 per year

51. 600 cases per $1000

Section 3.3

1. $\dfrac{2x}{\sqrt{2x^2 + 1}}$ 3. $48(6x - 1)^7$

5. $\dfrac{5}{2\sqrt{5x + 1}}$ 7. $5(y + 1)(\sqrt{y^2 + 2y})^3$

9. $\dfrac{3}{\sqrt{6x + 2}}$ 11. $10\left(3x + \dfrac{1}{x}\right)^9\left(3 - \dfrac{1}{x^2}\right)$

13. $\dfrac{105}{4}(5x + 6)^{-1/4}$ 15. $3\left(\sqrt{x} + \dfrac{3}{x}\right)\left(\dfrac{1}{2\sqrt{x}} - \dfrac{3}{x^2}\right)$

17. $\dfrac{-2}{(2x + 1)^2}$ 19. $\dfrac{4}{(2 - x)^3}$

21. $-(8x^2 + 4)(4x^3 + 6x)^{-5/3}$ 23. $x - 3y = -5$

25. $10x - 27y = -41$ 27. $4x + 5y = 5$

29. $\dfrac{x}{\sqrt{x^2 + 5}}$ 31. $\dfrac{5}{3}(5x + 9)^{-2/3}$

33. $6(2x + 1)^2 + 2$

35. $2(5x^2 + 3)(10x)$ is the same as $100x^3 + 60x$.

37. $(65,000 - 40w - 320\sqrt{w})\left(.2 + \dfrac{8}{\sqrt{w}}\right)$; $16,184

39. $\dfrac{50}{3}(w^2 + 30w)^{-2/3}(2w + 30)[40 - 4(w^2 + 30w)^{1/3}]$;
    $311 per day

41. $16,000 per week   43. $D_x[f^{-1}(f(x))] = \dfrac{1}{f'(x)}$

Section 3.4

1. $105x^2 - 28x + 20$ 3. $6x^2 + 22x + 7$

5. $\dfrac{x^2(7x + 18)}{2\sqrt{x + 3}}$ 7. $\dfrac{3(3x + 1)}{\sqrt{2x + 1}}$

9. $\dfrac{14}{(x + 5)^2}$ 11. $\dfrac{4 - 2x^3}{(x^3 + 4)^2}$

13. $\dfrac{3x^2 - 20x - 1}{2(x - 5)^{3/2}}$ 15. $\dfrac{5q^2 + 200q + 125}{(q + 20)^2}$

17. $21x[(3x^2 + 2)(x^3 + 5)]^6(5x^3 + 2x + 10)$

19. $\dfrac{-100(4z + 1)^4}{(8z - 3)^6}$ 21. $60x^2 - 54x + 37$

23. $\dfrac{-6x^2 - 4x - 19}{(3x + 1)^2}$ 25. $\dfrac{10x^2 + 24x - 9}{2\sqrt{x + 3}}$

27. $\dfrac{3(2 - 3x)(x - 12)}{(x + 5)^4}$ 29. $\dfrac{9x + 40}{2\sqrt{x + 5}}$

31. $\dfrac{-7}{(6x + 5)^2}$ 33. $1 + 3x^2 + \dfrac{3}{2}x^{1/2} + \dfrac{5}{2}x^{3/2}$

35. $16x + y = 24$ 37. $91x - 169y = -390$

39. $5x - y = -8$

43. $R(60) = $960; MR(60) = 7

45. a. $v(0) = 25; \lim_{q\to\infty} v(q) = 15$

b. $C(q) = \dfrac{15q^2 + 825q + 2250}{q + 3}$;

$MC(q) = \dfrac{15q^2 + 90q + 225}{(q + 3)^2}, q \ge 0$

c. $v(10) = $17.31; MC(10) = 15.53. Although the variable cost of making the tenth case of racquetballs is $17.31, the total cost increases by only $15.53.

d. Both limits are $15, indicating that for large production levels, the increase in the total cost when another case is produced is approximately equal to the variable cost of making that case.

Section 3.5

1. Increasing
3. Decreasing
5. Increasing on $(-\infty, -1)$ and $(1, \infty)$; decreasing on $(-1, 1)$
7. Increasing
9. Increasing on $(-4, 0)$; decreasing on $(0, 4)$
11. Decreasing
13. Decreasing on $(-\infty, 0)$; increasing on $(0, \infty)$
15. $(-\infty, \infty)$
17. $\left(-\infty, -\dfrac{3}{2}\right)$
19. $(-\infty, 1)$ and $(2, \infty)$
21. $(-\infty, \infty)$
23. $(3, \infty)$
25. $\left(-\dfrac{1}{3}, \dfrac{7}{3}\right)$ and $(5, \infty)$
27. $(0, 50)$
29. $(-\infty, 0)$
31. $\dfrac{dv}{dq} = \dfrac{-90}{(q + 20)^2}$, which is negative for $q > 0$. The graph of $v(q)$ declines from 12.5 at $q = 0$ toward a horizontal asymptote of $v = 8$ as q increases.
33. When $ac < b$
35. $v(0) = \$25$; $v(150) = \$20.50$; $v'(q) = -.06 + .0004q$, which is negative for $0 \leq q < 150$.
37. $C'(q)$ becomes negative at $q = 80$; the longest interval on which the function models an increasing function is $[0, 80]$.
39. $[0, 90]$
41. $\dfrac{dp}{dq} = \dfrac{.3q}{\sqrt{2500 + .3q^2}}$, which is positive for $q \geq 0$. $\$50$ per cord is the lowest price acceptable to the suppliers.
43. $\$360$ is spent and $\$140$ is saved.
45. $\dfrac{dS}{dI} = .05 + .012\sqrt{I} + \dfrac{.12}{\sqrt{I}}$. $\$154$ if the previous salary was $\$16,000$; $\$161$ if the salary was $\$25,000$.

Section 3.6

1. 0
3. $6x$
5. $1050(5x + 4)^4$
7. $-\dfrac{9}{4(3x + 1)^{3/2}}$
9. $\dfrac{16}{(z - 1)^3}$
11. $\dfrac{220}{(q + 10)^3}$
13. $\dfrac{3x + 6}{(2x + 3)^{3/2}}$
15. $\dfrac{225}{(5p^2 + 45)^{3/2}}$
17. Upward
19. Upward
21. Downward
23. Downward
25. Upward
27. Upward on $(0, \infty)$; downward on $(-\infty, 0)$; $x = 0$ is a point of inflection.
29. Upward on $\left(\dfrac{1}{2}, \infty\right)$; downward on $\left(-\infty, \dfrac{1}{2}\right)$; $x = \dfrac{1}{2}$ is a point of inflection.

31. Upward on $(6, \infty)$; downward on $(-\infty, 6)$; no point of inflection.
33. Upward on $(0, \infty)$; downward on $(-\infty, 0)$; $x = 0$ is a point of inflection.
35. Upward on $(-\infty, -1)$ and $(0, \infty)$; downward on $(-1, 0)$; $x = -1$ is the only point of inflection.
37. $x = -\dfrac{b}{3a}$
39. $p''(q) = .0625(.5q + 2500)^{-1.5}$, which is positive for $q \geq 0$.
$R''(q) = -(.1875q + 1250)(.5q + 2500)^{-1.5}$, which is negative for $q \geq 0$.
41. $C' = 1 - \dfrac{.05}{\sqrt{I}} - .004I$, which is positive for $8 \leq I \leq 48$.
$C'' = \dfrac{.025}{\sqrt{I^3}} - .004$, which is negative for $8 \leq I \leq 48$.
43. $v(0) = 60$; $\lim_{q \to \infty} v(q) = 20$; concave downward for $(0, 10)$; concave upward for $(10, \infty)$; $q = 10$ is a point of inflection.

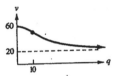

45. a. $q' = p(1.5p^2 + 400)^{-2/3}$, which is positive for $p \geq 20$; $q'' = (400 - .5p^2)(1.5p^2 + 400)^{-5/3}$; inflection point at $p = \sqrt{800}$.
b. $q' = .4p(.6p^2 + 110)^{-2/3}$, which is positive for $p \geq 5$; $q'' = .4(110 - .2p^2)(.6p^2 + 110)^{-5/3}$; inflection point at $p = \sqrt{550}$.

Chapter 3 Review

Drill Problems

1. 5
3. $2 - \dfrac{12}{x^3}$
5. $18x(x^2 + 8)^8$
7. $6x^{1/2} - x^{-1/2}$
9. $\dfrac{2}{(4x + 3)^2}$
11. $\dfrac{-5(3x^2 + 16x - 2)}{(x^3 + 8x^2 - 2x + 1)^2}$
13. $\dfrac{4x - 31}{(8x + 5)^{3/2}}$
15. $\dfrac{105x^3 + 126x^2 + 15x + 14}{\sqrt{5x + 7}}$
17. $\dfrac{1}{3}(8x - 7)(4x^2 - 7x + 8)^{-2/3}$
19. $\dfrac{224(6x + 1)^7}{(2x + 5)^9}$
21. $5x - y = 5$
23. $3x - 5y = -16$
25. $x - y = 0$
27. a. $(-3, \infty)$; b. $(-\infty, \infty)$
29. a. $(-\infty, 2 - 2\sqrt{3})$ and $(2 + 2\sqrt{3}, \infty)$; b. $(2, \infty)$

31. a. $(0, \infty)$;   b. $(-2, 2)$
33. a. $(0, \infty)$;   b. $(-\infty, \infty)$

Applications

1. a. $MC(q) = 191 - .58q + .003q^2$;
   $MR(q) = 229 - .64q, 0 \le q \le 200$
   b. 180 printers per day

2. a. $MC = \dfrac{20(9q^2 + 720q + 47,600)}{(q + 40)^2}, 0 \le q \le 200$
   $MR = 347 - .94q, 0 \le q \le 200$
   b. $q = 160$

3. 8 mo
7. $C = 18; .95$

5. When $t = 10$ mo
9. $122.50 per worker per day

Section 4.1

1. 3%

3. 9%

5.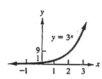

7.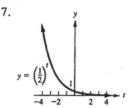

9.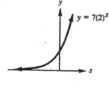

11.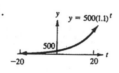

13.

15. 300% rate of growth
17. 80% rate of decay
19. 95% rate of decay
21. 20% rate of decay
23. 200% rate of growth
25. $f(x) = 500(1.1)^x$
27. $f(x) = 120(.7)^x$
29. $f(x) = 3(5)^x$
31. $f(x) = 1500(1.7)^x$
33. $1850.93
35. $30,720; $19,661
37. At 5%: $0.86, $0.74, $0.60; at 10%: $0.73, $0.53, $0.35
39. $2.88, $2.44, $2.07, $1.75, $1.49, $1.26, $1.07, $.90
41. $F_1 = 89.58 and $F_2 = 23.48; thus, after 12 yr the price is $23.48, not the original $30.

Section 4.2

1. 5.095%
5. 8.322%
9. 10.517%
13. 6.555%

3. 5.127%
7. 10.250%
11. 5.378%
15. $806.75

17. $1366.59
21. $22.53
25. $.80; $.89
29. $2573
33. 19.56%

19. $3612.22
23. $7408.18
27. $660
31. 8.73%

Section 4.3

1. $\log_2 8 = 3$
3. $\log_{81} 9 = \dfrac{1}{2}$
5. $\log_7 1 = 0$
7. $\log_3 \left(\dfrac{1}{3}\right) = -1$
9. $3^2 = 9$
11. $27^{1/3} = 3$
13. $3^{2.096} = 10$
15. $e^{.693} = 2$
17. 1.11   19. 1.36   21. .34
23. 5 yr, 3 mo; 7 yr, 9 mo
25. 10 yr; 9 yr
27. 4.3 yr
29. 4.4%
31. 11.65%
33. 14.87%
35. 1.4650
37. -2.7909
39. $-.6610$
41. 16.4863
43. $-.4055$
45. $y = e^{2.3026x}$
47. $y = 5e^{-.6931x}$
49. $y = 3e^{3.2188x}$
51. $y = 50e^{-.2231x}$
53. $t = \dfrac{\ln F - \ln P}{r}$

Section 4.4

1. $5e^{5x}$
3. $\dfrac{1}{x}$
5. $5^x \ln 5$
7. $\dfrac{1}{(\ln 5)x}$
9. $\dfrac{-5}{2(x + 4)(x - 1)}$
11. $12e^{4x}$
13. $2 \ln (2x) + 2$
15. $2(\ln 7)7^{2x+1}$
17. $\dfrac{2x}{3(x^2 + 5)}$
19. $2^x \ln 2 + 2x$
21. $\dfrac{2^x \ln 2 + 2x}{2^x + x^2}$
23. $2xe^{2x}(1 + x)$
25. $\dfrac{7}{x}([\ln x]^6 + 1)$
27. $\dfrac{1}{2x\sqrt{\ln x}}$
29. $x - y = -1$
31. $x - y = 1$
33. $2x - y = 4$
35. $(-1, \infty)$
37. $(0, e)$
39. $\left(\dfrac{1}{e}, \infty\right)$
41. $(-2, \infty)$
43. $(0, \infty)$
45. .15   47. $\ln 2$ 49. $\dfrac{3}{x}$
51. 2.956%; $y = 750,000e^{.02956t}, 0 \le t \le 7$
53. 6.761%; $3699
55. $6283; 22.1%

Section 4.5

1.
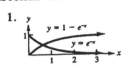

3.
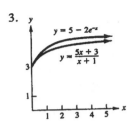

5.
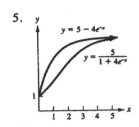

7.
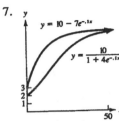

9. a. $y = 100 - 50e^{-.223t}$;   b. $y = \dfrac{100}{1 + e^{-.405t}}$

11. a. $y = 200 - 180e^{-.059t}$;   b. $y = \dfrac{200}{1 + 9e^{-.220t}}$

13. a. $y = 500 - 499e^{-.00182t}$;   b. $y = \dfrac{500}{1 + 499e^{-.2321t}}$

15. a. $S = 1000 - 990e^{-.022t}$;
b. $S(50) = 670$, $S(150) = 963$;   c. $t = 1.9$ days

17. a. $S = \dfrac{5000}{1 + 249e^{-.1t}}$;   b. $S(10) = 54$, $S(90) = 4851$;
c. $t = 37.8$;   d. $t = 55.2$

19. Approximately 63 wk   **21.** 2.68%

23. Natural growth: $P = 3.6e^{.02t}$; $P(20) = 5.4$, $P(30) = 6.6$,
and $P = 20$ when $t = 86$—in the year 2056

Logistic growth: $P = \dfrac{360}{9 + 91e^{-.02t}}$; $P(20) = 5.1$, $P(30) =$
6.1, and $P = 20$ when $t = 116$—in the year 2086

Chapter 4 Review
Drill Problems

1. $-.465$ **3.** 1.667

5. $\dfrac{3x^2 - 6}{2 - 6x + x^3}$ **7.** $\dfrac{1}{t} - \dfrac{5}{5t + 1} + \dfrac{6t}{4 - 3t^2}$

9. $5e^{5x} + 5(\ln 10)10^{5x}$ **11.** $\dfrac{3e^{3y} + 3y^2}{e^{3y} + y^3}$

13. $\dfrac{8e^{2x}}{1 + e^{2x}}\ln^3(1 + e^{2x})$

15. 10.5156%   **17.** 5.8 yr

Applications

1. 8.10% compounded quarterly, which yields an effective
rate of 8.349%

3. 15.43%

5. $P = P_0(.985)^t$, $0 \le t \le 5$; the instantaneous rate of decline
is 1.511%.

7. $S = 15 - 13e^{-.1t}$, $t \ge 0$

Section 5.1

1. None   **3.** $x = \dfrac{1}{2}$

5. $x = 0$ **7.** $x = -\dfrac{5}{3}, -1$

9. $x = 0, 8$ **11.** $x = 0, 4, 8$

13. $x = -2$ **15.** $x = 2$

17. $x = 5$ **19.** $x = \dfrac{1}{6}$

21. $x = 0, 4$ **23.** $x = 0$

25. $x = -3, 3$ **27.** $x = 2$

29. $x = \dfrac{1}{e}$

31. a. $x = 3$ is a critical point; $f'(3)$ is undefined.
b. $x = 3$ is not a critical point; it is not in the domain of f.
c. $x = 3$ is a critical point; $f'(3) = 0$.
d. $x = 3$ is not a critical point; it is not in the domain of f.
e. $x = 3$ is not a critical point; it is not in the domain of f.

33. $P(q) = R(q) - C(q)$, so $P'(q) = R'(q) - C'(q)$, and so
$P'(q) = 0$ when $R'(q) = C'(q)$—that is, when $MR = MC$.

35. $f'(x) = a$, which is nonzero, so f' is always defined but
never 0.

37. There are no critical points if $b^2 - 3ac < 0$, one if
$b^2 - 3ac = 0$, and two if $b^2 - 3ac > 0$.

39. $f'(x) = (ad - bc)/(cx + d)^2$, which is not 0 unless
$ad - bc = 0$ (in which case f is a constant function).

Section 5.2

1. Max: $f(7) = 23$; min: $f(0) = 2$

3. Max: $h(0) = h(1) = 4$; min: $h\left(\dfrac{1}{2}\right) = \dfrac{13}{4}$

5. Max: $g(5) = 84$; min: $g(2) = -24$

7. Max: $f(1) = 8$; min: $f(2) = 1$

9. Max: $p(-2) = 64$; min: $p(0) = p(2) = 0$

11. Max: $p(0) = p(27) = 0$; min: $p(-1) = p(8) = -\dfrac{4}{3}$

13. Max: $f(1) = \dfrac{17}{2}$; min: $f(4) = 4$

15. Max: $h(1) = h(-1) = e$; min: $h(0) = 1$

17. Max: $g(1) = e$; min: $g(0) = 0$

19. Max: $f(2) = (8 \ln 2) - 4 \doteq 1.55$;
    min: $f(4) = (8 \ln 4) - 16 \doteq -4.91$
21. Max: $p(4) = 5$; min: $p(0) = 3$
23. Max: $h(0) = 0$; min: $h(4) = -16$
25. 250 wallets (profit: $175)
27. 150 mufflers (profit: $1362.50)
29. 30 units (profit: $40)
31. $x = \$6561$; $P(6561) = \$1987$; $q(6561) = 583.2$ units
33. $400 per day (profit: $460)
35. 225 persons (revenue: $81,000)
37. 22 students (profit: $1936)
39. $k = \$50$ thousand (output: 142.9 tons)
41. $x = 4$ in. (volume: 1024 cu in.)
43. $l = 300$ ft; $w = 150$ ft (area: 45,000 sq ft)
45. $p = .2033$; $C_D(.2033) = 1.0577$; $C_S(.2033) = .0636$

Section 5.3

1. Relative minimum at $x = \dfrac{1}{2}$
3. Relative minimum at $x = 0$
5. Relative maximum at $x = -\dfrac{5}{3}$; relative minimum at $x = -1$
7. Relative minima at $x = 0, 8$; relative maximum at $x = 4$
9. Relative minimum at $x = -2$
11. Relative maximum at $x = 2$
13. Relative maximum at $x = \dfrac{1}{6}$
15. Relative maximum at $x = 4$
17. Relative maximum at $x = 2$
19. Relative minimum at $x = \dfrac{1}{e}$
21. Relative maximum at $x = 2$; relative minimum at $x = 3$
23. Relative minima at $x = -2, 2$; relative maximum at $x = 0$
25. Relative minimum at $x = 3$; neither at $x = 12$
27. Relative maximum at $x = -12$; relative minimum at $x = 0$
29. Relative minimum at $x = 0$ ($x = -4, 4$ are not in the domain)
31. Relative minimum at $x = 7$
33. Relative maximum at $x = 9$; relative minimum at $x = 15$
35. Relative minimum at $x = 2\sqrt{2}$ ($x = -2\sqrt{2}$ and $x = 0$ are not in the domain)
37. Relative maximum at $x = -5$; relative minimum at $x = 5$ ($x = 0$ is not in the domain)
39. Relative minimum at $x = \ln 4$
41. Relative maximum at $x = 2$
43. Relative minimum at $x = 2$; neither at $x = 3$
45. Relative minimum at $x = 1$; relative maximum at $x = 3$
47. If P has a relative maximum at q_0, then $MC < MR$ when $q < q_0$ and $MC > MR$ when $q > q_0$.

49. $f'(x) = (kx + 1)e^{kx}$; $f'(x) < 0$ when $kx + 1 < 0$ (i.e., when $x < -1/k$) and $f'(x) > 0$ when $kx + 1 > 0$ (i.e., when $x > -1/k$).
51. $f'(x) = (k/3)(x - a)^{(k-3)/3}$. If k is even, then $k - 3$ is odd and $f'(x)$ changes sign at $x = a$. If k is odd, then $k - 3$ is even and $f'(x)$ does not change sign at $x = a$.
53. Decreasing; min: $h(10) = 5 - \ln 10$
55. Increasing; min: $g(0) = -5$
57. Decreasing; min: $f(-8) = 4$
59. Increasing; min: $h(-4) = 3$

Section 5.4

1. Relative minimum at $x = \dfrac{1}{2}$
3. Relative minimum at $x = 0$
5. Relative maximum at $x = -\dfrac{5}{3}$; relative minimum at $x = -1$
7. Relative minima at $x = 0, 8$; relative maximum at $x = 4$
9. Relative minimum at $x = -2$
11. Relative maximum at $x = 2$
13. Relative maximum at $x = \dfrac{1}{6}$
15. Relative maximum at $x = 4$
17. Relative maximum at $x = 2$
19. Relative minimum at $x = \dfrac{1}{e}$
21. Relative maximum at $x = -5$; relative minimum at $x = 3$
23. Relative minimum at $x = -1$; relative maximum at $x = 1$. (At $x = 0$ the second derivative test fails. From the first derivative test we find f does not have a relative extreme value at $x = 0$.)
25. Relative minima at $x = -4, 6$; relative maximum at $x = 1$
27. Relative maximum at $x = \dfrac{2}{3}$; relative minimum at $x = 0$
29. Relative minimum at $x = 0$
31. There is a relative minimum at $x = -\dfrac{9}{2}$. The second derivative test fails, so the first derivative test must be used.
33. Relative minimum at $x = 2$ ($x = -3, -1$ are not in the domain of f)
35. Relative minimum at $x = 0$
37. $f'(x) = \dfrac{6}{x} + 3x^2 - 9$. $f'(1) = 0$, so $x = 1$ is a critical point. $f''(x) = -\dfrac{6}{x^2} + 6x$. $f''(1) = 0$, so the second derivative test fails. From the first derivative test we find that $x = 1$ is not an extreme point.
39. $f'(x) = 6 - 2x + 2(x - 3)e^{(x-3)^2}$. $f'(3) = 0$ so $x = 3$ is a

critical point. $f''(x) = -2 + 2e^{(x-3)^2} + 4(x-3)^2 e^{(x-3)^2}$.
$f''(0) = 0$ so the second derivative test fails; by the first
derivative test we see there is a relative minimum at $x = 3$.

Section 5.5

1. Increasing on $(-\infty, -2)$ and $(2, \infty)$;
   decreasing on $(-2, 2)$;
   relative maximum at $x = -2$;
   relative minimum at $x = 2$;
   concave upward on $(0, \infty)$;
   concave downward on $(-\infty, 0)$;
   point of inflection at $x = 0$.

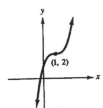

3. Increasing on $(-\infty, \infty)$;
   no extreme points;
   concave upward on $(1, \infty)$;
   concave downward on $(-\infty, 1)$;
   point of inflection at $x = 1$.

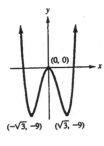

5. Increasing on $(-\sqrt{3}, 0)$ and
   $(\sqrt{3}, \infty)$; decreasing on $(-\infty, -\sqrt{3})$
   and $(0, \sqrt{3})$;
   relative minima at $x = -\sqrt{3}, \sqrt{3}$;
   relative maximum at $x = 0$;
   concave upward on $(-\infty, -1)$ and
   $(1, \infty)$;
   concave downward on $(-1, 1)$;
   points of inflection at $x = -1, 1$.

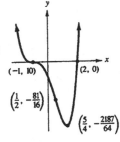

7. Increasing on $(5/4, \infty)$;
   decreasing on $(-\infty, 5/4)$;
   relative minimum at $x = 5/4$;
   concave upward on $(-\infty, -1)$ and
   $(1/2, \infty)$; concave downward on
   $(-1, 1/2)$; points of inflection at
   $x = -1, 1/2$.

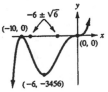

9. Increasing on $(-\infty, -10)$, $(-6, \infty)$;
   decreasing on $(-10, -6)$;
   relative maximum at $x = -10$;
   relative minimum at $x = -6$;
   concave upward on
   $(-6 - \sqrt{6}, -6 + \sqrt{6})$, $(0, \infty)$;
   concave downward on
   $(-\infty, -6 - \sqrt{6})$, $(-6 + \sqrt{6}, 0)$;
   points of inflection at
   $x = 0, -6 \pm \sqrt{6}$.

11. Increasing on $(-1, \infty)$;
    decreasing on $(-\infty, -1)$;
    relative minimum at $x = -1$;
    concave upward on $(-2, \infty)$;
    concave downward on $(-\infty, -2)$;
    point of inflection at $x = -2$.

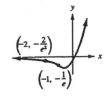

13. Increasing on $(0, \infty)$;
    decreasing on $(-\infty, 0)$;
    relative minimum at $x = 0$;
    concave upward on $(-4, 4)$;
    concave downward on $(-\infty, -4)$,
    $(4, \infty)$; points of inflection at
    $x = -4, 4$.

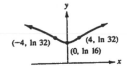

15. Increasing on $(-\infty, 0)$;
    decreasing on $(0, \infty)$;
    relative maximum at $x = 0$;
    concave upward on $(-\infty, -3)$,
    $(3, \infty)$; concave downward on
    $(-3, 3)$; points of inflection at
    $x = -3, 3$.

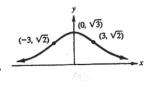

17. Horizontal asymptote: $y = 2$;
    vertical asymptote: $x = 3/2$;
    decreasing on $(-\infty, 3/2)$, $(3/2, \infty)$;
    no relative extreme points;
    concave upward on $(3/2, \infty)$;
    concave downward on $(-\infty, 3/2)$;
    no points of inflection.

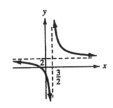

19. Horizontal asymptote: $y = 0$;
    no vertical asymptote;
    increasing on $(-3, 3)$;
    decreasing on $(-\infty, -3)$, $(3, \infty)$;
    relative maximum at $x = 3$;
    relative minimum at $x = -3$;
    concave upward on $(-3\sqrt{3}, 0)$, $(3\sqrt{3}, \infty)$;
    concave downward on $(-\infty, -3\sqrt{3})$, $(0, 3\sqrt{3})$;
    points of inflection at $x = -3\sqrt{3}, 0, 3\sqrt{3}$.

21. No horizontal asymptote;
    vertical asymptote: $x = 2$;
    increasing on $(-\infty, 1)$, $(3, \infty)$;
    decreasing on $(1, 2)$, $(2, 3)$;
    relative maximum at $x = 1$;
    relative minimum at $x = 3$;
    concave upward on $(2, \infty)$;
    concave downward on $(-\infty, 2)$.

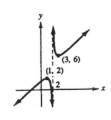

23. Horizontal asymptote: $y = 3$;
no vertical asymptote;
increasing on $(0, \infty)$;
decreasing on $(-\infty, 0)$;
relative minimum at $x = 0$;
concave upward on $(-\sqrt{2}, \sqrt{2})$;
concave downward on $(-\infty, -\sqrt{2})$, $(\sqrt{2}, \infty)$;
points of inflection at $x = -\sqrt{2}, \sqrt{2}$.

$\left(-\sqrt{2}, \frac{3}{4}\right)$ $\left(\sqrt{2}, \frac{3}{4}\right)$

Section 5.6

1. The only relative extreme point is a relative minimum at $x = 3$; so f has an absolute minimum of $f(3) = 1$ on $(0, 4)$.

3. The function does not have a unique relative extreme point on the interval; it has a relative maximum at $x = 1$ and a relative minimum at $x = 2$.

5. The only relative extreme point in the interval is a relative maximum at $x = 1$; so h has an absolute maximum of $h(1) = -1$ on $(0, 2)$.

7. The only relative extreme point is the relative minimum at $x = 1$; so f has an absolute minimum of $f(1) = 1$ on $(0, \infty)$.

9. The only relative extreme point in the interval is a relative maximum at $x = 6$; so g has an absolute maximum of $g(6) = 1/12$ on $(0, 8)$.

11. The only relative extreme point is the relative maximum at $x = 0$; so f has an absolute maximum of $f(0) = 1$ on $(-\infty, \infty)$.

13. $2 \times 2 \times (7/4)$ ft   15. 100 stools   17. 2 yr

19. $15^{2/5} \doteq 6.1$ yr

21. 60 pairs of boots   23. 150 shirts; 16 orders per year

25. 8000 filters; 12 runs per year

27. The optimal output is unchanged—profit is maximized at 400 tires per day.

29. Optimal output is reduced to 350 tires per day.

31. $9.48 per tire, at which the company's output is 222.22 tires per day and the revenue from the tax is $2106.65 per day

Section 5.7

1. $2400
              3. $30

5. $dy = 5\,dx$
        7. $dy = 4e^{4x}\,dx$

9. $dy \dfrac{-3x}{\sqrt{10 - 3x^2}}\,dx$

11. $dy = \left[\dfrac{t}{t - 2} + \ln(t - 2)\right] dt$

13. $dy = e^{-s^2}(1 - 2s^2)\,ds$ 15. $dy = -.06$; $\Delta y = -.06$

17. $dy = .03$; $\Delta y = .0305$ 19. $dy = .016$; $\Delta y = .0160$

21. $dy = -.008$; $\Delta y = -.0080$

23. $df = -.18$; $\Delta f = -.1782$

25. $df = 0$; $\Delta f = -.0015$ 27. $df = -.05$; $\Delta f = -.0513$

29. $df = .04$; $\Delta f = .0392$

31. $f(4) + dy = -48.768$; $f(4.032) = -48.7711$

33. $f(1) + dy = 1.014$; $f(1.0035) = 1.0141$

35. $f(1) + dy = 2.7202$; $f(1.0007) = 2.7202$

37. $f(1) + dy = -.12$; $f(.88) = -.1278$

39. $dV = 60(25)(-.5) = -750$ cu in.

41. $dC = \$328$ 43. a. 10,400;   b. 11,400

45. $p(30) = 26.42\%$; $dp = 2.94\%$

47. a. The price will drop by $dp = -\$.44$;
    b. $200 + dq = 183$ cases

49. a. $dp = -\$16.50$;   b. $R = 500q - 8q^2 - .005q^3$,
     $10 \le q \le 40$; $dR = \$181.25$

Section 5.8

1. .5, 2, 5
                 3. .083, .237, .5

5. .111, .667, 1.5
         7. .281, .889

9. 1, 1, 1
                   11. .5, .5, .5

13. .5, .5
                 15. 1.25, 1.25

17. 1% increase
         19. .25% decrease

21. 1.5% decrease
      23. 1% increase

25. 1% decrease
         27. .25% increase

29. 1.5% increase
      31. No change

33. $\eta = 1.6$

35. Demand increases by 50%; revenue increases by 40%.

37. Demand increases by 8.97%; revenue increases by 2.07%.

39. $\eta = 2.50$
           41. $\eta = .67$

43. $p = \$75$
             45. $p = \$30$

47. $p = \$15$

49. $\eta = \dfrac{pm}{b - pm} = 1$ if $pm = b - pm$, or $2pm = b$, so
$p = \dfrac{b}{2m}$.

51. $\eta = \left(\dfrac{p^2}{A}\right)\left(\dfrac{A}{p^2}\right) = 1$ for all $p \ne 0$; $R = A$ for all p.

Chapter 5 Review

Drill Problems

1. Relative maximum at $x = -3$; relative minimum at $x = \dfrac{5}{3}$

3. Relative minimum at $x = 6$; no relative extreme value at $x = 0$

5. Relative maximum at $x = \dfrac{2}{3}$; relative minimum at $x = 0$

7. Relative maximum at $x = -5$; relative minimum at $x = 1$

9. Absolute maximum: $f\left(\dfrac{2}{3}\right) = \dfrac{22}{3}$;

absolute minimum: $f(3) = -9$

11. Absolute maximum: $f(-2) = \dfrac{11}{3}$;

absolute minimum: $f(2) = \dfrac{3}{7}$

13. Absolute maximum: $f(1) = 12$;

absolute minimum: $f(4) = -15$

15. $-.1333$ 17. 4

Applications

1. $P = -.001q^3 - .03q^2 + 108q - 800,\ 0 \le q \le 200$; $q = 180$ maximizes P.

3. 15 min   5. $q = 40$

7. $dq = -10.42$; demand will decline by approximately 10.4 croissants per day.

Section 6.1

1. $8x + c$

3. $\dfrac{x^5}{5} + c$

5. $\dfrac{5x^{7/5}}{7} + c$

7. $\dfrac{x^{1.35}}{1.35} + c$

9. $\dfrac{5x^3}{3} - \dfrac{3x^2}{2} + 4x + c$

11. $\dfrac{2x^3}{3} + \dfrac{5x^2}{2} - 3x + c$

13. $\dfrac{2z^5}{5} + \dfrac{z^6}{6} + c$

15. $8x^{1/2} + \dfrac{x^{3/2}}{6} + c$

17. $\dfrac{2x^{7/2}}{7} + c$

19. $15y^{2/5} + c$

21. $\dfrac{2x^{5/2}}{5} + \dfrac{10x^{3/2}}{3} + c$

23. $5x + 3\ln|x| - \dfrac{2}{x} + c$

25. $5e^x + c$

27. $3e^5y + c$

29. $\dfrac{x^4}{4} + \dfrac{10x^3}{3} + \dfrac{25x^2}{2} + c$

31. $C(q) = 2000 + 700q - .9q^2 - .04q^3,\ 0 \le q \le 50$

33. $A = \dfrac{5}{q} + 12 - .15q - .0004q^2,\ 0 < q \le 20$

35. $v = 700 - .9q - .04q^2,\ 0 < q \le 50$

37. $v = 12 - .15q - .0004q^2,\ 0 < q \le 20$

39. $R = 5000q - 10q^2 - .09q^3,\ 0 \le q \le 50;\ p = \$44.56$

41. $C(I) = 7.50 + .96I - .02I^{3/2} - .003I^{5/3},\ 0 \le I \le 30$

43. a. $C(q) = 50 + 10q$ and $R(q) = 34q - .03q^2 - .0001q^3,\ 0 \le q \le 100$

b. $P = -50 + 24q - .03q^2 - .0001q^3,\ 0 \le q \le 100$

c. P is maximized when $q = 100;\ P(100) = 1950$

Section 6.2

1. 28   3. 88   5. -28 7. 4

9. -6 11. $\dfrac{1}{6}$ 13. $\dfrac{74}{3}$ 15. $\dfrac{4}{5}$

17. $2\ln 4$ 19. $e^2 - 1$ 21. $\dfrac{26}{3}$ 23. 154

25. $22 + 5\ln 3$ 27. 138   29. $\dfrac{14}{3}$

31. a. \$89.82;   b. \$64.68

33. a. \$1085.26;   b. \$915.24;   c. \$2000.50

d. $\displaystyle\int_{90}^{110} f(q)\,dq = \int_{90}^{100} f(q)\,dq + \int_{100}^{110} f(q)\,dq$

35. \$63.30   37. a. \$769.75;   b. \$750.25

39. \$59.21   41. \$1716

43. a. 0;   b. 4;   c. -4;   d. -14

45. $D_x\left[\displaystyle\int_0^{12}(x^8 - 2x^4 + 7)\,dx\right] = 0$;

$D_x\left[\displaystyle\int(x^8 - 2x^4 + 7)\,dx\right] = x^8 - 2x^4 + 7$

Section 6.3

1. $\dfrac{26}{3}$ square units

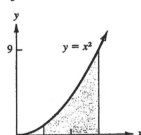

3. 17 square units

5. 6 square units

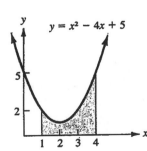

7. $\dfrac{101}{4}$ square units

9. $\dfrac{1}{3}$ 11. $\dfrac{143}{6}$ 13. $2e - 4$ 15. $\dfrac{52}{3} - \ln 9$

17. $\dfrac{4000}{3}$ square units

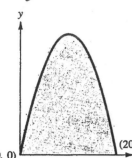

(0, 0)   (20, 0)

19. $\dfrac{9}{2}$ square units

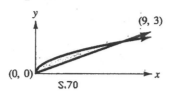

(9, 3)

(0, 0)   S.70

21. $\dfrac{15}{8} - \ln 4$ square units

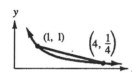

(1, 1) $\left(4, \dfrac{1}{4}\right)$

23. $\dfrac{1}{2}$ square unit

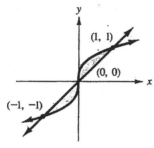

(1, 1)
(0, 0)
(−1, −1)

25. a. $\dfrac{4}{3}$; b. $\dfrac{3}{2}$

27. $\displaystyle\int_a^b \dfrac{a}{b}x \, dx = \dfrac{a}{b}\dfrac{x^2}{2}\Big]_0^b = \dfrac{ab}{2}$

Section 6.4

1. $\dfrac{(x-7)^5}{5} + c$

3. $\dfrac{(2x+5)^4}{8} + c$

5. $\dfrac{(3x^2+5)^4}{24} + c$

7. $\dfrac{(t^3+2)^5}{15} + c$

9. $-\dfrac{1}{3(x^3+5)} + c$

11. $-\dfrac{(4+5/x)^3}{15} + c$

13. $(x^2+3)^{3/2} + c$

15. $\dfrac{3}{2}(1+x^2)^{4/3} + c$

17. $-\dfrac{1}{6}(8x+2)^{-3/4} + c$

19. $\dfrac{(3x^2-6x+2)^2}{12} + c$

21. $(x^2+8)^{1/2} + c$

23. $-\dfrac{1}{2(x^2+4x+5)} + c$

25. $\dfrac{1}{2}\ln|2x+4| + c$

27. $3\ln(r^2+4) + c$

29. $\dfrac{1}{5}e^{5x} + c$

31. $\dfrac{1}{2}e^{x^2} + c$

33. $-\dfrac{1}{3}e^{-x^3} + c$

35. $\dfrac{(\ln x)^2}{2} + c$

37. $-\dfrac{\ln^5(3-x)}{5} + c$

39. $\dfrac{1}{3}\ln(e^{3x}+2) + c$

41. 320   43. 2   45. 0   47. $\dfrac{4}{3}$

49. $\dfrac{\ln 17}{8}$ 51. $\dfrac{e^4-1}{2}$ 53. $\dfrac{1}{3}$ 55. $\dfrac{64}{3}$

57. $\dfrac{32}{5}$ 59. $\dfrac{5}{2}\ln 5$ 61. $33.33

Section 6.5

1. Additional cost: $308.80

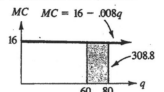

MC $MC = 16 - .008q$
16
308.8
60 80 q

3. Increased consumption: $2208.30

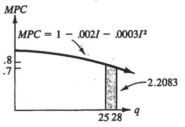

MPC
$MPC = 1 - .002I - .0003I^2$
.8
.7
2.2083
25 28 q

5. Equilibrium point: $q = 200$, $p = 42$; $CS = $800, $PS = $3200

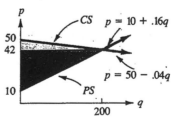

p
CS $p = 10 + .16q$
50
42
$p = 50 - .04q$
10   PS
200   q

7. Equilibrium point: $q = 30$, $p = 16$; $CS = $126, $PS = $189

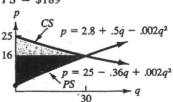

p
CS $p = 2.8 + .5q - .002q^2$
25
16
$p = 25 - .36q + .002q^2$
PS
30   q

9. Equilibrium point: $q = 40$, $p = 15$; $CS = \$77.26$,
   $PS = \$200$

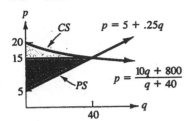

11. $CS = \$772.59$, $PS = \$1666.67$
13. a. \$39.9 million;   b. \$14.9 million

15. 7   17. 0   19. $\dfrac{13}{6}$

21. $2 + \dfrac{1}{4}\ln 5 = 2.402$ 23. 1.297   25. \$1370.20

27. \$15,836.88   29. a. $\dfrac{q}{3}$; b. $\dfrac{3}{4}q$

31. 4273 units per day   33. $\dfrac{L\ln\left(\dfrac{2a}{a+1}\right)}{\ln a}$

Chapter 6 Review

Drill Problems

1. $\dfrac{2}{15}(5x + 4)^{3/2} + c$ 3. $-\dfrac{1}{2}e^{-2x} + c$

5. $-\dfrac{1}{2}(1 - x^3)^{2/3} + c$ 7. $\dfrac{1}{2}x^2 + \ln|x| + c$

9. $-\dfrac{1}{x} + 2x + \dfrac{1}{3}x^3 + c$ 11. 12

13. $\ln\left(\dfrac{7}{3}\right)$ 15. $\dfrac{3}{80}$

17. $\dfrac{4}{3}$ square units   19. $CS = \$625$, $PS = \$166.67$

Applications

1. $C(q) = 45q - .05q^2 - .004q^3 + 50$, $0 \le q \le 40$;
   $C(30) = \$12.47$

2. $\displaystyle\int_{50}^{60}\left(3.5 - .02q - \dfrac{30}{q}\right) dq = 18.53$; \$18,530

3. $S(I) = .03I + .004I^{3/2} + .0006I^{5/2} - .1712$, $4 \le I \le 10$;
   $S(9) = .3526$ or approximately \$353 billion

5. 120 pies will be sold at the equilibrium price of \$2.50;
   $PS = 75\ln 5 - 60 = \$60.71$, $CS = \$360$

Section 7.1

1. 13.8; true value is 14   3. 72.256; true value is 68

5. 4.5; true value is $\dfrac{14}{3}$ 7. 1.10; true value is $\dfrac{1}{2}\ln 8.5$

9. 20.94   11. 3.145
13. 1.093   15. 21.37
17. $T_5 = 3.135$; $T_{10} = 3.140$
19. $T_5 = 3.268$; $T_{10} = 3.248$
21. 500   23. 982.5
25. .857   27. 1.249

29. $MV \doteq \dfrac{[f(c_1) + f(c_2) + \cdots + f(c_N)]\,\Delta x}{b - a}$

   $= \dfrac{[f(c_1) + f(c_2) + \cdots + f(c_N)]\,(b - a)/N}{b - a}$

   $= \dfrac{f(c_1) + f(c_2) + \cdots + f(c_N)}{N}$

Section 7.2

1. $xe^x - e^x + c$
3. $-x^2 e^{-x} - 2xe^{-x} - 2e^{-x} + c$

5. $2x(1 + x)^{1/2} - \dfrac{4}{3}(1 + x)^{3/2} + c$

7. $\dfrac{1}{2}x^2 \ln x - \dfrac{1}{4}x^2 + c$

9. $\dfrac{1}{10}x(2x + 1)^5 - \dfrac{1}{120}(2x + 1)^6 + c$

11. $2x^2(4 + x)^{1/2} - \dfrac{8}{3}x(4 + x)^{3/2} + \dfrac{16}{15}(4 + x)^{5/2} + c$

13. $x^2(1 + x^2)^{1/2} - \dfrac{2}{3}(1 + x^2)^{3/2} + c$

15. $x(\ln x)^2 - 2x \ln x + 2x + c$

17. $-\dfrac{4^{6-x^3}}{3\ln 4} + c$ 19. $-\dfrac{1}{2}\ln|4 - x^2| + c$

21. $\dfrac{1}{6}e^{3x}\sqrt{e^{6x} - 2} - \dfrac{1}{3}\ln|e^{3x} + \sqrt{e^{6x} - 2}| + c$

23. $\dfrac{1}{8}(1 + 4x^2)[\ln(1 + 4x^2) - 1] + c$

25. $\dfrac{1}{6}\ln(3x^2 + \sqrt{1 + 9x^4}) + c$

27. $6e^{-1/2}$ 29. $8\ln 4 - \dfrac{15}{4}$

31. $-\dfrac{64}{21}$

33. a. $5000(e^{.4} - 1) \doteq \$2459.12$
    b. $6000(e^{.4} - 1) - 400 \doteq \$2550.95$
    c. $50,000(e^{.4} - 1) - 20,000 \doteq \$4591.23$

Section 7.3

1. Diverges   3. Converges to 12

5. Converges to 5
9. Diverges
13. Converges to 0
17. Converges to $\frac{1}{4}$
21. Converges to 1
25. Converges to $\frac{1}{2}$
29. Diverges
33. \$18,000
37. \$100,000

7. Converges to 6
11. Converges to 0
15. Diverges
19. Converges to $\frac{1}{4 \ln 2}$
23. Diverges
27. Diverges
31. \$12,000
35. \$15,000

Section 7.4

1. $y = x^2 - 5x + c$
3. $y = .01x^3 - .5x^2 + 15x + c$
5. $y = \frac{2}{3}(x + 1)^{3/2} + c$
7. $y = 5x + 8 \ln|x + 2| + c$
9. $y = 10e^x + c$
11. a. $r = k \ln s + c$; b. $p = .5(\log_3 q + 1)$
13. $V = 100e^{.1t}$
15. $A = 1000e^{-.05t}$
17. $p = \dfrac{1}{50.1 - 50q}$
19. $S = 100 - 90e^{-.02x}$
21. $S = \dfrac{100}{1 + 9e^{-4x}}$
23. $y = x$
25. $V(t) = 500e^{.07t}$
27. $Y = Ce^{kt/h}$
29. $S(x) = 1000 - 990e^{-.00123x}$; 69,000
31. $N(t) = \dfrac{6500}{1 + 64e^{-.4908t}}$; November 1980
33. $q = 2.5(50 - p)$

Chapter 7 Review

Drill Problems

1. $-\frac{1}{2}xe^{-2x} - \frac{1}{4}e^{-2x} + c$
3. $\frac{1}{2}x^2e^{x^2} - \frac{1}{2}e^{x^2} + c$
5. $2x^2(1 + x)^{1/2} - \frac{8}{3}x(1 + x)^{3/2} + \frac{16}{15}(1 + x)^{5/2} + c$
7. $\frac{1}{20} \ln\left|\dfrac{2x - 5}{2x + 5}\right| + c$
9. $\frac{1}{6}x^6 \ln x^3 - \frac{1}{12}x^6 + c$
11. 9.314
13. $y = 4e^{3y}$
15. $S = 100 - 95e^{-.03t}$

Applications

1. \$200
5. \$57,390 per year
3. \$800,000
7. \$2 million

Section 8.1

1. $f(1, 1) = 7; f(-1, 3) = 1$
3. $f(1, 2) = 16$; $f(2, 1) = 17$; $f(0, 3) = 27$; $f(3, 0) = 54$
5. $f(1, 2) = 0$; $f(1, 8) = 0$; $f(2, 1) = \ln 2$; $f(2, -3) = 9 \ln 2$
7. $f(3, 1, -2) = -19$; $f(1, 0, 2) = 6$; $f(-1, 2, -3) = -5$
9. $7 + 4h$
11. $4xy + 4hy - 2x^2y - 4hxy - 2h^2y$
13. 6
15. $C = 1000 + 80q_A - .2q_A^2 + 100q_B - .2q_B^2 + .2q_Aq_B$, $0 \leq q_A, q_B \leq 250$
17. $R = 90q_A - .3q_A^2 + 112q_B - .4q_B^2 - .2q_Aq_B$, $0 \leq q_A, q_B \leq 250$
19. $P = -1000 + 10q_A + 12q_B - .1q_A^2 - .2q_B^2 - .4q_Aq_B$; $0 \leq q_A, q_B \leq 250$
21. a. $P = 800$;
   b. $P = 1106.5$ and $P = 867.6$;
   c. L must increase from 40 to 95, a 238% increase. K must increase from 40 to 1280, a 3200% increase.
23. $f(nL, nK) = C(nL)^\alpha(nK)^{1-\alpha} = CL^\alpha K^{1-\alpha}n = nf(L, K)$

Section 8.2

1. $f_x(x, y) = 2x$; $f_y(x, y) = -2y$
3. $f_x(x, y) = 5 + 2y$; $f_y(x, y) = 2x + 3$
5. $f_x(x, y) = 2x - 3y$; $f_y(x, y) = -3x + 2y$
7. $f_x(x, y) = 5e^{5x-2y}$; $f_y(x, y) = -2e^{5x-2y}$
9. $g_s(s, t) = \dfrac{2t^3}{2s + 3}$; $g_t(s, t) = 3t^2 \ln(2s + 3)$
11. $F_x(x, y) = \dfrac{3}{2y - 6}$; $F_y(x, y) = \dfrac{-2(3x + 5)}{(2y - 6)^2}$
13. $f_x(x, y) = \dfrac{x}{\sqrt{x^2 + 3y^4}}$; $f_y(x, y) = \dfrac{6y^3}{\sqrt{x^2 + 3y^4}}$
15. $f_x(x, y, z) = 2xz$; $f_y(x, y, z) = z^3$; $f_z(x, y, z) = x^2 + 3yz^2$
17. $f_r(r, s, t) = \dfrac{s^2}{2\sqrt{rs^2 + st^2}}$; $f_s(r, s, t) = \dfrac{2rs + t^2}{2\sqrt{rs^2 + st^2}}$; $f_t(r, s, t) = \dfrac{st}{\sqrt{rs^2 + st^2}}$
19. $f_p(p, q, r) = \dfrac{1}{p}$; $f_q(p, q, r) = \dfrac{3}{q}$; $f_r(p, q, r) = \dfrac{5}{r}$
21. $f_x(2, -1) = 11$; $f_x(1, 1) = 2$; $f_x(2, -1) = 7$; $f_y(1, 1) = 1$
23. $f_x(3, 2) = 6$; $f_x(1, 1) = 2e$; $f_y(3, 2) = -9$; $f_y(1, 1) = -e$
25. $f_x(0, 2) = -\dfrac{25}{2}$; $f_x(-2, 4) = -\dfrac{5}{4}$; $f_y(0, 2) = \dfrac{3}{2}$; $f_y(-2, 4) = -\dfrac{3}{8}$

27. a. $P_{q_A}(10, 20) = 100$;   b. $P_{q_B}(10, 20) = 0$

29. a. $q(18, 6, 9) = 34{,}979$;

    b. $q_x(18, 6, 9) = 972$;

      $q_y(18, 6, 9) = 1749$; $q_z(16, 6, 9) = 1555$;

    c. Radio ads

31. $f_{xx}(x, y) = 10$; $f_{xy}(x, y) = 0$; $f_{yy}(x, y) = 24y^2$

33. $f_{xx}(x, y) = 0$; $f_{xy}(x, y) = 21y^2$; $f_{yy}(x, y) = 42xy$

35. $f_{mm}(m, n) = 12mn + 2n^2$;

    $f_{mn}(m, n) = 6m^2 + 4mn + 12n^2$;

    $f_{nn}(m, n) = 2m^2 + 24mn$

37. $T_{ss}(s, t) = 2t^5 e^{s^2}(1 + 2s^2)$; $T_{st}(s, t) = 10st^4 e^{s^2}$;

    $T_{tt}(s, t) = 20t^3 e^{s^2}$

39. $h_{pp}(p, q) = 4e^{2p+1} \ln(3q + 2)$; $h_{pq}(p, q) = \dfrac{6e^{2p+1}}{3q + 2}$;

    $h_{qq}(p, q) = -\dfrac{9e^{2p+1}}{(3q + 2)^2}$

41. $F_{xx}(x, y, z) = 12x^2 z^2$; $F_{xy}(x, y, z) = 0$;

    $F_{xz}(x, y, z) = 8x^3 z$; $F_{yy}(x, y, z) = 0$;

    $F_{yz}(x, y, z) = 3z^2$; $F_{zz}(x, y, z) = 2x^4 + 6yz + 20z^3$

43. $f_{pp}(p, q, r) = -\dfrac{r}{4p^{3/2}} + \dfrac{3q}{4p^{5/2}}$; $f_{pq}(p, q, r) = -\dfrac{1}{2p^{3/2}}$;

    $f_{pr}(p, q, r) = \dfrac{r}{2p^{1/2}}$; $f_{qq}(p, q, r) = 0$;

    $f_{qr}(p, q, r) = 0$; $f_{rr}(p, q, r) = 0$

Section 8.3

1. $A = 9.96$, so 9960 people attend. $\partial A / \partial p = -4.98$, so an increase of \$1 in the ticket price would result in 4980 fewer attendees. $\partial A / \partial t = -.04$; thus, a 1° increase in temperature will result in about 40 fewer attendees.

3. $p = \$4.25$. $\partial p / \partial h = -.15625$; another 100 lb of halibut will decrease the price by about \$.16 per pound. $\partial p / \partial s = -.0625$; another 100 lb of salmon will decrease the selling price of halibut by about \$.06 per pound.

5. a. $P = \$49{,}142$; $\dfrac{\partial P}{\partial r} = .931$ (\$931);

    b. $\dfrac{\partial P}{\partial s} = 1.365$ (\$1365)

7. $C_x(20, 50) = \$12.30$;

    $C_y(20, 50) = \$15.40$

9. $C_x(50, 80, 40) = \$12.80$; $C_y(50, 80, 40) = \$14.30$;

    $C_z(50, 80, 40) = \$24.20$

11. $R_x(20, 50) = \$28.90$; $R_y(20, 50) = \$30.88$;   product X

13. $R_x(50, 80, 40) = \$26.36$; $R_y(50, 80, 40) = \$28.82$;

    $R_z(50, 80, 40) = \$36.49$; product Y

15. a. $C_s(60, 80) = \$32.60$;   b. $C_t(70, 40) = \$32.50$;

    c. Snow tires: $29.8 < 32.8$

17. a. $R_h(10, 60) = \$8.00$; $R_s(10, 60) = \$.40$;

    b. $R_h(10, 70) = \$7.00$;

    c. $R_s(15, 60) = -\$.10$

19. Complementary   21. Competitive

23. Competitive   25. Complementary

27. $Q_L(300, 500) = .48$; $Q_K(300, 500) = .34$

29. $Q_L(300, 500) = 3.3$; $Q_K(300, 500) = 1.83$

31. $Q_L(K, L) = \alpha C \left(\dfrac{K}{L}\right)^{1-\alpha}$ and

    $Q_K(K, L) = (1 - \alpha)\left(\dfrac{K}{L}\right)^{\alpha} C$ so

    $LQ_L + KQ_K = \alpha CL^{\alpha}K^{1-\alpha} + (1 - \alpha)CL^{\alpha}K^{1-\alpha} = Q$.

33. Raise the advertising budget: $3638 > 2425$.

35. Raise the advertising budget: $2681 > 2010$.

Section 8.4

1. $x = 0, y = 0$ 3. $x = 2, y = -1$

5. $x = 2, y = -4$ 7. $x = 1, y = 1$

9. $x = 5, y = \dfrac{1}{5}$

11. f has a saddle point at $x = 0, y = 0$.

13. f has a relative minimum at $x = 0, y = 0$.

15. f has a saddle point at $x = -4, y = -24$.

17. f has a relative minimum at $x = -3, y = 1$.

19. f has a saddle point at $x = 0, y = 0$, and a relative minimum at $x = 2, y = 2$.

21. f has a saddle point at $x = 0, y = 0$, and a relative maximum at $x = \sqrt{2}/2, y = \sqrt{2}/2$, and at $x = -\sqrt{2}/2$, $y = -\sqrt{2}/2$.

23. f has a saddle point at $x = 2, y = 4$, and at $x = -2$, $y = 4$, and a relative minimum at $x = 0, y = 0$.

25. f has a saddle point at $x = -1/2, y = 1/4$.

27. f has saddle points at $x = 0, y = 3$; $x = 1, y = -1$; and $x = -1, y = -1$; f has relative minima at $x = 1$, $y = 3$, and $x = -1, y = 3$; and f has a relative maximum at $x = 0, y = -1$.

29. $w = 30, z = 20$ 31. $q_A = q_B = 20$

33. 2×2 ft base, 1 ft height

35. $x = 40$ in., $y = z = 20$ in.

37. $t = 3, w = 4$ maximize N_t

39. $\partial z / \partial x = a + by$ and $\partial z / \partial y = bx + c$, so $x = -c/b$, $y = -a/b$ is a critical point. Also $\partial^2 z / \partial x^2 = \partial^2 z / \partial y^2 = 0$ and $\partial^2 z / \partial x \, \partial y = b$, so the test function equals $-b^2$ which is negative at this critical point.

Section 8.5

1. Maximum at $x = y = 3$; $f(3, 3) = 45$

3. Minimum at $L = 6, K = 3$; $g(6, 3) = 120$

5. Minimum at $q_1 = 25, q_2 = 75$; $C(25, 75) = 8850$

7. Maximum at $x = 10$, $y = 20$; $f(10, 20) = 300$
17. $L = 4000$, $K = 16,000$, where $Q = 4850$ gal
19. $L = 259$, $K = 62$, where $C = \$9308$
21. Revenue is maximized when $x = 100$ and $y = 60$. Corresponding profit is $\$2400$.
23. $x = 5$, $y = 200$, $z = 25$; number of pizzas: 5472
25. From the constraint, and $L = (T - bK)/a$,
    so $Q = c((T - bK)/a)^a K^{1-a}$ and

$$\frac{dQ}{dK} = c(aK)^{-a}(T - bK)^{a-1}[(1 - \alpha)T - bK].$$

This derivative changes from $+$ to $-$ at $K = ((1 - \alpha)T)/b$ where $L = (\alpha T)/a$. Thus Q is maximized when

$$\frac{K}{L} = \frac{(1 - \alpha)T}{b} \cdot \frac{a}{\alpha T} = \frac{(1 - \alpha)a}{\alpha b}.$$

Chapter 8 Review

Drill Problems

1. $f_x(x, y) = 3x^2 y + y^2$; $f_y(x, y) = x^3 + 2xy$;
   $f_{xx}(x, y) = 6xy$; $f_{xy}(x, y) = 3x^2 + 2y$;
   $f_{yy}(x, y) = 2x$

3. $f_x(x, y) = \dfrac{1}{x}$; $f_y(x, y) = \dfrac{-1}{y + 1}$;

   $f_{xx}(x, y) = -\dfrac{1}{x^2}$; $f_{xy}(x, y) = 0$;

   $f_{yy}(x, y) = \dfrac{1}{(y + 1)^2}$

5. $f_x(x, y) = \dfrac{y}{2\sqrt{x + y}}$; $f_y(x, y) = \dfrac{2x + 3y}{2\sqrt{x + y}}$;

   $f_{xx}(x, y) = \dfrac{-y}{4(x + y)^{3/2}}$; $f_{xy}(x, y) = \dfrac{2x + y}{4(x + y)^{3/2}}$;

   $f_{yy}(x, y) = \dfrac{4x + 3y}{4(x + y)^{3/2}}$

7. f has a saddle point at $x = 5$, $y = -1$.
9. f has a relative minimum at $x = 3$, $y = 1$, and a saddle point at $x = 3$, $y = -1$.
11. f has a saddle point at $x = 0$, $y = 4$, and relative minima at $x = 2$, $y = 4$, and $x = -2$, $y = 4$.
13. f has saddle points at $x = 2$, $y = 1$, and $x = 2$, $y = -1$. f has a relative minimum at $x = 0$, $y = 0$.

Applications

1. $q_A = 600$; $q_B = 350$
3. A $\$2$ cut in the fee causes an approximate increase of 25 members. A $\$100$ increase in advertising causes an increase of 6 members.

5. One more manager reduces the time by approximately 2.68 days; one more laborer reduces it by approximately 1 day. Total salaries paid will decrease by $\$320$ (assuming that the time T to complete the project is rounded to the nearest integer).
7. $x = 64$, $y = 4$, $z = 2$

Section 9.1

1. $a_0 = 0$, $a_1 = 1/10$, $a_2 = 1/5$; $\lim_{n \to \infty} a_n = \infty$, so $\{a_n\}$ diverges. ($\{a_n\}$ is an arithmetic sequence with common difference $1/10$.)
3. $b_0 = 100$, $b_1 = 50$, $b_2 = 100/3$; $\lim_{n \to \infty} b_n = 0$, so $\{b_n\}$ converges to 0.
5. $c_0 = -1$, $c_1 = 1$, $c_2 = -1$; $\lim_{n \to \infty} c_n$ does not exist, so $\{c_n\}$ diverges. ($\{c_n\}$ is a geometric sequence with common ratio -1.)
7. $a_0 = 2$, $a_1 = 2/5$, $a_2 = 2/25$; $\lim_{n \to \infty} a_n = 0$, so $\{a_n\}$ converges to 0. ($\{a_n\}$ is a geometric sequence with common ratio $1/5$.)
9. $b_0 = 11$, $b_1 = 19/2$, $b_2 = 41/4$; $\lim_{n \to \infty} b_n = 10$, so $\{b_n\}$ converges to 10.
11. $c_0 = 0$, $c_1 = 1/2$, $c_2 = 2/3$; $\lim_{n \to \infty} c_n = 1$, so $\{c_n\}$ converges to 1.
13. $a_0 = 1/7$, $a_1 = 1$, $a_2 = 29/11$; $\lim_{n \to \infty} a_n = 7$, so $\{a_n\}$ converges to 7.
15. $b_0 = 1/13$, $b_1 = \sqrt{2}/16$, $b_2 = \sqrt{5}/19$; $\lim_{n \to \infty} b_n = \dfrac{1}{3}$, so $\{b_n\}$ converges to $\dfrac{1}{3}$.
17. $a_n = 1 + 2n$ and $b_n = 3^n$
19. $a_n = 10 - 8n$ and $b_n = 10\left(\dfrac{1}{5}\right)^n$
21. $a_n = -1 + 2n$ and $b_n = (-1)^{n+1}$
23. Geometric with common ratio e
25. Arithmetic with common difference $\dfrac{3}{20}$
27. Neither; $\dfrac{a_{n+1}}{a_n} = \dfrac{n + 1}{2n}$, and $a_{n+1} - a_n = \dfrac{1 - n}{2^{n+1}}$
29. Geometric with common ratio $-\dfrac{3}{2}$
31. $a_n = 5000 - 400n$, $a_{10} = 1000$; $b_n = 5000(.92)^n$, $b_{10} = 2172$ (to the nearest dollar)
33. $y_n = 20,000(1.05)^n$, $y_{10} = 32,578$, and $y_{40} = 140,800$; $f_n = 20,000 + 1250n$, $f_{10} = 32,500$, and $f_{40} = 70,000$

Section 9.2

1. 11
3. 103
5. 14
7. 28

9. $\dfrac{4}{5}$

11. 70

13. 2499

15. 2047

17. $10\left[1 - \left(\dfrac{1}{5}\right)^{11}\right]$

19. 848

21. Converges to 27

23. Converges to $\dfrac{5}{8}$

25. Converges to $\dfrac{1}{3}$

27. Diverges

29. Converges; compare to the convergent p-series $\displaystyle\sum_{n=1}^{\infty}\dfrac{1}{n^5}$.

31. Diverges; $\dfrac{n+1}{n^2} > \dfrac{1}{n}$ and the harmonic series $\displaystyle\sum_{n=0}^{\infty}\dfrac{1}{n}$ diverges.

33. Diverges; the general term does not tend to 0—it approaches e.

35. Converges; compare to the convergent p-series $\displaystyle\sum_{n=1}^{\infty}\dfrac{1}{n^{3/2}}$.

37. \$493

39. \$13,255.90

41. \$500,000

43. \$60

Section 9.3

1. a. \$3600; b. \$6923
3. a. \$14,000, \$10,000, \$6000;
   b. \$11,600, \$6800, \$3600;
   c. \$10,400, \$6000, \$3500
5. a. \$2000, \$2000; b. \$3200, \$800; c. \$2500, \$1500
7. \$2543.20
9. \$4591.70
11. \$23,285.39
13. \$2256.29
15. \$2848.05
17. \$12,430.79
19. \$173.33
21. \$266.93
23. \$419.60
25. \$2992.83, \$292.83
27. \$911.89

29. $n = \dfrac{\ln(Fi/R + 1)}{\ln(1 + i)} = 20$ yr

31. \$14.44
33. \$7400 at 11%. The monthly payments are \$344.90, compared with \$347.04 for \$8000 at 3.9%.

Section 9.4

1. $1 + x^2 + x^4 + \cdots = \displaystyle\sum_{n=0}^{\infty}x^{2n}$, for $|x| < 1$

3. $\dfrac{2}{2+x} = \dfrac{1}{1+x/2} = 1 - \dfrac{x}{2} + \dfrac{x^2}{4} + \cdots = \displaystyle\sum_{n=0}^{\infty}\dfrac{(-1)^n x^n}{2n}$, for $|x| < 2$

5. $\dfrac{x}{x-1} = \dfrac{-x}{1-x} = -x - x^2 - x^3 - \cdots = -\displaystyle\sum_{n=1}^{\infty}x^n$, for $|x| < 1$

7. $\left|\dfrac{c_{n+1}}{c_n}\right| = \dfrac{n|x|}{n+1} \to |x|$ as $n \to \infty$, $R = 1$

9. $\left|\dfrac{c_{n+1}}{c_n}\right| = |4x|$, $R = \dfrac{1}{4}$

11. $\left|\dfrac{c_{n+1}}{c_n}\right| = \left|\dfrac{x}{7}\right|$, $R = 7$

13. $\left|\dfrac{c_{n+1}}{c_n}\right| = \dfrac{(n+1)|x|}{3n} \to \left|\dfrac{x}{3}\right|$ as $n \to \infty$, $R = 3$

15. $\left|\dfrac{c_{n+1}}{c_n}\right| = \left|\dfrac{x^2}{4}\right|$, $R = 2$

17. $\left|\dfrac{c_{n+1}}{c_n}\right| = \dfrac{x^2}{(2n+3)(2n+1)} \to 0$ as $n \to \infty$, R is infinite

19. $\left|\dfrac{c_{n+1}}{c_n}\right| = (n+1)\left(\dfrac{n+1}{n}\right)^n |x| \to \infty$ as $n \to \infty$, unless $x = 0$, thus $R = 0$

21. $f'(x) = \displaystyle\sum_{n=1}^{\infty}(-1)^{n-1}x^{n-1} = \sum_{k=0}^{\infty}(-1)^k x^k$, if $k = n - 1$;

$\displaystyle\int f(x)\,dx = \sum_{n=1}^{\infty}\dfrac{(-1)^{n-1}x^{n+1}}{n(n+1)} + c$

23. $f'(x) = \displaystyle\sum_{n=0}^{\infty}\dfrac{nx^{n-1}}{2^n} = \sum_{n=1}^{\infty}\dfrac{nx^{n-1}}{2^n}$;

$\displaystyle\int f(x)\,dx = \sum_{n=0}^{\infty}\dfrac{x^{n+1}}{(n+1)2^n} + c$

25. $f'(x) = \displaystyle\sum_{n=0}^{\infty}\dfrac{nx^{n-1}}{n!} = \sum_{n=1}^{\infty}\dfrac{nx^{n-1}}{n!} = \sum_{n=1}^{\infty}\dfrac{x^{n-1}}{(n-1)!} = \sum_{k=0}^{\infty}\dfrac{x^k}{k!}$,

if $k = n - 1$; $\displaystyle\int f(x)\,dx = \sum_{n=0}^{\infty}\dfrac{x^{n+1}}{(n+1)!} + c$

27. a. $\ln(1 - x) = -\displaystyle\int_0^x \dfrac{1}{1-t}\,dt$

$= -\displaystyle\int_0^x \left[\sum_{n=0}^{\infty}t^n\right]dt = -\sum_{n=0}^{\infty}\dfrac{x^{n+1}}{n+1} = -\sum_{k=1}^{\infty}\dfrac{x^k}{k}$;

if $k = n + 1$.

b. $\ln(1 + t) = \displaystyle\sum_{k=1}^{\infty}\dfrac{(-1)^{k-1}t^k}{k} = \sum_{k=1}^{\infty}\dfrac{(-1)^{k-1}(-x)^k}{k}$

$= \displaystyle\sum_{k=1}^{\infty}\dfrac{(-1)^{2k-1}x^k}{k} = -\sum_{k=1}^{\infty}\dfrac{x^k}{k}$

29. $\dfrac{1}{(1-x)^2} = \displaystyle\sum_{n=0}^{\infty}nx^{n-1} = \sum_{n=1}^{\infty}nx^{n-1}$

31. $\dfrac{1}{x} = \displaystyle\sum_{n=0}^{\infty}(-1)^n(x-1)^n$, for $|x - 1| < 1$ or $0 < x < 2$

Section 9.5

1. $\dfrac{79}{48} = 1.65$

3. 1.0955

5. $2(1.331) = 2.66$

7. $.0954$

9. $\displaystyle\sum_{n=0}^{\infty} \dfrac{x^{2n}}{(2n)!}$

11. $\dfrac{\ln(1 + x)}{x} = \displaystyle\sum_{n=1}^{\infty} \dfrac{(-1)^{n-1}x^{n-1}}{n}$

13. $e^{-x} = \displaystyle\sum_{n=0}^{\infty} \dfrac{(-1)^{n}x^{n}}{n!}$

15. $\dfrac{e^{x} - 1}{x} = \displaystyle\sum_{n=1}^{\infty} \dfrac{x^{n-1}}{n!}$

17. $\displaystyle\lim_{x\to 0}\left(\sum_{n=1}^{\infty} \dfrac{x^{n-1}}{n!}\right) = 1$

19. $\displaystyle\lim_{x\to 0}\left(\sum_{n=1}^{\infty} \dfrac{(-1)^{n-1}x^{n-1}}{n}\right) = 1$

21. $\sqrt{1 + x^3} \doteq 1 + \dfrac{x^3}{2} - \dfrac{x^6}{8} + \dfrac{x^9}{16}$

23. $.707, .715, .722, .730$

Chapter 9 Review

Drill Problems

1. Does not exist

3. 1

5. 4

7. 0

9. Convergent

11. Divergent

13. Divergent

17. 4

19. 1

21. $\dfrac{1}{3}$

Applications

1. $6154.91

3. $14,318.58

5. $400,000

7. Yes; the total interest would be $154.89.

9. $e^{r} - 1 \doteq r + \dfrac{r^2}{2}$

r	.06	.08	.10	.12
$r + \dfrac{r^2}{2}$	.0618	.0832	.105	.1272

Section 10.1

1. a. Discrete; b. Discrete; c. Continuous; d. Discrete;
   e. Continuous

3. a. .15; c. .15; d. .70; e. .55

b.

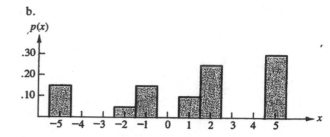

5. a. $\{-3, -2, -1, 0, 1, 3, 4, 6, 8\}$;   d. .45;   e. .45
   c.

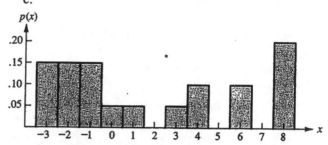

7. $\mu_X = 1.1,\ \sigma_X^2 = 11.49,\ \sigma_X = 3.39$

9. $\mu_X = 1.9,\ \sigma_X^2 = 16.99,\ \sigma_X = 4.12$

11. a. $\mu_X = 14.05,\ \sigma_X = 6.32$;   b. .85;   c. .99

13. $\mu_Y = 15.1,\ \sigma_Y^2 = 76.59$

15. $\left\{1, \dfrac{1}{2}, \dfrac{1}{3}, \dfrac{1}{4}, \dfrac{1}{5}\right\},\ E(Y) = \dfrac{1}{3},\ V(Y) = .0411$

17. a. $\dfrac{1}{3}, \dfrac{2}{9}, \dfrac{4}{27}$;   c. $\dfrac{8}{27}$

19. a. $E(X) = 8.65,\ V(X) = 3.1275$;
    b. $E(Y) = \$416.25,\ V(Y) = 1954.7$;
    c. $Pr(\$372.04 \le Y \le \$460.46) = .71$

21. a. $\mu_X = 1.8$ yr, $\sigma_X = 1.31$ yr;
    b. $\mu_Y = \$1161.58,\ \sigma_Y = \$132.38$

Section 10.2

1. b. .4;   c. .8

3. a. $\dfrac{1}{16}$;   b. $\dfrac{15}{16}$;   c. $f(x)$

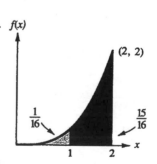

5. $\mu_X = \dfrac{11}{2},\ \sigma_X^2 = \dfrac{25}{12}$

7. $\mu_X = \dfrac{8}{5}$, $\sigma_X = \dfrac{2\sqrt{6}}{15}$

9. $\dfrac{1}{18}$

11. a. $\dfrac{1}{b-a}$; b. $\mu_X = \dfrac{a+b}{2}$, $\sigma_X^2 = \dfrac{(b-a)^2}{12}$

13. No; if $c > 0$, then $f(x)$ is negative on $[-1, 0)$; if $c < 0$, then $f(x)$ is negative on $(0, 2]$.

15. $\mu_X = 3$, $\mu_Y = \dfrac{12}{7}$

17. 4 yr, $2000   19. $625

Section 10.3

1. .3466   3. .7324   5. .1981   7. .9909
9. 1.45   11. 1.65   13. 1.17   15. 2.43
17. .3721   19. .1841   21. .0567   23. .3085
25. .9332   27. .7734   29. a. .3085; b. .8413
31. a. .8212; b. 4.65%   33. 34,900 mi
35. 621 to 685 points

Section 10.4

1. a. .0756; b. .2401; c. .9163
3. a. .0146; b. .1142; c. $(.1)^6$
5. $\mu_X = 1.2$, $\sigma_X = .917$, .6762
7. a. $f(x) = .2, 5 \le x \le 10$

   b. $\mu_X = 7.5$; $\sigma_X^2 = \dfrac{25}{12}$

   c. .4; d. .4
9. a. $f(x) = .01, 0 \le x \le 100$

   b. $\mu_X = 50$, $\sigma_X^2 = \dfrac{2500}{3}$

   c. .65; d. $1 - .01\pi$
11. a. $f(x) = 3e^{-3x}, 0 \le x < \infty$

    b. $\mu_X = \dfrac{1}{3}$; $\sigma_X = \dfrac{1}{3}$

    c. .9975; d. .1353
13. a. $f(x) = \dfrac{1}{8}e^{-x/8}, 0 \le x < \infty$

    b. .3834; c. $\sigma_X = 8$, .3679; d. .1353
15. .5443   17. .7065
19. $\mu_X = 20$ sec, $\sigma_X = 11.55$ sec, .375
21. a. $f(x) = \dfrac{1}{70}e^{-x/70}, 0 \le x < \infty$

    b. 18%
23. .6916

Chapter 10 Review

Drill Problems

1. $\dfrac{1}{40}$ 3. $\dfrac{4}{3}$ 5. .8906   7. .0427
9. .3446   11. .4817   13. .2304   15. .0778
17. .3935   19. .5507
21. a. $f(x) = \dfrac{1}{30}, -10 \le x \le 20$

    b. $\sigma^2 = 75$; c. $\dfrac{1}{3}$

Applications

1. $\mu = \$586$, $\sigma = \$18$ 3. .2177
5. Approximately $47,400

7. $p(x) = \begin{cases} \dfrac{1}{4200}(x - 5), & 5 \le x \le 75 \\ \dfrac{-1}{3000}(x - 125), & 75 < x \le 125 \end{cases}$

Section 11.1

1. $\begin{bmatrix} 6 & 4 \\ 4 & 1 \end{bmatrix}$, $\begin{bmatrix} -2 & -2 \\ -6 & 5 \end{bmatrix}$, $\begin{bmatrix} 6 & 3 \\ -3 & 9 \end{bmatrix}$, $\begin{bmatrix} 12 & 9 \\ 15 & -6 \end{bmatrix}$

3. $\begin{bmatrix} 4 & -2 \\ 0 & 6 \\ -11 & 8 \end{bmatrix}$, $\begin{bmatrix} 2 & 14 \\ 4 & -2 \\ 1 & 8 \end{bmatrix}$, $\begin{bmatrix} .3 & .6 \\ .2 & .2 \\ -.5 & .8 \end{bmatrix}$, $\begin{bmatrix} .1 & -.8 \\ -.2 & .4 \\ -.6 & 0 \end{bmatrix}$

5. $\begin{bmatrix} 11 & 8 & 5 \\ 8 & -6 & 9 \end{bmatrix}$, $\begin{bmatrix} -3 & 4 & -11 \\ 2 & 2 & -9 \end{bmatrix}$, $\begin{bmatrix} 40 & 60 & -30 \\ 50 & -20 & 0 \end{bmatrix}$,

$\begin{bmatrix} 70 & 20 & 80 \\ 30 & -40 & 90 \end{bmatrix}$

7. $\begin{bmatrix} 1 & 1 & 1 & 1 \\ 1 & 1 & 1 & 1 \\ 0 & 1 & 1 & 1 \end{bmatrix}$, $\begin{bmatrix} -1 & 1 & -1 & 1 \\ 1 & -1 & 1 & -1 \\ 0 & 1 & -1 & 1 \end{bmatrix}$,

$\begin{bmatrix} 0 & -1 & 0 & -1 \\ -1 & 0 & -1 & 0 \\ 0 & -1 & 0 & -1 \end{bmatrix}$, $\begin{bmatrix} -1 & 0 & -1 & 0 \\ 0 & -1 & 0 & -1 \\ 0 & 0 & -1 & 0 \end{bmatrix}$,

9. $\begin{bmatrix} 1 & 2 & 3 \\ 4 & 5 & 6 \\ 7 & 8 & 9 \end{bmatrix}$, $\begin{bmatrix} 1 & 2 & 3 \\ 4 & 5 & 6 \\ 7 & 8 & 9 \end{bmatrix}$, $\begin{bmatrix} .01 & .02 & .03 \\ .04 & .05 & .06 \\ .07 & .08 & .09 \end{bmatrix}$, $\begin{bmatrix} 0 & 0 & 0 \\ 0 & 0 & 0 \\ 0 & 0 & 0 \end{bmatrix}$

11. -1 13. 0   15. -9

17. $AB = \begin{bmatrix} -6 & -7 \\ 3 & 10 \end{bmatrix}$, $BA = \begin{bmatrix} 4 & 1 \\ 39 & 0 \end{bmatrix}$

19. $AB = \begin{bmatrix} -22 & 65 \\ 8 & 31 \end{bmatrix}$, $BA = \begin{bmatrix} 19 & -16 & 38 \\ 0 & -12 & 19 \\ 22 & 8 & 2 \end{bmatrix}$

21. $AB = \begin{bmatrix} 4 \\ 0 \\ -5 \end{bmatrix}$, but BA is not defined.

23. AB is not defined, $BA = \begin{bmatrix} 14 \\ 20 \\ 20 \end{bmatrix}$

25. Neither AB nor BA are defined.

27. $\begin{bmatrix} 35 & 7 & 0 & 13 & 20 \\ 52 & 44 & 22 & 0 & 0 \\ 18 & 0 & 0 & 160 & 90 \\ 155 & 155 & 110 & 14 & 22 \\ 70 & 20 & 5 & 0 & 0 \end{bmatrix}$, $\begin{bmatrix} 5 & 1 & 0 & 3 & 4 \\ 8 & 4 & 2 & 0 & 0 \\ 2 & 0 & 0 & 20 & 10 \\ 5 & -5 & 10 & 2 & 2 \\ 10 & 0 & -1 & 0 & 0 \end{bmatrix}$,

$\begin{bmatrix} 22 & 4.4 & 0 & 8.8 & 13.2 \\ 33 & 26.4 & 13.2 & 0 & 0 \\ 11 & 0 & 0 & 99 & 55 \\ 88 & 82.5 & 66 & 8.8 & 13.2 \\ 44 & 11 & 2.2 & 0 & 0 \end{bmatrix}$

29. $\begin{bmatrix} 64.6 \\ 75.5 \\ 60.9 \\ 57.8 \\ 68.9 \end{bmatrix}$

31.
	Job 1	Job 2	Job 3	Job 4	Job 5	
	42,500	36,500	24,500	19,750	13,500	Rough In
	66,800	58,400	38,400	32,000	23,600	Complete

33. $SA = \begin{bmatrix} 970 \\ 550 \\ 185 \\ 195 \end{bmatrix}$, $SM = \begin{bmatrix} 940 \\ 500 \\ 175 \\ 185 \end{bmatrix}$

Section 11.2

1. $\begin{bmatrix} 2 & -3 \\ 4 & 1 \end{bmatrix}$, $\begin{bmatrix} x \\ y \end{bmatrix}$, $\begin{bmatrix} 7 \\ 8 \end{bmatrix}$

3. $\begin{bmatrix} 1 & 3 & -5 \\ 3 & 6 & 1 \\ 5 & -3 & 0 \end{bmatrix}$, $\begin{bmatrix} x_1 \\ x_2 \\ x_3 \end{bmatrix}$, $\begin{bmatrix} 3 \\ 8 \\ 4 \end{bmatrix}$

5. $\begin{bmatrix} 1 & 0 & 8 \\ 2 & -3 & -8 \end{bmatrix}$, $\begin{bmatrix} x \\ y \\ z \end{bmatrix}$, $\begin{bmatrix} -2 \\ 14 \end{bmatrix}$

7. $\begin{bmatrix} 2 & 8 \\ -3 & -5 \\ 6 & 1 \\ 1 & -2 \end{bmatrix}$, $\begin{bmatrix} x \\ y \end{bmatrix}$, $\begin{bmatrix} -3 \\ 8 \\ 12 \\ 0 \end{bmatrix}$

9. $\begin{bmatrix} 1 & 3 & -4 & 2 \\ -1 & -4 & 0 & 7 \\ 2 & 5 & -3 & 6 \\ 6 & -4 & 5 & 0 \end{bmatrix}$, $\begin{bmatrix} x_1 \\ x_2 \\ x_3 \\ x_4 \end{bmatrix}$, $\begin{bmatrix} 21 \\ -8 \\ 3 \\ 10 \end{bmatrix}$

11. $3x + 5y = 8$
    $7x - 2y = 6$

13. $2x + 4y + 5z - w = -7$
    $3x - 2y + 8w = 13$
    $x - 7z + 9w = 6$

15. $x_1 + x_3 = -3$
    $2x_1 - x_2 + 5x_3 = 8$
    $3x_1 + 4x_2 = -6$

23. $x_1 = 3, x_2 = -1$

25. $x = 2, y = -2, z = 5$

27. $x_1 = 5, x_2 = 6, x_3 = 1$

29. $d = 1, \begin{bmatrix} 8 & 5 \\ 3 & 2 \end{bmatrix}^{-1} = \begin{bmatrix} 2 & -5 \\ -3 & 8 \end{bmatrix}$

31. $d = -2, \begin{bmatrix} 5 & 4 \\ -2 & -2 \end{bmatrix}^{-1} = \begin{bmatrix} 1 & 2 \\ -1 & -2.5 \end{bmatrix}$

33. $d = 0$, the inverse does not exist.

37. $B = BI = B(AC) = (BA)C = IC = C$

39. a. $a \neq 6$; b. $a = 6, b = 3$; c. $a = 6, b \neq 3$

Section 11.3

1. $x = -5, y = 7, z = 4$

3. $x_1 = 10, x_2 = 13, x_3 = -4$

5. $x = -3.5, y = -11, z = 4, w = -6$

7. $x_1 = 2, x_2 = -8, x_3 = 12, x_4 = -4$

9. $x = -2, y = 5$

11. $x_1 = -2, x_2 = 7$

13. $x = 2, y = 2$

15. $x = -2, y = 5, z = 4$

17. $x_1 = 0, x_2 = -1, x_3 = 2$

19. $x = 5, y = -3, z = 2$

21. $x \doteq 1.46, y \doteq 2.54, z \doteq -1.23, w \doteq 3.38$

23. $x_1 = 2, x_2 = -1, x_3 = 3, x_4 = -2$

25. $\begin{bmatrix} 2 & -1 \\ 3 & -2 \end{bmatrix}$

27. $\begin{bmatrix} -4 & 6 & -3 \\ 2 & -3 & 2 \\ 5 & -7 & 4 \end{bmatrix}$

29. $\begin{bmatrix} 12 & 16 & -13 \\ -1 & -1 & 1 \\ -8 & -11 & 9 \end{bmatrix}$

31. $\begin{bmatrix} 11 & -3 & -1 & 21 \\ -10 & 3 & 1 & -20 \\ -18 & 5 & 2 & -35 \\ -10 & 3 & 1 & -19 \end{bmatrix}$

33. 3 lb: $80, 4 lb: $100, 5 lb: $140

35. 150 lb celery, 120 lb cucumbers, 80 lb peppers, 200 lb tomatoes

Section 11.4

1. $x = \dfrac{2y + 5}{3}$; y arbitrary

3. No solution   5. $x = 1, y = 2$

7. $a = 2.15 + .3c$; $b = .7 + .4c$; c arbitrary

9. $x_1 = \dfrac{9 - x_3}{7}$; $x_2 = \dfrac{5x_3 - 10}{7}$; x_3 arbitrary

11. No solution

13. $x = 2z - 8w - 1$; $y = 5w + 1$; z, w arbitrary

15. $x_1 = x_4 + 1$; $x_2 = 2 - x_4$; $x_3 = -1$; x_4 arbitrary

17. $v = -8y + z$; $w = -2y + z$; $x = 15y - 4z$; y, z arbitrary

23. -4 25. 10

27. If C, S, and D denote the amounts in checking, savings, and the certificate, respectively, and if $6666.67 \le D \le 7500$, then $S = 30,000 - 4D$ and $C = 3D - 20,000$. When $D = \$7000$, $S = \$2000$ and $C = \$1000$.

29. a. $A = C = (110 - 2D)/5$ and $B = (180 - D)/5$, where $D \le 55$ is arbitrary.

    b. $A = C = 10, B = 30, D = 30$

Section 11.5

1. $\begin{bmatrix} 84.75 \\ 81.36 \end{bmatrix}$ 3. $\begin{bmatrix} 105.97 \\ 129.85 \end{bmatrix}$

5. $\begin{bmatrix} 140.17 \\ 96.36 \\ 130.74 \end{bmatrix}$ 7. $\begin{bmatrix} 2016.83 \\ 1481.97 \\ 2401.44 \end{bmatrix}$

9. $x_1 = x_2 = x_3$, with x_3 arbitrary

11. $x_1 = x_2 = 2x_4$ and $x_3 = x_4$, with x_4 arbitrary

13. $x_1 = 52.28, x_2 = 187.82, x_3 = 115.23$

15. a. 710 tons of grain and 180 head of cattle

    b. 1333 tons of grain and 222 head of cattle

17. a. 24 hr of repair, 34 hr of maintenance, 106 hr of custodial services

    b. 47.2 hr of repair, 67.7 hr of maintenance, 114.9 hr of custodial services

19. $x_1 = 143.2, x_2 = 15.6, x_3 = 99.1, x_4 = 41.3$

Section 11.6

1. -3 3. 15   5. 86   7. 0

9. -72 11. -26 13. $x = -2, y = 3$

15. $x = 5, y = -7$ 17. No solution

19. $x = -1, y = 0, z = 6$

Chapter 11 Review

Drill Problems

1. $\begin{bmatrix} 1 & -22 & 15 \\ 15 & 0 & 3 \\ -22 & 7 & 3 \end{bmatrix}$ 3. $\begin{bmatrix} -36 \\ -13 \end{bmatrix}$

5. $\begin{bmatrix} -7/2 & 31/2 & 2 \\ -3/2 & 13/2 & 1 \\ 1/2 & -3/2 & 0 \end{bmatrix}$

7. Verify that AB is the 3×3 identity matrix. Det $A = 2$, det $B = 1/2$.

9. $x = 1 + \dfrac{5}{14}z, y = 4 - \dfrac{3}{7}z, z$ arbitrary

11. $x = 4, y = 10, z = -2$

13. $x_1 = 300, x_2 = 400$

15. $x_1 = \dfrac{7}{17}x_3, x_2 = \dfrac{12}{17}x_3, x_3$ arbitrary

Applications

1. $40 for a term policy, $150 for a whole life policy, $50 for a universal life policy

3. 5 cases of rosé, 3 cases of burgundy, 6 cases of rhine, 8 cases of chablis

5. 177.52 units of oil and gas, 99.95 units of cotton, 228.80 units of cattle, 141.68 units of grain

Section 12.1

1. Let x and y be the number of cans of Florida Punch and Texas Cooler, respectively, that are made.

    Maximize $P = 10x + 9y$

    Subject to $40x + 44y \le 30,000$

    $15x + 12y \le 9000$

    $x, y \ge 0$

3. Let x and y be the number of MST-10s and MST-80s, respectively, that are made.

    Maximize $P = 60x + 80y$

    Subject to $5x + 8y \le 460$

    $\dfrac{1}{2}x + \dfrac{2}{3}y \le 40$

    $x, y \ge 0$

5. Let x and y be the number of loaves of French and cracked wheat bread, respectively, that are baked.

    Maximize $P = 4x + 5y$

    Subject to $3.5x + 4y \le 1260$

    $.25x + .5y \le 135$

    $x + y \le 336$

    $x, y \ge 0$

7. Let x and y be the number of grams of Vita-All and C-plus, respectively, used.

Minimize $C = 5x + 6y$
Subject to $50x + 25y \geq 125$
$50x + 150y \geq 500$
$x, y \geq 0$

9. Let x and y be the number of barrels of regular and unleaded gasoline, respectively, that are refined.

Minimize $C = 22x + 24y$
Subject to $x + y \geq 3600$
$x - 1.25y \geq 0$
$y \geq 1000$
$x, y \geq 0$

11. Let x and y be the number of basic and championship trophies, respectively, that are made.

Maximize $P = 5x + 18y$
Subject to $2x + 4y \leq 400$
$4x + 6y \leq 700$
$4x + 12y \leq 1080$
$x, y \geq 0$

13. Let x, y, and z be the number of cabinets, dressers, and chests, respectively.

Maximize $P = 80x + 100y + 50z$
Subject to $12x + 15y + 10z \leq 500$
$30x + 30y + 15z \leq 840$
$8x + 10y + 5z \leq 300$
$x, y, z \geq 0$

15. Let x, y, and z be the number of pounds of Sorbathane, Harvestonic, and XTR-Green that are used.

Minimize $C = 22x + 26y + 25z$
Subject to $.7x + .8y + .5z \geq 70$
$1.5x + 1.7y + 1.2z \geq 150$
$.9x + 1.8y + 1.4z \geq 100$
$x, y, z \geq 0$

17. Let x_1, x_2, and x_3 be the number of cases sent from Portland to Boise, Seattle, and Sacramento, respectively; let y_1, y_2, and y_3 be the number of cases sent from Tacoma to those cities.

Minimize $C = 5x_1 + x_2 + 12x_3 + 4y_1 + 4y_2 + 8y_3$
Subject to $x_1 + x_2 + x_3 \leq 7000$
$y_1 + y_2 + y_3 \leq 6000$
$x_1 + y_1 \geq 2000$
$x_2 + y_2 \geq 5000$
$x_3 + y_3 \geq 2000$
(all variables nonnegative)

19. Let x and y be the amount of tobacco from lot 1 and lot 2, respectively, used to make cavendish; let w and z be the amounts used in the aromatic.

Minimize $C = 5x + 7y + 5w + 7z$
Subject to $x + y \geq 200$
$w + z \geq 300$
$-.20x + .10y \geq 0$
$-.10w + .20x \geq 0$
$-.15z + .10y \geq 0$
$-.05w + .20z \geq 0$
$x, y, w, z \geq 0$

21. Minimize $Z = CX$
Subject to $AX \geq B$
$X \geq 0$

23. Minimize $Z = 7x + 3y$
Subject to $6x + 2y \geq 10$
$-x + 4y \geq 35$
$2x \geq 6$
$3x + 5y \geq 18$
$x, y \geq 0$

25. Four constraints; three variables. B is 4×1; C is 1×3; X is 3×1.

Section 12.2

1.

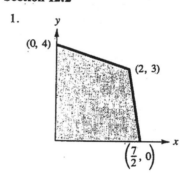

$Z = 17$ when
$x = 2, y = 3$

3.

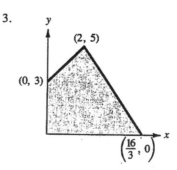

$Z = 19$ when
$x = 2, y = 5$

5.

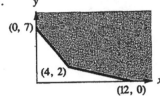

$Z = 28$ when
$x = 3, y = 2$

7.

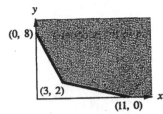

$Z = 40$ when
$x = 4, y = 2$

9.

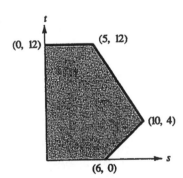

$P = 39$ when
$s = 5, t = 12$

11.

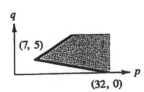

(The first constraint is not binding.)

$C = 41$ when
$p = 7, q = 5$

13.

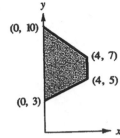

$Z = 11$ when
$x = 4, y = 7$

15.

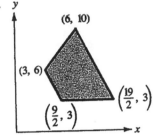

$Z = 68$ when
$x = 6, y = 10$

17.

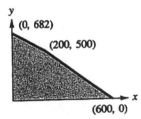

$P = \$65.00$ when
$x = 200, y = 500$

19.

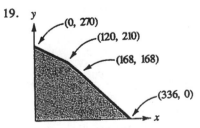

$P = \$15.30$ when
$x = 120, y = 210$

21.

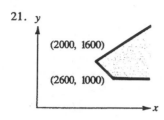

$C = \$81,200$ when
$x = 2600, y = 1000$

23.

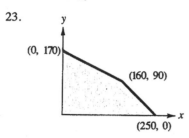

(The machine time is not binding.)
$P = \$2950$ when
$x = 160, y = 90$

Section 12.3

7. $Z = 40$ when $x = 10, y = 0$
9. $Z = 36$ when $x = 3, y = 6$
11. $Z = 80$ when $x = 3, y = 8$
13. $P = 900$ when $x = 36, y = 0, z = 6$
15. $Z = 160$ when $x_1 = 50, x_2 = 20, x_3 = 0$
17. $P = 105$ when $x = 0, y = 10, z = 0, w = 35$
21. Maximize $R = 2.5x + 3y + 1.2z$
    Subject to $40x + 60y + 20z \le 3600$
    $$-x + z \le 0$$
    $$x - y + z \le 0$$
    $$x, y, z \ge 0$$
    $R = 198$ when $x = 36, y = 36, z = 0$
23. Maximize $N = .15x + .20y + .45z$
    Subject to $x + 5y + 8z \le 400,000$
    $$x + y + z \le 50,000$$
    $$-.75x + .25y + .25z \le 0$$
    $$x, y, z \ge 0$$
    $N = 18,750$ when $x = 12,500, y = 0, z = 37,500$
    (All coupons are distributed at a cost of only \$3125.)
25. Maximize $R = .07x + .08y + .09z + .12w$
    Subject to $x + y + z + w \le 200,000$
    $$y + z + w \le 90,000$$
    $$x + y - z - w \le 0$$
    $$-x - y - z + 2w \le 0$$
    $$x, y, z, w \ge 0$$

$R = 16,200$ when $x = 90,000, y = 0, z = 30,000,$
$w = 60,000$
(There is \$20,000 remaining in the account.)

Section 12.4

1. Minimize $Z = 20y_1 + 25y_2$
   Subject to $y_1 + 4y_2 \ge 5$
   $$3y_1 + 2y_2 \ge 7$$
   $$y_1, y_2 \ge 0$$
3. Minimize $Z = 80a + 45b + 64c + 20d$
   Subject to $5a + 3b + c + 4d \ge 35 \cdot$
   $$2a + b + 7c - 3d \ge 15$$
   $$a, b, c, d \ge 0$$
5. Minimize $P = 70y_1 + 55y_2 + 60y_3$
   Subject to $5y_1 + 4y_3 \ge 1$
   $$y_1 + 3y_2 - y_3 \ge 2$$
   $$4y_1 + 2y_2 + y_3 \ge 4$$
   $$y_1, y_2, y_3 \ge 0$$
7. Minimize $Q = 24a + 16b + 35c + 28d$
   Subject to $2a - b + 3c \ge 5$
   $$5b + c + 2d \ge 2$$
   $$-a + b + 4c + 3d \ge 4$$
   $$a, b, c, d \ge 0$$
9. $Z = 31$ when $y_1 = 19/8, y_2 = 1/8$
11. $C = 155$ when $x_1 = 5/2, x_2 = 5/2$
13. $Z = 46$ when $y_1 = 1/3, y_2 = 13/3, y_3 = 0$
15. $Z = 104$ when $y_1 = 2/3, y_2 = 14/3$
17. $C = 300/7$ when $x = 0, y = 25/7, z = 15/7$
19. Minimize $C = 25x + 30y$
    Subject to $-2x + y \ge 0$
    $$x + y \ge 600$$
    $$x \ge 300$$
    $$x, y \ge 0$$
    $C = \$25,500$ when $x = 300, y = 600$
21. Let x_i denote the number of boards that are cut in pattern i
    for $i = 1, 2, 3, 4, 5.$
    Minimize $N = x_1 + x_2 + x_3 + x_4 + x_5$
    Subject to $4x_1 + 2x_2 + 2x_5 \ge 700$
    $$x_2 + 2x_3 + x_4 \ge 200$$
    $$2x_4 + 2x_5 \ge 100$$
    $$x_1, x_2, x_3, x_4, x_5 \ge 0$$
    $N = 300$ when $x_1 = 150, x_2 = 0, x_3 = 100, x_4 = 0,$
    $x_5 = 50$
23. $P = \$38.10$ when $x = 120, y = 210$
25. $C \doteq .2178$ (approximately \$.22) when $x = 0, y = 15/7,$
    $z = 25/14,$ where x, y, z are the number of grams of Vita-
    All, C-plus, and Organic ABC, respectively.
27. a. The profit is \$926.67 when $x_1 = 5.33$ and $x_2 = 11.$
    b. The profit is \$925.00 when $x_1 = 3.5$ and $x_2 = 12.5.$

Section 12.5

1. a. 2 to ∞; the basic variables are x, y, and the second slack variable.
   b. -4 to $+2$;   c. $-\infty$ to 6
3. a. $P = 30$; $x = 30$, $y = 0$, $z = 0$. The basic variables are x and the first and second slack variables.
   b. $P = 240$; $x = 45$, $y = 30$, $z = 0$. The basic variables are x, y, and the third slack variable. $P = 420$; $x = 0$, $y = 60$, $z = 20$.
   c. $P = 160$; $x = 46$, $y = 24$, $z = 4$
5. The solution is $P = 159.6$ at $x = 49.8$, $y = 19.8$, $z = 0$. The second and third constraints are binding; the basic variables are x, y, and the first slack variable.
7. $C = 870$ when $x = 20$, $y = 50$
9. No feasible solution   11. Unbounded solution
13. Multiple solutions; any point on the constraining line $x + 3y = 21$ between the points (3, 6) and (6, 5)
15. Multiple solutions; any point on the constraining plane $2x + y + z = 20$ that meets the other conditions. [This is a four-sided plane figure with corner points (8, 0, 4), (22/3, 0, 16/3), (0, 6, 14), and (0, 22/3, 38/3)—locating these points is beyond the scope of this textbook.]

Chapter 12 Review

Drill Problems

1. $Z = 28$ when $x = 14$, $y = 0$
3. $Z = 26$ when $x = 4$, $y = 3$
5. $Z = 45$ when $x = 0$, $y = 9$
7. $Z = 39/2$ when $x_1 = 5/2$, $x_2 = 0$, $x_3 = 3$
9. $Z = 26$ when $x = 1/11$, $y = 14/11$
11. $Z = 2100$ when $x = 150$, $y = 50$

Applications

1. Maximize $V = 4x + y + .5z$
   Subject to $x + y + z \le 74$
                      $150x + 45y + 15z \le 3000$
                      $x, y, z \ge 0$
   V is maximized at $x = 14$, $z = 60$.
3. Maximize $P = 10x_1 + 15x_2 + 30x_3$
   Subject to $8x_1 + 26x_2 \le 300$
                      $4x_1 + 8x_2 + 20x_3 \le 800$
                      $7x_1 + 4x_2 + 5x_3 \le 320$
                      $x_1, x_2, x_3 \ge 0$
   P is maximized at \$1290, when $x_1 = 18$, $x_2 = 6$, $x_3 = 34$.

5. Minimize $C = x_1 + x_2 + x_3$
   Subject to $12x_1 + 6x_2 + 2x_3 \ge 180$
                $-3x_1 + x_3 \ge 0$
                $x_2 - x_3 \ge 0$
                $x_1, x_2, x_3 \ge 0$
   The minimum C is 30 calls when $x_1 = 0$, $x_2 = 30$, $x_3 = 0$.

Section 13.1

1. $p(x) = 10 + 5x - x^2$
3. $p(x) = 100 + 30x - .2x^2$
5. $p(x) = 8 + 4x - 3x^2 + x^3$
7. $p(x) = -58 + 25.9x - 1.045x^2 + .0135x^3$
9. $A = 14$, $S = 50$

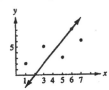

11. $A = 24$, $S = 160$

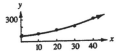

13. $A = 0$, $S = 0$

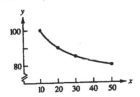

15. $v = 5.2\overline{3} - .02325q + .00003542q^2$, $0 \le q \le 500$
17. $P = -100 + 50q + .1q^2 - .002q^3$
18. $C = 200 + 50q - .2q^2 + .003q^3$
19. $q = \dfrac{20p + 4000}{p - 400}$

Section 13.2

1. $y = 4 + 1.5x$

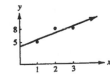

3. $y = 2.7570 + .5701x$

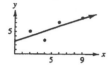

5. $y = .5 + .37x$

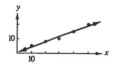

7. $y = .2833 + .0833x$

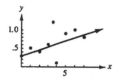

9. $y = 46.8541 - 13.0383x$

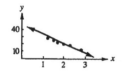

11. $q(p) = -560.8 + 152.8p$, $q(3.80) = 19.8$,
    $q(4.25) = 88.6$, $q(4.50) = 127$
13. $C = 174.32 + 63.92q$,
    fixed: $174.32,
    variable: $63.92/unit
15. $C = 46.55 + 2.09q$,
    fixed: $46.55,
    variable: $2.09/roll
17. $G(t) = 1.4971 + .2250t$,
    $G(-6) = .1471$, $G(10) = 3.7471$,
    annual increase: .225
19. $W(t) = 1.618 + .2444t$,
    $W(8) = 3.57$, $W(18) = 6.02$,
    $W(28) = 8.46$; $W = 10$ if $t = 34.3$, or during the year
    1994
21. $F(t) = 23.92 - .2190t$,
    decreasing by .219% per year
23. $T(y) = 14.18 + .338y$,
    $T = 25$ when $y = 32$, or during 1992
25. $B(t) = 1668 + 390.6t$,
    $B(3) = 2840$, $B(5) = 3621$,
    $B(9) = 5183$
27. .75   29. .59   31. .97   33. .43
35. .86   37. .98   39. .94   41. .98
43. .997   45. .89   47. .97   49. .91
51. .72   53. .9997   55. .79

Section 13.3

1.

q_i	C_i	$C_{i,\ i+1}$	$C_{i,\ i+1,\ i+2}$	$C_{i,\ \ldots,\ i+3}$
10	300			
		30		
20	600		.5	
		40		$-.008333$
30	1000		.1667	
		45		.0009524
50	1900		.2428572	
		62		
100	5000			

A second-degree fit is probably best.

3.

q_i	C_i	$C_{i,\ i+1}$	$C_{i,\ i+1,\ i+2}$	$C_{i,\ \ldots,\ i+3}$
6	100			
		13.3333		
12	180		$-.09259$	
		11.6667		.001653
24	320		$-.02315$	
		10.8333		$-.0002192$
48	580		$-.05208$	
		4.5833		
144	1020			

A second-degree fit is probably best.

5.

x_i	y_i	$y_{i,\ i+1}$	$y_{i,\ i+1,\ i+2}$	$y_{i,\ \ldots,\ i+3}$
0	20			
		80		
1	100		-17	
		46		3
2	146		-8	
		30		1
3	176		-5	
		20		5
4	196		10	
		40		
5	236			

A third-degree fit is needed.

7.

q_i	C_i	$C_{i,\ i+1}$	$C_{i,\ i+1,\ i+2}$	$C_{i,\ \ldots,\ i+3}$
0	50			
		18.8		
5	144		$-.16$	
		17.2		$-.056$
10	230		-1	
		7.2		.21067
15	266		2.16	
		28.8		$-.05195$
20	410		$-.7181$	
		3.67		
50	520			

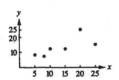

A linear fit is probably as good as any.

9.

x_i	y_i	$y_{i,\ i+1}$	$y_{i,\ i+1,\ i+2}$	$y_{i,\ \ldots,\ i+3}$
5	8			
		$-.3333$		
8	7		5.667	
		2.5		$-.09238$
10	12		$-.3571$	
		0		.05143
15	12		.26	
		2.6		$-.048$
20	25		$-.46$	
		-2		
25	15			

A linear fit is probably as good as any.

11. $C = 10.02 + 25.53q + .2438q^2$

13. $C = 16.49 + 14.05q - .04915q^2$

15.

q_i	v_i	$v_{i,\ i+1}$	$v_{i,\ i+1,\ i+2}$	$v_{i,\ \ldots,\ i+3}$
10	78			
		$-.25$		
30	73		.0025	
		$-.15$		.00002619
50	70		.004333	
		.06667		$-.00002698$
80	72		.2	
		.2		
120	80			

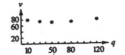

A quadratic fit appears to be best.

17.

q_i	C_i	$C_{i,\ i+1}$	$C_{i,\ i+1,\ i+2}$	$C_{i,\ \ldots,\ i+3}$
20	340			
		12		
30	460		$-.1$	
		10		0
40	560		$-.1$	
		8		.001952
50	640		.03667	
		10.2		
100	1150			

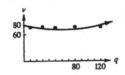

A linear fit appears to be as good as a quadratic fit.

19. $v = 81.00 - .3500q + .002861q^2$

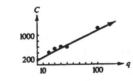

21. $C = 143.42 + 10.28q - .002256q^2$

23.

Y_i	S_i	$S_{i,\ i+1}$	$S_{i,\ i+1,\ i+2}$	$S_{i,\ \ldots,\ i+3}$
1960	1.296			
		.0428		
1965	1.510		$-.0051$	
		$-.0082$		$-.00514$
1970	1.469		$-.00514$	
		$-.0596$		.00091
1975	1.171		.00852	
		.0256		
1980	1.299			

A linear fit appears to be as good as a quadratic fit.

25. $M = 5648.27 + 75.6321t + 32.2737t^2$

27. $V = 9.424 - 1.646t + .2458t^2 - .00974t^3$

29. $B = 872.5 + 987.2t - 59.7t^2$

Section 13.4

1. $y = 9.6223x^{.319838}$

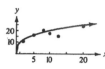

3. $y = 2.067x^{1.18962}$

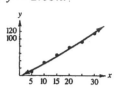

5. $y = 16.1679x^{.79712}$

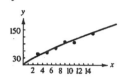

7. $y = 8.1222x^{2.2932}$

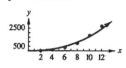

9. $y = 101.09e^{.0978x}$

x_i	$\ln y_i$	
5	5.1059	
		.1004
8	5.4072	
		.0993
10	5.6058	
		.0702
12	5.7462	
		.1953
15	6.1048	

11. $y = 499.96e^{.08x}$

x_i	$\ln y_i$	
2	6.3750	
		.0799
5	6.6147	
		.0806
8	6.8565	
		.0778
10	7.0121	
		.0805
15	7.4146	
		.0803
20	7.8160	

13. $y = 1195e^{-.089245x}$

x_i	$\ln y_i$	
2	6.9078	
		$-.0878$
3	6.8200	
		$-.0926$
4	6.7274	
		$-.0875$
5	6.6399	
		$-.0894$
8	6.3716	
		$-.0886$
10	6.1944	

15. $y = 19990e^{-.1997x}$

x_i	$\ln y_i$	
5	8.9038	
		$-.1998$
10	7.9047	
		$-.3900$
15	7.7098	
		$-.3593$
20	5.9135	
		$-.2016$
25	4.9053	
		$-.1987$
30	3.9120	

17. $S = 134.85x^{.766214}$ so $S(50) = 2702$
19. $S = 9.498x^{.8233}$
21. $V = 13788e^{.13854t}$;
    principal: $13,788;
    interest rate: 13.854%
23. $V = 37.99e^{.1t}$;
    $V(0) = 37.99$, and the appreciation rate is 10% per year.
25. $V = 65.094e^{-.19993t}$;

original value: $65,094;
annual depreciation rate: 19.993% nominal

27. Semilog Data   Log-Log Data

t_i	$\ln W_i$		$\ln t_i$	$\ln W_i$	
1	.8514		0	.8514	
		.0288			.0804
6	.9594		1.7918	.9594	
		.0505			.4166
11	1.2119		2.3979	1.2119	
		.0718			.9576
16	1.5707		2.7726	1.5707	
		.0826			1.5193
21	1.9838		3.0445	1.9838	

The first divided differences are more nearly constant for the semilog fit. Fitting these data in the least squares sense, we have $y = 1.934e^{.059t}$

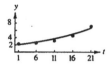

Section A.1

1. {1, 2}, {1, 3}, {1, 5}, {2, 3}, {2, 5}, {3, 5}
2. {1}, {2}, {3}, {5}, {1, 2}, {1, 3}, {1, 5}, {2, 3}, {2, 5}, {3, 5}, {1, 2, 3}, {1, 2, 5}, {1, 3, 5}, {2, 3, 5}, {1, 2, 3, 5}
3. {4, 7, 10, 13, ...}
4. $\{x \mid x = 2k - 1,$ where k is a natural number$\}$
5. {2, 4, 6, 8, ...}; $\{x \mid x = 2k,$ where k is a natural number$\}$
6. 1 with .01, 2 with .001, 3 with .0001; in general, k with the real number whose decimal representation has k 0s followed by a 1
7. 1 with 2, 2 with 4, 3 with 6; in general, k with $2k$
8. a. .25;   b. .166666...;
   c. 1.555555...;   d. .27272727...

Section A.2

1. a. $(-1, 8)$;   b. $(2, 10]$;   c. $[-4, -1]$;   d. $[0, \infty)$
2. a.    b.
   c.   d.
3. a.
   $\{x \mid x$ is a real number between 2 and 8, inclusively$\}$
   b.
   $\{x \mid x$ is a real number greater than or equal to -7 but strictly less than 2$\}$
   c.
   $\{x \mid x$ is a real number strictly between -10 and $-1\}$

d.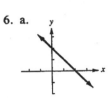

$\{x \mid x \text{ is less than or equal to } 5\}$

4. $(-\infty, \infty)$

5.

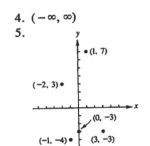

6. a. 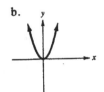   b.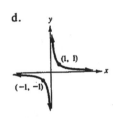

c. 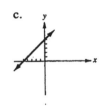   d.

Section A.3

1. -14	2. 3	3. -5	4. -4
5. 7	6. 2	7. -31	8. -14
9. 54	10. 67	11. 70	12. -32
13. $\dfrac{3}{35}$	14. $\dfrac{2}{9}$	15. $\dfrac{3}{10}$	16. $\dfrac{1}{12}$
17. $\dfrac{20}{9}$	18. 7	19. $\dfrac{5}{6}$	20. $\dfrac{1}{6}$
21. $-\dfrac{5}{16}$	22. $\dfrac{19}{30}$		

23. Commutativity of addition
24. Associativity of multiplication (write 12 as $4 \cdot 3$ and 20 as $5 \cdot 4$)
25. Commutativity of multiplication
26. Commutativity and associativity of multiplication
27. Distribution of multiplication over addition
28. Commutativity of multiplication and distribution of multiplication over addition
29. Distribution of multiplication over addition
30. 0 is the additive identity

Section A.4

1. 2^8	2. 2^{15}	3. 2^2 or 4	4. 2^{-2} or $\dfrac{1}{4}$
5. $\dfrac{y}{x}$	6. x^2y^2	7. $\dfrac{1}{x^2y^2}$	8. x^2y^{14}
9. $8x^3$	10. $\dfrac{27}{64}$	11. $\dfrac{x^4}{81}$	12. $x^2y^4z^2$
13. 1	14. $\dfrac{1}{27}$	15. 8	16. $\dfrac{1}{4}$
17. 2	18. 8	19. $\dfrac{1}{3}$	20. 64

21. $5^{1/2}$ or 2.236
22. $7^{1/3}$ or 1.913
23. $3^{5/4}$ or 3.948
24. $9^{4/7}$ or 3.510
25. $\sqrt{3}$ or 1.732
26. $(\sqrt[3]{5})^{-4}$ or .117
27. $\sqrt[10]{8^{213}}$ or 1.721×10^{19}
28. $-(\sqrt[10]{6})^{-32}$ or $-.003$
29. $5\sqrt{3}$
30. $2\sqrt{5}$
31. $3\sqrt{2}$
32. $10\sqrt{3}$
33. $7\sqrt{2}$
34. $2\sqrt[3]{3}$

Section A.5

1. 11	2. 2	3. 2	4. -19

5. 2.5   6. 2   7. $3x^3 + 12x$
8. $4xy^2 + 20y$ 9. $-2x^2y - 2xy^2 - 2y^3$
10. $3x^2y + 3x^3y^2 - 3xy^4$ 11. $2x^2 + 13x + 15$
12. $6x^2 + 13x - 5$ 13. $x^2 - 25$
14. $4x^2 - 1$ 15. $x^3 - a^3$
16. $x^3 + a^3$ 17. $2x^3 + 13x^2 + 31x + 35$
18. $x^3 - 5x^2 + 10x - 12$
19. $x^4 + 12x^3 + 54x^2 + 108x + 81$
20. $8x^3 + 60x^2 + 150x + 125$
21. $32x^5 - 80x^4y + 80x^3y^2 - 40x^2y^3 + 10xy^4 - y^5$
22. $x^5 - 10x^4 + 40x^3 - 80x^2 + 80x - 32$
23. $x^7 + 7x^6 + 21x^5 + 35x^4 + 35x^3 + 21x^2 + 7x + 1$
24. $x^8 + 8x^6 + 24x^4 + 32x^2 + 16$
25. $2x^2y(4y^2 + 2 + x^3y)$ 26. $6a^2b^2(4 - 3ab^2 - 6a^2b)$
27. $(x + 2)(x + 6)$ 28. $(x - 2)(x - 4)$
29. $(x - 3)(x - 5)$ 30. $(2x + 1)(x - 1)$
31. $(x - 6)(x + 5)$ 32. $(x - 6)(x + 7)$
33. $(x - 6)(x + 6)$ 34. $(2x - 7)(2x + 7)$
35. $4x(x^2 + 3x - 18) = 4x(x + 6)(x - 3)$
36. $5x(x^2 - 5x - 14) = 5x(x - 7)(x + 2)$
37. $\dfrac{(x-3)(x-1)}{x+1} \cdot \dfrac{(x-1)(x+1)}{x-3} = (x-1)(x-1)$

$= x^2 - 2x + 1$

38. $\dfrac{x+4}{(x-5)(x+5)} \cdot \dfrac{(x-5)(x+2)}{(x+5)(x+4)} = \dfrac{x+2}{(x+5)(x+5)}$

$= \dfrac{x+2}{x^2 + 10x + 25}$

39. $\dfrac{(x+2)(x+2)+(x+3)(x-1)}{(x-1)(x+2)}$

$= \dfrac{x^2+4x+4+x^2+2x-3}{x^2+x-2}$

$= \dfrac{2x^2+6x+1}{x^2+x-2}$

40. $\dfrac{(2x+1)(x+3)-(x-3)(x+5)}{(x+5)(x+3)}$

$= \dfrac{(2x^2+7x+3)-(x^2+2x-15)}{x^2+8x+15}$

$= \dfrac{x^2+5x+18}{x^2+8x+15}$

41. $\dfrac{(x-6)(x+2)}{(x-7)(x+2)} - \dfrac{x+1}{x-7} = \dfrac{x-6}{x-7} - \dfrac{x+1}{x-7}$

$= \dfrac{-7}{x-7}$

42. $\dfrac{x^2-3x-10}{(x+1)(x+1)} - \dfrac{(x-5)(x+1)}{(x+1)(x+1)} = \dfrac{x-5}{x^2+2x+1}$

43. $\dfrac{\frac{x-(x+h)}{x(x+h)}}{h} = \dfrac{\frac{-h}{x(x+h)}}{h} = \dfrac{-1}{x(x+h)}$

44. $\dfrac{\frac{2(x-1)-3(x+1)}{(x+1)(x-1)}}{x+2} = \dfrac{\frac{-x-5}{(x+1)(x-1)}}{x+2}$

$= \dfrac{-x-5}{(x+1)(x-1)(x+2)}$

45. $\dfrac{5(\sqrt{7}+\sqrt{3})}{4}$

46. $\dfrac{8(\sqrt{6}-\sqrt{10})}{-4} = -2(\sqrt{6}-\sqrt{10})$

47. $\dfrac{x^2-5}{3(x-\sqrt{5})}$ **48.** $\dfrac{x-7}{9(\sqrt{x}+\sqrt{7})}$

49. $\dfrac{(x+h)-x}{h(\sqrt{x+h}+\sqrt{x})} = \dfrac{h}{h(\sqrt{x+h}+\sqrt{x})}$

$= \dfrac{1}{\sqrt{x+h}+\sqrt{x}}$

50. $\dfrac{3(4+\sqrt{2})}{16-2} = \dfrac{3(4+\sqrt{2})}{14}$

Section A.6

1. $6x=12; x=2$ **2.** $7x=21; x=3$

3. $6x=-24; x=-4$ **4.** $20x=65+15; x=4$

5. $12x=4; x=\dfrac{1}{3}$

6. $8(x+1)=32; 8x=24; x=3$

7. $2(x+1)=4(x-3)$
$2x-4x=-12-2$
$-2x=-14$
$x=7$

8. $4(x+3)=3(x-2)$
$4x-3x=-6-12$
$x=-18$

9. $x=2(x-1)$
$-x=-2$
$x=2$

10. $2x=4(5-x)$
$6x=20$
$x=\dfrac{10}{3}$

11. $x=\dfrac{-8\pm\sqrt{64-24}}{2} = -4\pm\sqrt{10}$

12. $(x+2)(x+3)=0;$
$x=-2,-3$

13. $(x-9)(x+2)=0;$
$x=9,-2$

14. $(x-3)(x+2)=0;$
$x=3,-2$

15. $x=\dfrac{-3\pm\sqrt{9-4}}{2} = \dfrac{-3}{2}\pm\dfrac{\sqrt{5}}{2}$

16. $x=\dfrac{7\pm\sqrt{49+36}}{2} = \dfrac{7\pm\sqrt{85}}{2}$

17. $x=\dfrac{-7\pm\sqrt{97}}{4}$

18. $x=\dfrac{4\pm\sqrt{100}}{6}; x=\dfrac{7}{3}, -1$

19. $3x^2-11x+6=0;$
$(3x-2)(x-3)=0;$
$x=\dfrac{2}{3}, 3$

20. $2x^2-13x+7=0;$
$x=\dfrac{13\pm\sqrt{113}}{4}$

21. $x(x-5)(x+5)=0;$
$x=0,5,-5$

22. $x^2(x^2-x-20)=0;$
$x^2(x-5)(x+4)=0;$
$x=0,5,-4$

23. $x^2-x-6=x^2+4x+3;$
$-5x=9;$
$x=-\dfrac{9}{5}$

24. $x^2+4x-21=x^2+6x-16;$
$-2x=5;$
$x=-\dfrac{5}{2}$

25. $(x+5)(x+1)=(x+8)(x-2)$
$x^2+6x+5=x^2+6x-16$
$5\neq-16$, therefore no solution

26. $(x-3)(x-1)=(x+4)(x+2)$
$x^2-4x+3=x^2+6x+8$
$-10x=5$
$x=-\dfrac{1}{2}$

27. $6x + (x - 5)(x - 2) = 2x(x - 5)$
$6x + x^2 - 7x + 10 = 2x^2 - 10x$
$x^2 - 9x - 10 = 0$
$(x - 10)(x + 1) = 0$
$x = 10, -1$

28. $(x + 4)(x - 3) - 4x = 3x(x - 3)$
$x^2 + x - 12 - 4x = 3x^2 - 9x$
$2x^2 - 6x + 12 = 0$; this has no real solutions

29. $\dfrac{(4x - 1)(x + 1) + (2x + 3)(x + 3)}{x^2 + 4x + 3} = \dfrac{26}{x^2 + 4x + 3}$
Equating the numerators:
$4x^2 + 3x - 1 + 2x^2 + 9x + 9 = 26$
$6x^2 + 12x - 18 = 0$
$6(x - 1)(x + 3) = 0$
$x = 1, (x = -3$ is extraneous$)$

30. $(2x + 1)(x + 5) - (x - 3)(x - 2) = -61$
(the denominators are equal)
$2x^2 + 11x + 5 - (x^2 - 5x + 6) = -61$
$x^2 + 16x + 60 = 0$
$(x + 10)(x + 6) = 0$
$x = -10, -6$

Section A.7

1. $x < -11$

2. $2x > 6; x > 3$

3. $-9x > 27; x < -3$

4. $-4x \leq -23; x \geq \dfrac{23}{4}$

5. $-x - 10 \leq 3 + 7x$
$-8x \leq 13$
$x \geq -\dfrac{13}{8}$

6. $4x + 3 \geq 8x - 7$
$-4x \geq -10$
$x \leq \dfrac{5}{2}$

7. $(x - 6)(x + 2) < 0$

$$+++++++ \; ----- \; +++++++$$
$$\xrightarrow{\quad\; -2 \qquad\quad 6 \qquad\;} x$$

$-2 < x < 6$

8. $(x + 5)(x - 4) < 0$

$$+++++++ \; ----- \; +++++++$$
$$\xrightarrow{\quad\; -5 \qquad\quad 4 \qquad\;} x$$

$-5 < x < 4$

9. $(x + 2)(x + 5) \geq 0$

$$+++++++ \; ----- \; +++++++$$
$$\xrightarrow{\quad\; -5 \qquad\quad -2 \qquad\;} x$$

$x \leq -5$ or $x \geq -2$

10. $(x + 3)(x - 7) > 0$

$$+++++++ \; ----- \; +++++++$$
$$\xrightarrow{\quad\; -3 \qquad\quad 7 \qquad\;} x$$

$x < -3$ or $x > 7$

11. $x^2 - 3x - 18 > 0$;
$(x + 3)(x - 6) > 0$;

$$+++++++ \; ----- \; +++++++$$
$$\xrightarrow{\quad\; -3 \qquad\quad 6 \qquad\;} x$$

$x < -3$ or $x > 6$

12. $x^2 - 11x + 24 < 0$;
$(x - 3)(x - 8) < 0$;

$$+++++++ \; ----- \; +++++++$$
$$\xrightarrow{\quad\; 3 \qquad\quad 8 \qquad\;} x$$

$3 < x < 8$

13. $x^2 - 12x + 10 \geq 0$;
$x = \dfrac{12 \pm \sqrt{104}}{2} = 6 \pm \sqrt{26}$

$$+++++++ \; ----- \; +++++++$$
$$\xrightarrow{\quad 6-\sqrt{26} \quad 6+\sqrt{26} \quad} x$$

$x \leq 6 - \sqrt{26}$ or $x \geq 6 + \sqrt{26}$

14. $x^2 + 3x - 5 > 0$;
$x = \dfrac{-3 \pm \sqrt{29}}{2} = -4.193, 1.193$;

$$+++++++ \; ----- \; +++++++$$
$$\xrightarrow{\quad -4.193 \quad 1.193 \quad} x$$

$x < -4.193$ or $x > 1.193$

15.
$$------ \; +++++ \; ------$$
$$\xrightarrow{\quad -1 \qquad\quad 6 \qquad\;} x$$

$x \leq -1$ or $x > 6$

16.
$$+++++++ \; ----- \; +++++++$$
$$\xrightarrow{\quad -4 \qquad\quad 3 \qquad\;} x$$

$x < -4$ or $x > 3$

17. $\dfrac{(x - 5)(x + 1)}{(x + 1)^2} > 0; \dfrac{x - 5}{x + 1} > 0$

$$+++++++ \; ----- \; +++++++$$
$$\xrightarrow{\quad -1 \qquad\quad 5 \qquad\;} x$$

$x < -1$ or $x > 5$

18. $\dfrac{3}{x + 1} - \dfrac{5}{2x + 1} \leq 0$;
$\dfrac{x - 2}{(x + 1)(2x + 1)} \leq 0$

$$------ \; +++ \; --- \; +++++++$$
$$\xrightarrow{\quad -1 \; -\frac{1}{2} \qquad 2 \qquad} x$$

$x < -1$ or $-\dfrac{1}{2} < x \leq 2$

19.
$$++++++ \; ----- \; ++++ \; ----- \; +++++++$$
$$\xrightarrow{\quad -3 \quad -1 \qquad 2 \qquad 5 \quad} x$$

$-3 < x < -1$ or $2 < x < 5$

20.
$$++++++ \; ----- \; ++++ \; ----- \; +++++++$$
$$\xrightarrow{\quad -8 \quad -4 \qquad 1 \qquad 7 \quad} x$$

$x < -8$ or $-4 < x < 1$ or $x > 7$

21. $-2 < x < 8$

22. $6 \leq x < 9$

23. $4 < x \leq 10$

24. $x < 3$

25. $x \geq -1$

26. $-8 \leq x \leq -2$

27. $2x + 1 = 8$ or $2x + 1 = -8$;
$x = \dfrac{7}{2}$ or $x = -\dfrac{9}{2}$

28. $2x - 8 = 1$ or $2x - 8 = -1$;
$x = \dfrac{9}{2}$ or $x = \dfrac{7}{2}$

29. $-4 \leq 2x - 9 \leq 4$;
$5 \leq 2x \leq 13$;
$\dfrac{5}{2} \leq x \leq \dfrac{13}{2}$

30. $-9 < 3x + 4 < 9$;
$-13 < 3x < 5$;
$-\dfrac{13}{3} < x < \dfrac{5}{3}$

31. $3x + 2 < -2$ or $3x + 2 > 2$;
$3x < -4$ or $3x > 0$;
$x < -\dfrac{4}{3}$ or $x > 0$

32. $5x - 8 \leq -10$ or $5x - 8 \geq 10$;
$5x \leq -2$ or $5x \geq 18$;
$x \leq -\dfrac{2}{5}$ or $x \geq \dfrac{18}{5}$

INDEX

APPLICATIONS

Basic Rules of Differentiation
(b, k, and n are real numbers with $b > 0$)

1. $D_x[k] = 0$

2. $D_x[x^n] = nx^{n-1}$

3. $D_x[kf(x)] = kf'(x)$

4. $D_x[f(x) + g(x)] = f'(x) + g'(x)$

5. $D_x[f(x)g(x)] = f(x)g'(x) + g(x)f'(x)$

6. $D_x\left[\dfrac{f(x)}{g(x)}\right] = \dfrac{g(x)f'(x) - f(x)g'(x)}{[g(x)]^2}$, $g(x) \neq 0$.

7. $D_x\{(f(x))^n\} = n[f(x)]^{n-1}f'(x)$

8. $D_x[\ln f(x)] = \dfrac{f'(x)}{f(x)}$, for $f(x) > 0$

9. $D_x[\log_b f(x)] = \dfrac{f'(x)}{f(x) \ln b}$, for $f(x) > 0$

10. $D_x[e^{f(x)}] = e^{f(x)}f'(x)$

11. $D_x[b^{f(x)}] = (\ln b)b^{f(x)}f'(x)$

Basic Rules of Integration
(c denotes an arbitrary constant)

1. $\displaystyle\int k\, dx = kx + c$

2. $\displaystyle\int x^n\, dx = \dfrac{1}{n+1}x^{n+1} + c, n \neq -1$

3. $\displaystyle\int x^{-1}\, dx = \int \dfrac{1}{x}\, dx = \ln|x| + c$

4. $\displaystyle\int e^x\, dx = e^x + c$

5. $\displaystyle\int b^x\, dx = \dfrac{1}{\ln b}b^x + c$

6. $\displaystyle\int kf(x)\, dx = k\int f(x)\, dx$

7. $\displaystyle\int [f(x) + g(x)]\, dx = \int f(x)\, dx + \int g(x)\, dx$

A Summary of Notation and Formulas used in Applications

q: quantity or number of units

p: price per unit

v: variable cost per unit

k: fixed cost

$R = pq$: revenue

$C = vq + k$: total cost

$P = R - C = (p - v)q - k$: profit

$MR = D_q[R]$: marginal revenue

$MC = D_q[C]$: marginal cost

$A = \dfrac{C}{q}$: average cost

I: income

$C(I)$: consumption of income

$MPC = C'(I)$: marginal propensity to consume

$\eta = -\dfrac{p}{q}\cdot\dfrac{dq}{dp}$: price elasticity of demand

$PS = \displaystyle\int_0^{q_0} [p_0 - f(q)]\, dq$; $f(q)$ the supply function:

producer's surplus

$CS = \displaystyle\int_0^{q_0} [f(q) - p_0]\, dq$; $f(q)$ the demand function:

consumer's surplus

Financial Formulas

r: nominal rate of interest

n: compounding periods per year

t: time in years

$F(t) = \left(1 + \dfrac{r}{n}\right)^{nt}$: future value of \$1 after nt compounding periods

$F(t) = e^{rt}$: future value of \$1 after continuous compounding

$P(t) = \left(1 + \dfrac{r}{n}\right)^{-nt}$: present value of \$1 with nt compounding periods

$P(t) = e^{-rt}$: present value of \$1 with continuous compounding

$i = \dfrac{r}{n}$: interest rate per compounding period

$F = \dfrac{(1 + i)^n - 1}{i}$: future value of an annuity consisting of n \$1 payments

$P = \dfrac{1 - (1 + i)^{-n}}{i}$: present value of an annuity consisting of n \$1 payments

$R = \dfrac{Pi}{1 - (1 + i)^{-n}}$: annuity payment whose present value is P

Depreciation Methods

P: initial value of an asset

S: salvage value of an asset

V_k: value of an asset, with an n year life, after k years, $k = 0, 1, \ldots, n$

$V_k = P - \dfrac{k}{n}(P - S)$: straight line depreciation

$V_k = S + \dfrac{(k - n)(k - n - 1)}{n(n + 1)}(P - S)$: sum-of-the-digits depreciation

$V_k = P\left(\dfrac{S}{P}\right)^{k/n}$: fixed percentage depreciation

Definitions using limits

$e = \lim\limits_{n \to \infty} \left(1 + \dfrac{1}{n}\right)^n$: the natural base

$f'(x) = \lim\limits_{h \to 0} \dfrac{f(x + h) - f(x)}{h}$: the derivative of the function f

$\displaystyle\int_a^\infty f(x)\, dx = \lim_{b \to \infty} \int_a^b f(x)\, dx$: an improper integral

$\displaystyle\sum_{n=0}^\infty a_n = \lim_{k \to \infty} \sum_{n=0}^k a_n$: an infinite series

Summation formulas

$\displaystyle\sum_{n=0}^k (a_0 + kd) = \dfrac{(k + 1)(a_0 + a_k)}{2}$

$= \dfrac{(k + 1)(2a_0 + kd)}{2}$: finite arithmetic sequence

$\displaystyle\sum_{n=0}^k a_0 r^k$

$= \dfrac{a_0(1 - r^{k+1})}{1 - r}$: finite geometric sequence

$\displaystyle\sum_{n=0}^\infty a_0 r^k = \dfrac{a_0}{1 - r}$, if $|r| < 1$: geometric series